HEINEMANN
AVCE

ADVANCED

Leisure and Recreation

Ian Roberts

Heinemann Educational Publishers,
Halley Court, Jordan Hill, Oxford OX2 8EJ
A division of Reed Educational & Professional Publishing Ltd.

Heinemann is a registered trademark of Reed Educational & Professional Publishing

OXFORD MELBOURNE AUCKLAND
JOHANNESBURG BLANTYRE GABORONE
IBADAN PORTSMOUTH (NH) USA CHICAGO

© Ian Roberts 2001

First published 2001
2005 2004 2003 2002 2001
10 9 8 7 6 5 4 3 2

Typeset by 𝖙 Tek-Art, Croydon, Surrey

Printed and bound in Great Britain by The Bath Press Ltd., Bath

Contents

This book has been written to support students who are studying for an Advanced VCE in Leisure and Recreation. The book is divided into six units which cover the compulsory units of the new Curriculum 2000 National Standards.

The six compulsory units will form the core of the different Advanced VCE awards that will be offered by all awarding bodies.

The six units are:

Unit 1: Investigating Leisure and Recreation
Unit 2: Safe Working Practices in the Leisure and Recreation Industry
Unit 3: The Sports Industry
Unit 4: Marketing Leisure and Recreation
Unit 5: Customer Service
Unit 6: Leisure and Recreation in Action

Each unit of this book has been organised to follow the content specified for the corresponding unit of national standards. Headings are designed to make it easy to follow the content of each unit and to find all the knowledge and other details needed in order to achieve a high grade. It is worth noting that some topics appear throughout the book under several different headings.

Assessment

Units will be assessed either by an assignment or by an external test, which will be set and marked by the awarding body. Units 2 and 4 are the externally assessed units. Units 1, 3, 5 and 6 will be assessed through project work marked internally within the school or college delivering the Advanced VCE.

External tests are expected to take the form of an examination and will require short written answers to questions. These questions may often be based on case studies or brief descriptions of situations, some of which will be released before the exam.

Special features of the book

Throughout the text there are a number of features which are designed to encourage reflection and discussion and to help relate theory to practice in Leisure and Recreation. Some activities may also help to develop **key skills** such as numeracy. The features are:

Think it over thought-provoking questions or dilemmas, which can be used for individual reflection or possibly for group discussions

Try it out activities which encourage the general application of theory in practice

Thought for the page ideas, thoughts and situations that can be used for reflection.

Case studies brief stories or situations which help to explain the relevance of key issues and how theory relates to practice.

Check it out short blocks of questions, found in every unit at the end of sections, which allow you to check your understanding of the preceding text. The answers can be found in the text but in a few cases the questions require interpretation of the text.

References at the end of each unit there is a list of references, recommended further reading and useful websites.

At the end of the book is a comprehensive index.

Dedication

To my mother and late father, and to my daughters, Kirsty, Shona and Fay, whose loving support and tolerance of many lost leisure hours has made this book possible.

Acknowledgements

In trying to make this book fresh and up to date, I would like to thank the following people for their advice, support and information.

Margaret Berriman, Mary James, Gillian Burrell and the team at Heinemann, Sarah Lucas at HSBC, Stephen Studd and all the crew at SPRITO, Nicki Clarke at Virgin plc, Abbey Worsnip at Leicester City FC, Darrell Day at Quayside Leisure Centre, Roberta Stansfield at the Royal Academy, Nigel Hooke at CCPR, Richard Allen at the ETB, Guy Daines at the Library Association, Jane Denning at ILAM, ISRM, CIPFA, Bracknell Forest BC, Marc Hutton and the library staff at Sport England, Michael Taylor at the National Trust, Allison Henderson at Flagship Portsmouth, Christopher Dobbs at the Mary Rose Trust, Sally Maynard at LISU, Jacqui Meenan at Manchester 2000 Commonwealth Games, the RNID and Martha Murray at the Stoll Moss Group.

The publishers would like to thank the following for permission to reproduce copyright material:

p.15, p.17, p.32, p.43, p.46, p.54, p.57 and p.167 Social Trends 30/National Statistics © Crown Copyright; p.30, p.55 Chartered Institute of Public Finance and Accountancy; p.37, p.57 The National Trust; p.66 The Library Association; p101 Crown copyright material is reproduced with the permission of the Controller of Her Majesty's Stationary Office; p.107 © Royal Life Saving Society UK 1999; p.127 Safety Signs and Signals Regulations 1995; p.143 The Observer Newspaper, June 2000; p.156 British Betting Offices Association, pre-eminent in representing independent bookmakers; p.160 General Household Survey/National Statistics © Crown Copyright; p.164 Mark Rowe, A grim toll: holidays that turned to disaster/The Independent 30th April 2000; p.170 The Sports Industries Federation; p.193 Sportscan/IPSOS-RSL/Sports Marketing Surveys; p.217 McDonald, Marketing Plans, How to prepare them, how to use them/Butterworth-Heinemann; p.237 CACI's AreaData Service/Leisureweek; p.367 R M Belbin, Management Teams: Why they succeed or fail/Heinemann Educational Publishers 1981.

The publishers would also like to thank Ginny Stroud-Lewis, picture researcher and the following for permission to reproduce photographs:

Ace: Chris King – page 109 (top), 109 (middle)
Ace: Ian Hallows – page 109 (bottom)
Ace: Pavel Libera – page 289
Allsport – page 9, 116, 143, 152

Allsport: Julian Herbert – page 297
Allsport: Doug Pensinger – page 139
(bottom right)
Allsport/Stephen Dunn – page 182
Allsport/Dave Rogers – page 166
Allsport/Vandystadt – page 163
BBC Worldwide – page 288
Corbis – page 7, 28, 41, 139 (top), 139
(bottom left), 225, 317 (top), 361
Guildford Spectrum – page 274, 288, 294
David Lloyd Ltd – page 23
Meadowhall – page 14
Peter Morris – page 95
Photodisc – page 44, 210, 213, 216, 344,
357, 399

Popperfoto – page 156
Popperfoto/Reuters – page 205
Popperfoto/Reuters/Paul Sanders – page 353
Popperfoto/Reuters/Ian Waldie – page 388
R Smith – page 47
Frank Spooner – page 359
Sheena Verdun Taylor – page 65, 131, 172,
225, 271, 299, 301, 317 (bottom)

Every effort has been made to contact
copyright holders of material published in
this book. We would be glad to hear from
unacknowledged sources at the first
opportunity.

This unit is organised into six sections. You will learn about:

- defining leisure and recreation
- the development of the leisure and recreation industry
- the structure of the leisure and recreation industry
- the scale of the UK leisure and recreation industry
- working in the leisure and recreation industry
- pursuing your own progression aims.

Introduction

Since the Second World War there has been a massive change in work, communications, technology and travel. Apart from making the world of work unrecognisable from pre-war days these changes have also resulted in what is often called the 'leisure revolution'. The opportunities to enjoy leisure activities have increased for all of us, both in terms of the time available and the variety of ways in which we can spend this time. For us to be able to enjoy ourselves there has to be a structure and workforce supplying recreational activities – the leisure industry. In this unit we are going to look at how our behaviour in our free time has changed and the factors that affect it. We are also going to look at how the industry is organised and managed; its effect on employment and the opportunities open to anyone wishing to become a part of the industry.

1.1 Defining leisure and recreation

Defining leisure

Leisure and recreation are as old as human beings and were present in the lives of our Stone Age ancestors. Studies of the earliest sites where *Homo sapiens* first emerged in Africa showed that pigment powders such as red ochre were collected and used for body painting in preparation for ritual dances. Thus there is evidence from over 100,000 years ago of both art and physical recreation. Anthropologists are sure that early humankind had the same intelligence and instincts as we do. Our ability to enjoy ourselves and to develop recreational activities appears to be innate and may even be a distinguishing factor between us and the rest of the animal world.

Work is equally ancient. The work of early humankind can be defined as the activities

Ten-pin bowling is a major recreational activity today. Is there any evidence that early humankind played a game similar to this?

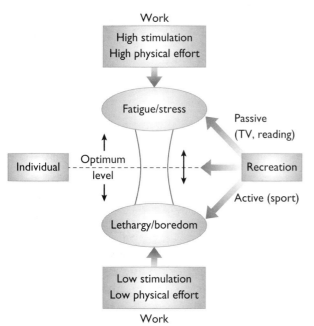

Figure 1.1 Chill out or work out? One function of recreation is to repair the balance between boredom and stress caused by work

required to survive, and was first simply a continuous, active response to the basic needs of hunger, warmth and safety. Gradually the development of skills in making tools, increasing production and storing resources meant that work was not necessarily continuous and there were times of relaxation. These were leisure times – **the available time we have when we are not working or carrying out essential activities**. In modern life, work is the time we spend in jobs or doing domestic chores; essential activities are things like sleep and travelling. Leisure time is the time when we have maximum influence on controlling and doing the things we enjoy (Figure 1.1).

Key terms

Work: The time or activity required to survive

Leisure: The time available when we are not working or doing other essential activities such as sleeping

Recreation: The activities we choose to undertake during leisure time.

Thought for the page

It is interesting to note that most people's work has always been controlled by others, whether by feudal lords or modern industrial corporations. The word 'leisure' is derived from the Latin for the word meaning 'permit' or 'licence'. In other words, people had to have permission to stop work and do other things. The practice still lives on. In many jobs employees have to ask for permission to take holidays, and their contract of employment will state when and for how long they are expected to work.

Classifications in leisure and recreation

Leisure providers, such as the Sports and Arts Councils, equipment manufacturers or cinema chains find it is helpful to classify recreational activities and put those with similar products into categories. Let's look at two examples of classification.

Active recreation

This is when an individual personally participates in an activity which involves physical or mental exertion to a significant degree:

- playing sport (e.g. netball, sailing, badminton, etc.)
- playing a musical instrument, acting in amateur dramatics
- gardening and crafts and other hobbies
- rambling.

Passive recreation

This is when an individual receives or consumes entertainment by other people or activities:

- watching television (including watching sport)

- listening to music
- reading
- playing computer games
- going to a restaurant or a pub.

Active recreation is especially stimulating and rewarding. The word 'sport' stems from the Latin *disportare* which means 'to carry away'. Sport to both the Greeks and the Romans was a means of achieving a sharper mental awareness and heightened consciousness. This aspect of physical exercise and the practice of physical skills is well recognised today. There are many accounts by top-class athletes of a heightened awareness and the deadening of pain when performing to their limits, while modern research shows that activity stimulates a variety of body chemicals that affect our brains, and particularly the emotional responses of pleasure or fear.

Passive recreation also takes up a large proportion of people's leisure time. Passive activity includes self-indulgence – 'the feel good factor' – and huge amounts of money are spent on activities such as drinking and eating, gambling, and entertainment such as the cinema and theatre.

Defining activities as active or passive is of particular importance to organisations who want to promote active leisure. Both the Sports and Arts Councils have an interest in getting people to play sport or take part in the arts. Manufacturers and retailers need to be able to identify trends in activity so that they can provide appropriate clothing and equipment. Likewise companies supplying passive recreation need to know about changing patterns, such as the uptake of Web-based activity.

Thought for the page

In sport the active/passive division is important.

Sports clothing and equipment are now fashion items as much as functional wear for sporting activities. It is important for footwear manufacturers, for example, to assess the number of customers who are serious, active sports participants who will judge the footwear by its performance, and the number that judge its fashion value.

Think it over

Many activities fall easily into the active/passive classification, but there are others which are could be classed either way. Games are particularly difficult. Chess and bridge, for example, are often regarded as sports (largely because of their competitive nature and mental discipline). Gambling, which often involves mental discipline and active effort on the part of the player, is seen as passive. Scrabble and crosswords when played competitively involve much the same mental energy as, say, bridge but are treated as passive. Football spectating is classified as passive but involves far more physical activity and mental involvement than going for a quiet stroll around the park (active).

Classify the following activities and identify any difficulties you have in doing so:

dominoes	refereeing
embroidery	yoga
bingo	do it yourself

Home-based and non-home-based recreation

This is another way of classifying recreation. Home-based recreation can be either active or passive. It is also the predominant form of leisure. This is simply because in general it is:

- cheaper (library books are free, eating a meal is cheaper at home than eating out, terrestrial TV costs nothing after the investment in a set and a licence)
- easier – as it does not involve time spent travelling, and it is not dependent on anyone else.

There are plenty of exceptions, though, as a stroll in the park will cost nothing compared to the investment in CDs or computer software necessary for in-home entertainment.

Figure 1.2 shows some of the more familiar, home-based activities and Figure 1.3 shows some non-home-based activities.

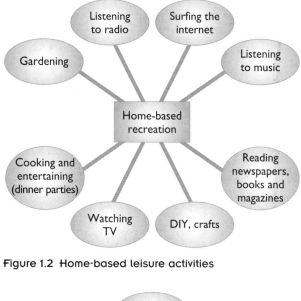

Figure 1.2 Home-based leisure activities

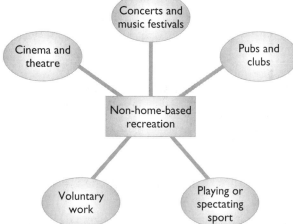

Figure 1.3 Non-home-based leisure activities

Home-based recreation is changing rapidly. For the past 80 years the mainstay of in-home entertainment has been the gramophone, television or the radio. Now the advent of digital TV, home computers and the Internet has opened up a new world of home entertainment and communications. Some people say this will cause a breakdown in society as people become increasingly insular in lifestyle, less inclined to participate in group activities and less able to communicate face to face. Others say that the speeding up of working processes will release more leisure time and encourage smaller communities. No one really knows where the electronic revolution will lead.

The home-based/non-home-based classification is used throughout the industry and for many sectors is more useful than the active/passive classification. For example, the tourist industry operators and leisure service providers are keen to know the trends and patterns of leisure behaviour, and to know what attracts people away from the home.

Try it out Try to find out how people spent their leisure time at home a hundred years ago and compare this with today's home-based activities. Discuss how the different leisure patterns would affect communication and a family life.

Scope of the leisure and recreation industry

The industry is very broadly based, encompassing three main aspects:

- the activities themselves – e.g. playing a game of tennis, going to the cinema, listening to music
- the products associated with leisure – e.g. sports clothes, videos, music equipment
- leisure services – e.g. leisure centres, restaurants or cafés, clubs, cinemas, stadia.

In general, home-based leisure is cheaper than leisure activities away from the home because it is less dependent on products associated with leisure. These products are classified as those that are consumable (e.g. food and drink, watching a film) and those that are non-consumable (e.g. a set of golf

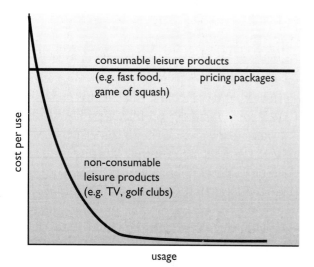

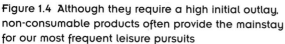

Figure 1.4 Although they require a high initial outlay, non-consumable products often provide the mainstay for our most frequent leisure pursuits

clubs, a book, a TV). The cost of consumables (a tennis lesson, pizza) remains the same each time the activity is done, whereas a non-consumable may cost more initially but is an investment for frequent future use – the more it is used the better value it becomes (see Figure 1.4).

An application of this can be seen in the health business. Many early gyms were run entirely on a consumable 'pay and play basis'. It quickly became clear that participants would stop and start their fitness programmes according to the money they could afford at a given moment. The industry responded by introducing annual membership schemes which shifted the product to being more non-consumable (large investment/unlimited use). As with many non-consumables this one-off payment was too much for many customers to pay. So the industry responded by introducing payment methods similar to that for other non-consumables – such as monthly direct debit payments.

Think it over

Television is an important home-based leisure activity. It is an excellent example of a non-consumable leisure activity requiring a one-off investment in a set. This has started to change with subscription viewing (e.g. Sky). The concept of 'pay as you view' for special events like boxing means that this specialist viewing has become a consumable activity. Many viewers cannot afford these costs despite wanting to view. This has created an opportunity for pubs to provide the service for nothing and at the same time boost sales of their own core product – drinks and, very often, food.

Conduct a survey amongst your friends and family to find out how many people have used 'pay as you view' television. How did they feel about having to pay to watch an event? Do you think this is the future for television?

Check it out

1 Give three examples each of active and passive leisure activities.

2 Note down any products or services associated with each one.

3 Which activity is likely to be most expensive? Give your reasons.

4 Explain why home-based leisure is so popular.

1.2 The development of the leisure and recreation industry

Today the leisure industry is dynamic and there are constant changes in the type of activities on offer, but up to the end of the Second World War in 1945, leisure in the UK had changed very little over a long period. Home-based leisure was predominant, with reading and hobbies, games, and then radio and television all being popular. Away from the home the cinema was a national passion, as were spectator sports and, in particular, football. To a lesser extent, people played locally in popular team games – cricket, football and rugby, and took part in

the amateur performing arts. Some of the key factors that determined this relatively long and static period of leisure were:

- a smaller proportion of earnings available to spend on leisure
- a culture that preferred habit rather than change
- limited holidays and free time
- more time-consuming chores
- few leisure goods, limited mass production
- limited personal transport (e.g. cars).

Leisure slowly started to change in the 1950s. Many people would say that the arrival of rock and roll and high employment created a new and distinct youth market, which blossomed in the 1960s. The new youth culture, with its emphasis on enjoyment and change, soon spread to all sectors of society. The new 'consumer society' saw the start of a period of continuous change in all areas, not least the leisure industry, where there has been little short of a revolution. In the process, some areas of leisure such as participation in team sports have declined, whereas other areas such as home-based computers have grown rapidly. These changes have not been coincidental, but can be explained by a variety of specific factors. Some of the main factors behind these changes are shown in Figure 1.5.

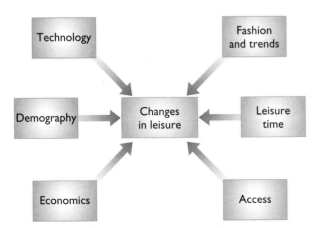

Figure 1.5 Changes in leisure in the 20th century

Fashion and trends
Spirit of the times

It is the prevailing cultural philosophy within a society that dictates how leisure time is spent. This prevailing philosophy will affect what people do, where they go, what products they want and their leisure patterns. Leisure providers try to understand and anticipate these trends, which seem to go very roughly in about ten-year cycles and can be conveniently described as the 'spirit of the times'.

Spirit of the times – the last fifty years

Post-war consumer philosophy was 'keep things simple, save before you spend money on leisure or luxuries'. This was a period when house ownership increased enormously as the older generation looked for the security they had missed in their youth. The 1960s saw the emergence of the young as major consumers of mass-produced goods with an emphasis on style and fashion. The youth culture started to dominate, but the start of consumer spending was also tempered by the rejection of material values for spiritual ones – this was the hippy age after all.

Throughout the 1970s consumption was seen increasingly as a sign of social and personal achievement. It was also a period when sport began to be seen as a serious consumer leisure activity. It saw the beginnings not only of private sector sports clubs but also the establishment of leisure facilities run by local authorities. The 1980s has become known as the 'me, me' decade. Plastic money and credit cards greatly increased consumers' buying power and allowed them to enjoy items that had previously been found only in the playgrounds of the rich, such as country clubs, flights on Concorde or safari holidays.

This riot of materialism was blunted during the late 1980s when the collapse of the

An increase in consumers' buying power has enabled people to enjoy items previously enjoyed only by the more affluent

housing market that had underpinned the economic growth reduced consumer confidence in this lifestyle. Because of the importance of the housing market this was a period that saw the huge growth of DIY and other home-based recreation.

Throughout the 1990s, while consumerism continued to flourish, people were increasingly focusing on activities that involved more personal development or private, social activity. For example, while the DIY market slumped and made only a gradual recovery, gardening enjoyed a boom that perhaps indicated a more creative attitude and a search for 'self' or peace of mind. Connected with this search is the rapid growth of the health and fitness business; and it is forecast that it will continue to grow and sustain its market for at least several years more.

What fashions fashion?

Some of the major influences on how we choose to spend our leisure time include:

- business
- media and communication
- consumerism
- marketing
- politics.

Business: Leisure has become increasingly controlled by large national or multinational corporations who have great power to influence what we do and how we spend our money. In the 1970s small, local, independent businesses such as breweries, cinemas and theatres or equipment manufacturers provided most of our leisure products and arenas, which were more individual and varied. Many of these firms, having made the initial investment and pioneered the designs, have been taken over by the increasing number of major multinational, corporate organisations. These large companies have the capacity to expand very rapidly, and having found a successful formula rely on repeating it everywhere. As a result products tend to be standardised and conform to the needs of national and international markets, rather than local ones. This is known as 'globalisation', and good examples are the chains of Disneylands and McDonalds throughout the world. Thus, taste and fashions in leisure are increasingly controlled by a small number of companies offering a small range of standardised products.

Media and communication: This area has been transformed since the 1960s with the

> **Think it over**
>
> Large companies are mainly concerned with the return on investment and the profit margins that a particular sector offers them. They may also be interested in acquiring companies that complement their existing companies. For example, MGM originally made films but by developing multiplexes they could also influence the distribution process.
>
> Try to think of a recent merger/acquisition in the leisure and recreation industry. Consider the implications for both the customer and the company.

development of new technology. There has also been a dramatic increase in the coverage of leisure and consumer pursuits on television, through advertising and programming, and in publishing in newspapers, magazines and information sheets.

Marketing: Marketing is now more sophisticated than it has ever been in identifying consumer behaviour and adapting or creating products to suit current trends. Computers allow businesses to maintain massive customer databases and to analyse survey data at speed to provide forecasts and analysis. Although marketeers would deny it, many people think that they can and do create desire for a product rather than simply supply an existing desire.

Consumerism: By the 1970s consumerism was prevalent in society. One feature of consumerism is its emphasis on the value of change, consumption and innovation. In other words, change is fashionable. There is an increasing desire to sample a wider range of leisure opportunities for short periods only. New is best; and old products are abandoned for new. Thirty to forty years ago many people would always go to the same place for their holidays, play with the tennis racquet they had had for the past fifteen years and stick to a small number of leisure pursuits over many years. At that time, spending half a week's wages on a sports shoe that would be out of fashion within a year would have been thought of as folly.

Politics: Another important influence on the leisure environment is a political one. Whether government policies and actions can create an overall 'spirit of the times', or whether they simply reflect the prevailing mood is difficult to say. What is certain is that political action can affect the leisure industry. Here are two important influences.

- *Legislation.* This can be directly aimed at the leisure industry; for example, the extension of the licensing hours, censorship, regulation of stadia design, and broadcasting regulations can all affect what providers can do and the resulting consumer experience.

- *Policy.* Governments have different policies and push through legislation to implement them. For example, in the 1970s 'Sport for All' was the policy endorsed by the government whereas now there is a greater emphasis on elitism and excellence. At the same time the welfare state, based on public sector provision, was seen as a basic foundation of our society. Since 1979 successive governments have taken the 'market economy' approach that reduces public sector expenditure and encourages business to identify, compete and provide for markets. In other words governments have encouraged the use of private sector services.

Short-term trends and fashion: Not all trends in leisure are long term and significant. There are plenty of short-term fashions that come and go, created by role models and events. Hair styles and drinking habits are obvious examples, but sports participation and product sales can be equally affected by, for instance, Wimbledon tennis (which provokes a flurry of tennis activity in the weeks around it), and a major football win. Films and television programmes also influence musical and reading habits in the short term. Who had heard of Herodotus before the film *The English Patient*? Yet for a few months this 2000-year-old classic became a best-seller in bookshops – 'as featured in *The English Patient*'. Another factor in leisure is happenstance – in other words we just don't know what is going to spark off a leisure fashion. Some things work, others don't. For example, in the 1980s the National Football League started a campaign in Britain which aimed to make American Football the national game by the year 2000. The League

Sales of products, such as football kit and accessories, can be influenced by role models

tried all the right marketing tactics but somehow it just didn't take off.

In stark contrast, the Chippendales entered Britain at a time when male stripping went totally against the grain of feminist philosophy that was prevalent at the time. Somehow, however, they hit the right note and hen parties and male strippers are now commonplace and include an audience that would have been demonstrating outside the venue 20 years ago.

> **Think it over**
>
> Think of a time recently when you bought a leisure item or went to a film or a show. Identify the various factors that influenced your decision to buy/go. What were the main considerations in your choice?

Leisure time

Leisure time is the time left over after work and other essential activities. Technological developments are said to have led to a decrease in working hours, and it is reasonable to suppose therefore that leisure hours will have increased. For many years, commentators have been forecasting the arrival of a leisured society.

However, the evidence is that work time is not decreasing but is in fact increasing. In 1998 (Labour Forces Survey) British men who were in full-time employment worked on average 45.7 hours a week while women worked 40.7 hours. Both these averages lie far above the 35-hour week that most contracts require. These high figures are particular to the UK; the average in the rest of Europe is 41.3 and 39.0 hours. There is concern that these long working hours are largely caused by a growing work ethic that has developed in this country (especially in offices) of 'good employees go the extra mile'. This can be seen in workplaces where the staff compete to be in first and leave last. The effects of excessive work are not healthy and there is official concern that these long hours lead to family breakdown and stress-related disease.

There is a paradox therefore, that leisure time appears not be on the increase but leisure consumption is increasing. Why is this?

The answer seems to lie not so much in the amount of time available, but in how it is managed. Moreover, different groups use time in different ways; for instance, there is a great variation between the way the employed and the unemployed spend their time.

The employed

These are the major consumers of purchased leisure and the group that the leisure industry focuses on. As a group they tend to have little time for leisure and are going to be tired or stressed after work. They will want to make best use of their leisure time and so the accessibility and availability of leisure activities will be a priority.

Accessible at any time: Working people increasingly want their leisure to fit in with their work schedules. They want leisure facilities to be open when it suits them rather than the staff working there. Gyms and pools that open at 6am and are still open late at night often do brisk business at each end of the day. Fast-food restaurants open until late at night and there will be a trend in the next few years for bars to stay open far later, as well as throughout the day. TV and radio scheduling has taken note of this need with programmes early and late and an increased number of repeats and omnibuses. The growth of video recording has also meant that the consumer can self-schedule. For example, you can record while you work or sleep and then watch at your leisure.

Accessible in any place: Generally, people do not have the time or inclination to travel far. At the top end of the market it is possible to arrange for trainers, therapists and cordon bleu food to come to the door. Much market research, shopping around and buying can be done on the Internet, particularly in the travel and tourism industry. And many health clubs and cinemas have sprung up near business centres to cater for workers at lunch time and before and after work, or else are positioned on busy commuting routes convenient for customers on their way home.

Designed to take up least time: The 1970s saw a boom in the number of squash players with over 4 per cent of the population playing (it is less than 0.4 per cent now). Sport was then a major leisure interest and one of the few high-energy activities that could be done in a short space of time. Nowadays there is more emphasis on personal development and the need for 'quick fix' activity is greater than ever. Health and fitness has largely replaced squash. Quite a few sports used to have extensive training programmes; now, off-the-shelf packages have greatly reduced the time needed. For instance, in sub-aqua, under the old BSAC system it would normally take

about 30 hours' training to prepare for a dive in open water, whereas under the PADI system which is used in many commercial diving centres, trainees are in the sea within hours. This need for a 'quick fix' is adversely affecting club and team sports, which require commitment by their members not only for the afternoon or day to play the sport but also to give up the extra hours for duties such as rolling pitches or washing the strip.

> **Think it over**
>
> Short and varied activities are increasingly becoming the regular pattern in many areas. Cinema programmes are half the length they once were, many plays are cut down in length, and the radio station Classic FM, which has a rapidly growing audience, focuses on musical highlights or short pieces of music rather than entire works. Even leisure hardware such as computers and hi-fi is now designed to plug in and play – whereas 20 years ago it was morning's work to decipher the instructions and assemble them. What conclusions can you draw from this? Is the modern concentration span becoming shorter and shorter?

Taken in blocks: People may work long hours in Britain but their working hours are more flexible than ever before. Nowadays short breaks of three or four days are possible, and sometimes leave can be taken all in one go to allow for extended trips lasting several weeks. In some industries, sabbaticals are encouraged so that employees can take several months off work, usually for a period of self-development. The leisure industry has been quick to provide for these blocks of time. The weekend and short-break industry is the major growth area in travel and tourism, and leisure organisers frequently provide themed entertainments (like murder mystery weekends) or cultural entertainments (like antiques or art courses and trips) as part of the 'break'. Sports 'breaks' are also popular. Hotels, travel operators and sports and leisure providers combine to produce a complete package with emphasis on one or more sports such as golf, tennis, sailing, diving and others. Intensive coaching courses in a wide variety of sports, including many unfamiliar to the general British public such as the martial arts, karate, fencing, etc., are now widely supported and seen as the mainstay of personal development.

Sampling: One feature of the leisure market that is on the increase is the customer habit of sampling various different activities and sports in quick succession rather than choosing and developing one or two skills or interests over a longer period of time. The trend now is to try something a few times and then move on to another activity. Many leisure products now have to be short and sharp and do not involve long-term commitment. This has partly come about because there is so much more on offer, and often within the same complex. Multi-activity is the next step. During one 'block' of free time you can, for instance, go to a gym, shop, eat pizza, go to a film and then out for a drink; or at home you can read and listen to the radio, watch TV, surf the Web and practise some yoga – almost all at the same time. Leisure providers are recognising this trend and, as a result, out-of-town centres such as Bluewater are providing a wide range of leisure activities on one site.

People are increasingly aware of the effects of stress and tiredness in their lives, and there is

Think it over
Thirty years ago, a seventeen-year-old with a job would have finished work at midday or later on a Saturday, gone home for a meal and then, on a 'good' day, gone out locally to the cinema, or more rarely, a party, either on public transport or on foot. Describe what you would regard as being a 'good' Saturday for a seventeen-year-old today, and compare the number of leisure activities involved, the distance travelled to them, and the time devoted to each one.

evidence now to show that they are tending towards passive activities or the less strenuous active ones. Participation in sport, as opposed to health and fitness, is on the decline. Even in a growth area like the fitness industry, many users appear to prefer light physical activity that will help them to unwind rather than achieve improved fitness. In many health clubs, pools, saunas, jacuzzis, and aromatherapy sessions are proving extremely popular.

Try it out
Look at six local leisure services in your area and assess them in terms of how 'time friendly' they are to users.

Non-employed

There is a cynical view that because they do not 'work' the non-employed have plenty of time for leisure. This is a simplistic view, and it is necessary to analyse what it means to be non-employed. There are two groups.

Non-employed people with an income: These are usually pensioners. In the years leading up to the seventies pensioners had little money to spend and entertainment was largely home-based. The increase in private pensions has meant that pensioners are becoming a major customer group often known as the 'Grey Panthers'. New products are being developed all the time to suit this market. Pensioners tend to take short breaks and they pursue leisure interests rather than sample them. They are also increasingly active and enjoy sport and health activities and buy leisure clothing to match it. This sector of the population will grow over the next 20 years and will be increasingly targeted by leisure providers.

Non-employed people with low income: Contrary to popular opinion this group does not have unlimited leisure time. People in this group develop activities that are equivalent to work.

For students this will be establishing a balance between education and part-time jobs. For the unemployed there are the tasks of looking for work, and visiting benefit offices. They may also 'work' by earning 'on the side' or by doing voluntary work. However, even if they do have more time for leisure than the working population, they will not have the income for many activities and will often concentrate on those that take up time but cost little.

Thought for the page

People are often judgemental about the unemployed and low incomed. You might hear or read comments like 'If they're so badly off why have they all got videos and TVs?' As we have seen, leisure is a basic need in our life whether we work or not. It could be argued that people on low incomes who buy TVs are in fact making sensible strategic choices on spending their leisure time cost effectively.

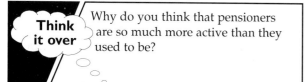

Think it over

Why do you think that pensioners are so much more active than they used to be?

Access

Access can be divided into psychological and social access; physical access and mobility; and financial access, which will be looked at later.

Psychological and social access

To be able to enjoy an activity you need to have the self-confidence to do it and to know that you will be made welcome. Thirty years ago this was not always the case.

Leisure providers were often elitist in their approach and deterred people they considered to be 'the wrong sort'. This is what is now known as 'exclusion'. It was exercised in several ways, such as vetting applicants for membership, insisting on expensive dressing or a certain etiquette. In many places it was intentional and there were certainly clubs around who would not accept people from the 'wrong' class, race or religion. More often it was institutionalised or unintentional; for instance, the Wimbledon Tennis Championships were largely watched by the middle classes who portrayed a very British style of spectating that was off-putting to anyone outside that group. With the advent of corporate hospitality (when companies block-book seats for clients and staff) and the promotion of tennis among the young, anyone can and does attend the Championships now.

In the 1970s in the inner-city areas, cricket was rarely played by the black community even though the game was popular. Studies by the Sports Council showed that the main reason for this was that the long-established white teams were not good at welcoming new black members and black people felt ill at ease in white clubs. The situation was not helped by the fact that public pitches were booked for the same teams every season. Since then, pressure from groups like the Greater London Council and the Sports Council has gone some way to rectifying this exclusion.

Many sports and recreational clubs (for example, golf and tennis clubs, choirs, dramatic societies) required applicants to be of a certain standard before they were accepted. Many novices felt that all sports associations were like this and the fear of not being sporty enough or of making a fool of oneself were major reasons why many people did not take up sport and other recreational activities. And it was not only novices; many women (who in the 1970s did not participate nearly as much as men), middle-aged and elderly people, and people with disabilities could feel that they were not suitable, or not welcome.

Leisure development workers and facility managers have, over the past 20 years, worked consistently at dispelling these ideas and obstacles. They have improved customer care and provided various methods to encourage people to take up sport such as 'taster' days and introductory courses. By the 1990s it was probably the exception rather than the rule to meet a provider who did not follow the philosophy of 'leisure for all'.

Physical access and mobility

Access to a product or service is largely determined by the factors shown in Figure 1.6.

Figure 1.6 Factors determining access to a product or service

Provision: It may seem obvious, but it is nevertheless an important factor, that it is difficult to pursue a sport or recreation unless there is facility near at hand. In the early 1960s sports provision was confined largely to swimming baths, playing fields and voluntary tennis and football clubs. It was difficult to play anything other than team games or racquet sports. Cinema, although still popular, was on the decline, and many cinemas were being converted into bingo halls. Supermarkets and retail parks did not exist and eating out was a luxury. The succeeding decades have seen facility provision grow and change with the prevailing spirit of the times.

In 1967 the first leisure centre was built in Crawley, south of London and this heralded the growth throughout the 1970s of new pools and sports halls. By 1995 there were 1,450 leisure centres and 1,300 indoor pools for public use in Britain. In the 1980s the rate of growth slowed as public funding declined, and instead there was, as a result of new technology, a big increase in the number of artificial outdoor surfaces.

The 1980s, as we have seen, was the 'me, me' decade and material consumption was high. This period saw the advent of shopping malls and retail parks with superstores that provided for the growing demand for home entertainment and DIY. At the same time, property development on a big scale caused land prices to soar, and this tempted schools and local authorities to sell off their playing fields for building, thus contributing to the decline in outdoor team games. So great was this decline that, in 1996, planning legislation was introduced to curtail the practice.

The 1990s can now be seen as a period when the leisure market was interested in self-development and small-group socialising. Gardening and outdoor entertainment (such as barbecues) flourished, and gyms sprang up to cater for the health and fitness revolution. In the mid-1970s health and fitness sessions were largely confined to multi-gyms in public sports centres but by 1999 there were at least 2,500 private health and fitness clubs, not counting those based in leisure centres. Outdoor activities have also expanded. Innovation and novelty were the rage and, consequently, many traditional leisure facilities were considered outmoded and in need of a rethink. Bars and clubs became increasingly popular, as did themed bars and multiplex cinemas, which began a renaissance of cinema-going that is likely to last into this decade at least.

Location: Leisure facilities have been built over the last 30 years on sites chosen for ease of access for the greatest number of potential customers. This has meant that they have sprung up in thickly populated areas – cities – and affluent areas of the country. They have also been built near the working areas specifically to attract workers, as well as in the residential areas. In the 1970s when public sector provision was high, new leisure facilities were built to serve whole communities. Although there were regional differences in how leisure provision was valued, it meant that leisure facilities could be found all over the country in both towns and rural areas. Now public sector provision is restricted and growth is mainly in the private sector that builds only where there is a commercial return. This has meant that there is an imbalance in location, and that there is a tendency for leisure facilities to be built in affluent, populated areas.

Access to a location can be on foot, by car for short or long distances, or by public transport. For those health clubs, gyms or squash courts built in city centres or business parks, walking distance for the surrounding workforce is the guiding principle. For leisure centres in residential areas and in major leisure and retail complexes, it has been found that roughly 80 per cent of consumers will travel up to half an hour by car, even for short-time activities. The problem here is that unless

Retail complexes, like Meadowhall in Sheffield supply ample parking, since the majority of customers come by car

there is a very good public transport service, customers have to have a car, and this can create exclusivity. It has also been analysed that for 'a day out' customers will travel two or three hours to, say, a theme park. These day trips are usually a one-off visit, and the parks therefore, in order to attract many thousands of customers and make a profit, need to be within reach of several large cities or residential areas, and, if possible, good transport links.

Transport: Obviously, transport is important because it will determine:

- the distance a person can travel
- the ability to get to a location
- the time it takes to get to a location.

Leisure providers are therefore interested in how their market travels and then will locate the facility in a place that is best suited to that means of travel.

Car ownership has increased dramatically over the past thirty years and about 80 per cent of the population has access to a car. This has meant that people can travel further to leisure facilities and are less reliant on public transport links. Public transport, however, is still important for certain groups (e.g. the elderly). Public sector provision is often concerned that facilities are near bus stops or stations, although some facilities are particularly hard to reach (e.g. the countryside, outdoor activities) and groups reliant on public transport may be excluded from enjoying them.

Think it over

Lack of access to the countryside is a serious leisure restriction for many people in the inner cities. Many outdoor activity teams like to work with this client group as it is frequently rewarding to introduce people, and children in particular, to the countryside.

How would you try to improve access to the countryside for low-income inner-city dwellers?

Air travel has been revolutionised in the 1990s, with massive price reductions making it competitive with other forms of travel. Short breaks are now possible by air, and distant events accessible for many people, so that sports fans may find it quicker and cheaper to travel to an away game overseas than to go to a match at the other end of England. Despite the criticisms about time keeping and service quality, the railways since privatisation in the late 1980s have steadily attracted more customers, mostly with the introduction of intercity day trips which include an attraction as well (such as shopping, theatre trips) at a discounted price. Many train journeys are faster now, thus increasing the distances that people will travel to leisure activities. The two leading examples are the East Coast line, and the Channel Tunnel which has opened up the continent to thousands.

Economics

The effect of the national economy on leisure is considerable. The leisure industry of today is immediately sensitive to the amount of money people have to spend, which is in turn the result of various interacting factors:

- economic wealth
- earnings and disposable income (money people have to spend on leisure)
- prices
- money supplies.

Economic wealth

The amount of money in a country determines the strength of its currency and the income and expenditure of its residents. In Britain the economy grew steadily after a recession in the early 1970s. Throughout this period Labour government policies encouraged public spending on projects such as leisure centres. The 1980s saw the rise of a free market economy under the Conservative government and private sector spending grew rapidly

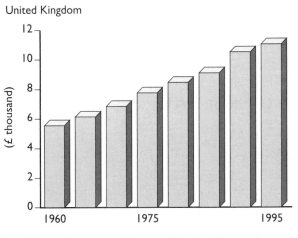

United Kingdom

[1] At 1997 prices. Figures up to 1965 are from Feinstein (1976).
Source: Feinstein; Office for National Statistics © Crown copyright

Figure 1.7 Gross Domestic Product per head at factor cost[1]

while public spending shrank. Eventually the economy overheated and went into recession at the turn of the decade. The 1990s saw a steady strengthening of the economy again with growth largely in the private sector or in partnership with the public sector.

One way of measuring this is the per capita Gross Domestic Product (GDP) which is roughly the average amount of goods and services every person in a country produces. The graph above (Figure 1.7) shows how this has almost doubled in the past 30 years.

Earnings and disposable income

Businesses usually borrow money to build facilities such as shops or cinemas or to manufacture products. When an economy is strong and interest rates are kept low, business can expand. This means that there are more leisure products and services on offer. In order to maintain this growth there has to be a sufficient number of customers earning enough in wages to pay for the leisure developments and products. Over the past 30 years there has not only been a steady growth in wages, after allowing for the effects of inflation, but there has also been a growth in the proportion of income that is available

Table 1.1 The growth of disposable income

	1989	1990	1991	1992	1993	1994	1995	1996	1997
Income per head (£)	8275	9184	9942	10592	11010	11439	12060	12759	13392
Disposable income per head (£)	5563	6184	6760	7313	7769	8020	8443	8870	9405
Disposable income as a percentage of income	67	67	68	69	71	70	70	69	70

Source: Office for National Statistics (ONS) © Crown copyright

to be spent on items other than necessities such as food, rent or mortgages. This portion of income is known as *disposable income*. It is the level of this disposable income that will determine how many leisure products and service can be sold.

Let's look at the way that disposable income has varied over the past decade (see Table 1.1). From these figures, adapted from Office for National Statistics (ONS) data, you can see that income has risen steadily. There has also been an increase in the proportion of household income that is disposable and can be spent on leisure activities as well as other consumer purchases. In other words, people have more to spend on leisure. This growth of the *leisure pound* (i.e the part of people's disposable income that they spend on leisure) has been significant.

There are considerable regional differences in income as well. In 1997, people in London and the Southeast earned 17 per cent and 12 per cent respectively more than the national average, while at the lowest end the Northeast was 16 per cent below and Wales about 13 per cent below the national average. In other words, the affluent areas will tend to attract more leisure provision than poorer areas. For businesses to succeed in poorer areas they will often have to find ways to provide their product more cheaply if they are going to attract the market.

For the first time, in 1998-99, expenditure on leisure goods and services was the largest element of household expenditure. Major changes had also occurred in the makeup of this expenditure – eating out accounted for

a large proportion and the average spent was £5.20 per week. TV and home entertainment were also important. People spent £8 a week on these, whereas in real terms they were spending only £2 a week 30 years before.

A flourishing leisure market creates a great deal of competition among suppliers who are constantly improving the quality of their products and/or dropping their prices. This means that consumers will be able to buy more of better quality for their 'leisure pound'. For example, Internet purchasing is bringing down the prices of CDs and other home entertainment products, and in clubs décor and special effects are of increasingly high quality.

Prices

We can see in Table 1.2 (opposite) how prices change each year for various purchase groups. The RPI (Retail Price Index) for all items is the average percentage increase for all purchases in a given year. We can see that throughout the 1990s leisure services increased more than the RPI, but that now the gap is closing. This is probably partly explained by the fact that in the early stages of the current boom providers were largely targeting the more affluent markets, while now they are increasingly hoping to attract the less affluent by keeping price increases low. Leisure goods are cheaper every year by comparison, and in 1998 were showing price decreases. Alcohol and catered food, on the other hand, were roughly in line with price increases overall.

Table 1.2 United Kingdom Retail Prices Index rates of change[1]

	1993	1994	1995	1996	1997	1998
Housing	−5.4	3.3	6.7	1.3	6.5	8.8
Motoring expenditure	4.3	3.5	1.8	3.0	5.3	3.1
Food	1.8	1.0	3.9	3.2	0.1	1.3
Household goods	1.2	0.3	3.7	3.3	1.2	1.2
Alcoholic drink	4.5	2.5	3.8	2.9	2.8	3.4
Leisure services	4.5	3.7	3.2	3.6	4.9	4.4
Clothing and footwear	0.8	0.5	0.2	−0.7	0.8	−0.6
Household services	3.6	0.1	−0.3	0.1	1.8	2.6
Catering	5.2	4.2	4.3	4.0	3.8	3.8
Leisure goods	1.4	−0.6	−0.1	1.6	0.2	−2.3
Personal goods and services	4.0	3.7	3.2	3.7	3.6	4.7
Fuel and light	−1.3	4.4	2.1	0.2	−3.1	−4.3
Tobacco	8.5	7.5	6.7	6.7	7.4	8.6
Fares and other travel costs	5.2	2.6	2.5	3.0	3.4	2.2
All items – RPI	1.6	2.4	3.5	2.4	3.1	3.4
All items except housing	3.1	2.3	2.7	2.7	2.4	2.2
All items except mortgage interest payments	3.0	2.3	2.9	3.0	2.8	2.6

[1] Annual average percentage changes on the previous year
Source: Office for National Statistics (ONS)

© Crown copyright

Money supplies

Disposable income traditionally meant cash in the bank. In 1970 credit cards were highly unusual, mortgages extremely difficult to come by, and loans usually granted only for essential investment such as repairing a house. Consumable goods could be bought on hire purchase, but again application procedures were tough. The idea of borrowing money to buy a boat or holiday was laughable. Today's economy has far higher levels of lending and credit, which means spending power has increased (Figure 1.8). For example, to buy a mini audio system for £500 will probably need only about £10 a month to pay for it. Someone with £100 a month disposable income could afford to purchase goods worth ten times as much (£5000) instead of the £100 of goods for a cash sale. It sounds good, but the interest payable over the repayment period will put the value of the goods up to about £700. Furthermore, if you lose your disposable income and cannot make the repayments, you are saddled with an unpaid debt.

The credit industry is booming and has risen by about 300 per cent since the last recession in 1992. Not only are more people borrowing, but the opportunities to borrow have increased with the emergence of credit banks and card companies – by 1998 these accounted for 24 per cent of the credit market, double their share in 1987. At present there is a period

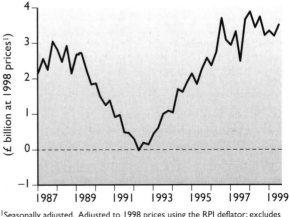

[1] Seasonally adjusted. Adjusted to 1998 prices using the RPI deflator; excludes lending secured on dwellings.
Source: Bank of England

© Crown copyright

Figure 1.8 United Kingdom net borrowing by consumers in real terms[1]

of low interest rates and there is high competition in the credit industry. Therefore credit-generated purchases are attractive. Because the economy goes through cycles it is highly likely that at some point over the next few years interest rates will rise. As a result, there will be a decline in leisure expenditure as people will find it harder to pay the interest on their purchases.

Thought for the page

Despite the opportunities available to purchase goods and increase wealth outlined in the tables, these figures are averages – that means, by definition, that there are people who are not part of the leisure boom because they cannot afford it. It is interesting to note that the often-held view that the low-income worker or non-employed person is more likely to watch Sky TV is a myth. They are least likely to watch it because of the charges.

In the past, local government has been responsible for making leisure services available to all, but for the past decade they have been financially weakened and have been unable to build new facilities or maintain many of their existing ones. They also have been tempted to follow the commercial market and increase prices. The idea of a Local Authority charging £500 a year for club membership would have been fantasy 20 years ago. Unless this trend is reversed, it is likely that we will see an increase in the divide between the 'haves' (those who eat out, join clubs, go to the cinema) and the 'have-nots' (those who watch terrestrial TV, have a kick-about in the park).

In conclusion, greater wealth and purchasing power is a major factor in the increase in leisure activity. However, regional and class variations in income and expenditure will mean that commercial providers will tend to target the more affluent at the expense of the less well off. Those without purchasing power

will miss out on the leisure revolution unless other provision can be made that is not so price related.

Demography

Demography is the study and classification of a population or groups of people. Population is often defined by:

- age
- gender
- class or social economic group
- car ownership.

There are other factors that may be interesting such as religion, disability, and where people live.

Age

The number of older people in Britain is increasing. This is due to a fall in the birth rate and the fact that people are living longer, so that older people are becoming a larger percentage of the population than they used to be. This has several effects on the leisure industry. The first is that there is a new market for products and services for the older person, and their disposable income will increase with better pension schemes. The other likely effect will be that the labour market will shrink. Unless technology dramatically improves and decreases the amount of work required by human workers, there will be a shortage of skilled workers and income will increase but so will working hours. Leisure spending for the economically active will probably increase and so will the products designed for this age group.

For various reasons, there are occasional surges in the number of births in a year. Known as a 'baby boom', this group will remain larger compared to younger and older groups until it dies. The 'baby boomers' born after the Second World War in the late 1940s and early 1950s are now approaching middle age and there may well be a correspondingly larger older market in the near future. Thereafter, the numbers in all age groups will even out, unless there should be another baby boom. A mini baby boom was forecast by the media, for the millennium year. In this case, leisure providers can be ready to cater for an increase in demand for leisure activities for babies and children in everything from baby swimming classes and 'tumble tots' to Suzuki violin lessons.

Try it out	Carry out your own survey on attitudes towards leisure across the generations. Find out and record what activities are enjoyed by two friends of your own age, two of your parents' age and if possible, two from your grandparents' generation. Ask them why they have chosen these activities and how often they do them. What conclusions can you draw from your findings, and how far do they bear out what you have just been learning?

Gender

The dramatic developments in the leisure industry in the 1970s were concurrent with, and partly the result of, the changing behaviour and role of women in society. During the last 30 years many women have changed their lifestyles and their leisure habits, and this has had considerable impact on the leisure market.

- Women have largely reconsidered the importance of the domestic role that previously took up their time. Although men do now play a greater part in domestic life, and in particular in the care of children, women have also off-loaded domestic work by using labour-saving equipment, finding other ways of getting the work done (using dry cleaners buying services, buying pre-prepared food), or by changing their domestic standards (less cleaning, fewer large, formal meals).

- Women have merged into the entire labour market and increasingly compete for salaries and jobs traditionally held by men. Thus female spending power is increasing.

- Statistics show an increase in the numbers of single women, either because women are not marrying or marrying late, or are divorced. Single women, and single men, have greater independence to follow their leisure activities when and how often they want.

Women now can pursue activities that 30 and 40 years ago were not considered suitable or appropriate; for instance, drinking, going out to pubs, and partaking in sports that were until recently men-only preserves – football, rowing, cricket, judo, to name but a few. There is a new self-image of the fit, toned woman, who exercises and is competitive. At the beginning of the 1970s women's participation in sport (as measured in terms of participation in the past four weeks, according to the *General Household Survey* or *GHS*) was about 30 per cent. By 1987 it had risen to 52 per cent (as against men 70 per cent) and in 1990 it increased to 57 per cent (men 73 per cent).

While participation rates have grown and gender differences have decreased, the pattern of activity remains distinctly different between the sexes, as can be seen from Table 1.3 (page 20) which shows age and gender difference in sport.

The *General Household Survey* for 1996 also sheds light on gender differences for leisure activities as a whole: for example, it was found in the period of four weeks before the survey, that 8 per cent of women go to leisure classes, as against only 4 per cent of men; 71 per cent of women read as opposed to 58 per cent of men. The National Day Visits Survey

Table 1.3 Leisure patterns of men and women

Activity	1986–87		1996–97	
	Male	Female	Male	Female
Watching TV	97	97	99	99
Reading books	52	58	64	71
Gardening	54	58	39	45
Walking	41	49	35	41
Snooker/billiards	24	20	5	4
Cycling	10	15	7	8
Swimming	14 (1990)	13	15 (1990)	17
Darts	14	11 (1990)	4	4 (1990)
Soccer	10	10	<1	<1
Golf	7	8	1	2
Running	8	7	3	2
Keep fit/yoga	5	7	12	17
Tenpin bowls/skittles	4	3	3	2
Badminton	4	3	3	2

Source: adapted from GHS

in 1998 showed that men prefer to eat or drink (21 per cent males, 15 per cent females), while women tend to visit friends more than men. However, it was also found that men are approximately twice as likely to take part in sport than women.

Try it out Carry out another survey into the activities of your own age group but this time identify the similarities and differences between the sexes and explain why they exist.

Class

Class affects our consumption of leisure in three ways:

- Class is often associated with disposable income. Generally, the higher classes will be able to buy the more expensive products on offer, e.g. opera tickets and subscription TV. To take the example of satellite TV, in 1999, about 18 per cent of subscriptions to satellite TV were taken from skilled manual households, while 16 per cent were from

managerial households and 15 per cent were from professional households. Unskilled households represented only 12 per cent of subscriptions (*Social Trends*, 2000).

- Class is often associated with education, and activities that require more learning tend to be pursued by the higher classes (e.g. foreign cinema and opera).

- Classes often have patterns of leisure behaviour which they conform to. One of the most commonly used measurements of this is newspaper readership. The *Sun* and *Mirror* tend to be read by manual workers, the *Daily Mail* and *Daily Express* by clerical and managerial workers, whilst the 'broadsheets' tend to be read by professionals.

Ethnic group

There is remarkably little research data available about the leisure patterns of ethnic minorities – which is surprising, since in major population areas like the big cities 30 per cent of the population comes from this group. Work has been done on sports participation, and the Sports Council, using *GHS* data for 1996, gave the rates shown in Table 1.4. Arguably, similar patterns would be found for the performing arts.

Table 1.4 Leisure patterns of ethnic groups

Participation in at least one sport and/or physical activity in the four weeks before interview by ethnic group (% of population)

All persons aged 16+   *Great Britain*

Ethnic group	Percentage participating in the four weeks before interview		
	Excluding walking	Including walking	Base
White	45.8	64.0	14,972
Any ethnic minority group	40.9	55.9	721
Indian	37.0	51.6	192
Pakistani/Bangladeshi	25.0	37.9	124
Black (Caribbean, African, other)	41.3	55.9	213
Other (Chinese, none of above)	54.7	69.8	192
Total	45.6	69.6	15,694

Source: Sports Council: New Horizons

Cultural attitudes have long been felt to affect participation in leisure activities, and this certainly seems to be the case within the Muslim community. Women often find it difficult to comply with religious requirements. Considering the high profile of black athletes it might be supposed that black participation would equal or be greater than white. As can be seen from the table, this is not the case, and only the Chinese community has a higher participation rate than the white community.

Two reasons for this might be problems with access and economics. The black community as a whole is poorer than the white and therefore has less disposable income and less personal transport. A survey run by the London Borough of Southwark found that black customers were less likely to use indoor centres than white customers, but were equally if not more active in outdoor sports. The survey found also that black customers were more likely to find activity charges off-putting and ventilation in leisure centres to be unsatisfactory. It would

seem, however, that black athletes achieve despite the obstacles they meet in access.

Technology

Advances in technology affect product and service design and the pace of change is accelerating. Products that are claimed to give a better performance are constantly appearing, for example graphite tennis racquets, advanced sports shoe design, sportswear with better moisture or heat retention properties, and digital sound on radio and TV. Such improvements often persuade consumers to upgrade their equipment.

Technological improvements reduce prices all the time. The silicon chip replaced valve-based electronics and greatly reduced the price of home entertainment equipment. Canoes used to be made of wood, but glass fibre replaced wood, which in turn was replaced by carbon technology. These changes have made canoeing an accessible and relatively cheap sport. In the musical world, mass production

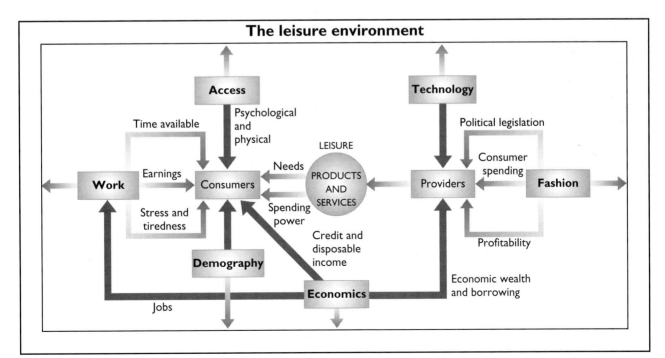

Figure 1.9 Influences on leisure choices

and use of synthetic materials have greatly reduced the price of instruments.

Finally, new technology creates new leisure experiences, and perhaps the best example of this is the computer. Computers were originally designed for work, but leisure manufacturers have adapted the concept to produce entirely new leisure concepts with computer games, game-based learning and of course the Web. Virtual reality machines are just a step away for the mass market. In sport, the health and fitness club is largely a result of advances in engineering and computer technology that have replaced the free weights and circuits that previously comprised the aids to fitness.

We have come a long way in this section. Before looking at the questions, you might like to look at the diagram on page 21 (Figure 1.9) which summarises the way the various factors covered here combine to influence how we spend our leisure time.

! Check it out

1 Describe three ways in which leisure has changed over the past 30 years.

2 Name the main factors influencing the leisure and recreation industry.

3 Explain the economic reasons behind the boom in the leisure industry in the 1990s.

4 What three factors affect access to leisure?

5 Faced with a choice of several sites what would you want to know when locating
   a) a health club aimed largely at professional workers in a city,
   b) a cinema aimed at evening and weekend entertainment,
   c) a new theme park.

6 What are the main demographic variables that affect leisure participation?

7 What is the 'leisure pound'?

8 'The leisure boom of the past 30 years is directly related to the decrease in the working hours.' Do you agree with this statement?

1.3 The structure of the leisure and recreation industry

Sectors

Traditionally, leisure facilities and activities have been provided by three sectors as shown in Figure 1.10.

Figure 1.10 The sectors providing leisure facilities

In recent years the differences between them have become less pronounced, and a provider in one sector may have characteristics which are usually associated with another sector. Such overlap is normal, but it is useful to recognise these variations when carrying out assignments. Here are two examples:

- Wimbledon Lawn Tennis and Croquet Club and Queens Club are voluntary sector clubs where for most of the year their ordinary members play tennis. Yet for three weeks of the year they stage two of the biggest and most commercial tennis events in the world.
- The water companies are private sector companies that own large areas of land for their reservoirs. These are of major recreational value for watersports, and are often provided free of charge to the public. This is a case of a private sector company providing services on a non-profitable basis.

Despite overlaps, each sector still maintains a distinctive profile as a result of its purpose and the way each is controlled and funded.

The private sector

The primary objective of private sector organisations is to make a profit. If they fail to make a profit they eventually go out of business. To make a profit they need to produce services and goods at a cost that is less than that at which they sell them. They are also in competition with other leisure providers and need to maintain value for money and keep prices down in order to retain their market share.

Private sector operators can locate wherever they want. Consequently, in areas where there is a small market there will be a lack of

Try it out Walk down your local high street or round your main shopping centre and make a list of the stores that provide records and CDs, videos, books and magazines, television and home entertainment goods and artist's materials. Now ask yourself questions, such as 'Why are there so many competing shops in one area? How many of these are large chains and how many local traders? What examples of competitive selling are they each showing?'

The past ten years have seen a national growth in health clubs and tennis centres, although this may not be evident in some less affluent regions

Think it over The West Country has, compared to other built-up areas, a sparse rural population which is less affluent than, say, the concentrated populations of London and the Southeast. In the past ten years there has been a national growth in health clubs and tennis centres, but while these are numerous in the wealthy Southeast they are less so in the Southwest; for instance, the first private sector tennis centre west of Bristol was due to open in 2000. Health clubs tend to be small if privately owned and are more usually provided by the public sector. Where large gyms do exist in the private sector they are often in hotels run by national chains in the few major towns and cities. The general conclusion is that the smaller and less affluent the population, the more likely it is for the public or voluntary sectors to be the main providers of active leisure. Does this generalisation apply in the area where you live?

operators, while in areas where there are large markets there is a great deal of competition and numerous firms will jostle beside each other to win customers. There are two types of private sector organisation – non-limited businesses and limited companies – and they operate in slightly different ways and have slightly different products to offer.

Non-limited businesses

Sole traders: These are people who set up and run a business which they own themselves. The business is usually small, with few or even no staff. Being a sole trader can be a precarious business, as the owner can raise money only from conventional sources such as personal savings, loans and mortgages, and is also personally liable for any damage or debts incurred by the firm's activities. The advantages are that the trader owns the company and can keep all profits and make all decisions. To operate legally the sole trader simply needs to declare trading to the Inland Revenue and exhibit a notice of trading on the premises. In other words, this is a convenient way to set up a small business for the first time.

Partnerships: Sometimes a group of people get together and contribute funds and expertise in order to set up in business as a partnership. Partnerships can accommodate up to 20 people. To be recognised they have to sign a *deed of partnership*. Like sole traders, the partners are personally responsible for the liabilities of the firm, to the extent that if one partner dies or breaks the agreement, the remaining partners are liable for any actions of that partner.

Small firms like these are common in the leisure industry. Many consultants, professional coaches and teachers are sole traders. So too are many actors, street and circus performers and aerobics instructors. In rural areas there is a long tradition of 'honey pot traders' – people who have set up a business that will attract the incoming visitor. Sole traders or family partnerships often own small visitor attractions, tea gardens, beach shops and cafés. In towns and popular tourist sites mobile food vendors and souvenir sellers are most likely to be sole traders.

In many cases sole traders become limited companies to avoid personal liability, but it is surprising how many long-established businesses of this sort still operate as sole traders.

Limited companies

Private limited companies: These are privately owned firms where control is passed to a board of directors. The chief benefits are that the owner/directors are not personally liable for any business debts or any damage caused by the firm unless they have been negligent of laws such as Health and Safety. In addition, in a limited company the staff and owner are paid a set salary and cannot use the company funds for any personal expenditure.

The assets of the company are owned by shareholders. In a private limited company these are usually the owners and a close circle of associates who have put money into the firm, or are on its board of directors. In some firms shares are also given to workers in the company – this is a great incentive, as staff members who work well will see the price of their shares rising. If the company is doing well these shares will increase in value and pay dividends to the shareholders. Because the firm has assets it has the security to raise money from various sources apart from high-street banks. If the company is big enough these sources will include merchant bankers and venture capitalists who will invest large amounts in a firm in exchange for shares and repayment of the loan. Increasingly, Government partnership money is also available to limited companies.

To be legally recognised, limited companies must have a certificate of incorporation. This is obtained by producing a 'memorandum of association' (which describes the name, address, objectives and capital of the company) and 'articles of association' (which describe the powers and responsibilities of the directors, the accounts, share transactions and company meetings). In a private limited company there is a board of directors (which must include a Chairperson, Treasurer and Company Secretary). Details of all limited companies are kept at Companies House (www.companieshouse.gov.uk), where this information and also the annual reports and accounts of the companies are recorded.

Private limited companies are often family firms where the directors are from one family or connected to it; or they may be partnerships that have proved successful and become too big for partners individually to risk personal liability. Some do grow very large, and the largest was the Littlewoods Pools group, which was sold in 2000 for £161 million. No matter what their size, limited companies can be recognised by the letters 'Ltd' that appear on their literature.

With the exception of a few Premier League soccer clubs, most professional sport clubs are limited companies with a small board of owner/directors. Sports clubs like these are interesting in that many of them are not successful businesses and make only small profits or even losses. The chairperson and major directors of these clubs are often wealthy local business people who have a love of the club or feel they gain status from their role. In minor league clubs these directors are often asked to lend the business money to keep it afloat.

Try it out

Return to your shopping centre list on page 23 and identify which of the companies you noticed are limited.

Are there other firms that are not in the shopping centre that you might have expected to be there? You might use a trade directory like Thomson's to identify them. What proportion of them is limited? Give any explanations you can of the differences you find between the locations.

Public limited companies (plcs): When a company becomes large and successful it needs to raise money to expand further. How does it do this? Sales income is often not enough to fund expansion and borrowing is expensive, so other methods are needed.

One way is to reduce expenditure, but usually successful companies are already efficient and cannot release significant extra funds. Occasionally, expenditure can be reduced in effect by government incentives – subsidies, for example, which might reduce, say, the rates for several years if the company locates to new business premises in a deprived area. (This is another example of how political factors can influence leisure provision.)

The conventional way to raise funds is to 'go public'. This means that the company offers shares to the public, and the income from the share issue is then used to fund further development. To be able to sell shares the company has to become 'listed' on the Stock Exchange which is the marketplace for shares of all sorts. The company is now called a public limited company or 'plc'. While providing extra cash, the issue of shares means that the board of directors loses some of its control and is now answerable to the shareholders. In the leisure industry this can be an important factor. In private companies the directors are frequently personally concerned and wrapped up in the business and what it does, whereas shareholders are primarily interested in making a profit on their investment. This means that shareholders will sometimes make decisions that will result in radical changes of the product or even result in selling it off.

Thought for the page

Contradiction in terms: A 'public' company is not so called because it is in the public sector like local government, nor does it mean that the company is no longer a commercial organisation. The term 'public' simply means that anyone can buy shares in the company – in other words the shares are not limited to a few individuals.

Central to the success of any public company is that it must make a profit – largely from sales but also from other sources like selling off parts of the business. Good profits means that the value of shares goes up, which keeps the shareholders interested in the company. In addition, while a large proportion of profits is reinvested in the company, a proportion (dividend) is given back to the shareholders as an annual cash bonus. The board of directors determines policy and strategy for these companies and in this respect is independent of shareholders. However, once a year there is an Annual General Meeting in which the board reports back to shareholders who can take this opportunity to elect to continue or change the board or request a change in its strategy.

Public limited companies, while few in number, play an important part in the leisure industry. They usually do this by operating in a variety of sectors and by supplying the market through chains of outlets.

They do this in two ways. One way is by making strategic decisions such as what sort of companies will complement their existing ones or what sectors of the market are going to be profitable. They then go and either make offers to other plcs to buy a part of their organisation, or they look around and find private limited companies that are doing well and buy them. By doing this they are entering their desired market and eliminating competition that may come from a successful private company operating in the same market.

Plcs that own lots of other businesses are known as 'parent companies'; very often they do not refer to their identity but prefer to maintain the brand images of the companies they own – for example, the Pearson Corporation owns Alton Towers and Madame Tussaud's both of which have very strong brands of their own.

The other way is to make *economies of scale* that can be passed on to the customer. Many plcs, for example, will carry out the administration and accounting for the entire operation through a central point, and buying decisions are made by a central buying team. Possibly the most important of these economies of scale is that they have enormous buying power and can achieve significant reductions

CASE STUDY – Aquaria

Sea Life Centres were originally a small chain of aquaria and sea life interpretation centres set up in resorts by an entrepreneur called Ian Cunningham. They were fairly low-key affairs but highly enjoyed by the public. They were then acquired by Vardon plc, a major player in the leisure industry. Vardon took the original concept and expanded it by building new purpose-built centres in premier locations including London, Birmingham and Blackpool. After only a few years Vardon found that other areas of leisure such as bingo were more profitable and that indoor wildlife attractions are particularly prone to fluctuations in the weather. For instance, in a bad summer there is a fall in the number of visitors to resorts while in hot spells visitors stay on the beach. Major public companies do not like fluctuations of this sort and much prefer sustained growth. Meanwhile Ian Cunningham, like many entrepreneurs, maintained an enthusiasm for the sector he started in. First, he developed another chain of wildlife centres. Then, in 2000, he became the operations director for the biggest wildlife project in Europe – the Eden Project in St Austell.

Strategic development of this sort is frequent and when researching businesses you should check the latest information about ownership and company results rather than rely on textbooks and older sources, which will quickly go out of date.

Questions

1 What type of organisation were the original sea life centres?

2 What type of company is Vardon?

3 Why did Vardon build sea life centres at inland sites like London?

4 What is Vardon's principal aim?

in the prices charged by their suppliers. This is an important reason why high-street plcs, despite having to pay high rents for their sites, can still offer customers the lowest prices in town.

The big players in the leisure industry

While there are thousands of leisure businesses in the country, the lion's share of the business is conducted by a few giants who build up and break down their businesses to find the best mix of products to achieve maximum profits and means for expansion (see Table 1.5). Theme parks are an exception to this as there is only one product or outlet. The secret of success is to find a formula and brand it by having chains of outlets, which normally are identical in the services and products they provide. In other words plc ownership normally means less variety of product and service. On the other hand, tried and tested formulae mean that there is often a higher consistency of service.

In the limited company, customers will determine turnover. To find extra funds to expand the services, the company relies on shareholders and lending institutions. (Figure 1.11)

Plcs that are dedicated to active leisure are few and far between. The leader is First Leisure which owns nightclubs, ten-pin

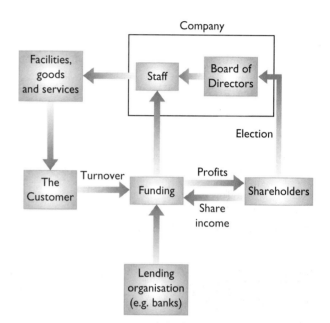

Figure 1.11 Information about the private sector changes daily. You can keep up to date with changes by looking at websites and the business pages

Table 1.5 Some of the biggest players with their 1999 turnover in £ million

Company	Profits	Turnover	Interests
Granada	1056	4102	TV, motorway services, hotels, Spirit health clubs, TV rental
Scottish and Newcastle	324	3294	Breweries (28 per cent of European brewing), pubs, Pontins, Center Parcs (being sold in 2000)
Bass	572	4686	Hotels and pubs, catering, Hollywood Bowl, Coral bookmakers (breweries sold in 2000 to Interbrew 32 per cent of European brewing)
Whitbread	325	2966	Pubs, restaurants, hotels, David Lloyd Centres (breweries sold in 2000 to Interbrew)
Hilton	163	4299	Hotels, Ladbrokes bookmakers, Living Well health clubs
Rank	108	2041	Gambling, publications, cinemas, restaurants, holidays
Pearson	480	3332	Internet (AOL) publishing, theme parks (Alton Towers)
News Corporation	N/a	N/a	Broadcasting, publishing

Note: N/a = not applicable

Source: uk.biz.yahoo.com/p/ukie/i/545a.html

bowling centres, health and fitness clubs (Esporta and Riverside), family entertainment centres and theatres.

Try it out

Have a look round your town and identify six private sector outlets in a variety of leisure sectors. Now either enquire or research what sort of companies they are and who the parent company is, if any.

You can read about the cut and thrust of public companies in the financial pages of the national newspapers but probably the best source is *Leisure Week* (**www.leisureweek.co.uk**).

The public sector

Figure 1.12 shows the bodies which make up the public sector.

Figure 1.12 The bodies which make up the public sector

Its main functions are:

- to develop policy
- provide facilities and services that are not adequately supplied by the private sector and are for the 'common good'
- provide funding and other help to the voluntary sector (and sometimes the private sector).

Local government

In Britain the philosophy of the 'common good' has existed for about 200 years. Today it is accepted that it is in the common

The public sector supplies services, such as museums, that benefit all the community, which the private sector tends not to supply

Thought for the page

Providing recreation is expensive and if the cost was passed on directly to the customers they would be in for a nasty shock. For example, the cost of a swim might be as much as £10, while hiring a good-quality grass football pitch might cost as much as £100 per hire. Entry to a park might be 50p, and libraries would have to charge maybe £1 a loan for each book borrowed. Of all the services provided in the public sector only dry indoor sports facilities and artificial turf areas charge something like a profitable price.

interest of the community that facilities and services are supplied free or at subsidised cost to everyone. In other words access is not determined by ability to pay. The 'common good' encompasses rights such as the right to education and the right to health and the freedom of assembly. In leisure, public provision for the common good is interpreted as the provision of culture, health and exercise. Traditionally, this meant the provision of libraries, museums and galleries, parks and recreation grounds, swimming pools and baths and assembly rooms. These facilities are expensive to create and maintain and because they had to be priced as cheaply as possible to allow all the people access they were non-profit-making. Private enterprise would therefore not be interested in providing them – although there were exceptions, such as Boots the Chemists, who ran a penny lending library in their shops until the 1950s.

Local government is the organisation that provides services, facilities and other support for the common good that other sectors cannot provide. It is managed by an 'executive' of officers who work in various departments answerable to a Chief Executive. In many Local Authorities there are separate Leisure Service Directorates. There is, however, a trend to amalgamate these into super-departments under big umbrellas such as education or community services. The officers' role is to advise councillors on policy; they in turn decide policy and the officers then devise objectives and deliver the policy.

Councillors are members of the local community who stand for election to the Local Authority (often but not always representing a political party). They are unpaid and part of their job is to make sure that local people get the services they need or want. This may be a multi-million-pound swimming pool, but it is more likely to entail making sure that potholes in park paths are filled or that vandals are kept out of a children's playground. So the work of a Local Authority is controlled by councillors who in turn are answerable (through the ballot box) to the local residents.

Who controls the Council? The Council is in control of a Local Authority. It sets policy and fixes budgets, which the executive has to

identify ways to achieve. In most Councils this means a constant cycle of Council meetings when officers get approval from councillors to carry out their work proposals.

The investors in a Council, and therefore services, are the local community who pay their taxes (Figure 1.13). They tend to judge the worth of the Council by the size of their taxes and the value of the services they get for them. Very often their judgement is very personal – for example, the success or failure of the Council to remove an overhanging tree. In the private sector people are more likely to register their dissatisfaction with their board by selling their shares. In local government taxpayers will register their dissatisfaction by voting out the councillors. Councillors can therefore be very sensitive to public opinion, so there is a potential weakness in the system in that they will tend to make decisions to keep voters 'sweet' rather than attend to the strategic development of the community even when it is in the common good. They will always manage to offend someone.

Local Authority income: The vast majority of council services are loss making and need to

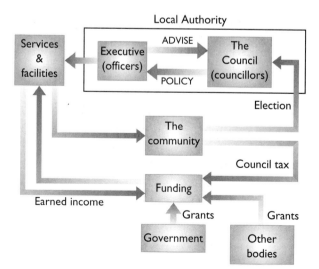

Figure 1.13 The public contributes to services, as well as using them, by entry charges and tax. Indirect influence can be the result of electing councillors

Try it out

- Go to your library and find out the following about your Local Authority:
- the name of your local councillor and the size of the vote in his/her ward in the last election. Is the councillor vulnerable to small changes in voting?
- who is your Chair of Leisure?
- who is the Director of Leisure and what services does she/he control?

be subsidised by income. This comes from three main sources (Figure 1.14).

- *Local taxes*: Local residents pay the council tax, a tax based on the type of home they live in (which is determined by the Council). This accounts for about 25 per cent of income. Local business pay a non-domestic rate set by central government.
- *Government funding*: Central government determines on an annual basis the amount of money (about 48 per cent) it will give individual Local Authorities, based partly on their needs but also on how economic they have been in their past spending. Central government also sets the non-domestic rate. This means that local government has control of only about 27 per cent of its income which is why it extremely difficult to maintain or expand its services.

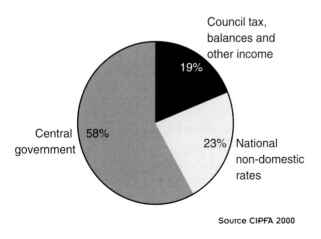

Figure 1.14 Local Authority budgets

Council tax, balances and other income 19%

Central government 58%

National non-domestic rates 23%

Source CIPFA 2000

- *Earned income*: Some council services are paid for at point of use. Leisure services directorates are often the major income-raiser in a Local Authority and will charge for most entertainment and sporting activities. Earned income makes up about 2 per cent of Local Authority income in all.
- *Grants*: Grant aid is increasingly available to develop and improve services. Occasionally, central government grants are available, such as Partnership Funding. Most grants come either from quangos, such as the Sports and Arts Councils or English Heritage, or European social and economic funding programmes. A major injection of grant aid for leisure has come from Lottery funding and, to a lesser extent, the Foundation for Sport and Arts (FSA). Both of these organisations have a responsibility to fund not only sport and art but also culture and heritage projects. Since 1998, Lottery funding has been increasingly diverted from its original targets and is now being used for educational and health projects.

Restrictions on local government activity: Borrowing, which is a common source of income for private sector firms, is legally forbidden to Local Authorities as a source of funds. This means that they are often unable to build facilities which, while expensive, would have a profitable business future. If they had been able to borrow to develop it is likely that the health and fitness business would now be largely a public sector one.

A second legal restriction is that Local Authorities can build only within their administrative boundaries. This means that they cannot set up chains of facilities. It also means that they cannot always locate a facility in the best place.

A third restriction is that they are not allowed to trade except to sell their normal services. For example, many Local Authorities have plant nurseries and could over-produce in order to sell to the public as well as plant up the parks. Central government would consider this a threat to private enterprise and therefore deters such activity.

At the end of the 1980s the Local Government Act required Local Authorities to compete against the private sector to run services such as ground maintenance and sports facilities (other than dual-use ones), which, until then, had been run entirely by local government. This was called Compulsory Competitive Tendering (CCT). Many Councils wished to maintain their workforces and therefore had to increase their efficiency by reducing expenditure and raising income. One result of this is that many Local Authorities concentrated on their revenue-generating skills at the expense of providing for the common good. The 1990s therefore saw steep rises in charges for usage and the deterioration of many higher-cost services, resulting, for example, in fewer flowers in parks, shorter library opening hours, fewer book purchases and the closure of smaller sports facilities in poorer communities.

Legislation has now changed and CCT is kept as a last resort for poorly performing authorities. What has replaced it is a series of performance targets ('Best Value') that are government approved. These are not just financial and many of them are concerned with achieving social objectives and ratepayer satisfaction with services. Best Value will still require Local Authorities to run their services efficiently, but it will also require them to satisfy their residents. This can be done by:

- providing: high-quality services
- enabling: providing contacts and resources to allow the community to access funding and support
- empowering: giving responsibility for resources to community groups.

It is quite likely that over the next 20 years we will see the decline of the Local Authorities' involvement in the direct provision of facilities. The emphasis will be on brokering agreements between the private and voluntary sector organisations and the community. This should result in high-quality facility provision that still can be accessed by using development programmes and concessionary pricing.

> **Think it over**
> Look at your local community and identify what leisure activities the Council provides directly. Which ones do you use? Do they offer good value?

Central government and public bodies

Central government is responsible (among other aspects of government) for creating policies for the national governing of a country. As with Local Authorities, the balance of power is divided between the policy-makers (ministers) and an executive of civil servants who put the policies into action. For leisure the principal department is the Department for Culture, Media and Sport (DCMS) (**www.culture.gov.uk**).

The full extent of the DCMS input into leisure can be seen from Table 1.6 (page 32).

There is often tension between local and central government because the latter has no direct control over the former. Thus a national government can have difficulty in persuading Local Authorities to perform in a way that reflects its national policies. For example, working in partnership is central to the government policy at present, but some Local Authorities prefer to be the sole provider of a service, or wish to protect the employment of their substantial workforces.

Table 1.6 Expenditure by the UK Department for Culture, Media and Sport

£ millions

	Museums and galleries (England)	Libraries (UK)	Museum/ library archives (UK)	The arts (England)	Sport (UK)	Historic buildings, monuments, and sites (England)	The Royal Parks (UK)	Tourism (UK)	Broadcast-adverting and media (UK)
1991/92	204	129	-	212	47	-	-	44	22
1992/93	217	133	-	235	50	-	-	46	79
1993/94	212	114	9	235	54	164	23	46	85
1994/95	223	146	9	195	53	164	24	44	93
1995/96	228	171	9	200	54	164	25	45	98
1996/97	214	114	10	195	52	162	23	46	97
1997/98	211	104	12	196	50	156	22	45	43
1998/99[1]	204	89	12	199	49	144	21	45	99
1999/2000[2]	220	90	16	228	52	148	26	48	104
2000/01[2]	223	91	20	238	52	144	22	48	104
2001/02[2]	247	95	19	253	52	142	22	47	105

[1] Data are Estimated Outturn

[2] Data are plans

In other cases, a local council will have a majority of councillors with different political allegiances from that of the government and will not want to follow central policies.

In order to overcome inertia and resistance, central government exercises considerable direct power by its control of grants and of Local Authority spending. Grant aid and policy implementation are largely achieved through quangos (quasi-autonomous non-governmental organisations) or non-departmental public organisations, to give them their official title. They are currently often referred to simply as Public or National Bodies. These are policy-making organisations which usually exist separately for Scotland, England, Wales, and Northern Ireland – an important fact to remember when researching, as each organisation will provide totally different information.

The main purposes of public bodies is to:

- influence thinking and practice about all aspects of their selected areas, including leisure

- redirect funding from the Department in the form of grants to local government and voluntary sector groups
- advise ministers on policy and the needs of the sector
- manage certain services and resources that fall beyond local interest. (English Heritage looks after sites of historical significance, UK Sports Institute runs drug testing in sport, Sport England operates the national sports centres).

As with other public sector organisations there is an executive that advises on and implements policy and which is directed by a council. In this case the council members are not elected publicly but are appointed by the chairperson and the council. The chairperson is directly appointed by the government minister. The selection criteria appear to be a mixture of expertise in the industry, capability as a policy-maker, political persuasion and demographic group. Public bodies are meant to be independent, but it is likely that, overall, their strategies and policies will reflect those of the ministry involved.

Most funding by the DCMS is made through the public bodies. For example in 1998-99, DCMS funded the arts to the sum of £199 million, of which £191 million was directed by the Arts Council. Grant aid is therefore a major source of income for public bodies. However, there are other sources, for example conference fees, publications, sponsorship and one-off grants for special projects. Look at the figures below (Table 1.7) for the two major recreational quangos.

Table 1.7 Income for Arts Council and Sports Council

Income 1998-99 £m	Arts Council	Sports Council
Government funding	190	31.5
Sponsorship and grants	0.34	0.0
Other	0.25	5.5

(Source: annual reports)

Public bodies normally have a chain of regional offices that work with leisure providers. They give advice and administer grant funding to predominantly local government or voluntary sector providers (e.g. local authority sports clubs). However, with the Arts Council there is significant funding of the private sector especially in the performing arts. Public bodies also direct grant aid to other major public sector organisations. Sometimes these are smaller public bodies (the Environment Agency is funded by the Countryside Commission) or government-initiated Trusts which technically fall within the voluntary sector. For example, the National Coaching Foundation and the Youth Sports Trust are funded in this way. The National Parks Authority is likewise funded by the Countryside Commission.

Leisure covers a wide range of activities and attracts the involvement of several quangos. Some of the more important ones are shown in Table 1.8 in the next column. For convenience we have listed the English organisations, but links to the other bodies can easily be made through their websites or the DCMS site.

Table 1.8 Organisations in the leisure industry

Organisation	Main responsibility
Arts Council (www.artscouncil.org.uk)	Develop and fund the arts
Sport England (www.english.sports.gov.uk)	Develop and fund sport
English Tourism Council (www.englishtourism.org.uk)	Support and promote tourism
Council for Museums, Archives and Libraries (www.resource.gov.uk)	Develop and fund museums, archives and libraries
Countryside Commission (Agency) (www.countryside.gov.uk)	Development and funding of countryside, water and waterways. Develop activities on them
(English) Heritage (www.english-heritage.org.uk)	Manage and promote ic histor sites

National training organisations (NTOs):
A major concern of national government is that skills and performance in British industry are slipping behind those of other countries. It is government policy that all industry should have the highest standards and that the workforce should not only be highly trained and skilled but that individuals should constantly refresh and extend their existing skills and knowledge. This is known as 'lifelong learning'.

In order to meet this aim, NTOs have been created to identify the competence and needs of the workforce in all sectors of industry and develop training programmes to achieve the required high standards. With regard to active leisure the following NTOs are particularly important:

CHITO – museums, galleries and heritage www.myi.org.uk

HTF – hospitality www.htf.org.uk

METIER – arts and entertainment
www.metier.org.uk

SPRITO – sports and health and fitness coaching and management, play, caravanning, piers, theme parks, stadia, equipment manufacturers www.sprito.org.uk

! Check it out

Try surfing the Internet. While annual reports are very useful, you will find instant and up-to-date information available on the many websites. Research the following:

1 Who is the Secretary of State for Culture, Media and Sport and who are the ministers?

2 What are the priorities of the Arts Council?

3 How much grant aid is given to village halls?

4 What are Sport England's key responsibilities?

5 What percentage of sports and recreation organisations have become Investors in People?

The voluntary sector

The voluntary sector is divided into two parts. In the first are the many activities that are run by volunteers – these are local voluntary organisations. In the second are charitable organisations that use volunteers but have a salaried administration.

Local voluntary organisations

The British are renowned for their involvement in voluntary work for the public good. Virtually every village in the country will run a cricket or football team, arrange dances and events to raise money for the village hall and organise a fête which may also act as a visitor attraction for the day. It is the same in towns and cities. Street carnivals are organised by volunteers, as are amateur operatic and drama groups. If you look at the programme of a public community centre

you will see that most of the performances will be by amateur groups, and likewise in a sports hall most of the block bookings will be from local sports clubs.

The impact of this work is impressive. For example, in sport alone the Sports Council estimate in their 1995 survey that 1.5 million people volunteer their help, giving on average 125 hours service a year. This is the equivalent of 108,000 full-time workers. Put another way, if these volunteers were paid at, say, the minimum wage, the sports industry would have to find a wages bill of around an extra £0.65 billion!

Despite the huge and unrecorded number of voluntary clubs and organisations, almost all are guided by the same set of principles and organise themselves in similar ways. Voluntary organisations work on limited budgets. They need to minimise the costs to their members but at the same time they must work in credit if they are not to become bankrupt. In other words, they need to keep running costs to a minimum, keep membership fees within the pocket of their members and constantly seek other sources of income, such as grants. This requires dedication and co-ordination, and to work successfully groups depend on elected committees who organise the programme of activities, seek out new resources, administer the organisation of the club and maintain the club's equipment and buildings.

The budget is usually based on membership fees and regular grants. Most clubs will have particular goals to aim for besides the everyday running of the club; things like new showers, a lighting rig or sound system or stage. They will often then apply for grant aid from funding agencies such as public bodies, charities or Local Authorities; or they will have fund-raising events such as a dance, fête, dog show, car boot sale, sponsored ride, etc.

Like all boards, the committees are responsible for the legal and financial affairs of the club and therefore produce an annual report and audited accounts. They also represent the group at meetings with, say, the Local Authority. In larger clubs the committee might appoint a small number of paid workers. For example, a golf club might appoint a ground staff and club secretary, a tennis club might employ a professional coach, and an amateur theatre group with its own premises might employ a steward.

Many voluntary clubs have run for many years on short-term planning and without long-term policies. Their activities suit the needs of the members and need no more regulation than perhaps a set of rules and regulations about conduct and behaviour and the election and powers of the committee. Many clubs continue happily in this way. However, the arrival of the Lottery as a source of funding for arts, community and sports clubs has meant that clubs have had to become more 'professional'. When applying for a Lottery grant a club now has to produce a business plan, with detailed drawings (if appropriate) and costings, and details of suppliers. The club must also identify how it is meeting the needs of the community as a whole, and whether it is supplying the activities that the Lottery Public Bodies regard as priority. The impact of this is that clubs are increasingly being run like small businesses. Committees are composed of professional members; clubs have long-term policies and business plans with well-defined financial targets.

Voluntary organisations normally measure their success in achievement not profit. Depending on their aims, achievement might be measured against the competition, or by critical acclaim, the size of the club or simply the enjoyment it gives members. If they do make profits, the money is invested in development or maintenance or held back for a rainy day.

Volunteers in some leisure sectors may also become involved in the organisation of their activity away from the local area. This is particularly the case in sport where governing bodies represent the needs of players and organise the sport as a whole. For example, the secretary of a local football club may sit on a series of committees going right up to Football Association headquarters.

Try it out Identify a local voluntary club that has received grants and explore the path of funding back to its original source. What changes (if any) did they have to make to club practice to achieve the grant?

Voluntary institutions – governing bodies and charities

Governing bodies: Sometimes voluntary organisations with a common interest will get together to create a governing body. They do this in order to fulfil certain needs, sort out common problems or seek arbitration on disciplinary problems or interpretation of rules. The English Cricket Board is an example. Often the governing body will take on a life of its own and develop activities not normally associated with the voluntary sector. It will often employ waged staff and it may develop its own profit-making trading activities. For example, several governing bodies have their own web servers, and credit cards available to their members.

Whether governing bodies are in the private or voluntary sector is a matter of debate. They serve the needs of voluntary organisations, but they are often non-profit-making limited companies (i.e. companies that make profits but invest them back into the company). The English Cricket Board controls sponsorship and broadcasting rights for the game, and the income from these contributes to its turnover of £83 million with profits of £6 millon.

However, much of this is ploughed back into the Cricket Foundation – a trust that is set up to put money into the grassroots of the game. Apart from trading profits, governing bodies also earn income from a levy applied to member clubs and from grant aid from quangos like the Central Council for Physical Recreation or the Arts Council.

Charities and Trusts: Charities used always to be seen as non-profit-making organisations that raised money for good works, using volunteers. Because of a relaxation of the laws governing the meaning of charitable status it is now much easier to register as a charity. There are also significant financial and tax advantages for private and public sector organisations if they do so. Thus, several public bodies have been set up recently as Trusts (e.g. the Youth Sports Trust). Organisations like this, despite their good work, are perhaps quangos in sheep's clothing and best thought of as in the public sector. Even Local Authorities are following this route – for example, Torbay Council in 1999 placed all its countryside assets and services in trust, while High Wycombe for many years has run its sports centres as Trusts.

The objectives of a charity are often to provide resources and opportunities for people who would otherwise not have access to them. In other words, where Local Authorities serve the common good, charities serve the special need (which the public sector cannot afford to do) – for example, a person in a wheelchair requires a full-time personal helper at certain times. Charities can reduce staff costs by using volunteers, and can therefore provide support more easily than Local Authorities.

Many charities now buy material resources such as vehicles, and invest in training workers rather than relying so much on volunteers. This makes these particular charitable services expensive because of the equipment and professional staff required.

Thought for the page

St John Ambulance provides an essential service on many thousands of occasions which could not run without their presence. Despite using volunteers, vehicles and the training of the staff cost a great deal. The charity offsets the costs by fundraising, donations and by sometimes charging the event organisers to whom they are providing a service.

In the heritage industry, conservation and maintenance costs are major items of expenditure, as is the purchase of collections and buildings. Flag days and membership fees are frequently insufficient to meet these costs and a more commercial outlook is being taken. This new direction means that charities are becoming more entrepreneurial and commercial. Charities cannot themselves trade but they can set up 'trading companies' that can open shops, sell merchandise (e.g. Oxfam, Age Concern, Cancer Research and many others) or even offer accommodation and operate at a profit. This can greatly increase the funds they raise.

In some cases this approach is taken to extremes and the organisation has much of the appearance of a private sector organisation. For example, the National Trust operates shops in both the high street and on their properties, which are very similar to companies in the private sector like Past Times. In the leisure sector the National Trust is probably the most successful example of a 'profit making'

Try it out

You can identify a charity by the registered charity number on its letterhead and other documents. Identify three charities you have become aware of as a result of their marketing and commercial operations. Find out (e.g. from annual reports) how they raise funds, and the importance of the various sources.

CASE STUDY – The National Trust

Major charities require an increasingly business like approach to funding their charitable activities and have a different financial profile from traditional or smaller charities that may fund themselves more from gifts, 'flag days' and grants. One of the most established and successful charities in leisure (heritage and countryside sectors) is the National Trust. Their income for 1999–2000 is shown below:

	£m	%
Membership	60.0	31.0
Property income		
Admission fees	8.5	4.0
Rents and other income	23.3	12.0
Grants	5.6	3.0
Trading	11.7	6.0
Investments	26.3	12.0
Gifts and appeals	10.0	5.0
Legacies	36.0	19.0
Other income	12.0	6.0
All income	192.0	100.0

Just over 25 per cent of income comes from the traditional charity sources of gifts, appeals and legacies. The National Trust like any organisation is required to make the best use of its assets and it does this in two ways. It has large-scale investments in stocks and shares, which provide a major source of income. Being a major landholder it can also raise considerable sums by renting out farms and houses on its estates.

Providing public access is a major charitable aim of the Trust and is also a major source of income. The Trust gets income in three ways that have direct parallels with both public and private sector leisure providers.

- *Admission fees:* These are point of entry income.

- *Membership fees:* Many visitors find that they get better value by subscribing as members of The Trust (magazines, free entry, access to special events). As the subscription is a *charitable donation* the Trust is able to claim tax back. Membership fees also produce a stronger regular cash flow.

- *Trading:* This is secondary income produced by its trading company from gift shops, restaurants and holiday cottages.

Like the private sector it also has a sizeable marketing (or communication) budget of £19 million. The view that charities are run by volunteers and therefore have low staff overheads needs to be reconsidered. Although there are 38,000 volunteers the Trust also employs 3,700 staff whose wages account for 50 per cent of total expenditure – a proportion that is not dissimilar from many private sector leisure providers.

Despite these similarities with the private sector the Trust still maintains a key characteristic of all charities in that surpluses are put back into the charity and not distributed to members.

charity. In 1999 it was staffed by 3,381 paid staff and 38,000 volunteers, which is a far higher ratio than many charities, such as the British Paralympic Association who often have only a handful of paid staff.

In conclusion, this section has covered a good deal of information and you may find it useful to refer to the summary shown in Table 1.9 (page 38). Look out for the exceptions.

Table 1.9 Summary of how the various sectors in the leisure and recreation industry operate

Attribute	Voluntary	Public	Private
Income	Membership fees Donations (Increasingly) Trading Loans Grants	Taxes Grants Sales Government funding	Share issues Owner's capital Sales Loans Government incentives (unusual)
Expenditure	Kept low (e.g. use of volunteers)	Kept low (e.g. wages)	Higher if justified by results
Budgets	Income driven	Expenditure driven	Income driven
Market control	Recipients and customers	Electorate Customers	Customers
Policy and financial control	Board of trustees Committee	Elected representatives Central government	Board of directors Financiers (banks, shareholders)
Overall objective	To provide for specific needs	To serve the common good	To make profits
Staffing	High voluntary component	Occasional voluntary component	Minimal voluntary component
Operational area	Can extend	Restricted (quangos nationally, Local Authorities locally)	Can extend
Trading	Charities and trusts can trade through a trading company	Trade restricted to normal services only	Trade essential

Check it out

1 What is the difference between a limited and a public company?

2 Identify a major leisure company and the interests it has.

3 What are the principal objectives of private, public and voluntary organisations?

4 Explain why local government leisure provision cannot expand easily.

5 Give other names for a quango – what are the principal roles of these bodies?

6 Which bodies lead policy and funding for the countryside and for museums?

7 Which organisation determines policy and funding for leisure?

8 Comment on the statement: 'Because they are charities, organisations like the National Trust are not allowed to trade and compete with the private sector'.

Key components in the leisure and recreation industry

Recreational activities fall into six key components (often referred to as industries, e.g. the heritage industry), which are in turn divided into sectors (e.g. the museum sector). The classification is somewhat arbitrary and sometimes activities will fit into more than one category, and other activities are hard to put into any category, such as bridge clubs – are they sport or a home-based leisure activity?

The main components are shown in Figure 1.15.

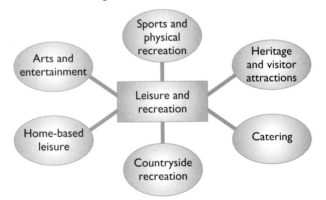

Figure 1.15 The main components of the leisure and recreation industry

Arts and entertainment

This is a huge industry that includes many sectors. The main ones are shown in Figure 1.16.

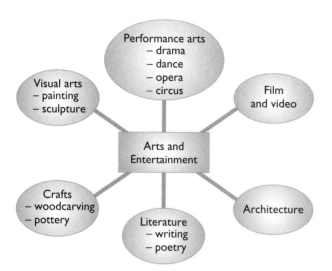

Figure 1.16 The main components of the arts and entertainment industry

Arts

The arts, apart from commercial cinema and theatre is a precarious industry where losses are easily incurred due to high costs and a very fragmented market. Consequently, sponsorship and grant aid plays an important part. The public sector plays the most significant part in funding the arts. At the top is the Arts Council, which in 1999 gave out £188 million in grants. Much of this came from the National Lottery. Some of it was given out to Regional Arts Boards who then fund local projects. Much of the grant aid is given directly to organisations and individuals. They range from the prestigious (The London South Bank complex – £13 million, and English National Ballet – £3.8 million) to the less well known but just as important innovative ventures (such as the Red Shift Theatre Co. which received a writing commission of £2,500, or the Tabernacle Children's Costume Band at the Notting Hill Carnival which received £700).

Try it out Try to find a copy of the annual report for the Arts Council to see just how huge and varied the grants programme is!

Thought for the page

The private sector sees good commercial value in associating itself with the arts. Private sector sponsorship of the arts is massive. Many productions are supported by local business, and national companies like Barclays Bank have funded initiatives that encourage new audiences to support the arts. In recent years there has been a shift by many firms from using sponsorship as a vehicle for corporate hospitality to using the arts to demonstrate social responsibility. The Barclays Full Houses scheme, for example, offered 10,000 people the opportunity to visit their local theatre for the first time.

The Arts Council is not the only national public sector organisation to be involved in the arts. One important group is The British Film Institute (BFI) (www.bfi.org.uk) which is responsible for supporting film-makers, and the promotion of the British film industry. Local Authorities play an important part as well. They employ arts development officers who promote the arts locally and will support local artists. Some larger authorities employ established artists 'in residence', who work in the area promoting their art and creating commissioned pieces. Local Authorities are major providers of galleries and performance space such as town hall stages or community theatres or even parish halls. In some cases, such as the Lyric Theatre at Hammersmith, London, or the Alhambra in Bradford, the Local Authority is a part-owner of a commercial theatre.

Voluntary sector groups also contribute to this sector. Numerous trusts and collectives exist to develop minority arts or provide for specialist audiences. For example, Wolf and Water in Devon is a drama trust dedicated to working with people with special needs. You will often find that small performance groups such as travelling drama companies are registered as educational trusts, as much of their work will be in schools.

Charitable trusts are an important source of funding. Many of these, such as the Gulbenkian Trust and the Getty Foundation, were set up by the super-rich of past years (the Bill Gates of their time). A recent newcomer on the scene is the Foundation for Sport and Arts. Amateur groups are another example of groups in the voluntary sector. Such groups include choirs and musical ensembles, some of which have an international reputation (e.g. Glasgow Tabernacle Choir).

Entertainment

Classified as entertainment are popular performing arts and spectacles. The voluntary sector is important here as nationwide participation in amateur dramatics and music is a popular pursuit. Public provision is also in evidence but has changed in recent years. Thirty years ago most town halls had a civic entertainments programme of films, theatre and musicals. This has largely disappeared now and has been replaced by events programmes that are organised by various departments. For example, many sports centres will host travelling theatre and ballet companies such as the Royal Exchange Theatre Group, while arts officers will book in tourism exhibitions. In the streets and parks outside, groups are invited to put on events such as the hot-air balloon events in Bristol's parks.

It is the private sector that monopolises entertainment. There is a flourishing small-business sector that includes pub

entertainments and single artistes such as party and street entertainers, but the bulk of the market is contained within three areas:

- cinemas
- theatre
- stadia/arenas (these have a dual role in also providing for sport).

Cinema: Cinema was in its full glory in the first half of the 20th century. Then the establishment of colour television, followed by the arrival of video players, meant that cinema was losing its appeal. The cinema companies were not updating their buildings, most of which were built in the 1930s, and were finding more profit in selling them off as bingo halls or DIY warehouses. Some survived this decline by aiming at niche markets (e.g. Corner House in Manchester). These 'art house' cinemas show foreign-language and art films. Another specialist approach has been the promotion of Asian cinema, which is locally popular. The main market is, however, for commercial English-language films. In the late 1980s there was a major review of how films were presented. This resulted in the invention and rapid growth of multiplexes. They have the following features:

- modern luxurious buildings with high-quality projection and sound
- multi-screens to show several films with a small audience for each

Think it over The multiplexes are a major growth area in the leisure industry. In 1996 the major players were:

- Showcase with 18 multiplexes
- UCI with 31 multiplexes
- Odeon with 60 multiplexes
- Virgin with 30 multiplexes.

Would this growth in cinema have been possible without the appearance of major national holding companies? Do you think this market will continue to expand? What will be its main competition?

- easy access often at out-of-town centres
- good customer care, such as advance booking facilities
- focus on key viewing markets with good disposable income (e.g. the 18–30-year-old market).

The formula is working and cinema has recaptured its place in our leisure life. The night out at the cinema is once again becoming a regular feature in many people's lives.

Theatre: The British are quite conservative in their choice of theatre. The London theatres are highly profitable with a city audience and a huge tourist market. Even then, they increasingly stick to a formula of musicals or familiar plays with big-name actors. Out-of-London theatres have to focus even more on a popular menu if they are to survive. The package largely consists of touring West End shows, nostalgia and tribute bands, comedians and spectacles like circus and ice shows.

The main London theatre companies are:

- Delfont Mackintosh Theatres (2)
- Ambassador Theatre Group (8)
- Really Useful Theatres (13)
- SFX (Apollo) (4).

Apollo Leisure is the leading national chain.

However, the fine performing arts (opera, theatre, ballet) often need to be subsidised despite the media coverage and sponsorship they attract, and Lottery money is a major part of ballet and opera funding. Lottery money also subsidises regional and national theatres. One of the problems is that theatres are concentrated in major towns and cities away from much of the population. Over the past 20 years several theatre companies such as the Royal Exchange, the National Theatre and the Royal Ballet have started to go on tour. For several weeks they go on the road taking portable stages with them, which they erect in sports halls and similar venues in places distant from theatres. Other small

touring theatre companies have also sprung up and play in smaller, unusual venues.

Arenas and stadia: These are essentially large multi-purpose buildings for very large audiences (e.g. several thousand upwards). Arenas (indoor) for example are just as likely to put on conferences and trade exhibitions as they are concerts, while of course stadia (outdoor) are principally designed for sport. A new type of stadium is being built that lends itself more to entertainment, and in some cases the stadia are covered to allow all-weather performances (e.g. the New Den at Millwall FC).

Many arenas are owned by Local Authorities or development corporations (especially in towns where conferences are a major source of income). Good examples of this are the various halls and centres in Birmingham, including the National Arena and National Conference Centre, which, while owned by the City, are managed by the NEC group. Other major arenas include the Royal Albert Hall, Wembley Arena, Earls Court and Olympia in London, the SECC in Glasgow and GMEX in Manchester. As arena entertainments slowly expand, it is likely that larger companies will take over the management of several facilities. One firm that is doing so already is the American group Ogden

The Royal Albert Hall hosts a variety of events from classical music concerts to indoor sports events

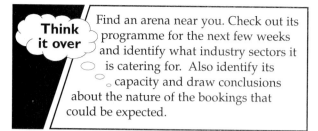

Think it over — Find an arena near you. Check out its programme for the next few weeks and identify what industry sectors it is catering for. Also identify its capacity and draw conclusions about the nature of the bookings that could be expected.

Entertainments, which focuses on arena and theatre management.

Sports and physical recreation

These activities can be grouped as follows:

- informal recreation (play, walking, gardening)
- competitive sport (e.g. football, tennis, golf, motor racing)
- outdoor activities (e.g. sailing, climbing, gliding)
- health and fitness (e.g. jogging, yoga, gym-based activities).

As with other areas of the industry, activities can often be put into more than one category. For example, swimming in the sea or a leisure pool is informal, swimming in a conventional pool is informal or health and fitness, and swimming with a club can be competitive. There can also be many more categories such as wheel-based sports, indoor games, and outdoor games.

The role of the sectors varies (as shown in Table 1.10) and depends on the context of the activity, and this will determine the 'profit – common good – special need' continuum we

Table 1.10 The role of the sectors in various sports and recreational activities

Component	Private	Public	Voluntary
Informal recreation	Equipment Magazines Clothing	Provision and upkeep of public facilities such as parks and footpaths Occasional development projects	Support organisations
Amateur competitive sport	Equipment Magazines Clothing Profitable facility service provision (tennis centres)	Facility provision Support development (inc. instruction) Funding	Facility provision Instruction Coaching Administration and regulation
Professional competitive sport	Owned and managed Equipment Magazines Clothing Broadcasting	Some funding Regulation Some broadcasting (BBC)	Sports Clubs rules of the game Sells events (e.g. Olympics)
Outdoor activities	Equipment Magazines Clothing Profitable facility and service provision (ski slopes, dive centres)	Provision and upkeep of public facilities e.g. wilderness areas Funding Regulation Instruction (e.g. youth service activities)	Facility provision Instruction Coaching Administration and regulation
Health and fitness	Equipment Magazines Clothing Facility and service Provision when profitable (gyms)	Facility and service Provision (pools, gyms, yoga) Funding Development	Little involvement (although the YMCA is a major provider)

identified earlier. For example, professional sport, because of its live and broadcast spectator market is run by private sector companies. In amateur competitive sport the private sector restricts its role largely to selling equipment and clothing. The public sector supports the voluntary sector by providing facilities and support services.

Each component has a different profile in the type of facilities and services it produces.

Informal physical recreation or exercise: This is the most popular activity throughout the country. The General Household Survey (*GHS*) shows that in 1996 44 per cent of adults went for a walk of over three miles at least once a month, while 88 per cent of children went swimming at least once a month. Nobody knows the hours children spend playing or adults spend in the garden or doing strenuous hobbies. We pursue these activities because they are cheap, readily available and don't require a great deal of skill. The enjoyment we get from them often depends on the quality of the environment we do them in. This means that the work of Local Authorities or public bodies like the National Parks Authorities in maintaining public parks, beaches and open spaces is very important.

Competitive sport – professional: Most people immediately associate sport with the professional game. This means that they are spectators, and it is the spectator money from the gate and broadcasts that underpins professional sport. For many years professional sport was supported by personal investment by local businessmen and it was not always very profitable. Facilities were often run down to the extent that some were dangerous for crowds. In the past decade the situation has improved as professional sport has become far more profitable. Providers have found that profits increase when standards of customer care and corporate hospitality are improved and other entertainments like concerts are

catered for. This has led to the building of a new generation of high-class stadia and race tracks and other facilities where the key services are:

- presentation of the core event
- merchandising
- catering
- safety and security
- large crowd and customer handling.

In addition, professional sport is increasingly conscious of its public image and often involves itself in sports development services in the community. Sometimes the professional clubs (e.g. Arsenal FC) make facilities like sports halls and facilities available to the public.

Competitive sport – amateur: Amateur sport is geared around participation and voluntary clubs. However, because land and buildings are expensive, many clubs use the facilities provide by Local Authorities. You can see in Table 1.11 just how many people are members of voluntary clubs.

Many outdoor sports clubs have their own facilities although there is an even greater number of players who use recreation grounds. In all there are about 78,000 pitches in the country. Thirty years ago amateur

Table 1.11 Sports club membership and clubs

It is estimated that there are 150,000 sports clubs in the country covering a wide range of sporting and recreational activities. The top ten sports in terms of club membership (and respective club numbers) in 1995 were:

	Members	Number of clubs
1. Football	1,650,000	46,150
2. Billiards/Snooker	1,500,000	4,500
3. Golf	1,217,000	6,650
4. Squash	465,000	1,600
5. Bowls	435,000	11,000
6. Sailing	450,000	1,650
7. Angling	392,000	1,750
8. Rugby Union	284,000	3,250
9. Lawn tennis	275,000	2,800
10. Swimming	288,000	1,950

Source: Individual Sports Organisations; Keynote, *UK Sports Market; 1996 Market Review*

sport was largely centred on outdoor team games. Since then, the invention and rapid rise of the sports centres and other indoor facilities have meant that many indoor clubs have opened or existing clubs have expanded. There are now about 1,500 such centres and another 1,300 swimming pools in public ownership. In the past ten years there has been a move to private sector provision in certain profitable areas, notably tennis. Examples are Invicta plc's County Rackets and David Lloyd, who claims the distinction of becoming the first 'active leisure' company to go public; and to be then subsequently acquired by a giant, Whitbread.

Competitive sport means participation and developing skills and there is a sizeable industry (largely in the voluntary and public sectors) for coaches and instructors. However, despite its profile, competitive sport is on the decline and organisations like Sport England are concerned that as a nation we are losing our sporting skills and becoming less fit and healthy. To fight against this there is an extensive industry of sports development that targets and works with all sorts of groups to promote sporting activity. For example, many governing bodies have big school-based programmes, and Local Authorities will run schemes in deprived areas where people cannot afford to play sport or go to health suites.

The concern shown by public sector bodies and the voluntary sector for development is not just centred on attracting new participants. It also focuses on the entire range of skills needed to produce the training and competitive opportunities that are required to achieve excellence in any sport. Indeed, the pursuit of excellence and of high achievement at international level is part of the sports policy of the current government.

Outdoor activities: Facility provision is also essential for outdoor sports, meaning the upkeep of the environment, and this is

Private sector companies are the main providers in profitable areas of the industry

regulated by the organisations under the Countryside Agency umbrella, such as the Forestry Commission, Local Authorities or the National Trust. For most participants activity in the natural world is occasional, and more time will be spent in training in built facilities such as pools or climbing walls. In most cases these are provided by Local Authorities. Once again, in profitable areas such as skiing, sailing or sub-aqua, private sector companies are the main providers.

Accommodation is an important part of outdoor activities since people are away from home. Usually this is provided by the private sector in campsites and holiday parks or hotels. One major exception is the Youth Hostel Association (**www.yha.org.uk**), which provides accommodation in the form of 230 youth hostels and is a voluntary sector organisation.

Health and fitness: Finally, we come to the health and fitness business. There are now at least 2,500 private health and fitness clubs in the UK – it is a boom industry that many young people see as the exciting, glamorous and profitable place to work in leisure.

There are also several hundred publicly owned health suites in leisure centres. Although there are many exceptions these health suites often lack the investment to be as attractive or as well equipped as private sector gyms. Because of funding and the inability of Local

Authorities to operate outside their area, it is probable that the private sector will increasingly dominate the market and eventually also manage and invest in public sector facilities on behalf of Local Authorities.

The central product of these clubs is the fitness room consisting of cardiovascular equipment (the machines) and perhaps free weights; the activities areas for aerobic exercise; and, frequently, areas with small pools, jacuzzis and saunas. There is a large female market, and beauty treatment rooms are also often included, as is a bar with catering. Whereas leisure centres and pools emphasise facility provision, fitness suites emphasise instruction and coaching. Aerobic activity is led and there is a high level of assistance and training for those using the fitness room.

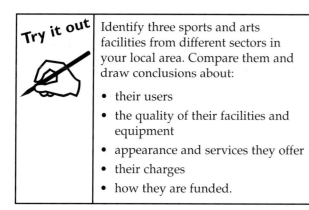

Try it out

Identify three sports and arts facilities from different sectors in your local area. Compare them and draw conclusions about:

- their users
- the quality of their facilities and equipment
- appearance and services they offer
- their charges
- how they are funded.

Heritage and visitor attractions

The heritage industry concerns buildings and materials that have historical value. Thirty years ago these were largely stately homes, castles, ruins such as Stonehenge, battlefields, or the museum collections of artefacts. Major arts collections were also included, but these now fall into the arts sector. Heritage was often about how the rich and famous had lived or what they had collected, or about culture (e.g. Shakespeare). Now this category has expanded to include a much wider interpretation of what is of historical value, and also to provide accompanying entertainment. This has meant that:

- The definition of historical value has changed, and the history of ordinary people is of as much if not more interest than that of the rich. Industrial heritage is also particularly important, as is seen for example in the Beamish Open Air Museum, or Telford Gorge Industrial Museum, which is now designated as a world heritage site.
- These sites are now brought to life in an entertaining and not just educative way. For example, at sites like Wigan Pier, actors in period costume interact with visitors, and at Portsmouth Dockyards there is a host of interpretation materials and guides to answer questions.
- Because of the importance of the visitor market new facilities are built that have no historical significance, but are simply based around a heritage theme, for example, the World of Beatrix Potter or the London Dungeon.
- The owners of existing heritage sites add on visitor attractions to the extent where the attraction features more than the initial historical monument. For example, Longleat Safari Park has combined visiting a stately home with seeing exotic animals.

Whether the attraction is a theme park or a museum, the organisers will do their best to employ all the techniques of facility management to look after the customer and make the product interesting and exciting. In a theme park the excitement of the rides is a key feature. In a museum finding new ways to present information and items is essential, and these include hands-on experiences, quizzes, actors and films. The difference between a visitor attraction and a heritage site is that the latter involves considerable work behind the scenes which the public never sees. Table 1.9 shows the most popular tourist attractions in Britain between 1981 and 1998.

Table 1.12 Visits to the most popular tourist attractions in Great Britain

Museums and galleries	1981	1991	1998	Historic houses and monuments	1981	1991	1998
British Museum	2.6	5.1	5.6	Tower of London	2.1	1.9	2.6
National Gallery	2.7	4.3	4.8	Windsor Castle	0.7	0.6	1.5
Tate Gallery	0.9	1.8	2.2	Edinburgh Castle	0.8	1.0	1.2
Natural History Museum	3.7	1.6	1.9	Roman Baths, Bath	0.6	0.8	0.9
Science Museum	3.8	1.3	1.6	Stonehenge	0.5	0.6	0.8
Theme parks				**Wildlife parks and zoos**			
Blackpool Pleasure Beach	7.5	6.5	7.1	London Zoo	1.1	1.1	1.1
Alton Towers	1.6	2.0	2.8	Chester Zoo	-	0.9	0.9
Pleasureland, Southport	-	1.8	2.1	London Aquarium	-	-	0.7
Chessington World of Adventure	0.5	1.4	1.7	Edinburgh Zoo	-	0.5	0.5
Legoland, Windsor	-	-	1.5	Knowsley Safari Park	-	0.3	0.5

Source: National Tourist Boards

© Crown copyright

Many heritage sites are owned by Trusts and limited companies that have been set up to manage individual sites, while many stately homes are owned and run by two big organisations:

- **English Heritage (www.english-heritage.org.uk)** is the national body responsible for the management, promotion and conservation of 400 archaeological sites and the historic environment
- **The National Trust (www. nationaltrust. org.uk)** is a trust set up in 1895 to preserve places of historic interest or natural beauty. Its sites include a range from Paul McCartney's teenage home to stately homes like Waddesdon Manor. Table 1.13 shows a list of its top ten sites by number of visitors:

Table 1.13 Top ten National Trust sites by visitors

	99/00	98/99
Fountain's Abbey and Studley Royal	297,201	275,831
Wakehurst Place	295,942	282,699
Polesden Lacey	252,275	234,540
Stourhead	220,817	213,285
St Michael's Mount	191,364	204,596
Quarry Bank Mill	171,262	186,927
Bodiam Castle	170,755	164,063
Corfe Castle	166,508	163,618
Sissinghurst Castle Garden	163,740	171,885
Lanhydrock	158,951	166,193

Source: National Trust Annual Report 1999/2000

Theme parks and many visitor attractions are usually private sector organisations. In the major conurbations the owners are often public limited companies like Whitbread. In the traditional holiday areas such as the Southwest they are often family concerns. In south Devon, for example, most of the leading visitor attractions such as Kent's Cavern, Babbacombe Model Village and Woodlands Theme Park are all family owned.

There has been a rapid growth in visitor attractions in the past 20 years but there are now indications that it is slowing down. This is because there is a limit to the number of day visits tourists will make or can afford and it would seem the market is becoming saturated. Recently, following Millennium funding, several facilities, such as the Royal Armouries in Leeds, have got into serious difficulties as a result of low visitor numbers. The theme park sector is also near saturation. The 'white knuckle ride' is at the core of many theme parks' success, taking several years to develop at a cost of millions. The concept was imported from America where the more consistent climate encourages regular visitors. In the UK operators have literally caught a cold. A bad summer can mean a huge drop in profits, which the major companies that usually own the parks do not welcome. Furthermore, theme parks are very competitive and, to keep their markets, massive investments are needed for new rides.

However, the leading theme parks are too big to close down and as long as a particular company owns a park it is likely to make further investment. This is especially so with the 'white knuckle rides' and these will continue to get bigger, scarier and more fantastic for many years to come.

'White knuckle rides' at the core of theme parks' success will continue to get bigger and scarier

CASE STUDY – The Royal Dockyards

In Portsmouth, several heritage trusts exist within the naval dockyard. They include HMS *Victory* and *Warrior*, the *Mary Rose* Tudor warship, the Royal Naval Museum, apprentice workshops and an interactive IMAX display of a modern naval warship. These Trusts have created a joint marketing and ticketing organisation, Flagship Portsmouth, which coordinates these functions and gives the impression, to over 400,000 visitors a year, of an integrated operation, achieving economies of scale.

Visitors can choose to visit one or more of the exhibits, where guiding, interpretation, display and merchandising are run by each separate Trust. The purpose of these activities is to provide income for the behind-the-scenes activities which are the core mission of each Trust and of primary importance.

These activities include:

- conservation – protecting the collection. The *Mary Rose* hull is constantly sprayed with preservatives and kept under low lighting in a polythene tent
- collection and cataloguing – collecting, storing, displaying and recording items
- archives – storing records, samples of documents and items of interest
- education – providing educational services and products (e.g. loaning items to schools)

- academic research – (e.g. forensic examination of the *Victory's* sails showed where the flax came from).

To give you some idea of the significance of the above activities, the following table shows the abbreviated income/expenditure account for the Mary Rose Trust in 1999.

£000

Income		Expenditure	
Visitor related	752	Visitor services	389
Net income from trading	138	Collection	86
Grants	328	Conservation	238
Donations	191	Education	56
		Publications	116

Questions

1 What is the core mission of Flagship Portsmouth?

2 HMS *Victory* is a wooden battleship. Identify three concerns that the Trust may have in letting 319,000 visitors come aboard every year. How might these concerns be addressed?

3 Using the figures above, explain the importance of promoting the *Mary Rose* as a visitor attraction.

4 Give three benefits of creating a joint marketing and ticketing organisation.

Museums: Museums are not usually run by the private sector, largely because of their high costs. These are due to necessary conservation, staffing, security and buying new items for the collections. Many museums started life as private collections which were later donated to the nation or the local community. They therefore tend to be one-off institutions run as Trusts (the national museums) or owned by the Local Authorities. They are registered with the Museums Commission.

Libraries: Apart from their lending services which we will look at later, libraries are heavily involved in the heritage sector. As with museums they have a back-room role of collecting important documents and publications including maps, and making these available to the public. This is known as the records and archives service. In some cases these records are kept nationally at the Public Records Office and other similar buildings. Local libraries keep local records and are much used by local historians and researchers and those who pursue the growing hobby of genealogy. They may include parish records and rate books, land deeds, and collections of letters.

Catering

Leisure catering includes pubs and clubs, restaurants, cafés and takeaways and fast food. It is the giant of the leisure industry and with a small number of exceptions is firmly placed in the private sector. Outlets often stand in high streets, on highways or near to visitor attractions, and sometimes companies will operate a 'concession' within a visitor attraction under their own name – for example McDonald's at Alton Towers. Not so apparent, but nevertheless important is contract catering. A catering company provides a service according to the specification of the 'client' and often under the client's name. Many leisure centres and theatres buy in service in this way. Contract catering may be behind the scenes but it is big business – for example, Compass plc is a world leader and the highest-placed leisure sector company on the Stock Exchange.

The catering sector has various components that make eating out an enjoyable experience: the provision of food and drink; entertainment, such as jazz at Pizza Express, games or almost anything in a pub; and security in the form of door staff. Eating out is an increasingly important and available leisure experience and consumer tastes are changing rapidly in response. The fast-food business is booming with a current growth rate of 30 per cent. This growth is at the expense of takeaways and cafés, and especially of pubs and clubs. Despite the fact that in 1999 about a fifth of all adults visited a pub every day, the pub industry is fighting to survive. It is under direct competition from new-style bars which are often preferred by drinkers in their twenties and who are the major market segment. But there are also changes in drinking habits, 'drink/drive' laws have crippled the country pub trade, and lunchtime drinking at work is increasingly frowned upon. To combat this decline, theming is being introduced into pubs to provide a wider range of services. These include:

- family pubs with child-friendly drinking, meals and play facilities
- Irish pubs with live music
- super-pubs which rely on space and music
- real ale pubs (e.g. Slug and Lettuce) that accentuate the quality of the beer, as well as reading, board games and ambience
- sports pubs with large-screen broadcasting of popular games.

Fast food tends to be run by chains that can make economies of scale by producing the same product in each outlet. Many breweries have followed this trend and operate chains like Harvester restaurants within their pubs. In contrast, cafés, restaurants and takeaways tend to be family owned and single outlet, although sometimes such ventures flourish and grow into chains such as Café Rouge.

Try it out — Look at catering in your area and identify evidence of how the trade is changing.

Countryside recreation

The countryside is the natural, national playground and one which is used by walkers, ramblers and those involved in more active outdoor activities. A survey in 1998 by the National Centre for Social Research showed that 1,427 million day visits to the countryside were made and a further 241 million to the coast, and this excluded figures for those on holiday and activities by those living in the countryside. Table 1.14 shows their estimate of what people do when they get there.

Like any leisure facility such usage will have an impact which in turn will lessen, and even threaten, the leisure experience itself. Organisations working in countryside recreation are therefore primarily stewards who maintain, manage, and regulate the

Table 1.14 Day visits: Main activity by destination

	All visits (%)	Town/ city (%)	Country- side (%)	Seaside/ coast (%)
1. Eat/drink	18	20	14	10
2. Visit friends	17	19	13	9
3. Walk	15	8	34	27
4. Shop	12	15	3	5
5. Entertainment	6	7	2	2
6. Hobbies	5	5	5	1
7. Indoor sport	5	7	2	4
8. Outdoor sport	4	3	6	4
9. Drive, sightsee	3	2	5	17
10. Swim	3	3	1	3

Source: NCSP 1998: Day Visits Survey

environment and also produce information and education. In most cases countryside organisations do not provide leisure activities themselves, but they will allow others to do so if they are sure that they will treat the environment with respect.

Two national bodies are especially important. They are the Countryside Commission (CC) and the Forestry Commission. They work under the umbrella of the Department of the Environment and execute government policy and assess direct grant aid. A third group that is funded by the Countryside Commission is the Environment Agency (EA) which has a major role in controlling the quality of water in inland water sites such as rivers and canals. The EA has strong regulatory powers and their permission is needed for any recreational activity that concerns water.

Another important organisation funded by the Countryside Commission is the National Parks Authority. This is responsible for the regulation and interpretative service inside twelve National Parks, which are designated areas of significant natural beauty and wilderness. They form the premier locations for many adventure activities. While these parks are unspoilt they are lived in by villagers and owned by a variety of landowners (mainly private, but also the National Trust, the Water Authorities or the Ministry of Defence). Apart from the Brecon Beacons National Park, the Park Authority itself is an insignificant owner. The Commissions and their agencies therefore control the countryside with a carrot of grants backed by a whip of enforcement. They also have a strong managerial function and are responsible in particular for keeping open and expanding the footpaths and cycle and bridle paths.

The Local Authority has a part to play in managing and regulating country parks. In many cases it also owns the land and will act as landlord to any tenants in the park, such as farmers. As with the National Parks they also have a strong mission to advise the public about correct usage of the countryside, and this is carried out by countryside rangers – who not only work in the parks but go out and visit local groups and schools.

Home-based leisure

Home-based leisure is cheap, easy and relaxing. The equipment most popularly used – radios, videos, TV sets, HiFis, computers, books, CDs, games, DIY and gardening materials, and home fitness machines is normally provided by the private sector. The main exceptions are the library lending services (books, videos and audio) in the public sector and the Talking Book voluntary service for the visually impaired.

Thought for the page

There is no legal obligation (statutory duty) for Local Authorities to provide leisure services. Local libraries are the exception, and are required by law to be provided. Local libraries are directly controlled and funded by Local Authorities but have a national body that represents them – the Libraries Association (**www.la-hq.org.uk/index.html**).

Except for broadcasting this component is retail based. The BBC is the only other public sector body apart from the libraries and is controlled by its governors who are responsible to the DCMS. The other broadcasters are in the private sector and are responsible to the Independent Broadcasting Commission for maintaining standards. All broadcasters have a duty to educate, inform and entertain. The BBC as a public broadcaster has a duty to deliver to all sections of society and not just those sections who will produce the largest viewing figures. Hence the difference in the content and style of programmes. The BBC is funded largely by the licence fee, supplemented by its sales of programme-based merchandise, while independent broadcasting is funded by advertising and its programme planning is directly affected by viewing figures. The situation produces a similar tension to that found in other public/private competition. The BBC is finding it increasingly difficult to bid for broadcasting rights to popular events or programmes.

! | Check it out

1 What are the main sectors of the arts?

2 Why does the private sector tend to provide entertainment and not art?

3 What is the most popular form of active recreation?

4 Give examples of public and voluntary organisations that are involved in the countryside.

5 What services do heritage and visitor attractions share?

6 Name a major public body and a charity that are involved in the heritage industry.

7 What are the four main sectors of leisure catering?

8 Give an example of a themed pub and explain why they have been introduced.

9 Describe your own home-based leisure activities.

1.4 The scale of the UK leisure and recreation industry

Any industry such as the leisure industry has an impact on a national economy in that it circulates money and employs people who in turn spend their wages. Knowledge of this impact is not just of statistical interest but has real practical importance for three reasons.

• It identifies where there are shortages or over-supply of provision. This allows the private sector to seek out new markets, while other sectors can plan the scale of provision of services and facilities. For example, pub drinking sales are declining so the breweries are turning to bars and clubs, or theming pubs. In the sportswear industry manufacturers know that the market is turning away from trainers to outdoor sports footwear.

- It supports the case for the importance of the industry and its impact on the economy. Most grant aid decisions involve consideration of the effect of a sector or project on the local economy. In deprived areas of the country leisure has been used both to reduce unemployment and increase income. One of the major claims of the Countryside Alliance in their support for the minority leisure pursuit of fox hunting is that the sport supports a huge rural economy.
- It allows us to estimate the needs for the supply of labour and the training required to improve the standards of service in the industry. Most NTOs are currently running surveys to measure the workforce so that they can plan training courses.

Knowing why you want to know about the scale of the industry is easy, but calculating it is difficult because of inevitable doubts as to the validity of data and insufficient knowledge of how it was extracted. The main problems are to do with classification and recording.

Classification: Statistics are defined by the categories you use to put them in. For example if you are looking at book sales and include all books, then you could not say that the total sales represented leisure reading because there would be academic textbooks, which is work. Neither could you say the sales represented home-based leisure as a proportion of books are bought by businesses and institutions. Another example of the difficulty of categorising arises in catering.

It is very difficult to find out if someone eating a Big Mac is doing so because they are eating out with friends or eating their meal at work. However, for convenience fast food is included together with pubs and clubs in the leisure catering category.

In countryside activities similar problems occur. For example, there is little or no information about sales of leisure activities such as pony trekking or numbers of people taking part in sailing. In contrast there are good sales data on clothing used for outdoor activities. Can we therefore use this as an indicator for the growth of the outdoor activities industry? Probably not with great confidence. The reason for this is that most sales of outdoor clothing are for fashion reasons. A quick inspection of the City of London is likely to reveal more Helly Hansens and Barbours than you would find in a yachting marina or a riding stables respectively. Therefore, if you are going to use secondary data to reflect participation you have to be very sure about how associated the data is with the activity concerned.

Try it out	Conduct a survey amongst your fellow students to find out how many people own fleeces. Find out if the fleeces were bought for outdoor pursuits or as fashion items.

Classification is a particular problem when it comes to workforce data. The government sets the standards for this classification and uses a system called Social Occupational Classification (SOC). It was designed many years ago before the leisure industry was so significant. As a result, workers in leisure are often classified in sectors that bear no relation to leisure. For example, in the caravan industry there are three sectors of the workforce – manufacturers, sales staff, and holiday park staff. The first of these are classified and mixed in with coachbuilders and automotive workers, and the second in car sales. Only the holiday park staff are put into a leisure industry category.

Measurement: To add to these problems there are difficulties in measurement. By and large, retail sales statistics are accurate even though they may not indicate participation rates; for example, most sports clothing is not used for sport. In the service sector visitor statistics are often used. There are problems here, however, as in areas where there is high repeat business (e.g. sports centres, live spectator sports) entrance figures do not indicate the number of individual customers. Thus, when the figures from 1995 state that there were 115 million visits, this obviously does not mean people as there are just over 50 million people in the entire country.

In some areas of the industry there are no gates through which to count participants. Many of the English Heritage sites are free and open, the countryside is totally free, and there are no measurements of outdoor activists, day trippers, ramblers or participants in field sports.

Sales units and attendance figures are often collated by trade associations or government bodies such as the Chartered Institute of Public Finance and Accountancy (CIPFA) which monitors Local Authority leisure usage. In many cases the only way to measure is to run surveys, but these are expensive and give only a snapshot view of the time and occasion when they were carried out.

Apart from the *GHS* and other 'rolling' surveys much survey data quickly becomes out of date. Even the *GHS* has problems, because small samples are used and they cannot be sub-divided into categories. For example, *GHS* in 1996 showed that 6 per cent of the population attended leisure classes, but there is no information as to what the 6 per cent did in these classes (learning a language? playing

sport?). Similarly, despite the large following of martial arts it is still not big enough to feature as a significant activity in the survey, let alone be separated into the various fighting styles.

The measurement of the workforce is even more problematical. The leisure industry has high proportions of casual, part-time and temporary workers, who, if they are asked to say what they do for a government survey will often give their main job which is not leisure related. For example, a bar attendant working evenings in a leisure centre might work as a shop assistant in the day; and a theme park assistant is often likely to be a student working part time in the vacation.

Other workers do not show up in the data at all. Volunteers are an obvious example and they are often a significant, if unpaid, part of the workforce. In some areas of the industry such as caravan parks, fairgrounds, and small visitor attractions where family businesses abound there is often a good deal of employment on the 'black economy'. For example, there may be benefit claimants working on the side, and employers failing to declare employees and paying them under the counter without declaration to Social Security, let alone to a government survey.

A final comment on measurement is that a survey of direct spending (e.g. ticket prices) is not the end of the matter. In many cases the provision of a leisure facility or service will result in spin-off or indirect expenditure. For example, a theatre may get its programmes printed by a local printer or buy food for its restaurant from local suppliers. These in turn may well buy from other local suppliers and so on. This effect is called the multiplier effect and it needs to be calculated rather than measured. In some parts of the country, such as resort towns or where there are major visitor attractions, the multiplier effect from leisure is a major component of the local economy.

When looking at data:

- be wary of how you interpret data
- try to use the source data and not extracts
- use various sources of data to draw a conclusion
- always check the small print: date, size of sample, what was being measured and how it was classified
- state your assumptions and reservations when using data
- when comparing between data sources it is often better to look at relative data (rank, trends and proportions) rather than the absolute (sales figures, usage).

At this advanced level of study you should not be accepting lists that make sweeping statements. Instead, challenge what you read and learn to draw your own conclusions. With this warning in your mind, read the following brief overview of the industry. When preparing your assignment you should return to source materials to allow for a full assessment of the area you are focusing on.

Consumer spending

Overall leisure spending is estimated by Mintel to have risen from £49.1 billion in 1994 to £57.5 billion in 1997 and to £60.3 billion in 1999. How is this broken down?

One way of measuring the economic impact is to look at the average household expenditure for which there is long-term data. Since 1968 leisure services and goods have increased more than any other sector of household expenditure due mainly to the service sector. The proportion of household expenditure spent on leisure goods has remained much the same.

It is the service sector that has largely accounted for the growth in leisure. The

growth of pay TV, visitor attractions, spectator sports, and sports/health clubs has meant that there are more opportunities to spend money in the service sector, resulting in substantial growth in household expenditure. The major part of growth is accounted for by the growth of holiday expenses which accounted for 44% (13% on incidental holiday expenses) of leisure service expenditure in 1998 compared with arts and admissions 2%, sports admissions and fees 6%, TV charges 9% and gambling 9%. These figures are, however, taken from the Household Expenditure Survey which seems to have some anomalies of classification.

Table 1.15 Leisure spending as a percentage of weekly household expenditure

	1968	1978	1988	1998
Leisure goods	4	4	5	5
Leisure services	4	5	9	12
Average total weekly Expenditure (£)	25	80	204	352
Of which the percentage of all leisure goods:				
Reading	9	12	10	8
Electrical goods	18	15	12	12
Holidays	19	20	25	31

Source: Household Expenditure Survey
These findings are reflected in a more detailed analysis, by Mintel, of the growth of key non-domestic service markets in terms of turnover.

Try it out

Cinema continues to become more popular with the expansion of multiplexes. In 1988 there were 495 cinemas with 1,117 screens; by 1998 this had risen to 481 cinemas with 1,975 screens. In recent years, not only have takings increased but entrance fees have also gone up. Cinemas have become more efficient by having more screens, smaller auditoria and shared reception areas and have almost doubled the return on a screen.

Discuss the implications of these changes.

It includes educational fees as a leisure expenditure but not eating out or drinking or the purchase of bikes, boats, DIY, gardening goods, and sports clothing.

Cinema going is about the only arts and entertainment activity to have increased significantly over the past decade (Table 1.16). As with any industry, underneath the average statistics there are winners and losers. For example, theatre looks steady, but on closer inspection provincial theatre has undergone a decline that is counterbalanced by the growth of the London theatres which showed a turnover of £186 million in 1991 and £238 million in 1995.

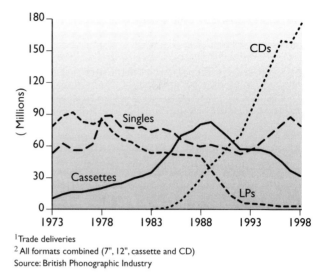

[1] Trade deliveries
[2] All formats combined (7", 12", cassette and CD)
Source: British Phonographic Industry

Figure 1.17 United Kingdom sales [1] of CDs, LPs, cassettes and singles[2]

Table 1.16 Attendance[1] at cultural events (Great Britain)

			Percentages
	1987-88	1991-92	1997-98
Cinema	34	44	54
Plays	24	23	23
Art galleries/exhibitions	21	21	22
Classical music	12	12	12
Ballet	6	6	6
Opera	5	6	6
Contemporary dance	4	3	4

[1] Percentage of resident population aged 15 and over attending 'these days'
Source: Target Group Index, BMRB International

The areas which the big players in the industry are really interested in these days are:

*   ten-pin bowling which will increasingly be linked with family entertainment centres
*   gambling
*   nightclubs and bars which are replacing pubs
*   health and fitness clubs and tennis centres which will eat into the public sector provision of team-based recreation in particular.

As you can see from the household expenditure table (Table 1.15), listening to music, watching TV and reading are all moderately high in terms of expenditure. This is confirmed by

looking at sales figures; for example, the total retail sales in 1995 for durables (e.g. audio) and consumables (e.g. tapes) were £902 million. The major expansion in this area has been CDs, as can be seen from Figure 1.17. However this may be a temporary surge as new products like minidisks and DVD become popular. Computers continue to expand; in 1986 only 16 per cent of households owned one, and by 1997 the figure was 26 per cent.

Reading is a national pastime which is growing rapidly with an estimated sales growth of books and magazines between 1996 and 2000 of 9.3 per cent (Table 1.17). Sales may boom, but patterns change. For example, newspaper readership is facing a decline and sales figures are dropping, especially of the local weeklies as they are increasingly hit by free newspapers. The numbers of books produced are increasing steadily. Perhaps the biggest changes have been in magazine readership. There has been a general shift towards special-interest and consumer magazines. But it is male readership that has been the phenomenon of the 1990s. *FHM, Loaded, GQ, Men's Health* and *Esquire* have all made a significant impact on the magazine market.

Table 1.17 Forecast reading sales (£m)

	1996	1998	2000
Books	1,600	1,700	1,900
Newspapers	2,450	2,450	2,400
Magazines	1,300	1,420	1,550

Source: Mintel

It is interesting to note that three out of the six most-read magazines were TV guides. *Sky TV Guide* is the most popular and read by 12 per cent of adults. This reflects our love of TV and radio. The question now is not who has TV (98 per cent) but how long and what they watch. On average we watch about 25 hours a week and listen to the radio for about 16 hours, but this does not take into account that a lot of time is spent with either medium as background to other activities.

Thought for the page

Once viewing figures were the guide to advertising companies as to where to place their advertisements. These are no longer so useful. Our viewing habits include having the TV on in the background, turning the sound down, channel hopping, and turning the advertisements off. Catching our attention is increasingly difficult.

The major impact on broadcasting has been the introduction of new channels. In radio, Classic FM, Talk Radio and Virgin Radio have all been successful newcomers. In TV the impact has been more significant still. With a new terrestrial channel (Channel 5) and the introduction of cable and digital it is hard to see who will win the broadcasting battle or what form TV will take in the near future. One outstanding success has been satellite, and particularly Sky. By 1999, 13 per cent of households subscribed to satellite – a figure that will surely grow in the future.

The emergence of the Web will also make a huge difference to broadcasting and it is quite possible that the war between satellite and terrestrial TV is simply a warm-up bout before the main event, which will be the emergence of the Web in the next decade as the main communication medium. There are already signs of this happening with mergers between multinational companies that aim to bring the relevant resources into play. For example, in 2000, Time (publishing), Warner (films and TV), and AOL (web server) merged to form the first of the super communication-entertainment companies.

We now move on to areas where it is more difficult to measure the size of the industry in terms of sales figures, either because there are no fees or no measurement of activity. These areas are the public and voluntary sectors and countryside activities.

Local Authority arts and leisure: Local government is monitored by the Institute for Public Finance (IPF), which produces detailed tables of expenditure on leisure services including indoor sports, outdoor sports including parks, cultural facilities and other services. In 1999-2000 the 410 Local Authorities in England and Wales will have spent in total £2066 million on leisure provision. The pie chart in Figure 1.18 gives the proportions spent on the various sectors.

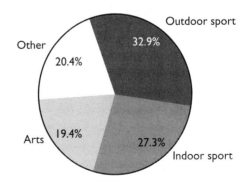

Source: Chartered Institute of Public Finance and Accountancy

Figure 1.18 Expenditure on leisure provision by all authorities in England and Wales

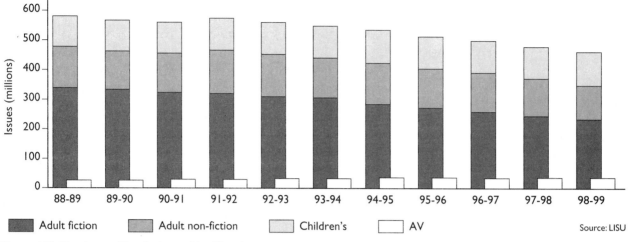

Figure 1.19 Numbers of books issued by libraries

Libraries: We know from surveys of reading and retail sales of books that reading is a favourite and ever-growing home leisure activity – in 1987 60 per cent of adults read at least once a month, and in 1996 this had risen to 65 per cent. Library statistics come then as a surprise, as over the past ten years there has been a steady and significant (10 per cent) drop in issues (i.e. books borrowed) from public libraries. This is especially so in adult fiction (Figure 1.19).

> **Think it over**
> Why do you think there has been this drop in library book issues but a rise in audiovisual (AV) loans?

Countryside: The major data source on countryside activities was the national Day Visits Survey – a biennial survey held since 1994. Although this looked at all day visits it separated out trips to the countryside or coast. In terms of visits it is estimated that 65 per cent of us visit the countryside in a year and 51 per cent the coast.

Not surprisingly, people spend less on countryside trips than they do for other destinations – after all, there are fewer shops and places to spend your money. What is interesting is that, after prices have been adjusted for inflation, average countryside spending is showing a significant increase; in 1996 the average spend per person was £5.40, and it had increased by 20 per cent to £6.50 in 1998. The survey used these figures and calculated the total spend made by visitors to the countryside, which came out at £13 billion, of which £9 billion was for the countryside, £2 billion for sea and coasts and £1 billion for woodland and forest. This seems a lot but it is not all. The sample should be treated with caution, because in this survey the sample was of 'people going on trips outside their normal environment'. In other words the survey excludes country people enjoying themselves on their own patch doing things like going for a walk, clay pigeon shooting, going to a gymkhana or going to the village fête. The £13 billion is therefore likely to be an underestimate of the total economic impact of countryside activities.

Workforce size

It has already been seen that there are problems affecting estimates of workbase size. Our understanding of the workforces is particularly fragmented. Although you can research

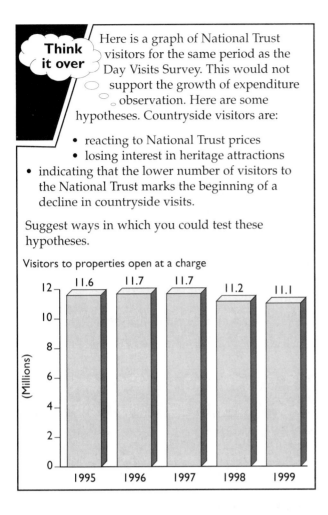

Think it over

Here is a graph of National Trust visitors for the same period as the Day Visits Survey. This would not support the growth of expenditure observation. Here are some hypotheses. Countryside visitors are:

- reacting to National Trust prices
- losing interest in heritage attractions
- indicating that the lower number of visitors to the National Trust marks the beginning of a decline in countryside visits.

Suggest ways in which you could test these hypotheses.

Visitors to properties open at a charge

government statistics such as are found in the *Employment Gazette* they should be used only as a general guidance. Perhaps the best sources are the studies that the National Training Organisations (NTOs) are producing. These dissect the structure of the industry using specially designed surveys. It is worth while checking if they have published their results.

As a general observation the following profile applies to the industry.

- The vast majority of jobs in the industry are service jobs (although there are a minority of trade-based jobs such as plant engineers, stage electricians, countryside crafts such as hedge trimming).
- Most work is unskilled or semi-skilled (for example cleaners, receptionists, play leaders)
- Most of the workforce is non-graduate. Many managers are graduates but there are still many opportunities to 'come up through the ranks'. The main exceptions to this are libraries and museums where graduate entry is usually required.
- There are high levels of seasonal and temporary work.
- Pay levels are on the whole low up to and including junior management level.

Table 1.18 gives an idea of employment trends in the industry over the past ten years.

Table 1.18 Employment in tourism-related industries (Great Britain)

At June in each year   Thousands, not seasonally adjusted

	Hotels and other tourist accommodation	Restaurants, cafés, etc.	Bars, pubs, clubs	Libraries, museums, culture	Sport and other recreation	All	Estimated self-employment
1989	299.2	283.4	428.2	82.8	294.7	1,644.2	191.0
1990	314.4	303.0	445.8	80.0	311.5	1,714.7	190.0
1991	307.9	297.7	435.0	75.6	316.5	1,685.4	183.0
1992	311.0	303.0	414.2	74.8	320.8	1,671.0	178.0
1993	317.6	298.0	370.6	75.6	316.5	1,643.6	196.0
1994	375.5	372.3	399.4	77.4	356.0	1,872.8	208.6
1995	385.9	386.6	445.4	80.3	363.1	1,752.0	215.4
1996	370.8	394.5	437.9	78.4	355.8	1,949.5	215.4
1997	344.1	410.4	479.5	80.0	363.1	2,003.8	217.8
1998	332.6	413.7	467.3	86.4	357.8	1,951.7	183.9
1999	306.0	357.7	428.8	84.5	337.7	1,787.5	158.6

Source: Office for National Statistics, short-term employment survey

It gives the figures for June which is the maximum employment period. (NB the leap in 1994 is due largely to a reclassification.) What is interesting is that although the industry is expanding overall in usage and spending, the past few years have seen an overall contraction of the workforce. One reason for this may be that the industry is designing service and buildings that require fewer staff (e.g. new-style health clubs or cinemas have a far greater capacity for customers but require proportionally fewer staff. Another reason may be that there is a greater reliance on casual staff.

The exceptions to this are libraries, museums and culture. Libraries probably do not feature in this increase as the number of librarians is fairly constant and not related to issue numbers. The Local Government Association estimates that there are about 22,000 employed in local lending libraries, while the NTO estimates 26,000. The growth is therefore probably taking place in museums and other cultural activities. Two reasons may account for this. The first is that this is an area which is heavily funded by the Lottery. In other words there are many new facilities and activities coming on line. The other reason may be that the nature of the service is changing, with more interaction taking place between guides and visitors; for example, at the Royal Armouries at Leeds, there are numerous people employed to demonstrate fighting techniques.

> **Think it over**
> Sport is also an area which is heavily funded by the Lottery. However, this has not been accompanied by a rise in employment. Why does this observation not contradict our suggestion about museums?

Check it out

1. What are the three main measurements used to determine the size of the industry? Give an example of each.
2. In terms of consumer spending what are the three biggest areas of leisure activity out of the home? Which area has shown the biggest growth since 1993?
3. How has cinema become more profitable in the past decade?
4. What sector of the newspaper industry has declined, what sector of the magazine industry increased?
5. What threats does terrestrial TV face?
6. What is the total best estimate of spending on countryside activities? Why is this an underestimate?
7. Describe the characteristics of the leisure service workforce.

1.5 Working in the leisure and recreation industry

A great deal of the leisure industry is either made up of home-based leisure or concerned with selling equipment and clothing for out-of-home leisure activities. This part of the industry is largely about retailing and sales and really falls into the retail sector. What we are going to concentrate on in this section is service and provision within the main leisure industry, and the sort of work that this entails.

The nature of employment

Seasonal work

Seasonal work is a common feature of the industry and is usually associated with tourism-related sectors. Thus visitor attractions, countryside activities, bar work in resorts all show high levels of seasonal employment, with summer and Christmas being likely peak times. Major events such as county shows will also cause short-term uptake of temporary staff.

Outdoor sports and activities workers have adapted to a seasonal way of life. For example, there is a tradition among outdoor activity instructors to go south for the winter or work as instructors in ski resorts.

Temporary work

Temporary work is work that is offered for a fixed period of time as opposed to permanent work where the employee can expect to work for the employer indefinitely. There are those among leisure employers who think it keeps the workforce on its toes and gives greater flexibility to the firm to offer employees temporary contracts. In fact, the net result is usually that the staff has little loyalty or motivation and moves on to jobs that have more security.

Seasonal and temporary employment has both advantages and disadvantages. On the upside it means there are plenty of opportunities to enter the industry through weekend work or summer jobs. If you are suited to the work, this is often a way of being noticed by the manager and retained on a permanent contract. If you are studying, this practical work can also be important in providing experience. A disadvantage is that employers are often less likely to invest money on training temporary staff. It is common to hear employers justify this by saying 'Why should I spend my money on training when they will be working for someone else in six months' time?' For the industry this means that the competence and performance of the workforce does not reach its full potential.

Long-term employment is more common in sectors not affected by the weather or tourism, such as in swimming pools or cinemas. If they have a surge of business, they will tend to bring in workers from a 'bank' of casual or part-time staff.

Unsociable hours

Employees in the leisure industry are at work when other people are having fun. Leisure work involves unsocial hours, working at weekends, bank holidays, evenings and even early mornings. Being able to handle this is an essential part of any employee's makeup. Round-the-week operations and working hours regulations also mean that you have to be flexible in the hours you work.

Most leisure providers work rosters. These are schedules of shifts that allow the facility to be fully staffed. They come in all shapes and sizes. For example, you may work seven days continuously and then have three days off, or you may work three days of ten hours followed by a short day and then three days off. You need to be flexible to accommodate these sorts of rosters.

Pay

Pay in leisure is usually low. For example, a typical attendant's wage outside the Southeast will probably be around £10,000 p.a., while a manager of a facility will probably rarely earn above £22,000 p.a. Overtime is becoming rarer. In most areas of the industry apart from some Local Authorities there has been a great reduction in enhanced extra pay for working overtime or unsocial hours. You can expect to receive the same rate whenever you work.

A 'people business'

Because your job is to ensure that the customer is happy and has an enjoyable visit, it is essential that you have good people skills. This means that you have to able to respond in a pleasant and helpful way no matter how you are feeling or how obnoxious you find the customer.

Finding a job in leisure and recreation

Skills and qualifications

It is still possible to come into many areas of leisure without qualifications and work your way up. While this will continue for some time, the opportunity is fast being eroded as qualification and training is now becoming a life-long experience. With the exception of information management (i.e librarians) where five GCSEs is the normal entry qualification, the minimum entry point for most leisure jobs will remain largely influenced by personality and experience rather than qualification. This does not mean qualification will be unimportant at this level, as it will indicate knowledge and interest in the industry. At this level employers want the employee 'to hit the deck running'. It is likely therefore that vocational awards (e.g. NVQs) will become valuable qualifications.

Once in work many employers will offer continuous professional development (CPD) which is a programme of training opportunities (e.g. courses) or additional qualifications allowing you to improve your performance and progress in the industry. Again the NVQ system will be a good route to follow when the knowledge gained from training can be demonstrated in work.

Alternatively, entry can be at a higher level based on qualifications like HND or degrees (e.g. leisure management or arts

management). This is particularly so with culture and information management where many jobs will depend on academic knowledge gained from higher education. In some areas of leisure, competition is extremely high and you will often find that possession of these qualifications does not necessarily mean that you will enter at the level that they are intended for. For example, it is common for a person with a degree in recreation management to come in as a supervisor or duty manager rather than as the manager of a sports centre. It is not unknown for graduates to work as recreation assistants to get on to the career ladder. In contrast to this, the major private sector players may have fast-track schemes for a limited number of outstanding candidates.

Structure

In some areas of the industry, career paths and job types are fairly easy to identify. For example, in any facility (theme parks, leisure centres, cinemas and, nowadays, pubs) there is normally a three-tier system of receptionists and attendants, shift supervisors and duty managers and managers (Figure 1.20). Away from the service outlet there will

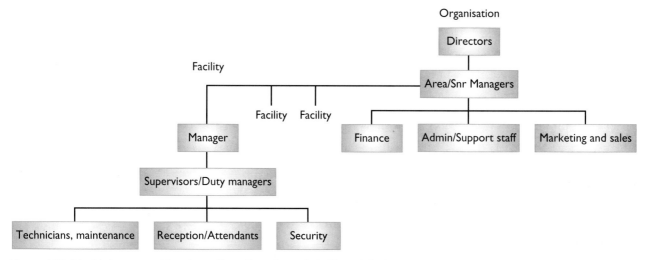

Figure 1.20 Most leisure providers have three/four tiers of staffing at facility level, with the manager reporting to an area or senior manager who is responsible for several facilities

be an administrative system supporting the outlet and a senior management structure that will determine policies, budgets and marketing.

In the countryside the key people are the rangers. There are two main types – rangers who are trained and qualified with craft and trade skills, and ones who specialise in interpretation and education. The teams are normally managed by a head ranger.

In libraries and museums the library assistants are the people on the desk; they will be managed by qualified graduate librarians. Librarians and museum staff often work behind the scenes in their main duties of managing the collections (by acquiring, cataloguing and conserving) and the service (budgets and staff).

In all sectors of the industry there is a split between operational and strategic work. For most employees who want to progress in the industry there will come a time when they have to decide to leave front-of-house services and be promoted across to the strategic side of the business which leads to senior management.

In sport and culture there is a huge range of jobs which it is beyond the scope of this book to cover in detail. All the public and professional bodies such as the Arts Council or the Library Association produce lively guides to their sector and allow you to investigate the many specialist areas within it. A general overview can be had by reading several publications such as a *Brief Guide to Careers in Leisure*.

Despite the long hours and poor pay a lot of people want to work in leisure and the competition is fierce. Getting a qualification is therefore often only the first step and does not guarantee work. Employers are looking for key skills and qualities that will help them decide to employ you.

Key skills
Personal skills

If you are working in leisure, especially on the public side of the industry, then you need to have:

- good personal presentation (clean hair, smart clothes)
- good interpersonal skills such as eye contact, clear voice, nice smile
- patience and consideration for your customers
- good time keeping and reliability.

Whether you are on front of house or behind the scenes you will also have to be able to:

- work in a team
- be enthusiastic and positive about your work
- show loyalty
- follow instructions but show initiative
- be cheerful.

You may think all these are fairly obvious but many candidates let themselves down when being interviewed, and it is worth thinking about all these factors.

Technical skills and experience

All sectors of the industry have qualifications that allow you to do the job better or will mean you do not have to be trained. A good example is a first aid, life-guard or coaching certificate. It is always a good idea to obtain some of these while still in education. A lack of experience is a major stumbling-block when competing for a job. For the employer, experience means that you have:

- tested yourself in the field and found you enjoy it
- developed some work skills
- acquired knowledge.

A person with experience probably has an advantage over someone without. Given the part-time opportunities available there is really no reason why you cannot obtain experience through paid work – so keep up the Saturday job. Voluntary experience is especially well thought of as it indicates a genuine interest in leisure rather than simply a financial one. Activities such as the Duke of Edinburgh Award, voluntary sports leadership or working with local charities will demonstrate your commitment. In the countryside and heritage industries there are numerous activities such as wildlife trusts, environmental improvement schemes or archaeological digs. If you can't get a part-time or seasonal job, then make the best use of work experience. In leisure, work experience can often lead to a job at the organisation you work in. Try to select an organisation that you would want to work for rather than just going for any workplace that happens to turn up.

One of the great fallacies about leisure is that it gives you the chance to practise your particular talent. Forget it. Most of your working life will be about serving customers or cleaning up after them. While knowledge and enthusiasm for the leisure activity are a great asset, your employer is really interested in how you will pull your weight and get on with your workmates and customers. Watching a film, playing a sport or performing music will usually remain part of your personal leisure life not your work life.

In some cases personal excellence may be a handicap for employment. For example, international athletes would on first sight appear to be excellent candidates for a job.

> **Think it over**
>
> Find some job advertisements, from the local press, websites and trade publications, for positions in the leisure and recreation industry that you are interested in. Look at the skills needed for the job and identify whether you already have the skills. If not, consider how you will gain them.

Although there is some status from having a known sportsperson in an organisation, many managers are wary about employing them as they may ask for time off to train and compete, or may be self-absorbed in their quest for personal achievement.

Time out: Taking time out to travel and perhaps more importantly work abroad does seem to increase many people's maturity and self-confidence. This is an attribute that will allow them to work more effectively in leisure and will also give them the edge at interview.

> **! Check it out**
>
> 1 Explain the differences between part-time, temporary, seasonal and permanent jobs.
> 2 How does a job in the leisure industry often differ from a job in another industry such as retailing?
> 3 Identify three personal skills that are important in the leisure industry. Explain their relevance in relation to a particular job.
> 4 Why is experience important in getting a job?
> 5 What is CPD?

1.6 Pursuing your own progression aims
Planning your career development

Faced with the options for employment in the industry you may feel somewhat confused and need to bring order to your decisions. This section will try to give some practical advice.

Look at the industry

It is easy to have a restricted view of the industry and see it in terms of the public image. Think of sport, and you think of professional players, coaches and leisure centres. Think of libraries and you think of public or college libraries. This is seeing it from the consumer's viewpoint and is missing the greater part of the industry which is below the surface. Research the industry and you will find many less public jobs – for example, a sports scientist, a psychologist or a business librarian for a large company.

Exploring opportunities

It pays to explore the field and find out the sorts of jobs that are available, what they involve and the qualifications and routes needed to be employed. In Figure 1.21 are shown some of the factors to think about.

As we have already said there are plenty of sources of information about careers in the industry. However, it is well worth doing a bit of first-hand research. A careers adviser is an excellent source of information and may help you to structure your career planning. Your course tutors and other teaching staff

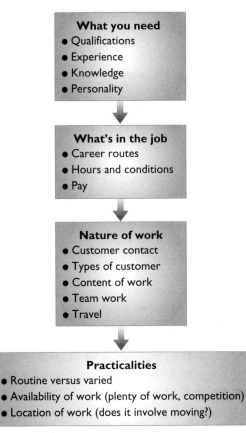

Figure 1.21 Planning your career means researching your desired area of work and matching it against your own profile

may be of help, especially if they have worked in the industry. But nothing can really beat talking to the people who do the job. Hopefully, your school or college will arrange for speakers to come along. If so, use them to your advantage.

You may also want to take direct action by phoning up workplaces and asking if you can talk to someone or even come in for a shift and shadow someone doing a job. Sometimes you may meet with a refusal, but providing you are enthusiastic and have good interpersonal skills it is likely that someone will give you half an hour of their time.

Self-assessment

The ability to assess yourself objectively is a great help in choosing a career. For most of us there are three obstacles – fantasy, self-perception and habit.

- *Fantasy*: Fantasising about what you are going to be is no bad thing. There is a large school of thought that says if you want to do something you need to imagine that you are doing it, but if you are going to turn a fantasy into a reality, you need to be sure that you have the capability or talent. For example, if you are short it is highly unlikely that you will become a professional basketball player. You have to be able to assess if your fantasy is an achievable goal with hard work, or one where your own ability is not going to be sufficient.
- *Self-perception*: Most people have only a limited ability to see themselves and their talents as they are. We also often put ourselves down. We fail to see our strengths and think our talents and good points are ordinary.
- *Habit*: Some people accept a job because it is a well-defined route or they can't think of anything else. For example, people often go into jobs because their

family is already involved or their friends work in that area. Falling into a job in this way does not allow you to explore other options that might better suit your profile.

If you can assess yourself objectively you can draw up a profile of yourself in terms of strengths, weaknesses and interests. You can do this by yourself but it is far better to talk to a range of people. Family is a good starting point as they will have an intimate knowledge of you and be able to remember things about you that others do not know about. However, there is a danger that they will be locked into, and even the cause of, your self-doubts. You know the sort of thing – 'Well, you can't even keep your room tidy let alone a leisure centre!' Spread your net wider and talk to close friends who will be enthusiastic for you but may not be very well informed. Finally, talk to professionals who know you. Careers teachers are an important source of information and guidance and so will be your course tutor who will have seen you in action. If you work as a volunteer or in a part-time job ask your employers for their views on your strengths or weaknesses.

Figure 1.20 (previous page) identifies factors you may want to consider in relation to particular jobs.

You can add or change this list, but what you are trying to do is analyse the sort of person you are. It is a good idea to make a table out of your answers, giving a column for each of the people whom you asked, including yourself. You may notice that other people see you differently from how you see yourself. If they do, you would be well advised to note what they say, especially if there is a degree of consensus. After all, this is how the world (customers and employers) sees you.

At this stage you can start to match your profile against a variety of jobs and industry sectors that have struck you as being interesting. You

might also want to consider some you have rejected – with a second view against your own profile, you might discover some surprises. All this planning will take up some time and you can short-circuit it by talking to a careers adviser who will be able to carry out a match using computer models. These are well worth doing, but they have one drawback in that they do not involve you as much as doing it yourself. Only when you have gone through a soul-searching and sometimes painful process of assessing yourself, will you be truly convinced and committed to what you are doing.

Preparing for the future

Once you have worked out what you want to do you will probably find that your goal is in the future and that you can achieve it only by making certain moves to gain the necessary experience and qualifications. You need to make a career plan (Figure 1.22). When aiming for any goal you have to work backwards from that goal and ask yourself key questions about each preceding stage until you get back to the present.

Ask these questions to reach your goal.

- What qualifications do I need for this stage?
- What experience do I need for this stage?
- What other skills do I need?
- How will I ensure that I have the necessary qualifications and experience?
- How will I develop myself ?
- How long do I need to achieve these?
- What life changes do I need to make? (e.g. move house, cut down socialising, save)
- What sort of jobs or employers would be suitable to this stage?

Most career maps are fairly straightforward and involve only a few steps. Normally it is sensible to think in terms of between five and ten years for the map. Any less and you will not be able to make enough steps, any more and the plan becomes obscure and unrealistic.

Figure 1.22 It is a good idea to look at your strengths and weaknesses in relation to a particular job

Overleaf (Figure 1.23) is a map for becoming a librarian. Career planning is an active process and you cannot expect to achieve objectives by just drifting by. Generally speaking, your progress will be quicker if you are prepared to move to work and change employers when appropriate.

In the past it was generally good advice to go for companies with long-term prospects. In today's world change is to be expected both by employee and employers. This may mean that you must occasionally consider taking on a so-called 'dead end' job if you can gain experience or qualifications from it that will let you take the next step. For example, working as an activity leader in a holiday park will almost certainly be a short-term contract offering little training, but the experience of organising and entertaining several hundred children over the space of six weeks will probably give you more customer handling experience than a year working in a leisure centre. The secret of using these short-term opportunities is to work out what you want to gain from the experience and, if the job offers it, go for it with the full intention that it will be a short-term stop on the career path.

Throughout your career path there will be major steps like going to college. For students, part-time jobs are normal. The vast majority of students look for work unrelated to their intended careers such as shelf stacking. It is well worth investigating the local leisure market to see if you can work within it. Bar work is obviously one area but it is surprising how many other opportunities exist. You may be able to get a job in the local radio as a cleaner, or assist with sports or arts development with

Experience gained from part-time work may open up career opportunities

65

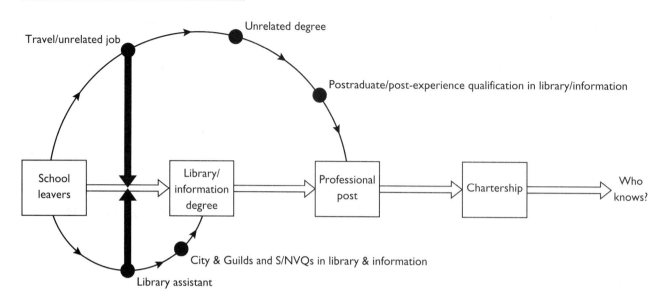

Travel/unrelated job – unrelated degree	Take some time off ... Do a degree in a completely different subject ... Work in other areas. Librarians can work as subject specialists and in all sorts of workplaces, so none of this previous experience is wasted.
City & Guilds and S/NVQs in library & information	Learn while you earn! S/NVQs are competence-based qualifications which you can do while working.
Library assistant	Employers expect assistant to have a minimum of 5 GCSEs. Other ask for A-levels or equivalent.
Postgraduate/post-experience qualification in library/information	For full-time courses, colleges ask for some experience of library and information work.
	Part-time and distance learning courses expect students to be working in a library or information service while they study.
City & Guilds and S/NVQs in library & information	You can take a City & Guilds library and information assistant's certificate before you start working in a library or information service.
Chartership	Write your Professional Development Report with the Library Association and become a Chartered Librarian.

Source: The Library Association

Figure 1.23 Career map for becoming a librarian

the local council. There may be a need for casual recreation assistants or receptionists in a local health club. If you are lucky, the experience will lead directly to a job. If not, you will be able to observe the industry in action and meet contacts who you can tell you about your aim in life.

Finding a job

You now know what you want to do and are ready to make the first step. You need to find the job, prepare yourself and handle the interview.

Despite equal opportunities, jobs in leisure often appear as a result of a personal contact and this is particularly the case at entrance level. A typical career path for first-level entry is work in a service either through volunteering, work experience, a training placement or knowing a friend who can put in a good word. A 'good friend' may be a real friend or it may be a contact such as a relative of your course tutor (who will probably have an excellent network amongst local employers). Providing your work is good and you make it known that you want to continue to work there, you will often be invited to apply for a vacancy.

It makes a great deal of sense therefore to be proactive and not wait until the advertisements appear – if they ever do. A good strategy is to identify specific places where you want to work and ask for an interview with the aim of discussing how you could work there either in a paid or unpaid capacity. If you get turned down, ask when you should contact them again. If you repeatedly get turned down, have the nerve to ask them if there is anything about yourself that is stopping you from getting in. At least you will have got another source for your self-assessment.

At higher levels of qualification the same principles apply, but much less so. With your extra skills and expertise and with the responsibilities of the job in mind, managers are more concerned about their investment. Although being in the organisation will no doubt help, you must expect that the job will normally be advertised and competed for openly. Supervisor posts and below appear in job centres and local papers when they are advertised. They may sometimes be advertised in specialist publications. More senior posts tend to be advertised in specialist newspapers such as *Leisure Week* or The Institute of Leisure and Amenity Management (ILAM) weekly listings, more senior ones are advertised in national newspapers as well.

Increasingly, Local Authorities have a website that shows all local jobs in the public sector – this is a trend that the professional bodies are picking up on and the Arts Council and Central Council for Physical Recreation (CCPR) (www.ncf.org.uk) for example, have vacancy sites.

Job applications

Do what it says in the advertisement. There is a reason – for example, if they think they will be flooded with phone calls they will say write. If it says phone, phone; if it says write, write a simple request for details of the job. When you have the details, you first need to see if the job will match your career plan. If it does not, do not necessarily abandon it. Having an interview may be a valuable learning experience for when you do go for the job you want. If you do apply, the key piece of information you need to look at is the person specification. This is a description of the ideal candidate in terms of skills, qualifications, expertise and personality. If done well, it will be prioritised into what is 'essential' and 'desirable'. Some companies provide only a job description in which case you will need to invent your own person specification for the job.

Now you have a person description you need to match it against your own profile. Don't be too concerned about the term 'essential'. If you cannot give evidence for several essential items, the job is probably not for you, but if there is only an odd point you cannot fulfil you should phone the employer and check if lack of evidence would debar you. This is because sometimes employers over-write the person specification and include what is 'desirable' as 'essential'.

Your next job is to prepare a CV (curriculum vitae) and application.

Curriculum Vitae

A lot has been written about composing a CV. Here is some more. The purpose of a CV is to show an employer at a glance who you are, your qualifications and experience.

Tips for writing a CV

- Keep it concise (no more than two sides of A4 and preferably one side).

- Keep personal details relevant: name, age, and contact point. Gender, nationality and ethnicity are irrelevant under equal opportunities but may give you an advantage if the company is recruiting by quota.

- Do not add your photograph. Visual impressions can often act against you.

- Qualifications should list institution, subjects, grade and date achieved.

- Other qualifications should include technical (e.g. first aid) and vocational (Duke of Edinburgh).

- Experience: this should be custom designed for each job you go for and focus on experience that matches the person description. At an early stage in your career this is a difficult section. You can be assured, though, that most other candidates' CVs will probably look like yours in terms of qualifications. The tie-breaker in being selected could well be that you have more experience than the others.

- Interests: the main point of this section is either to provide the interviewer with an ice-breaker or to show that you can demonstrate your interest in the industry from your own leisure life. So don't make things up.

Try it out

If you do not already have a CV, try putting together a draft copy. When you have your CV exchange it with someone you know. Is their CV a good representation of them? Identify the good points about their CV and suggest possible areas for improvement.

Applications

When shuffling through hundreds of CVs managers find it hard to make judgements. It is a good idea to make your CV stand out. A subtle way of doing this is to use a high-quality, heavy paper. Not only does this show that you care about presentation but the physical handling of the paper will make it stand out.

In order to standardise applications many companies ask you to fill in an application form which may ask for all these details. They will sometimes ask you not to send a CV, in which case comply with their wishes. Usually these forms will contain a space for you to say why you want the job and how you are suited to it. If the employers are doing their job they will read this and match it against the person specification. In other words, when you write this section you write

---

curriculum vitae of Emma Phipps

Personal details

Name: Emma Phipps   **Date of birth:** 23 April 1983   **Age:** 18 years

Gender: Female   **Marital status:** single   **Languages:** English, French, Spanish

Address: 23 Ley Road, Surbiton, Surrey KT6 3NY

Telephone/fax no: 020 8546 3983

E-mail: ephipps@hotmail.co.uk

Education and qualification

Institution	Dates	Awards	Grade
Hincley Wood School	1999-2001	AVCE Leisure and Recreation	Merit
		A level Drama	B
	1994-1999	GCSE:	
		Maths	B
		English Language	A
		Drama	A*
		History	C
		French	B
		Spanish	A
		Art	A
Red Cross	1998	First Aid at Work Award	

Work experience

I have worked part time for two years in the Kingston Theatre, front-of-house in the ticket office and as a customer assistant. I have been stage manager for several school plays and assistant stage manager for a National Youth Theatre summer school.

Interests

My main interests are in arts and entertainment where I see my career lying. My aim is to become an Arts Centre Manager. I was involved in stage productions at school and was lucky enough to be selected as assistant stage manager for the NYT millennium summer tour. I love films and regularly go to the cinema. I play the keyboard in a pop group I formed. I enjoy working with people and am captain of my school netball team. I also like walking and the countryside and have recently started working towards my silver Duke of Edinburgh award.

it so that you cover as many points in the specification as you can. If you want to, you might save the employer time by using the person specification points as sub-headings. Some companies do not provide forms but ask you to submit your own application. If this is the case, definitely supply a CV and a piece similar to the one above describing your suitability for the job.

When returning applications it is polite to include a short covering letter that states how you heard about the job, confirms your interest in it and briefly says why you want to do it.

Unless otherwise stated (some companies like to see handwriting and judge personality by it), type all application materials – handwriting is tiring to read and the employer may well skip over important points you have made.

Printed application forms are sometimes folded and difficult to get through a printer. If so, it is a good idea to make some photocopies of the blank form and practise until it prints correctly every time. On the other hand, you may be advised to complete the form in black ink with clearly written capitals. Again, practise a few times; if you don't, you will find that you will be more likely to make mistakes and make a mess of the form.

The interview

The interview is the only opportunity you will have to convince an employer that you should be taken on.

Before the interview

Although things can always go wrong on the day the chance of this happening can be minimised by careful planning.

Strengths: In the interview you will be reinforcing the point that your strengths will match the criteria for the job. You need at

this stage to identify what strengths the job requires and if you have them. For example: you note that the employer has sessions for the elderly. So you would note that you have worked as a volunteer with a local residential home and got on well with residents. You might then note some things which you would need to be aware of when working with them, such as hearing problems.

Of course you may not have worked with old people and this begs the question of what you will say if they ask you about this area. You should not invent things, but do a little bit of research so that you can say 'You are quite right, I have not worked with old people, but I do enjoy their company and know the following things about working with them...'.

A question that is often asked is 'What is your main weakness?' Avoid answering with ones that cut you out from the job – such as 'I've got a really evil temper.' Either answer 'None that affects my work' or turn it into a strength such as 'I tend to attend to detail too much, but I don't mind being told to ease up.'

Rehearse questions: A good interviewer will start with easy social questions such as 'did you find us all right?' Treat them as openers and give brief answers. Often the first serious question is 'Why do you want this job?' Again, this is a bit of an ice-breaker to which you should have prepared a non-controversial answer: 'I have always wanted to work in the leisure industry and I know that you are generally regarded as an excellent provider and I want to learn from the best'.

You may also be asked what you can bring to the job. Think what they want from you and tell them that. This may be very simple requirements like commitment, enthusiasm and reliability, or it may be more specialised like coaching skills or knowing a lot about the countryside. If possible, highlight one point on which you think you are really strong. These are typical questions you may be asked and you will answer them all the better if you have thought about them and composed short answers that highlight your strengths. Even better is to ask a friend to help you simulate the interview so that you are actually speaking your answers rather than saying them in your head.

Getting there

Getting to an interview in the right state of mind is all-important. Here are some tips.

Interview tips

- Research where the interview is and plan in detail how you will get there and what time you will need to leave. If tickets are required, buy them in advance. You should aim to get to an interview about half an hour early – wait near by and then enter the building about 20 minutes before the interview.

- Materials and clothes: decide what you need for the interview, such as notebook and pen, and decide what clothes you will be wearing. Put on your clothes just prior to leaving home. If possible, don't eat or drink on the way – the coffee cup is bound to drip!

- Personal presentation: this is the first chance that the employers will have to judge your personal appearance. Remember that their judgement will often be from their perspective and not necessarily what you think looks cool, although in some cases, such as working on an arts project, coolness might be the preferred form to adopt.
  - Make sure your hair is cut (if necessary), and washed, your finger-nails clean. It is a good idea to remove any body piercing, partly because some employers won't like

it but also they may regard it as a health and safety hazard. Clothes should be smart and conventional. It is best for males to wear a tie, and whatever sex you are, clean your shoes. Power dressing in suits is not really necessary. The interviewer can see that you would not normally do this and you will probably feel self-conscious and unrelaxed.
  - Sexiness is normally not a good thing in dress style as it is more likely to be threatening to an interviewer than an asset to the interviewee.

- Finally, try not to be tired. Being tired may show in your face and it will certainly take the edge off your answers.

At the interview

You have arrived at the interview and you are rehearsed and ready to go. If you stick to your preparations the interview should go well. Your main problem now is the choreography – that is getting in and out the room without mishap and creating a good impression. Many interviews are sold on the first minute and the impression you give in that time. Here is some advice.

Relax before the interview: This may mean chatting to the other candidates, or keeping to yourself and maybe reading a magazine. Hiding in the toilet and getting focused is not a bad idea. It is whatever you prefer. Just before the interview take a few slow breaths and let your shoulders relax.

Trip ups: Leave your bag and coat or any other items in the waiting area. They are only designed to trip you up in the interview. If you need to take anything in to the interview, perhaps certificates or a notepad, then make sure they are contained. Loose papers have a

What is your first impression of this interviewee?

habit of sliding all over the place when you are nervous. When inside, put them at the side of your chair.

Presentations: By and large it is not a good idea to present materials while in the interview. If for example, you hand over your National Record of Achievement the interviewer now has to pay you the courtesy of looking at complex material which he/she has already noted in your CV. Materials that demonstrate a point can be acceptable. For example, if the job involved producing graphics it might be an idea to pass across an example of something you had done already. Unless specifically asked, avoid being slick and using a flipchart or overhead projector. They are notoriously temperamental and you risk them collapsing on you or your slides appearing upside down.

Making an impression: The interviewer often comes out to you to invite you in. You're off. Stand up, shake hands firmly, look him or her in the eye, smile and say 'Hello, how are you'. You have just made a good first impression. If someone else has taken you into the interview or there are others on the

panel then repeat the introduction process. Shaking hands is never inappropriate and denotes that you are feeling confident and have good social skills.

Handling the interview: Now sit down. Women often feel more comfortable with their legs crossed at the ankle and towards one side, men should sit with their legs slightly apart. Hands are best placed in the lap but do not worry about making gestures to emphasise interest and the points you are making. You will want to sit up straight and slightly forward. But the sooner you can settle back and relax the shoulders the easier you will find the interview.

When answering the questions try to stick to your plans. Don't rush into answers, but pause for a couple of seconds or so. Don't be afraid to be natural and say things like 'I thought you might ask me that and I have spent some time thinking about it'. This shows that you have gone to the trouble of planning the interview, and that confirms that you are sincerely interested in the job.

Maintain eye contact and smile at the panel. It is a great temptation to look only at the person who asked you the question or whom you like most. This puts that person in an awkward position as they have to keep returning your look. Meanwhile the rest of the panel feel left out. So pass the looks around.

Keep answers fairly short. Make your point with an example, then leave it. In most cases an answer will be between one and no more than two minutes.

Time to leave: Leaving can be difficult, especially if the room is big. Normally the interviewer will give you the cue to go. Something like, 'We will let all the candidates know by next week. In the meantime thank you for coming'. All you have to do is stand up (no handshakes needed now) and thank the panel for their time and say it has been pleasant meeting them. Often they will not get up to show you out, so you should half turn and walk to the door and say goodbye as you exit.

That's all you have to do. Now for some 'don'ts'.

Interview don'ts

- Don't try cheap tricks. Squeezing the interviewer's hand when shaking it to show intimacy is a non-starter.

- Don't fill the silence. It is inevitable in an interview that there will be short silences as the interviewers gather their thoughts. In your nervousness it is tempting to fill these and this is when the unrehearsed answers and the slips are most likely to occur. If you have said your piece, stick there and don't dig a hole for yourself.

- Don't assume the interviewers know what they want. There are a lot of poor interviewers about and if you let them have their way they won't see the best in you. Whenever you can, turn the question so you are making your prepared point that you are the best person for the specification they have given.

- Don't freeze up. Interviewees that don't change the tone of their voice or move are hard work and tiring for interviewers. If you are not lively and don't try to catch their attention you are quite capable of sending them to sleep. This is deeply embarrassing to them and they are not going to thank you when they feel their eyelids dropping.

- Don't play off the other candidates by criticising them. Play to your strengths alone and let the interviewers decide who is the best candidate.

Try it out

Now try conducting your own mock interview in pairs, with each person taking turns to play both the role of interviewer and interviewee. Think of a position you are going to interview for and the type of questions you will ask. Create an interview setting. If you can, try to record the interview on video. One person should do a 'bad' interview and the other a 'good' interview. Play back the tapes and analyse both interviews. Don't worry if you don't get it right the first time.

Well that wasn't so bad, was it? We would like to invite you to join us in the world of leisure.

! Check it out

1 What are the four key areas that you need to assess when planning your career?

2 What are the three obstacles that most people face when trying to assess themselves objectively?

3 Who are the best people to give you advice on your career?

4 Identify three sources of information on vacancies.

5 Identify three questions you might ask yourself when planning your career.

6 What is the purpose of a CV?

7 How would you prepare for an interview? Give three examples of things you would do in preparation.

Sources of information and further reading

The leisure industry is constantly changing and most books become out of date very quickly. For example, if you were reading a textbook for the first series of GNVQ you would probably have read that DIY is the boom home leisure sector for the foreseeable future and the Web would probably have not been mentioned. If you want to know about the leisure world, you need to investigate it, using the latest materials. The following is therefore not a list of further reading but a list of sources which will need to be updated.

Government statistics

Government offices produce a huge number of statistics such as the *Employment Gazette*, *Social Trends*, *General Household Survey* often with interpretation and commentary. You will also find that the Government websites for the Office of National Statistics provide many tables. While extremely useful, they are also selective and you will often find the information you really want is only in printed form.

Press and magazines

Leisure Week is perhaps the best general overview of the industry and particularly the private sector. The professional bodies, trade associations and public bodies often have monthly magazines that are valuable sources. For example, ILAM produces *The Leisure Manager*.

The broadsheet newspapers often provide articles about the leisure industry in their business pages and increasingly in their sports and leisure sections. Sometimes these may be snippets – for example about one company merging with another – but often they will have a long detailed articles about a sector or a particular company that provides current statistics, views and forecasts.

Annual reports

Although in some cases these contain the bare minimum of information they are more often an opportunity for the organisation to promote itself and provide statistics and articles about their work. The National Trust, Arts Council and Sport England are excellent examples of bodies that issue high-quality reports.

The Web

Increasingly, websites provide statistics and documents. Some are immediately available on your web server which will almost certainly have a business page for example. There are also many other sites. You may find the following list useful as points from which to start a search through the links they provide. Major organisations and public bodies run some of these sites while others are created by smaller organisations such as trade associations. As organisations may not be geared up to student enquiries, it is courteous to use websites first, and to write rather than telephone if you have further enquiries.

Reading

Houston C. *Creating Winning CV Applications*, Trotman, 1998

Sansregret M. and Adam D. *Assess Your Skills, Personality and Ability For The Job You Want*, Kogan, 1998

Foster V. *Developing Employment Skills*, Trotman, 1998

Useful websites

Association of Business Sponsorship of the Arts: **www.absa.org.uk/index.html**

Audit Bureau of Circulation: **www.abc.org.uk**

Brewers and Licensed Retailers Association: **www.blra.co.uk**

British Audience Research Board: **www.barb.co.uk**

British Audio Federation: **www.british-audio.org.uk**

British Casinos Association: **www.british-casinos.co.uk**

British Hospitality Association: **www.bha-online.org.uk**

British Phonograph Industries:
www.bpi.co.uk

British Radio and Electrical Equipment
Association: www.brema.org.uk

British Toy and Hobby Association:
www.btha.co.uk

British Video Association:
www.bva.org.uk

CEDEA (home entertainment):
www.cedea.org.uk

CHITO: www.myi.org.uk

CIPFA: www.ipf.gov.uk

Companies House:
www.companieshouse.gov.uk

English Heritage:
www.english-heritage.org.uk

HTF: www.htf.org.uk

Leisure Week: www.leisureweek.co.uk

LISU: www.lboro.ac.uk

METIER: www.metier.org.uk

Sports Industry Federation:
www.sportslife.org.uk

SPRITO: www.sprito.org.uk

The Local Government Association:
www.lga.gov.uk

The National Trust:
www.nationaltrust.org.uk

The Youth Hostel Association:
www.yha.org.uk

Safe working practices in the leisure and recreation industry

This unit is organised into five sections. You will learn about:

- working within the law
- health and safety legislation
- hazards and risk assessment
- ensuring a safe and secure working environment
- security in leisure and recreation.

Introduction

Think of the leisure industry as a large tree: what you see is an attractive display of leaves, branches and fruits that provide a base for the birds and insects that live there. It is all dependent upon the massive root system that is out of sight below ground and responsible for keeping the whole structure in place and thriving. The tree is like the facilities and services that make up a leisure service. The root system is the administration, mechanical plant systems and, above all, the health and safety arrangements that exist to make sure the customers, staff and all who use the facility are protected from harm.

Anyone working in the industry needs to be saturated with health and safety awareness and practice. Many leisure activities involve, at various times, large numbers of people, hazardous machinery, and potentially hazardous pursuits in water, the air or unfamiliar environments. People working in the industry therefore need to be vigilant. You should be aware of the relevant laws (but do not need to be a walking encyclopaedia of law) and be able to take action to avoid or rectify and control unsafe practice. After a while these skills will fall into place naturally and become second nature. Furthermore, many of the tasks you do will be ones that have been designed to maintain good health and safety.

2.1 Working within the law

What is health and safety?

What is meant by the terms health and safety?

Health can be defined as a state of personal well-being. It means you are free of injury, illness or disease. It is important to note that this refers to both:

- *physical health* – the absence of diseases (such as AIDS or hepatitis) or injuries (cuts, breaks and fractures)

  and

- *mental health* – the absence of mental illness such as depression. It also includes the absence of anxiety resulting from bullying, stress from overwork, and trauma such as post-traumatic stress syndrome.

Recreational environments can hold some major health risks unless they are controlled, for example:

1   The spread of infectious disease:

- swimming pools must have sterilisation systems to prevent transmittable diseases being spread from one swimmer to another

- poor hygiene in food preparation can cause food poisoning
- orienteers can contract hepatitis and other diseases from scratches.

2 The risk of injuries:

- all sports participants are prone to trips, falls and collisions
- cinema swing seats on strong springs might cause a crushed finger
- in holiday parks faulty gas cylinder connections can result in fatal explosions.

Safety can be defined as the prevention of accidents. In the leisure industry our aim is to provide safe conditions for all who use or work in our services and facilities. It would be ideal to say that we are totally safe, in other words that there would be no accidents. However, this is not possible, for the following reasons:

- the unexpected or unlikely event (e.g. a lightning strike at a sports event)
- the customer acting in a reckless way (e.g. drunken guests using a hotel pool in the middle of the night)
- the cost of making things safe (e.g. replacing an entire sports centre roof because there is one leak on to the hall floor)
- the failure of materials (e.g. a hidden fracture in compressed air cylinders)
- the failure of operative staff or contractors to provide and maintain safety (e.g. not checking a bouncy castle for hidden children when deflating it)
- the activity itself requiring an element of risk to be enjoyable.

The principal responsibility of anyone working in the leisure and recreation industry is to protect the health and safety of anyone using the services and facilities provided. Many would say that this comes before customer service or the leisure experience

Think it over

Recently there has been a tightening up of safety standards in outdoor activities. Some companies now restrict activities to facility-based pursuits with no activity in natural environments. The aim is to maximise safety.

However some experts (such as Chris Bonington) have said that this has removed the excitement and the recognition of hazards that are part of outdoor activities and self-development. What do you think?

itself. Many recreational situations have the potential to cause accidents or be injurious to health. This is because leisure activities often involve:

- an inherent health and safety risk to the customer, especially when physical effort is involved as in sport (e.g. white-water rafting, martial arts, over-50s keep fit)
- a large numbers of customers (e.g. at discos, concerts, football matches)
- customers doing things that are new to them or stretch their capabilities (e.g. bungee jumping, holiday sub-aqua)
- customers who are unfamiliar with the recreational surroundings (e.g. when walking on cliffs or rocks)
- the use of plant and equipment with significant potential to cause injury or damage to health (e.g. chlorine gas in pools, amplifiers at concerts, fairground equipment)
- customers who may tend to relax their normal standards of self-protection (e.g. when drinking and swimming, showing off).

Inadequate organisation of leisure can mean injury, harm and, at worst, death for customers and workers. No matter how much fun the leisure activity provides, no one will thank you for killing their loved ones or taking away their livelihood. There are many health and safety regulations which you will have to

Look at the picture of a school party on a day trip. Identify three potential hazards. What actions would you take to try to prevent these? What would you do if there was an accident?

Now look at the picture of the fun session in a pool. What potential dangers to the children can you identify? Who should the session be open to? Suggest two changes that could be made to improve safety.

know. You do not have to be an academic, but rather appreciate the key roles played by common sense and observation. At Advanced Level you are acquiring knowledge that a junior manager in a leisure company would use. This means that you will need to know the main requirements of the law in this area and be aware of where and when the laws and regulations will apply. You don't need to know the intricacies of legal debate or case history. It is more important to develop your awareness of hazards and your ability to take action to minimise them. You will need to become familiar with the training and information materials which are readily

available from the Health and Safety Executive (HSE) and many of the organisations that advise on health and safety. Try to develop a health and safety instinct inside yourself so that you become permanently alert.

Health and safety regulations are not static – they represent an on-going crusade to minimise risk and protect health and safety. Within a leisure service any incident or near miss should be evaluated and actions taken to reduce the risk of it happening again. Failure to protect safety or respond to incidents can lead to loss of business, or civil or criminal prosecution. In particular, any problems with hygiene can damage customer relations and it can take many months to bring customers back.

In the main, the industry is highly competent in managing risk. However, standards have to be continually maintained or improved and the pressures on the industry become greater every year. This is largely because, as a society, we are becoming more litigious and will sue if we are injured or suffer ill health, while at the same time high risk activities grow in popularity. Many judgements turn upon the extent to which the leisure provider has taken care to manage risk and to inform customers of any remaining risk.

Thought for the page

- People today are more likely to sue. One reason for this is that most people live in a world where danger and risk have been removed by good health and safety practice. They develop a belief that whatever they are offered will be without risk.

- They are also more likely to place themselves at risk. This may be because their actual experience of risk and danger has been minimal, and they are starved of excitement. Their knowledge of danger from the media is sanitised and remote from the real thing. Unrealistic impressions of what is safe, and a reduced ability to identify danger, lead to heightened expectations as to what the leisure provider should allow them to do.

- This places staff under pressure to provide activities that are exciting and appear dangerous, while at the same time managing the considerable increase in risk.

The quality of health and safety culture and practice has numerous implications apart from the direct effect on health and safety.

- *The organisation, its facilities and events*: A good record will enable the service to be run efficiently without having to spend time and money dealing with incidents and their after effects, such as legal costs. A good safety record will be reflected in lower insurance premiums. It will also enhance the reputation of the organisation and indirectly increase sales through customer confidence and therefore use of the service. On the other hand, a poor record may lead to prosecution, loss of trade and possible closure.

- *Staff*: Well trained staff will feel confident working in a safe environment. Their increased awareness of health and safety issues will mean that they manage health and safety better.

- *Customers*: Knowing that wellbeing is of concern to the organisation will make customers feel more secure and valued. Health and safety is a sign of good customer care and customers who are looked after will become loyal.

- *Environment*: Good health and safety often promotes good environmental practice. Maintenance of plant and machinery minimises fumes, and safe disposal of effluent and waste reduces pollution.

Our working aim is therefore to maximise safety on all occasions without affecting the enjoyment of the leisure experience. Surprisingly high levels of safety can be achieved in all of the categories in the above case study as demonstrated by many organisations. However, this is not always the case and there are still organisations which, for various reasons, do not place the safety of staff and customers above all other considerations. In order to support good practice among the majority, and regulate and punish those who are unsafe, a massive raft of legislation has come into existence.

It may be massive but this legislation is not just red tape. It is effective strategy for informing people how to be safe and to

CASE STUDIES — Playgrounds, activity sports and stadia

Playgrounds

In the 1970s serious accidents to children in specific public playgrounds showed that many injuries were a result of poor design of the equipment, the quality of surfaces and the overall arrangement. Investigation showed that the majority of playgrounds were in a similar state, based on very outdated designs. Since then there has been a major overhaul of playground specifications and, in particular, of surfaces and equipment.

Activity sports

Activity sports had for a long time had voluntary 'understood' codes of practice to prevent accidents. Since the 1970s there has been a growth in commercially run activity centres, governed by the same codes. Incidents had occurred, but the high-profile deaths of several Plymouth schoolchildren while canoeing in Lyme Bay led to investigations which showed that, as a result of commercial expediency and operational pressures, basic safety had

been compromised. Further inquiry revealed that other centres might operate in similar ways. So great was the concern that licensing legislation was introduced.

Stadia

Large crowds are particularly exposed to the dangers of fire or stampede. The enclosed nature and fire risks of many older stadia in the UK were highlighted by the fire at Bradford City's ground. Also, the disaster at Hillsborough further exposed the dangers of crowds in confined spaces. In spite of the huge costs involved, legislation prompted by the public inquiries was introduced to require improvement and, for older grounds, compulsory refurbishment.

Questions

1 For each case study identify two safety features associated with the facility/activity.

2 Identify two hazards for each facility/activity.

maintain health. Whether you are a leisure provider or a customer you cannot afford to be ignorant of it nor avoid the implications of getting it wrong.

Check it out

1 With examples, identify two areas health and safety is concerned with.

2 What is the difference between health and safety?

3 Why can't 100% safety be guaranteed?

4 Why is there a high risk of accidents in the leisure industry?

5 What does HSE stand for?

6 Why are accidents bad for business?

2.2 Health and safety legislation and regulations

Before studying the legislation it is worth looking at some terms and their explanations.

Laws are passed by Parliament and published as *Acts of Parliament* after debate in both Houses. Before an act is passed it will be published as a *Green Paper* (it is actually printed on green paper!) which is debated and amended and then finally published as a

White Paper. The White Paper is usually pretty dry and tells us little about the details of how the act will be applied. To help us know what we are meant to be doing there is usually a set of *Regulations* that go into greater detail. Sometimes because circumstances change there will be further White Papers which are called *Amendments* (changes or additions) to the original act.

Laws are one thing; making them work is another. Who enforces them? Sometimes it is the police, but in health and safety that is not common. Instead, the laws are policed by *an enforcing authority.* This can be a department of a local authority (as is the case for the food and environmental health laws), or it may be a new agency specially set up to make sure the law is obeyed. The most notable of these is the **Health and Safety Commission** which advises on the law and policy and the **Health and Safety Executive (HSE)** which polices health and safety. There are other enforcing authorities. Football stadium safety is controlled by the **Football Licensing Authority**, while commercial adventure activities are policed by the **Adventure**

Activities Licensing Authority. Fire Certificates are issued by the **Fire Service.**

Enforcing authorities such as these have several rights and duties (Figure 2.1).

Figure 2.1 Rights and duties of enforcing authorities

Laws tell us either what we must do or what we must not do. Sometimes the law uses words that have only one meaning, for example the term 'absolute' means something must be done, and you will read expressions like 'employers must' or 'employees shall'. But

CASE STUDY – Reasonable care at the farm

A farmer has opened up his farm as a country interpretation centre. There is a children's corner with rabbits, guinea pigs and chickens with a notice saying 'Parents please note that it is the nature of animals to occasionally nip or peck. If you are concerned about this, please allow your children only to look at the animals'. Three incidents occur in the first season of opening.

a   A child hurts the tip of her nose when a guinea pig bites her as she kisses it.

b   A child contracts an infection that can be attributed to chickens.

c   A rambler is cutting across the fields of the farm and breaks his leg falling in a rut caused by a tractor.

In all three cases the people sue the farmer.

Questions

1   In each case say whether you think the farmer took reasonable care.

2   If you think he did not, what other precautions do you think he should have taken?

legal documents also use words that need interpretation. Two words frequently used are *reasonable* or *practicable*. For example, would it be reasonable to expect a provider to re-roof the premises if there was a small leak that customers might slip on? The answer is 'no'; but putting up signs and cleaning up would be reasonable actions. If, however, the leak was into a chemical store where there was the possibility of a reaction, then it would be reasonable to expect the roof to be repaired.

The final judgement on the interpretation of these relative terms is made by courts, usually after an accident has occurred and the provider is being prosecuted or sued, or there is an inquiry. Obviously it is far better to avoid an accident and to determine what is reasonable by taking advice and seeking guidance from the Health and Safety Inspector or other enforcing authority.

Other sources of information which, while they are not law, should be taken into account. These are:

- guidelines
- professional papers
- codes of practice
- standards
- manufacturers' instructions
- labelling

and would be taken into consideration if there was an investigation or trial.

The official guidelines are most important. These give detailed interpretations of the law and recommend ways of doing things. The HSE publishes its own guidelines such as 'Managing health and safety in swimming pools' – the bible for pool managers – and ROSPA (the Royal Society for Prevention of Accidents) has produced guides for safety on British beaches and also for inland water sites. Professional bodies such as Sport England, ILAM (Institute of Leisure and Amenity Management) and ISRM (Institute of Sport and Recreation Management) also produce professional papers that interpret the law and give examples of good practice. These tend to be general documents that go into considerable detail over issues affecting a broad area of provision.

Safety is a matter of individual responsibility and people need to be aware of hazards and actions that put them at risk. Codes of practice are often available to inform people working or participating in specific activities. These codes are simple, easy-to-read documents produced by organisations involved in the activity such as governing bodies, charities or local authority departments such as education. Codes of practice are not 'absolute', but a litigant who had not followed these would have to justify why he or she had ignored them.

The Department of Trade and Industry and the British Standards Institution set standards for virtually every construction, piece of equipment and many services. One of the criteria they use is 'Is the item safe?' Thus if we use only approved methods or resources we can be seen to be taking reasonable care. The British Standards are all given a number starting with BS and approved items also show the 'kitemark' symbol. For example, gymnasium equipment has the standard BS1892. The British standards are continually reviewed and may in the future be replaced by European Standards.

Another source of guidance is the manufacturers' instructions. Manufacturers of

Check it out

1 What are Acts of Parliament?
2 What are Green and White Papers?
3 What is an enforcing authority?
4 Name five sources of written guidance to help leisure providers keep within the law.
5 What is meant by 'absolute'?

equipment, machinery and products that contain chemicals provide labelling that gives safety warnings and treatment advice.

Health and Safety at Work Act (1974)

In the United Kingdom the legal foundation of health and safety rests upon the Health and Safety at Work Act (1974) (HSWA). It is important to realise that:

1   HSWA is an *enabling act*. This means that additional pieces of related legislation (regulations) can be introduced as and when they become necessary without full parliamentary process. Unfortunately, the need to add further legislation has often arisen as a result of major incidents or an increase in court verdicts in favour of the victims of an accident. A good example is the Activity Centre (Young Persons' Safety) Act (1995) which came into effect after the deaths of four young canoeists at Lyme Bay in 1993. In many cases the introduction of legislation of this sort is the direct result of a *public* or *judicial inquiry* set up to investigate the causes of an accident and to suggest measures to ensure that it does not occur again. These inquiries are headed by a judge who will gather evidence and question witnesses and others involved. To do the job thoroughly, an inquiry needs time to gather evidence, so it is usually about six months to a year, or more, before it will have considered all the evidence and made recommendations. Another parliamentary session is then needed to push through new legislation. So you can see that three years from accident to new legislation is pretty quick in parliamentary terms!

In other cases legislation or guidelines are the result of pressure from the public or pressure groups. A good example of this is

the action taken over safety in children's playgrounds. For many years, playgrounds were built on concrete or other similar, hard surfaces, which broke up easily causing many falls, and worse still, were so hard to fall on to from the playground equipment that children had serious accidents. This situation was originally highlighted in the BBC consumer programme 'That's Life'. This led to a major public campaign that pressured for the resurfacing of playgrounds with soft materials. Although this did not result in legislation it did lead to HSE recommendations on good practice.

2   HSWA is a general act that affects all working environments and not just leisure. It is supported by other legislation that affects health and safety in the leisure industry. This may:

   - relate directly to the leisure environment (e.g. Safety at Sports Ground Act [1985])
   - be relevant in the leisure environment in question (e.g. Use of Abrasive Wheels Act, which provides regulations that are used throughout the engineering industry but are relevant in ice rinks where skates are sharpened).

3   HSWA is a *criminal law*. In other words, those breaking it are subject to criminal prosecution and if found guilty can be fined or imprisoned. As you will see later the employee can sometimes be the guilty party as well as the employer. This is a good reason why health and safety is the concern of everyone.

HSWA core principles

The Act is aimed at the management that provides the leisure activity. It covers the health and safety of all involved with the organisation:

CASE STUDY – Duty of care

The scene: You work in a leisure centre and there is a spillage on the floor.

1 Action: You have been trained and therefore you will rope off the area and place a warning sign nearby. A customer then steps over the rope and slips and breaks an ankle.

Outcome: You have satisfied your duty of care and any action against you would be unsuccessful.

2 Action: You have been trained but can't be bothered to rope off the area as you will miss your tea break. The customer fails to see the liquid and slips and breaks his ankle.

Outcome: As you have failed in your duty of care you will be personally liable.

3 Action: Your manager has never trained you nor informed you of procedures for clearing up spillage. The same accident happens.

Outcome: You may be sued successfully for not taking 'reasonable care' but it is more likely that the manager will be found to have failed in his/her duty of care by not training staff to be aware of their responsibilities and duties.

Question

You will note that the word reasonable is used above. Do you think an untrained person should have been able to take 'reasonable care' in these circumstances?

- staff (full- and part-time, permanent and temporary such as holiday workers)
- customers (participants and spectators)
- contractors (e.g. builders, servicing engineers, casual instructors and coaches)
- trespassers.

It is up to the employer and employee to ensure that legislation is followed. Both are affected by a common law principle – *duty of care* (see page 87). This means that all individuals are responsible for the effect of their actions or their omissions on other people. This means that if an accident occurs due to your action or failure to act then the injured party can seek compensation in a civil court.

Employers' responsibilities

The employer's key duties refer to

1 Conditions of employees (Section 2 of the Act)

2 Duties to non-employees (Sections 3 and 4 of the Act)

The employer, as far as is *reasonably practicable* must ensure the following conditions for employees:

- a safe place of work with safe access (e.g. fabric of the premises, paths and car parks in good condition)
- safe plant and equipment (e.g. heating, ventilation, ice and pool plant in good condition)
- safe use, handling, storage, and transport of articles and substances (e.g. for chemical storage, handling beer kegs)
- safe systems of work (safety checks and procedures, evacuation routes, notification of disease)
- information, instruction, training and supervision of employees
- a safe working environment (e.g. good conditions of ventilation, heat, light, hygiene).

Employers need to look at all these areas in detail and co-ordinate them. To ensure this, the Act (section 2[3]) places upon the employer an *absolute duty* to produce and revise *a Health and Safety policy* and *inform employees* of it. Where the organisation is larger than four employees, the policy has to be written.

The employer, so far as is *reasonably practicable* must ensure that non-employees are not exposed to risks to their health and safety. This can be achieved by:

- managing the health and safety of the facility and the services it provides (e.g. restricting spectators to seating areas, having first aid equipment available, having shower temperatures comfortably regulated)
- Informing (verbally and non-verbally) non-employees of hazards and correct procedures to reduce risk (e.g. telling swimmers to keep within safe water flags on a beach, signs saying no running or deep water signs in pools).

It is important to remember that the employer has to do both these things. For example, if a company warned visitors about a dangerous situation but did nothing further to reduce the risk, it would be liable.

Think it over There is a damaged swing in a children's playground. What action would you take?

Who are non-employees? HSWA is supported by other legislation, such as the Occupational Liability Acts (1955, 1984) which are laws that define non-employees as 'all visitors to a site'. The OLA enforce on the employer (occupier) a duty of care to all visitors. These include:

1   Customers who are using the facilities

2   Contractors working at leisure facilities (e.g. visiting instructors, engineers or building contractors carrying out repairs). The employer needs to inform and manage the work environment for them. For example, a stage manager will check that actors in a pantomime have used a trap door before and instruct them on the safety arrangements before they rehearse.

Thought for the page

Managing the safety of outside contractors can pose problems for the leisure provider. On the one hand, you need to protect their safety and the safety of others. On the other, you don't want to annoy them by constantly supervising them. Checks on references and qualifications and an interview will enable you to assess their competence and how much supervision is necessary.

You should always inform contractors of any features that may be temporary or unusual to a facility. For example, many sports halls leak and it would be good practice on a wet day to remind casual instructors that they should check the surface before they start teaching. It would be common sense to think ahead and warn any builder working on site of electrical cabling, water pipes or other existing, unseen hazards, that you are aware of.

It is important to remember that it is the employer or organisation that is held responsible for health and safety overall. If a contractor causes an accident and the victim decides to sue, he/she will initially sue the organisation even if it is the contractor's fault. It is then up to the organisation to sue the contractor for negligence. If the employer has not carried out full safety checks and safety management then it could be difficult to find the contractor liable.

Trespassers: OLA (1984) introduced a duty of care of trespassers. The occupier not only has to inform them but needs to discourage trespassers from putting themselves at risk.

For example, if a teenager breaks into a swimming pool and swims under a pool cover and drowns, the centre could be held liable unless it could show that it had taken reasonable care to warn the trespasser of the danger (e.g. 'Danger' notice) and had protected the trespasser from danger (e.g. had secured pool covers down as normal).

A problem organisations face is how to protect their grounds from trespass. Too low a boundary wall can be interpreted as an implied invitation to enter, while a wall that is too high or topped with wire or glass can be interpreted as dangerous for trespassers. The normal practice is to opt for a medium-height boundary of 3.3 metres, although boundaries at sports grounds are 2.2 metres.

A well-known situation arises in pubs and clubs when customers outstay their welcome and in effect become trespassers. Bouncers or security staff are very much under a duty of care to remove them safely and to be aware of the fine line between safely escorting the trespasser off the premises and common assault.

A recent development in the laws dealing with trespass is the Countryside Act (2000) which gives the public the right to roam on private countryside. This means that recreations like rambling and countryside quests and other activities can take place as legitimate pursuits all over the country.

Thought for the page

Many trespassers are children whose main aim is to have a bit of fun rather than cause damage. Unfortunately, for many having fun means taking a risk that they wouldn't be allowed to do under supervision at school or home. However, the fact that they are not used to taking these risks means they stand a greater chance of having an accident. As leisure providers we have to think ahead and anticipate things that would happen in this situation that would not occur with customers.

Landowners are worried that they will be liable under OLA for any accidents that occur to ramblers – this means that they could be sued by someone who twisted his ankle down a rabbit hole. This is an unfeasible situation and the Government has indicated that it will make visits of this sort exempt from occupiers' liability.

Children: OLA (1957) also introduced the concept that applies to all health and safety legislation – that children are less responsible than adults. A child is someone under the compulsory school-leaving age. An employer must be aware that children are likely to be:

- ignorant of dangerous materials and other dangers
- attracted to dangerous substances
- less aware of dangerous situations
- less able to take evasive action
- unable to understand or take notice of information provided for adults
- able to enter spaces that adults cannot.

Because children play such a major part in our industry either as customers or trespassers leisure staff need to be ever-vigilant of the heightened risks for children.

Similar vigilance is needed for customers with learning difficulties or physical disability. It is also important to ascertain before the start of any activity if any of the participants has a disability which is not immediately apparent; for instance, deafness.

Employees' responsibilities

When an employee starts work the law requires that he/she is informed about health

Think it over

One of a group of swimmers tells you that he is partially deaf. Make a list of what this is going to mean a) for him, b) for you, c) for the rest of the group. What else would you ask him before starting the activity?

CASE STUDY – Abseiling

A primary school party went abseiling with a reputable activity centre. They had to abseil down a cliff, then make their way in pairs along a beach and up a steep but safe path with a fixed rope to help them climb up. One of the girls was deaf. The instructions were signed to the girl who made the abseil successfully and then proceeded back with one of the others.

A few minutes later, the leader saw a group of tourists looking over the cliffs where the return rope was. Wondering what they were watching and whether there was anything wrong he ran over to find the deaf girl had ignored the path and was climbing unaided up a sheet cliff face, where she was stuck, unable to look up or down and therefore out of communication. The leader made a rapid unroped descent and managed to escort her safely down to the beach.

Questions

1   Who was at risk in this incident?

2   What lessons were there to be learnt?

! Check it out

1   What does HSWA stand for?

2   What four groups of people does HSWA protect?

3   What is 'duty of care'?

4   What are the employer's two key duties?

5   Give three of the conditions that must be provided for employees, and give an example for each.

6   Give two ways in which employers protect non-employees.

7   What does OLA stand for?

8   How does OLA affect duty of care?

9   Give three reasons why children are more at risk.

and safety procedures and recognised hazards within the organisation. Good practice on the part of the employer is to provide this in the form of a formal 'induction' package that will include written notes, verbal instruction and a physical demonstration and which will identify any need for training. A briefing for a new employee should ensure that he/she is:

- made aware of the health and safety systems in practice
- fully aware of any hazards in the place of employment
- checked for knowledge and competence on health and safety matters and that any training that may be necessary is identified
- assigned responsibilities and tasks for health and safety
- brought up to date about any changes in practice and regulations.

Armed with this information the employee is now in a position to maintain the health and safety of that organisation. It is expected under the HSWA (sections 7 and 8) that they will:

1   co-operate with the employer in carrying out the statutory provisions

2   take reasonable care of their own safety and the safety of others in so far as it may be affected by their actions or omissions (principle of *duty of care*)

3   refrain from reckless or intentional misuse of anything designed to maintain health, safety and welfare.

If employees follow these principles, they will be contributing to the maintenance of health and safety. If there is an accident they will not be liable. It is only if they ignore these duties that they could be dismissed, prosecuted or sued for criminal liability.

In most cases the law intends the employer to develop good health and safety practice. This practice is dependent upon the employees to carry it out; they are the ears, eyes and hands of the organisation. It is the employees who are often the first to notice hazards, take action to remove them, and report back and inform colleagues. At the same time the practice will work only if the employees support it to the full and carry out its intentions. They must work according to the dictates of the safety practice in place, and with the other employees.

In some cases, unfortunately, the employer has not provided adequate health and safety and the employee or others are exposed to risk. In such cases the duty of care (principle 2) will override the principle of co-operation (principle 1) and the employee may have to take alternative action.

Duty of care

All leisure environments are potentially hazardous and all employees must be able to recognise and anticipate hazards, and to take action to avoid or reduce them. A good employee needs to be aware of and responsive to conditions (the duty of care) not only for personal safety but for everyone in the area.

Taking care involves four key stages (Figure 2.2).

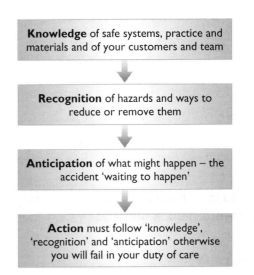

Figure 2.2 The four key stages of taking care

Taking care of yourself and others is not difficult if you keep this model in your head throughout your working day. Experienced leisure operators will often work intuitively and thinking like this is second nature to them.

The opposite of responsibility and care is misuse and negligence. There are always some people

---

Think it over

You are asked to help with the creation of theatre sets. You are given aerosol adhesives and paint. What would you check out first before starting work?

Try it out

Tim is taking a party of active pensioners for a 'beachcombing' walk along a coast of sandy picturesque beaches under towering cliffs. Their plan is to follow the tide line for a couple of miles looking for wreckage and items of natural interest. In most parts the tide line is well down the beach but in one of two places it comes right up to the cliffs. At these places he will make sure the less active in the group stay on the flatter sandy beach. Tim is familiar with the walk which he does regularly with schoolchildren. The walk normally takes two hours and he reckons that leaving at 10am will mean they are back well in time for lunch.

Using the four criteria shown in Figure 2.2 (knowledge, recognition, anticipation, action) analyse how Tim should take care in this situation.

SCENARIOS

Situation: You are asked to get some racquets out of a store. You find that the racquets are on a high shelf under a pile of heavy metal signs and gym mats.

Knowledge: You know how this equipment should be stowed in a store.

Recognition: You can see that the heavy items are piled high on the top.

Anticipation: If you attempt to move them by yourself they might fall and crush you. There is no one around to hear you if this happens.

Action: Go and get others to help you put the store into a safe condition.

Situation: You are taking a party of children for a walk on the moors on a warm day.

Knowledge: You know that children are more susceptible to chilling than adults, and you know that wind is expected later in the day.

Recognition: You realise that you are in charge of a group of children in exposed conditions.

Anticipation: Although it is warm now the children will be chilled when they get up high. They may become hypothermic, exhausted and there will be an increasing chance of follow-on accidents.

Action: Insist children have warm clothing or shorten or change location of walk.

---

who seem to have to do things differently from the herd. They want to be daring, individual or simply want to be the centre of attention. The laws and codes of practice are there to protect us and them from their actions.

Failure of care

Equipment and systems are designed to be as safe as possible. Generally speaking, the more dangerous the hazard, the greater the controls there are to prevent mishap. This means that most accidents occur when the situation and the materials are of the simplest, or they occur as a result of stupid behaviour. For instance, plugging wires into a socket using a matchstick, playing air guitar with a badminton post, not asking someone to help you put a trampoline into a locked position, standing on a chair to stack mats on a shelf.

Failure to follow safety systems or procedures can have dangerous consequences not only for the perpetrator but also for others. Disregard of simple good practice, such as warming up a group of participants in a keep fit class,

may have minor consequences such as a pulled muscle. In other areas, disregard of safe practice may have more serious results.

We said at the beginning of the unit that health involves mental as well as physical health. Thus

Think it over Children are being delivered for a playgroup session in a hall situated on a busy road. What checks will you make before the activities begin?

Thought for the page

Swimming pools. Sodium hypochlorite granules react with water to produce bleach and chlorine gas (used in chemical warfare) which, when diluted, is used to sterilise swimming pool water. These granules are delivered in drums. If the drums are placed anywhere near the pool and any were spilt the result would resemble a gas attack. Normal operating procedures would prohibit this happening, but there have been cases of pool staff ignoring these safety precautions with disastrous consequences.

bullying, racist and sexual harassment could all be interpreted as intentional disregard of the health of others, especially in cases where this has resulted in stress-related outcomes. This has been known to surprise individuals and companies who, while protecting the physical safety of staff, have harassed them and thus fallen foul of HSWA.

> ! **Check it out**
>
> 1 Describe the various stages of a health and safety induction.
> 2 Describe the three basic responsibilities of the employee.
> 3 What do you need to be able to do to care comprehensively for colleagues and visitors?

Support legislation to HSWA – the European Six Pack

This is a set of six laws set out by the European Community in 1992. The laws support HSWA and spell out in more detail duties and responsibilities in particular areas. Think of HSWA as the canvas for health and safety and the Six Pack as the painting.

These laws are shown in Figure 2.3.

Figure 2.3 The six laws that support HSWA

We shall look at each in turn.

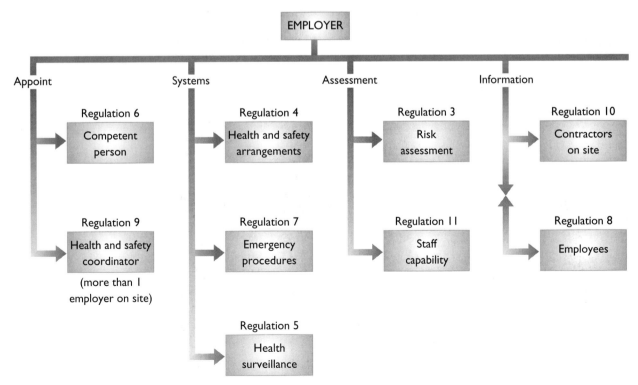

Figure 2.4 MHSW Responsibilities of Employers

Management of Health and Safety at Work Regulations (MHSW)

These regulations set out how employers and employees should manage the health and safety of their facilities (Figure 2.4). The following are of particular relevance to leisure management, and, as in the HSWA, the regulations focus first on the employer and then the employee.

Employers' duties

Risk assessment (Regulation 3): The regulations specify three key requirements for safety:

1 recognising hazards

2 assessing the risk (likelihood) of an accident occurring

3 assessing the potential seriousness.

These are followed by:

1 action – suggesting a course of action and implementing it

2 recording the assessment (required in law for employers of over five staff).

Risk assessments are not one-off projects; they are *dynamic* in that they are carried out regularly and include updated plans of action. The reasons for this are:

- conditions change. Whenever there is a significant change in design or practice a new risk assessment should be done
- knowledge and technology changes. For example new materials such as safety glass may become more easily available or cheaper. Staff may be better trained or advised and be able to propose better action plans.

Health and Safety arrangements (Regulation 4): The employer must document the health and safety procedures. These will include:

- normal operating procedures (i.e. the safe day-to-day running of the facility)

- emergency procedures (e.g. in case of evacuation, fire, bomb alerts, major failure of plant)
- procedures for monitoring and reviewing health and safety performance.

Again, these are dynamic arrangements that are continuously updated. The regulations also require the arrangements to be integrated into the other management systems operating in the organisation. In other words there is no point having a wonderful plan for safety training unless it can be resourced from the budget.

Health surveillance (Regulation 5): If there is risk of an identifiable disease or condition that is related to work, formal health surveillance should be set in place. In most cases, such as AIDS or hepatitis, prevention of infection is extremely well controlled. One disease that does occur, albeit very rarely, is legionnaires' disease. This is carried in contained hot-water systems. Water testing can and does identify it and when it occurs stringent surveillance and control procedures are put in place.

Participants in certain outdoor activities, such as canoeing, should be aware of the possibility of water-borne diseases such as Weil's disease (leptospirosis) or entero-gastric disease. It is sensible to avoid closed water sites or water with an effluent discharge where these diseases might occur. On water that is used regularly it is good practice to seek information from environmental services as to the bacterial content of the water.

Appointment of a competent person (Regulation 6): Health and safety law is a complex body of regulations that are constantly changing. Therefore there is a requirement to employ a suitably trained person who can advise on good practice and ensure compliance with the law. Many firms will seek advice from a specialist such as the Company Health and Safety Adviser or the local authority Health and Safety officer. However, they still also need to have a competent person on the premises who is assigned to this role. This is nearly always a senior official such as the manager or deputy manager.

Emergency procedures (Regulation 7): All employers and employees must know what to do when there is serious and imminent danger. In leisure facilities these emergencies will include fire, bomb alerts, explosions, structural failure, major plant failure, major injury, gas emissions and pool rescue. The complexity of these will vary from facility to facility. Outdoor leisure activities require emergency plans based on the natural environment; for example, marine sports have specific codes and procedures to deal with shipwreck and severe weather conditions.

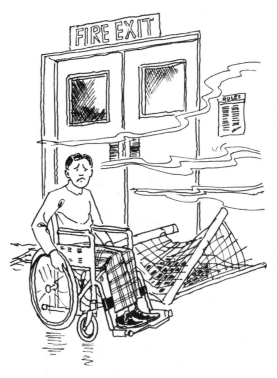

Would this fire exit allow for speedy evacuation of the building?

> **Think it over**
>
> Theatres, nightclubs and cinemas all have similar characteristics: they are dark and hold a lot of people. Sports halls usually have easy access to the outside. Stadia hold even more people but are not necessarily enclosed. Think about what different procedures might be suggested for speedy evacuation in each case.

> **Thought for the page**
>
> Never assume that a leisure facility is easy to evacuate. You need to be alert for temporary blockages, such as faulty catches on emergency doors, or rubbish or equipment being left behind a door.

Information for employees (Regulation 8): Communication in the organisation must be two-way. Employees must go through induction training on all health and safety procedures at the start of their employment and they should be retrained as appropriate. Non-employees and temporary workers need also to be informed but not trained by the organisation.

Co-operation and co-ordination (Regulation 9): Where there is more than one employer using a site (dual-use facilities such as a shopping mall with a nightclub, a multi-activity centre for outdoor activities, a church hall where playgroups, keep fit classes and rehearsals take place), then all the employers must work together over health and safety procedures and regularly meet to exchange information. It would be normal to appoint a health and safety co-ordinator.

Persons working in host employer's undertakings (Regulation 10): This means contractors. The employer needs to inform them of risks to health, health and safety procedures and, in particular, to risks specific to the site. For example, contractors working on the landscape should be informed of the whereabouts of underground electric cables.

Capabilities and training (Regulation 11): Employers need to consider the competence and capability of employees when assigning tasks involving health and safety. When circumstances change (for instance, the introduction of new equipment) appropriate training is required.

Employees' duties

This section of MHSW is an expansion of the HSWA. There are three main duties:

- to use all equipment/machinery in accordance with instructions/training
- to inform the employer of any situation where there is an immediate or serious danger to health and safety to oneself or others
- to inform the employer of any deficiencies in the health and safety arrangements.

These responsibilities are so important because the staff are the people who monitor the systems and check for new hazards. The attitude 'That's not my job' should never be found in a leisure facility. To leave a hazard unreported and unattended is to shirk responsibility and risk an accident, very possibly to someone else.

Personal Protective Equipment at Work Regulations (PPE)

There are many jobs in leisure that involve dirty or hazardous conditions for which protective clothing is necessary. Working with fibreglass requires a mask and gloves, grinding skates requires goggles, handling pool chemicals involves wearing aprons, gloves and boots. In outdoor activities there is a vast range of protective clothing which both staff and participants need to use. Where there is heavy plant, such as compressors, ear defenders/plugs need to be used.

PPE regulations simply require the employer to provide and ensure use of protective clothing when a risk cannot be controlled by other measures.

Manual Handling Operations (1992) (MHO)

The leisure industry is one where handling of heavy or unwieldy equipment is often an

---

CASE STUDY— Routine checks at the swimming pool

Kaylee is a shift leader in a swimming pool. At the beginning of her shift – which is a quiet one with usually about a dozen people in the pool – she does a routine check of the pool area. She has a checklist which she will hand in to the duty manager at the end of the shift. Here is what she finds.

- The pool hall seems in good order except that someone has put all the safety lines in a jumbled pile instead of leaving them ready for use at the lifeguard stations.

- She also notices that a tile has come loose at the top of the pool steps. It is not very hazardous but could give a

nasty scratch if a customer did not notice it.

- She goes into the first aid room where everything is in place except for the eyewash bottle which is missing from its unit.

- Passing the lockers she sees that an eye-level locker door has been vandalised and is hanging off its hinges.

Questions

1 Identify who should be told about these hazards and when.

2 What other actions should Kaylee take?

everyday part of work, whether it is moving beer kegs around the cellar or erecting football posts. This can lead to employees suffering from backstrain and having to take time off work. Frequently employees suffer because they have not been properly trained or have ignored their training in manual handling.

MHO works on a scale of responsibilities which both employer and employee should follow.

Avoid: Hazardous manual handling operations should be avoided where reasonably practicable. This means finding ways to make the job less hazardous. Obvious solutions are to find extra people to tackle the task (e.g. lifting gym mats with a colleague), break the task down into a smaller, less hazardous one (e.g. lifting one mat at a time), and if practicable, introduce mechanisation such as a trolley or a hoist.

Assess: If a hazardous situation cannot be avoided, the situation should be assessed. A plan should be made to decide the least hazardous way of handling.

Reduce: Reduce the risk of injury as far as is reasonably practicable. This may mean using more people or mechanisation. In many cases it will mean ensuring that people know what they are doing and follow through their training.

Health and Safety (Display Screen Equipment) Regulations (1992) (DSE)

Over recent years, working at a computer monitor has become an everyday experience for many people. In the leisure industry there are some people who spend long hours at a screen. Receptionists and booking personnel are probably the largest group in leisure but managers are becoming increasingly bound to work stations. There are numerous injuries that poor work station design can create. These include sight-related problems such a headaches, repetitive strain injury and postural problems such as back injuries. There is evidence for and against radiation-related injury. The HSE advises that there are now no damaging radiation effects, but some employers prefer to take precautions for the peace of mind of their staff.

> **Think it over**
> As facilities such as Internet cafés and arcades develop, a duty of care will arise towards customers who spend long hours at screens and risk affecting their health. How would you react?

The DSE regulations are aimed at employees who rely on using monitors for long periods to do their jobs. The regulations are intended to remove or manage the risks mentioned above by requiring employers to:

i carry out risk assessment of work stations

ii ensure work stations conform with minimum standards

iii provide a suitable environment (e.g. well-ventilated, heated, and with reduction of glare)

iv provide work breaks

v train the work station users

vi provide eyesight tests

vii inform and train employees.

Workplace (Health and Safety and Welfare) Regulations (1992) (HSW)

These regulations concern the environment in which we work. They replace the old Factories Act and the Offices, Shops and Premises Acts. They cover most leisure situations with the exception of outdoor activities – there, if the activity is sited away from main buildings in the countryside, the regulations do not apply.

Employers have to provide:

i   a good working environment (e.g. one with lighting, ventilation and heating maintained)

ii safety of pedestrians and vehicles, windows, gates and doors, escalators and floors

iii facilities such as rest areas, toilets and wash rooms, clothing storage

iv housekeeping and hygienic conditions for the storage and removal of waste.

Provision and Use of Work Equipment Regulations (1992) (PUWER)

We use equipment throughout the industry not only for providing the activity but also for maintaining the buildings and plant, and for providing administration and support (guillotines for cutting posters, binding machines, staple guns). It is essential that all work equipment is suited to the job and maintained in a safe condition.

The regulations cover 24 categories and sum up the employer's responsibilities as follows:

i   equipment is used only for its intended use and is suitable for that use

ii equipment is properly maintained in accordance with guidelines and instructions

Thought for the page

When doing a risk assessment it is a good idea to use the full list of 24 categories of PUWER to serve as a checklist.

iii working conditions and hazards are considered when selecting equipment

iv there is training and information made available.

Check it out

1   List three of the responsibilities of the employer under MHSW – give an example of how each of these might be applied.

2   What are the responsibilities of the employee under MHSW?

3   Describe the scale of responsibilities under MHO.

4   Give two possible effects on health covered by DSE and identify ways of rectifying them.

5   Summarise the responsibilities of the employer under HSW.

Beyond the Six Pack .... more regulations

Anyone working in the leisure industry will come into contact with three major potential hazards:

* Electricity
* Noise
* Chemicals.

Poor maintenance or misuse of electricity and chemicals can lead to serious, even fatal consequences. Regulations have come into force that have been designed to minimise this risk.

Electricity: This is particularly important in the leisure industry. In sport there are many situations where the combination of wet conditions and electricity could be particularly hazardous. Similarly, the use of portable electrical apparatus at events such as rock concerts can be dangerous. In theatres there are complex lighting systems, while in fairgrounds and theme parks there is the combination of high-voltage cabling and complex machinery. To reduce these hazards

DANGER OF DEATH
ELECTRICITY
KEEP OUT

IN CASE OF EMERGENCY
PHONE 0800 626555
EAST MIDLANDS ELECTRICITY

the Electricity at Work Regulations (1989) require various precautions such as inspection, testing and certification as well as the training of staff by independent inspectors. Electrical work must be done by recognised contractors or a qualified technician.

Noise: This may be a hazard in certain leisure situations. A pool plant room can be unpleasant when a wave machine is in action, while most people know all too well the effect a rock concert will have on the ears for some hours after you leave it. The Noise at Work Regulations (1990) come into force in the workplace if you cannot hear a person from two metres away.

Control of Substances Hazardous to Health Regulations (1989, 1994)

Throughout the industry there is a range of chemicals used for hygiene and disinfecting.

Household cleaners such as bleach or ammonia, floor polish and aerosol sprays are all familiar. Facilities may have a problem with pests and therefore rat poison or insecticide may be used. Although they are familiar they can be hazardous, especially when stored with other industrial substances.

In swimming pools chlorine or ozone is used to disinfect the pool water. Both chemicals are extremely dangerous in concentration and strict control is necessary over their storage and use. There is also a range of chemicals that is used to create the gas chlorine, such as hypochlorite granules or liquid and acids and other chemicals used in 'dosing' the water. These may react with water or other chemicals to produce corrosive reactions or create chemicals that are dangerous to health.

Solvents are also a problem as they may be an irritant if touched, and poisonous or asphyxiating if swallowed or inhaled. Many solvents are highly inflammable. Solvents range from specialist adhesives used for glass fibre in canoe repairs or set building in theatres, to everyday products such as paint or glue either in liquid or aerosol form. Clearly regulations are needed to minimise risk and this is where COSSH comes in. A hazardous substance is one that is toxic, harmful, corrosive or an irritant. It can have either immediate affects (acid) or delayed ones (such as radiation). The regulations require employers to do the following:

i   appoint a COSSH assessor who is given the time to train to be able to assess risk

ii obtain the code of practice for COSSH

iii inform the staff of the organisation's practice using published guidance material

iv keep a record of hazardous substances that are used or produced on site

v   obtain up-to-date hazard data sheets from the supplier of the substances

vi   ensure the use of hazardous substances is absolutely necessary, and undertake to replace them if reasonably practical

vii   identify the control measures used (for example, chlorine gas has now been largely replaced by chloride salts and acid which are inert until mixed)

viii train staff who will be in contact with chemicals in the safe use, storage and disposal of the substances, and in the use of personal protective equipment and emergency procedures

ix   create and implement a system to maintain the control of substances (e.g. how they will be delivered, how long they will be stored and in what conditions)

x   monitor the handling of substances by staff and their adherence to control measures.

Of these, regulation ix above is very important in three respects:

1 Storage

In most facilities there will be one or more storage rooms where substances that are not being used pose no danger.

a   store rooms should be well away from public areas, clearly marked and kept secure

b   substances that would react if combined need to be separated

c   inflammable materials must be kept away from areas where there may be a fire risk (e.g. close to electrical points)

d   store rooms should be ventilated so that stored substances will not be affected by damp or sunlight

e   first aid remedies should be at hand.

It is worth remembering that fireworks, which are occasionally obtained for parties or Guy Fawkes Night, are regarded as explosives and subject to different regulations. They need to be kept in their own store apart from hazardous substances.

2 Handling

Once chemicals are being used there is an increased chance of spillage or contact with the handler or other people. To minimise this:

a   only trained people should handle substances

b   they should follow the instructions for use and handling

c   they should wear the appropriate protective clothing

d   they should have appropriate first aid remedies near the site

CASE STUDY – An emergency at the pool

Kaylee has had a bad morning on her shift. A group of lads came into the pool and started clowning about. After several warnings she asked them to leave. Unnoticed by her, one of them came back carrying a foam fire extinguisher which he had pulled off its wall fitting. He thought it would be a laugh to pretend to set it off. Unfortunately he did just that by accident. The foam squirted in his face causing him to drop the extinguisher in the pool. The pool is staffed by two experienced lifeguards and an apprentice placement who started work that morning as a shadow.

Questions

1 What are the dangers?

2 What should Kaylee do to manage this emergency?

e they should be trained in how to take immediate action should something go wrong.

Emergency

What happens if something goes wrong and the substances threaten to harm people?

- move people out of harm's way and give first aid to casualties
- enact procedures to contain the situation (e.g. automatic close-down of the systems, fire extinguishers).

Working Time Regulations (1998)

These regulations are enforced by the HSE or Environmental Health Department and are essentially employment legislation which is designed to prevent exploitation and overworking of the workforce. There are, however, considerable health and safety concerns when staff work long hours and become tired, less vigilant and less competent as a result.

In some areas of leisure the work may involve long hours. Before these regulations came in it would be common for workers to do double shifts. In the events sector unforeseen circumstances can extend already long working days into round the clock operations. In outdoor activities leaders may be responsible for their participants over several days or longer on expeditions.

The industry is a low-paid one and uses large numbers of part-time staff. It is often likely that these employees will have other part-time jobs which may include night work. So although it may appear from the leisure employer's records that staff are working short hours, the truth of the matter is that they are working excessive hours and are arriving in an exhausted condition.

The regulations state that there is no obligation for any worker to work more than

Thought for the page

Good employers are aware of the possibilities of part-time staff becoming over-tired. They will find out what other work the part-timer is doing and alert shift supervisors to notice if anyone is particularly tired.

an average of 48 hours a week. However, if an employee wants to work longer hours he/she can do so legally by signing an 'opt-out' clause. Because of this clause and the fact that many employers in the leisure industry are now employing part-time staff these regulations have not really affected the industry.

 Check it out

1 Name three regulations that apply directly to specific hazards at work.

2 Describe and give an example of a hazardous substance.

3 What do you need to get from the suppliers of a hazardous substance?

4 Describe the three aspects of day-to-day management of hazardous substances.

Health and Safety (First Aid) Regulations (1981) and RIDDOR

Providing first aid

Despite all the precautions you have taken to ensure safety, unforeseen accidents will occur.

1 this might be because someone did not follow the rules

2 sometimes the activities themselves have an element of risk

3 sometimes the participants have a hidden problem, such as a person having an undetected heart complaint

4 sometimes there are chance circumstances such as a lightning strike or a gust of wind.

It is important that a procedure for treating injured people is in place and that all the staff know it. It is also important to keep a record of any incidents, covering the immediate circumstances and possible causes. A record will allow:

- analysis of causes which may lead to a review of the risk assessment and control measures. In other words, we can stop the accident happening again.
- the government agencies to collect statistics and identify key areas of concern for health and safety. Recently the number of drownings in small commercial swimming pools has become a cause for concern.
- provision of evidence should there be legal proceedings.

The main regulations outlining these procedures are the Health and Safety (First Aid) Regulations (1981). These are primarily designed to protect employees but, because the leisure industry has customers and is liable for them (occupational liability), the spirit of the regulations passes to visitors to the premises. This can create problems, because most leisure facilities do not have many staff on duty and there will normally be only one first aider. If the facility has a large event, that may be inadequate and extra trained staff or auxiliaries like St John's Ambulance may be needed.

The regulations require the employer to provide first aid within the context of the workplace. In other words, not only should general first aid be available but also devices, specific aids and procedures necessary to the particular site. For example, in sports centres there is a heightened risk of heart attacks, and many centres will provide a defibrillator to help steady the heart in the event of a

customer having an attack. In night-clubs, staff should be trained to be able to recognise and treat alcohol overdose or other drug-related conditions. In stadia or clubs first aiders should know how to treat crush injuries in case of a panic evacuation.

Assessment

Employers need to assess what first aid requirements are necessary in the context of their facility. Figure 2.5 shows the factors influencing these requirements.

Figure 2.5 Factors influencing level of first aid requirements

Provision

Having assessed the situation, the employer should provide the following:

1 A *list* of likely accidents and how these will be dealt with. This goes beyond the initial first aid to consider how a casualty will reach treatment and the contacts with and access for emergency services.

2 *Personnel*: two types of person are needed. The first is a qualified first aider (usually the First Aid at Work Certificate is the approved award). Secondly, there must be

a 'first aid co-ordinator' who initially determines the risks and commissions training, and who, at the site of an accident, sets the first aid process in motion and contacts the emergency services.

Special equipment

If the first aid assessment shows a need for special equipment such as breathing aids, eyewash or spinal boards, the employer must provide these.

First aid rooms

It is good practice to provide an area designated for first aid where treatment and recovery can take place, and where materials and records can be stored. While not compulsory, such a room features in most first aid assessments in leisure situations.

First aid materials

There has to be adequate provision of first aid materials at various points on the premises.

These need to be marked, checked and restocked regularly. The materials are stored in a standard green box with a white cross on it. First aid boxes are normally stocked with simple bandages, gauze, eye patches and sterile washing solutions. There should be no creams or painkillers as this may affect medical treatment. This is because the aim of first aid is not to treat but to control and maintain the injury until medical help arrives.

Notices

First aid rooms, points and boxes should be signposted. There should be a notice to say who is the first aid co-ordinator and to list the first aiders.

Reporting accidents

In order to ensure that correct procedures are followed these are the stages laid down by the regulations:

First aid should be given only by a qualified first aider. Sometimes there seems to be a

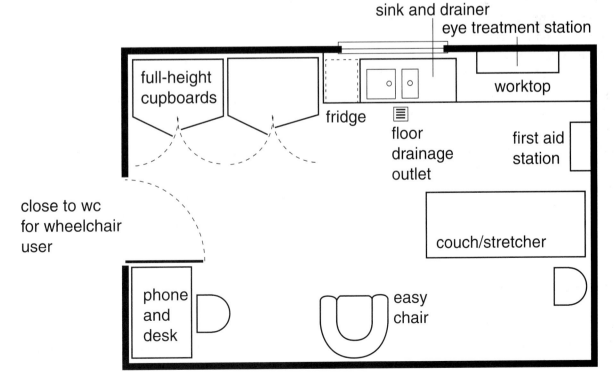

First aid rooms should be spacious and accessible. This is the sports council recommended layout

rush of members of the public claiming that they are first aiders. Be wary, what proof is there? If you have let someone give first aid who is not qualified, you may be liable later in any legal prosecution. It is better to know if possible from the outset where the nominated first aider is to be found and then in an emergency fetch that person only. If possible, you need to find witnesses of the accident and discover how first aid was given. This is in order to support a statement that treatment was given correctly. It also protects the first aider against any claims of improper behaviour. Remember there is a fine line between loosening clothing and improperly exposing a person.

These days, cross-infection of diseases like AIDS or hepatitis B is a possible problem both for the first aider and the casualty. Protection should be taken to prevent any exchange of bodily fluids such as saliva or blood. Using gloves, aspirator tubes or masks is now standard practice. Practices like these should also be recorded.

Recording accidents

All leisure facilities carry an accident book in which the details of any accident and near accidents are reported. The book is principally designed to keep a record of staff accidents and is designed to be of use to social security and accident claims. However, because of the presence of customers, the book may be modified or another book used for accidents to them.

Investigating the accident

Recording the accident is the start of the investigation into why it happened, which should be carried out in order to prevent it from happening again. So you need to visit the scene, talk to anyone who was involved or knows the circumstances. You can then draw conclusions as to the cause of the accident, assess the circumstances and try to outline a plan to prevent its re-occurrence.

Trend analysis: Accidents that are more than a chance occurrence often re-occur over a period

CASE STUDY – A crisis at the sailing club

Jenny is a sailing instructor who works part time for a sailing club. Her club regularly runs sessions for children, teaching them to sail. In each session several boats go out, each with an instructor and three children. The entire fleet is supervised by two safety boats skippered by senior club members.

Today Jenny's group has been slow and is the last to get on to the water. The children have to pull the dinghy down to the water on a trolley. As they do so, one of the children traps his finger between the boat and the trolley, crushing and losing the nail and possibly the tip. The child is screaming.

Several bystanders come forward to help. Jenny has no first aid qualifications and is thankful that one of the bystanders informs her that he is a qualified first aider. Relieved, she takes him into the clubhouse where he takes charge of the situation. Seeing that everything is all right, Jenny resumes her duties.

Question

Review this situation and explain what actions and decisions Jenny could have made to improve her handling of the crisis.

of time, although not always in the same place or in the same circumstances. If this is the case, you will see a pattern emerging. For example:

- one particular location seems to produce a variety of accidents. Is this something to do with the design or environment there?
- accidents often occur at the same time, such as at the end of a shift when staff are tired or in a hurry to get home.
- the same type of accident is re-occurring, for example, customers complain of skin irritation and rashes which might mean that the protective clothing is too hot.
- one member of staff is always having accidents. Has he/she been trained sufficiently? You should question capability and also investigate any possible handicaps such as poor eyesight or ability.

Trend analysis is an important procedure when sufficient data has been collected. It is used to identify key accident issues, to find out their causes and establish the means to rectify them. It will often highlight failings in such things as the design and condition of the building or equipment, training and information procedures or work practice.

Serious incidents

Some accidents or outbreaks of disease are sufficiently serious to warrant more than a trend analysis by the employer. They have to be reported to the appropriate authority, which in the case of sport and leisure is the local authority's environmental health department. RIDDOR (the reporting of injuries, diseases and dangerous occurrences regulations, 1995) are the regulations that determine what is reported and how. They apply to all staff and users of a facility.

There are four classes of incident that must be reported to the enforcing authority. The form that is used is either an accident report

Think of three situations in which you would need to complete a form like this

form (F2508) or a disease report form (F2058a); this has to be returned within ten days, and the employer is also required to keep copies of it for three years.

1 Death or major injury

If an employee or person working on the premises is killed or suffers a major injury, or a member of the public is killed or needs to be taken to hospital, the enforcing authority must be informed by telephone immediately and a completed accident report form sent to them within ten days. Major injuries include:

- fracture other than to fingers, thumbs or toes
- amputation
- dislocation of the shoulder, hip, knee or spine

101

- loss of sight (temporary or permanent)
- chemical or hot metal burn to the eye or any penetrating injury to the eye
- injury resulting from an electric shock or electrical burn leading to unconsciousness or requiring resuscitation or admittance to hospital for more than 24 hours
- any other injury leading to hypothermia, heat-induced illness (e.g. sunstroke, dehydration in discos), unconsciousness, or requiring resuscitation, or admittance to hospital for more than 24 hours (e.g. heart attack, diver's bends)
- unconsciousness caused by asphyxia or exposure to harmful substances or biological agents
- acute illness requiring medical treatment, or loss of consciousness arising from absorption of any substance by inhalation, ingestion or through the skin
- acute illness requiring medical treatment where there is reason to believe that this resulted from exposure to a biological agent or its toxins or infected material.

2 Over-three-day injury

If an employee or person working on the premises suffers an injury that is not major but results in them being off work for over three days, the employers must send in a completed accident report form within ten days. Injuries, in this case, include those resulting from attacks on staff.

3 Dangerous occurrences

If something happens which does not result in a reportable injury, but which clearly could have done, then it may be a dangerous occurrence which must be reported immediately (e.g. by telephone). Again this must be confirmed within ten days using an accident report form. Here are some examples of dangerous occurrences and how they might apply in the leisure industry:

- electrical short circuit or overload causing fire or explosion (e.g. amplifier at a rock concert)
- explosion, collapse or bursting of any closed vessel or associated pipework (e.g. boiler burst in pool plant)
- failure of any load-bearing fairground equipment
- accidental release of any substance which may damage health (e.g. chlorine escapes in swimming pools).

4 Reportable diseases

If a doctor notifies you that your employee suffers from a reportable work-related disease then it must be reported using a completed disease report form.

With the use of protective clothing and other devices, work-related diseases are not common in leisure. However, there are some diseases which are reportable, e.g.:

- infections such as leptospirosis (Weil's disease), hepatitis, tuberculosis, legionellosis (legionnaires' disease), tetanus, food-related disease including *E. coli* and salmonella
- decompression illness (divers' bends)
- some skin diseases such as occupational dermatitis, skin cancer.

> **! Check it out**
>
> 1 What two sets of regulations govern injury and disease?
> 2 What is the role of the first aid co-ordinator?
> 3 Why is it not a good idea for a member of the public to give first aid in a workplace?
> 4 What is trend analysis?
> 5 What are the four categories of dangerous incidents and reportable injuries and diseases?
> 6 What are the health and safety benefits of the Working Time Regulations 1998?

Other legislation in relation to health and safety

There are several laws that are not central to health and safety legislation but which have important implications for it. These include the Disability Discrimination Act 1994, the Children Act 1989, the Food Safety Act 1990 and the Data Protection Act 1984. The first three of these are covered below. You will find information abut the Data Protection Act on page 133.

Disability Discrimination Act (1995) – DDA

This act makes it illegal for a business to discriminate against disabled people in terms of either:

- employment, or
- provision of goods and services.

First, what do we mean by 'disabled'? The DDA concerns itself with disability that needs some support to enable the person to carry out day-to-day activities. DDA covers the familiar categories of physical (using a wheelchair, co-ordination problems), sensory (hearing and sight impairments), learning difficulties and problems of mental illness. It also includes people with severe disfigurement, where there is a history of disability as with recurring mental health problems, and progressive conditions such as cancer.

Employment

DDA applies only to firms of 20 employees or more. In these organisations employers cannot discriminate against disabled people. This means they must also take reasonable measures to change arrangements and remove barriers which would place disabled employees at a disadvantage. For example, they would have to provide a ramp for access, or provide adapted telephones for hearing-impaired people.

DDA covers all stages of employment, including recruitment, promotion, training and dismissal. It also covers working conditions, and it is these that have the greatest health and safety implications. This is because a disabled employee working in an unsuitable workplace might be exposed to hazards and increase the risk of accidents.

There are very few jobs that disabled people cannot do providing there is some modification to the task or the working environment. Apart from some tasks where a particular sense is essential (like sight or hearing) it would seem that disability is not an intrinsic barrier to working in the leisure industry.

Goods and services

DDA makes it an offence for any organisation to:

- refuse to serve a person on grounds of their disability
- provide a lower standard of service or a service on worse terms.

The Act has been successful in persuading some firms with outdated attitudes to change them. Such attitudes are now illegal and case law is developing to show that prosecutions do occur.

Review and adaptation

Many pressure groups have seen the DDA as a weak act for several reasons:

- there is no enforcing authority so that anyone suffering from alleged discrimination has to take a civil action against the employer.
- it relies on employers making adjustments after a situation arises rather than before. Compare this to stadium safety where operation can occur only after the completion of a successful inspection.

- it does not require the employer to make an assessment of provision and practices for disabled people.

The Act does encourage providers to make reasonable adjustments to provision so as to serve disabled workers more successfully. This involves:

- reviewing and changing policies and practices that may have been discriminatory
- providing auxiliary aids such as adjusted signs, induction loops, cassette information, adapted equipment and facility design (e.g. ramps)
- removal of physical barriers and improving access.

In 1999, codes of practice were introduced for the improvement of policies and auxiliary aids, while similar guidelines for the removal of physical barriers are scheduled for 2004.

Sensory disability has major health and safety considerations. Blind people cannot see emergency exit signs, so an auditory alarm is required. The visually impaired require better contrast, larger print and better lighting for

The Disability Discrimination Act encourages organisations to provide adjustments to serve disabled workers such as hearing induction loops

signs and information. Deaf people cannot hear alarms but the provision of a hearing loop in a facility or flashing lights would help them to be alert.

While many disabled people cope well with day-to-day activity they are at much greater risk in emergencies. Moreover, staff and other customers may not react in the best interest of a disabled colleague. A well-intentioned attempt to lift a wheelchair may end in

Thought for the page

There are exemptions from the DDA which would apply if the health and safety of the disabled customer is genuinely at risk. For example, climbing with children with severe behavioural problems would be too risky even with one-to-one supervision. Many outdoor activities can create problems for the disabled, and these problems can create exemption. Such a case would be when a leader of a group would have to attend to the disabled customer to such an extent that it precluded the other members of the group from continuing.

It is encouraging to note that it is these areas of the industry where exemptions operate that are usually most enthusiastic about developing provision for disabled people.

Think it over

These codes of practice may appear to have greater relevance to customer service but there are also numerous health and safety considerations. For example, someone in a wheelchair will find the heavy doors and fire doors in an office difficult to manage, and too risky altogether with a cup of hot coffee. Again, wheelchair drivers are far safer when getting out of their vehicle in a dedicated area of a car park, as opposed to the main car park with narrow bays. These are the sorts of considerations that will be implemented over the next few years. Can you think of other ways in which premises can be improved for disabled people?

CASE STUDY – Woodville Gymnastics Club

Norman has been running the Woodville Gymnastics Club for the past ten years. It is a competitive club that provides a wide range of activities for children aged from three to sixteen years as well as running senior squads. The club is registered with the Governing Body of Sport and runs five sessions a week in the local Council's sports centre. Norman is an experienced and qualified coach as are his team of coaches who have been with him for years. He likes to run the club in a traditional way and only allows parents to drop off and collect their children for the session. It is a small friendly club and he and his staff know all the kids. He feels this adds to the family atmosphere and means he can do away with formalities like keeping a register of who's present. He prides himself on the fact that the children regard him as an 'Uncle' and he feels that this helps him to relate to the kids – for example, if one of the girls is feeling sulky he will often give her a tickle until she smiles.

It is a warm summer's evening and the under-eights session is underway with Norman, Gary and Steve taking the session. Thirty girls have turned up and the hall is getting warm – in fact Norman opens up the fire exit doors onto the car park to get some fresh air in. One thing that puzzles him is that Stacey, a shy seven year old, always keeps her tracksuit on even on a warm evening like this. Norman is beginning to feel that there may be a reason for this and that she may be hiding bruises or bug bites (i.e. signs of abuse or neglect). At the end of the session he decides to investigate further and on the pretext of fixing a faulty shower in the changing rooms he gets a chance to see that as she changes she has indeed several large bruises on her arms and back.

Questions

1 Identify two of Norman's actions that are not appropriate in terms of child abuse issues. Suggest alternatives that he could take.

2 Describe how Norman has been negligent in ensuring the children were physically safe and secure.

3 On confirming his suspicion that Stacey has bruises, what action should Norman take?

4 What improvements would you suggest that Norman makes to the way the club is run.

---

jettisoning its occupant down the stairs. As we have already seen under MSWW there is a need to plan and train for emergencies. It is advisable to review evacuation and emergency policies and training so as to take into account the special problems resulting from disability and how they are best dealt with by staff.

Children Act (1989)

Child abuse is a recognised problem in many areas of the industry where close physical proximity and a position of trust is common. While incidence of abuse is low, all organisations involved in leisure should do their best to eliminate it.

People working in the leisure industry must be aware that they can accidentally become targets for allegations of abuse. They should therefore follow the codes of practice in order to protect themselves from malicious accusation. For example, workers should not get into isolated situations with children, room inspections should be done in pairs, and physical contact should be cut to a minimum and involve only non-sensitive areas such as hands, elbows and shoulders.

The Children Act (1989) was introduced essentially to protect children in a wide range of supervised situations. It applies only to activities where parents or guardians are not present. It applies to all children in these circumstances aged under sixteen, although many of the safeguards are aimed at the under-eight age group. Although it is mainly concerned with childcare, the Act also has major implications for leisure. The Act covers:

1   the protection of children from physical, sexual and emotional abuse

2   the provision for children to be placed in a safe environment.

The enforcing authority is the local authority social services who will inspect and register a leisure provider working with children aged under sixteen.

The Act focuses only on three situations in which the parents are *not* present:

1 Closed access: Out-of-school clubs, crèches or holiday play schemes, where the children are registered in advance of the activity.

2 Supervised activities: These include special-interest activities such as sports or hobby clubs, coaching courses, and residential outdoor activities. Similar situations occur in other sectors of the industry. For example, zoos have junior nature clubs, parks and countryside reserves run a wide range of interpretation, arts and crafts projects, and museums run heritage days. Any activity of this kind is subject to the Act.

3 Open access: Children come and go as they please. There is often no control on numbers and supervision is limited, for example an activity day in the park, an adventure playground, a children's holiday club in a hotel or holiday park.

The Act has power over the following areas:

- number of children
- maintenance of premises and equipment
- staffing quality and numbers
- maintenance of records
- notification of changes.

Number of children

In situations involving large numbers of children, such as a ballet school festival or a taster day, then all children should be divided into self-contained groups not exceeding 30. If the children are under eight, groups of ten are appropriate.

A staff ratio of 8:1 is required for children under eight regardless of group size, and at least half the staff should be experienced or qualified. Staff numbers cannot be made up with people like the receptionist or work experience students.

Maintenance of premises

The Act concerns itself with *fitness* of premises and staff. Fitness in this sense is defined as being able to do the job or fit for the purpose. Premises need to be big enough to allow for at least 2.3 m^2 per child and there should be separate areas for changing and rest. In play schemes for under eight-year-olds there should be areas dedicated to particular activities such as sand and water play, arts and crafts or story telling. There should be a toilet for every ten children and all equipment should be fit for the purpose and well maintained. This applies to activity equipment such as tumble tots gymnastics and support equipment like low-level urinals, and child-friendly seating.

Staffing

Adults are similarly checked out for their attitude and style of working with children. In both the private and public sectors checks are made with the police to see if the adult has a clear record with respect to child-related offences. Voluntary organisations do not have to make these, but they are increasingly and voluntarily carrying out similar checks.

Keeping records

For any activity, three sets of records must be kept (Figure 2.6).

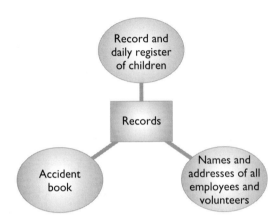

Figure 2.6 Records which must be kept for any activity

Notification of changes

Finally the Act requires the employer to inform social services of any changes in its provision since the inspection, such as changes in staff, in the numbers of children, and nature of activities.

So far we have covered the requirements of the Act. However, the security of children can also be maintained by operating according to codes of practice and through awareness training both for helpers and for the children themselves.

For example, helpers are advised to:

1   show good role model behaviour by not showing off or taking risks, not shouting or swearing

2   avoid drinking and smoking before and when on duty

3   always be in the company of other adults

4   listen to children and act on reliable information (e.g. about bullying)

5   take training on various aspects of child protection and to be able to recognise and manage it (e.g. abuse, bullying)

6   follow professional guidelines

7   be alert to the presence and whereabouts of the children

8   use physical restraint only in emergencies that threaten the safety of the child

9   restrict physical contact to the minimum.

Children can be made aware of safety through a variety of well-supported campaigns such as:

* stranger danger
* road safety and cycle proficiency
* water safety codes and rescue

The Royal Life Saving Society UK's Water Safety Code is an example of a voluntary code of practice that is widely used in the leisure and recreation industry

- anti-drug campaigns
- first aid.

Adventure activities

The Children Act is not the only law concerned with the well-being of children. In general, it is understood in all safety legislation that children are at greater risk and that this needs to be taken into account.

Outdoor adventure activities for children are of special concern. While the vast majority of providers have an excellent regard for safety, there has always been an uneasy balance between maintaining profits without compromising safety. In 1993, new legislation was introduced following the loss of four children in a canoeing accident in Lyme Bay. The Activity Centre (Young Persons' Safety) Act resulted in certain adventure activities centres becoming subject to inspection and licensing by the Adventure Activities Licensing Authority (Figure 2.7).

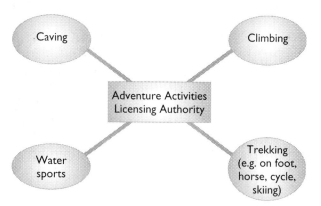

Figure 2.7 Areas covered by the Adventure Activities Licensing Authority

The licensing scheme is aimed at organisations that sell adventure activities to children of pre-school and school age. This includes commercial centres like stables or adventure holiday companies. It also includes local authority leisure departments. It does not include schools and colleges, or activities where the parent or guardian is present or voluntary associations such as the Scouts.

This is regrettable because both schools and voluntary organisations have a varied record of safety in adventure activity safety. Groups such as the Scouts who are aware of this shortcoming are providing their own assessment and codes of practice.

At present the onus appears to be on the organisations to apply for a licence. In many cases this self-registering works because commercial centres find it hard to sell to corporate customers like education authorities without being licensed. In some areas, particularly riding, customers are often individual members of the public who are unaware of the licence. As a consequence it is likely that many smaller businesses will remain unlicensed for some time to come.

Food Safety Act (1990) and Food Safety (General Food Regulations) (1995)

Nearly all leisure providers provide food and drink for their customers in some form or other. This may be on an occasional basis such as a hamburger stall at a fairground, or on a more substantial basis as in corporate catering or a permanent café or restaurant. Food is a real hazard if it is not prepared and stored in the correct way. There are three major sources of hazard when:

- materials such as glass, hair, stones or even animals get into food
- a toxic substance (poison) has got into the food. Did you know that cyanide smells like the almond essence used in cakes?
- microbes are present in food. Food is food for bugs just as much as it is for us. Unfortunately, many microbes and parasites find humans a wonderful place to be if eaten in food. While food poisoning can be a mild discomfort, it can also be a fatal health hazard. *Escherichia coli* (*E. coli*) is a well-publicised killer, but there are other diseases caused by worms and fungi which are just waiting for us to relax our food hygiene.

Food poisoning and its avoidance

In most cases, good food processing means that food reaches the leisure provider in good condition and the presence of foreign materials is not common – and if present, the effects are usually not too serious. On the other hand, food poisoning (that is a disease of an infectious or toxic nature caused by the consumption of food or drink) can at best be unpleasant but can, in some cases, kill the victim. What are the microbes that are involved?

- *Campylobacter* is the most common (about 40,000 cases of poisoning a year) and is found in unpasteurised milk or raw poultry and, occasionally, in eggs.
- *Salmonella* is the second most common (about 30,000 cases of poisoning a year) and is found in raw meat, eggs and poultry.

- Others include *Clostridium perfringens* found in meat, and *Staphylococcus aureus* and *Bacillus cereus* both of which are found in rice.
- These bugs are found in open conditions but there is another group which is related to the bacteria found in animal guts (including our own). One of the nastiest of these is *E. coli* 0157 and it is a potential killer.

The preparation, transportation and selling of food are all governed by legislation – name some of these laws

Food poisoning can be avoided without resorting to the law by some very simple precautions:

- cooking and reheating at a sufficient temperature and for an appropriate time will actually kill *Salmonella*, *Campylobacter* and *E. coli*
- bacteria do not grow if food is stored at below 5°C (but they will spread rapidly if chilled food is left out in a warm place like a sunny windowsill)
- keep hands and equipment washed, especially after handling food, rubbish or having been to the lavatory
- before reusing utensils, wash any that have had meat or eggs in them with hot water and detergent and do not let juices and spillage from these utensils contaminate other food
- wash salads
- avoid unpasteurised milk and raw eggs.

As with any disease, babies, elderly people, the sick and pregnant women are often the worst affected. Food preparation should be especially considerate of them. For example, eggs should be hard-boiled rather than soft-boiled.

Food legislation

Although the above methods are common sense and straightforward, they can be difficult to enforce when faced with the circumstances found in a leisure provider (e.g. numerous staff perhaps unaware of what utensils have been used for, food standing on serveries for hours before being served to the customer, or a variety of suppliers supplying food of differing quality). Furthermore, because leisure providers sometimes serve hundreds or even thousands of customers in a day, the presence of contaminated food could be very serious indeed. In order to minimise risk and bring order to the catering sector, laws have been introduced known as the Food Hygiene Laws.

As with other health and safety legislation there is the enabling Act, the Food Act (1995), that is supported and expanded by regulations, The Food Safety (General Food Hygiene) Regulations (1995). These apply to anyone who prepares or serves food whether for profit (e.g. restaurants, a hot-dog stall) or fundraising (e.g. charity fetes).

The laws cover the following activities:

- preparation
- handling
- processing
- manufacturing
- storage
- transportation
- selling
- distribution
- supplying.

In other words, everyone who handles food or whose action might affect it are obliged under the Act to follow certain procedures.

As usual, while employees have certain responsibilities under the regulations, it is the employer who has overall responsibility for seeing that the law is enforced. Ensuring that this is done is the enforcing authority, which for food is the Environmental Health department of the local authority, who inspect, advise and otherwise control all stages of the process from preparation and processing to selling and supplying.

The regulations (Table 2.1) cover several areas which are:

1 General requirements for food premises (that is the design and environment of the workplace is safe and hygienic). This means that food premises should:

- be clean and maintained in good repair
- be designed and constructed to permit good hygiene practices
- have an adequate supply of potable (drinking) water

Table 2.1 Requirements of the Food Act

Requirements of the Act	Equipment and premises	Action
Food premises		Keep clean, and in good repair and condition.
Washbasins	Must have hot and cold (or appropriately mixed) running water and materials for cleaning and drying hands. Where necessary, there must be separate facilities for washing food and hands.	Provide soap and suitable hand-drying facilities.
Washing of food	Where appropriate, provide adequate facilities for washing food. Supply with hot and/or cold water as required.	Wash food properly where necessary.
Equipment	Articles, fittings and equipment that can come into contact with food shall be made of such materials and maintained so that they, and the surrounding areas, can be kept clean and, where necessary, disinfected.	All equipment and surfaces that come into contact with food must be kept clean.
Personal hygiene	Food handlers must wear suitable, clean and, where appropriate, protective clothing.	Everyone in a food-handling area must maintain a high level of personal cleanliness.

- have suitable controls in place to protect against pests
- have adequate natural and/or artificial lighting
- have sufficient natural and/or mechanical ventilation
- provide clean lavatories which do not lead directly into food rooms
- have adequate hand-washing facilities
- be provided with adequate drainage.

2 Specific requirements for food preparation rooms (design, hygiene of equipment, washing food). For example, surfaces should be made of materials that are smooth and easily washable, such as stainless steel. In particular these rooms should have:

- adequate facilities for washing food and equipment
- adequate facilities for the storage and removal of food waste.

3 Requirements for moveable/temporary facilities (marquees, and mobiles such as burger vans and vending machines). Obviously conditions will vary with these, but the two basic principles are:

- there should be adequate facilities to prepare and serve food safely
- food-handling procedures should avoid exposing food to any risk of contamination.

For example, with a hot-dog van, the owner should not have the food preparation area near the selling counter where dirty hands and money are being exchanged and hands should be washed between taking money and recommencing food preparation.

4 Transport (containment, contamination, equipment). When being transported, food needs to be maintained at the correct temperature and in clean conditions without spillage or contamination (e.g. fumes).

5 Equipment needs to be fit for purpose. For example, it needs to be washable or disposable, and it must not harbour germs.

6 Food waste (containers, removal). Essentially, waste needs to be contained in a place and vessel that will minimise its contact with food and food handlers. It needs to be removed and stored outside

in a vermin-free store for collection at regular intervals.

7 Water supply. Water or ice should come from a drinkable (potable) source and be stored safely.

8 Personal hygiene (clothing, handling, infectious handlers). Anyone working with food must have clean personal hygiene and dress appropriately. The golden rules are:

- observe good personal hygiene
- routinely wash their hands when handling food
- never smoke in food-handling areas
- report any illness (e.g. infected wounds, skin infections, diarrhoea or vomiting) to their manager or supervisor immediately.

9 Provision (raw materials). Fresh food should be used and stored in a way that will prevent contamination or the build-up of bacteria, for example it should be stored in cool airy conditions. Foods which have a high risk of cross-contamination such as raw and cooked meats must be separated. Table 2.2 shows the precautions that need to be taken to prevent contamination of food.

10 Training (supervision, instruction and training). As with other aspects of health and safety, staff must be appropriately

trained. You may have noticed in many catering outlets that the food hygiene certificates of the staff are displayed on the wall.

Food hygiene, as with most areas of health and safety, is achieved by having the right equipment combined with the right actions. Here are some examples:

Food storage and temperature control

Accompanying the general regulations, is a variety of specific ones for various food types such as dairy produce or meat. Particularly important are the temperature control regulations. This is because temperature is a

Think it over

You are the manager of a heritage attraction with a country food shop. Most of the food in it has a long shelf-life, such as jams and preserves. You do, however, have two cool units, one for cheese, the other for fresh meat such as sausages. A lady called Mrs Sue Todd comes in one day with a sample of home-made meat pies she makes to original historic recipes. She explains that she has only just started up this part-time business and would be able to supply you with about thirty pies a week. The pies look and taste appetising and you know they would sell well.

What actions would you need to take under the Food Act? What checks would you make about Mrs Todd? If there was an outbreak of food poisoning resulting from the pies who would be liable?

Table 2.2 Precautions for the prevention of food infection

Food group	Examples	Temperature
Dairy products	Dairy desserts such as yoghurt, mousse, milk and cream, soft and semi-hard cheese	At or below 8°C
Smoked/cured/ready-to-eat flesh	Ham, salami, kippers, smoked salmon, sliced beef	At or below 8°C
Prepared ready-to-eat foods	Prepared vegetables, salads including dips, and mayonnaise-based salads such as coleslaw	At or below 8°C
Uncooked/part-cooked foods	Pizzas, pies, dough products, meat, fish	At or below 8°C
Hot prepared food	Cafeteria food, fish and chips	At or above 63°C, and must be discarded after two hours

major factor in biological contamination. The regulations basically state that the food groups in Table 2.1 should be held either at or above 63°C or at or below 8°C.

Staffing and inspection

As with all health and safety, the employer is obliged to train and inform staff. Risk assessment is also required.

Any premises supplying food for public consumption for a period of over five weeks will be inspected by an Environmental Health Inspector from the local authority. The result of this inspection is a letter from the inspector asking for improvement or saying that the firm is satisfactory. Unfortunately, there is no licence or certificate scheme, as there is in fire inspection or health and safety.

This poses problems for leisure providers. While you can keep a tight grip on your own facilities, you always depend on suppliers of at least raw materials or prepared food – even if it is a packet of crisps. In most cases it would be sensible to use established suppliers and ask to see:

• their letter of approval from the enforcing authority
• original copies of staff certificates for food safety training.

Events and the use of mobile catering are often risky as suppliers may be amateurs (e.g. cake sales at fêtes) or semi-professional caterers or restaurateurs who may not be used to working in a mobile food environment. Whether it is a goat curry stall at a Caribbean Carnival or the Women's Institute stall at a church fête, the organisers may be responsible for any unfortunate outcomes. In the absence of guidelines and inspection of suppliers, the following checks might be sensible:

• provide all contributors with food hygiene literature and ask them to follow it
• wherever possible inspect the preparation premises
• insist on basic containerisation (e.g. clingfilm, airtight containers)
• check that storage and display at the event are adequate
• ensure food handling at the event is hygienic
• give a member(s) of the event team the task of checking that food procedures are being followed
• if possible keep a list of contributors' names and contact information.

Events legislation

Licensing laws

There are several licensing laws that require leisure providers to gain a licence to operate from the local authority or magistrates.

Gambling

The Lotteries and Amusements Act (1976), the Gaming Act (1968) for gaming machines, and the Betting and Gaming Duties Act (1981) for bingo apply here.

Consumption of alcohol

The Licensing Act (1964) is the main piece of legislation that governs licensed premises. The person responsible for selling liquor and ensuring the law is kept is the licensee who needs to display the licence at the entrance to the premises. The licence is available from local magistrates and is renewed on an annual basis

The Act has three main implications for health and safety:

1   To gain a licence, inspection of the premises includes an assessment of health and safety issues.

2   The Act restricts alcohol sales to minors and this can be seen as a control on early dependence on alcohol as well as a control on the affects of excessive drink on young people.

3   Possibly the most important implication is that the licensee can refuse to sell to anyone he/she chooses. In health and safety terms this means the licensee might refuse:

•   customers who are about to be active where alcohol might endanger their

health (e.g. swimming, squash)

•   customers who are drunk and may injure themselves

•   customers who are drunk and are likely to become aggressive and hurt themselves or others.

The licensee also has the right to ask a customer to leave and use reasonable means to make him do so.

The application of these laws is confusing to say the least. In the sports sector, one would not normally find experienced people drinking before exercise. However, on some occasions drinking may be part of the activity. For example, players or supporters may have had a few drinks before a local fundraising football match. Swimmers relaxing by outdoor pools at hotels may also have a few drinks. Both practices contravene good health and safety common sense. The latter contravenes the HSE guidelines on swimming pool safety.

Is this swimming pool following the HSE guidelines on swimming pool safety?

Drinking often leads to aggression which is potentially a serious problem. At large-scale events which traditonally have an association with violence, such as football, drinking is no longer allowed in the public parts of a stadium. Even when a licence is granted for a one-off occasion, event organisers need to consider to what extent and when alcohol will be sold. Drinking is a recreational activity in itself for nightclubs and pubs. Staff have to be sensitive to the distinction between customers having a good time and going too far. Good bar staff are the secret to this and through a blend of tact, diplomacy and group psychology can often deter unpleasant scenes. If this fails, door staff are used. If the licensee cannot control antisocial behaviour, the licence may be revoked. The licensing laws are about to be reviewed and three changes are likely:

- the licensing authority will become the local authority
- there will be no licensing hours and publicans can have flexible hours
- the publican can close the pub if there is trouble of any sort.

The aim of the amendments is that it will reduce the British habit of drinking right up to closing time and that drinkers will drink less, or the same over a longer time. Thus injury and health problems associated with excessive drinking may be reduced.

Events legislation – safety at events

When people are in danger they become anxious and frightened and may panic. When they are alone, or in small groups they tend to freeze or run. In crowds, on the other hand, they may panic and stampede or fight each other. Thus, apart from the original hazard that provoked the danger there is now the added hazard of crush injuries or personal attack. This aspect of human behaviour has been known for years. Theatres in particular have long recognised the consequences of a fire and introduced safety measure such as exit doors and fire curtains long before health and safety became the science it is now.

At the beginning of the last century we saw the creation, for the first time since Roman times, of large stadia. In these, thousands of people could gather to watch sport and in particular soccer. The early stadia were often huge and could cater for many thousands of spectators, most of whom would be standing. Furthermore, there was little control of numbers.

Disasters started early, and in 1924 the Cup Final crowd, which was an overcapacity one, panicked and fights and injuries were incurred. In 1946, there was a disaster at Bolton Wanderers ground. Growing crowd control problems coupled with old and poorly designed stadia led to another disaster at Ibrox Park. This resulted in a public inquiry out of which came the Safety at Sports Grounds Act (1975). Ten years later, further disasters, first at Bradford 1986 and then the horrific tragedy at Hillsborough, led to reports by Lords Popplewell and Taylor. These led to the Fire Safety and Safety of Places of Sports Act (1987). The enforcing authority for these acts is the Football Licensing Authority for football grounds and the local authority for other stadia and sites.

Safety at Sports Grounds Act (1975)

The Safety at Sports Grounds Act is concerned with larger sports stadia (i.e. 10,000 spectators or more) and makes the managers/ owners of stadia criminally liable if they do not implement the Act. It requires that:

- the stadium can be used only after a safety certificate has been issued
- the certificate applies only to the activities initially applied for in the stadium
- the Act defines the number of spectators allowed in the stadium (before the Act people were packed in like sardines)

- the owners keep records of attendance
- the owners keep records of maintenance to the stadium.

Fire Safety and Safety of Places of Sport Act (1987)

The Fire Safety and Safety of Places of Sport Act greatly expands the scope of the earlier Act:

- both fire and safety certificates have to be issued (the Fire Authority is the enforcing agent for this)
- the granting of the fire certificate is based on facilities for both prevention and control of fire, and escape from it (e.g. the use of fire-proofed materials, fire barriers and fire exits)
- it extends the Safety at Sports Grounds Act (1975) to all sports grounds
- it allows prohibition notices (closure) of hazardous grounds
- it includes the safety of stands in grounds which are not designated sports grounds (e.g. temporary stands for a sports event)
- it includes licensing for indoor sports venues (the National Arena and the Royal Albert Hall are major venues that require licences).

The Act has had a major impact on sports grounds. The recommendations of the Taylor Report highlighted areas of safety concern that produced fundamental changes in stadium design and brought in new safety standards. Together, rugby and football stadia make up most of the stadia in the country and have the greatest problems of crowd control. To focus on this the report recommended actions which have largely been undertaken. Some of these are summarised here but the Green Guide, which contains the guidelines for the Act, names 76 recommendations in detail:

- the creation of the Football Licensing Authority (FLA) (www.flaweb.org.uk/fla) as the enforcing authority (although inspections and safety certificates are issued by the Local Authority).
- the creation of an Advisory Design Council to develop good practice and provide information
- defined maximum capacities for terraces and control of numbers
- terraces should be stewarded and monitored during events
- crowds outside stadium should be monitored using CCTV
- gangways should be kept clear
- barriers such as fences and gates should be less hazardous (e.g. maximum height of fences 2.2 m, with gates; barbed wire and obstacles should not be on the top of walls)
- crush barriers should be regularly inspected and safely sited
- turnstiles must be in adequate condition
- signing and information (including information on tickets) should be clear
- police need to designate a named officer in charge of policing the stadium

Under the Fire Safety and Safety of Places of Sport Act police involvement should be planned and take crowd safety into consideration

- police involvement should be planned and take crowd safety into consideration
- police communications to be effective and interlinked
- emergency services need a planned and co-ordinated approach
- first aiders should be available at a ratio of 1:1,000
- a doctor should be present if the crowd exceeds 2,000.

As terraces presented a heightened safety risk, a principal recommendation of the report was that there should be a move to all-seat grounds. Given the state of many grounds it could not be expected that safety changes could be brought in overnight. The FLA thus drew up a plan that began in 1993 with high-risk matches requiring all-seat stadiums. In successive seasons there has been a gradual programme with two strategies:

- Premier and First Division English League and Scottish Premier League grounds to reduce terracing by 20% a year. For other leagues there should be a decrease by 10% a year.
- existing grounds to bring in modifications in order to obtain safety certificates.

Check it out

1 Who are the enforcing authorities for the Licensing Act and the Safety at Sports Grounds Act?

2 What are the principal health and safety issues connected with drinking alcohol?

3 Why are crowds in a particularly hazardous situation?

4 What two Acts govern safety in sports grounds?

5 What aspects does the fire certificate cover?

6 What happens if the ground does not meet the requirements of the Acts?

7 How are grounds being brought into compliance with the law?

2.3 Hazards and risk assessment

Risk assessment plays a very important part in the management of health and safety. The degree of competence you show in carrying out risk assessment will to a large extent determine your eventual performance in the AVCE assessment for this unit. Identifying hazards, assessing the risks attached to them and deciding on a course of action is essential procedure in any leisure facility. What exactly is meant by 'hazard' and 'risk'?

- a hazard is anything that has the potential to cause harm to people or places
- a risk is the chance that someone or something will be harmed to a greater or lesser degree by the hazard
- when the risks of hazards are reduced to a minimum we hope that maximum possible safety has been achieved.

Accident statistics

Before we look at hazards we shall look at some figures to show how safe the industry is as a whole.

Fatalities

Staff

You will be glad to know that you are not likely to get killed working in leisure. According to the HSE report 'Key fact sheet on injuries within the consumer/leisure service industry' published in 1998, there were only seven fatalities between 1991 and 1997. Even better news is that three of those fatalities took place before the Six Pack came in, although five took place in the sport and recreation industry (three of which were due to falls).

Customers

The public have not fared so well, but remember that there are far more people participating than providing. There were

24 fatalities in the same period, but after 1995 the annual figures were lower (e.g. in 1996/97 there were two deaths). Of these, 21 took place in sport and recreation. Ten deaths were from falls (four from a horse), and four were caused by a moving vehicle.

Note: Figures have to be put in context, and do not tell the whole story. These deaths were reported through RIDDOR and therefore do not include deaths in non-workplace situations such as voluntary sports clubs, or accidents from private informal recreations such as climbing, swimming, walking, etc. Also, since RIDDOR came into force the reporting of deaths has increased but it is not known how reliable the reporting from the different sectors is likely to be. Finally, the figures for deaths and injuries should be looked at as a percentage of the numbers of people employed in the industry and of the numbers of customers.

As an example, RoSPA estimates that there are over 440 drownings a year.

Of these, in 1997:

- 24 (5%) occurred in swimming pools
- 108 (24%) on the coast
- 58% on non-domestic inland water such as rivers.

Drowning during impromptu swims is often a result of drinking or dares and peer pressure.

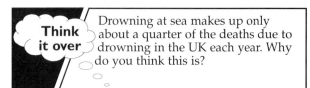

Think it over
Drowning at sea makes up only about a quarter of the deaths due to drowning in the UK each year. Why do you think this is?

Clearly these drownings are not all a result of recreational accidents within the industry. But it should be noted that many authorities have a duty of care over their estates, which can include for instance, parks and country parks.

Non-fatal injuries

Staff

Accident statistics appear to show that the number of injuries is growing. This is explained by the fact that there are a greater number of people partaking in leisure activities every year and that many more reports of accidents are being filed. Taking one year (1996/97), there were 346 major injuries and 1159 over-three-day injuries for the entire working population.

If we compare the figures in different sectors, we can see that the leisure industry is either a risky area or reports better than other sectors (Table 2.3). Retailing recorded 90.3 accidents (major injuries), wholesaling 59.1, offices only 23.6, hotels and catering 70.8, but consumer/leisure came in at 102.6. This is about half the rate found in manufacturing or a quarter of the rates for construction. Most of these injuries were fractures. Where an injury resulted in absence from work for three days or more (over-three-day injuries) the industry was a little safer compared with other sectors and in fact came behind retailing with a figure of 294.9.

Table 2.3 Injury to employees 1996/97 adapted from HSE statistics

Industry	Major injury	Over-three-day injury
Retail	90	384
Wholesale	59	200
Offices	24	75
Hotel and catering	70	205
Consumer/leisure	103	295

Source: HSE

In the consumer/leisure sector, sport and recreation accounted for 76% of major injuries and 68% of over-three-day injuries. Membership organisations (e.g. golf clubs) accounted for most of the rest. Of these, 35% of major injuries were a result of a slip or trip, and 26% the result of a fall (over half from a horse). Twenty eight per cent of over-three-day injuries were from slip and trips, but 22% were a result of manual handling, 12% from a fall and 12% from being struck by a moving object.

Customers

Nearly all (94%) of the 1077 major injuries in leisure were in sport and recreation. Fifty two per cent resulted from a slip or trip and another 33% from a fall (of which over a third were from a horse). Eighty two per cent of these injuries were fractures. (Over-three-day injuries to the public are not reportable.)

The message seems clear. Despite our efforts, leisure, and particularly sport and recreation, is a risky business for employees and customers. We need to be vigilant all the time.

It may seem a simple conclusion, but so good is the control of safety in leisure that the accidents people are likely to have are ones of their own making. People have a habit, especially when relaxed and enjoying themselves to misjudge, trip, lose balance or drop things. Think of some classic examples:

- jumping over a low barrier or running down a slippery slope to take a short cut
- carrying too many things to avoid another journey
- leaning over a barrier to see something
- showing off – for instance when revving up a jet ski
- not paying attention.

Think it over
List as many probable slips and trips and their causes as you can think of, taking different facilities and circumstances into account. Why do you think that these are the greatest causes of accidents?

Risk assessment

What is the purpose of risk assessment? It is to try to prevent accidents from happening. Risk assessment is the technique by which you measure up the chances of an accident happening, anticipate what the consequences would be and plan what actions could prevent it.

We carry out assessments to check if our policies, procedures and practice are working. The risk assessment process always follows the same five-stage path:

1 look for hazards

2 identify who might be harmed and how

3 evaluate the risks and decide if existing safety measures are adequate

4 record your findings

5 review and revise assessment.

1 Look for hazards

The best way to look for hazards is to examine the area under assessment. Ask other staff and the customers what they have noticed or witnessed. It is possible that accidents may have occurred or nearly occurred but people did not report them. Manufacturers and suppliers of facilities and goods will have a long track record of knowing what hazards their products may have. They will have recorded these in the labelling and in manufacturers' instructions, and you should at the outset have familiarised yourself with them. This will enable you to spot any peculiarities in working in the future. Use your other senses as well to detect the symptoms of a hazard that are hidden. For instance, you may smell damp in a store room or the pungent smell of old wiring. You may hear water or liquid dripping, or the changed note of a motor in a plant room or at an event. You may sense that a room or piece of equipment is too hot, or too cold. Many experienced pool managers can smell if dosing systems are keeping water quality up to standard. You will be able to do an assessment yourself in most cases, but if you are in any doubt as to your knowledge, you should call in an expert.

It is easy to see that some accidents are more common than others. Here are some of the more frequent ones:

- trips and falls
- object falling from a height (e.g. lighting rigs)
- fire
- explosion
- electric shock
- water-related
- crushes by people or objects

- poisoning by toxic substances
- asphyxiation, by dust or fumes
- disease
- missiles (balls, javelins, darts).

It is perhaps a credit to our management in the industry that most of these hazards are controlled. For example, in 1996/97 there was only one recorded injury from each reportable area attributed to fire, and only one incident of an explosion causing injury. Even a relatively common hazard such as electric shock caused only eight injuries to employees and none to the public.

These hazards can and will always happen unless everyone is constantly vigilant. Vigilance means not only seeing and noticing, but also interpreting what you see so as to anticipate what could happen in the future.

You work in a leisure centre, and have been asked to complete a risk assessment for the gym in this picture. What factors would you need to consider?

When first starting to assess you may tend to put everything down as a hazard. For example, you might think that all the fruit in a fruit cocktail should be seedless because a customer might choke on the seeds. Try to get things in perspective and concentrate on the real not the trivial.

2 Identify who might be harmed and how

Staff and customers will behave in different ways. Not only do the staff have the knowledge of the premises and the equipment and the safety training behind them, but they are aware of their responsibilities. The customers do not have prior knowledge and, cushioned by the feeling that it is not their business, will react very slowly.

Think it over | Having identified the risks in the picture of the gym on page 120, how would you eliminate them?

People will also vary in their ability to recognise or respond to hazards. For example, children and people with learning difficulties may not read notices and have a lessened sense of risk. A youth worker leading a group may have less experience in recognising hazards than an instructor.

Circumstances will also change throughout the day (entrance lighting will be needed in the dark) and over the year (a room might be unpleasantly hot in the summer).

Let's look at some groups for whom hazards may be different.

Trained staff
Trained staff should be highly aware of risks and know what to do. There are times though when they may take short cuts (e.g. leave off protective clothing, not clear up

rubbish because they are in a hurry). The temptation to do this needs therefore to be anticipated and controlled.

Outside staff and temporary staff
Never make assumptions about what people know and understand. Check out first the extent of their knowledge in general and then you will know how much you can rely on them to be hazard-aware – if at all! They will not necessarily know about any hazards that are particular to your facility. They will also not know what standards you expect, and might try to cut corners. The conclusion is that it is wise not to take anything for granted.

Untrained staff
Untrained staff will not be any more aware of risks nor know what to do in an emergency than an ordinary member of the public. However, they are working for you and so should be happy to co-operate and learn.

Members of the public
Customers may:

- be unable to understand information and instructions (e.g. they do not speak English, or are children, or have learning difficulties)
- have health or mobility problems (e.g. members of a cardiac rehabilitation club, pregnant women, people with disabilities)
- have varying expertise (members of a swimming club are more likely to be able to cope with hazards in a pool than people who have hired the pool for a party)
- be in different emotional and physical states (plenty of customers arrive for adventure activities with a hangover, the old and the young are more prone to falls, exhaustion or even heart attacks in the case of the old).

Trespassers

Trespassers will often be on the premises in an anxious or excited state with no supervision and will be operating in unsuitable conditions – most probably the dark.

3 Evaluate risk and decide if safety is adequate

You now need to assess the likelihood of a hazard causing injury and how this risk can be controlled. Many assessors have a scale of hazard, for instance:

- *serious* where the outcome would be death, a long-term injury or a spell in hospital
- *moderate* where the hazard incapacitates, is treatable, and recovery is likely in the short term
- *minor* where the injury is easily treatable and does not incapacitate.

You now know the potential hazards and who they are likely to hurt and how they will hurt them. What we need to know next is how great the risk is of the hazard leading to an injury or disease. We also need to assess if existing precautions to control the risk are adequate.

Like hazards, risk can be graded:

- *high risk* a good chance of it happening
- *medium risk* might happen occasionally
- *low risk* not likely to happen or happen only very occasionally.

If we multiply the hazard score by the risk score we get a scale ranging from 1–9.

	Risk		
Hazard	High	Medium	Low
Serious	1	2	3
Moderate	2	4	6
Minor	3	6	9

This scale gives a guide to the seriousness of the situation and the urgency and scope of any necessary action. There is no definite rule, but the lower the score the greater the need for serious review of the situation and speed of attention.

CASE STUDY – Two examples of hazard and risk

In a theatre, scenery and curtains are heavy and would be likely to injure or even kill someone should they fall – a major hazard! So an inspection of the mechanisms and counterbalances used to control and slow their movement, of the maintenance records and the necessary signs, together with a check that all the actors and staff are aware of potential dangers should mean that the risk is reduced to a low level.

In another example, a sharp edge to a locker door could cause scratches. Usually this would be a minor hazard with a high risk. However, it could be a serious hazard with a low risk if it so happened that this was a country rugby club where the pitch was grazed by cows when not in use: then a scratch could lead to a chance of tetanus. In these circumstances, hazard control would be to advise all players to have a tetanus jab, and of course, to fix the sharp edges of the locker with tape as well.

Question

For a swimming pool, think of examples of a minor hazard with a high risk and a serious hazard with a low risk.

You now have identified and graded the hazards. The second stage of your assessment is to judge if the existing management of the hazard is sufficient. This means you want either to remove the risk or reduce it to a low level. To do this you need to investigate control measures.

You need to ask:

1 What controls are being used already?

2 Are they satisfactory and if not how can they be improved?

3 What other options are available?

Removing the hazard

In some cases hazards are a problem because they are in fact redundant (e.g. foot baths at the entrance to a pool are relics from days when the disinfecting process in the pool was not very effective, and are now places where it is easy to slip) or the hazard is so dangerous that it needs to be decommissioned or removed (e.g. old playground equipment that is badly corroded – if it is not removed it is almost certain that some children will ignore notices and play on it).

Replacing or modifying facilities/equipment

Some items become dangerous with wear, for example, steps, or hand-rails. Others can be replaced with new, safer versions (e.g. trampolines are now made with counterbalanced tension, glasses can be made of plastic rather than glass, and material can be fire-proofed). Very often a simple design change can reduce the hazard, such as putting a mirror on a blind corner.

Introducing barriers to the hazard

Keeping users away from the hazard can often be an effective solution. But remember that temporary barriers must be securely in place and well signed, and that a permanent barrier (such as high fencing) can in itself present a hazard, particularly if speedy evacuation is necessary (as was found at Hillsborough). Good examples of introducing barriers are: a safety railing on steps, a logo on glass doors to stop people walking through them, and an important one, the use of effective protective clothing.

Limiting damage that might result from a hazard

For example, the provision of nearby first aid, sprinkler systems, fire doors.

Informing staff and users

This can be done by using hazard warning notices, posters and brochures, training, alarms.

Supervising the hazard

Lifeguarding is an excellent example of this, as is the use of video surveillance. Other examples of automatic surveillance are alarm systems, print-out from plant rooms, and measuring equipment in ski resorts to monitor avalanche activity.

Changing the work patterns

Hazards are created if staff are overstretched or exposed for too long in certain conditions. Lifeguards should not spend too long in a warm pool hall, receptionists should not stay at the desk for too long, and leaders should not have to clean or repair outdoor equipment for hours in the cold and wet. It is important to vary tasks and ensure that breaks are taken.

Recording the assessment

Strictly speaking, if a company employs less than five people it does not need to record its findings. However, as people can forget what they said – or forget to do things – it seems sensible that every firm should record the assessment.

You can write a long report or present your findings in the form of a table. The example here is for a sub-aqua course. It is a good idea to show the report to the staff, particularly as they have probably been involved in the assessment and will need to know about recommended future action. Remember to keep your assessment records. They will be useful in analysing any accident, or as evidence that care has been taken. Finally, remember that as circumstances change, so the assessment will need to be regularly reviewed, and any new equipment, schedules, or working practices subjected to interim assessments which can be absorbed into the main report when next revised.

The system for risk assessment is simple; it is your knowledge of health and safety and your ability to turn your observations into practical action that is difficult. This chapter has provided you with the background behind assessment, you will now need to read around the subject and expand your knowledge. Some sources to look at are:

Risk Assessment report

Site_Budmouth Bay_____**Date of assessment**_3.6.00__ **Date for review** next dive

Main activity (ies)___sub-aqua dive **Assessor Name** Ian Roberts____**Assessor signature** Ian Roberts

Hazard	Who might be harmed?	Is risk adequately controlled?	What further action is required to control risk?
Expedition management Moderate hazard: low risk	Group of able-bodied teenage divers and their teacher (pool trained) on first open water dive	Qualified BSAC instructor present with assistants Top copies of Insurance, AAL and other certification checked	Check credentials with BSAC Ask for customer references Long term: teacher to become instructor
Equipment (is equipment adequate and fit for purpose?) Serious hazard: low risk	"	Check on issue Checked by buddy and instructor on entry	Visually check date stamps on air bottles
Terrain, steep wet tarmac slope to shingle beach which encourages trips and slips Moderate hazard: high risk	" "	No. No special instructions given	Use trolleys to transport equipment to beach Wear footwear with good grip
Climate: exposure a likelihood Minor hazard: moderate risk	"	Yes. Use of neoprene suits and warm clothing advised	Teacher to have space blanket and spare fleeces available Hot drinks to be available
Depth of water: participants in unfamiliar environment Moderate hazard: low risk	"	1:1 participant/instructor ratio Expedition to be cancelled if water conditions are poor	Instructor to stay on land but kitted up
Stress in individuals Moderate hazard: high risk	"	Yes. Instructor is alert to stress signs	

- the excellent model assessment in *HSE's managing health and safety in swimming pools*.
- the wide range of health and safety leaflets produced by HSE for employers and staff.
- health and safety literature produced by organisations. An excellent series are those produced by Scriptographic Publications which are used by 'blue chip' organisations like the Chase Manhattan Bank. Extremely simple in design, they effectively point out many hazards in relation to the appropriate legislation.

Try it out

Think of a facility (this could be a built structure or the natural environment) or a service you know well. Using a risk assessment form similar to the one on page 124, plan a risk assessment for a particular user group of the facility doing a specific activity. You can use either a situation you have actually experienced or invent one for an imaginary group.

! Check it out

1 Why do you have to be careful when comparing RIDDOR statistics over several years?

2 What is the most common form of recreational accident?

3 What are the major types of accident involving employees?

4 Give the five stages of risk assessment.

5 How would you grade hazards and risks?

6 What control measures do you need to investigate to reduce risk?

2.4 How to ensure a safe and secure working environment

It is the leisure managers who are responsible for ensuring that their premises constitute a safe and secure working environment.

Inspection, advice and control

We already know that enforcing authorities have a right to inspect premises. They can also close them down if they consider them to be unsafe. They can suggest improvements and a timescale for their completion and re-inspection. As well as the general inspections for health and safety, specialist inspections are also suggested to look at the provisions for fire prevention, and to check specialised equipment, in particular electrical equipment and cabling. These are carried out by qualified contractors.

The enforcing authorities see themselves as advisers first and foremost. They prefer that a hazard is controlled or an accident avoided rather than having to take action after the event. Employers can make use of the wide range of information the authorities produce, as well as seek the advice which they will give free of charge. It is as well to approach more authorities than you might think you need, especially when running outdoor events where a large number of people may be involved. Very often discussion will throw up issues that you haven't thought of. Here are some of the more common authorities:

- HSE
- Environmental Health
- Social Services (child protection)
- Police (crowd and traffic issues)
- Fire
- Ambulance
- Local Authority Chief Executive (lotteries and gambling licences)
- Mountain rescue service

Think it over

You are organising a carnival procession through the middle of your town. What authorites would you contact in advance? Would there be anybody else you should contact?

- Aviation authority (fireworks, ballooning)
- English Rivers Authority (waste discharge)
- Football Licensing Authority (stadium safety)
- Adventure Activities Licensing Authority
- Coastguard
- Magistrates (liquor licences) for the time being.

Increasingly, many facilities find it cheaper in the long run to pay private contractors to do more specialised inspections and assessments of, for example, electrical equipment, playground equipment and water quality.

Inspection by the organisation and staff

Inspection is also the job of both employer and employee. There are several levels of inspection:

Informal

All staff are expected to be constantly on the watch for hazards (e.g. broken glass) and breaches in safety practice, such as a displaced sign. Remember that circumstances change all the time and staff should be able to recognise what action to take. For example, a heavy frost overnight might necessitate the gritting of access paths. A disabled customer might need some special help. Cleaning staff are often in a position to notice wear and tear or damage and should report any faults (this applies, for instance, in theatres, cinemas and stadia). Very often hazards are instantly rectifiable or can be corrected easily by setting in motion the normal operating procedures. For instance, a spillage is taped off and a notice put up until it is mopped up; or a piece of gym equipment malfunctions, so a notice is put on it and it is turned off.

Daily

Most leisure providers will carry out daily inspections of the facilities. This is essentially to check that the facility is operating normally both in terms of service and safety. If inconsistencies are found, the problems have to be identified and dealt with. A good example of this is periodic (often every two hours) water-quality checks of pool water.

Daily inspections are made at the opening and closing of the facilities and are often also repeated at shift changes. Any changes or issues should be passed on to the incoming shift as hazards don't leave the building when you do. Daily inspections are usually recorded on a checklist which the staff member signs. Inspections of this sort are often combined with security checks. Staff need to be on the watch all the time to ensure the smooth running of everything to do with the premises and the people there – from turning off a tap (is the washer faulty?) to helping a distressed customer.

Periodic inspections

These are more detailed and carried out to see if, for example, fire extinguishers are in place and operational. Their frequency will vary according to the risks and safety policy and procedures of each individual facility.

Automatic inspection

Most heavy plant has built-in fail-safe systems and monitoring devices to prevent leakage or pressure build-up, to check temperature and humidity, to correct control of current in case of a short circuit, to measure and regulate the automatic injection of chemicals and so on. In advanced systems this is computer-regulated with monitoring reports which are printed out. However, with older systems a regular vigilant eye should be kept on all machines to check for any unusual developments. As with a car, so with plant; once you are familiar with the normal running sounds, sights and smells, you will be quick to notice anything different, and take steps to find out why.

In some facilities video is used to monitor the centre. This is of limited use as it depends on staff looking at the screen which, if they are also doing another job, such as receptionist, they cannot do all the time. It takes only a moment to miss a customer incident – a fall, a faint, or even an altercation.

Public inspection

Unstaffed facilities such as outdoor activity areas and children's playgrounds present particular problems. They can be hazardous – children can fall and hurt themselves. They can be subject to vandalism, and may attract undesirables such as muggers or paedophiles. It is very difficult to keep these places supervised continuously and the public's vigilance and feedback is important. Such areas should have notices giving a contact number, details of the nearest phone, and encouraging people to report faults.

Commissioning

Before a new facility can be opened it has to be inspected by the relevant enforcing authorities. Similarly, if there is a new development to existing premises, such as a gym or a restaurant, a full inspection has to be made.

Information

The employer is obliged to provide information for employees and customers in the form of leaflets, posters and signs. Although information leaflets can be designed by the management and staff, signing can not and needs to follow the European regulations (Health and Safety Regulations (1996) [Safety signs and signals]) and be displayed in key places. The six most common signs are:

Where might you see some of the signs shown above? In what way do you think they help ensure people's health and safety?

Other signs and posters are used to demonstrate good practice – for example, many surf beaches will have fairly detailed advice to swimmers on how to swim safely. Countryside parks often have interpretation boards which may include the country code or other pieces of safety advice.

There is no set format for these but they cannot be used instead of formal health and safety signs, only as well as. Employers must also display a standard poster (that outlines the details of HSWA) in a prominent place for staff to see.

Training staff

Staff must be trained. Most training can be done in-house with the health and safety officer as the trainer, or by a specialised external trainer. All staff must receive adequate induction training when they start working for the employer and this will:

- explain their legal responsibilities
- define and explain organisational health and safety policy and procedures
- identify particular hazards.

Thereafter much of their training will be in the form of updates with other staff, and occasional specialised training or courses which will bring them up to date on any new issues on health and safety such as:

- changes in legislation and what they mean
- implications of new resources and procedures
- outcomes of risk assessments and trend analysis.

Sometimes training will involve release from work, such as lifeguard and first-aid-at-work training, and in other sectors such as the

theatre, training in working with large objects or at heights.

Implementing health and safety legislation and codes of practice

Neither the law nor codes of practice apply specifically to any one facility. Much time has to be given by each administrator to applying and interpreting the laws and codes in a way that creates good working procedures and practice for a safe and healthy facility.

The manager will need to produce the following:

- risk assessment
- safety policy
- normal operating procedure
- emergency procedures
- records of accidents and near-misses
- trend analysis reports (analysis of the occurrence of incidents and their causes)
- a policy for public liability insurance (to cover the costs of damages payable as a result of any action brought against the organisation, the cost of damage to people or property on the premises).

Budgeting for health and safety

It is rare for facilities to have a separate budget for health and safety. Instead, they tend to take money from the budgets for training, maintenance, and the purchase of equipment. Costs however, can be considerable:

Staff training: Many providers prefer to keep training costs down by hiring qualified instructors or lifeguards. However, because of changing circumstances (e.g. new equipment) or changes in the law, there will be a need for an ongoing programme of training.

Staffing levels: In most leisure facilities staff numbers are determined by health and safety factors. The Children Act and Governing Body guidelines affect the ratio of instructors to their classes. Stadium Legislation determines

Thought for the page

When leisure pools were first built in the late 1970s no one had really thought about the staffing levels. Early designs, while exciting for the user, proved a headache for safety as there were so many obscured sight lines – meaning that large numbers of lifeguards often had to be used to supervise small areas like a hidden jacuzzi or a rapid. After a series of accidents, it was soon realised that even a flume will take two lifeguards (one at the top and one at the bottom) to safeguard the user. Modern designs are far more open and have fewer features than their exciting predecessors.

stewarding numbers, while in pools HSE Guidelines determine life-guarding numbers.

Purchase and maintain safe resources: As safety levels are raised so new equipment is designed to meet them. In swimming, for example, expensive equipment such as spinal boards, medi stations, and resuscitation equipment which is fairly commonplace today, were unheard of 15 years ago.

Although it is expensive to invest in safety measures and new equipment, there are conspicuous advantages. Table 2.4 shows the advantages of good safety and disadvantages of poor safety.

Table 2.4 The advantages of good safety and the disadvantages of poor safety

Advantages	Disadvantages
A safe facility gains a good reputation and this will bring increasing sales	Loss of earnings if the premises have to be closed
Savings on insurance (a good accident record will generate lower premiums)	The cost of replacing sick and injured staff
Avoidance of unnecessary damage to the facilities and equipment	The costs of litigation and damages.
A reputation for good safety and security will attract good staff.	

Check it out

1   Name the enforcing authorities you would consult to put a music event on in a park.

2   Give examples of different types of inspection.

3   Draw an example of four types of sign used in health and safety

4   What costs are incurred in health and safety?

5   What are the savings to be had from good health and safety practice?

6   What procedures and records does an employer have to produce?

2.5 Security in leisure and recreation

Security is the protection of people and materials from attack, damage or theft.

Part of the leisure experience is to be able to relax, knowing that you, your friends or family will not be threatened by other people and that your personal belongings will be safe. For the managers and staff of a facility much the same principle applies. No one wants to be in a job where there is a risk of abuse from customers or colleagues. Part of the pleasure of working in a team is the trust you can place in your team-mates.

While there are no statistics, it seems likely that the leisure industry is one where there are relatively few security incidents. Probably the main exception to this has been urban parks, but even here major advances are being made.

The three factors we try to control or prevent are shown in Table 2.5 on page 130.

Violence to staff and visitors

Thankfully, violence is relatively rare, and in many facilities staff know their customers and work in harmony with their team-mates. There is still cause for concern though. In 1996/97 20 attacks resulted in major injuries on employees and 34 in over-three-day injuries (HSE statistics).

With the tensions of modern living it is possible for customers to lose their self-control very easily and quickly. This tendency inevitably becomes more pronounced when people have been drinking. In most situations control of drinking will reduce the risk, but there are occasions in leisure where having a drink is the prime recreational activity. Although door or security staff can be used, in many cases sensitive customer service can resolve the situation before it escalates out of

Table 2.5 Factors involved in controlling security

Problems	Examples	Prevention
Temptation (when the circumstances make anti-social behaviour easy)	Deserted reception area due to staff shortages Handbags and money-belts left in the sports hall Equipment left lying around	Design of the premises – heavy furniture, with tills hidden under the counter, secure changing arrangements and good sight lines
Provocation	Staff attitudes can provoke or anger customers, customers can upset each other	Customer service – providing a welcoming attitude, and patient, non-aggressive complaint handling
Protection (when layout of the premises invites anti-social behaviour)	Dark areas, deserted corners out of the public view can invite vandalism	Security – providing safes, security lighting, locks, alarms Monitoring and surveillance – patrols and CCTV

Source: HSE

control. At some older pools or cinemas the receptionist is still sitting behind a glass screen. Barriers like this are unfriendly. The fact that the customer has to shout to be heard immediately provokes an aggressive reaction, and such screens are not much use in the face of a hammer or sawn-off shotgun in any case.

Cash security

Cash is an obvious reason for aggressive attack. Modern designs now have open reception desks with tills and cash facilities hidden below them. In centres where there is a high cash flow, money can be sent down a chute to a secure area or removed by security guards at regular periods, thus removing the temptation for thieves. If there is a strong chance of physical attack, pneumatic shoot-up screens and concealed panic buttons can be installed. Taking the cash to the bank is a particularly vulnerable moment, and there are sensible precautions that can be taken (see the 'thought for the page').

Deterrents

Close circuit TV can be monitored by security or other staff who will take action if there is an incident. It can also be linked to a

video which will give a record of the culprit. In isolated situations such as parks, where there may be a real fear of rape and assault, new designs, installing lighting, removing railings and dense shrubbery in order to provide sight lines, and the use of close circuit TV have greatly improved security.

Theft of property or money

In many recreational situations we are parted from our possessions; coats at clubs and restaurants, all clothing and valuables in the

Thought for the page

Cash control

- Bank frequently – to avoid keeping large amounts of cash on site
- Encourage credit cards
- Bank irregularly – do not develop a schedule
- Use different people, to protect them and to avoid a pattern
- Try to arrange for two people to go
- Carry a personal alarm
- Carry the money in an everyday bag
- Go by car if possible.

CCTV and lighting are effective deterrents against theft

changing rooms at sports centres. The temptation to steal can, however, be largely reduced by design and monitoring.

- CCTV is once again an effective deterrent, both in car parks and indoors in locker rooms, but removing the temptation is even more effective. In car parks, lighting deters thieves, as do security racks for bicycles and security barriers for cars
- secure lockers are important and some centres will have a clothes locker in the changing room and then another smaller one in the activity area to secure personal effects such as jewellery, money and watches. The same principle applies to

staff who, under the HSWA, have a right to personal locker space in the staff areas. The Victorians used to have the changing rooms by the pool – an excellent security device. Modern locker design has copied this at some pools where the locker corridors are ideally at right angles to the poolside so swimmers and staff can see down them and spot any suspicious behaviour

- theft of equipment is a problem in some centres. Using unusually coloured or logo-marked equipment helps to prevent this. Some items can be security marked with special paint or even with etched security codes.

Most centres have a rigid end-of-day closing and security procedure, which involves setting alarms and security lighting, and securing locks. One of the simplest devices in any facility in populated areas is to have large windows and leave the lights on when the facility is closed. Increasingly, CCTV is being used. There are three types:

- systems that simply monitor. These are of little use if evidence is needed, but a good deterrent when the facility is unstaffed
- systems that are linked to video (VCR). When staff are not present this system means that there is a record that can be used to identify intruders when staff return. Although useful, these systems sometimes suffer from poor quality
- systems linked to control centres run by specialist security firms or which will alert local security forces.

Theft by staff

Stealing from your employer can lead to instant dismissal and possible criminal prosecution. Most employees are honest and are more likely to find themselves accidentally in a position where they might be accused of theft due to careless actions:

- taking a book from work to prepare for a course
- taking entry money from a customer and putting it in your bag to keep it safe for the time being
- borrowing some money from the till until you get to the bank.

Think it over

You and one other staff member are responsible for clearing up at the end of the day. You find a £20 note on the floor of the sports hall. The till is locked. What would you do?

In most organisations there will be *standing orders* that define how you handle money and property in all situations. These should be followed. If the case is not clear, always seek your line manager's approval and/or get a witness to what you are doing.

Fraud

Fraud is the obtaining of goods or money by deception. Minor fraud (like using stolen credit cards) does not occur a great deal in leisure because the nature of our services and goods doesn't make the reward worth while. However, in some areas such as home entertainment retailing, the risk is much higher. Wherever credit cards are presented they should be checked carefully and the signatures compared. Public fraud such as passing forged notes is often unintentional but still needs to be detected. Large denomination notes should be looked at (the foil strip is one device that indicates whether the note is genuine; they can also be scanned with UV light or marking pencils). Many facilities do not scan notes all the time as it may be insulting to the customer. However, if the police notify the facility that there is an increase in false notes, these devices may have to be used. Credit card fraud is more difficult to detect. The police issue lists of cards known to be active in the area and on-line referral by telephone will detect stolen cards. However, many centres still do not or cannot operate on-line referral.

Fraud by staff is possible at all levels within organisations and indeed the more senior the employee, the more possibilities for fraud and the harder it is to detect. Fraud is usually achieved by changing or falsifying documents or having control of resources, particularly food and drink. For example, a staff member and the drayman could collude and not deliver the full number of beer barrels – the drayman then sells on the extra barrels and they split the difference. Bar fraud may also include watering spirits and then keeping or selling the bottles that have been saved. Many sophisticated techniques are used to detect fraud:

- automated tills and staff codes make till fraud very difficult.
- separating processes makes collusion less likely. For example, in some centres it is staff from the next shift that will bank the money taken from the last shift (who counted and bagged it).
- transactions over a certain amount can be authorised only by named staff signing for them. In other words you can't go on a spending spree with the company cheque book.
- cheques and audit claims, stock counts and cash collection will be checked several times by various departments. In many companies the accounts department will act as an internal audit ('the money police') and they will do spot enquiries to check claims.

One overlooked area of fraud is people applying for jobs with false documents. This could have serious consequences. Imagine a personal trainer who had no real knowledge of health and fitness, or an untrained outdoor activities leader taking some kids climbing. It is good practice by employers therefore to inspect the original copies of awards that applicants are claiming.

Theft of information

For any leisure company information is highly valuable. Here are some key examples:

- *customer databases*: If these are stolen you will not be able to charge or contact your customers. The thief can use the information to 'steal' your customers.
- *financial information*: This can be valuable to your competitors.
- *product information*: Designs of equipment or information on suppliers and

manufacturers can lead to copying. The most serious case of this is in record and video piracy.

- *data*: Although most information these days is kept on computer, the computer programme data itself is extremely valuable. The best example of this is the electronic game industry where many millions of pounds may go into producing the software programmes themselves.

The Data Protection Act (1998)

This Act makes it illegal to use information about individuals for any purpose other than that for which it was intended. The organisation that holds the information legally is responsible for securing it – so both paper records and data records will be held in a secure place or accessible only to authorised users. If customer records are stolen, it is likely that the thief could be prosecuted under the Act. However, the situation is confused, because many companies in seeking a prosecution would also be opening themselves up to a counter-prosecution that they had not secured the data.

The situation is even more confused with other types of record involving company information to which the Act does not apply. Existing industrial law has not fully caught up with the idea of electronic information. This lack of clarity and the potential damage means that companies take theft seriously.

Securing information

- all records should be kept under lock and key when they are not being used.
- computer databases can be electronically locked by encoding them to allow only certain people to see certain information. Usually access is controlled by a password name or number. It is essential that staff

don't tell people this or leave it written down, and that they choose codes that are not easy to guess, such as date of birth.

- it is normal practice for anyone leaving the organisation to lose his/her authorisation to access information. In some cases this will mean the employee leaving the workplace immediately it is known he or she is leaving.

- E-mail may be checked to see the type of information that is being sent. Some companies will encrypt certain files so as to make it impossible for them to be copied or downloaded. Others will keep a record of any user who has accessed the file.

Damage to property – sabotage

Sabotage is deliberate action by the staff to damage the facility they work in. One reason employees damage equipment is to get out of working. Anyone who has worked in a factory or on a building site knows that work can be brought to a halt by breaking or loosening a small component on a piece of machinery. But work in the leisure industry is very different; we are in control of our work process and the work itself is pleasant and rewarding. Sabotage is therefore very unusual. The only time there might be a risk of sabotage is when an employee has a chip on the shoulder, or is resentful as a result of a lost promotion or a dismissal.

Most people can handle this but occasionally a member of staff will become belligerent. In rare cases these people are extreme in their behaviour and do serious things like setting fire to the building or trashing the manager's office. It is more likely to be a case of someone removing papers or vandalising the manager's car. Such actions are hard to control, and can be difficult to prove. If possible, it is as well to try to anticipate any problems and try to avoid them by talking things over.

Vandalism – intentional damage by the public

Unlike sabotage, vandalism is a major problem. In some areas it is so bad that it has resulted in the closure of facilities. It occurs mainly in open spaces and to the outside of buildings. Sometimes damage is malicious, such as setting fire to pavilions or destroying flower beds. Sometimes it is stupid or misplaced, such as drinking in a playground and then smashing the bottle, spray painting a wall, or cycling over bowling greens. Opening up areas and lighting spaces makes it harder for vandals. Park patrols and neighbourhood watch schemes have also proved an effective deterrent.

Vandalism also occurs indoors. Cinema seats are often cut or jammed, changing cubicles have holes drilled in them, lockers get kicked or sprinkler systems set off. Vandals seem to vandalise where there is already damage, it is important to get rid of the signs of vandalism as soon as they appear – if a wall has been sprayed, paint over it right away. If this is done, vandalism indoors can usually be kept to a minimum by CCTV and regular patrolling of the known trouble spots such as the changing rooms.

Education can be effective and some providers go into schools to talk not only about vandalism but also about how young people can become more involved in their parks and open spaces. Far-sighted authorities have empowering and enabling policies, where they will find out what young people would like to find in the parks and then help to provide it, such as a skating or biking area. Experience shows that this kind of approach can encourage young people to take pride in an area and help police it against others who might want to destroy it. This is not a new idea and 'Interaction', a major youth and adventure playground project in North London, helped to pioneer it in the 1970s when they recruited local gang leaders on to their committee.

Another approach has been to work with vandals who have been given community service, and to get them working on projects connected with the area they vandalised. It is a method that does appear to have an effect in some cases, especially when there are social improvement schemes taking place at the same time.

Accidental damage

Theoretically this should not happen, but in reality it does. No matter how well trained or co-ordinated we are, there are times when things go wrong. People make mistakes, drop things, break things. Sensible design of facilities can help to prevent accidental damage to a certain extent. Cinema seats are designed to make it difficult to put your feet up on the row in front. Netting is draped over the decorated surfaces and windows at sports halls to prevent ball marks and breakages, and car parks are designed for one-way traffic to avoid scrapes. The materials used are increasingly accident-proof. Pub glasses are made of glass that will shatter rather than shard, chairs are often moulded to avoid fracture points and weaknesses, squash rackets are increasingly made to be virtually unbreakable, and carpets can be protected against cigarette burns and spillage.

Final word

Throughout this chapter we have largely assumed that you are an employer or at least the manager of a facility. In fact, should you decide to work in the industry you would normally enter at a more junior level, but the more aware you are of health and safety matters at any level the more you can act in a responsible way and be a better employee.

We have concentrated largely on the sport and recreation industry because the likelihood of hazards is far higher here than it is in other areas of the industry. Should you wish to expand your knowledge of other areas, you should extend your reading, and it would be a good idea to compare health and safety procedures of two different organisations from different sectors.

Further reading and practice is essential for this unit. Sources of information are excellent and nearly all you want can be taken from the Web, where most of the agencies have good sites with lots of information and many links. Many HSE publications are free. Telephoning is often not very productive as many of the organisations are huge and it is not always easy to find the right person, or they are small and could do without endless calls from students. It is far better to let your course tutor order publications in bulk.

Sources of information and further reading

There are many brochures and pamphlets available. Websites are also very good and have many guides and links on them as well as copies of legislation. Books are available but they tend to be expensive and are probably best obtained from a library.

> ## ! Check it out
>
> 1. What three factors need to be controlled with regards to security?
> 2. What are the main methods of risk reduction?
> 3. How can customer service reduce violence?
> 4. Give three design features for protecting staff.
> 5. What precautions would you take when taking cash to the bank?
> 6. How is CCTV used in reducing risks?
> 7. What is fraud?
> 8. How do organisations deter fraud?
> 9. Describe some methods used to reduce vandalism.

DfEE *An introduction for small and medium sized businesses*

HSE/HM Stationery Office publications list has a wide range of pamphlets/brochures, many of them free

British Pyrotechnists Association *Guidelines for organisers of professionally fired firework displays*

HSE *Managing health and safety in swimming pools*

HSE *Guide to Health and Safety and welfare at pop concerts and other similar events*

ILAM fact sheets. There are a variety of fact sheets dedicated to health and safety

ILAM & Pantry, S. *Health and safety in the leisure industry* CD-ROM (£450 annual licence)

NSPCC/NCF *Protecting Children – A guide for sports people*

Passingham, S. *Organising local events* Directory of Social Change

RoSPA *A guide to European Playground Equipment – Children's playgrounds*

Safety at Inland Water Sites

Safety on British Beaches

Scriptographic Publications Ltd *Health and Safety Guides*. Tel. 01420 541738

HM Stationery Office *Sport England – factfile – safety*

HM Stationery Office *Guide to Safety at Sports Grounds*

Take Ten National Centre for Playwork Tel. 01242 532949

Ward, Ted *An ABC of Hygiene and Safety –* Society of Licensed Victuallers Tel. 01344 884440

Useful websites

HSE: www.hse.gov.uk/hsehome.htm

Office of National Statistics: www.ons.gov.uk/

RoSPA: www.rospa.co.uk/

British Safety Council: www.britishsafetycouncil.co.uk/

Royal Institute for Public Health and Hygiene: www.riphh.org.uk/

Sir Norman Chester Centre (football trust): www.le.ac.uk/snccfr/fo.html

Centre for Accessible Environments: www.cae.org.uk/index.html

NSPCC: www.nspcc.org.uk/homepage/

NCF: www.ncf.org.uk/whats.html

AALA: www.aala.org.uk

The sports industry

This unit is organised into five sections. You will learn about:

- the nature of the sports industry
- the scale of sport and its contribution to the UK economy
- the organisation and funding of sport
- sport and the mass media
- trends in sport.

Introduction

Unit 1 made the point that the leisure industry is wide ranging and that you can follow a varied career in many of its sectors. For example, a facility manager's main role is to manage space and programming. It is perfectly feasible for someone to run an art gallery, a sports centre or a cinema without a great deal of extra technical training. The same principle can be applied to development workers. While their specialist knowledge and interest may mean they exclusively pursue the arts or sports, the techniques they use are almost identical. Consequently a sports development officer should be quite capable of becoming a leisure development officer.

This unit will provide you with information about the sports industry, how it is organised and the work people do in it. Furthermore, in the modern world sport is becoming a major factor influencing society in terms of politics and broadcasting.

3.1 The nature of the sports industry

Sport: what it is and why we do it

Before we look at the industry in detail it is a good idea to think about defining sport and why we do it.

Active recreation is any physical activity that we do in our leisure time. For many people it may be part of an activity such as gardening or dancing. For others it is the central activity, such as going for a walk or playing a game of tennis. Within active recreation comes the theme of this unit – 'sport and physical activities'. Sport is defined as physical activity done to a set of rules and which may or may not involve competition. Physical activities can be defined as activities involving physical effort that are intended to develop mental and physical well-being and skill. Straight away you will see that this is not a watertight definition, as a sport can fall into any category, usually depending on whether competition or scoring is involved.

For example, riding a mountain bike along a cycle way would be a physical activity, while entering a hill race would be a sport. Generally speaking, we tend to refer to any physical activity that *may* have a competitive element at some time as a sport. It is usually the competition that defines sport, more than the physical effort involved, and sports therefore include both snooker and chess. But in the main, exercise is a key part of the activity.

Physical activities tend to include such things as:

- health and fitness activities (e.g. jogging, going to the gym, aerobics)

137

- artistic dance, such as contemporary dance (ballroom dancing is recognised as a sport because of its competitive element)
- relaxation activities, such as yoga, and non-fighting forms of the martial arts (e.g. t'ai chi).

Sports are generally also slotted into certain categories (see Table 3.1). Again these are not watertight but refer to the main form in which the sport is played competitively. These are fairly useful categories in that they not only link activities but also indicate the facility they require. Netball is a good example of a sport that falls within more than one category. Of course, other classifications may be used, such as team and non-team sports, or high, medium and low aerobic value. As is often the case, the classification system you choose will be the one that best fits your purpose. For example, personal

trainers would probably use the aerobic classification when advising clients on the range of activities they could choose from to burn off calories.

The reason people do sport is important to know when we want to analyse trends or design programmes. Some of the reasons outlined below will be useful in understanding the popularity of sport, either through participation or watching sport.

Try it out Take a look at your local area, identify five different sports facilities, and classify the types of sports that are played in them. Now identify a facility that is not present locally and how this affects participation in sports that it offers. Finally, compare a rural and inner-city location and explain why certain sports are likely to be played and others not.

Table 3.1 Different categories of sports

Sports group	Activity	Facilities
Indoor sports	Snooker, weight-lifting, basketball, volleyball, ten-pin bowling, ice skating	Sports halls, weights rooms, bowling alleys, ice rinks
Outdoor sports	Football, rugby, hockey, netball, cricket, athletics	Grass pitches, artificial turf pitches, tarmac/redgra surfaces, tracks
Wet or pool-based sports	Swimming and diving, water polo, synchronised swimming	Swimming pools, diving pits
Racquet sports	Tennis, badminton, squash, real tennis, table tennis	Tennis centres, squash courts, sports halls, real tennis courts
Turf-based sports	Bowls, croquet, golf	Bowling and croquet greens, golf courses, driving ranges
Aerial sports	Gliding, flying	Aerodromes
Martial arts	Boxing, judo, karate	Dojos, boxing rings
Wheel-based sports	Cycling, motor racing, quad biking	Tracks
Target sports	Shooting, archery, fencing	Targets, shooting ranges
Equine sports	Driving, eventing, horse racing	Stables, arenas and rings, tracks
Outdoor activities	Canoeing, skiing, sailing, sub-aqua, rambling	Natural features, waterways outdoor activity centres, climbing walls
Non-physical sports	Bridge and chess	Halls and rooms

Participation

Until recently, modern sport has been largely about competitive games, often involving teams. Competitive games are often enjoyed most when you win, and for many years certain physical and mental characteristics made some people more likely to enjoy this type of sport than others. Physically these traits include strength, speed and co-ordination, while mentally, aggression, competitiveness against opposition, team-working skills with team members, self-determination and confidence, foresight and focus are all key components.

In recent years other sporting options have emerged, such as outdoor activities, fitness activities and non-competitive sports that allow other characteristics to be of importance. In other words, with a better balance of options, these days 'Sport is for all'.

Many people do sport for personal development. Some people for example find they learn a lot about themselves through the challenges of sports – such as dealing with exhaustion, problem solving, learning to win

Sport and physical recreation comes in all types and forms that provide enjoyment and exercise for everyone

and lose. For those who are insecure about themselves, who have low esteem or self-confidence, sport can be a way to achieve and improve self-esteem and confidence.

Lifestyle and well-being are also important factors now. A general preoccupation with health and longevity has meant that looking after your body and mind are worthy aims. For many, participation in competitive team games is not a good way to achieve this aim – with the tensions and injuries that are often associated with them. This is one reason why health and fitness and outdoor activities are increasingly popular.

Dreams, careers and rewards

Until the 1990s sport was predominantly amateur. The professionals made a good living but not a fortune. It was their dreams that drove them on – not fame and wealth. These dreams were a desire to play for the team they worshipped, their country or in an event they dreamt about (e.g. playing on Centre Court). Fantasy and the inner dream often seem to be the processes that drive athletes and are often factors that sports psychologists use when motivating athletes.

Nowadays the rewards of sport may include excellent cash rewards, fame, and opportunities to develop a career after playing. However, few elitist performers seem to start off with material objectives. Players like Beckham or Owen in interviews often say that it was always their dream to play for a particular club that drove them, not the money or fame. The difference now is that once players have achieved success, ambition and playing decisions appear often to be affected by material rewards and the advice of agents.

Many people play sport because it gives them the opportunity to meet like-minded people and make friends, to play with their children or relatives, i.e. the social aspect is important.

Players vary in the seriousness with which they pursue excellence and fitness in a sport. However, most enjoy the camaraderie and social life that revolves around any sports activity. It is interesting to note that for many years health clubs emphasised the activity side and the social life was minimal. More recently, the larger centres are starting to provide excellent social areas, catering and children's play areas that cater for the social life of their members.

For some people, belonging to a club is seen as a reflection of social status or a reflection of lifestyle and self-image. These days it is important not only where you play but how you look. As we shall see later, the sportswear industry has exploded since 1990 and the choice of the latest equipment or logo appears to have some magical power to improve your sporting performance.

Fashion also can affect the popularity of individual sports. Before health clubs became popular, squash was seen as a sport that active trendy people did. Now people wanting to make a lifestyle statement will be members of a health club, running marathons or doing one of the more glamorous outdoor activities.

Watching sport

The passion people feel for supporting a sport is sometimes a mystery to others. But let's start with the simple explanation: watching sport or following a team can often be a way of life. Research by 'When Saturday Comes' in 1991 showed that in a sample of football fans over 60 per cent had been introduced to the 'match' by their father or other male relative and 43 per cent supported a club because their family did. Much the same probably applies to viewing habits. In other words, a young person grows up in a household, absorbing the rituals and behaviour associated with watching a game on television, and then continues these in adult life to pass them on

to the next generation. So our sporting passions can be a learnt behaviour that for some people is very deeply ingrained.

Many sports fans have learnt to enjoy sport by participating in it. When they watch they can to some extent experience the feelings of the player, interpret the game and appreciate the skill of player. They may even enjoy the recollection of their own performance.

On the other hand, some people become fans because it is the 'cool' thing to do. In soccer, young white middle-class men are now the biggest market segment – especially with Premier football clubs. They are far less likely to have experienced the spectator habit in their middle-class childhood so it seems that they have acquired the passion as a lifestyle accessory.

Female spectator numbers have increased as well, not only in soccer but also in rugby, cricket and tennis. Again we do not know the reasons but it is probably a mixture of lifestyle association and liking the players. Certainly the teenage girl fans of Manchester United are often driven by the connection from the Spice Girls to David Beckham; any love of football often seems to be acquired afterwards. Football is the new rock 'n roll.

Corporate hospitality, where companies book seats, rooms and marquees at prestigious events, is another source of spectators. In some circles it looks good to say you were at Ascot or the Henley Regatta. However, the large-scale presence of 'instant' fans can be an annoyance to grassroots fans who are often denied access due to corporate hospitality block-booking seats.

A sense of belonging

Many people seem to have a basic urge to want to 'belong' – whether to a group of similar people, our town or country. For example, in the survey mentioned above

48 per cent of fans supported their club because of local pride. Sport can often supply this need and indeed the whole structure and ritual of sport encourages this; for example, consider the Olympics and the martial aspects of the uniforms and flags of the competitors in the opening ceremony, or the emotion when medallists hear their national anthem.

This sense of belonging and identity with others can affect the mood of supporters and it is one reason why politicians support sport. Another is that if politicians show support for clubs they are seen as belonging to that community and more likely to get votes.

Thought for the page

Our sense of belonging and loyalty has sometimes had tragic consequences. In the First World War, in order to help recruitment of the troops, the authorities encouraged men to join up with their workmates and other groups to form fighting units that would stay together throughout the war. One such group was the football fans of Accrington Stanley FC, one of the founding teams of the FA. They became known as the Accrington Pals. In the holocaust of the trenches the Pals were annihilated and the small town of Accrington lost an entire generation of menfolk.

Symbolic war

Many commentators have suggested that sport is a simulated form of war and that society has a need for simulated aggression. 'When two sides go to war' we see typical behaviours of armies such as the use of chants and colours, ritual celebrations, aggressive behaviour and irrational stereotypical thinking about the opposition. Some politicians see the value of this and, if they can encourage national teams to win, they are more likely to gain votes in the euphoria of victory.

While the battle itself is meant to be a symbolic one between the players, it can turn into real violence among the supporters. In soccer and boxing, in particular, things can spill over and hooligans from opposing sides turn on each other.

> **! Check it out**
>
> 1 Classify in three different ways the sports of squash, golf and cycling
> 2 How might a person benefit from playing rugby?
> 3 How do we learn to enjoy watching sport?
> 4 What is corporate hospitality?

The sports industry

The phrase 'sports industry' first conjures up a picture of professional sport and its players and managers. Then think about the meaning of 'industry', which means 'people working' and think about all the people who work or make a living out of providing sport and who through their work allow you to participate in it or watch it. The list starts to grow and includes facility provision, coaches, people in sports medicine, the retailers and manufacturers who supply clothes and equipment, holiday companies specialising in sport, people who work in health and fitness and those who deal with sports injuries. The industry is huge.

Sporting goods

Once upon a time if you had a pair of baggy cotton shorts, a pair of plimsolls and a piece of equipment you were set to play your chosen sport for some time to come, without spending any more on clothes or equipment. To extend the life of your equipment you would maintain it by oiling it or storing it in the right conditions. You would extend the life of your kit by wearing it only when you played sport. This was the norm well into the 1970s.

THE SPORTS INDUSTRY

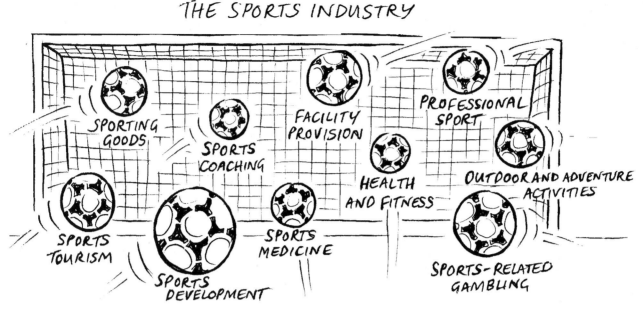

SPORTING GOODS

SPORTS COACHING

FACILITY PROVISION

PROFESSIONAL SPORT

HEALTH AND FITNESS

OUTDOOR AND ADVENTURE ACTIVITIES

SPORTS TOURISM

SPORTS DEVELOPMENT

SPORTS MEDICINE

SPORTS-RELATED GAMBLING

The sports industry contains a variety of components

Today the sports goods market is probably the largest single market in the entire sports industry. So why did it change? There are two important reasons.

First, technology: the invention of new materials such as Lycra, neoprene, carbon fibre and fibreglass have drastically opened up new opportunities in design that allow the player to perform better. Both clothing and equipment are affected and, in particular, improvements have been made to make them:

- more responsive (as with basketball boot soles, archery sights)
- more comfortable (sweat-absorbent clothing, lighter football boots)
- stronger or lighter (lighter racquets, more flexibility in golf clubs).

The rate of invention is breathtaking. Whereas thirty years ago technology had left most sporting goods virtually unchanged for fifty years, it now produces major shifts on a regular basis – making last year's design or materials outmoded.

The second reason for the change in the sports goods market is fashion: there has long been a fashion value to wearing sports clothing. Two sports that were particularly prone to this were tennis and golf. As early as the 1920s, the bandana worn by tennis stars like Suzanne Lenglen caught on as a major fashion accessory. Fred Perry, the last (1936) British Wimbledon champion, pioneered the logo which is still popular. On the golf scene the knitwear company Pringle produced distinctive sweaters that told the world that the wearer played golf – which for many years also implied you were well off.

Thought for the page

Technology is expanding so rapidly that it can outpace the game. A basic principle of any sport is that it is meant to test the performance of the participant and this means that any variation caused by playing conditions or equipment needs to be controlled. With expanding technology a player can obtain a huge and possibly unfair advantage by being the first to use an improved technology. For example, the use of lightweight materials for tennis racquets and golf clubs, while allowing greater performance by the user, have been banned by the governing bodies of sport.

Until the 1980s, wearing sports clothes as a fashion item was usually restricted to participants of a small number of sports. The rise in sport as a leisure interest in the 1970s, accompanied by the new materials available, meant that more people were playing sport and starting to wear their sports clothes away from play. Particularly dominant at this time was the track suit.

The growth of the sports shoe has also been spectacular. Since the 1980s sports shoe technology has produced a range of different and improved shoes designed for increasingly specific use. Furthermore, because of their style and comfort they have become the favoured footwear for many people in everyday use. For many types of sports shoe (e.g. trainers, sailing or deck shoes) the majority of sales are for non-sports use.

This fashion trend has been fully exploited by the manufacturers in the marketing of sports shoes for general wear. Marketing campaigns have included:

- identifying products with sporting heroes through endorsements and advertising
- promoting the status of logos and designer labels
- focusing on the technical properties of shoes.

Speedo Fastskin

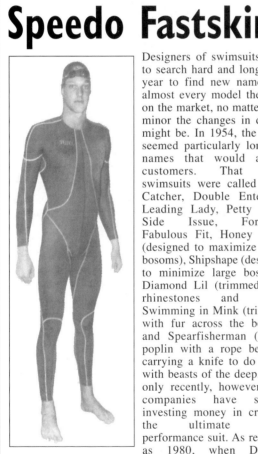

Designers of swimsuits used to search hard and long each year to find new names for almost every model they put on the market, no matter how minor the changes in design might be. In 1954, the reach seemed particularly long for names that would attract customers. That year swimsuits were called Beau Catcher, Double Entendre, Leading Lady, Petty Foxy, Side Issue, Forecast, Fabulous Fit, Honey Child (designed to maximize small bosoms), Shipshape (designed to minimize large bosoms), Diamond Lil (trimmed with rhinestones and lace), Swimming in Mink (trimmed with fur across the bodice) and Spearfisherman (heavy poplin with a rope belt for carrying a knife to do battle with beasts of the deep.) It is only recently, however, that companies have started investing money in creating the ultimate high-performance suit. As recently as 1980, when Duncan Goodhew splashed to glory for Britain in Moscow, he was still wearing a pair of simple Adidas nylon trunks. But Speedo have spent three years, 450 different types of fabric and 10 prototypes – each costing £15,000 – developing the Fastskin Suit. It has tiny ridges on the body similar to those found on a shark. In the water, the ridges glow white, making them look like fish scales. Each suit takes 21 times longer to make than a conventional suit, with the scales of the material having to run down the body.

Source: *Observer Sport Magazine*, 2000

Sporting products become identified with sporting heroes through advertising

CASE STUDY – Rip off or strip off

A major consumer fashion in the 1990s has been the emergence of team strip replicas which in Britain have been largely marketed by Umbro (football) and Cotton Traders (rugby). Marketing rights are agreed with the clubs and it is in their financial interest to make changes to the official strip so that replica sales will be boosted. This practice has been heavily criticised in the media, but research from the Centre for Football Research shows that the supporters themselves are more tolerant. In 1995 about 10 per cent objected to merchandising but this had dropped to less than 9 per cent two years later. In the same period their average spend per head had risen from £85 to £132.

Endorsement of equipment is also big business. However the problem with this is that many top professionals use personalised equipment designed to a specification that the amateur player could not handle. For example, tennis players string their racquets at a higher tension than club players. This can lead to charges of misrepresentation such as Nike's embarrassment when it was revealed that Tiger Woods did not use the golf balls he endorsed.

Questions

1   Look through the advertisements of a sport magazine and identify clothing and equipment that is associated with clubs or individual players.

2   Identify the merchandise range of your nearest or favourite professional football team.

3   Try to get hold of the annual report of this team and identify what proportion of income comes from merchandising and manufacturing rights.

4   Apart from football clubs which other organisations benefit from replica kit?

In the past ten years, sports equipment and sports wear have become a worldwide phenomenon. Participants pay more now than they have ever done on buying equipment and clothing that extends their performance. In addition to this, the majority of the population that does not play sport will invariably have at least trainers and a 'track suit' in their wardrobe.

Sports coaching

Coaching is teaching, i.e. advising, training and motivating sports participants to enable them to improve their performance. Properly done, coaching involves a variety of skills (see Figure 3.1).

Think it over

In groups, discuss what the key factors are when deciding to buy a pair of sports shoes of a particular brand. How much are you influenced by the performance boost they give you and how much are fashion and marketing involved?

Figure 3.1 The skills involved in sports coaching

Strictly speaking, a coach works in competitive sport and aims to improve the performance of participants. In recreational or non-competitive areas the people who show you how to do the activity are called **instructors** (e.g. health and fitness and outdoor activities) or **teachers** (swimming, yoga). Teachers and instructors are generally more concerned with their clients' developing technique. Just to confuse things, many people who teach recreational sport are in fact qualified coaches who find it easier to make a living by teaching.

Coaches usually work long and often unsocial hours because their clients need them when they are competing or training which is often at weekends and in the evenings. Despite the media coverage of professional sport, participation in competitive sports is primarily in the voluntary sector, organised through many small clubs. Not surprisingly, these clubs cannot afford to pay coaches, so about three-quarters of coaches in the country work on a voluntary basis. For the remaining quarter the following opportunities arise:

- clubs that wish to achieve elite status increasingly pay senior coaches on a part-time (or sometimes full-time) basis.
- the governing bodies of sport have a hierarchy of paid full-time coaches. This normally consists of regional coaches who answer to a national coach. In popular sports, or ones where there are several events like athletics, there may be a group of national coaches responsible for their specialities and answering to a Director of Coaching.
- professional clubs and players in sports like tennis or snooker will usually employ a professional full-time coach.

In terms of pay, a junior coach will earn about £15,000 a year (2000 rates) and opportunities are rare and heavily competed for. With professional sport there is also the option of bonuses for success based on a share of prize money or a fixed rate. The vast majority of employment for paid coaches and instructors comes not from coaching but from instruction in recreational sport (such as swimming, tennis courses or aerobics).

Qualifications

Qualifications for coaches are controlled by the governing bodies of sport themselves and co-ordinated by the National Coaching Federation. Entry requirements are rarely academic and usually depend on the coach having a love and understanding of the sport and a degree of skill in it.

Qualifications usually consist of a series of graded courses that build up to club or senior coach level. Until recently these had a wide variety of names and standards. However, increasingly the governing bodies are redesigning their awards to fit the standardised NVQ framework. Apart from the various levels of sports-specific awards there are also (generic) awards that show competence in coaching children, adults and people with disabilities.

 **Try it out** Identify a coaching award of your choice. Find out what requirements there are to do it. Why are these important? What skills and knowledge are required other than being able to play the sport? What do you think about this qualification?

Facility provision

The growth of participation in sport and active recreation over the past thirty years has largely been the result of building indoor facilities such as racquet centres, health clubs, sports centres, swimming pools and ice rinks. These sports are also catered for by the provision of outdoor facilities such as pitches and courts. Most significant has been the development of artificial surfaces and floodlighting that have boosted the growth of hockey, five-a-side football and tennis.

Table 3.2 gives an estimate of how many facilities there were in 1991. Because of the restriction on public sector spending there has been little growth since, but there has been considerable growth in the private sector.

Table 3.2 Provision of different facilities

Facility	Number
Swimming pools	1300 + 3351 school pools
Sports halls	1500
Indoor tennis courts	470 but rapidly expanding in the private sector and now probably above 1000
Indoor bowls	300 (has probably risen significantly)
Ice rinks	40
Ski slopes	99
Athletics tracks	412
Golf courses (18-hole equivalent)	1270 (probably a significant increase in driving ranges and some courses)
Health clubs	1999 estimates: 2500 (Mintel), 3500 (Keynote)

Source: Sport England

There are also other types of outside built facilities for spectator sports, such as tracks that include horse racing, dog tracks and motor racing. Not only do these have large outdoor areas that need to be maintained but also large indoor facilities such as the grandstands, hospitality areas, function rooms and animal accommodation. The crowds, which are often large, require special expertise in crowd control.

One of the weaknesses behind the growth of leisure centres for indoor sport in the 1970s was that they were designed principally for participation. With professional sport becoming so commercially successful there

was a need for arenas that could hold sufficient audiences to make spectating and broadcasting profitable. In the same period there has been an increasing demand to stage large-scale entertainment events like pop concerts, exhibitions and conferences. As a consequence there has also been a healthy growth of new arena and conference centres. Sometimes these have been from the conversion of existing buildings like stations (GMEX) or from older buildings like the Royal Agricultural Hall in Islington, London.

There has also been new building. Because of inner-city traffic congestion and the fact that audiences will travel many miles, these new sites are often located on or near motorways. The National Exhibition Centre at Birmingham is a good example of this. These areas are built to be flexible. One night you may see an international basketball or tennis event or a TV programme like *Gladiators* – which was broadcast from the National Exhibition Centre. The next day the arena is stripped down ready for a rock concert at the weekend.

Whatever their size or function, sports facilities require special skills in management which are known as:

- *operational management*: which is managing services and facilities such as bookings, customer handling, marketing, staging events, cleaning and routine maintenance
- *technical*: this is the management of the plant, security systems and grounds within a facility
- *service delivery*: the programming and development of activities.

Although leisure centre managers often have a sports training and qualifications, the managers of arenas and stadia may have no specific technical training but might have come from retail management or from an events and conference background.

You can find out more about facility management from the professional bodies such as the Institute of Leisure and Amenity Management (ILAM) or the Institute of Sport and Recreation Management (ISRM).

Stadia

In 1991, two-thirds of the football league clubs were playing in stadia that had been built before 1910. The recommendations of the Taylor Report (1990) to improve stadium conditions made clubs legally obliged to turn to all-seater and refurbished stadia. The Football Foundation was created by the FA to put money into helping clubs meet this requirement.

The 1990s also saw a growth in demand for events, conferences and corporate hospitality. It was quickly discovered that the prestige of association with a professional sports club meant that there was a commercial market for going far beyond simply the provision of seating. Nowadays, conference and function rooms, corporate hospitality suites and sports facilities and gyms are all part of the facilities offered in a stadia, especially those

in the top divisions of soccer, rugby and cricket.

Refurbishment has not been the only solution and in the 1990s ten new stadia have been built in England alone, with others coming up such as the new Molyneux stadium in Wolverhampton. The new Millennium Stadium in Cardiff was also opened in 1997 for the Rugby World Cup. The stadia are listed in Table 3.3.

Sports development

Sports development programmes are about increasing participation in sport or pursuing excellence. Usually employed by local authorities or governing bodies of sport, the concept of sports development was started with the 'Glasgow Sports bus' that was operational in the late 1960s. It tackled the problem that people often do not participate in sport for reasons of access. The basic idea was that sports leaders took sports equipment into the local community to encourage local participants to take part in sports activities. These would be locations that the locals felt

Table 3.3 Stadia built in the 1990s

Stadium	Main user	Capacity	First used
Pride Park	Derby County FC	33,258	1997
Britannia Stadium	Stoke City FC	28,000	1997
Stadium of Light	Sunderland	42,000	1997
Riverside Stadium	Middlesbrough FC	35,000	1995
Reebok Stadium	Bolton Wanderers FC	27,800	1997
Alfred McAlpine Stadium	Huddersfield Town FC/Huddersfield/Sheffield RLFCs	24,000	1994
JJB Stadium	Wigan Athletic FC/Wigan Warriors RLFC	25,000	1999
Madejski Stadium	Reading FC	25,000	1998
The New Den	Millwall FC	20,000	1993
The County Ground	Durham CCC	5,000 for county matches and up to 20,000 for internationals	1995

Source: Sports Council Planning Bulletin no. 7, 2000

happy with, at prices they could afford and with few constraints on what people wore.

The first principle of sports development is that it tends not to be focused on formal sports facilities but will use what is available locally (e.g. parks, church halls).

The second principle is 'the pyramid of participation' or to give it its new name 'Sports development continuum model' (see Figure 3.2). This focuses on the fact that most adults are non-participant, often as a result of their lifestyle or even an active rejection of sport resulting from their school experiences. This prompts two lines of strategy:

* to work with schools to ensure that the next generation of adults are sports friendly
* to reintroduce non-participant adults to sport in a way that makes it fun.

In some cases, having established the primary goals the development process provides opportunities for individuals should they wish to progress further up the pyramid until a few will have reached excellence.

Many development workers carry out most of their work at the bottom of the pyramid, providing basic courses and activities or

setting up promotional events like taster days. They will also organise routes up through the structure, for example by setting up development squads, master classes or creating leagues and competitions.

A third principle is that sport is a means of helping to reduce social and personal issues found in communities. Sports development projects may, for example, aim to tackle unemployment problems by using sport to develop self-esteem and confidence, or produce skills that can be transferred; or they may use activities to reduce loneliness among old people.

Development workers fall into two categories:

* generic: who work with a variety of activities with one or more target groups which are typically those who do not participate or are socially excluded. For example women, youth, the elderly, the deprived, people with disabilities and ethnic minorities
* sports-specific: whose job is to increase participation in one sport only.

Development work has become a main plank of government policy to work within the community and fight exclusion. It is consequently increasingly well funded by the Sports Council's schemes like Top Club or Top Sport.

Sports development is unusual in that it is one of the few public sector areas that makes extensive use of volunteers. An important scheme that has turned helpers into skilled leaders has been the Central Council for Physical Recreation (CCPR) The British Sports Trust's community sport leaders awards: junior, sports leader, higher sports leader and basic expedition. Their estimates are that they will have trained over 50,000 leaders by 2000.

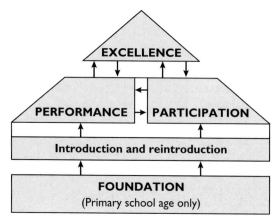

Figure 3.2 Sports development continuum model or pyramid of participation

> **Think it over**
>
> Sports development often has to play down the competitive nature of sport or the emphasis on fitness if it is to attract clients. Do you think sport loses something in this or can it be enjoyed simply as a social activity?

! Check it out

1 What is the difference between a coach and an instructor?

2 What opportunities are there for professional coaches?

3 What national organisations are especially involved in coaching development?

4 What sorts of services do stadia provide?

5 Explain with examples how the sports development continuum model works.

6 What is the difference between sports-specific and generic sports development?

7 Other than increasing participation, what are two other benefits of sports development?

8 What are sports leadership awards and how do they help sports development?

Sports tourism

Sports tourism is an important sector of the tourism market. The British Tourist Authority has even created a new department dedicated to promoting and developing sports tourism. The aim is to build up a database that identifies the extent of sports-specific tourism.

Sports tourism is about making day trips or taking longer breaks to be involved in either spectating or playing sport or visiting venues that have particular sporting interest. Perhaps biggest of all is recreational participation like skiing holidays. We will look at the four areas.

Spectator sports

Britain hosts many famous sporting events that are unique to our country and which are known as 'icon' events. The Grand National and the Derby, Henley Regatta, Wimbledon, the British Grand Prix and the Cricket Test Series are examples. As well as people in Britain, tourists will come from all over the world to watch these famous events.

Icon events are annual ones but there is a circuit of 'world class' or international events which countries and cities bid for or which come to countries on a cyclical basis. The Olympic Games is the most famous, but others include the Commonwealth Games (in Manchester in 2002), Euro 2000, FIFA World, and Rugby World Cup.

At the other end of the scale is the huge number of 'domestic events'; for example regular fixtures of football and rugby clubs, local and regional competitions of amateur sports clubs, such as martial arts. Premier Division soccer excepted, most of these events in themselves do not attract huge crowds but because of their frequency they account for many of the sports tourism trips made each year.

There has always been a steady market in sports fans travelling away to watch professional teams. However, with cheaper travel and the increase in international competition at club level, there is also a growing market in international away matches that fans follow. These tend to happen in sports that have a degree of universality. Football is the prime example but the widening of rugby at club level throughout Europe will no doubt increase fan travel. Increasingly, cricket's 'Barmy army' regularly travels to test match venues which until recently would have been considered as exotic and a 'once in a lifetime' trip.

Competitive participation

While the number of professional sports players travelling to matches is relatively

149

CASE STUDY – The multiplier effect – sport boosts the economy

Any sports project will have spin-offs for the local community and economy in terms of jobs, wealth and community spirit. The Commonwealth Games will be the biggest sports tourism event held in the UK since Euro 96. Here is a forecast of their impact:

Before the games

Apart from the development team of several hundred employees for the Games, the event also has a major building programme (51,000 square metres of floor space) to create facilities like new stadia, pools and a competitors' village. This capital expenditure will be paid for by contributions from the public sector (e.g. the Lottery), the private sector (Manchester City FC) and the voluntary sector (e.g. the Lawn Tennis Association, LTA). Development will result in 40 hectares of derelict land being reclaimed at a cost of £200 million. This will increase employment for a wide range of people from builders to architects and surveyors. It will also result in increased business for suppliers to the industry (e.g. builders' merchants) and the various firms that will support workers (e.g. corner cafés, newsagents). In addition, the equipment of these buildings and administration of the Games will involve many other suppliers (e.g. office supplies, IT).

The Games reflect the importance of broadcasting and sponsorship in modern events. Income from these will be a major contribution to paying for the revenue costs, as will ticket sales and merchandising. A far cry from the last (1978), loss-making Commonwealth Games in Edinburgh when broadcasting and sponsorship were still undeveloped.

During the Games

Over two weeks the Games will attract one million spectators and 10,000 participants. Many spectators will spend large amounts on travel costs to Manchester, and both national and local firms will develop packages to attract this market. For the Games themselves, there will be some temporary work, although one of the features of the Games is that they will employ 15,000 volunteers. There are also social benefits, as the Games will use themselves as a vehicle to promote multicultural understanding and to celebrate the richness of Manchester's own culture.

After the Games

There will be impressive long-term benefits. A major benefit is that the areas regenerated as a result of the Games will offer £36.7 million of discounted development allowing new businesses to set up and create an employment base in these areas of Manchester. The Games will also create various sports-related projects including the relocation of Manchester City FC. The creation of the United Kingdom Sports Institute (UKSI) academy will not only allow regional athletes to further their careers but also provide local youth with the support and training which will not only improve sports participation but also enrich local communities. Overall it is thought that approximately 1,000 new permanent jobs will be created.

Questions

1   The multiplier effect is the indirect impact that a project or industry has on the local economy. Suggest the types of business or job that will be directly and indirectly affected by the Games.

2   Identify a sports event or new facility in your area and suggest ways it has affected the local economy and community.

small, the number of amateurs doing this is huge. This is particularly the case with team sports such as hockey, rugby and soccer, where the annual tour is an important social and competitive fixture in the year. Often these trips are treated as mini-holidays and there is a great deal spent on accommodation, food and entertainment – all essential ingredients of the tourism industry.

Table 3.4 shows the number of major events for different sports and their attendance.

Table 3.4 Event attendance in the UK 1998

Sport	No. of events	Attendance (millions)
Football	2193	25.4
Athletics	6	0.085
Tennis	12	0.66
Cricket	379	1.7
Golf	9	0.5
Rugby League	516	1.2
Horse racing	1137	5

Source: Mintel

(*Note* Professionalisation of Rugby Union will mean an expansion of spectators from its previous lower levels)

With the exception of rugby and soccer fans, who probably incur an average of about £25 per league match, most fans attending these events are going to spend perhaps £100 in all for their trip. This is speculation but it does not seem far-fetched and may well be more for events that require long trips and stay-overs, such as internationals. If this is so then the estimated value of sports tourism from

Try it out

What was the average attendance at football matches in 1998?

Does horse racing attract bigger or smaller crowds than cricket matches?

Name two of the big six athletics meetings in the UK.

Think it over

Think about the last time you travelled out of your area to watch or play sport. Work out your expenditure for the trip, including food and travel, tickets, accommodation and other spending, such as souvenirs. How typical are visits like this in your life? How much do you think you contribute to the sports tourism industry spend in a year?

these sports alone is £1,459m or about 11 per cent of total tourist income.

Visiting venues

Britain's sporting legacy means that many of our venues are the 'homes' of international sports or have a sporting heritage that interests tourists. Examples include St Andrews, the home of golf, Wembley, Lords Cricket Ground, Twickenham, Manchester United and the All England Lawn Tennis Club at Wimbledon.

Personal leisure activities

Probably the biggest area of tourism is where people simply go on holiday or take a short break to take part in sport; for example, going on a residential course, going to a hotel to play golf or tennis, going on a pony trekking holiday.

In some cases people will go to an area and arrange their own participation, for instance a walking weekend in the Fells. But activities can be packaged – a tradition that goes back to the 1680s when Scarborough offered sea bathing and spas, coupled with accommodation and entertainment. The spa package expanded enormously over the next two centuries, while in the nineteenth century hydros (health orientated) and golfing hotels became very popular.

With modern marketing, the growth in wealth and the interest in sport this packaging has grown. Not only are traditional golf holidays still expanding but also packages that offer participation in many other sports. Tennis is particularly popular, as are residential outdoor activity holidays and chartered sailing.

There is a growing trend for people to sample sport and also a growing interest in participating in 'exotic' sports such as hot-air ballooning or those in remote areas such as white-water rafting. Because people in this market will have neither the skills nor the knowledge to arrange their own schedule they will be particularly responsive to package deals that offer a short and entertaining introduction to the sport, and companies offering packages like this are rapidly expanding.

Also expanding is the youth market. Increasingly, we are adopting the American idea of the summer camp, and residential sports and activity courses for youth are an important niche market. Bobby Charlton was a pioneer of this product with his sports schools. In adventure activities, the business is sufficiently important that major international companies are buying into it.

Companies offering 'exotic' sport packages have expanded rapidly in recent years

For example, the 3D group has been bought by Center Parcs which themselves are owned by Whitbread.

Britain has a reputation for sporting excellence that is attractive to the overseas market. In terms of excellence we have the centres of excellence and the national sports centres which may well expand their market for overseas visitors. It is likely that the existing and extensive language school industry that already attracts many thousands of overseas youth every year will see sports participation as an important 'bolt on'. Sports activities have always played a part in their stay; more recently there is an interest in providing sports coaching as a major part of the product.

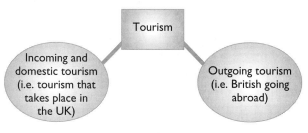

Figure 3.3 Classification of tourism

While the UK can compare well with other countries in terms of spectator events and can probably outdo them in terms of sporting heritage, it faces stiff competition with participation. This is because enjoyment in participation is often enhanced by appropriate climate and the quality of facilities. Apart from golf where there are excellent courses, and the soft aspect of our natural environment which lends itself to walking, most other sports are better provided for abroad. This is particularly so where overseas resorts have developed facilities to best provide for sport. Ski resorts are a long-standing example, but more recently the arrival of the 'sports hotel' offering top-class facilities and teaching, as well as accommodation, provides a powerful attraction which few British facilities can offer.

Traditionally, sports tourism was not marketed well and it became fragmented as a result. Until fairly recently it was a 'do-it-yourself' operation. You would buy your ticket for the match from the Club, make your own travel arrangements and then find accommodation and food when you got to the venue. This is now rapidly changing and sports tour, event and participation operators are numerous. They provide all-inclusive packages for a vast array of sports. Many of these operators form trade associations, such as the International Association of Golf Tour Operators.

It is not only tour operators who see the value of sports tourism. Local councils and chambers of commerce often recognise its economic impact and will make efforts to encourage tourists for their first visit, hoping that they will enjoy it sufficiently to return or recommend the place to their friends. Cardiff city is a case in point, and for the 1999 Rugby World Cup designed a special web page to provide information and booking for almost anything the visitor to the World Cup could need.

CASE STUDY – The big fight economics vs ethics

In 2000 Mike Tyson fought twice in the UK, in Manchester and Glasgow. As it turned out both fights were short-lived and disappointing to the fans. More memorable was the controversy that was created – which demonstrates the complexity of the impact of sport on society.

At issue was the fact that Tyson is a convicted rapist and, under British law, convicted foreign criminals are not allowed entry into the country. For both fights, the Home Secretary, Jack Straw, gave special exemption to the law and allowed Tyson entry and a work permit. Just as controversial was the decision by the Civic Authorities in both cities to approve the fights. There was a huge outcry from the press and women's groups who took the view that letting Tyson in condoned rape and gave credibility to the behaviour that Tyson was associated with both inside and outside the ring. Support for him came from groups who saw him as a successful athlete who could inspire youth, and from sports fans who felt that it was the sport that counted and not the player's private life. Another powerful lobby that supported the fights was the the local politicians and business people in both cities who weighed up the situation and decided that the fights would make a significant economic contribution. In the case of Glasgow it was claimed by the promoters that the fight would have a 'multiplier effect' and would bring in £30 million to the local community. A more conservative analysis suggested £3 million – still a sizeable input.

The Tyson fights demonstrate that sports tourism is not just about 'staging a sports event' but that there are often complex political, moral and economic issues involved.

Questions

1   What contribution did the appearance of Mike Tyson make to British sport?

2   What impact did direct income from the fights (e.g. ticket sales, broadcasting rights) have on the local economies of Manchester or Glasgow?

3   What income from the fight would have gone into the local economy?

4   What other examples do you know of where the decision to stage a sport event has caused controversy in political or economic terms?

> **! Check it out**
>
> 1 Explain what an 'icon' is in sports tourism.
> 2 What are the top three best-attended sports?
> 3 What activities are particularly important in personal leisure activities?
> 4 What are 'packages'? – identify a specific example from another source of reading.

Professional sport

Professional sport was once clearly defined as sport where:

- the participants are paid either in terms of a salary or prizes

and/or

- players could be bought and sold and contracted to teams.

Until the 1970s the distinction from the amateur game was obvious and only a few sports were significantly professional. They included football, Rugby League, golf, tennis, snooker, and motor and horse racing. At this time taking payment in the amateur game was a serious offence and could lead to a life-long ban. A sport that was particularly affected by this was rugby where the codes – League and Union – meant that Union players had to give up their Union career if they were tempted to play League, say in Australia during the British summer.

Competitive sport, including soccer, had evolved from the leisured classes and the public schools. Central to their class and sporting ethic was that sport was something done for the love of the game. To introduce payment dirtied the ideal and subjected sport to all the pressures of the world of commerce. This sporting ethic was very important well into the twentieth century and was adopted by the vast majority of sport participants. By the 1970s it was under threat and the concept of 'shamateurism' arose in which amateur sports participants were finding ways around the payment rules by:

- accepting sponsorship deals in the form of trusts
- being given paid but nominal jobs by sponsors and sport officials
- being given inflated travelling expenses
- being given payment in kind (e.g. a free car, clothing, house).

Given the importance of the amateur ethic, shamateurism provoked heated debate which was to last into the 1990s. By this time the huge growth in the income potential of professional sport had become too much of a temptation for all but the most traditional, especially when the governing bodies found that they could attract large sums of money to fund the sport.

Today the debate hardly seems important, with virtually every sport from archery to volleyball having a professional side to its game, or where amateur players, while not being paid or receiving prize money, can make a living from endorsements, sponsorship, book writing and media appearances. For example, the top Olympian Steve Redgrave belongs to the Amateur Rowing Association – one of the remaining entirely amateur sports – and receives support of the kind described above although he is not paid to row.

Structure

Most sports are divided into leagues of some sort. These are defined by the skill shown by the participants or teams; and promotion depends on competitively challenging others in the league. For example: in English soccer there are four fully professional leagues, in cricket the sixteen major counties fall into two professional leagues.

Professional leagues are usually separated from the amateur ones and it is the players who make the move from amateur to professional status if they choose or are selected. In some sports the division is seamless and a team can slowly evolve into a professional one if it can afford to do so. Soccer is the best example of this, running from the Sunday morning league team to the top professional level, in which case the team can rise and make the slow transition to professionalism. In fact, very few make the change, with Wimbledon being the great success story of the last thirty years when it came from semi-professional to Premier League status.

In professional sport there are only two levels of play – either as an individual or team; or at international level where a club player is released to play for the national squad. Playing opportunities at either level are increased by having reserve teams or teams for different age groups (for example, under-21 youth teams). In contrast, the amateur game provides a wider spread of opportunities to develop. Most sports provide competition at local, county and national level but others may have district and regional levels as well.

With few exceptions, both professional and amateur sport is divided between the sexes. There are some sports such as tennis, badminton and volleyball where both sexes can compete and this may account for their enduring popularity as social games. In most sports, however, even when the sexes are in the same team (e.g. athletics) they compete in different gender-based events.

There is considerable debate about this division. It is generally agreed that men are, on average, stronger and faster than women and that women would be at a disadvantage in sports where these traits are important. In some sports (e.g. gymnastics) the differences have been balanced by having a totally different set of events. These allowances are largely accepted in professional sport. What is not acceptable is the different treatment that female competitors receive compared with male competitors.

In some sports (such as horse racing or Formula 1 motor racing) there appears to be social exclusion – the sports themselves in theory allow for women to compete with men but few women do. In many other sports the real question is funding. Sponsors are less willing to fund women's sport and team or event organisers have a tendency to award smaller prizes or pay lower fees to female players.

Sports-related gambling

Gambling and sport have a long tradition. The Romans used to wager vast amounts on the outcome of chariot races and gladiatorial fights. In Britain the tradition continued and probably reached a zenith in the late eighteenth century when prize fighting, horse racing and cock fighting all attracted huge wagers. In Victorian times restrictions were introduced on many forms of gambling and until the 1960s it was illegal to place bets anywhere other than the venue of the contest.

Sports-related gambling is largely focused on horse and dog racing. This is carried out at

Think it over The argument put forward for lower prizes and sponsorship is that women's sport is less entertaining, less skilled and attracts smaller crowds than the man's game. What are your views on this justification? Discuss this in a mixed-sex group.

Try it out Where is it legal to place bets in the UK nowadays?

Find out what you can.

59 horse race tracks and 34 dog tracks (Perry Barr in Birmingham is the most popular). The most popular meetings for horses are held at:

- Ascot (67,326)
- Cheltenham (59,016)
- Epsom (47,550)
- Aintree (46,679).

These are 1999 figures. Interestingly, the Grand National at Aintree, which is the most bet on and viewed race, is only the eleventh most attended meeting. Unlike other spectator sports that are steady or slightly growing, spectating at tracks is in decline. For example, in 1993 horse track attendance went down from 4.2 million people and in 1995 this had dropped to 3.8 million.

The industry, particularly horse racing, is huge and offers extensive employment for breeders and trainers and their stable/kennel staff as well as support staff like vets and farriers. In horse racing there is a significant workforce of jockeys and stable riders. In all, there is thought to be about 60,000 employed. The websites of the national bodies will give further insight.

On-course 'bookies' are colourful characters who contribute to the lively atmosphere of a race meeting

There is also a sizeable market for gambling on the outcomes of other single events, such as tennis championships or boxing title fights. These bets are normally placed through betting shops and phone/Internet lines with bookmakers. Table 3.5 shows the principal bookmakers in the UK.

Table 3.5 Principal bookmakers

Bookmaker	Approx no. of outlets
Ladbrokes	1900
William Hill	1550
Coral	900
Stanley	800
Tote	300

Source: British Betting Offices Association, 2000

In Asia there is an even bigger gambling market and controversially this has affected British sport. 'Fixing' is where gambling syndicates bribe participants to 'throw' the game, thus making bets certain. It has long been a problem in horse and dog racing, which have stringent controls on doping and inquiries on jockey or horse performance that have largely controlled the practice. In the past ten years there have been several cases involving match fixing, in sports such as cricket and football. There was the celebrated case where Bruce Grobelaar, the Southampton goal-keeper, was acquitted of charges. International cricket has also been under a cloud, with several players accused of accepting payments from the Far Eastern betting syndicates to fix matches.

The pools

Another type of sports-related gambling is the pools. This is essentially a game of chance like the Lottery, whereby the gambler bets on the combination of draws or other outcomes from matches in the FA league. The pools for the past seventy odd years have been a major industry and Littlewoods, Vernons and Zetters were

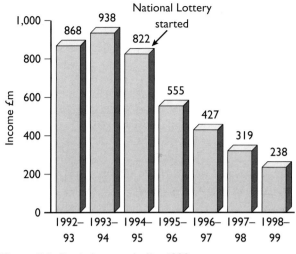

Figure 3.4 Pools income in the 1990s

Look at the figures in the table.

Approximately what percentage of gambling is sports-based gambling?

Try it out

The figures above give a somewhat false impression since the 1995 drop represented the impact of the National Lottery being introduced. Like the pools, horse racing and other gambling through bookmakers, there was a move away from traditional forms of gambling to try the novelty of the Lottery.

Unlike the pools, betting shops have recovered, partly because they are transferring to electronic as opposed to shop-based distribution. It can also be expected that the pools will regain some of their former popularity – especially if the government relaxes its tax levies on the industry, as is thought likely.

household names. The introduction of the National Lottery changed all this and in the past six years the turnover of the pools has crashed (Figure 3.4). Because the pools firms are located in areas of high economic deprivation this decline has had a serious impact on employment in these areas. It also had a serious indirect effect on recreational funding because the Football Trust and the Foundation for Sport and the Arts are largely funded by the contributions made by the pools companies.

Obviously, gambling is a major part of the leisure industry. The amounts involved are huge and bookmaker-based gambling accounts, which are largely sports-related, hold the biggest share of the market (Figure 3.6).

Check it out

1 What was the 'shamateurism' debate about?
2 How can elite amateurs supplement their costs?
3 What are the three main areas of sports gambling?
4 Which are the top three bookmakers? If gambling is increasing why are there fewer bookmakers?
5 What is match fixing?
6 Explain why pools sales have dropped and the effect this has had on sport.

Sports medicine

Sport by its very nature is risky and injuries will occur. For example, players will be bruised, tear muscles and tendons, strain or break joints and bones. Participation also affects our body chemistry or physiology. When we sweat, we lose water and salts from our body and can become dehydrated. When

Table 3.6 Gambling sales £m

	1990	1995
Betting shops	9530	8800
Bingo	1011	950
Casinos	120	118
Lotteries	1003	1200
Machines	234	225

Source: Mintel

we become exhausted the chemistry of muscles and nerves goes out of balance and both begin to malfunction. This is why you sometimes see marathon runners losing control of their legs at about the twenty-mile mark. Sports medicine aims to keep athletes in peak condition, and to prevent and treat injury and disease.

Maintaining condition and prevention

Nutrition is an important aspect of training and achieving desired body mass and physiology. A combination of people work on this issue, including sports nutritionists, sports scientists and sports doctors. Their research findings may be used to develop other nutritional products, such as vitamins, but they also design dietary regimes that suit the players' needs.

Recently, a new profession has emerged. Sports therapists, while often not medically qualified, have a combined knowledge of the above areas; and they can advise clients on their training and nutritional programmes.

Sports doctors will also become involved in analysing the training programmes of the top athletes who can apply for this service. They will monitor heart pulse and blood pressure as well as many other tests (such as blood sugar levels) that will indicate not only levels of fitness but if the training is having any damaging side-effects on the athlete.

Sports doctors are used to check whether an athlete is fit to play or participate. In some sports this is essential, for example boxers need medical approval for a licence to fight.

'Doping' or the use of banned performance-boosting drugs affects nearly all sports. A huge number of drugs are available and they are used for all sorts of purposes, such as to deaden pain, prolong stamina, develop body mass (anabolic steroids), improve response

times or steady nerves. Testing has to be carried out independently by UK Sport. Although they do not use doctors to take urine and blood samples, they are often used in interpreting the results. In 1998-99 there were 5,147 tests made, in over 38 sports, with 98.5 per cent proving negative.

Another aspect of preparation is body conditioning through massage, stretching and manipulation and also, sometimes, alternative medicine like acupuncture. The purpose of this is basically to reduce tension or minor injuries, such as inflammation, so that when the athlete performs there is less risk of injury. This sort of work is largely done by physiotherapists, osteopaths and masseurs.

Treatment

Sports injuries generally tend to produce the same types of injury, such as bruising, skeletal breaks and fractures, and tears to soft tissues. However, specific sports will have certain types of injury more associated with them, and these are often increased by the repetition of certain actions (e.g. brain damage in contact sports, torn Achilles tendons in squash, decompression sickness in sub-aqua).

Sports medicine practitioners will usually be specialised in treating these groups of injuries. In some cases they will further specialise in sport-specific issues. Nearly all sports will employ doctors who are specialist in that sport to advise them. This may be at governing body level or at a club or player level. For example, Global Challenge sailors will be especially advised on nutritional matters and self-help treatment.

Many sports injuries are less traumatic if they are treated immediately. This is why first aid is so important. The unsung heroes of sports medicine are often the volunteers from the Red Cross and St John's Ambulance Brigade who might be first on the scene to give trauma-reducing help within seconds of an injury. In professional sport and major amateur events physiotherapists will be on standby to diagnose and treat injuries. For example, very often the 'man with the sponge' who comes on to the pitch in soccer or rugby matches is a highly trained physiotherapist or sports paramedic rather than a lay person.

Many sports injuries result in a trip to the outpatients department of the local hospital, and also follow-up treatment in the form of physiotherapy. Any nurse in a hospital will tell you that Saturday afternoons and Sunday mornings see a queue of sport injuries being wheeled in. In some health authorities it has been seen as efficient management to separate these sporting casualties from other accidents and to provide a specialised sports injury clinic that is equipped and staffed with specialist resources. These clinics have proved popular and there is also a large private sector provision, often staffed by self-employed physiotherapists.

Although most injuries are short-lived and heal, there are unfortunately some which have longer recovery times or in some cases are permanently disabling. In the professional sports sector there is a good deal of specialised private medicine available that provides expensive drugs, surgery and other treatment. For the amateur injured player such specialisation is not normally available and treatment would normally be by a doctor not specialising in sports injury. There are exceptions to this. For example, the Stoke Mandeville Hospital in Buckinghamshire which is the leading spinal injuries hospital, also has a centre dedicated to serious sports injuries.

Despite the huge number of injuries resulting from sport there are relatively few career opportunities in sports medicine. Most treatment is given by doctors and physiotherapists as part of their general duties or as an aspect of their work – for

example, some osteopaths will set aside a Saturday afternoon for sports injuries. Jobs that are entirely in sports medicine are largely restricted to professional sport; many football clubs employ a sports physiotherapist and a masseur, for example. Alternatively, they are in the academic or research field – for example, Exeter University has a department of Sports Medicine.

Health and fitness

It could be argued that there are four components to being healthy (Figure 3.5)

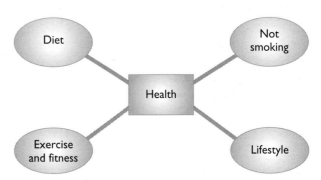

Figure 3.5 The four components to being healthy

- Smoking has dropped significantly in the past thirty years. In 1972, 52 per cent of males and 42 per cent of females smoked; in 1999 it was about 26 per cent of males and females.
- Despite rising wealth and opportunities as a nation we have not been able to organise our lifestyle or diet to help our health. Generally we live more inactive lives, and work and the threat of redundancy increase stress levels for many.
- Diet is a particular and rapidly increasing problem. In 1993, 57 per cent of males and 48 per cent of females were overweight; in 1999 the figures were 62 per cent of males and 48 per cent of females. The numbers of people who drink too much are also increasing.

- Exercise and fitness is the fourth factor and the good news is that we are taking more of it. Since 1990 female participation rates have risen from 52 per cent to 57 per cent, the rates for men, while more active, declined slightly from 73 per cent to 71 per cent. This quest for health through exercise can be provided in several ways.

The first and most popular is through **informal** exercise and, in particular, walking and cycling. For example, most of the female boom in participation was accounted for by walking, while cycling participation expanded from 8 per cent to 11 per cent in a similar period.

Tables 3.7a and b show the trend to get fit and keep healthy is not reflected by the statistics. We can see how we are getting fatter and drinking more than we should.

Table 3.7a Body mass[1]: by gender and age, 1997

England	Underweight	Desirable	Overweight	Obese	Total
		Percentages			
Males					
16–24	17	56	22	5	100
25–34	4	40	43	13	100
35–44	2	32	48	18	100
45–54	1	25	52	22	100
55–64	1	25	47	27	100
65–74	1	25	56	18	100
75 and over	4	34	50	12	100
All aged 16 and over	4	34	45	17	100
Females					
16–24	17	56	19	9	100
25–34	8	51	27	15	100
35–44	7	44	32	18	100
45–54	4	38	37	23	100
55–64	4	29	37	30	100
65–74	4	27	44	25	100
75 and over	8	30	41	22	100
All aged 16 and over	7	40	33	20	100

[1]Using the body mass index. © Crown copyright.

Source: Health Survey for England, Department of Health

Table 3.7b Percentage of adults consuming over selected weekly limits[1] of alcohol: by gender and age

Great Britain	Percentages		
	1988	1994–95	1998–99
Males			
16–24	31	29	36
25–44	34	30	27
45–64	24	27	30
65 and over	13	17	16
All aged 16 and over	26	27	27
Females			
16–24	15	19	25
25–44	14	15	16
45–64	9	12	16
65 and over	4	7	6
All aged 16 and over	10	13	15

[1]21 units for men and 14 units for women. © Crown copyright

Source: General Household Survey, Office for National Statistics

Traditionally, the other way of getting exercise was through **organised** sport. Figures from different sources would suggest that this sort of sport is probably declining slightly. For example, a study by Mintel in 1999, the results of which can be seen in Table 3.9 on page 166, suggested that sports club membership declined by about 250,000 between 1990 and 1995 and that much of the decline was accounted for by drops in high-aerobic sports like squash or soccer. Despite this decline, it would seem that exercise rates outside walking and cycling are remaining fairly constant. In other words, people are transferring from sport to the new growth area of health and fitness.

Health and fitness is the sector of the industry that provides opportunities to exercise without playing sport or competing. Health and fitness activities fall into two camps: floor-based and equipment-based exercises.

There are two types of exercise that maintain our fitness:

- aerobic (where the heart and lungs are exercised and oxygen is heavily metabolised) and which include aerobics, boxercise and dance-related exercise. Line dancing has partly enjoyed its popularity for its aerobic benefits.
- anaerobic (where oxygen uptake is not greatly increased but strength, stretching and breathing control are important) and which include yoga, t'ai chi, weights.

Floor-based activities require no complex equipment and for that reason can be done in any building providing there is a suitable floor. Because these exercises can be done anywhere they probably form the greater part of the industry and can be seen at any time of the week in church and village halls, sports centres and clubs and even in offices. Generally speaking, it is freelance instructors who promote their own programmes, or who are employed by organisations such as sports centres who provide them.

Equipment-based exercise takes place in gyms and health clubs, which have boomed in importance. Both the private and public sectors can provide these but the equipment is very expensive and the private sector is increasingly more important.

The typical gym will consist of:

- cardiovascular stations (e.g. bikes, rowing machines, step-ups, treadmills) that are used for aerobic exercise. These are very expensive and often computerised to allow individual users to insert a smart card and receive instructions about their exercise regime.
- free weights: these are banks of dumbbells that are used for aerobic exercise and primarily to body build or develop muscle.
- pool: gyms often have small pools, which can be used for aerobic swimming but also for toning and relaxing after a workout.

- floor area: for floor-based exercise this will often be mirrored and usually have a sprung floor to save impact injuries on the joints.
- ancillary areas: many gyms will have non-exercise areas such as jacuzzis and saunas, shops, beauty therapy and catering areas, which are a major source of income.

This is the major growth area for the next few years. Most health clubs are expensive and often have large turnovers as people get the fitness 'bug' and then lose the habit. Only a small percentage of the population (about 5 per cent) belong to these clubs, and despite the publicity surrounding health clubs, they probably have a limited impact on the health of the nation.

Personal trainers

If we read magazines like *Hello!* or watch the lives of celebrities it is possible to get the impression that the world is full of personal trainers. These professionals are essentially health and fitness coaches who advise their clients on health matters, diet, exercise and fitness. Personal trainers have to fit into their clients' lifestyle and will visit them as required at home or work and accompany them in their exercise. Such services are expensive (perhaps typically £30 to £40 per hour). Personal trainers will therefore be employed only by the wealthy. However, because clients need only a small number of hours of service a week, the personal trainer needs a large clientele. These factors mean that personal trainers are not very numerous and they tend to work in large population centres.

Far more common are the trained staff in gyms and health clubs who will provide personal attention to clients who come to the gym. Typical services include fitness assessment and devising and monitoring exercise programmes.

Health and GP referrals

The main reason why many people exercise is to keep healthy. At the start of the 1990s the view was developed that exercise could be used to supplement the health services by promoting fitness and healthy lifestyles in order to:

- reduce the factors that contribute to ill health such as obesity
- help people recover from illness.

As a result, a new concept – the GP referral scheme – came into being, and that has now become reasonably common. In GP referral, doctors, instead of prescribing drugs or even surgery, prefer to recommend patients to attend local leisure centres and gyms, where trained staff develop an exercise and lifestyle regime that will help to alleviate the causes of illness. Schemes vary around the country. In some case patients are simply recommended to attend, but in others they are actually given a prescription for a course of exercise which is claimed back from the health authority – just as a pharmacist would for prescribed drugs. When run properly,

these schemes can work well. There are many people whose recovery from heart attacks has been helped by referral schemes and probably many more who did not develop illness because of the schemes. Sport England gives an example that showed, in a deprived area of Sheffield and after a drive on participation in sports that 23 per cent of residents rated their health to be better, while in a control area only 16 per cent felt the same.

Outdoor and adventure activities

Outdoor or adventure activities are the group of activities that involve the natural environment as their focus and challenge. They are loosely grouped and there are some borderline categories. They should, however, not be confused with competitive sports that are done in the open air such as golf, road cycle racing, horse eventing or mechanised sports, such as motorbike scrambling. Outdoor activities are often non-competitive but some do have a competitive element, such as canoeing or sailing.

Table 3.8 includes a variety of traditional and 'new wave' activities.

For those who like adventure there is always the need to try new activities that provide new experiences and which test skill and fear. This need for adventure coupled with new technology and travel opportunities mean that outdoor activities can now fall into three categories: traditional, new wave and extreme activities.

Traditional

These are the long-standing activities which form the foundation of outdoor activity. Many outdoor activities stem from the nineteenth century. They are essentially survival activities, often borrowed from native cultures. The Victorians were eager to emulate the exploits of their heroes such as soldiers and explorers. Probably because of

> **! Check it out**
>
> 1 What are the main types of sports injury?
> 2 Give a sports injury that is sport-specific.
> 3 What are the functions of sports medicine?
> 4 What is the voluntary contribution to sports medicine?
> 5 What famous hospital is the centre for sports injuries?
> 6 What impact on the economy does health and fitness have?
> 7 What are the ingredients of a healthy lifestyle?
> 8 Explain whether you think the health and fitness boom is making us a healthier population.
> 9 What is a GP referral scheme? Explain how these schemes may affect health at a local level.

Table 3.8 Some different types of adventure and outdoor activities

Traditional	New wave	Extreme
Canoeing	White-water rafting	Canyon rafting
Sailing	Board sailing, Water skiing	Challenge races
Surfing	Boogie boards	Great-wave surfing
Winter sports	Snowboarding	Off-piste, Cresta
Sub-aqua	Vacation diving	Free diving (without equipment)
Cycling touring	Mountain biking	BMX
Climbing		Free climbing
Caving and pot-holing		Cave diving
Rambling and walking	Trekking	
Pony trekking		
Horse riding		
Aerial sports (gliding)	Ballooning, hang-gliding	Bungee jumping Free-fall parachuting

this, many traditional outdoor activities had until recently the ring of the 'services' to them, with long training periods, set procedures and a great deal of physical discomfort. Outdoor activities were further encouraged by the Scouting movement which was founded on military principles (the word scout refers to Army scouts who would go ahead of an army into enemy territory to get intelligence on the enemy and the terrain). Throughout most of the last century the Scout movement was the main organisation to train young people (usually boys) in adventure pursuits.

New wave

In the 1970s, with the new sports ethos, we began to see that there was a different way of doing adventure activities. New technology allowed new sports to be developed such as mountain biking or hang-gliding.

Commercial providers and educationalists saw that skills could be learnt and practised in short bursts rather than the prolonged training that clubs insisted on. Facilities such as sailing or diving schools and outdoor pursuits centres began to appear.

Making outdoor activities fun and easy to access through specialised holiday firms and dedicated facilities, such as diving centres, has resulted in major growth area in this sector of the industry. This can be seen in the growth of the outdoor activities goods market which between 1992 and 1998 increased by 59 per cent to £623m (Mintel).

Extreme sports

Many outdoor activities are enjoyed solely at a recreational level, such as a gentle ramble. For many participants, however, there is a challenge in testing personal response to overcoming fear. Some individuals need the 'buzz' of adrenalin from extreme danger and fear. These participants are often highly skilled and argue that they have advanced risk management that reduces the actual

Extreme sports provide an adrenalin rush which participants thrive on

Switzerland

JULY 1999: Three Britons and 14 Australians were among 21 people killed when a raging wall of floodwater and debris engulfed a group taking part in the 'adrenaline activity' of canyoning in which adventurers jump and abseil down a steep gorge into a white-water river and then bodysurf along the fast current. Locals near the Saxeten Gorge above Interlaken in the Swiss Alps claimed the party ignored storm warnings, prompting an investigation by Swiss prosecutors.

Source: Independent On Sunday, 2000

Sometimes extreme sports can be too much for participants who are not sufficiently experienced

danger as opposed to the perceived danger. Nevertheless, serious injury and fatalities are recognised realities.

The benefits of outdoor activities

Most people, regardless of age, fitness, wealth or location, can do outdoor activities. It is no coincidence that working-class people from the northern cities, accessing the moors and countryside and eager to get fresh air in their lungs, started the rambling movement. For many participants, simple activities such as off-road cycling or walking are great for general well-being. They relax people and take their minds off things, they encourage relaxed and deep breathing and allow people to appreciate the natural world.

As we travel along the spectrum and begin to take on more active and skilled activities, we can appreciate the high level of fitness that is required. It is interesting to note that the cardiovascular stations in health clubs simulate many of the actions required for outdoor activities such as climbing or skiing.

The importance of these outdoor activities has been recognised by the public sector and in many parts of the country, including urban areas, efforts have been made to improve access and quality of provision. Perhaps the most impressive scheme has been the Sustrans programme that is developing a national network of connected cycleways often involving the utilisation of old railway lines. Likewise, the Countryside Commission and its agencies are constantly improving and connecting local and national footpaths like the Pennine Way. Its agencies (Forestry Commission and Environment Agency) are establishing recreational access to forest and woodlands and waterways. Private sector companies like the water companies are also increasingly providing recreational facilities on reservoirs, including horse routes or bridle-paths.

Outdoor activities can often depend on facilities in outdoor areas which have the specialised equipment and expert tuition required to learn new skills. These began to be provided in the 1970s by the public and voluntary sectors. As popularity grew, these centres have become increasingly supplied by the private sector. Although most were excellent facilities, there was a temptation for profits to outweigh safety or for incompetent people to set up centres. Following several deaths, the government intervened and started a licence scheme enforced by the Adventure Activities Licensing Authority.

Outdoor activities are recognised by the Sports Council as important sporting activities and, as for other sports, there are centres of excellence. They are at Plas y Brenin in Snowdonia and Glenmore Lodge in the Cairngorms in Scotland. Here, top-class instruction is provided which allows instructors and skilled participants in climbing and canoeing, in particular, to gain higher-level qualifications and experience.

While outdoor activities should be enjoyable, they are also associated with self-development. Outdoor activities by their nature constantly put us in situations that we are unfamiliar with or which can frighten us. If we can overcome these, there is automatically a great feeling of achievement.

Self-development of clients is a major goal for both commercial and public sector activity centres. The objective is to provide activities that, while presenting a challenge, do not frighten to such an extent that the person cannot do them. Activity leaders will spend a lot of time encouraging the individual to take on the challenge, and when they succeed, they help people to relate their physical achievement to their work or self-image. Activity leaders apply this principle to all sorts of groups. For example, outdoor activities have been used to help women develop assertiveness skills and self-confidence, managers to perform better in teams or at problem-solving, and children with behavioural problems to understand themselves better and adopt different behaviours.

! Check it out

1 How has technology and tourism affected outdoor activities?

2 How do outdoor activities benefit the individual?

3 Why is golf not classified as an 'outdoor' activity?

4 Give two examples of informal outdoor activities.

5 What is Plas y Brenin?

3.2 The scale of sport and its contribution to the UK economy

There are many ways in which sport is provided and participated in. Many people are involved in industries that support sport. In addition to this there are many more people involved, for example, in broadcasting sport or writing in the press about it, as well as the thousands of businesses that supply

sports providers, such as maintenance engineers, gardeners, breweries and food suppliers. In this section we are going to look at:

* participation – the number of people who take part in sport
* workforce – the number of people employed in sport
* economics – the economic contribution that sport makes to the economy.

Note: Throughout this chapter and in Unit 1 we have visited and revisited various aspects of the above themes in a general leisure context and within a sports one. Sometimes it has seemed more appropriate to include information there and not in this section; for example, figures on broadcasting or participation. You may therefore want to refer back to expand on what is included in this section.

Statistics for participation, employment and economic impact are notoriously difficult to use, and they are often difficult to locate or out of date. Sometimes there is no classification system to identify statistics – for example, the English Tourism Council has no data on the extent or economic impact of sports tourism. Sometimes data has ceased to be produced: for example, the 'yardstick' *General Household Survey* cancelled its participation survey in 1999 and may reinstate it in 2002 and publish in 2003, producing a six-year vacuum in statistics. In other cases estimates are made on the basis of surveys, which may have asked different questions of different samples.

Perhaps the biggest problem is that most of the government statistics are based on classification systems that were invented before leisure acquired an important identity of its own. Thus someone who sells sports goods will be classified as a retailer, a cricket-bat maker will probably fall into joinery and carpentry, a steward in a sports club will be in the hospitality and catering industry. By and large, government statistics seriously underestimate the size of the sports industry.

We have tried to use only the most valid or latest available data. You will no doubt find different answers if you research other statistics. So tread carefully and be prepared to question and challenge.

Participation

A convenient starting-place when looking at participation is in terms of membership of sports clubs. One study by Mintel in 1999 looked at the most popular sports and showed that there was an overall decline here, largely due to a decrease in the high-energy team games like football, although swimming showed good growth in this period. Numbers for sports that involved less energy (golf/sailing) and/or the opportunity to play other individuals (golf/tennis), rather than in teams, were looking healthy. Even so, these figures are still impressive with over five million people belonging to clubs (Table 3.9), and this does not include membership of minority sports clubs. Using different sources, the Sports Council estimated that in

1992, 20 per cent of the male population and 12 per cent of females belonged to sports clubs.

Table 3.9 Membership of sports clubs (000s)

	1990	1995
Football	2350	1650
Golf	1002	1217
Squash	513	465
Sailing	300	450
Rugby Union	297	284
Lawn tennis	250	275
Swimming	217	280
Athletics	261	248
Martial arts	99	177
Badminton	101	84
Total	5390	5130

Source: Mintel

Think it over How do the figures in the table (above) demonstrate participation? What trends can you see?

Clearly, club membership is not the only way we do sport. There are health and fitness activities, outdoor activities, casual sport with a friend at the park or sports hall, a social swim in the pool or sea, or a walk in the park.

In other words, many of us do sport to a varying extent – and sometimes we would not really call it sport. Probably the best measurement we have is the General Household Survey, which asks a sample of adults what activities they have done in the past four weeks. The results show the most popular activities. You can see from Table 3.10 how the health boom has changed over the ten years of the survey. Keep fit and weight-training (i.e. gym-based activity) and cycling show a steady increase, while the health fashions (jogging, yoga) of earlier years start to fade away.

Why has there been a decline in participation in team games?

It is also interesting to note that identifiable traditional sports do not feature much in this list. Cue sports and darts feature highest but are declining, presumably due to the drop off in broadcasting of these sports from its height in the 1980s. After that, only golf and football feature. On the full list of sports, other sports such as tennis feature down the line but most sports such as hockey or squash involve fewer than 1 per cent of the adult population.

Table 3.10 Participation in sport and leisure activities

Percentages

	1987	1990	1993	1996
Sports, games and physical activities				
Walking	37.9	40.7	40.8	44.5
Swimming	13.1	14.8	15.4	14.8
Cue sports	15.1	13.6	12.2	11.3
Keep fit/yoga	8.6	11.6	12.1	12.3
Cycling	8.4	9.3	10.2	11.0
Darts	8.8	7.1	5.6	1.3
Weight-lifting/training	4.5	4.8	5.5	5.6
Golf	3.9	5.0	5.3	4.7
Jogging	5.2	5.0	4.6	4.5
Football	4.8	4.6	4.5	4.8
Any activity other than walking	44.7	47.8	47.3	45.6

Source: Social Trends 1999

All in all, by 1996 about 46 per cent of adults participated in sport or active leisure on at least a monthly basis. This is quite impressive at first glance; it means that there are at least 21 million occasions a month when people are involved in some form of active leisure. When you think that many of these occasions will involve some expenditure you get some idea of the economic impact that sports participation might create.

That's not all. These surveys involve adults, but about 20 per cent of the population (12 million) is aged under 16. These days large numbers of toddlers go to swimming classes and activity classes such as tumble tots; by the time they go to school they will participate in curriculum-based sport for at least two hours a week. On top of this there are large numbers of children who go to sports clubs and activities out of school.

The workforce

Tip for the future

In 2000, SPRITO, the national training organisation for sport and recreation (covering sport, theme parks, piers, holiday parks and play), completed the first survey of the industry upon which this sector is based. For students who wish to expand their knowledge of the industry in general this report is one of the most comprehensive to date. For other areas of leisure the relevant training organisations will be producing similar reports over the next few years.

As already mentioned, in many areas of sport people are classified under different codes or are not in jobs that are entirely to do with sport. For example, many people working in sports goods sell other types of clothes and shoes. Perhaps the most striking example is that some government statistics have shown a downturn in the size of the gym businesses, which we know to be growing rapidly. One explanation for this is that in the past few years the major brewers like Whitbread have been buying up gyms to form their own chains. The result is that the same fitness workers are now statistically part of the brewing industry!

One estimate of the total workforce size has been made by Sportdata and they propose, 'Employment in sport was 437,460 in 1998, compared to 425,056 in 1995. Employment in sport accounts for 1.6% of total employment in 1998 compared to 1.68% of total employment in 1995.'

The latest and most refined data refers to those employed in those sectors that directly provide sport and who have been especially surveyed by SPRITO. They split the sports sector into two sectors:

- the sports and fitness industry (active leisure)
- outdoor activities.

The sports and fitness industry

This consists of three areas of work:

- sport, fitness and leisure facilities, e.g. local authority leisure centres, swimming pools, sports and fitness clubs
- stadia and arenas, e.g. football stadia, field and track stadia and facilities for outdoor or indoor sports events
- professional sport, e.g. athletes and players, coaches, and officials.

About 255,000 people were involved in these three sectors in 1998. It is expected that by 2008 the workforce will have expanded to 347,000, a 36 per cent growth rate (Table 3.11).

These figures do not take into account the substantial volunteer force involved in this sector. The Sports Council has estimated that there are 1.5 million volunteers, but SPRITO estimate the figure to be more in the order of 1.9 million.

The outdoors

The SPRITO survey was concerned with outdoor activities as described earlier. Unfortunately, government statistics include a whole mixture of non-sports activities within their codes – for example, training animals for TV! These figures were difficult to filter out and the figures shown in Figure 3.6 probably slightly overestimate the size of the outdoor industry; but they probably describe its structure and predict its trends well.

In 1998 the workforce was probably about 177,000. As we have already seen this is a growth industry and by 2008 it is expected that it will have grown by 28 per cent to 226,000 (Table 3.12). It is a small-business sector, with one-third of firms having fewer than five staff. It is also heavily affected by weather conditions and by spending patterns in the public at large, as well as the education

Table 3.11 Breakdown of employment in sport and fitness (active recreation)

| | 1998 | | 2008 | |
	No.	%	No.	%
Male	131,000	51	167,000	48
Female	124,000	49	180,000	52
Part-time	107,000	42	168,000	48
Full-time	123,000	48	147,000	42
Self-employed	25,000	10	32,000	9
Total employment	255,000	~	347,000	~

Source: SPRITO Skills Foresight 2000 from *Business Strategies Forecast*, 2000
(derived from AES, 1997)

Think it over
Look at Table 3.11 and describe three trends between 1998 and 2008 in the sport and fitness labour market.

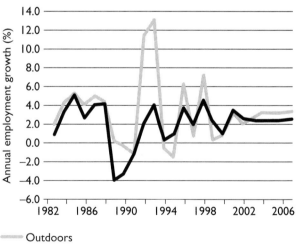

Outdoors
Active Leisure

Figure 3.6 Employment growth in the sports and outdoor industry

Source: SPRITO Skills Foresight 2000 from Business Strategies Forecast, 2000
(derived from AES)

sector. Consequently, growth is far more erratic than in the active recreation sector.

Employment marginally favours women in the industry. The good news here for the girls is that there are few female qualified outdoor leaders and you will be snapped up like gold dust. The bad news for the lads is that there are thousands of ex-Scouts and others dying to get into the industry – so you will have to work hard to compete.

Table 3.12 Workforce trends in the outdoors industry

	1998		2008	
	No.	%	No.	%
Male	84,000	47	104,000	46
Female	93,000	53	122,000	54
Part-time	80,000	45	93,000	41
Full-time	93,000	52	129,000	57
Self employed	4,000	2	4,000	2
	84,000	47		
Total	177,000	~	226,000	~

Source: SPRITO Skills Foresight 2000 from Business Strategies Forecast, 2000 (derived from AES, 1997)

Another good bit of news is that it is commonly believed that the outdoor industry is largely about part-time and seasonal work. Although the figures for these areas of work are higher than in other industries it is good to know that 52 per cent of workers are in full-time employment. However, for anyone working in the industry you should be aware that it is becoming increasingly competitive and with a good supply of workers – 'firms are

becoming leaner, making use of volunteers, flexible workers, lower pay and short-term contracts'. Perhaps with this culture it is not surprising that there is a tendency for workers to regard this as a gap-year type of employment. A fifth of workers had no qualifications, while 13 per cent were educated to degree level.

Economics

Defining the economic impact of sport can be difficult. The data concerning participation are particularly difficult as they are often not collected or, when they are, they are not often comparable. Instead, round figures are often stated without sources being given. For example, we have already seen from a survey regarding 'leisure day visits from home' that the average sum spent per visit is around £9.10, contributing to an approximate £7.8m in 1996. But this is a statistic that covers all trips out and not just sports trips.

In most areas of provision, income breakdowns tend to be rounded because precise figures are often seen as commercially sensitive. However, for the private health club sector it estimated that in 1999 the market was worth about £2.2 billion (Keynote, July 1999 *Sports Market (UK)*). In the voluntary sector large amounts of money are spent at club bars every weekend, as well as membership fees and match fees – and yet there is no record of the total for the country as a whole.

The Sports Industries Federation produces one comparative summary that may serve as a guide (see Table 3.13). It is probably fairly accurate as regards goods and gambling but immediately there is some question over the participation expenditure, which is given as £2.3 billion for 1998; this is only slightly more than the SPRITO estimate for the health business alone.

> **Think it over**
> Look at Table 3.12. Describe three trends you can see between 1998 and what is forecast for 2008 in the outdoors labour market.

Table 3.13 Consumer expenditure on sport-related goods and services

(Constant 1995 prices-£million)

	1995	1998	1995/98 Change %
Participation sports:			
Subscription and fees	2,010.81	2,373.27	18.0
Clothing sales	1,400.00	1,679.10	19.9
Footwear sales	900.00	979.48	8.8
Travel	453.03	548.47	21.1
TV rental, cable & satellite subscriptions related to sport	453.86	887.91	95.6
Gambling:			
Football pools	419.82	249.41	−40.6
Horse racing	2,211.41	2,352.97	6.4
Other consumer expenditure on sport	2,716.16	3,119.57	14.9
Total	**10,565.09**	**12,190.19**	**+15.4**

The figures are impressive. By 1999 there had been further growth of 7 per cent and total expenditure was £13,067.88 million, or 2.5 per cent of total consumer expenditure. Put another way, economic activity added value to the economy of £12,350.71 million, or 1.69 per cent of Gross Domestic Product.

These figures confirm the general trends about the sectors mentioned earlier. The large growth in participation is mainly due to the expansion of private sector sport. We can also see for the first time the growth of the sports tourism market and how it is growing more rapidly than participation in sport. However, although originally a small market, it is 'subscription fees for broadcasting' that is the boom area.

Think it over

Refer to Table 3.13. What areas of the market declined between 1995 and 1998?

In terms of market size what are the two most and two least important sectors?

Explain why subscription TV is a major growth area but not the largest market.

Sporting goods

The sporting goods sector is either the largest or possibly second-largest sector of the industry and the data is sufficiently reliable to explore it further. So we will look at the three main areas:

- equipment
- clothing
- footwear

Figure 3.7 shows the broad trends in growth of the markets.

Equipment: Sales of equipment in the UK in 1995 can be broken down, as seen in Table 3.14.

As might be expected, golf is the largest market as a result of the popularity and growth of the market and the price of kitting up to play. It will be interesting to see over the next few years if aerobics takes the lead with the growth of this sector. Remember that the gyms and not the customers usually buy aerobics equipment, so growth will depend on new gyms opening and technological advances in machinery.

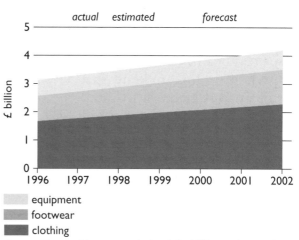

Source: Competitiveness analysis of the UK sporting goods industry 1999 (Taylor/Sports data original source Mintel)

Figure 3.7 Sales of sporting goods: equipment, footwear and clothing

Table 3.14 Sales of sports equipment in the UK, 1995

	1995 Sales £m	% of market	Forecast sales (£m) 2002
Outdoor/waterproofs	65	13	
Golf	180	35	
Aerobics	125	24	
Football kit/boots/trainers	10	2	
Swimwear	10	2	
Racquet sports	60	12	
Snow sports	10	2	
Snooker/billiards, darts	30	6	
Other	35	7	
Total	**520**	**100**	**694**

Source: Competitiveness analysis of the UK sporting goods industry 1999 (Taylor/Sports data original source Mintel)

Clothing: Whereas most equipment is used for a sporting purpose, the use for clothing and footwear is often for non-sports purposes. In fact, with items like trainers or fleeces probably the majority of use is non-sporting.

Table 3.15 Sales of sports clothing in the UK, 1998

	1998 £m	% of market %	% change in sales 1992–98	Forecast sales (£m) 2002
Outdoor/waterproofs	400	22	+51	
Track suits	360	20	+43	
Football kit	210	12	+250	
Swimwear	180	10	+48	
Aerobics/indoor fitness	140	8	+186	
Golf	120	7	+52	
Snow sports	90	5	+125	
Racquet sports	50	3	+9	
Other	250	14	+3	
All	**1800**	**100**	**+56**	**2260**

Source: Competitiveness analysis of the UK sporting goods industry 1999 (Taylor/Sports data original source Mintel)

As one might expect with the British weather and our national game being what it is, waterproofs, track suits and football kit are the market leaders. As we noted earlier, football participation is on the decline.

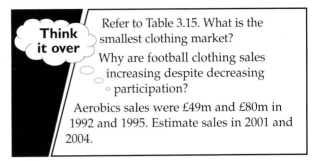

Think it over

Refer to Table 3.15. What is the smallest clothing market?

Why are football clothing sales increasing despite decreasing participation?

Aerobics sales were £49m and £80m in 1992 and 1995. Estimate sales in 2001 and 2004.

So why the huge increase in sales of football kit?

Footwear: As with clothing, sports shoes are often used for street use – this is particularly so for trainers and in recent years there has been some transference to wearing outdoor shoes such as hiking 'boots' (e.g. Timberland) and deck shoes. Table 3.16 shows sales of sports footwear in 1998.

Table 3.16 Sales of sports footwear 1998

	Sales (£m)	% of market	% change 1992–98	Forecast sales (£m) 2002
General sports/leisure design	250	24	+16	
Running shoes	200	19	+67	
Outdoor boots	170	16	+63	
Football boots/ black trainers	135	13	+59	
Aerobics/indoor fitness	110	10	+16	
Racquet sports	70	7	+8	
Golf	35	3	+21	
Snow sports boots	10	1	+67	
Other	70	7	+37	
Total	**1,050**	**100**	**+36**	**1,200**

Source: Competitiveness analysis of the UK sporting goods industry 1999 (Taylor/Sports data original source Mintel)

As might be expected, trainers and general sports shoes are the most important items but their growth is slowing off. At first it may seem surprising that aerobics growth is small compared with that for clothes and equipment. The reason for this is that there is little specialised footwear and most customers will use trainers.

Think it over Consider the sales of skiing and snow sports goods. Do a little research of your own about the holiday industry and explain the sports goods figures.

Outlets

Sports goods are distributed through the following outlets:

- independent generalist sports retailers (single shops or very small chains)
- multiple outlet generalist sports retailers
- specialist sports shops – the main examples being for golf, fishing (sometimes combined with other field sports), outdoor pursuits (walking, climbing, camping)
- department stores and others
- club outlets (e.g. golf 'pro' shops)
- mail order.

The major change in retailing in the last decade has been the rise of the multiple shops, especially in their sales of sports wear. They increased their market size by 239 per cent between 1992 and 1996. This

Why has there been such a growth in the big multiple stores?

was largely at the expense of the independent sport shops that saw a decline of 16 per cent over the same period.

The big multiple stores are Sports Division, JJB Sports and Allsports (see Table 3.17).

Table 3.17 Sales from the big multiple stores in 1996–97

	Sales (£m) 1996–97	No. of outlets
Sports Division	260	250
JJB Sports	130.8	185
Allsports	109	200

One of the ways in which the small independents are fighting back is to form a consortium that allows them to buy large orders at cheaper prices and then redistribute the products among themselves. A familiar brand name for a major consortium is Intersport that operates across Europe. In 1997 there were 367 shops using it, with a turnover of £190m in 1996.

Think it over At the opposite end of the scale from the independents, Nike rules supreme. In 2000 Nike plan to introduce a worldwide network of brand-based shops, where only Nike products will be sold. Discuss how strong your brand loyalty is for sporting goods and what the advantages and disadvantages of such a shop are to Nike. How do you feel about it? Would you be keen to shop there? Why?

Manufacture

Overall, we import more sports goods than we export – see Figure 3.8. With the import of goods from Asia and other low-wage economies this gap is set to increase.
In particular, the mass markets of trainers and track suits are supplied by Third World countries.

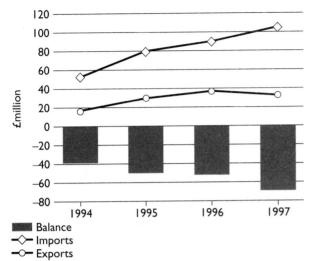

Source: Competitiveness analysis of the UK sporting goods industry 1999 (Taylor/Sports data)

Figure 3.8 Trade balance of track suits

The main reason for this trade gap is that:

- manufacturing costs are cheaper in the Third World
- USA (in particular) produces certain high-specification goods such as gym equipment.

But it's not all bad news. Britain has a good reputation for certain niche markets, such as golf equipment, which is our biggest export, and angling goods. Firms like Dunlop Slazenger (the tennis ball manufacturers) have also created successful niche markets.

The biggest supplier of sports wear is the conglomerate Pentland plc, which owns several British brands like Ellesse, Mitre and Speedo; their turnover in 1996 was £755m. Behind them, with single brands, Nike lead the field with a turnover £240m, then Adidas at £213m and Reebok with £145m. These firms are American or German. The biggest single-brand British company is Umbro, at £123m, which has effectively cornered the replica kit market in soccer. HiTec is the leading British manufacturer of footwear.

When it comes to equipment the giant is Grampian Holdings, which own several well-known brands and specialise in golf; they own, for example, Patrick and Glenmuir and had a turnover in 1996 of £244m. The golf-based Acushnet takes second place at £51m with the household names of Wilson (US) and Dunlop Slazenger (UK) being the other major single-brand suppliers.

The fitness boom is largely (about 40 per cent) supplied from the USA by firms such Weider, Gold's Gym, and Universal Gym. European firms like Tunturi (Finland) and Powersport (UK) are also important players.

! Check it out

1 What are the two most popular physical activities according to research?

2 What is the most popular sport?

3 What workforce sectors make up the sports industry?

4 Give examples of the two factors that have influenced the rise in sports good sales.

5 What British firm is the major player in the replica kit market? What are the main categories of sports goods? Give the market leader in each group.

6 Describe how outdoor clothing sales reflect the interest in outdoor activities. What caution should you take in making this link?

7 What is the trade balance? Describe it for sporting goods.

8 How do small independent shops compete against the major chains?

3.3 The organisation and funding of sport

In Unit 1 we looked at the overall structure, funding and organisation of leisure. We are now going to focus on sport. The first part of this section looks at the organisation of sport and its funding at local and regional level. The second part looks at how government and national organisations are funded and organised, and how they influence sport through funding and policy.

Local and regional level

Sports organisations obviously need to fund themselves. They will have access to different sources of funding according to their size and which sector they are in. These sources are shown in Figure 3.9.

Figure 3.9 Sources of funding for sports organisations

- grants, which are funds made available by the European Union, national public bodies or local government that help organisations fund new projects such as buildings and equipment (i.e as capital grants) or to fund personnel like coaches (i.e revenue grants). They often pay only part of a project's costs and the organisation needs to make up the rest (this is called match funding). Grants are usually available only to the public and voluntary sectors but in large important projects the private sector may also receive grants. They also have strict conditions on what can be funded.

- subsidies: local authorities cannot cover the costs of provision by charging the full rate; if they did, the price of a swim in your local pool might be as much as £10 or a football pitch hire up to £100. They

therefore operate by subsidising their losses using money from local taxes. In the voluntary sector, clubs with their own ground and premises can be financially crippled by having to pay high rates and taxes. Some enlightened councils give a subsidy known as discretionary rate relief, which reduces or eliminates these charges. There are also plans being considered by the Chancellor of the Exchequer to reduce VAT on bar income and pitch hire for clubs.

- the National Lottery is essentially a grant, which in the case of sport has largely replaced previous grant schemes given by the Sports Council.

- sponsorship is money given usually to professional clubs, events and voluntary clubs to use as they wish. Normally sponsorship is contractually defined and the recipient pledges to give publicity and access to the sponsor.

- charging for activities: all sports organisations can charge for their activities, such as playing or being instructed. The amount they charge and the importance of this as a source of income will depend on the popularity of the activity and their articles of association and marketing objectives (compare a voluntary club with a professional club). The public and private sectors are often heavily dependent on these charges.

- charges for spectating: this is entrance money to watch sport. It can be a major source of income for professional sports clubs and event providers such as racetracks. Most significant in the private sector, both voluntary and public sector organisations may also occasionally earn money in this way.

- merchandising: this is income from souvenirs and other items associated with an organisation. It is most significant in professional sport, where major clubs will not only sell their own merchandise but also earn money from giving other organisations the right to market it.

- membership fees: any organisation that has a membership will be able to earn from charging fees. Public sector organisations tend not to charge membership fees. In the voluntary sector it is a major source of income in selected private sector clubs such as gyms or tennis centres. Membership fees are usually charged on an annual basis. In voluntary clubs it is also normal to pay match fees; those are paid every time a member plays in a competitive game match.

- broadcasting fees: these are a major source of income for professional sport and private sector events. Often they are not taken into consideration in the public and private sectors, although certain amateur events like Henley Regatta can attract fees.

Apart from the sources of funding available, sports organisation is heavily influenced by four other factors that will determine which types of organisation can or will want to provide for sport:

- the cost of the facility required and its maintenance (indoor sports hall, pool, playing field, golf course)
- the amount participants are willing to pay to play
- the number of people required to play the game (team sports, individual sports)
- the formality of playing (competition or casual – like a friendly game of tennis).

Commercial enterprises

The private sector will generally become involved only in the provision of facilities and services for which the public will pay a sufficient return. Usually private sector facilities are less interested in organising activities and tend to encourage informal activity although some facilities – like tennis centres – will run competitive teams and

squads. Examples of private sector facilities include ski centres, golf driving ranges, indoor bowls halls, snooker halls, tennis centres and, of course, private gyms and health clubs. The private sector can borrow large amounts of money, which means it can often build better and bigger; they can also build anywhere there is a market. The downside is that such facilities have to make a profit and will tend to be built only in affluent populated areas and in sports where there is a paying public. So a minority sport, like trampolining, will not be provided for by commercial enterprises.

Professional clubs

There may be a professional club in your area. With traditional sports like soccer and cricket these started off as amateur clubs and grew bigger, although newer clubs like basketball and ice hockey have been created as professional clubs from the beginning. Professional clubs are private sector organisations and are usually limited companies, or sometimes – as in the case of many Premier Division soccer clubs – public companies.

In Figure 3.10 we can see how professional clubs fund themselves.

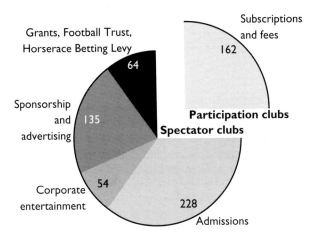

Total £643 million

Source: Henley Centre, 1992, *The economic impact of sport in the UK in 1990* in Sports Council New Horizons Part 2

Figure 3.10 Commercial clubs' income 1990 (£m)

With regard to professional sport, match admissions were traditionally the major source of funding. Over the past ten years things have changed significantly, especially at the top of club competition. New sources of income have been established, including:

- merchandising, including replica kit
- share-related income
- broadcasting income
- sponsorship.

The effect of this can be seen be seen by comparing the gate income for soccer. In 1990, 47 per cent of total revenue of all commercial clubs was admission fees. The latest figure (1998–99) for football's Premier Division is that this income is about 37 per cent of total revenues. Broadcast revenues grew faster than commercial/other revenues, making up 29 per cent of the total (contrasting with 21 per cent in 1996-97). The relative contribution of commercial/other revenues has decreased from 41 per cent in 1996-97 to 34 per cent in 1999 (Deloitte Touche, 2000), but much of this decline was in areas other than merchandising which has remained steady. We shall return to the impact of broadcasting later but, as a general statement, it can be said that for the top professional clubs and events in all major sports, gate money is declining in importance.

Commercialism in football has many implications, some of which we will look at later. So serious are these that there is a Government committee called the Football Task Force that has produced four major reports including one on the 'Commercial Interests in Football'. These are downloadable from the DCMS website.

Public sector facilities

Not everyone can afford to pay for activities provided by the private sector. Neither can small sports clubs raise money to buy the facilities they need for their sport (e.g. swimming pools and sports halls). The primary role of the public sector is therefore largely to provide facilities for hire and provide instruction at affordable prices. It does this by providing purpose-built facilities and also community facilities that can be used for sport, such as village halls and community centres, where groups like community associations, freelance instructors (e.g. in martial arts or aerobics) or sports clubs organise activities. It is funded largely by the council tax, but hire charges and course fees also play a significant part, as do grants.

Not all facilities have local significance and grant aid is often used to subsidise local authorities to build regional centres such as tennis centres, gymnastics centres and so on that will allow participants who are developing excellence to improve their skills using high-grade facilities and equipment.

Development and coordination

Local councils are also responsible for encouraging sport in their area. They do this in several ways:

- sports development activities like courses and creating new sports clubs
- advising sports clubs and helping them to get resources such as grants (this is called enabling)
- creating a network of sports organisations (e.g. local sports councils).

Try it out

Annual reports are an excellent way of getting first-hand financial data. Try to obtain the annual report of a professional football club other than in the Premiership. Look at the amount of income from different sources. Compare this with a Premiership side.

CASE STUDY –

Open-air leisure centres – the return of parks and open spaces

Active recreation comes in many forms from a quiet stroll, a game of tennis with friends or a local derby between two Sunday league football teams. All of these activities are largely provided in the nation's parks and open spaces. Sometimes these may be the large parks and recreation grounds dating from Victorian times or the green areas and recreational spaces in inner-city areas which may provide the only recreational activity for local people. Parks and open spaces provide for the casual participant (playgrounds, skate ramps, boating lakes, open grass, trim trails and cycle paths) or for the more competitive player (pitches, courts, tracks and grandstands, basketball nets, bowling greens and golf courses).

Open spaces are hungry for money (grass needs cutting, pitches marking and playgrounds need daily maintenance to keep them free from litter). Even though some charges are made (e.g pitch hire) they are basically free to everyone and reflect the principle of the 'common good'. For many people without the means to pay entry and membership fees, the park is the mainstay of recreation.

As a result of the costs of running parks, they have been in decline for many years. Increasingly, though, local authorities are recognising their value and applying the principles of leisure management to make the park an 'open-air leisure centre'. Boroughs like the London Borough of Newham, Swansea and Middlesborough are changing provision by:

- upgrading sport and play facilities (changing rooms, playing surfaces) to make them customer-friendly

- providing leadership in the form of park rangers and sports development officers

- improving security (parks' police, lighting) to eliminate vandalism and threatening situations (drunks, muggers)

- involving local communities in the design and running of parks

- finding ways of raising income to provide a better service. For example, from: special event hire (big trucks, strongest man contests), tours, sponsorship (e.g. the Weetabix basketball scheme) and grants.

Questions

1   Look at your local area and identify all the places where you can play football, bowls and tennis. How significant are public sector parks and open spaces in this provision?

2   What ways can playing surfaces and facilities be improved in a park?

3   You are the manager of a local netball league. What are the advantages and disadvantages of using your local indoor leisure centre and a local open space or park?

4   There can be conflicts of interest between different users of parks, such as children, participants in sport and dogs. Suggest ways in which both dog walking and active recreation can take place in harmony in parks?

5   Vandalism and antisocial behaviour have been a problem in many parks and have led to the destruction of many facilities (pavilions) and lack of use by the community. Suggest ways in which the trend can be reversed.

Education

Schools, colleges and the youth service have a crucial role in establishing the 'sports habit' in young people, which hopefully will last through their lifetime. Throughout the 1970s and 1980s there was a general decline in the value and time given to school sport. The factors that contributed to this were:

- less extra-curricular sport (e.g. inter-school and after-school sport)
- reductions in curriculum time
- a change in sporting values with competitive sport in particular becoming politically non-correct
- restrictions on school transport
- selling off playing fields
- lack of funding for facilities.

It is now being realised that a whole generation has lost the sports ethic and that, apart from the health and social benefits of sport, there is a real chance that the pool from which sporting excellence springs is drying up. International competitive success may well become harder to achieve. Consequently, there are now some schemes and grants which involve partnership between local authorities and the Sports Council that are designed to rekindle the spark of sporting enthusiasm.

The other role of schools is that they often have significant sports facilities and playing fields. Prior to the 1980s these facilities were often retained for sole use of the school. Since then it has been realised that this is a wasted resource

and, increasingly, facilities are hired out to the public. In some cases school sports halls have been designed specifically with this ideal in mind. They are called dual-use centres. So important is shared usage that the Sports Council will not give schools Lottery grants unless they can show substantial (40 per cent) public usage.

Voluntary sector

Finally, we come to the voluntary sector. Three types of organisation play a significant part in the organisation of sport:

- the churches
- voluntary youth organisations
- sports clubs.

Churches

The churches are a major provider of halls that often lay the foundation for recreational sport (e.g. badminton) in many communities. They pay for themselves through a mixture of church subsidy, hire fees and sometimes grants.

Voluntary youth organisations

Voluntary youth organisations (e.g. the Scouts, voluntary youth clubs) provide facilities for a wide range of sports. The Scouts and related organisations are central to the development of outdoor activities, and many adult participants first developed their interest with such groups who took them out of towns and into the countryside. These groups are funded by their reserves, grants and members' donations.

Sports clubs

Voluntary sports clubs are the main providers and organisers of competitive formal sport. They may also take an active role in developing their sport by offering courses. They often divide into two types of organisation: indoor and outdoor sports clubs.

Indoor sports: These require expensive purpose-built facilities to best compete. As they often

> **Think it over**
> Note down how much time per week you spend doing sport at school or college. Now ask someone of an older generation how much time they spent doing sport at school. Check the type of sport involved in both cases, e.g. competitive sport, team games, non-team games, keep fit, school teams, outdoor activities. What conclusions can you draw from the comparison?

cannot afford these they need to hire facilities from the local authority. They are largely funded by membership fees and what sponsorship and grants they can attract.

Outdoor sports clubs: Years ago land was cheaper and more available than it is now. Team games like soccer and cricket were the most popular sports. At that time many sports clubs bought land to play on. Nowadays many of these sites still consist of only a field and a changing hut. But, equally, many clubs developed their land and built pavilions and clubhouses that in turn would generate extra income from hires and bar income. Many professional clubs started in this way. There are also many amateur clubs who now have substantial clubhouses that generate income to supplement the membership fees and sponsorship. Because of their assets they are also in a favourable position to attract loans and grants should they wish. This does not automatically mean, however, that clubs are well off. Providing equipment and facilities is expensive. So despite this extra income, the majority of clubs run on tight budgets and modest surpluses.

Voluntary sports clubs are the cornerstones of developing excellence. Many players develop their performance or become coaches to bring on the next generation, some of whom will become professional or get to the top of the sport. This work is largely voluntary and clubs depend on members cutting running costs by helping to maintain and run the club. Figure 3.11 shows the contribution of volunteers to UK sport.

Competition is essential to these clubs and they can contribute to the overall organisation of their sport by sending representatives to organising bodies, such as local leagues (discussed in the next section).

The pie chart in Figure 3.12 typifies how a voluntary club funds itself.

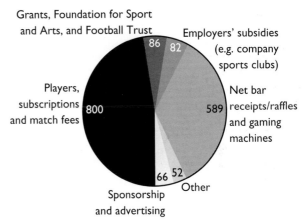

Total £1,675 million

Source: Henley Centre, 1992, *The economic impact of sport in the UK in 1990* in Sports Council New Horizons Part 2

Figure 3.12 Voluntary sector income, 1990 (£m)

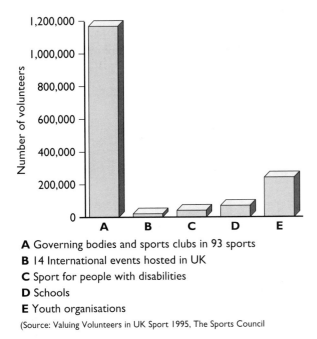

A Governing bodies and sports clubs in 93 sports
B 14 International events hosted in UK
C Sport for people with disabilities
D Schools
E Youth organisations

(Source: Valuing Volunteers in UK Sport 1995, The Sports Council

Figure 3.11 The size of volunteering in UK sport

Try it out Look at Figure 3.12 above and answer the following:

1 What is the largest source of income for voluntary sports clubs?
2 Approximately what percentage of the total income comes from the two largest sources?
3 What percentage of income comes from grants and subsidies?
4 What is the relative importance of grants and income to bars and membership?

National and international organisation and funding

National governing bodies

Because sport is competitive there is a need to:

- define the laws of the game and arbitrate on disputes
- identify and discipline irregularities throughout the sports
- provide and train neutral officials such as referees
- provide and organise workable competitive structures (e.g. leagues and competitions) for the amateur and professional games from local to national level
- select, manage and 'own' the national team.

In addition there is a need to:

- attract funding that will benefit the whole game (e.g. league sponsors)
- develop the game
- represent the interests of the game (e.g. lobbying government).

This role at national level (that is England, Scotland, Wales and Northern Ireland) falls upon the governing bodies of sport (for example, the Football Association or the English Cricket Board). Governing bodies are limited companies that solely represent the needs of a specific sport. Their status as a governing body is determined by the Sports Council and in most cases there is only one such body. There are some exceptions, particularly in the martial arts, where more than one governing body exists.

The organisation and funding of governing bodies is varied and often affected by the popularity of the sport and its commercial appeal. It is not possible therefore to be specific about individual aims, programmes and structure. For example, the English Football Association owns and takes the income from the FA Cup and other competitions, the England team and the broadcasting rights of the leagues (except the Premier). In all, it is a cash-rich organisation which does not greatly depend on the levy charged to its 219 members. The pie chart in Figure 3.13 shows how their £65.7m turnover was made up.

On the other hand, a smaller governing body with little professional or commercial interest will be far more dependent on levies made on member clubs, sponsorship and grant aid, such as the annual grant from the Central Council for Physical Recreation.

Governing bodies do not just operate at a national level but represent the pinnacle of organising their sport throughout the country. At the base of the pyramid are local affiliated clubs and teams which register to play in competitions and leagues recognised by the governing body. Above them are local committees, to which clubs often send representatives, and above them will be a series of district, regional and national committees that all contribute up the line to the national governing body. At their best, governing bodies are dynamic organisations that support their members through organisation, the supply of materials and

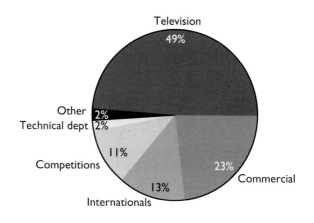

Source: For annual report 1998

Figure 3.13 Football Association sources of turnover

training, magazines, legal advice and insurance. Examples of good practice can be found with the English Cricket Board or the Royal Yachting Association. Figure 3.14 shows the functions of the Football Association.

Figure 3.14 Governing bodies of sport all have similar structures and functions through which they organise and promote the sport nationally. One of the largest – the Football Association – produces a handout that expands on this chart

There are criticisms as well. One common criticism is that clubs tend to have older people on their committees and it is the oldest (who have free time) who get sent on to higher levels. This results in some governing bodies being largely governed by older people who are traditionalist, not in touch with the modern game, and determined to keep their place on committees.

International organisation and funding

The governing bodies belong to international federations of sport such as FIFA for soccer, the ICB (International Cricket Board) and International Rugby Board. In many ways they have the same roles and responsibilities

at an international level as do the governing bodies at national level. For example, they will organise world cups and other international competitions.

The Olympic Games

The biggest and most prestigious of all events is the Olympic Games which is divided into the Summer Olympics and the Winter Olympics, each of which is held every four years with two years between each event. Being an Olympian is the ultimate goal of any competitive sportsperson and it is possibly the most exciting competition both for spectators and for viewers who can see a huge variety of sport.

The Olympics are organised by the International Olympic Committee (IOC), which is based in Lausanne, Switzerland. The modern Olympic Games were revived in 1896 and first held in Athens, the home of the first classical Olympic Games in 1360 B.C.

Here is an extract from the founding principles:

'Olympics is a philosophy of life, exalting and combining in a balanced whole the qualities of body, will and mind. Blending sport with culture and education, Olympism seeks to create a way of life based on the joy found in effort, the educational value of good example and respect for universal fundamental ethical principles . . . The goal of Olympism is to place everywhere sport at the service of the harmonious development of man, with a view to encouraging the establishment of a peaceful society concerned with the preservation of human dignity. To this effect, the Olympic Movement engages, alone or in co-operation with other organisations and within the limits of its means, in actions to promote peace.'
Source: IOC website, 2000

Practice quickly deviated from the ideal. The Games have been complicated by politics and commercialism for many years. In 1936 Hitler tried and failed to use the Berlin Games as a platform for Aryan supremacy; the 1972 Munich Games were the target for a terrorist attack; and the 1980 Moscow Games were boycotted by the American and British teams in protest against the USSR's invasion of Afghanistan.

The temptations of personal and financial rewards of success for competitors have also eroded the Olympic ideal. Certainly, as early as the 1960s the Russians and East Germans were placing their squads on intensive drug regimes and probably the Western countries were not far behind them.

The Olympic flame is a symbol of the olympic ideal

In 1984 Los Angeles won the Games. Through broadcasting, sponsorship and the development of the Games facilities as saleable real estate they showed that the Games could be immensely profitable, not only in themselves but also with the multiplier effect on the national or local economy.

The role of the International Olympic Committee: The IOC is essentially a negotiator and organiser and is not involved in building the facilities, marketing or any of the other income and expenditure involved. The main exception to this is that the IOC maintain the substantial broadcasting rights (see Figure 3.15). The smaller portion of this income goes to the IOC itself while the rest funds the organising committee (the

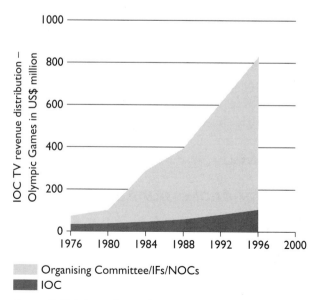

Figure 3.15 International Olympic Committee Broadcast Income Distribution Data

selectors), the international federations of sport and the national Olympic associations.

This commercialism has often had its critics. For example, the selection of Atlanta, Georgia, as the second American Games in a decade has often been attributed to the fact that Coca-Cola, the sponsor at the time, had its headquarters in that city. There have also been numerous scandals about corruption of the Olympic Committee that selects the host city from competition. Several members have been disqualified for taking bribes or excessive presents and services.

Even after a purge of corruption, and a 'Charter of Truce' that is meant to rule out political issues, these problems arose again with the 2000 Games in Australia. Petty corruption occurred when an Australian Olympic official tried to substitute his own daughter to carry the Olympic Torch instead of a schoolgirl. However, political sensitivity to Aboriginal issues in particular, meant that in the end, the games were successful and without controversy.

Each competing country has its own Olympic Committee – in the case of the UK it is the British Olympic Association (BOA). This is responsible in conjunction with the governing bodies for selecting the Olympic squads from each sport, managing and training the teams and raising funds to support them. In addition the BOA puts forward an official to sit on the IOC.

> **Think it over**
>
> Look at Figure 3.12 and then answer these questions:
> 1 What was the total income from broadcasting in 1996?
> 2 How is the income divided?
> 3 What changes have occurred in the distribution of the income between 1984 and 1996?
> 4 Why do you think that income from broadcasting began to expand in 1989?

National funding of sport

For many years, sports organisation in the UK was not centrally coordinated and individual bodies worked independently. From the 1960s onwards there was a shift in governmental thinking about its role and successive governments have increasingly become involved in sport.

Two particular events may have contributed to the government becoming more involved in sport. The first was the World Cup win over Germany in 1966. The celebrations and increase in morale and productivity that resulted from this showed that sporting success can be a major social catalyst. Support of such success by government would be a great vote-puller and the late 1960s and 1970s saw the growth of public provision of facilities in particular. The other factor was that in the early 1980s there were numerous urban riots in cities such as London, Liverpool and Bristol. They were seriously threatening to the government and one of the results was a release of funds into projects and facilities that would mend the social fabric of these communities. This period was probably the time at which sports development and community sports became seen as part of social policy and within the remit of central government.

Current government funding of sport

Sports funding is largely controlled through the Department for Culture, Media and Sport which channels funds through the Sports Council for redistribution to other organisations. Other funds sometimes come through the Department for Education and Employment for the building of educational sports facilities or specialist projects – such as rehabilitation of offenders using sport that may be funded by the Home Office. Figure 3.16 shows the distribution of public sector funding to sport by the British government.

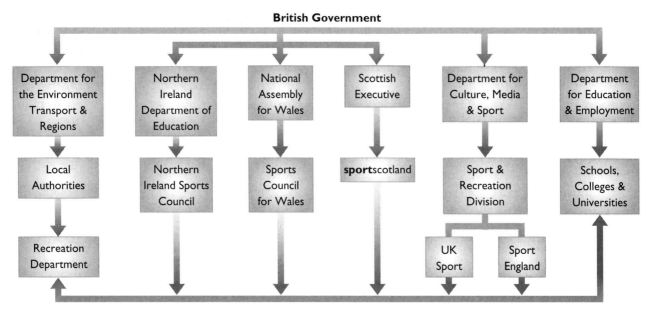

Figure 3.16 British government distribution of public sector funding of sport

It is interesting to note that whereas arts funding from the government has risen in recent years, the contribution to sport has slightly decreased. For example, see Table 3.18.

Table 3.18 Grant aid from the Department for Culture, Media and Sport (£m)

	1997-98	1998-99
English Sports Council	33	31
English Arts Council	186	190

Source: annual reports

There are some variations across the UK on how much is spent per person. For example, see Table 3.19. For the year 1997–98 the £ per capita spend was as shown in the table.

Table 3.19 Spending on sport per person

1997–98	
Wales	2.25
Scotland	1.91
N Ireland	1.66
England	0.67
(UK Sport was allocated 20p per person Across the entire UK)	

Source: CCPR *'An opportunity for change'*

The total subsidy that is given to sport is a matter of government decision and the effectiveness of lobbying by the Sports Council. What actually gets to sport depends on the efficiency of each national Sports Council and how it manages its affairs. One way of measuring it is the per capita spend for a country. In the case of Sport England, 34 per cent of their income was spent on administration, premises and staff in 1997-98, and that had risen to 40 per cent the following year. In other words, of the 67p per person in England that in theory would have been spent on sport, 27p was spent on administration and 40p got through to sport.

Grant aid

Grant aid is a major tool in determining that sport is developed according to policy. Several bodies give grant aid but the major source of grant aid is from the Department for Culture, Media and Sport and allocated by the Sports Council. The flow chart (Figure 3.17) may be useful in seeing the overall routes of funding in the UK.

CASE STUDY – Grant aid

Sport England issued 257 grants in 1999 from Lottery funds, 43 per cent of these were for over £100,000. You can see from the table below how much went to the various sectors.

Sector	Amount	No. of Awards
Local authority	£31,970,796	45
Education	£14,322,927	18
Voluntary	£14,259,228	174
Other	£11,662,825	20
Total	£72,215,776	257

Typically these grants are for capital projects, usually in the form of buildings. Sport England awarded £1.5 million for a new community pool to be built in Cotgrave, in the East Midlands, to complement the other pools in the borough, where community use was restricted throughout the day. The new pool is available to the wider community on a full-time basis.

The Foundation for Sports and Arts (FSA) on the other hand provided 1,288 grants for sport worth £5 million. Nearly all these grants went to individuals or voluntary clubs and were used for non-capital spending (e.g. minibuses, equipment, promotion costs) and some small capital projects such as floodlighting. For example, Sleaford Sword Club gained £3,000 for new fencing equipment.

Questions

1 Discuss the situation regarding distribution of funding to the voluntary sector as shown by the figures for Sport England and FSA.

2 The lottery has been criticised for paying only for public sector buildings to be built and not for developing sport. Give reasons to support and reject this view.

3 Think of a sports club you know or belong to. Explain how Lottery and FSA grants could be used to help it.

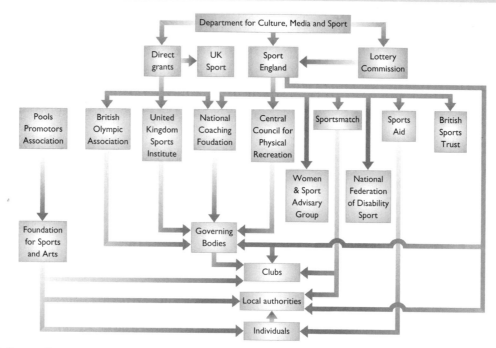

Figure 3.17 Supporting sport – major funding paths for sport in England

The Sports Council and the National Lottery

Grant aid is divided into two parts: 'Exchequer' funding, which is grant aid taken from the government subsidies, and 'Lottery' funding which comes from the allocation made by the Lottery Commission. Table 3.20 shows what they include.

The National Lottery was started in 1994 with the express aim of boosting arts, sport, heritage and community projects. Although health and education have been added to the 'good causes', the Lottery has succeeded in contributing over £1 billion to sport over its first five years. In other words, the Lottery is substantially bigger than the total government subsidy of sport and should thus be seen as the powerhouse behind sport. The Lottery Commission is the public body responsible for running the Lottery as a whole. It then allocates a portion of the receipts of the Lottery to each of the good causes. The Sports Council has a dual role in that it is first responsible for advising on sports Lottery applications. Secondly, it is responsible for deciding which applications receive funding. Figure 3.18 shows the schemes run by the Sports Council in 2000 aimed at encouraging youth participation in sport.

Capital grants were the only grants available in the 1990s and will remain the lion's share of funding for the future. These are the grants that often catch the eye of the media. Many of the grants are enormous as they fund major sports buildings. The biggest to date is the new English National Stadium at Wembley where a grant of £120 million has been put towards a total expenditure of £475 million.

> **Think it over**
>
> Look at Figure 3.16 on page 184. It is estimated that in 2002, the majority of lottery funding for sport will go to community projects. What a re the benefits and disadvantages of the use of lottery funds for such projects? Think of other ways in which this money could be spent on sport and the benefits that could result.

Table 3.20 Sources of grant aid from Sport England

Exchequer	Lottery
Total expenditure 1998-99 £34m	Total expenditure 1998-99 £72m towards 277 projects costing £112m
Block grants to governing bodies (through the Central Council for Physical Recreation and other representative organisations such as the National Coaching Federation or the National Federation of Disability Sport.	Community projects, including capital (buildings and facilities) awards grants of over £5000. Applicants are expected to part-fund projects themselves and while the norm is about 50 per cent, exceptions can be made for schools and deprived projects where 20 per cent is sometimes acceptable.
Project-based funding: the Sports Council has developed numerous schemes designed to tackle specific issues. The regional offices encourage local providers to develop projects that will become part of these schemes and such projects are part or wholly funded, often in the form of staffing or equipment.	Small projects (under £5000) to schools and community groups for small capital and revenue (staff/equipment)
	Revenue awards (£5,000+) aimed at tackling social exclusion
	The World Class Fund administered by the United Kingdom Sports Institute

Sport England leads the development of sport for young people in England. It coordinates the work of a wide range of agencies all of which share a concern for our young people's sporting future.

Source: Sport England 2000

Figure 3.18 Sports Council schemes aimed at youth in 2000

Figure 3.19 shows a forecast of the lottery structure for 2002.

Although publicity would suggest that it is the voluntary sector that most benefits, it is in fact the public sector that gets most of the money (Table 3.21). This is because although

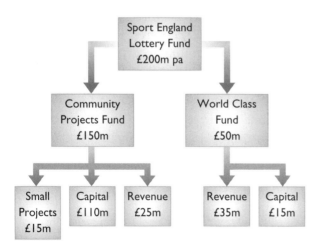

Source: Sport England Annual Report 1999

Figure 3.19 Forecast Lottery structure for 2002

Table 3.21 Lottery grants in 1998–99

Recipient	Number of grants	Value of grants (£m)
Local authority	45	31.97
Education	18	14.32
Voluntary	174	14.26
Other	20	11.66
Total	277	72.22

more clubs receive grants their projects are smaller in value. Also, there are fewer than three hundred grants a year. Applications far outstrip supply and many applications are rejected on technicalities in the application before the content is examined.

World Class Fund and the pursuit of excellence

From 2000, the second part of the Lottery is the World Class Fund. Some of its funds are capital based and will go to the provision of facilities that will aid world-class competition or preparation for it. However, much of the funds will support the United Kingdom Sports Institute and its programmes to develop strategically British elite performance.

UK sports organisations

Foundation for Sport and Arts (FSA)

The FSA is an anomaly as it is one of the few grant-aiding organisations that is not funded in some way by Sport England. Maybe for this reason it has a totally different approach to grant aid. It is a charitable trust that was set up in 1991 prior to the Lottery. Its funding is based on a compromise that was found to allow pools companies (The Pools Promoters' Association) avoid paying higher levels of betting duty by putting a proportion of their profits into funding leisure in the community. Before the Lottery went live the FSA was in a healthy state, distributing over £20m in grants every year. However, the

Lottery has hit pools' profits hard and so Trust funds have dwindled although even in 1999 they gave over £8m of grant aid. Changes in Treasury regulations may now see a rise in its importance as pools are helped to recover.

You may see the FSA logo on plaques in sports buildings that have been given grant aid by it.

The grants are decided on by a board of trustees, some from the pools industry but the majority are famous names in the arts, entertainments and sports world. Sir Tim Rice is the chairperson. Unlike the Sports Council the FSA is not strategic and gives grants on the basis of each applicant's worth and need as perceived by the trustees. This gives a different flavour to the funding – the voluntary sector is the majority recipient and the public sector receives less. Unlike the Lottery, commercial sector operators are sometimes funded when there is significant public gain. For example the FSA has funded several theatres. The trust also has other advantages:

- it funds very small projects (e.g. bibs and strip for a netball team)
- it funds transport, such as minibuses
- it will fund up to 100% of a project
- it will fund talented individuals for tuition fees and expenses (e.g. bursaries)
- it will fund talented individuals for expenses incurred in competing.

Sportsmatch

This organisation was originally formed by the English Sports Council but is now independent. Its role is to encourage sponsorship by matching sponsorship funding from between £500 to £50,000. It largely supports community-based projects, especially schools. The scheme works by sports organisations obtaining sponsorship from a commercial sponsor and then

doubling this amount by a matched grant from Sportsmatch, which in turn is funded by a Department for Culture, Media and Sport (DCMS) grant channelled through Sport England.

| Try it out | Look up the DCMS website and find out who the current Secretary of State and Minister of Sport are. |

Public bodies

The Department for Culture, Media and Sport releases funds through a hierarchy of public bodies at the top of which is the Sports Council. In this section we look at the most important of these and the areas of work they are involved in.

The Sports Councils

In 1972 the government set up the national Sports Councils (England, Scotland, Wales and Northern Ireland). In their original form their role was to:

- define policy and strategy for sport
- provide funding for governing bodies and local sport provision
- run promotional campaigns
- coordinate sports activity and practice
- advise government.

Although influenced by the government of the day, the Sports Councils were ostensibly independent and set policy. This position slowly changed as central government became more involved in leisure policy and funding. By the 1990s government had created a separate ministry (The Department of National Heritage to become the Department for Culture, Media and Sport – DCMS – in 1998) for leisure. In the late 1990s the government began publishing well-defined policy papers, e.g. 'Raising the Game' (Major government 1995), 'A Sporting Future for All' (Blair government 1999). These policy papers are the key to understanding where sport in the UK is going as they summarise the thinking of government and the Sports Council. 'A Sporting Future for All' promotes the following key points:

- more people *participating in sport*
- more places *to do sport in*
- more medals *to be won in international competition.*

 Try it out | Access the DCMS website and identify the main programmes and their targets for sport.

In 1996 the Sports Councils were reorganised into:

- the National Sports Councils
- UK Sports Council or 'UK Sport' (see below).

Each national council took the title of Sport England, Scotland etc. The biggest of these and most complex is Sport England. Like all public bodies, it is headed by a committee of leading figures from the sports world who in the main are volunteers, apart from the chairman. An executive body of paid officers reports to the council.

Because of its size, the structure is repeated in ten regions where there are regional offices and a regional council that advises the executive on decisions and priorities. They are:

- East
- East Midlands
- Greater London
- North
- North West
- South
- Southeast
- Southwest
- West Midlands
- Yorkshire.

Until 1990 the Sports Council emphasised long-term marketing campaigns underpinned with grant aid as its major approach to implementing policy. These campaigns were aimed at raising awareness and participation at specific market segments; they included 'Ever thought of sport' for youth and '50+' for the over-fifties.

Since then the approach has been to define specific projects and target groups. By making sure that facilities and services are funded in order to supply the needs of target groups, it is felt that people will start to use them without a great deal of promotion. Its current programme is well summarised in the Annual Report. Strategic planning requires selectivity and prioritisation and the subdivision of the overall programme into many sub-programmes. Each sub-programme is focused on:

- a **place** – which may be geographically or demographically defined
- an **activity** – which sports will be focused on
- a **target group** – such as children, ethnic minorities
- a **working ethos** – for example, partnership, elitism, sport development.

Here, for example, are the priority sports for UK Sport and their world-class performance programme:

Sports on the UK world-class performance programme	
Athletics	Modern pentathlon
Bobsleigh	Orienteering
Canoeing	Paralympic sport
Cycling	Rowing
Disabled table tennis	Sailing
Diving	Swimming
Equestrian	Triathlon
Gymnastics	Water skiing
Ice skating	Wheelchair basketball
Judo	

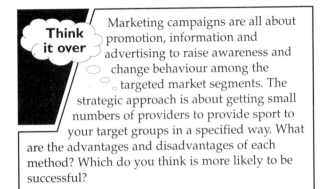

Think it over Marketing campaigns are all about promotion, information and advertising to raise awareness and change behaviour among the targeted market segments. The strategic approach is about getting small numbers of providers to provide sport to your target groups in a specified way. What are the advantages and disadvantages of each method? Which do you think is more likely to be successful?

UK Sport

One of the reasons for the reorganisation of the Sports Council was that some areas of its work were of national and international significance. These issues were:

- doping and ethical issues
- excellence and elitism at international level
- promotion of British sport abroad.

Therefore UK Sport was created to manage and coordinate this work.

The United Kingdom Sports Institute (UKSI)

This organisation was set up in 1999 to provide the best competitors with support and facilities. It will be fully operational by 2002. At its core are the National Sports Centres. These are specialised facilities to provide coaching and playing facilities that are the best in the country.

The ones in existence at the time of writing are outlined in Table 3.22 below.

Table 3.22 National sports centres

Centre	Key sports
Crystal Palace	Indoor and outdoor sports
Bisham Abbey	Indoor and outdoor sports
Lilleshall	Soccer and other outdoor team games
Holme Pierrepoint	Water sports
Plas y Brenin	Outdoor activities*

This is not part of the network as these activities are not competitive; they remain within the Sports Council Trust, a section of the Sport England.

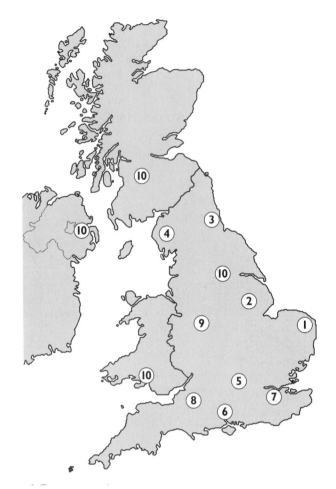

1 **East:** various locations
2 **East Midlands:** Loughborough University & Holme Pierrepoint National Sports Centre, Nottingham, and Rutland Water
3 **North:** Gateshead International Stadium
4 **North West:** Sportcity
5 **South:** Bisham Abbey National Sports Centre; Stoke Mandeville Guttman Sports Centre
6 **South coast:** Southampton University
7 **South East:** Crystal Palace National Sports Centre, Bexley, and Canterbury (University of Kent)
8 **South West:** University of Bath
9 **West Midlands:** Lilleshall National Sports Centre, Wolverhampton, and Birmingham Universities
10 **Yorkshire:** Don Valley Stadium
Northern Ireland: University of Ulster
Scotland: 4 sites being considered
Wales: Glamorgan CC, University of Wales, Swansea City and University

Figure 3.20 The national network of sports institutes

In 2000 the National Sports Centres were absorbed into a new national network of ten institutes in England, four in Scotland and two in Wales. These institutes are regional networks of expertise and facilities that will be co-ordinated by the Sports Council. They often are focused on one specific facility, such as Gateshead International Stadium, but in some cases they consist of a network of sites.

The institutes can be seen in Figure 3.20.

These centres will largely concentrate on elite sport – that is, participants who are destined for high levels of achievement, such as representing a county or the country. The Department for Education and Employment will also become involved in supporting this development of excellence in sport by 110 'sports colleges' which will be schools that select aspiring young people and provide first-class training and facilities.

In addition, the national governing bodies of sport will have centres of excellence throughout the country that allow aspiring participants to get high-level coaching and facilities reasonably close to their home. You should note that the sports colleges and centres of excellence replaced the concept of Academies of Sport that were conceived by the Major government.

The Central Council for Physical Recreation (CCPR)

This organisation was the forerunner of the Sports Council, and was formed in the days when sport was largely about the amateur game. Its role was then to represent and lobby for the common interest of the governing bodies. Although largely funded (80 per cent) by Sport England it has managed to retain a high degree of this independence and is well regarded for its persistent lobbying of government on behalf of its members.

For example, many voluntary clubs have extensive grounds such as playing fields for which they pay high business rates. Although some councils do give rate relief, many do not and this is a major headache for club finance. The CCPR is currently engaged in getting government to review the situation, with the aim of making rate relief mandatory rather than discretionary. Another campaign has been to reduce VAT payments made by sports clubs, which has resulted in an estimated saving of £40m to clubs.

The CCPR has several other functions. Perhaps two of the most important are:

- the development of the sports leadership awards in the 1980s, which have developed into a major national project for first entry into voluntary sport and sports development. These awards and other youth-centred programmes have now transferred to the British Youth Sport Trust.
- the Sports Sponsorship Advisory Service: this is a service that advises sports organisations on how to raise sponsorship and which researches sponsorship opportunities.

National Coaching Foundation (NCF)

As with the Sports Councils, the four countries of the UK each have an organisation dedicated to the promotion, coordination and development of coaching. They are:

- The National Coaching Foundation
- Northern Ireland Institute of Coaching
- Scottish Coaching Unit
- Welsh National Training Coaching Centre

We will look here at the largest – the NCF. As with other organisations in sport, the organisation is divided into ten regional offices but most of its work stems from headquarters in Leeds (all other public bodies in sport are in London). It is predominantly grant funded by Sport England (£1.631 million in 1999), but UK Sport also significantly give it grant aid (£0.836 million). It also has substantial additional income of £0.924m in 1999 much (£0.528m) of which was generated by its trading arm (Coachwise) through courses and publications.

The aims of the NCF and the other coaching bodies are to:

- develop national standards (NVQs) for coaching, teaching and instructing
- provide educational and training products and services for coaches (e.g. local coaching centres and workshops)
- provide information and support for coaches (e.g. publications, website)
- work with other sports organisations such as the BOA, Sports Councils, local authorities, governing bodies and educational institutes.

! Check it out

1 Give an example of an informal outdoor team sport and an indoor organised sport.

2 What are two ways that local authorities support local voluntary clubs?

3 Explain how two factors have caused a decline in school sport.

4 What are the two main sources of income for voluntary clubs?

5 How are the Olympic Games organised and funded?

6 Why was the DCMS set up?

7 What does UK Sport do?

8 Apart from the Lottery, name two sources of grant aid for sports clubs.

9 Explain which sector most benefits from Lottery funding.

10 Who funds the Scottish and English Sports Councils?

3.4 Sport and the mass media

In addition to participating in sport, many of us gain our sporting experiences by watching or listening to professional sport on TV or radio. Professional sport and the media are increasingly interrelated. As we will see this relationship has major implications for sport as a whole, our perception of it and the development of individual sports.

The mass media consists of:

- television (terrestrial, cable, satellite and video)
- radio
- the press (newspapers, magazines and books).

Television

Although cinema newsreels were once an important medium for sport, it is television that rules sport today. Sport watched on TV is called 'viewed sport' ('spectator sport' refers to the live audience at a sport event).

Television is the most powerful of the mass media because it simulates being a spectator at home. In recent years technology has made it even better than being a spectator, as it provides action replays and an expert commentary. With digital television the power increases, with multi-screen action and the opportunity to call up any action from the past.

The power of TV provides a new dimension on sport. Increasingly, large stadia are bringing in large screens so that they too can give the effects that the viewer has at home. At sports events spectators are often looking at the screen and not the live play. Event-based TV is undermining the referees and crowds will boo if a decision is made that goes against the evidence of the screen. It is likely that in the near future the referee will need to have the right to consult the replay or be advised from a control room through radio headphones. If so, this will create an opportunity for broadcasters to find lulls in the game where advertising can be inserted. Away from the ground, fans are even deserting their traditional viewing place – the living-room. The rise of the sports pub provides digital TV on large screens which would not be available to the household subscriber.

For many people, their only experience of sport is watching it on TV. With the exception of tennis it is men who are significantly more interested in viewing sport. Table 3.23 shows some figures from Mintel for a survey in 1999 of the most popular viewed sports.

Table 3.23 Percentage of adult population 'interested in watching specific sports' in 1999

	All	Males	Females
Football	56	71	43
Motor racing	33	50	17
Snooker	33	43	24
Tennis	32	33	31
Athletics	30	34	26
Cricket	28	40	17

Source: Mintel

In the same way as with spectator sports, the popularity of particular viewed sports changes with viewer taste. At present Rugby League has entered a period of difficulty in

> **Think it over**
>
> Look at Table 3.23 and answer the questions below.
> 1 Which is the most popular viewed sport overall?
> 2 What are the 'top three' viewed sports for women?
> 3 In which sport is the greatest gap in interest between men and women?
> 4 Why do you think there is this gap?

maintaining its popularity. Boxing, racing and snooker, all once top attractions, are steadily declining and are thought to be hard to revive as taste changes. The two national games, football and cricket, are probably going to increase in audience. Football is already doing so. Cricket has also made a great comeback and it is likely that, with Sky and Channel 4 becoming major broadcasters, they will revamp the presentation of the game and make it more attractive to the younger audience who view these channels. Tennis is also a winner as both the Grand Slam and indoor circuits, as well as club tournaments like the Stella Artois, are increasingly televised whereas ten years ago Wimbledon was about the only tournament that was covered. Table 3.24 shows the 'top ten' TV sports coverage in 1998.

The increase in watching a sport can be heavily influenced by the image of the sporting stars. Gymnastics flourished during

Table 3.24 TV coverage of sport, 1998 (Top 10, in minutes)

Sport	BBC 1	BBC 2	ITV	CH4	Eurosport	Sky	CH5	Total %
Football	4800	650	7475	2930	29725	102765	2815	16.54
General sport	935	295	215	7705	10610	76106	16610	12.31
Golf	1485	3548	0	60	2160	83900	90	9.98
Motor sports	390	1680	5620	0	26065	31945	645	7.26
Cricket	3042	9327	135	0	0	44970	0	6.29
Tennis	1130	2466	0	0	21035	15955	0	4.44
Motor-cycling	175	90	0	0	14880	11310	0	2.89
Horse racing	2581	1161	60	7635	0	13460	0	2.72
Boxing	95	0	140	0	7845	16260	0	2.66
Rugby League	40	160	0	0	0	22910	0	2.53

Source: RSL Research Services, RSL Sportscan July–December 1998

the years when Olga Korbut and the Eastern Bloc starlets worked their charms. Athletics soared as Coe and Ovett slogged it out in middle-distance running. Ice skating was established as a viewable sport after the success of Torvill and Dean and other British skaters.

The Olympic Games are a major influence on the popularity of various sports. The Olympic success of the British hockey team resulted in coverage of the sport for some time afterwards. Athletics for some time lost its way following the bankruptcy of the governing body in the 1990s. It has now been revived as UK Athletics. New deals have been secured with the BBC and the success of British athletes in the 2000 Olympics may well be crucial in ensuring that these deals are successful in revitalising the sport.

The broadcasting revolution

For many years the broadcasting companies had a cosy relationship with sport. Until 1955 there was only the BBC – which first started regular sports broadcasting in 1936. The Coronation in 1953 was an event that boosted television set sales and for the first time the medium could be said to have mass appeal. In 1954 *Sportsview* was launched as the first sports-dedicated programme, later to be replaced by *Grandstand.* In 1955 ITV was launched and the BBC, knowing how sport could boost audiences, was quick to fight the competition by signing up long-term contracts with many sports events. This enabled the BBC to dominate until the 1980s, despite other terrestrial broadcasting channels coming on line (BBC2, Channel 4 and Channel 5).

The arrival of subscription broadcasting in the form of BSkyB and, more recently, other satellite and cable companies has put paid to the traditional hold of the BBC. In 1992 BSkyB was struggling to survive and made the strategic decision to acquire sole rights to many major sports events, especially football.

Their idea was that the need to watch such events would allow them to form an audience core on which to hang their full programme package. They were right, and the packaging of Sky Sports channels has been a major reason for the survival and success of the company.

Data on television audiences is commercially sensitive and difficult to obtain. However, the following data shows that Sky also appealed to a different audience. Sky TV has mainly attracted the C1/C2 classes, in other words the more affluent. For football at least, and probably other sports, they also attract a young audience with more disposable income. In 1995 54 per cent of their audience were under 34, compared with 32 per cent for ITV and 29 per cent for BBC.

The entrance of Sky into the market shook up some of the ground rules. Their broadcasting was international and their potential was far bigger than terrestrial channels. This meant that:

- sponsors would be more willing to sponsor clubs and events getting this sort of coverage of their name
- clubs and events would be more recognised and therefore be able to merchandise themselves more profitably
- advertisers would pay broadcasters and clubs more for a larger audience.

The clubs also realised for the first time that the commercial importance of sport to the broadcasters was significant and they therefore could expect higher broadcasting income from the companies they signed with.

Apart from the BBC, the broadcasting companies are in the private sector, and so the amount they could bid for a contract was determined by the income they would make from subscriptions or advertising income – which would increase the bigger and more exclusive the event was. The BBC, on the other hand, being a public company could only bid using funds fixed by the licence revenue. The BBC was now less able to compete for contracts. As can be seen from Table 3.25 the main winners in the competition for sports viewing figures are Channel 5, ITV and Sky.

Table 3.25 Sports viewing hours

	1996	1998
BBC1	868	720
BBC2	881	1028
ITV	299	528
C4	694	803
C5	0	1290
All terrestrial	**2742**	**4369**
Sky	11738	19418
Eurosport	6304	6307
All subscription	**18042**	**25725**

Source: Mintel 1999

Sky TV focused on football as its foundation and dwarfed other companies with the size of its bids. Table 3.26 below shows the rise of Sky in controlling soccer.

Table 3.26 Milestone deals betwen TV companies and English footballing bodies

	1983	1985	1986	1988	1992	1997
Length of contract (yrs)	2	0.5	2	4	5	4
Broadcaster	BBC/ITV	BBC	BBC/ITV	ITV	BSkyB	BSkyB
Rights fee (£m)	5.2	1.3	6.3	441	91.5	670
Annual rights fee (£m)	2.6	2.6	3.1	11	38.3	167.5
Number of live matches per season	10	6	14	18	60	60
Fees per live match (£m)	0.26	0.43	0.22	0.61	0.64	2.79

Source: FA Premier League

The impact of television

When thinking about the impact of television, the first reaction of a sports fan

Think it over

Look at Table 3.25 again and then answer these questions.

1 By what percentage has Sky viewing increased?
2 How does this compare with the combined figures for the BBC (BBC1 and 2)?
3 What market share does Sky have overall?
4 What share does the BBC have?

might be 'great – we have never had so much sport so who cares who's providing it or what the standards are'. But there are some issues worth considering.

Players' behaviour and careers: Sports competitors play under conditions of high tension and sometimes snap. They swear, they hit each other, they break things. To some extent this has always gone on. In the 1930s, the legendary Dixie Dean, who had a swarthy complexion, once hit a spectator who made a racist remark to him. Apparently, a police officer on duty congratulated Dean because 'the bloke deserved it'. In those days there were no cameras. Fast-forward sixty years and Eric Cantona is caught on camera taking very similar action which provided TV with hours of debate on his behaviour and many hours of community service for himself.

Television seems to work in two ways for players.

1 It can pick up and exaggerate behaviour that would go unremarked without broadcasting. John McEnroe was famous for his tantrums but maintains that this was his nature and not the need for self-promotion that made him behave in this way. By all accounts he was similarly bad-tempered when playing off-camera. However, broadcasting focused on this behaviour and provoked the authorities to take action.

2 It can encourage a player to 'play to the camera' and adopt a certain image both on and off the field. This may be the 'bad boy'

image, such as Vinnie Jones, who went on to become an actor using the same persona. Conversely it can be the 'good guy' image, such as Gary Lineker. In many cases the media, especially the newspapers, follow the players into their private lives and publicise what they find. As such behaviour is normally negative it can have ramifications for the player because it is considered to be conduct that brings the game into disrepute. For example, both Paul Gascoigne and Geoffrey Boycott have been charged with beating up their partners. Press revelations about the golfer John Daly's alcoholism led to his sponsors dropping him.

For some players, their persona means that they can follow a career in the media after they finish playing – Ian Wright is an excellent example. Football, rugby and cricket are especially conducive to this. It is ironic to note that these sports often revert to using 'laddettes' as presenters to fill in on their teams rather than using players or commentators with deep knowledge of the game. This is a reflection on the lack of status given to the women's game. The main exception here is tennis where the game has always had women players who become commentators, such as Sue Barker and Virginia Wade.

The effect of TV on sports funding: Sponsorship is a big issue here. Television has swollen sports funding by directly increasing broadcasting income but also indirectly by making sponsorship more attractive, as the sponsors' names go to millions of viewers. Because of their combination of popular appeal and broadcasting potential, sport is the major target for sponsors – for example, 64 per cent of all sponsorship in 1995 was for sport.

The size of deals can be impressive. In 1999, for example, of the sixteen companies in the UK that entered new sponsorship deals of over £1 million only three were *not* soccer or Rugby Union. In international sport the deals get

bigger. Gateway, for example, has sponsored the 2002 Winter Olympics for £30 million.

Broadcasting fees: With regard to broadcasting fees there is a large gap between the top and bottom clubs, resulting from a combination of match fees and the number of broadcasts. In soccer, for example, an average Premier League club receives around £7.5 million a year from broadcasting fees, while an average Third Division team receives £250,000. This gap between top and bottom is widening. For example, in 1987 the top clubs in the British leagues earned about five times more from broadcasting than the bottom clubs. By 1999 the ratio was about 30:1 and maybe as high as 100:1 between the Premier clubs getting most coverage and those lower division clubs with least coverage – Leyton Orient, for example, was broadcast only once in two seasons.

What is the effect of TV on grassroots sport? While such deals benefit individual clubs and bodies and professional players, there has been increasing concern that this money is not going back to grassroots sports where all players will have come from. The CCPR lobbied on this score for some years and in 1999 drew up a code of conduct for broadcasting rights. This initially involved the governing bodies of athletics, tennis, horse racing, golf, rugby (both codes), cricket and soccer. A key element is that these bodies have agreed to contribute no less than 5 per cent of broadcasting fees back into the development of their sport.

So what's the problem? All the clubs are earning more than they ever did and money is going back into the sport.

The real problem is that the smaller clubs (and this is particularly so in soccer) get a disproportionately smaller share of fees. This means that they cannot improve their facilities at the same rate as top clubs – fans therefore tend to drift away to bigger clubs with better facilities. Worse still, as the top clubs can afford to pay more for players so the smaller clubs are less able to buy players they need to get promotion in the league. There is a real fear that smaller clubs will increasingly get into financial difficulties and at best simply become the nursery grounds for young players to develop before going on to the big time.

A second problem is that this division may well start to occur in the voluntary sector. Sports that are funded by broadcasting will increasingly be better promoted and have better facilities. The 'also rans' will be perceived as unglamorous and unpopular because they are rarely seen on TV – and increasingly, they will find it harder to attract participants. This will have a knock-on effect for excellence as the pool of talent from which to draw international competitors will start to dry up and it will become harder to find an elite.

In addition to this, where local professional clubs decline there will be less of a local link or model for the outstanding amateur to move up to the professional game. It is increasingly likely that progression in the sport will be a result of school-based programmes feeding the better athletes into centres of excellence. Despite the attempts to popularise participation it is possible that participation will be increasingly seen as something those who are 'good at sports' do, while the rest of us stay at home and become viewers.

> **Think it over**
> Many commentators feel that one effect of television on sport is that football will become a trans-global sport with only the richest clubs around the world being able to compete with each other. Home leagues and tournaments will come to be seen as second best. What do you think?

The effect of sports broadcasting

The power of television was first envisaged in 1954, prior to the British two-channel system. The Broadcasting Act stated that with certain listed events no one broadcaster could claim exclusive rights. This was on the grounds that the event was part of the national way of life and there should be free access to these events. The Act was revised in 1996 to take account of the invention of subscription broadcasting. Two years later the Home Secretary announced a revised list of sporting events for which live coverage must be made available to free-to-air terrestrial television. These are:

* Category A, where coverage must be made available to free-to-air terrestrial television, i.e. the Olympic Games, the FIFA World Cup Finals Tournament, the FA Cup Final, the Scottish FA Cup Final (in Scotland), the Grand National, the Derby, the Wimbledon Tennis Finals, the European Football Championship Finals Tournament, the Rugby League Challenge Cup Final and the Rugby World Cup Final
* Category B, for which live coverage might be shown on pay TV, provided there were satisfactory arrangements for secondary coverage by a free-to-air broadcaster, i.e. the cricket Test matches played in England, non-finals play in Wimbledon Tournament, all other matches in the Rugby World Cup Finals Tournament, Five Nations Rugby Tournament matches involving home countries, the Commonwealth Games, the World Athletics Championship, the Cricket World Cup (final, semi-final and matches involving home nations' teams), the Ryder Cup, the Open Golf Championship.

You will notice that the Act has relegated some events that are very much part of the British way of life (e.g. Test matches, Five

Nations Rugby) to the B list for which free live coverage is no longer guaranteed. Furthermore, for those sports that are especially popular (i.e football), live League coverage is not covered in the Act and has virtually disappeared from free television.

Television changes the game

The American experience is that TV has changed the game. It is said that in games like American football, ice hockey and basketball there is manipulation of the various breaks that exist in these sports to allow for advertising breaks. The staging of venues has also been affected. In the 1970s, the Ali/Foreman 'rumble in the jungle' fight was staged in the early morning in Zaire to make prime time TV in the USA. It has also been said that the timing of the Winter Olympic events in Japan were scheduled to catch American TV prime time.

Major British sports, by chance, do not have such breaks or there are plenty of natural gaps for advertising, such as in horse racing or tennis. Despite the fear, there is not much evidence of major changes in play so far. But it is frequently said that, with the growing dependency of top soccer clubs on broadcasting income, the time is not far off when we shall see a 'game of four halves'.

There have, however, been changes to the structure and presentation of sports. In the 1970s Kerry Packer introduced evening flood-lit cricket in Australia. Because of the lighting, traditional cricket whites and the red ball showed badly on the screen and to get a better picture we saw the introduction of the multicoloured strip.

Cricket: There have been many other changes in cricket in the past twenty years. The full extended game is now a relative rarity and various modified games have been brought in, such as one-day and floodlit cricket – the latter being invented solely for broadcasting

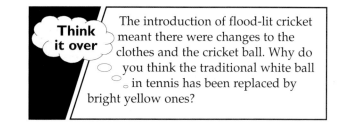

Think it over

The introduction of flood-lit cricket meant there were changes to the clothes and the cricket ball. Why do you think the traditional white ball in tennis has been replaced by bright yellow ones?

and to expand the appeal to a less patient market segment.

Rugby: Rugby League has made drastic changes to attract both the spectators and viewers. In 1998 the RFL faced competition from football and a lack of serious interest by broadcasters who were, in the main, following the soccer leagues. Changes included:

- restyling of the players' strip
- promotion of player profiles, especially by the introduction of many southern hemisphere players
- conversion of the season from winter to summer, thus sidestepping the football competition
- revamped League structure to give a streamlined Super League and a Premier League.

The ideas worked, and with heavy marketing they succeeded in increasing the average attendance from 6,420 to 6,901 between 1990 and 1999. TV coverage rose for a time from 6.5 million viewers in 1998 to 9.2 million in 1996, after which there has been a decline to 7 million.

Football: Soccer has also changed its programme. The extension of the home season and the inclusion of various out-of-season competitions and matches has almost certainly been encouraged by broadcasting and brings with it the problem of players suffering injuries and becoming exhausted.

Broadcasting has certainly affected the home game. Traditionally, soccer was a Saturday game and this meant there was limited opportunity for live football and for clubs to

Where will he play next?

get exposure. The move to Sunday games immediately doubled this opportunity and, more recently, the increase in mid-week games significantly extends the chance of being on TV. At £300,000 for a Premier team or £40,000 for lower divisions there is a great temptation to reprogramme the game.

With soccer, broadcasting is also changing the structure of the game. The Premier League originally broke away from the FA partly because its superior play could get it better broadcasting deals. The reality of the premiership is that it is itself two leagues: the half-dozen super clubs who are world players and the rest who will come and go. The world leaders can command even more fees and buy better players – and yet again the gap widens. Almost certainly within the next ten years they will have all but left British football to play in continental and world leagues created by the international federations and the broadcasting companies.

TV 'stinging' the viewer

The cost of securing broadcasting rights is expensive for the broadcasters and there are two sources of income to make a profit: advertising revenue and, for subscription, the viewing fee. The satellite companies have an advantage in that they have a wider audience for live coverage because of their international audience. Increasingly, however, terrestrial companies sub-let their rights and link up with overseas terrestrial channels.

Although controlled ultimately by what the market will pay, subscription broadcasting has not been slow in increasing its fees substantially. Sky originally charged £9 a month for a subscription; this has since risen to £32. It is also experimenting with 'pay as you view' charges for major events like World Championship boxing. But the natural consequence of this will be a section of the market who will want to watch sport but will not have the means to do so. In other words, subscription broadcasting restricts access to a proportion of viewers.

TV controls the clubs

More and more Premier League clubs are becoming public limited companies. This means they can be influenced if other companies buy significant shareholdings in them. If the major shareholders are broadcasters, there are two worrying implications.

The first is that the broadcaster may require changes to the club that are not in the best interests of the fans or game. For example, they may want to buy players not only because of their skills but for their audience rating. They may want to overrule management decisions in favour of the broadcasters' interests; for example, by deciding to play in a competition that brings a bigger audience or playing an injured player to get a good story out of it.

The second implication is that they could influence the club on how to use its voting rights on the Premier League executive when it comes to consider broadcasting bids. News International (Sky's parent company) tried in 1998 to take over Manchester United with a £623m offer. However, because this would give Sky an undue influence in the bidding process for broadcasting rights and control of broadcasting, it was considered that the deal was not in the public interest and it was blocked by the Monopolies and Mergers Commission.

The lessons of Sky's attempt were not lost. The next round of broadcasting licences for soccer is coming up with estimated packages of £2bn. This time there are more competitors in the marketplace from subscription and commercial terrestrial channels.

The advantages of having share ownership by broadcasters in top clubs are becoming clear and are controlled only by an FA ruling that 10 per cent is the ceiling for share ownership by any one company. Share ownership of this size is still influential, and the aim of the strategy almost certainly involves being able to influence the Premier Division clubs in making favourable decisions for their major shareholders when discussing both club issues and broadcasting rights for the League. According to the BBC's *Panorama* programme this is how they line up in 2000 (see Table 3.27).

Table 3.27 Broadcasting companies with shares in the top clubs

Broadcasting company	Club share ownership
Sky satellite	Man. Utd. 9.9%, Leeds 9.1%, Sunderland 6.1%, Chelsea 9.9%
NTL cable	Newcastle 9.9%, Aston Villa 9.9%, Middlesboro 5%
Granada terrestrial + joint ownership with Carlton of On Digital cable	Liverpool 9.9%

Source: BBC *Panorama* 'The £2billion game' May 2000

It is likely that TV broadcasting is an interim step to the Internet broadcasting which is beginning to emerge. It is probably significant that the £17 million sponsorship deal between Manchester United and Vodaphone involves an offer for Man. U. fans globally to have free mobile phones. At first this seems a good deal for Vodaphone as they will increase their call-based income. Within weeks of the deal we saw the introduction of a new generation of mobiles capable of handling e-mail; so it is just a short step away from them being able to handle full Web services. The vision of the near future is that Manchester United and other clubs will be able to broadcast over the Web into Vodaphone or other mobiles which can be plugged into your TV to provide a totally interactive service. What will be Sky's next move in response to this?

Radio

Radio was the birthplace of sports commentary, with cricket, football, Wimbledon tennis and horse racing all being broadcast from the 1920s onwards. It held dominance until the onset of television overshadowed the importance of radio. But radio broadcasting continued and, without competition from commercial stations, settled down into a format which in many ways remains unchanged and institutionalised. The rise of commercial radio in the 1970s provided little competition as it was often music-orientated. This monopoly was finally broken in 1999 with Talk Radio which for the first time took a Test Match away from the BBC by directly negotiating with the South African Cricket Board.

Although there is a shifting between which channel broadcasts which national event, programming largely still remains within the BBC – who incidentally will not reveal their audience figures for sport. BBC local radio broadcasting is an important service as it is increasingly the only way local people can hear local sport being broadcast or commented on in the broadcasting media.

In many ways this 'quiet monopoly' is a good thing:

- it provides commentary to people with no access to television. This is not just people who do not own a television but also those who cannot get to it: for example, those people listening to the Test Match in a car or to Wimbledon in the garden
- it provides regular local match commentary for local football clubs and other sports which are often missed out by television
- it provides a traditional style of broadcasting which many people associate with the enjoyment of listening to a sport.

Change is in the air, however. While event broadcasting has not been significantly eroded, more local radio stations are providing editorial comment and in particular 'phone-ins' on sport. Even more radical is the trend that major sports clubs, and in particular football, are beginning to run their own dedicated radio stations. Whether this will mean that local radio will lose this service no one can yet say.

The press

From the start of the popular press in the late nineteenth century it has always been known that sport sells papers. Until the 1980s, sport was always carried on the back pages of newspapers and its content was largely match results and commentaries. At that time the weekend nationals started to segment their papers and many of them had sports sections that not only carried the sports news but started to introduce feature articles, such as profiles of clubs and competitions, interviews with the stars and

investigations of scandals, such as doping or match bribery. Sports journalism had taken on a new image and could now be ranked alongside investigative journalism, to which it had traditionally taken second place.

The other arm of the press is the local papers, which by and large have kept the traditional approach to sports journalism, packing their back pages with every conceivable result from the local leagues. The commercial reason for this is that local sports competition is always tight and players want to know how other teams did. Furthermore, the prospect of a minute of fame by seeing a friend or yourself mentioned or even photographed in an article boosts sales of these papers.

Market research figures on sports journalism are seen as commercially sensitive and are not readily available. Likewise, according to the National Press Association, there are no public figures of column inches dedicated to sport or even sports readership figures.

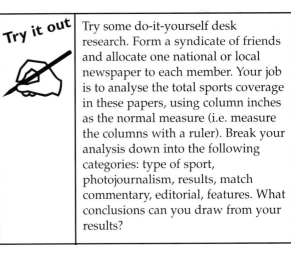

Try it out Try some do-it-yourself desk research. Form a syndicate of friends and allocate one national or local newspaper to each member. Your job is to analyse the total sports coverage in these papers, using column inches as the normal measure (i.e. measure the columns with a ruler). Break your analysis down into the following categories: type of sport, photojournalism, results, match commentary, editorial, features. What conclusions can you draw from your results?

Magazines

Magazines are another aspect of sport journalism. These had been popular in Victorian times but slowly disappeared with the *Sporting Life* or the 'Pink 'un' being the last to go in the 1980s. In the early 1990s there were a few magazines in the newsagents that specialised in the top sports of the time such as angling, boxing, horse racing, sailing and golf. However, most magazines were restricted to those produced by the governing bodies of sport who mailed them to their members.

The Taylor Report on football commented on how football clubs let down their fans with a lack of investment and high prices. These comments rang true and for some time before the report there had been the emergence of the first 'fanzines'. These had actually started as part of the punk movement in the 1970s, with magazines like *Foul*. These prototypes flourished in the 1980s and went national with *Off the Ball* and *When Saturday Comes*. Fanzines were soccer-focused and looked at what the fans were interested in and not what the clubs or broadcasters gave them.

The popularity of many of these magazines, plus the change in the reading public's taste in magazines, began to show the commercial publishers that new-format special-interest and lifestyle magazines could be successful. There are now dozens of special-interest magazines focusing on particular sports.

3.5 Trends in sports

In this brief section we look at the 'top ten' issues affecting sport today.

1 The drift towards health and fitness

The general indication is that people tend to see non-competitive activity as a preferred option which they do when it suits them. We are tending to sample more activities and often prefer to take up non-competitive activities for their health benefits. The fitness industry recognises this and, knowing that the lifecycle of various activities and services is short, is constantly reinventing or repackaging itself. For example, a current theme is 'Wellness', which is a holistic approach towards health and fitness, combined with a good diet and nutrition, to achieve all-round health and well-being.

2 Increase in outdoor activities

Outdoor pursuits are becoming more popular. The industry is rapidly becoming customer orientated and provides activities that the customers want. Perhaps the best exponents of this are the children's adventure holiday companies, such as 3D and PGL. A sign of their future prospects might be that the multinationals are buying up companies like these. Likewise, for adults, there is a rapid growth in adult products that can combine excitement with good food and accommodation.

> ## ! Check it out
>
> 1 Describe the main stages in sport broadcasting in the UK.
>
> 2 What are the three main forms of sports journalism?
>
> 3 To what extent does BBC radio have a monopoly on sports radio broadcasting?
>
> 4 How has television affected the way we spectate sport?
>
> 5 Name five of the most popular broadcast sports.
>
> 6 Explain the relationship between broadcasters, sponsors, advertisers and professional sports clubs.
>
> 7 Giving examples, what statutory control is there of broadcasting live events?
>
> 8 Explain how lower League clubs are affected by subscription broadcasting.
>
> 9 Describe how broadcasting has changed a particular sport.
>
> 10 How does broadcasting help the grassroots game?
>
> 11 How could share ownership be used in negotiating broadcasting deals?

3 Decrease in competitive participation

There is a serious possibility that in the long term there will be a drift away from many of the traditional team games, although individual competitive sports (such as tennis) where you can arrange your own playing time will be able to expand. There are several reasons for this:

- competitive team games require regular commitment to playing at set times, often for extended periods. In a fast-moving age this is difficult for many people.
- related to this is that people are often unable to keep to the time-consuming routine of training that is necessary in so many sports.
- minority sports clubs will find it difficult to recruit members from a public used to televised sports.
- broadcasting emphasises the major sports at the expense of minority ones – for which it is increasingly difficult to promote a public image.
- school sport has declined and the emphasis on the competitive instinct and the need to win played down. This means that skill levels and the numbers attaining them have probably dropped amongst young people.
- competitive sport depends on a level of fitness. As a nation we are becoming less fit, and fewer people will want to cope with the strain of playing. This may result in a drift towards recreational playing. This will benefit 'gentler' sports like badminton and ten-pin bowling but not sports like squash, rugby and soccer, which require a high level of fitness.

4 The squeeze on funding

The squeeze will come from three directions:

A While the Lottery has been a welcome addition to funding, much has been spent on prestigious public leisure facilities. It has not tackled the question of under-funded local government that has difficulty in maintaining the majority of facilities that were built in the 1970s and 1980s and which still form the basis for indoor competitive sport. Similarly, Lottery aid has touched only a handful of voluntary clubs. The next few years will see whether the injection of money into schools and youth development will occur and result in changing lifestyles.

B At the same time, most voluntary clubs will continue to struggle along on minimal finances and small-scale sponsorship. The exception to this will be clubs with assets such as land and buildings. This favours the older-established sports such as hockey, cricket and soccer. It is likely that they will be able to find ways to use these assets better and build new or improved facilities. It is also likely that they will evolve into semi-commercial sports clubs catering for the current market – for example, hockey clubs building artificial multi-use pitches or tennis courts.

C It is unlikely that grant aid from the government to governing bodies will increase and their membership will often be shrinking. Survival for the governing bodies and their ability to support their member clubs will depend on their ability to increase event income but, more importantly, broadcasting rights. In other words, sports that do not stimulate the viewing public or are difficult to broadcast (e.g. squash) will have to change their game (e.g. squash courts of smoked glass that allow full arena viewing plus all-angle camera shots).

5 Stimulating the public

The Roman circuses were based on a mass market appeal of sex and violence. Today, sex appeal is one reason why people watch some sports although this is frequently denied. It is also a key ingredient of broadcasting. Already offers have been made to women's beach volleyball teams to play topless – they were declined. Not so for darts! In athletics and swimming, Lycra and synthetic materials provide a second skin for participants; women athletes and tennis players have continually reduced their clothing. How likely is it that within a few years we will see the return of the classical Olympic ideal and the appreciation of the human form being used as the excuse for broadcasting companies and minority sports to put a different spin on 'Team strip'?

It is the same with violence. Sport gives us the vicarious excitement of watching human power and anger that sometimes results in injury. Although broadcasting rightly condemns violence this does not stop it being broadcast. In Euro 2000 probably more television coverage was given to violent fans than to the few hours of England playing football. More sinister is the outright promotion of violence. In UK there are programmes like the 'Bad boys of football' which look at the hard men of the game and shows fouls and fights. In the USA 'extreme fighting' – that is, no-holds-barred any fighting style allowed – is highly popular.

6 Broadcasting and sponsorship influences

Broadcasting has become the main influence on sport. 'He who pays the player, plays the game' is a new twist on an old proverb. Let us look at some of the effects:

- funding outweighs government sources. In soccer, a 5 per cent contribution of premiership fees alone back into the grassroots sport is £15 million. The entire Sport England's total budget spend on projects is £16 million, while CCPR's grants to governing bodies is approximately £117 000.

- televised sports will prosper over others. Governing bodies with huge turnovers, like the FA (£65m) or the ECB (£84m) – twice the turnover of Sport England – receive a vast proportion of their income from broadcasting and sponsorship. Sports like soccer, cricket, golf, rugby, athletics, basketball, riding and tennis should flourish. For example, the English Cricket Board, when faced with a decline in participation, has invested heavily (£8 million a year) in its development programme. But for a minority sport which is rarely televised, turnover will be largely from small grants and member subscriptions. Unless a sport can project a more televisual image (hockey, volleyball and netball probably have the necessary qualities here) it is possible that they will start to fade away.

- the traditional structure of the game and even its rules may start to change to accommodate TV. Almost certainly, football will lose its home league emphasis and trans-global teams and leagues will emerge. New games will emerge with new rules. For example, the growth of one-day cricket and the abandonment of the traditional dress code makes this form of sport far more attractive to a younger and mixed-gender audience.

7 Technologies

The growth of technology is escalating and we still have not seen its full potential. New materials make sports equipment less expensive or better performing, bringing sport to new markets or allowing records to be broken. Some amazing things may become possible in the next twenty years; for example, new gravity-free sports which could be developed as space tourism becomes established.

8 The ageing population

Demographically, the Western population is ageing. One effect of this will be that Third World countries, with increasingly larger young populations to draw from, will become the outstanding athletes of the world.

At home, it seems likely that the new elderly will carry through their attitude towards the sports that they enjoyed in the last half of the twentieth century. Traditional games like bowls will probably not expand much, but it is likely that the new elderly will want to keep healthy and fit by going to the gym, playing tennis, or walking and swimming. One interesting aspect of this may be that those activities which younger people do now will be full of oldies – a sure reason for young people not to use them. (How many teenagers do you know who belong to a bowls club or line-dancing club?) The question is what will the new young substitute for these?

9 Sport in fashion

Although currently still huge, the trend towards wearing sports clothing is starting to wane, and it is likely that in the future trainers and track suits will become less fashionable. It is likely that soccer and basketball will tend to dominate future sportswear fashion as these are the most televised sports worldwide. It is also very apparent that clothing associated with outdoor activities is expanding; trail shoes, surf shirts, hiking shorts and ski glasses are all standard street items.

Perhaps more predictable is that the materials and techniques used in sportswear will become integrated into main fashion on account of properties like colour, lightness, washability, durability and comfort. Lycra and sharkskin are already well established. Nike's wrap-around shoe technology could soon become part of all casual shoe wear.

10 New facilities

Advances in technology and architecture have ensured the steady growth of amazing buildings. While there will probably not be many new local sports halls, you can expect to see the growth of prestigious and awesome spectator facilities, with hi-tech information devices, sliding roofs and superb lighting and sound, great seating and catering.

In the private sector, firms will compete to provide to all their members the luxury and technology that would have been the domain of the super-rich a few years ago. Even in the public sector the few buildings that will be built are likely to be designed to a high specification and will want to reflect their importance in promoting the image of the area.

Advances in technology and architecture will ensure a growth in prestigious and awesome spectator facilities

! Check it out

1 Give examples of recreational activities that you think will increase or decrease over the next ten years.

2 What factors are going to be important in the survival of voluntary sports clubs?

3 Give three examples of how technology has affected or created a recreational activity.

Sources of information and further reading

Although there are books on certain aspects of the sports industry, these often date quickly. However, should you want to use books, it is worth contacting ILAM who produce suggested reading for particular topics. Their magazines also feature book reviews every month. Your college or school may pay for corporate membership which will mean that their magazines will be in your library.

But overall you are probably best advised to use current sources of information. Here are some suggestions:

The Internet

We have given many sites which we feel are worth while; in fact you should be able to gain sufficient information for this unit simply from the Web. Investigate them and use them as a starting-point for developing links.

A useful guide to the Web is *Internet Resources for Leisure and Tourism*, W. Theobald and H. Dunsmore (Butterworth-Heinemann 2000).

Company annual reports

With careful reading you will be able to tease out a lot of useful information about the people involved at the top, funding and expenditure paths and influence on other organisations. Annual reports will also often outline programmes, policies and strategies being used by the organisation.

Government statistics

These can be useful for getting generalised information about aggregates and trends. However, you should always check how the statistics were constructed in the first place. *Social Trends* is worth investigating as it provides a commentary on the statistics.

Policy documents

We increasingly live in a world that is strategically planned on the basis of policy documents. Essential reading is the DCMS strategy. Sport England is also a valuable source of numerous documents including policy documents and fact sheets. You should get a list on their website. Particularly useful is the 'New Horizons' series on sport in the 1990s, which is an excellent introduction to understanding the organisations and funding of sport provision in England. 'Young People in Sport' is also good. Remember, however, that these documents were largely written before the current government came to power and they may already not be relevant in certain areas. Furthermore, changes in society may be missed out – for example there is no mention whatsoever of the impact of broadcasting.

Newspapers and magazines

Newspapers and magazines are also an excellent source, especially regarding competitive and professional sport. We have hardly touched on players and their profiles here because it is far more entertaining to read about them in the press and see how they are presented. A promising new arrival on the scene is *The Observer's* monthly sport magazine, which is full of statistics and commentary on sport and society.

Useful websites

ILAM: www.ilam.co.uk

ISRM: www.isrm.co.uk

Horse racing: www.bhb.co.uk

Dog racing: www.thedogs.co.uk

Deloitte Touche: www.deloitte.co.uk

Football Association: www.the-fa.org

The English Cricket Board: www.ecb.co.uk

IOC: www.olympic.org

The English Sports Council:
www.english.sports.gov.uk

UK Sports Council or 'UK Sport':
www.uksport.gov.uk

The United Kingdom Sports Institute – no
website at present

The Central Council for Physical Recreation
– website due Autumn 2000

NCF: www.ncf.org.uk

British Sports Industries Federation:
www.sportslife.org.uk *and*
www.sportsdata.co.uk

British Olympic Association:
http://www.olympics.org.uk

World Cup Rugby:
www.wales99.com

International Association of Golf Tour
Operators: www.iagto.com

This unit is organised into four sections. You will learn about:

- marketing leisure and recreation

- the marketing mix

- market research

- marketing communications.

Introduction

Trade is probably as old as humankind and the principles that make one seller successful and another not, have probably existed down the ages. Traders and buyers (*the market*) have always had to go to the place where *the product* is being sold. For a *sale* to be made the product must be attractive to the customer. Being attractive means that the product must do what the customer wants (design), be at the right *price* and be available where and when it is needed (*place and distribution*). Of course, all this is a pointless exercise if the market is not aware of where the marketplace is or what is on offer there, so the trader needs to inform the market (promotion). If you were the only trader selling the product, life would be easy. However, in the marketplace there will be other traders (*competition*) selling similar products or different ones which are more appealing to the market. To compete successfully, you will have to work hard to make your product more suited to the market's needs.

A church poster campaign selling the benefits of worship

4.1 Marketing leisure and recreation: principles and processes of marketing

The principles of marketing apply to all businesses in every industry, even churches now have poster campaigns to sell the benefits of worship. They apply just as much to an individual selling a second-hand bicycle, as to big organisations like Nike and Adidas competing to sell you trainers.

As with all aspects of management and business we no longer rely on native shrewdness on the part of the trader but instead develop theories and terms that help us understand what we are doing and shape our plans in a highly competitive and complex trading world.

So what is the key objective of marketing in the leisure and recreation industry? M. McDonald, a marketing guru, wrote in 1995 that marketing can be defined as:

'The matching of an organisation's capabilities with the wants of customers in order to achieve the objectives of both parties' (*McDonald 1995*).

The examples below show how some organisations in the leisure and recreation industry match their activities to meet the changing needs of their customers:

Theme parks

Visiting a theme park is expensive for the customer and is therefore a once-only or occasional purchase. High prices are necessary to raise money for reinvestment in new features and to make their park more attractive to future customers. As prices cannot drop too much, emphasis needs to be placed on maximising value for money, in other words making the customer's day out enjoyable, exciting and interesting. This can be done by improving the rides, improving customer service (reducing queues, hospitality) and by making the environment attractive (disabled facilities, park and ride).

Theme parks have high capacity and their customers are scattered all over the country and abroad. To attract sufficient numbers they need to advertise both nationally and internationally using expensive techniques. The market is also limited and companies need to use various devices (vouchers, discounts, special events) to make themselves more attractive than their competitors. Since they know only a small proportion of customers will return, theme parks are also keen to use first-time customers to influence their friends when they decide to visit a theme park. Promotions such as 'come back free if you bring a friend' may help, but probably most important is ensuring that the customer's leisure experience is something worth remembering to tell friends about.

Country parks

Country parks face a different set of circumstances. Both the customers and the managers want a quiet unspoiled environment that will not be damaged by overuse – this is to some extent a non-renewable product and has to be sustained. Parks do not charge, so pricing and profits do not affect marketing decisions. Country parks usually keep their advertising to a minimum and often promote special events only where they know they will want to attract increased numbers. On the other hand, larger amounts are spent on providing information and education about the park which will allow users to gain maximum pleasure with minimum impact.

Theme parks can justify the high prices they need to charge, as long as they provide enjoyable and exciting rides

Cinemas

Traditionally, cinemas have advertised only in local papers and have relied on critics' reviews and the publicity machine of the film distributors to attract customers. In most towns, cinemas have been in the same location for decades. Customers have got into a familiar buying habit. The arrival of the multiplexes has broken these habits. The old cinemas have closed down and the new multiplexes are sited out of town. The cinema operators are concerned about losing the old market which may lose the habit of cinema-going and drift away with the change. They are also concerned about convincing a young market (who may not have gone to the old cinemas, and who are looking for a good place to spend the evening), that the multiplexes are the 'cool' place to be. To achieve this they have broken with the tradition of not advertising and instead have launched intensive press and poster campaigns to attract the local market.

Sports clothing

Sports clothing manufacturers like Nike and Adidas have a huge international market and the ability to expand production to meet demand. Their products are, in the main, well made and durable. This presents a problem because a customer, having bought the goods, need not buy more for some time. The secret of new sales is sometimes to make new products better-performing (the air bubble sole being an example), but there is a limit to what a shoe can do. More likely, it is to link the product with fashion which changes continuously and therefore makes an old product out of date and unwanted. The industry both creates and supplies the customer's fashion needs by regularly discontinuing old lines and introducing new ones, using fashion icons such as sports stars to endorse the products and using distinctive logos to make their products stand out from the competition.

> **Think it over**
>
> Reread the section above on sports clothing. Why do you think manufacturers like Nike and Adidas decided to link their products with fashion? How might this have resulted in higher sales?

Organisational cultures

It is interesting to note how different organisations develop cultures which influence the way they market themselves. Here are some examples.

Market-led culture

Many companies in the leisure and recreation industry have what is known as a *market-led* culture. This means the values, systems and operations of the company are based around the principle that if you supply customers with what they want, then the business will be successful. In such companies there will be great emphasis on customer care, marketing and market research. Staff are encouraged to value the customer and all departments within the organisation are encouraged to think how their actions help the customer. For example, the accounts department will not send threatening payment letters but, instead, advise the customer that they are passing the transaction to a debt agency.

Cost-led culture

An example of a *cost-led* culture is when schools let their halls to outside user groups such as sports clubs. Often they will simply

Traditionally, local government has been a cost-led culture

work out what it costs to run the hall (e.g. heating, caretaker time) and add a percentage on to it and charge that as a hire price, regardless of what local clubs are charging. In a poorer area this means there would be little use, while in a richer area the school could charge more. This approach shows an accountancy or *cost-led* culture.

One of the problems that faces small visitor attractions in established holiday areas is that they are based on the tradition that tourists always turn up and, because of the lack of competition, will invariably visit the attraction not because of its quality and enjoyment value, but because there is nothing else to do. These attractions have come to be seen as 'nice little earners' and operate on a basis of minimising costs (low-paid staff often have less pride in their work, tatty décor spoils the customer experience).

Local government traditionally has been a cost-led culture and officers have often been judged on their ability to keep within expenditure limits rather than maximise profits. Although there are an increasing number of exceptions,

many local authority leisure facilities do not maximise the customer experience because of a lack of investment.

Product-led cultures

This is where there is a belief that the product itself will be sufficient to sell and that there should be an emphasis on achieving high standards and specifications for the product. The attitude towards customers tends to be that they should consider themselves fortunate to have access to such a wonderful product – and indeed this may be a selling point for customers who relish gadgetry or the elitism of having 'the best'. Customer care and after-sales service is often poor. On the fringe of the leisure industry, computers and electrical entertainment products such as video cameras, digital cameras, radios and TV will often suffer from being product-led. For example, many computer adverts dwell on technical specifications and anyone who has spent hours on an expensive technical support line will

There are still some areas of the leisure industry where a product-led culture operates

know that after-sales service can be so poor that it deters you from buying again from the firm.

There are still some swimming pools where managers are more concerned about the technical aspects of the pool such as water quality rather than how customers use the pool. There used to be a standing joke where a manager would look at the empty sparkling pool and say 'it's a pity the customers are going to mess it up'. Such a view is reflected in brochures for pools and other facilities. If the photograph shows an empty but sparkling pool rather than happy customers, it is likely that a *product-led* culture is operating.

Traditionally, libraries have been examples of organisationally led cultures but are now moving towards making their services more suited to the needs of the market

Organisationally led cultures

Some organisations are *organisationally led.* This is where the product is marketed to suit the needs and system of the organisation and its staff. In the fitness industry and swimming pools, there is often a sizeable number of customers who want to use the facilities early or late in the day. Similarly, there may be a demand for single-sex sessions. It is not unknown for some managers to resist such a demand because of the inconvenience or because they don't believe in the principle. Some gyms may reflect a macho image of 'grunt and sweat' to attract a male rather than a female market. Similarly, in the public sector, Councils may set a political policy that actually goes against market-led forces. They will insist that prices are kept low even though customers would be prepared to pay more. They are perhaps more likely, these days, to insist that sports services make a profit. If so, participation by poorer individuals and groups will be restricted.

Local authorities are often organisationally led and one aspect of this has been the complex negotiated system of extra pay for overtime and unsocial hours. Until the 1990s, the cost of working to suit market needs was

prohibitive. Compulsory Competitive Tendering (CCT) broke this mould when it was realised that, to be competitive, staff would have to be prepared to work without enhanced payments. Libraries, although traditionally organisationally led cultures, are now moving towards making their services more suited to the needs of the market. Despite limited funding, which in the past has meant that opening hours often didn't meet the needs of the public, many libraries are now seeking to make opening hours sensitive to the needs of users. Public libraries are increasingly opening on Sundays and evenings. The London Borough of Sutton was the first library service to introduce Sunday opening in the mid-1990s.

Private gentleman's clubs such as White's, Boodle's and the Reform Club were formed in the 18th century and maintenance of traditions is important to their often white, male, upper-class membership. In the modern world the market has different needs. Women and people from ethnic minorities wish to join, men are less formal than they were and values have changed in society as a whole. Such clubs frequently find themselves in the dilemma of 'not changing and keeping existing members' or 'changing to attract new members but at the risk of losing their old ones'.

Artistic policy will often drive the repertoire of the smaller performing arts groups to provide challenging work for the audience. While admirable in challenging the blandness and conventionality of mainstream arts, it often means the product attracts only a small market.

Sales-led cultures

Sales-led cultures are ones where sales are all-important. Companies tend to overmarket their products, making claims that will not be substantiated. They may also have poor after-sales service and focus on persuading the customer to buy the product without assessing their needs or means. The caravan industry has been prone to this. Maximum profits can often be made by high-pressured selling of caravans which often ignores the customers' needs and how much they can afford. Needless to say, this can produce unsatisfied customers who feel they have lost out and will not buy again. This situation has been recognised by the industry itself as being poor practice and dealers are increasingly taking a marketing rather than a sales-led stance.

> **Think it over**
>
> Working in pairs, identify a local leisure organisation in your area. Decide what type of culture it has; is it organisationally or market led? Suggest at least two examples to support your decision.

Taking an integrated marketing approach

If an organisation adopts the marketing culture it will be most successful if all departments are involved and adopt the same view. This is called *integrated marketing*. In some organisations that have a market-led culture this is achieved by allowing the marketing

department to control things. A good example of this is the reliance by some organisations and companies on spin doctors to influence the customer.

This approach may have limited success because the marketing department will soon act in a vacuum. It is far better for all departments to have a belief in supplying the needs of the market and work with each other to make sure that there is a seamless fit. This is *integrated marketing.* Departments such as frontline services, sales, production and personnel will all work together to ensure that

> ## Some key marketing terms
>
> Marketing uses a language that can cause confusion. Here are some definitions:
>
> - **market:** the population you will offer your product to
> - **marketplace:** the environment in which rival organisations compete (this is often an abstract concept like 'Cool Britannia' or 'Virtual retailing' but may be a real location such as a resort town where leisure providers compete for the visitor market)
> - **marketing:** the process of matching products to the market
> - **customers:** the people from the market who consume your product
> - **promotion:** the process of communicating with the market
> - **a promotion:** a technique used in the short term to attract the market
> - **product:** the package of goods and services presented to the market (product can mean the material aspect of the product as opposed to the service aspect)
> - **market share:** the percentage of all sales achieved by any one company
> - **market segment:** groups within the market with distinctive consumer behaviour and attitudes.

the customer is getting what has been designed and 'promised' to them. If, for example, a marketing department is promoting a discount scheme for a fitness centre, the reception staff will need to be fully aware of it so as to tell the customers and assess whether the scheme will suit their needs. For example, 'Well Sir, given that you intend to use the gym during the day you will probably find that our standard off-peak membership will work out cheaper than the discount scheme.' In return the marketing department needs to know from reception whether the customer thought the promotion met their needs or whether there was other information that would affect their marketing strategy. In this example, price may not concern the customer but the provision of 'Well-being' classes might influence their decision to join.

Try it out	1	Define marketing in your own words.
	2	Give an example of one kind of organisational culture. Describe the culture.
	3	How can organisations integrate marketing?

Setting marketing objectives (planning)

In a market-led culture, the first step is to know the customers and understand their needs. Once the customer's needs are recognised and understood, then an organisation can set about fulfilling those needs by developing a marketing strategy. For a full analysis of the processes involved in researching customer needs, see the section on **market research** (page 243).

As with all business, marketing requires systematic planning that:

1 identifies corporate aims and objectives

2 analyses the organisation, its market and the world it exists in (the internal and external environment)

3 develops marketing objectives and plans.

Firstly, we will look at aims and objectives:

1 Missions, aims and objectives

Modern organisations are governed by their 'mission' – this means the purpose of the organisation's existence. Here are some sample mission statements that apply to leisure and recreation:

Some mission statements

- 'to improve the quality of life for the people of South Park' (local government)

- 'to show people their dreams' (film company)

- 'to let young people realise their full potential' (outdoor activities).

While there is only one mission for the entire organisation, there is a hierarchy of aims, objectives, targets and tasks that will be created at all levels within an organisation. At each stage these become more precisely defined and focused on individual workers or smaller teams, each of whom will be making their own contribution to the overall mission. Thus, a recreation assistant who is given the task of leafleting door to door in South Park is making a small but important contribution to improving the 'quality of life for the residents'.

At the top of this hierarchy there is a series of *aims* which will generally indicate the markets and type of provision that will achieve the mission. With the South Park example above, Figure 4.1 shows two possible aims.

Aims are normally defined by the use of a verb that denotes intent (to change, to achieve, to

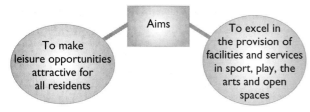

Figure 4.1 Two aims for the South Park example

dominate, to become, to make). The end result of a successful aim is a *goal* which is what you will have done to achieve that aim. If you want to excel in sport as an organisation then your goal may be to 'develop nationally successful sports clubs', if you want to make leisure opportunities available, your goal may be to 'provide new facilities and services'.

Next there is a need to define the *objectives* for the aims and their goals. These state specifically what is needed to achieve an aim. These are usually defined by doing verbs (to provide, to achieve).

To achieve a goal will mean involving numerous departments or processes. When building a new facility, architects would design the building, financial managers would have to make decisions about raising funds, the marketing department would have to find out what the local people wanted from the facility and personnel would have to recruit and train staff. In other words, for a goal to be achieved, numerous groups of people have to work in harmony pursuing their own set of objectives. Very often people work in their own work groups to achieve their goals but sometimes they will ask other groups to contribute. In the previous example, the marketing manager may ask the architect to take on board the results of a focus group.

Another feature of objectives is that they are serial. This means that the outcomes have to be achieved before moving on to the next stage. Thus, if you have a final objective of providing a sports hall, you will need to design it, contract a builder, then build and equip it.

A marketing department might hold focus groups to find out what the market would want from a new facility and its services

None of these objectives can be achieved without first doing the one before it.

SMART objectives

To be successful an objective has to be SMART:

Specific: It is well defined. 'To build a four-court sports hall with gym and 25 m pool' is better than 'build a sports hall'.

Measurable: You need to be able to measure an objective if you are to know whether you have achieved it. The measures you decide upon to signify you have achieved your objective are called *targets*. Objectives like sports halls and sales are easy to measure. More abstract concepts like 'all the residents of South Park' may require more thought.

Achievable: Can an objective be achieved with the time and resources available? To build a sports hall based on Lottery funding within a year is not possible because of the time it takes to process a Lottery bid.

Realistic: Will the objective achieve the goal? If the people of South Park are interested only in swimming, building a sports hall will not be a realistic objective.

Time-bound: An objective must be tied into being completed by a given time.

SMART objectives are:

Specific
Measurable
Achievable
Realistic
Time-bound.

The role of marketing in business planning

The contribution marketing will make to the achievement of corporate goals and objectives will be identified by producing a marketing plan (Figure 4.2). The aim of any plan is to allow you to make informed decisions about where you need to go and with this in mind, the exact method you use does not matter too much.

Malcolm McDonald (1995) describes a straightforward marketing planning process in the flow chart below (Figure 4.2). Let us look at the main stages. An understanding of these will help you organise your own marketing activities when you come to do your project in 'Leisure in Action'.

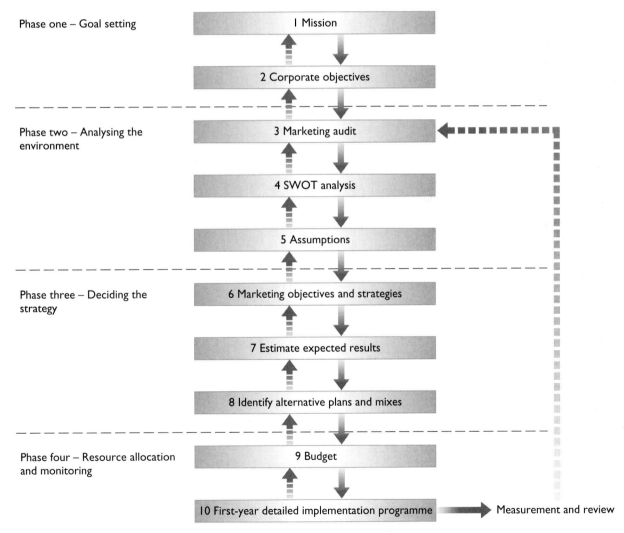

Phase one – Goal setting
1 Mission
2 Corporate objectives

Phase two – Analysing the environment
3 Marketing audit
4 SWOT analysis
5 Assumptions

Phase three – Deciding the strategy
6 Marketing objectives and strategies
7 Estimate expected results
8 Identify alternative plans and mixes

Phase four – Resource allocation and monitoring
9 Budget
10 First-year detailed implementation programme → Measurement and review

Adapted from McDonald, Marketing Plans, How to Prepare Them: How to Use Them, 1995. Reproduced with permission.

Figure 4.2   The process of marketing planning

Phase one – Goal setting

Marketing needs to satisfy both the market needs and those of the organisation. It would make no sense if Alton Towers or Sky TV, whose primary objective is to make a profit, drastically underpriced their products. Whilst it would win a huge market share, it would also fail to make a profit. However, for a local authority committed to providing recreation to those ratepayers who cannot afford the private sector, it could legitimately provide subsidies and perhaps run at a loss.

Therefore, the first step in the plan is to identify what your organisation is trying to achieve and how it intends to do this. In many organisations this will already have been developed and written down. In smaller businesses it may simply be in the owner's head.

Phase two – Analysing the environment

At this stage it would be normal to carry out an **audit** of:

a   the organisation or internal environment
b   the external environment.

The purpose of this is to obtain the information you know you will need to make good decisions about marketing.

a   For **the organisation** you need to know:

- the company profile
- the resources available in house or from outside suppliers such as advertising agencies
- the state of products and services – are staff customer-friendly?
- organisation – do front-line staff get briefed on the company's mission?
- communications such as PR
- sales and market share data
- sales and marketing procedures
- distribution procedures.

b   The **external environment** refers to:

- the market: its location and profile, trends in consumer behaviour and expectations, customer research
- competition: Who are the competitors? What is their size? What are their methods and operations? What are their strengths and weaknesses?
- the environment the organisation operates in: particularly legal, social and cultural features and technology (e.g. health and safety legislation, advertising standards, trends towards women making spending decisions, and the development of smart card technology).

Using SWOT

At this point you have all the information about the organisation and the world it operates in. You need to be able to analyse and summarise the implications of what this means in terms of marketing. The standard management tool for this is SWOT (Figure 4.3) and this section looks at a simplified method of carrying out this analysis.

The purpose of SWOT is to find out what is causing success or failure in competing in and meeting the needs of your market. Your answers will focus on the objectives and a strategy that will improve your performance.

It is a simple model that often has powerful effects.

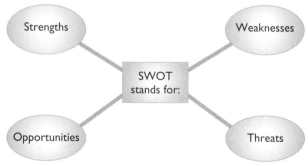

Figure 4.3 Definition of SWOT

CASE STUDY – A SWOT analysis

Many local authorities have taken the political decision to increase leisure participation in older age groups. In many cases, their main tactic was to provide leisure concessions (e.g. leisure cards) for certain groups such as pensioners, on the assumption that pensioners are poor and that cost is a factor acting against their participation. Many centre managers in more affluent communities noticed little change in uptake. The more astute of them who knew their communities, undertook SWOT analyses to find better ways to deliver the Council's goals.

They could see that in affluent areas there was no real financial need and therefore the so-called strength of effective pricing that included leisure cards was in fact irrelevant. As one manager said 'The first ones to use the leisure cards were the ones with the Jaguars and the Volvos, who have been coming here for years.' Discussions between staff indicated that the real needs of their market were:

- a warm environment, especially in pools
- activities that were scheduled for daylight hours
- activities that avoided pension days
- swimming sessions that excluded children and teenagers
- a quiet environment
- good lighting and paths
- many people felt the centre didn't meet their needs and was not for them.

Strengths and weaknesses
A strength was that the manager was a well-respected local person with good networks in the community. The action point here is that it would be relatively easy to set up consultation groups with the local elderly population which could accurately identify needs and involve the market in developing better means to supply these.

A weakness in provision was that the programming was based largely on function rather than needs. For example, 'over-50' activities were put into empty spaces in the programme rather than at times when they were wanted. The programming was also unimaginative, with the same product being offered to all people at all times.

It was also felt that the centre was youth-dominated with most staff being under 25 years of age.

Finally, it was felt that the centre was weak in promoting itself and relied on a strong base of local customers who were already aware of what the centre offered. As for the rest of the market, they thought the centre was for young sporty types only.

After consultation, the action points that were decided on were:

- to alter radically the programming and improve the physical environment. 'Over-50 only' sessions were introduced, where piped music was turned off. The pool temperature was brought up a couple of degrees (at the end of the week) and new sessions were introduced at convenient times
- to launch a promotional campaign aimed at the older market that emphasised the comfort and social benefits of using the centre
- to employ some more mature staff, especially when there were 'over-50s' sessions on.

As you can see, SWOT resulted in totally different and more effective marketing objectives than the original programme of promoting leisure cards which no one really appreciated.

CASE STUDY – A SWOT analysis (cont)

Questions

1 Why did some local authorities introduce leisure cards?

2 Why did this strategy fail to expand leisure participation among the over-50s?

3 What were the key results of the SWOT analysis?

4 How did SWOT show that the leisure card approach was not the best strategy?

5 Can you suggest other ways that local authorities could have adapted to meet changing customer needs?

You need to ask certain key questions such as:

- who is the market?
- what does the market want in terms of the marketing mix?
- to what extent do we supply this?
- to what extent do our competitors supply this?
- what are we good at doing?
- what are we poor at doing?
- how do we compare with our competitors?

These questions largely focus on the strengths and weaknesses of the organisation in its current state and often refer to issues such as adequacy and availability of resources, sales methods, quality of service, market domination, customer and staff loyalty, research and development, the market mix, innovation, image, and brand strength.

You should aim to identify about five key issues which you feel would most improve the performance of your organisation if you took action on them.

You may arrive at this answer by simply comparing your list of what the market wants with what you are offering and seeing if there is a gap.

Another way to arrive at your answer is by noting where your competitors are matching needs and supplying them more appropriately – the lesson here is to copy them and do it better. Another option is to note what your competitors are doing less well than you and

to increase your performance in that area – this is playing to your strengths. The lesson here is that by managing a key issue better than they do you will attract their market segment.

The second stage of SWOT is to look at threats and opportunities which may arise in the future. They will come from:

Internal pressures (e.g. organisational structure, resistance to change, levels of morale, funding).

External pressures

- The business environment (e.g. changing markets, state of competition)
- Environmental pressures (e.g. legislation, economic change, technology and resources, changes in market behaviour and attitude).

PEST analysis

Analysis of the external pressures is often called PEST analysis (Figure 4.4).

It is used to analyse external pressures affecting opportunities and threats.

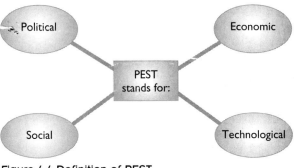

Figure 4.4 Definition of PEST

Many marketeers now include:

Environmental pressures (e.g. pollution, erosion, health).

You now should ask some different questions:

- how do threats and opportunities affect the market need?
- how do threats and opportunities affect your ability to supply the market?
- how and when are you going to respond to change?
- how and when is the competition likely to respond to change?
- how do your strengths and weaknesses affect your ability to respond?

Again, you should identify only up to five key issues that will allow you to take advantage of opportunities and avoid threats more effectively than the competition.

Managing a SWOT session

Handling this information can be confusing; the following method can make it easier.

The planning group brainstorms using SWOT categories. Every suggestion is taken on board and recorded on the top line of one of four grids (one for each category) or alternatively it could be for each question. It is a good idea to put the grid on a flipchart or board so that everyone can see.

When ideas are running out the brainstorming is stopped, and each member of the group is asked to rank or score each suggestion. A scoring system might be 5 – very important – to 1 – unimportant. The names of the contributors are written in the left-hand column of the matrix and the scores entered under the suggestions they and the others have made.

At this stage there should be many more suggestions than can be dealt with. The group has to decide a strategy to reduce them down into the key issues. A simple way is to add up the scores and select the five with the highest totals.

Try it out Take a facility or service you know well, for example, a local sports centre (you may or may not be a customer). Now analyse the strengths and weaknesses of the centre with the aim of attracting the market that you represent. Come up with action points/objectives and practical ways you could achieve these.

If you want to compare your organisation with others, then a grid like the one below may be useful.

Using SWOT and PEST in marketing plans

The SWOT analysis will by now have produced a series of action points or objectives that will be the targets of marketing in its contribution to achieving the overall corporate goals which were

Key issue	Our company (Market share 15%)	Company 1 (Market share 30%)	Company 2 (Market share 25%)	Company 3 (Market share 20%)	Company 4 (Market share 10%)
Prices too high	£350 annual fee	£420 direct debit	£450 direct debit	£300	£100
Customer service	Very good	Very good	Poor	Good	Very good
After-sales service	Good	Poor	Poor	Poor	Good
Company image	Undeveloped	High profile	High profile	Good	Negative
Up-to-date equipment	Good	Good	Very good	Good	Poor

Table 4.1 Example of a grid for comparing Winners Health Club's strengths and weaknesses following SWOT analysis

Using the analysis above for Winners, a Health and Fitness Club (Table 4.1), the SWOT results might read:

Our assessment of the market showed the following key issues:

Price: Annual membership appeared to have some effect, but the crucial element appears to be monthly direct debiting options.

Action point: Review pricing and payment options.

Customer service: This is fairly important and it is our greatest strength.

Action point: Continue to maintain and improve customer service.

After-sales service: This does not appear significant even though it is one of our strengths.

Action point: No review needed.

Company image: The major competitors are chain companies with powerful promotion and branding. We are weak in this area and feel we cannot copy their success here. However, we are aware that the local market responds well to locally run businesses.

Action point: Develop the company's image by improved promotion based on the theme of local business for local people.

Equipment: The market wants reasonably up-to-date equipment. We are moderately strong here.

Action point: Continue current renewal programme.

PEST analysis can be performed and written up in the same way. The data behind each statement is not given because one of the points of a good SWOT analysis is that it can be read and understood by people outside the analysis group. The following results are also based on the imaginary world in which Winners Health Club operates.

Political: It is felt likely that the Government will introduce statutory controls on the use of qualified fitness instructors. Eighty per cent of our instructors are qualified already. Company 4 has no trained instructors and will probably 'go under'.

Action point: Ensure our staff are qualified and prepare a promotional campaign focused on the customers of Company 4.

Economic: Hogan Homes is building 800 up-market houses in the area next year.

Action point: Link up with Hogan Homes to provide a free trial membership scheme as a welcome pack to new home owners.

Social: National Health surveys show that overweight, middle-aged people are put off from using health clubs and are an untapped market.

Action Point: Prepare a research project to show whether attracting this market would cause a fall away of existing members.

Technological: Anti-gravity trainers are now being marketed in the USA. They are very expensive and our competitors will be investing in them. They will be a market winner.

Action point: Investigate funding options to make this investment.

identified at the start of the planning process. Obviously the marketing objectives will vary according to SWOT, but the following are examples of some typical objectives:

In the private sector, companies often take a profit-led view. Typically the corporate aims (and their accompanying objectives) for the organisation as a whole might be:

- to achieve a specific market share
- to penetrate new markets
- to eliminate competition
- to achieve an increase in sales.

While there are many public and voluntary providers that take a similar view, political and social aims often play a part:

- inclusion of all sectors of the community
- development of excellence in competition and performance
- provision of facilities not provided by the private sector
- reduction of net expenditure.

Phase three – Deciding the strategy

You are now in a position to take each of the marketing objectives in turn and develop a strategy (plan) to achieve it. As with all plans it needs to be SMART. This means you need to take account of the resources open to you in the form of:

- human resources – who can do the job?
- physical resources
- finance
- time available.

The marketing plan will often consist of the following sections, each in turn with its own objectives, targets and tasks:

- communication (promotional) plan
- pricing plan
- distribution and sales plan
- product plan.

Communication plan

This will contain:

- what you hope to gain from communication (e.g. awareness, loyalty, transferred custom)
- the audience (market segment, buyers and consumers within the segment)
- communication methods that will be used

- where communication will occur
- timing (total time, phasing of different aspects of the programme)
- budget.

It is important that the plan links communication used in promoting the product to that used for selling it. How often do you set out to buy a product you are dying for, after having seen it advertised, only to be told by a sales assistant that it is rubbish and the one she had fell to pieces the first time it was used?

In many cases you will want to train sales staff, have suitable sales points and information displays, and ensure that sales and promotional information tell the same story. In many leisure facilities the operational staff are the sales staff and need to be trained just as much as the reception staff. This again is the integrated marketing approach.

Pricing plan

Price can be affected by factors such as competition, costs, value, and product life cycle. Factors like this will give a range of prices from which the organisation can trade successfully in a given market segment. Overall you need to know the pricing strategy or what you are trying to achieve through pricing. For example, if you need to *penetrate* an existing market to capture a market share from the competition, then you would enter the market at the lower end of the price range.

An alternative strategy might be to *skim* the market and enter the market at the higher end of the range. The reasons for doing this might include:

- demand is not being supplied by the competition
- there is not strong customer loyalty to the competition
- demand is not price-sensitive
- the capacity of the provider is low, with a limited customer level.

Distribution and sales plan

In many industries distribution is a major component in the marketing process. It means that goods need to arrive at the sales point in a fresh and marketable condition. In the leisure industry, it is primarily about where to locate the facility.

However, if you take the view that the satisfied customer is your product, then you must consider how to get the customer through their leisure experience in a marketable condition. For example, one of the main aims of an arena concert promoter is to tap into the network of tour companies that provide all-inclusive transport, accommodation and ticket deals. Such deals need to get the fans to the arena in a fresh state (happy and comfortable) just as much as the band needs to be able to play when it goes on stage. The situation is analogous to how a supermarket gets fresh produce (e.g. cabbages) from all over the country by taking it to distribution depots (warehouses) and then transporting it to the sales point (supermarket). In the case of the concert promoter, the fresh produce is the fans, the distribution depots are the coach stop and the sales point is the arena.

When they get to the arena there is the whole question of audience handling which aims to get the rock fans on to the seats in a fresh condition. This might include a rapid transport system from the car park to the arena, friendly helpful reception staff, low-profile security and reasonably priced merchandising and catering.

At a less glamorous level, an outdoor activity centre has to plan how customers will get from their homes to the centre and then from the centre to the outdoor environment.

Booking

Another aspect of distribution peculiar to industries such as leisure is booking. In many cases, such as events or where membership is required, the sales transaction may take place at a different time and place from the activity itself. How do you get tickets to customers, ensure that there is no overbooking, and ensure that they can book when they want? In other words the booking distribution system may be different from the distribution of the product. In some activities this can be a major logistical challenge. For example, booking agencies will take blocks of tickets to sell on. If these sales are not monitored, underbooking can take place if sales in one agency are low. Measures then have to be taken to transfer those tickets to agencies where demand is high.

Capacity

Capacity is also an important factor in leisure and the distribution plan needs to ensure that customers get the service they want when they want it. Currently salsa classes are popular community education courses and are often held in classrooms or gyms which are lacking the right atmosphere. They are often heavily oversubscribed, which means lost and disappointed markets. Perhaps a better distribution plan would be to do a deal with local nightclubs (with their large capacities and better atmosphere) and run the classes early in the evening before the club starts.

In leisure, packaging is about how staff and buildings are presented, rather than how products are wrapped. Distribution plans involve packaging as well. Do the staff reflect the company and product image? In many leisure activities staff should have attractive personalities, good personal appearance and adopt the dress code of the company. Premises should be inviting, clean and attractive. Packaging is not just about looks, other senses can be involved. Many traditional sports participants enjoy the locker room smell of liniment and other typical smells, but many new customers prefer fresher aromas such as citrus and pine that suggest cleanliness and nature. Saunas are more popular with certain

Capacity is an important factor in leisure. Popular community education classes are often held in rooms or halls lacking the right atmosphere

scents in the steam. For cinema-goers, the sound of the theme music and the advertisements add to the anticipation of the film starting, while many fitness freaks would grind to a halt without MTV.

Sales plans are often not well developed in leisure because marketing has often made the sale, and sales merely concern issuing a ticket. This in itself is not a simple process as you will see in the unit on customer service.

Where selling is required, the sales plan will need to consider:

- the most appropriate sales style
- the location for selling (on premises, at the customer's home)
- sales procedures and administration
- sales presentation (leaflets, demonstrations, information, video samples)
- selling points.

Selling points are worth a special mention. These are the features of the product and service that most meet the customers' needs and which will most serve to persuade the customer to use the product. Selling points don't just appear at the sales stage. As a result of market research, they will have been thought of and integrated into the:

- price (payment by direct debit spreads the financial load)

- product (the use of sweat-absorbent materials such as latex foam on fitness equipment)
- place (out-of-town cinemas make it easy to park near the entrance).

They will also be stressed throughout the promotion (e.g. exclusive offers for limited periods only, such as half-price membership).

These points will be identified in the sales report. In particular there are USPs (unique selling points). These are selling points that are unique to that organisation or which are substantially stronger than that of the competition.

USPs are important not only in helping make a sale; if they are truly unique, they will justify a higher price being charged.

Having a USP is a valuable sales tool and companies have to defend it strongly. For example, if you have made a claim in your sales information that you are the market leader and you lose that lead, then not only have you got the cost of redesigning your sales and promotional materials which would

Endorsement by role models is often used as a USP

now be erroneous and therefore illegal, but you also have the embarrassment of explaining to a shrewd customer why you have lost a USP.

Product plan

The planning process will often identify where the product can be improved. Improvement and change are key factors in the industry. As you have seen, they are important in prolonging the life-cycle, reflecting changes in customer needs and fashions and keeping ahead of the competition. Even something as traditional as Sunday morning football can be improved by having better changing facilities and spending more on pitch maintenance. The input of the Football Foundation's millions of pounds to be used for improving grassroots soccer will no doubt prove this point.

Examples of Unique Selling Points (USPs)

Lowest price: Many health clubs use this.

Best after-sales services: Hawkshead offers lifelong replacement guarantees on some walking boots

Own technology: Zzig tennis racquets produce soft-ball racquets (of their own invention) for children.

Endorsements by role models: Cotton Traders endorse the national rugby team.

Staff quality: Personal trainers rely on being highly trained and up to date.

Facilities: Plas y Brenin would claim to have the best natural climbing coupled with state-of-the-art equipment.

Reputation: Many firms will have USPs that stress that they have been trading a long time or that they are the market leader.

Status: Holme Pierrepont stresses that it is the National Rowing Centre, Blackpool Pleasure Beach claims (in 2000) to have the best roller-coaster in the UK.

Exclusiveness/snobbery: Many golf and country clubs restrict their membership to a certain kind of customer. A lot of mail shots and telephone selling emphasises that you have been specially chosen.

Performance: Most sports equipment is sold by emphasising how it will help the player play better. For example, the 'sweet spot' in a tennis racquet.

Technical specification: In some cases, high standards of technical specification are an important USP. Artificial turf manufacturers will go to great lengths to supply details and performance measure (bounce coefficient) about their product's performance.

Design: It's not what it does but what it looks like that often persuades us to buy one product over another. In the diving world, the use of colourful fashion design for wet-suits and equipment has appealed especially to female divers.

Try it out Identify two contrasting leisure products, for example a theme park and a piece of sports equipment. For each one write down 3 USPs.

Product life also affects product planning. A good manager will be able to forecast the likely decline of an activity and replace it with other services. A good example is the conversion of squash courts to gyms, quiet rooms or play centres.

In marketing it is assumed that products will be packaged and promoted over a period of time. Many leisure providers will plan ahead, change their products and package their attributes. For example, a sports centre will often have a seasonal, promotional showing of its new products to customers, such as 'spring into summer with a host of new courses plus your old favourites'.

Presenting the plan

The final plan is usually a short document as managers tend to prefer short documents. It briefly summarises the findings of the audit and highlights issues that are extremely important or problematical. It defines the product to be marketed and the profile of the markets it is to be aimed at.

The bulk of the plan consists of an overall marketing summary that looks at the strategy, aims, objectives and targets for marketing the product. Following this, there are separate subplans also with aims, objectives and targets. Each subplan also provides specific tasks of how the objectives are to be attained, such as a door-to-door leafleting campaign to 1,000 local households or provision of 6 new computerised cardiovascular stations.

Check it out

1 What is a mission statement? Identify one for an organisation you know well.
2 Why are objectives SMART?
3 Why are objectives fixed?
4 What does a marketing audit do?
5 What is the purpose of SWOT?
6 Look at the PEST analysis and identify threats and opportunities.
7 What are the four components of the marketing plan?

4.2 The marketing mix

A market is made up of actual or potential buyers and the people selling the goods to meet the buyers' needs. A market requires a process of exchange between buyers and sellers. This is called '**the marketing mix**' (Figure 4.5).

The building blocks of the marketing mix are the Four Ps:

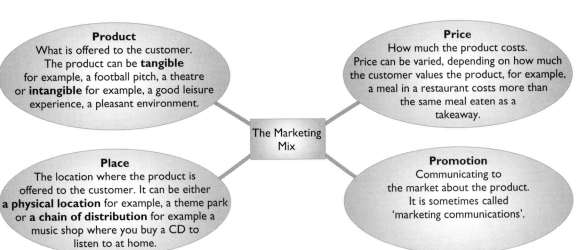

Product
What is offered to the customer. The product can be **tangible** for example, a football pitch, a theatre or **intangible** for example, a good leisure experience, a pleasant environment.

Price
How much the product costs. Price can be varied, depending on how much the customer values the product, for example, a meal in a restaurant costs more than the same meal eaten as a takeaway.

Place
The location where the product is offered to the customer. It can be either **a physical location** for example, a theme park or **a chain of distribution** for example a music shop where you buy a CD to listen to at home.

Promotion
Communicating to the market about the product. It is sometimes called 'marketing communications'.

The Marketing Mix

Figure 4.5 The marketing mix

- product
- price
- place
- promotion.

Marketing theorists differ on the components to the mix. We have focused on four but you may come across other writers who also include:

- branding
- distribution
- packaging
- selling
- display
- servicing
- communications and information seeking.

You should also be aware of the role of competition. Competition is the spark that sets the mix alight. If you find a product the market wants and you are the sole provider, then you can probably do a variety of things to maximise your profits. You can keep it in short supply and thus be able to charge more for it; you can make cuts to the product costs; or you can increase your price until you have taken the market as high as it can go.

A *competitive market* is characterised by many traders dividing the market, with frequent entries and exits from the marketplace as they succeed or fail in the competition for sales. After a flurry of activity the marketplace settles down and it is found that it can accommodate a few traders who will normally continue to compete heavily for the market.

Not surprisingly, traders would like to remove competition. One way they do this is to enter trade agreements with the governing bodies for the market. For example the Governing Body of a sport might recognise only one brand of equipment for its events, or traders can try to control the sources of raw materials and so stop other companies manufacturing the product.

Product, place, price and promotion in the leisure industry

Product

1 *The input model*

One way of defining the product is in terms of what you put into it. This is called '**the input model**' (Figure 4.6). In a service industry the input model divides the product into *tangible* and *non-tangible* products.

Tangible (can be touched): These are materials, for example, a stadium, a theatre, the seats in them, lockers or showers. Since tangible products are physical they have certain properties:

- products can be seen and handled by the customer before purchase and can be easily measured
- products last over time
- customers gets the same product every time they purchase it
- the product can be stocked ready for use.

These characteristics give tangible products an advantage in that customers can easily assess how they like them, while providers can monitor and check deterioration, and designers can adapt them to suit customer needs.

Non-tangible (can't be touched): In leisure, customers participate or are involved in the leisure experience itself. To provide the best experience we need to add a non-tangible component to the tangible one. This means providing:

- services
- good staff attitude and behaviour
- ambience or atmosphere created by the interaction of physical products, customers and the natural and built environment.

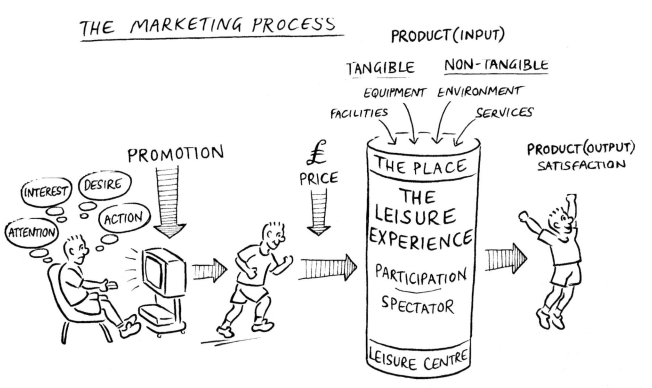

Figure 4.6 The production process – input model

For example, a well-designed leisure facility will have a welcoming, clean reception area with good lighting, plants and seats. It will be designed so that the customer has minimal waiting time and there is clear information about prices and directions. All these non-tangible products enrich the service and reduce stress or inconvenience to the customer. They make the customer feel valued.

The non-tangible product is largely about experience and feeling. Since customers and circumstances are constantly changing, the product has to continually adapt.

In the leisure industry the non-tangible product is vitally important and we normally provide the tangible products combined with a complex variety of non-tangible products. These include:

- customer handling and care (reception, queuing, complaints, hosting)
- cleaning, safety and maintenance practices
- management of the environment (heating, lighting, music, décor)
- information services (notices, telephones, e-mail, fax, staff expertise)
- specialised services for (families, infants, elderly, disabled, unisex, beauty and sports therapy)
- access management (car parks, public transport access, disabled access)
- security services (CCTV, guards)
- recreational services (competitions, leagues, modified games such as short

Think it over

You are a customer at the following entertainments:

- a rock concert in an arena
- a romantic meal in a restaurant
- the final basketball competition in a sports hall.

Identify some important tangible and non-tangible features that will make your customer experience a good one. Suggest the form in which the management could provide for these features.

tennis, wheelchair basketball, fitness induction)
- privilege (membership packages, loyalty schemes, leisure passports, special offers).

Try it out

A male customer at your sports centre wants to take up an aerobic sport or activity. List the product requirements (tangible and non-tangible) that would make his experience fully enjoyable.

As a customer, you may take such services for granted but in any well-marketed leisure facility they will be adapted and designed to give the greatest possible satisfaction to the customer. Remember that because customer needs vary, these services are not always the same for different facilities and services. For instance, professional boxing gyms may have fairly shabby facilities, with only basic equipment because aspiring boxers value the expertise of the coaching staff more. In contrast, users of a prestige health club will be looking for luxury and a minimum of inconvenience. At a rock concert lighting and sound effects and the quality of the band are all-important in providing the right atmosphere for the audience.

In the same way services can differ within one facility. In a sports centre, it is likely that the staff will be adapting their service to accommodate different types of customer groups and even individuals. On a Saturday morning, recreation assistants might be welcoming small children for a play session, and in the evening they may be putting on bow-ties and waistcoats to welcome the audience to a performance of a travelling theatre company that has rigged a stage in the main hall.

What are the tangible and non-tangible products at the Bluewater Centre?

The product also depends upon the interaction of staff with the customers and will change with individual disposition. If the customer is feeling good, a light-hearted welcome by the receptionist is fine. If the customer has had a bad day the same comment will be seen as sarcastic and rude.

The key point is that to be really successful, marketing has to be integrated. There is no point in promoting a product such as a friendly women-only swimming session if the staff are not friendly and aware to the needs of such a group.

The output model

The most successful leisure providers view the product in terms of an *output model*. They regard the tangible and non-tangible products mentioned above as two raw products which they mix with another raw product – the customer. Mixing these with participation or spectating by the expectant customer produces the final product – a satisfied customer.

Thought for the page

The leisure industry has helped pioneer the output model. For many years marketing was concerned with tangible manufactured goods. Even ten years ago it was hard to find texts on marketing services. The success of the output model has meant that manufacturers and other service industries are learning from our success. In the USA companies are now into 'total marketing', which goes beyond marketing to actually extending the scope of the product to meet needs.

To take an example, a breakdown company will assess the customer's needs and then service these as well as the breakdown. Thus, they will arrange a replacement car, provide blankets, coffee or food for the customer, and will try to turn a stressful experience into one of least possible discomfort and inconvenience. The company's *mission* is to 'save the customer from the perils of breakdown' and not 'to sell breakdown cover'.

This model has powerful advantages over the traditional input model:

- It concentrates attention on making sure the customers get what they really want. This is often a non-tangible outcome such as making friends, feeling good and affluent.
- Focus as to what makes the customer use the product, and then this information can be used to help us promote the product. For example, advertisements that simply show the facilities and use slogans like 'Why not come to' or 'First class facilities' are often far less attractive than those that use atmospheric pictures of customers enjoying the experience and words like 'Pamper yourself' or 'Have the experience of a lifetime'.
- It is a reminder of the corporate aim – 'We create customers' and not 'We provide pools'. It means staff need to note and think about *how* they have satisfied the customer rather than simply trusting that the provision of raw ingredients will provide an acceptable service.
- It provides a direct measurement (customer satisfaction) which shows whether or not the inputs have worked. This is especially important as far as non-tangible products are concerned, because of their transitory, non-physical nature which makes measurement difficult.

Branding

If you have a successful product that has recognisable features, it is likely that customers will continue to buy it rather than test out other similar, but unknown ones. This aspect of buying behaviour can be successfully used as an important marketing tool. What marketeers do, is to use a brand which automatically signifies the qualities which the customer values – these are known as core values. This brand, like the one used on cattle, is stamped across the entire product range. The most obvious brand is the name of the company (e.g. Madame Tussaud's, Rank or Sega). In many cases the branding is carried through to the whole design, such as using a logo, distinctive colours or design features.

Once a brand is established it can be used to influence the customer into making the decision to buy. The intention will be:

- To achieve sales across a range of goods and services within a sector: e.g. Head skis and racquets, Nike sports wear

and Panasonic home entertainment goods.

- To attract sales in different locations: e.g. David Lloyd Tennis Centres, Cannons Gyms and Sea Life Centres.

- To attract sales in new industries: e.g. Boots. Occasionally, larger companies step out of their industry and enter a new one using the brand as an assurance to the customer that the standards they offered in the parent industry will apply to the new one. An example of this is shown in the case study of Virgin's move into the fitness industry.

CASE STUDY – Use of the Virgin brand in developing Virgin Active

The four core Virgin values which feature in every Virgin business:

- fun
- innovation
- value for money
- great customer service.

Virgin have made the decision to enter the health and fitness market because:

- They feel that there are no good-value products available and that the public are being ripped off by joining fees, high subscriptions, limited facilities and poor service.
- Only 5% of the British population are members of health clubs and they feel that clubs currently are not offering what people really want. The equivalent membership figure for the US is 10%.
- It is an opportunity to offer a totally new concept which research has shown that people want.

The application of the marketing mix has meant that:

- There has been a break from the traditional ways of advertising. They are using non-stereotypical images (overweight, older people) to reinforce the fact that Virgin Active does not judge its members and it is a fun, non-intimidating place to visit. (The success of this approach can be seen in Preston, the first club to open, where over 60% of the members have never been members of a health club before).
- Non-threatening language and tone is being used through all marketing communications. For example, fun signs in the club like 'if you want to break your leg, please run along the poolside' rather than traditional 'No running' orders.
- Joining fees and annual membership commitments have been abolished. As a result a healthier lifestyle has been put within the reach of many more people.

CASE STUDY – Use of the Virgin brand in developing Virgin Active (contd)

Virgin has tried to incorporate aspects of its already established brand into the new health and fitness clubs by:

- Innovative design features which make the clubs fun to visit, especially for nervous, first-time exercisers.
- Inclusion of many 'non-fitness' facilities e.g. libraries including Internet access, medical centres and large relaxation areas. These ensure that members don't have to exercise to have a great time.
- Making the interiors of the clubs cheerful, colourful and welcoming. All fitness activities are upstairs, so new members aren't confronted by a sea of fitness equipment as soon as they walk in the door.
- Bringing the company ethos into the clubs. For example 'Virgin goes the extra mile' to ensure customer satisfaction, by ensuring all changing rooms have large lockers so that work clothes can be hung up and won't get crushed.

The company sees several advantages to this brand-led marketing approach:

- Widespread recognition of Virgin's brand values and the fact that the company has a reputation of doing things differently to benefit its clients has assisted in the level of interest in this product.
- Based on what customers see, membership sales for their Leeds club (before it has even opened) have reached extremely high levels.

However, there are also some disadvantages to brand-led marketing:

- members have very high expectations which MUST be surpassed
- there is potential vulnerability if another Virgin company generates bad publicity.

Questions

1 What was one main result of applying the marketing mix?
2 How has this benefited Virgin?
3 How has the brand-led marketing approach worked to Virgin's advantage in its entry into the fitness market?

Life-cycle

The consumption of any product will vary over time. The standard curve is shown below in Figure 4.7 and consists of four stages:

- introduction
- growth
- maturity
- decline.

This cycle exists in leisure services but the problem is that it varies with different services and is difficult to predict. However,

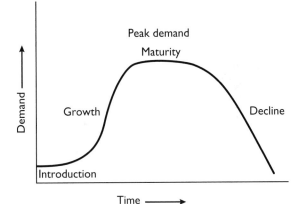

Figure 4.7 Product life-cycle curve

it can still be used as a guide to marketing planning. Here are some basic ploys:

Repetition

We know that some products have repetitive cycles and that promotions and product launch can be easily planned. These are usually the old favourites, such as seasonal sports and pantomime in the theatre. But care should be taken to watch for long-term changes in these cycles. For example, squash traditionally takes off in September and grows throughout the winter before declining in the summer months. Over successive years this cycle has been repeated, but every year has seen a drop in demand or sales. In the 1970s about 4 per cent of the population played the game. It is now about 0.4 per cent.

Length

Life-cycles vary considerably from a few months to years. Roller- and ice-skating seem to follow approximately a twenty- to thirty-year cycle. Some activities might last only a year or so (e.g. BMX biking). It is important to have some idea of the likely cycle when deciding marketing strategy. In the case of BMX biking, the rapid growth of its popularity led some local authorities to build tracks at large cost only to find that there was an equally rapid decline. This meant that the return on investment was often very low.

Sometimes a sporting success prompts a rapid growth period. Experienced managers know that this may see little maturation and decline after a short while. The successful marketing strategy in such cases is to set up short-term provision with minimal investment until the nature of the demand becomes clear.

Extension

Life-cycles are not fixed and can be extended by manipulating the marketing mix; for example, by changing the packaging,

Life-cycle benefits!

improving or adding to the product, pricing offers, and extra promotion. Successful managers tend to revitalise their products before they go into decline. In the health business new activities replace old ones every few months. If the product is the whole gym package, these changes serve to invigorate it and keep it fresh and fashionable for a market that wants change. If gyms had stayed at just providing aerobics their life-cycle would have probably gone into decline.

While the cycle length and shape are difficult to anticipate, extension is a principle that can be put into action. For successful leisure providers the motto is 'Don't let the grass grow under your feet – always look for change'.

Place

The place is where the product is distributed to the customer. The two main concerns are:

- how the product is distributed
- where it is located.

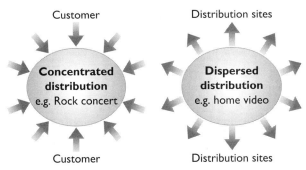

Figure 4.8 The distribution matrix

Distribution

Distribution decisions will vary according to two dimensions (see Figure 4.8).

- A *concentrated distribution* is where the consumer needs to come to the organisation.
- A *dispersed distribution* is where there are many delivery sites. For example, a rock concert is concentrated as it can be experienced only at the arena. Whereas buying CDs of the concert from record outlets would be a dispersed distribution.

However, if you are buying a CD of the concert to listen to at home, then the distribution techniques employed will have little effect on your enjoyment of the record.

Sport and sport spectating

The home entertainment industry is the major distribution point for sports spectating and is dispersed (through TV sets) and integrated (through strong control of broadcasting standards and programming). In other words, customers view sport when and how they want to, but the industry has to make sure that broadcasts get through on

> **Think it over**
> In some sports shops, goods like racquets and trainers are stacked high. In other shops they are displayed individually. How does this affect the customer's experience?

time and that they are of sufficiently good quality. BBC Radio's outside broadcasts have suffered in recent years from occasional breaks in transmission because the cost of a backup line is too great. This is therefore a case of poor distribution spoiling the leisure experience. For sports retailing there is a diverse choice of distribution points such as shops, e-mail and mail order, and the consumer's experience of a product such as trainers is largely independent of the distribution process.

Leisure and recreation

The main point of distribution is the facility itself, or perhaps a few facilities if the provider operates a chain. The customer's experience is totally dependent on the delivery of the facility and its services. Thus, leisure and recreation distribution is usually concentrated and integrated.

There are some exceptions. For example, children's playgrounds usually consist of standard equipment in many unstaffed sites. Think of these as distribution outlets. The child's experience of play will, however, depend on distribution, particularly in terms of maintenance, security, health and safety, landscaping and design, and the distribution is therefore a dispersed integrated one.

Location

Whatever the distribution process the provider will need to consider if its physical location:

- falls within a sufficient market size
- is accessible to customers
- fulfils other customer needs.

There are usually three market types of location that apply (solely or in combination) to the place.

Local markets: Where a facility is serving a market within, say, a five-mile radius. This distance will vary, for example a housing estate might form the market for a community sports hall and an entire town for a minor football club.

Extended markets: Specialist centres such as tennis centres, country clubs or health and fitness suites and centres of excellence will expect their market to come from a wider but well-defined area. Health suites might typically regard a 30-minute driving time as their market radius, while a centre of excellence will be looking at an entire region or even an entire country.

Niche markets: Some sports and recreation centres serve a niche market (that is, a small market of customers with very specific needs). Customers are often prepared to travel great distances to these facilities. Outdoor activity centres and early music consorts fall into this category.

For any of these markets there will be need to consider other features of the site. These include:

- *market size*. Is there a sufficient population of the targeted market segments?
- *access* (to the public, to staff, to contractors). It is fairly obvious that customers need to be able to get to the site. So roads, public transport and parking availability have to be considered in relation to the market. So also do other factors such as hills or major roads which restrict pedestrian access. Social access can be a factor. For example, there are numerous cases of leisure facilities failing because they are surrounded by hostile communities who 'frighten off' customers.
- *aesthetics*. The physical nature of architecture or surroundings can be off-putting. For example playing fields near sewage works, health clubs in heavy industrial areas.

- *logistics*. Where there are a number of distribution points, consideration may be given to ensuring that they can be accessed by head office staff. For example, one of the strategies used by contractors for local authority leisure facilities is to tender for sites in a small area. Staff can then be spread over a variety of sites, thus increasing efficiency.
- *other*. Political and financial factors often determine the choice of place. Community centres may be championed by a politician and thus situated in his constituency, and property prices and rates may determine the site financially.
- *happenstance*. Don't always expect there to be a marketing rationale behind the location of sites. Many facilities are where they are because that's where they are. Market research has not played a part. For example, many parks are located where they are simply because a rich Victorian donated some land for public use. Many smaller private facilities are where they are because the rents were cheap, or it was close to the owner's home, or it was the only site available.

Deciding where to locate products

The industry often assesses certain locations or populations and decides what service (e.g. a swimming pool) will be needed. Sport England uses a highly sophisticated **needs-based model** founded on many thousands of measurements of recreational behaviour. The public sector uses a **facilities model** which combines many factors and can identify if there is a need for a particular facility in an area, and where the ideal place to locate it would be.

Using the facilities model, Sport England suggest a minimum population figure within a radius of a 30-minute drive to warrant a new facility being built (Table 4.2).

Table 4.2 Geographical criteria for people using sports facilities

Facility	Population
A swimming pool	30,000 within 30 mins drive
A four-court sports hall	4,000–6,000 within 30 mins drive
A small community recreation hall	3,000–6,000

Source: Sports Council Sports Hall Design Guidance Notes; SCRC fact sheet.

Surprisingly useful estimates of market size and need can also be made from simple demographic mapping. Until recently, this was a laborious business of mapping census districts within the required radius and then adding the data from census tables.

Recently the National Office of Statistics has begun to provide digital population maps which make analysis easier and more accurate.

When these populations are multiplied by participation rates taken from sources like the National Household Survey, you can work out how many people from the population should be playing a specific sport and then compare this with the number of facilities in the area, and where new ones would be best located. Figure 4.9 shows an example of analysis of the population within the Croydon area.

Demand-led model: More often used in the private sector, these models identify the number of customers they need to make a profit and the market segment they occupy. They would then identify where these markets are located. They would also research the competition in the area, the transport, and other relevant factors.

Price

To understand price in marketing terms you must appreciate three concepts:

- price is affected by competition
- price is more determined by the value the customer places on the product than the cost of producing the product

Analysis of population within the Croydon area

Unemployment in the Croydon area is, at 6.5 per cent, slightly higher than the national average of 6.1 per cent. The current population of 330,930 people was growing at a higher than average annual rate in 1995 – 1.4 per cent compared to 0.9 per cent nationally – but is expected to fall in line with the UK average annual growth of 0.3 per cent through to 2005. The area has a higher than average proportion of people aged four and under, at 7.1 per cent against 6.5 per cent nationally, and 33.1 per cent of residents fall in the 25 to 44 years age bracket compared to 29.6 per cent UK-wide. There are lower than average numbers of those aged 45-plus. These trends are set to continue to 2005.
Data provided by CACI's AreaData Service. For further details contact the AreaData Group in London on 0171-605 6008

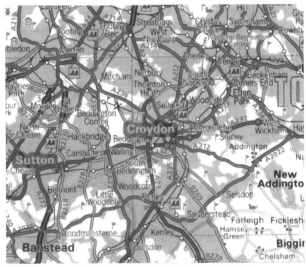

Figure 4.9 An example of analysis of the population within the Croydon area

> **Thought for the page**
>
> You can see the results of demand-led location decisions when you look at the siting of country clubs, tennis clubs, health and fitness centres and other high-profit earners. These are mostly located in the more affluent areas or on the access roads to major cities or towns, where activity is part of the predominant lifestyle. Rural and depressed areas do not attract these facilities so much – which is a paradox, as the need for improved fitness and health is greater among the communities living there who, by and large, will suffer more from the effects of poor diet and insufficient exercise.

- price is subject to the economic laws of supply and demand.

Competition

Prices are affected by the prices of other providers competing in the same market place. In order to compete successfully a provider will need to improve the product and/or drop the price.

Value

The first question most buyers ask themselves is, 'Is it worth it?' This is known as 'value' and it constantly changes with the customer's needs and the availability of the product. For example, if you are at a club and you are hot and thirsty from dancing, £2 for a bottle of water will seem good value if it is the only supply, whereas the next day in the supermarket you would be prepared to pay only 80p.

Some golf or country clubs market themselves as having members only from elitist groups (e.g. class, business connections). Although the golf course or facilities may be no better than at other clubs they charge large membership fees to reassure members that they are going to be only with people like themselves who can afford the fees. Interestingly, the reverse was found to be the case when sports development started. Twenty years ago, many sports development schemes provided sport in underdeveloped areas free of charge. It was found, however, that clients did not value the activity because they did not associate value with something that was free. When a nominal price (say 50p a session) was charged, clients psychologically put a value on the activity and were more committed to it.

Adding value

Competition pushes prices down, but a point comes if prices fall too low when providers cannot operate successfully, and income is not sufficient to cover costs. One obvious thing to do in these circumstances is to make

> **Think it over**
>
> Adding value. Lucozade for years manufactured glucose-based 'health' drinks. In the 1980s they redesigned the product by adding minerals and salts to make it isotonic. With only a small increase in the cost of adding minerals they now could access the fitness market where a drink that counteracted dehydration was valued, and the price that could be charged was significantly higher than the price of the plain old glucose drink. Why did Lucozade want to access the fitness market?

production more cost-efficient and therefore reduce costs. The alternative – and this is the marketing solution – is to improve the product to meet the customers' needs more exactly and attract a larger market segment. This is known as adding value. However, for this to work, the cost of adding value must be less than the extra sales it generates.

Just what the customer values is difficult to identify and managers will spend a lot of time listening to customers talk about their experiences at various facilities and gauge what could be added to improve their experience and hence the value. Larger providers may do research in the form of focus groups.

Ability to pay: While customers may appreciate the value of the product they may not have the ability to pay for it. Leisure and recreation providers have found lots of ways of 'taking the pain out of paying'. Method of payment is important. As well as cash transactions, many organisations now accept cheques (this is convenient for the customer) while most accept credit cards (which allow the customer to defer payment). In fact some sports organisations (e.g. the Royal Yachting Association, ILAM) now produce their own credit cards with benefits to members. Providers may also accept transactions by telephone or e-mail. Possibly more important is the *pricing policy* or packaging of payments.

CASE STUDY — Adding value

In a health and fitness centre there are some small things to be done that would cost little or nothing to do and would add value to the service. This would allow a higher price to be charged, and the customer would hopefully value this product more than the competitors' close by.

For instance:

- all staff to be particularly friendly, informed and helpful.

- high standards of hygiene and cleanliness to be maintained (e.g. change the scent of the air freshener, provide cologne in the washrooms).

- food and refreshments to be more attractive (e.g. concentrate on presentation and add garnish)

- documentation for the customer to be personalised (use a database when generating letters)

- invite certain types of customers to previews of new equipment

- select the right décor (e.g. change the colour of paint, have fresh flowers in reception)

- use crockery instead of plastic cups

- put down carpet instead of vinyl

- promote club information/'customer of the month' type displays

- introduce a club newsletter.

Questions

1 Which items on this list would you promote? Which would you reject, and for what reason?
2 What other improvements can you imagine would be useful and inexpensive?

Here are some common methods which spread payment or reduce price:

- season tickets
- packages (e.g. two for the price of one)
- pay as you play (pay on the door)
- ticket books (e.g. twenty tickets for the price of eighteen)
- concessions (standard reductions for certain groups such as claimants)
- family or group membership
- corporate membership (a company pays a one-off fee and charges its staff a lower price or gives them free entry)
- monthly payments or an annual fee
- market segmentation: chains of leisure facilities may sometimes have different prices for outlets in different parts of the country where disposable income varies.

Think it over

Think of the following products and identify how value could be added to them.

- a CD
- a session of carpet bowls for pensioners
- corporate hospitality entertainment at a big sporting event, e.g. Henley Regatta.

The economics of supply and demand

The pricing of a product is governed by economic principles or laws.

The *law of supply* is that suppliers of the product need to charge a certain amount to make a profit. The smaller the profit becomes (i.e the lower the price) the less prepared the supplier is to supply the product. Thus low prices will mean low supply.

Working against this law is another – the *law of demand* – the higher the price the less people will buy it. Thus low prices mean high demand but if prices go up sales go down.

The tension between the two laws results in an equilibrium of the ideal price that satisfies both demand and supply (see Figure 4.10). If you go above that price you end up with lower demand and over-supply, while if you go below it there is an excess of customers for a lack of products. In practice, managers recognise these symptoms by raising the price if there is over-demand by customers and by lowering the price to meet a lack of demand.

A third law is that volume (sales) × price = income. This means that 100 members at £10 produces the same amount as 10 members at £100. Most leisure facilities have a maximum capacity for use – so there is a point where sales cannot be increased. To maximise income the provider needs to manipulate the price to create a demand somewhere near that capacity.

In practice this can be difficult because:

• Other factors do not remain constant. A competitor might appear and undercut, or there is a lay off at the local factory and disposable income of customers falls. It should also be remembered that the life-cycle of the product will affect demand and if its novelty wears off, so will demand.

The relationship between price and volume is rarely smooth because of *elasticity* of demand as shown below. This is defined as the relationship between the percentage change in sales or demand and the percentage change in price. If the change in sales is less than the change in price then demand is *inelastic*, but if it is more then it is *elastic*. In practice this means that in an inelastic situation sales will not decline proportionally to price increase, and so there is some scope to raise prices and to retain turnover even though there is a drop in sales. In an elastic situation, raising prices would mean a greater drop in sales and declining turnover. Elasticity is a headache to all concerned with pricing. This is because it is affected by many factors. Different market segments may value the product differently and accordingly react differently in terms of elasticity. Or changes in disposable income might occur at the time of price change or the marketplace become more competitive.

Market equilibrium. A concept that helps us focus on the ideal state we want but rarely achieve is the market equilibrium. This is

My accountant suggested I should make my prices more elastic...

Elasticity of demand

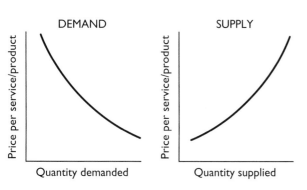

Figure 4.10 Supply and demand

when the price curve crosses the demand curve, as can be seen in Figure 4.11. We already know that demand will grow with reduced prices. Supply on the other hand will increase with price until capacity is reached, simply because suppliers will usually be increasing their return on costs as sales grow. In the graph of the health club we can see that the area below the intersection represents a greater demand than there is supply. Above the intersection there is excess supply, i.e. unfilled memberships and unused equipment. In this case the manager is charging £600 per annum and this is causing under-demand. By dropping the fee to £400 she would achieve an equilibrium where the number of members would match the club's capacity. Such planning is often hypothetical and in practice it is difficult to estimate the market equilibrium, unless there is the sort of research data that only a major company has to make such calculations. In most cases providers make judgements based on local knowledge but keep the principles in mind.

A private leisure club with a long waiting list knows that it is operating above capacity. Therefore it can afford to charge members more, earn more income and hopefully maintain a shorter waiting list. But what happens if demand is less inelastic than supposed? A price rise might then result in the departure of existing members and also of those on the waiting list who are disillusioned with the new prices. In

Think it over

The prices charged by leisure facilities cause annual concern at local government level. This is because a rise in prices will provoke a drop in usage or membership, and this will provoke criticism that the service is inaccessible to the ratepayers; or that the drop in income will mean budget targets are not met.

Think of a council facility that you use. What percentage price rise would a) stop you using the facility b) decrease your use?

contrast, another club may be failing to attract customers. Are its prices too high? If the demand is inelastic then it might take a considerable price drop to attract customers and that would lead to a drop in income.

Price determination: In other industries such as manufacturing it is common to price in relation to cost. The cost of each unit to produce is worked out, a percentage for profit added on (the profit margin) and the price is reached. The market then judges if the product is worth the price. The cost-based method of price setting is difficult in the leisure industry because it is extremely difficult to work out the cost of producing a unit or a satisfied customer. Furthermore, the product varies over the day and between customer types, because of the different equipment and varying cost of staff. The cost of producing a satisfied child in a play group is probably less than the cost of producing a satisfied badminton customer. However, the customer would probably expect to pay less for the play session than for the badminton court. Cost-based pricing is thus not often used in leisure and recreation although obviously costs must be kept in mind to ensure that profits can be maintained.

Instead, we tend to use one of these methods:

- Look at the local successful competition and charge similar prices. Charge lower prices if there is need to expand

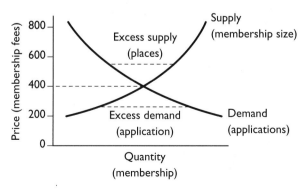

Figure 4.11 Market equilibrium – health clubs

the market share, and greater if there is over-demand in the area which the competition is failing to supply.

- If there is no local competition look at the prices being charged for similar products in similar markets elsewhere.
- Ask the market. Either informal questioning of the market, or more formal market research such as focus groups, will provide a good idea of the range within which people will be prepared to pay.

An important factor in price setting is the analysis of the market segment that is being served. Different segments will have different abilities to pay and will also value the product in different ways. Many health and fitness clubs in Britain have decided that they want to go for an affluent, young market where prestige of belonging to an exclusive gym is valued. This is a relatively small market but it is willing to pay high prices.

Promotion

When a product has been developed, the price set and the place where it will be distributed worked out, the next stage is to tell the world about it. Promotion is communicating to the market about the product. Many people now refer to promotion as marketing communications and this avoids the confusion there is sometimes between the terms 'promotion' and 'promotional events' or 'promotions'. It has four aims (often called AIDA) which are shown in Figure 4.12.

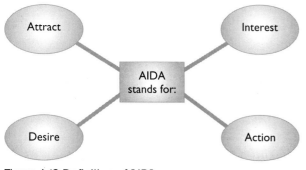

Figure 4.12 Definition of AIDA

Attract *the market*. In order to sell something to someone you need to attract their attention. This is why market traders shout a lot. Promotional material should stand out and make people take notice, so striking use of sound and colour, strong images, attractive distribution and display of information are all important and frequently used.

Interest *the market in the product*. This is essentially providing information that will be of interest to the customer, such as what the product is, how much, where and when it is. Sadly, many leisure providers do not go further than this stage.

Desire *to have it*. This is showing the customer the benefits of having the product. More often than not these benefits are psychological, such as 'you will become attractive, you will feel healthier, people will think a lot of you'. Promotions often represent this by using role models and representing fantasy situations. An effective TV advert for Nike featured Carl Lewis running over water in his trainers. The message? 'Wear these trainers and you will become a living god'.

Action *to buy it*. A promotion will often remind you to act now, as in the slogans 'Closing offer', 'Only six days left', 'Phone us now on…'. It will also offer the means to buy such as phone bookings or using credit cards or hire purchase. Why wait a year when you can have it now?

Promotion therefore means recognising the needs and desires of the market for the product, and communicating the product to that market in order to persuade it to buy. This may be achieved directly as in the case of an advert. It may also be achieved indirectly through public relations. For example the launch of the Millennium Dome was accompanied by poor media reception which in effect reduced the desire of the market to visit it. A major objective of public relations in the following months was to reverse this poor image.

Promotion takes several forms that include:

- advertising
- promotional events
- promotional packages
- public relations
- direct mailing
- self promotion.

We will return to these later.

Thought for the page

In as much as market segments vary so will their needs and desires differ. Care needs to be taken not to mix the message. For example, business people use many country clubs, to entertain clients. But these clubs also want to attract family membership. Just as these two types of customer need to be kept apart within the club so should the promotional messages be separated. Two separate promotional campaigns focusing on the needs of each market will be more effective than trying to mix them up in one campaign that is meant to please all the people all the time.

Check it out

1 Apart from the four Ps, identify three other components that are sometimes included in the marketing mix.
2 Why is competition important in marketing?
3 What are the differences between tangible and non-tangible product?
4 What is the benefit of the output model of the product?
5 Give three factors that might affect the choice of location for a facility.
6 Give two advantages and disadvantages of brand-led marketing.
7 Give three examples of pricing policy.
8 Explain how elasticity can affect pricing.
9 Why is AIDA important in promotion?

4.3 Market research
Market definitions

You will by now have realised that marketing requires planning. Planning needs to be based on facts about the needs of the market, the competition and the environment. This information is gained from *marketing research* which gathers data about the competition, the mix, the environment and all the other factors involved in the planning process. An important area of this research is *market research* which concentrates on the people who are or who we hope will become our customers – the market.

In any population there will be small groups of people with similar interests and ways of behaving, and if we can identify them then we can make more accurate assessments of what they want from the marketing mix. These groups are called *market segments* and they:

- respond in the same way to promotions
- have similar pricing requirements
- have similar needs for the product
- will use the same place
- provide consistent responses to market research.

We tend to use market information in two ways:

1 The first is to find out which segment is appropriate to a given product.

For example, the house that belonged to Agatha Christie, the great detective story writer, has recently been given to the National Trust. Their Marketing Officer (who we will call Jeff) will need to find out the selling points of the house and then identify market segments that will be attracted by them. He will do this by talking to managers of other similar houses but also by looking at market research data or conducting surveys of his own. Obviously, one market segment will be Agatha Christie fans and the manager will have to find out where they live, what sort of publications they read and what interests them about Agatha Christie. One selling point is that the house has magnificent gardens. The gardening/garden-lovers market is a huge one and the manager, working for the National Trust as he is, will know this market segment and what they will find attractive. This information can be used to:

- refine the product. (e.g. selling plants, having guided tours and themed entertainment)
- determine the price
- design the promotion
- indicate the probable number of visitors
- identify any conflicts between the market segments. (The gardeners want peace and quiet, but the Christie fans might want enactments of her books. If so, a balance needs to be found in the use of the product by each group.)

2 **The other way the information is often used is to design the mix to meet the needs of a specific market segment.**

For example, one role of a community development officer (Debbie) is to develop social and recreational activities for the local community. In this case she has close contact with the market but no product as yet. She needs to research the needs of the community and to do this she simply has to ask them what they want and to offer them the options available. With their answers, she will probably discover that even in this small market there are market segments (e.g. the elderly, the young, a small community of Somali refugees) who have different needs. She can now devise a marketing mix that will, hopefully, suit all the different segments. Perhaps a concert in the park for teenagers, old-time dancing for the pensioners?

Market segments can be fitted into one of four categories:

- customers
- geographical
- psychographical
- demographic.

Customers

Customers can be crudely put into three categories:

- first-time (new) customer who has been attracted by promotions or referred by existing customers, or other reasons
- retained/repeat customer – first time customers who return
- non-customers.

Many leisure organisations rely on repeat and referred business. If they are doing their job and pleasing the customers this may easily

Promotional material must be aimed at a defined market, in this case, holiday makers

represent 80% or more of their custom. A typical marketing strategy would be two-staged:

1 at set-up of the service: a promotional strategy aimed at the key market segments in the non-customer population

2 on establishment: a research and promotional strategy aimed largely at retained or referred customers.

Jeff at the National Trust would be well placed to do this. He would have a good idea of the profile of his market from the Trust's database. He might also introduce tickets that can be used more than once or at discount price, thus encouraging repeat business or referred business if people handed the ticket on to their friends. The use of these used tickets would be an indicator of the extent of this sort of business. Debbie might have a different problem with her concert in the park. She will want the stall holders invited to set up at the concert to return next year as they provide a sizeable income. She should take care that they feel they have made a good return on their investment. To help this she does not charge a set fee but takes 10% of their takings, thus ensuring that they know she trusts them and that they will not be out of pocket if it rains during the event.

Establishing a sizeable repeat or referred custom base is an excellent foundation for marketing, especially for the smaller provider with limited budgets. Market research is simplified in that the customer is always accessible and can be researched, not only by the more sophisticated methods of surveys, but also through inexpensive methods such as talking to the customers and watching them. An astute manager will encourage the staff to talk frequently to customers and ask them what they like or do not like. The staff will then be encouraged to report back at staff meetings.

Secondary research can be used to reinforce market knowledge. Having established a customer base, a manager will often then classify the customers into other market segments and look at other information associated with those groups. For example, a manager might have a high proportion of divorced men using the service. She might come across a research report on lifestyles of divorced men showing that they tend to eat out a lot. Would this be a clue that the manager might improve the catering service at the facility by introducing light meals as opposed to snacks?

Back in the park, Debbie has been doing some research reading the *Rough Guide to World Music* and finds that Somali music is really lively dance music. She has found an excellent way not only to attract the Somali segment of the community but also to achieve her overall objective of bringing the community together.

Geographical

Location has a big influence on people's behaviour, including their spending potential and patterns. This is seen at various levels; the national north/south divide is commonly accepted as one division or, at a local level, a golf club will market to the more affluent community who can be easily defined because they will live in certain residential areas.

Psychographical

Different groups in society have well-defined characteristics, such as their buying patterns or how they travel. In some cases there is a link between their leisure preferences and their buying of other products. For example, vegetarians may be more likely to climb than play football; non-smokers may be more likely than smokers to belong to fine wine clubs. One psychographical observation is that people with similar psychographical profiles tend to live close to each other. So strong is this correlation that very small areas such as enumeration districts or postcode areas can be associated with certain consumer types. Systems such as *ACORN Analysis* are highly sophisticated and can give detailed profiles of the population in these areas and their consumer patterns and preferences. This does away with the need for primary research by the leisure provider who can use the system by:

- providing the location of the market and asking what its profile is likely to be
- defining the market segment and asking where it will be located.

Unfortunately, access to these systems is expensive and only the major providers such as large councils or private sector chains can afford to use them.

Demographic

The census provides the main base for market segmentation. As with the groups above these indices are often closely associated with behaviour, attitudes and needs. The indices that are commonly used are:

- social class
- gender
- age
- socio-economic group
- ethnic status
- disability
- car ownership.

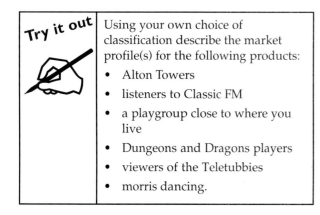

Try it out

Using your own choice of classification describe the market profile(s) for the following products:

- Alton Towers
- listeners to Classic FM
- a playgroup close to where you live
- Dungeons and Dragons players
- viewers of the Teletubbies
- morris dancing.

Thought for the page

Niche markets

Most markets are large and generalised in the needs of the consumer. They are easily recognisable, and as a result, many providers will compete for their custom. Some will become highly successful and large if they can survive. Good examples are the high-street bookshops that cater for the popular reading and audio markets. In contrast, smaller companies, by aiming at smaller more specialised markets called niches, can find a marketplace where there is less competition but also less demand. Niche markets are small and often hard to locate as they are spread thinly through the population. Advertising in specialist magazines and mail order are typical strategic solutions to this problem. Niche markets have specialised, individual and often well-defined needs that the provider must match exactly to get their business. To succeed, the provider is often also a consumer and therefore personally knows what the market wants. Since niche market providers offer value, they tend to charge relatively high prices but the volume of their sales will be low in comparison to high-street stores. In the book trade antiquarian booksellers and technical booksellers are good examples.

Of these, social class and socio-economic group (SEG) need some clarification. The population is divided into groups that will reflect their economic and social status. Both these classifications measure socio-economic status as shown in Table 4.3.

Research methods

A wide range of methods is used to collect data. They are often divided into:

Primary research: This is when the researcher collects data from its source. It has a great advantage in that it can focus exactly on the population in question and on what needs to be researched. However, it has the disadvantage that it usually has to be precisely and extensively planned and managed and is often expensive.

Table 4.3 Measures of socio-economic status

Social class		SEG	Typical occupations
I	Professional occupations	A	managing director
II	Managerial and technical	B	cinema manager, leisure centre manager
III Skilled			
	non-manual	C1	projectionist, supervisor
	manual	C2	electrician
IV	Partly skilled	D	recreation assistant
V	Unskilled	E	cleaner

Secondary research: This is 'second-hand data' as it is often other people's primary research collected from published and other secondary sources.

- It has several advantages in that it is often cheap and plentiful and will look at the problem from a variety of viewpoints and circumstances and therefore allows for comparison and inference.

- Its main disadvantage is that it often does not focus on the issue you want to examine so you often have to go for the nearest fit. For example, the results of a study on elasticity to swimming pool pricing in Doncaster in 1998 may not be applicable to an assessment of customer response to changing pool prices in Basingstoke the next year. When using secondary data it is advisable to get as close a match as possible of all the factors involved.

You also need to be critical of the pedigree or provenance of secondary recorded data you are using. Is the source reliable? Were the methods used to generate data valid? Is the analysis of the information partial? Web-based information is particularly susceptible to doubt as to its validity.

Primary research

Censuses

A census is the recording of characteristics in the population. Normally we think of the Census as being the national census which is held every ten years. But there can be many other censuses of any population. Where the population is small, it is feasible for a small organisation to carry out the census itself. For example, there are about 800 holiday parks in Britain and it would be perfectly feasible to contact all of these for information. Censuses are the best means of acquiring accurate statistics of simple items such as age, occupation, and residence. However, because they are often large and entail the handling of a huge amount of data, they often need to be restricted to just a few questions.

Surveys

Research that asks the same questions of a sample number of a population is called *sample surveys* or surveys for short. Surveys are useful because they are a quick way of getting detailed information at a fraction of the price of a census. The extent we rely on the sample to reflect the characteristics of its population is called the *level of confidence*. The level of confidence grows with the sample size. However, at some point this growth levels off and there is little to gain from increasing the sample. Surveys can be used at all levels, ranging from national surveys using vast numbers of field staff (like the ones who stop you in the street) to small in-house surveys of your customers. The basic tool of a survey is a

questionnaire. This is a schedule of questions about a person:

- what they do (*behaviour*)
- what they know (*awareness and knowledge*)
- what they think about something (*attitudes*).

The researcher may be present to help the respondent interpret the questions, but sometimes the questionnaire may be sent by post when physical distance makes interviewing impossible (see page 252). The answers that are received are grouped together to build up the sample.

Because questionnaires are fixed in size and content they are excellent for finding out about behaviour, awareness and knowledge. They are also used to measure attitudes and feelings, but because they offer only a limited opportunity to respond they may skim over the significance. Attitude questionnaires often limit themselves to asking respondents to rate their feelings on a scale – for example:

> 'Was the customer service you received':
>
> ❑ very good ❑ good ❑ average
> ❑ not very good ❑ bad

Questions about behaviour or personality are often simply 'yes' or 'no' choices, or ask the candidate to choose from a series of categories. e.g.:

> 'How often do you go the theatre?'
>
> ❑ never ❑ more than once a month
> ❑ more than monthly but less than once a year
> ❑ once a year or less

'Fixed-choice' or closed questions like this channel the respondents' thoughts and allow for easy handling of the data.

'Open' questions can also be used where the survey records the respondent's response.

Postal questionnaires can reach people too far away to interview

Survey design

In designing a survey it is wise to follow some basic rules:

1 The *sample size* should be big enough to have at least 95% *level of confidence*. If it has not, the results may not give the correct picture. There are various simple statistical means of determining this, but they depend on having results from similar studies or pilot results from your own survey. These tests would be used in large surveys, but when doing small surveys (e.g. customer satisfaction in a country club) you may well throw scientific caution to the wind and take a stab at selecting a suitable sample. As a rule of thumb a 10 per cent plus sample will often serve. But you must remember that the larger the population is, the sampling fraction can become smaller, and with smaller populations it will become larger. Having started the survey you may be able to apply statistical tests to the data and adjust the sample size if appropriate.

2 The number and type of factors that will be used to identify the data are important. The more factors there are, the bigger the sample you will need.

Say the country club has 1,000 members of which 100 are sampled. If there was just one factor (e.g. satisfaction of members expressed as a five-point scale) then you would have an average of 20 responses for each level of satisfaction which is probably adequate for analysis. A split for gender reduces average response by half, which may be adequate. However, if you now introduced five age groups then there would be an average of only two responses to each combination of factors, which is far too small to pick up significant differences. For example, you would be foolish to infer that three retired female members expressing a level of satisfaction were significantly different from two male retired members expressing the same level, even though 50% more females expressed this response than did males.

3 Seek to get a high response rate (i.e. a high number of completed questionnaires). *Respondents* (people answering questions) may refuse to take part for all sorts of reasons. The questionnaire is too long, they don't like the interviewer, or they have been approached at the wrong time. It may be that the people who refuse are different from those who don't and you have therefore got distorted data due to *response bias*. Sometimes if you have good information about the sample (e.g. membership lists) you can simply check for bias by seeing if the profile of the respondents is different from the non-respondents.

4 Be sure that the people in the survey reflect the population that is being looked at as a whole. For example, in a survey of all members, it would not be accurate to sample only weekend customers as they might have different characteristics from weekday customers. Distortion of this sort is known as sample bias.

5 Check that individuals in the sample are treated in the same way and are asked the same schedule of questions in the same order using the same approach. Questions need to be pre-tested to see that they are understood by all the sample and elicit consistent response. If this is not done the data is distorted by *schedule bias*.

6 When interviewers are used they must all use the same approach and ask the questions in the same way. If not, the data may be distorted by *interviewer bias*. For example, if an interviewer feels sorry for old people in the survey and helps them to answer the questions then there could be bias.

7 Market researchers usually deal in big differences in data. Tests of statistical significance which other scientists prefer are rarely used in everyday work. When analysing results, look for differences of at least 5 per cent between groups and preferably for double-figure differences.

Finding the sample: Before carrying out a survey you first need to ask who the target population is (for example, customers aged over 60, women, customers working in a town, people with disabilities, people from ethnic minorities). You then need to decide where you can find a cross-section of that population. The population from which you draw the sample is called a *sampling frame* (Figure 4.13). Sampling-frame characteristics are given below with examples of how *Yellow Pages* telephone directory might have weaknesses if you were doing a survey of sports equipment manufacturers in an area.

Some lists are an excellent choice of sampling frame: for a general population the electoral roll is a good choice, or even the telephone directory (but only if your population will consist of phone owners who are in the directory). Membership and customer detail lists are ideal when looking at customers. If you are looking at non-customers then your

Ensure the sample is:	
Complete	Not everyone pays to be put in *Yellow Pages*. Smaller firms are less likely to be included.
Up to date	Towards the end of a directory's life some people may have changed address.
Not duplicated	Some addresses might have more than one phone number or there may be more than one entry as in *Yellow Pages*.
Identifiable	There is no standard classification, so manufacturers might appear under several categories of their own choice.
Easy and inexpensive to use	The layout of the directory makes sampling difficult.

Figure 4.13 Sampling frame based on publicised lists

sampling frame might be to contact the next-door neighbour of your customers.

Sometimes lists are not available or not practical to use. This is the case when a rapid response is needed, as in political opinion surveys. A way round this is to sample in places where large numbers of the target population go. Street interviews are a common example of this. In the leisure industry we often do *exit polls* when we ask customers what they think of the service they have received. If, as in many cases, the poll is a questionnaire which is left for the customer to fill in if they choose to, the results are often biased as it usually the customers with complaints who return them.

Sampling strategy: This is the way the sample is chosen. Here are the most frequently used types:

- *random samples*: If you think the characteristics you are looking for are spread evenly through a population and the population can be identified in advance, say by a list, then a random

sample can be taken by selecting at random the number needed for the sample from the population list or the sampling frame. If a cinema chain wants to know about the viewing preferences of its audience, it could interview 2,000 customers in the areas around its chain of 100 cinemas. In principle, this means interviewing 20 people in each area. The normal method for household interviews is to take the electoral rolls for each area. These are complete and about 95 per cent accurate lists of all households living in an area. You give each household a number and then select at random 2,000 of these numbers as the interviewed households.

- *systematic non-random sampling*: To avoid the problem of chance bias you may decide to choose the sample at regular intervals. The interval is known as the sampling fraction (size of sample/size of population). For example, if the population of the audience areas at the cinema was 2 million and you required 2,000 interviews, then you would select one in every two thousand households.

- *stratified sampling*: Sometimes a survey will want to focus on certain groups in a population to emphasise certain aspects of the population. This may be because the groups which are important to you are not well represented in the population, in which case you want to boost the sample size. Or it may be because these are groups which you are primarily interested in (e.g. cinema-goers) and there is no point in wasting time on those you have no interest in. There are two common ways of stratifying the sample:

Try it out Suggest 3 ways in which the population at a college or school could be sampled to find out about their leisure preferences.

- The first is at sample selection and you may choose to exclude certain areas of the list. If you were selecting high-income households, for example, and you were using a council tax list as the sampling frame, you might exclude the lower tax bands on properties as these would tend to represent the low-income households.
- The second way is at the interview stage. If looking at teenage viewing habits for instance, the interviewer can ask straight away on starting the interview 'Are there teenagers living in this household?' If not, the household can be dropped from the sample.

- *cluster sampling*: It is useful that people of similar profiles act in similar ways. Thus it is likely that manual workers living across a particular area will have similar TV viewing patterns, for example. You can therefore select a smaller district (a cluster) which has a profile similar to the whole area, and the answers you receive should reflect those of the area as a whole. The advantage of this is that smaller samples are required as the population in the sampling frame is lower, and the costs and logistics of doing the survey are greatly reduced. However, there is always a risk of unexpected regional or cultural differences when adopting cluster sampling, which may mean the cluster is unrepresentative of the greater population of the area. Researchers tend therefore to hedge their bets and opt for a series of clusters spread over the whole area. At data analysis they can then look out for these unexpected effects.

An alternative approach to planning samples in advance is to place interviewers in key locations (e.g. shopping centres, leisure centres) where the population is likely to go and for them to interview without pre-selection. When the results go

back to the researcher they can be processed, and interviews from outside the sample definition can be rejected. There are two types of sampling that are often used:

- *quota sampling.* If the sample size (*quota*) of a type of respondent is known and the respondent can be identified, a percentage (of the quota) number of interviews can be decided on as being representative of

---

Analysis and reporting – making sense of the results and reporting back

Bias – the degree to which the survey produces results that do not truly reflect its population

Census – measurement of an entire population

Clustered samples – where sampling is made from selected areas (often geographical) within the population that are thought to represent the population as a whole

Data processing – transferring the data from questionnaires into accumulated data (e.g. tables)

Fieldwork – implementing the survey, i.e. training interviewers and managing their work

Non-random samples – where sampling is carried out on a regular or fixed frequency (e.g. every tenth address)

Pilot survey – the testing and review of survey design or questionnaire by testing it on a small sample of the sample

Population – all the people that live in a defined area or have specified behaviours

Quota samples – where the sample size and characteristics are determined in advance and interviewers identify suitable interviewees at the point of interview until the sample size is reached

Random samples – where the sample is chosen at random

Sample – a proportion of the population

Sample survey – measurement of a sample

Sampling fraction – the proportion of the population selected in the sample

Sampling frame – a list of the population from which the sample is drawn

Significance – the degree to which results of a survey truly reflect the population and are not produced by the chance effects of the sampling

Stratified samples – where the sample is divided into subgroups within the population (e.g. different age groups, ethnic groups)

Survey design – identifying the sample and designing the questionnaire

Glossary of terms

CASE STUDY — Sampling

A cinema chain wants to research its viewers' preferences, and management decide that there is a distinct difference between northern and southern audiences. Based on this recognised assumption, it is further decided that there is no need to sample all the cinemas in the chain, and that cinemas in Manchester, Leeds and Newcastle will represent the north, while Brighton, Oxford and Bristol will be typical of the south. The sample will therefore be clustered in these outlets but the results will apply to the entire northern and southern areas of the chain.

Questions

1 What are the advantages to the cinema chain of carrying out this type of sampling?
2 Do you think that the clusters chosen are representative of the wider audience?

the whole. The interviewer can approach these known types and interview until the sample number is reached.

- *convenience sampling*: Sometimes it is difficult to pre-define or identify the characteristics of the sample. On other occasions catching the sample is difficult, for example, if the sample is a crowd leaving an event. On other occasions you may need information quickly and cannot plan samples. An example of this is if you were tracking the public response to a promotional campaign week by week.

The best strategy here is to sample anyone who will answer and then reconstruct the sample at the data analysis stage. For example, the cinema chain might be promoting a blockbuster movie and will want to know if the public has heard of the film and if they intend to see it. Street interviews in various locations on a daily basis would provide this information in time for the promotional campaign to be modified.

Methods of surveying

Surveys are carried out with or without interviewers. Interviewers need to be trained and briefed as a group to make sure they are working consistently. Interviewers are used for:

- telephone interviews
- household (doorstep) interviews
- street interviews.

Using interviewers is expensive unless you use volunteers or your own team. If you can do this, it becomes a very cheap survey method. Interviewers, if they are doing their job well, will get high response rates. Both household and street interviews should get response rates of above 90%. Interviewers are particularly useful for complex questionnaires, for dealing with sensitive issues or where clarification is needed.

Questionnaires can also be used without interviewers. For example, mail surveys (postal, e-mail and fax) do this, as do hand-outs such as customer response cards. Mail

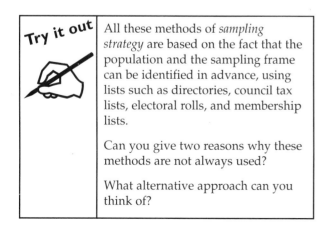

Try it out

All these methods of *sampling strategy* are based on the fact that the population and the sampling frame can be identified in advance, using lists such as directories, council tax lists, electoral rolls, and membership lists.

Can you give two reasons why these methods are not always used?

What alternative approach can you think of?

surveys are particularly useful as they are far cheaper than using paid interviewers and can be used for large samples. They are often seen as having low response rates (e.g. 20%). However, if well managed and if incentives such as vouchers are used, response rates of up to around 80% are possible.

Using postal surveys is more expensive than first appears. A well-run postal survey will normally consist of three stages. An initial letter, a follow-up to non-respondents and then a final follow-up. The first and final letters should contain a stamped addressed envelope and a questionnaire. Stamps should be first class to show that you are placing importance on the survey. Just on postage alone a mail survey will cost more than £1 a head. For many smaller leisure providers this will prove to be outside their marketing budgets.

Focus groups

Surveys are basically about measuring the combined responses of many people and this type of research is also known as *quantitative research*. It is fine for finding out the more superficial things we do or feel, or simply describes us (age, weight). In order to explore emotions, motivation, experiences, more time and variation has to be taken. This is *qualitative research* and involves small, representative groups of people who are interviewed over a longer period of time by a sensitive interviewer. These *focus groups* usually involve small numbers of people (no more than twelve) meeting for one to two hours on perhaps three occasions. Here they are asked to discuss their feelings and interact with each other on about ten questions. The interviewer analyses, categorises and interprets their responses and makes a report that depends more on interpretation than the data tables that are used in surveys.

It is perhaps surprising that small groups of people can indicate feelings and produce ideas that will represent those of a far larger population. However, the evidence is that they do work and are excellent in helping the design of products, in improving customer service and in dealing with community and development issues. They are also excellent at reaching a deeper level of understanding than surveys about what people mean. For example, a survey might show that 90 per cent of a community when asked 'do you want a new leisure centre?' said 'no', while a focus group asked 'What do you like and what don't you like about leisure centres?' elicited the fact that what people do not like is the traffic associated with it. Moreover they might all say that if the traffic could be managed (i.e. by a new access road) then they would love a new centre. The focus group thus produced a very different outcome from that generated by the survey.

Qualitative interviews: In any industry there are experts who can provide large amounts of insight and knowledge. Usually these are senior managers, but they can also be people like experienced front-of-house staff, technicians or even customers. Researchers who are involved in a study and understand its objectives usually carry out qualitative interviewing of these experts. The interviewing follows a similar format to that used by some TV interviewers but is carried out in an encouraging rather than hostile manner, either in person or by telephone. Developed from a framework of questions, an interview can last up to a couple of hours. The conversation is taped and later analysed and sometimes quotations are taken from it. The results may be used in their own context or to help plan other research such as surveys. Qualitative interviewing is comparatively cheap and in the right hands can reveal data that would be difficult to obtain in other ways. It can also provide contact networks for further research. Often interviewees will refer to other experts or even recommend them to the interviewer. There are disadvantages: interviews tend to be selective and their interpretation can be subjective.

Checklist: The secrets of qualitative interviewing

✓ plan the visit (maps, transport, arriving on time, when to eat)

✓ adopt a personal appearance and body language similar to the interviewee. (Professional interviewers travel around with a trunk of different outfits in their boot.) People interview best with people like themselves

✓ plenty of subject preparation (e.g. investigate the subject and possibly the person and organisation being interviewed)

✓ preparation of the interview pattern and its content

✓ good social skills (being relaxed and putting the interviewee at ease)

✓ manage the interview (encouraging the reticent, closing down and focusing the garrulous)

✓ make notes or better still record the interview

✓ listen more than you speak (controlled silence often provokes valuable information).

Observation

Most leisure managers have neither time nor money to use on research. Instead, a great deal can be done through quiet observation. One option is to observe not only their customers but also people outside their organisations. Simple observation of, for instance, some

customers being irritated by the presence of babies could lead to the development of special facilities for them away from the other customers. Observation is used in more analytical ways. Analysis of freeze-frame tapes from security cameras can indicate how crowds behave and allows the provider to adapt the facility and services to reduce vandalism and injury and increase enjoyment of the event. Similar observation can provide information on how to manage traffic control from large events. Overall observation costs nothing and can be done at any time. On the other hand the observer, unless trained, can easily be subjective and confirm existing prejudices.

Secondary research

A great deal of information is available from other people's primary research which includes:

• research papers (e.g. *Journal of Leisure Studies*, Sports and Arts Councils' research projects)
• textbooks (e.g. AVCE Advanced leisure and recreation!)
• trade summaries (Fact Files available from the Sports Council)
• articles (e.g. in trade magazines such as *Leisure Manager*, or in newspapers)
• organisational reporting (e.g. company reports, marketing plans, council yearbooks and minutes)
• government statistics (e.g. the Census, *General Household Survey, Social Trends*)
• market research reports (e.g. Mintel reports).

Secondary or *desk* research is a major part of the marketing manager's toolbox. It has strengths in that it:

• is often cheap (although some market research reports can cost several hundred pounds)
• is easy to set up
• reveals facts that would never be shown in survey research (e.g. newspaper, articles, letters)

- **The Census.** The British Census is held every ten years on the first year of the decade. It is highly accurate and has data limited to demographic variables. Data is geographically well defined and ranges from enumeration districts of a few hundred households to regional and national breakdowns. It has a weakness in that it takes a couple of years to process it fully and the data becomes less reliable towards the end of the Census period.

- **The General Household Survey.** A rolling survey of adults with a total sample of 19,000. It is the main source of leisure participation rates which are specially included every three years (apart from 1999). It is useful but not totally reliable as the data is national and will not account for local variations.

- **Social Trends.** A quarterly digest of statistics from many sources. A useful guide as to how we behave in all aspects of our lives.

- **Mintel.** This is the market leader in providing research reports on consumer behaviour. The reports are very expensive but can be viewed in specialised libraries.

- can bring together large amounts of data for cross-comparison.

There are also weaknesses:

- *Is it valid?* Has the primary research used correct methodology such as sampling and analysis? While most academic and market research sources are valid there are other resources which may not be. In particular, data from the Web is frequently unsubstantiated and newspaper articles are notoriously unreliable.
- *Is it current?* Secondary data will always originate from the past. It is necessary to assess whether the data is still valid.
- *Is there like for like?* Any piece of research must relate as closely as possible to the population and circumstances being studied. Two studies of cinema-goers might have no relation to each other at all if one

has been done in a small country cinema and the other in a multiplex in a major city.

Analysing and presenting data

Data analysis is a hard discipline which must be practised and studied at length. Like most of this chapter on research, this section will guide you to further reading. However, the following points may be helpful:

- Use graphics and tables where appropriate. It is normal practice to convert all data into this form and for the researcher to draw conclusions from it. When reporting back, include graphs and tables, but only sparingly to make a point.
- Use percentages and rates, as well as actual figures as this allows two samples to be compared. In some cases this data can be weighted to balance out differences in, say, age or gender in two samples.
- Use extrapolation and interpolation: this technique can be done mathematically, but is easier to do on a graph. By extending the curve of a graph one can predict where current trends will lead.
- Practice forecasting. Data extracted from a survey can be applied to the population as a whole to give estimates of market size (see 'Try it out' on page 256).
- Check that the methodology is valid. Never use data from too small samples or surveys with low response rates unless you are confident they have some significance – in which case inform your audience. Check for currency and compare like for like where possible. Be extra wary of facts from the Web!
- Balance qualitative and quantitative evidence in the face of survey data. Local knowledge and expert views can reveal data not picked up by surveys. For example, a graph might show that swimming pool use slumped at the start of a price rise. The lesson is that the local

market is sensitive to price rises. However, the real reason is that the pool was closed for repairs at the same time. It is a good idea to discuss results with local 'experts' before you draw conclusions. Consider all possible interpretations and understand why you have made your conclusion.

- Big differences and unexpected results are often the result of faulty data, so check the data processing. You will probably find that someone put the wrong code on the data when it was being punched into the spreadsheet.
- Present data clearly. Be concise, use bullet points, and present only relevant facts and statistics. Don't use gimmicks such as excessively distorted 3D graphs.
- Always quote sources as this allows the readers to make up their minds about the validity of your findings.

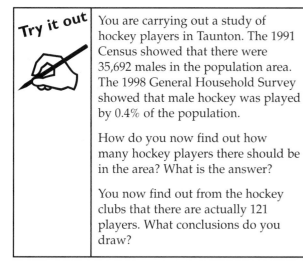

Try it out

You are carrying out a study of hockey players in Taunton. The 1991 Census showed that there were 35,692 males in the population area. The 1998 General Household Survey showed that male hockey was played by 0.4% of the population.

How do you now find out how many hockey players there should be in the area? What is the answer?

You now find out from the hockey clubs that there are actually 121 players. What conclusions do you draw?

Check it out

1 Explain the difference between primary and secondary research.
2 What is qualitative research?
3 What is qualitative research good at measuring?
4 What is a sample?
5 Give four examples of good data presentation.

4.4 Marketing communications

Advertising

Kieron Walsh describes advertising as 'the communication of images and information in total messages'. This covers a huge range of activities including:

Localised advertising

Notice boards, posters, brochures, leaflets and fliers are for many providers the main form of advertising. They are the cheapest way of providing publicity and can be distributed in all sorts of ways, such as in shop windows, on notice boards, on windscreens, and door-to-door or street distribution. With the exception of the major corporate providers

Promotions need AIDA

most organisations have very limited promotional budgets and so localised advertising is their sole or main form of advertising. Until recently, materials were often poorly produced or did little more than inform and could even put off customers because of the poor image. However, as desktop printing has developed, so providers have produced more professional materials that are geared towards the market. Most recently, blank high-quality posters are being used which individual providers can overprint. Distribution is important, as adverts placed in the right outlets for the market segment work well. For example, for women aged over 60, flyers in hairdressers' and doctors' waiting rooms would reach a high proportion of the market.

> **Think it over**
>
> Where might be good places to put up posters aimed at:
> - mothers with young children?
> - unemployed people?
> - teenagers?

Media advertising

Advertising through the mass media can use a variety of channels including:

- local and national press and magazines
- cinema and video
- the Web
- bill boards and poster sites.

Leisure and recreation providers do not often use most of these advertising outlets. This is because their markets are usually localised and their capacity to supply demand is limited. In other words, there is little point in attracting people who are too far away to use the service, or in raising expectations through advertising only to disappoint customers by not being able to supply the service. It is interesting to note that service-based industry with its lack of capacity generally restricts advertising compared with product-led sectors (e.g. records, books, gyms, restaurants) where supply of the product is limitless and means large-scale advertising is profitable.

The providers who extensively use the mass media are usually:

- large-capacity facilities and spectator events (e.g. stadia, cinemas and theatres)
- providers with visiting markets (e.g. tourist attractions)
- activities with significant sponsorship
- activities that operate in a chain of facilities (cinemas, some health clubs, fast-food chains).

The driving force behind all advertising is budget. To be viable the cost of advertising must be less than the increase in profits it will create.

The provider will need to ask:

- what is the cost of *advertising space*?
- what are the *production costs* of the advert?
- will the increase in custom pay for the cost of advertising?
- where do adverts need to be placed to best reach the intended market?

Advertising rates vary and are often negotiable. For example, national TV will charge according to expected audience size. Here are some rates to give some idea of advertising costs in 2000:

Television advertising rates	£
TV (Carlton West Country) 30-sec advert	1,500
Virgin Radio (national) 30-sec advert	3,000
Gemini Radio (local) 30-sec advert	66
Daily Mail (national newspaper) 15 × 2 cm advert	4,500
Herald Express (local newspaper) 15 × 2 cm advert	150
Poster sites (60" × 40" per week)	30

The effectiveness of the advert is affected by other factors:

- penetration of the market: the proportion of the market who will see it
- impact: the effect on the audience (AIDA).

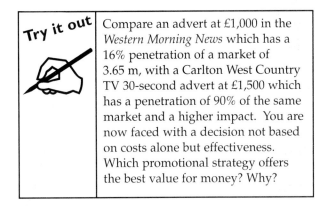

Try it out

Compare an advert at £1,000 in the *Western Morning News* which has a 16% penetration of a market of 3.65 m, with a Carlton West Country TV 30-second advert at £1,500 which has a penetration of 90% of the same market and a higher impact. You are now faced with a decision not based on costs alone but effectiveness. Which promotional strategy offers the best value for money? Why?

Local advertising rates are not prohibitive and sometimes warrant advertising for smaller providers. For example, providers sometimes launch new products such as the opening of a facility or an event or course in the local newspapers, or on the local radio station. They will also use them for special promotions, for example health clubs will often run a discount promotion just after Christmas or about three months before the summer holidays.

The Web is untested ground as yet. A website is inexpensive and can be seen equally by local markets and by international ones. However, at present the media is not sufficiently understood either by consumers or providers. It is probable, though, in the near future that it will be a major advertising medium for all leisure providers. One site that is already developed is the Health Club Network (**http://www.health-club.net/index.html**), while some Governing Bodies of Sport such as the Royal Yachting Association (RYA) are providing web servers that focus on that sport.

Promotional events

Providers sometimes stage events to promote their businesses. Sometimes an event is simply to provide information about the product but more often it is designed to provoke interest and attract sales (membership). One purpose of a promotional event is to reflect the core values of the product, and in leisure this usually means demonstrating activities that are fun, exciting, healthy and social.

Promotional events can be used to create immediate sales but they can be used for other objectives. Many leisure providers will stage events to maintain awareness or to promote goodwill in the community as an investment for the future should the provider need the support of the community. Typical events of this sort are floats in carnival processions or taking part in a Telethon fundraising event.

To achieve the right effect the product is often 'dressed up' for the event, such as:

- employing attractive representatives/demonstrators to promote
- employing celebrities
- holding competitions
- supplying goody bags or free gifts
- letting prospective customers try out the products
- having 'actors' dressed up as mascots such as cuddly bears or cheeky foxes (see case study opposite).

Promotional events take many forms but often include:

- taster and open days when people can visit the facility and use the service
- stands or demonstrations (e.g. test your fitness) in public places like shopping malls and at other organised events (trade exhibitions, professional football matches)
- publicity stunts (bungee jumps for charity, Children in Need presentations).

CASE STUDY – Mascot magic

Football clubs are particularly proud of their wide range of special links with their local communities. Leicester City's progressive and on-going programme of community initiative has earned plaudits from all quarters, making a real difference to the community at large. Club mascots, first introduced in 1993, Filbert Fox, Vicki Vixen and Cousin Dennis have provided a useful link between the club and the community. They act as both a powerful marketing and public relations tool and are also a great way to enhance customer loyalty and the Club's brand. All mascots are the property of the Club and as such, are registered under trademark. In order for a mascot to bring awareness and excitement, it must be energetic, interactive and personify the image of the club. The larger-than-life characters have a fun-loving attitude and act as a figurehead for both children and adults. They are highly interactive with both the LCFC supporters and the general public. Filbert Fox is one of the best known mascots in the Premier League.

Reasons for having a mascot include:

- to create team loyalty
- to market to children (future fans)
- team recognition
- to represent Leicester City Football Club in the community
- for merchandising and licensing opportunities.

Mascot conduct is tightly controlled as they not only represent the Club but also the Club's sponsors.

From appearing at first team games and family night football, Filbert and the other mascots have become synonymous with Club events and community schemes across the county. Filbert Fox is the figurehead for the Club's junior supporters club. The mascots are involved with schools, community groups and charity campaigns throughout Leicestershire and also at the sponsor's events. As well as Club business, the mascots are available for hire for birthday visits and parties.

The mascots' popularity is measured through newspaper coverage, repeat bookings and recommendations. It is estimated that all three mascots make more than 500 visits per year.

Questions

1 Approximately how many visits do the mascots make in a year?

2 Apart from appearing at team games, what other events and activities are the mascots involved in?

3 What are the main reasons for Leicester City Football Club to have mascots?

(Photo courtesy of Leicester City FC)
Leicester City mascot Filbert Fox

Promotional events can be highly effective as they can be accurately targeted to market segments and may have the added benefit of attracting free press coverage. On the down side they can be expensive to set up, time consuming to manage and can miss the mark.

Promotional packages

Special incentives can be used occasionally to drive up sales over a set period. Promotional packages therefore differ from pricing policies in that they are short term. They also differ from promotional events as they are aimed solely at achieving immediate sales. Frequently they involve price offers such as 'two for the price of one', or discounts. Other incentives such as free gifts, prizes and competitions may be offered. You may have wondered how organisations can offer such lavish prizes as luxury weekends or colour TVs. The answer is quite simple. Invariably there are other providers who have surplus stock who will sell it on at greatly reduced prices. Weekend breaks are normally in hotels where there are frequently empty rooms. Because the prize winner pays for meals and drinks extra profit will be gained from this. Promoters offer vouchers to provide new customers to the supplier of the voucher. With large events (e.g. the Greater Manchester Youth Games) the organisers will sell space in their promotional package to the discount supplier. For this payment the suppliers have the right to trade, distribute their vouchers and have advertising in the event programme. This technique of charging others to take part in your promotional package is called *cross-marketing*.

Public relations

The goodwill of customers, the public at large and people in authority such as politicians plays an important part in maintaining a successful business that is supported by the community. It is important to build up goodwill with these groups over time, to persuade them to recommend the product and to gain support in times of need. Public relations are a continual process. Four techniques are involved:

- maintaining good relations with the media and local politicians by providing hospitality and inviting them to events and promotions
- keeping local communities happy by minimising any inconvenience (e.g. noisy customers and traffic), making donations to local good causes, contributing to community events
- entertaining VIPs. People respond well to the 'party' rather than the business atmosphere. Entertaining means people meet new contacts important to them and spread the word to other influential people about the product
- maintaining good relations with the customer. Customers will always be the best ambassadors for a product.

Good public relations can help promote the business by acquiring *free publicity*. If journalists are well disposed to the provider they will invariably cover stories about the facility and give it a positive image. A manager who is successful at public relations can often generate publicity which would be worth thousands of pounds over a year. This type of coverage is known as *editorial space*. Sometimes you will see an article in a newspaper which looks like a series of articles featuring the product. In fact, these are a type of adverts known as an *aditorial*. The newspaper often commissions them, approaches the provider and makes a charge

Try it out Find a copy of a local newspaper and see if you can find an example of an 'aditorial'. Discuss how it has been put together. Do you think it works well?

for printing the aditorial. Good practice dictates that the word 'Advertisement' must be featured on the page and you will usually find it in small print at the top of the page.

Press releases are often used in PR work with the media. This is a document where the provider writes what they want the world to know. It is distributed to all media in the market area and often has an *embargo* (date and time) on it which dictates when the press will be able to announce the story. Press releases are usually about events and courses, change of staff or image, or new facilities.

'Spin' is now an everyday term. It comes originally from the spin that baseball pitchers put on a ball to make it go where they want. Although it is often associated with politics, it is what all public relations work involves. For example, when building a new leisure facility there will always be a section of the public that do not want it – for example, local people who do not want the traffic or the view of the building. The provider will put 'spin' on the proposals by emphasising the social benefits of the proposal.

Sponsorship

To be successful sponsorship needs to be a mutual arrangement that centres around the marketing benefits for both the sponsor and sponsored.

Here are some common benefits:

- The sponsor has an image that it wishes to reinforce or it seeks prestige. For example it may want to be youth-associated or seen as caring. It will therefore be attracted to organisations that reflect this image.
- The sponsor may wish to increase product awareness or increase sales. It will therefore want an opportunity to have product placement with the sponsored group's activities. The Vodaphone sponsorship of Manchester United is a marketing first. One aspect of the deal is the display of the Vodaphone name on products of the club. However the genius of the plan is to distribute free mobile phones to the fans (the club has the world's biggest fan base) this will give them Internet access (which they pay for) to keep up to date with the club.
- The sponsor may consider the publicity associated with the sponsored group will offer opportunities for its own publicity. The sponsor may want assurances that its name will be mentioned in all publicity and that there will be coverage of its involvement. Perhaps most familiar are product logos or names on players' shirts. The sponsor sees the sponsored group's activities as a means for corporate entertainment. Thus a sponsor of a professional football club may expect the use of an executive suite for its entertainment.

For the sponsored group there may be advantages other than having more resources to perform their activities. For example:

- A corporate sponsor may have a powerful public relations and publicity machine that can be very useful. It may be able to provide influential contacts and subsidiary sponsors.
- The image of the sponsor may make the activity itself more exciting or attractive to the audience or participants.
- Sponsorship money can increase marketing power in terms of being able to improve the product (better prizes, better participants), extend promotions or affect price by subsidising pricing or adding value.

As a consequence, sponsorship deals are normally complex and often contracted.

Sensitivity and compliance is crucial even for simple deals. It should also be remembered that sponsorship compliance extends not only to the organisations but also to their members. Consequently, poor images presented by players or officials in their private lives can result in sponsorship being withdrawn.

Direct marketing

Direct marketing is when potential customers or prospects are personally contacted by the provider by mail or telephone (*telemarketing*). The prospects are selected because they are known to have certain characteristics that indicate that they are likely to be interested in the product. For example, people aged between 20 and 30 with high income are most likely to be interested in health and fitness products. Residential homes and GPs are more likely to be interested in sports therapy for the elderly.

Mail lists of such people can be bought from Direct Marketing Agencies, who will also manage the mailshot or telephone calls. Some providers in leisure and recreation use these but many more compile their own lists. One commonly used target group is the provider's own customers. Many providers will get details about members and if they use smart cards can track what those customers like and use. When a new product becomes available they can filter out the customers who are most likely to be interested and contact them. Direct mailing is also expensive, each mailshot contact probably costs around a pound. Thus a provider needs to pretty sure that there is going to be a high return to make it worthwhile.

Direct response advertising is where the prospect sees the advert and then can immediately purchase the product using a credit card. For many years direct advertising and marketing has been used. You may be familiar with mass marketing such as the advertising channels on TV where, having seen the product demonstration, the viewer can telephone and purchase it using a credit card. The method has been refined to become directly marketed using mailshots.

The growth of the Web is drastically increasing the power of the method. This is partly because the Web is universal and can be approached by all market segments that have access. More disturbing is that it is a self-selecting process since every hit on a Web site identifies the sender and means their address can be used for further e-mailshots. The Web is also an important site for distribution because it allows the customer to view the promotion, purchase and sometimes consume all in the same action.

At present Web-based direct response is largely used by the manufacturing industry for selling physical products. However, the Web is already expanding this method for services – recently the gambling industry has gone on line! Websites have been created for other sectors such as the fitness industry. The customer can sample services such as fitness testing and then subscribe to gain entry to membership and a full service. If the trend continues it will become normal practice for all leisure facilities to advertise in this way and accept on-line booking.

 **Try it out** Look up the website for a leisure consumer product, for example Nike or Adidas. How easy is it to buy directly from the website? Have you or anyone you know ever purchased this way? What were the advantages, if any, over traditional methods of buying?

Customer promotion

Most leisure providers find that '*word of mouth*' is often the only promotion they need.

If the service and products are good and what the market wants, customers will come back (*repeat business*) or tell their friends who then buy it (*referred business*). With many leisure providers, 80–90 per cent of business comes from this category. If operating near capacity, a provider may therefore only need to use other forms of promotion to keep existing customers attracted or to penetrate new markets for new products. Customer promotion has to be earned and means that standards have to be high and maintained. This may concern the physical side of the facility such as the state of the equipment or the landscaping, as well as the intangibles such as customer care.

! Check it out

1 Give two examples of localised advertising. What are its two main advantages?

2 What is market penetration? Explain how you would apply it when advertising a new boy band album on television?

3 Explain the difference between promotional packages and events.

4 What is public relations?

5 Explain why attractive demonstrators are used at promotional events?

6 Why is editorial space a good form of promotion? How does it differ from aditorials?

7 Explain two ways in which sponsors benefit from sponsorship.

8 Give two ways of direct mailing.

9 How do you achieve effective word-of-mouth promotion. Who does it?

Ethics and control of marketing

Marketing intrinsically intrudes into people's private lives and if not regulated can have damaging affects. Controls are either made by the industry itself (i.e. *self-regulation*) or by law (*statutory control*).

The most important areas of control are:

Research

Primary research can expose facts that can embarrass respondents or even endanger them. Interviewers also can have access to people's homes or workplaces. Here are the ground rules of good practice.

Interviewers must:

• Always carry ID and explain the purpose of the research (ideally give out a pre-printed letter).

• Explain how confidentiality will be maintained. For example, no link will be made between the person and his/her answers. This can sometimes be hard to do in reports where it becomes obvious who the person is. For example, if you quote an ice rink manager in the Southwest, it is obvious who it is as there is only one ice rink in the Southwest.

• Give people a contact to verify who you are or to follow up any queries they might have a later date.

Researchers must always:

• secure data. Lock questionnaires and tapes away. Do not show them to people who might have a vested interest

• ensure that, when logging reports, respondents cannot be identified if anonymity has been assured.

Many researchers are professionals and their companies belong to the Market Research Society (**www.mrs.org.uk**) which has a code of conduct that expands on these points and to which its members subscribe. Even when researchers are not members it is still good practice to follow these principles, some of which are summarised here:

Checklist: The principles of good market research

✓ research is founded on willing co-operation. It depends upon the confidence that it is conducted honestly, objectively and without unwelcome intrusion or harm to respondents. Its purpose is to collect and analyse information, not directly to create sales or to influence the opinions of anyone participating in it.

✓ the general public and other interested parties shall be entitled to complete assurance of confidentiality anonymity, and data should be used only for the purposes of the research

✓ wherever possible, respondents must be informed as to the purpose of the research and the likely length of time necessary for the collection of the information

✓ research findings must be accurate and never misleading

✓ respondents' co-operation is ntirely voluntary. They must not be misled when being asked for co-operation

✓ researchers must take special care when interviewing children, young people and other potentially vulnerable members of society. The informed consent of the parent or responsible adult must first be obtained for interviews with children

✓ respondents must be told if observation techniques or recording equipment are used

✓ respondents must be enabled to check, without difficulty, the identity of the researcher

✓ researchers must not undertake any non-research activities involving data about individuals which will be used for sales or promotional activity. Any such non-research activities must always be clearly differentiated from marketing research activities.

The growth of computer-stored data has increase the opportunity for abuse of data storage. For example, many companies that have lists sell them on to other companies to be used for direct marketing. More sinister, is that such data could be used to find out personal things about individuals such as their medical or criminal records. So great is the possibility of abuse that legislation (the **Data Protection Act 1998**) has come into force that must be followed if you are using computerised data. Full details can be found from the Data Protection Registry (**http://www.dataprotection.gov.uk/dprhome.htm**), but here are the main regulations:

To comply with the Act anyone handling personal data is subject to various controls. All data-handling organisations have to comply with this and register with the Data Protection Registry. They are also bound to use data properly, store it securely, retain it and make it accessible to the person to whom the data relates. From a personal point of view the Act means that you will:

- keep data secure
- not pass it on to other organisations/ individuals without the data owner's permission
- use it only for the purposes it was intended for
- not use it for your personal gain or interest.

Advertising

Advertising is a major influence in all our lives. It has the power to persuade us to buy things and, because it needs to attract our attention, it can potentially use images that are offensive. The advertising industry is long established and all professional advertising is governed by the Advertising Standards Authority (**http://www.asa.org.uk/**). There are also statutory controls such as **The Control of Misleading Advertisements Regulations 1988**. The Authority has drawn up three codes for Advertising, Promotion and Cigarette advertising – the last has a direct relevance to the leisure industry because of the involvement of tobacco sponsorship with major sporting events.

There are two major principles of these codes:

1   All advertisements should be honest, decent, legal and truthful.

Honest: Advertisers should not exploit the credulity, lack of knowledge or inexperience of consumers. An example of this is in the publicity for lotteries and draws where the term 'you could win' should be used as opposed to 'win'.

Decent: Advertisements should contain nothing that is likely to cause serious or widespread offence. Particular care should be taken to avoid causing offence on the grounds of race, religion, sex, sexual orientation or disability. An advert for lunchtime fitness sessions for women with an image focusing on a male athlete in Lycra shorts and the slogan 'Girls, what's in your lunchbox today?' might fall into this category.

Legal: Advertisements should contain nothing that breaks the law or incites anyone to break it. An advert advertising football shirts and picturing crowd violence would be deemed to be inciting civil disorder offences.

Truthful: No advertisement should mislead by inaccuracy, ambiguity, exaggeration, omission or otherwise. The classic example here is saying something is the best. Probably!

Promotional material must be honest and true!

2   All advertisements should be prepared with a sense of responsibility to consumers and to society. Sony computer entertainment had complaints brought against them after a direct mailing campaign of three successive official letters that featured a mock medical marked 'private and confidential' and stated 'test results' inside. This alarmed people who were awaiting genuine medical tests and the complaint was upheld.

Sales

The final stage of the marketing process is when the promotion becomes a reality for the customer and he/she buys the product. This end of the process is strictly controlled by law with a variety of acts, most of which are regulated by the Office of Fair Trading (**http://www.oft.gov.uk/**) or in cases of criminal fraud and deception by the police themselves. The relevance to marketing and sales is that the legislation all links to what has been promised, the way the sale was made and if the product lived up to what had been promised. The implication of this is that your advert, promotion or sale will be illegal or unethical if somehow it:

- leads the customers to think they will be getting something which they do not in fact get
- pressures the customer into buying the product.

You may notice that on some promotions and sales literature there will be a notice to the effect that 'This offer does not affect the consumer's statutory rights'. This means that the following laws that affect consumers' rights will still be adhered to:

Trade Descriptions Act 1968

This Act prohibits misdescription of goods, false claims for services, accommodation and facilities. It is particularly relevant in the leisure industry. Unless there is evidence to support the claim a provider cannot claim, for example, that that he is providing luxury or relaxing conditions, improving the client's personal relationships, state-of-the-art equipment, easy access to the town centre or qualified staff.

This is the legal requirement for your promotions to be honest and true.

Sale of Goods Act 1979 (amended with Sale and Supply of Goods Act 1994):

Goods and services must fit the description used in any advert, label, or packaging, etc. that relates to them – such as the year or make, type, colour, size or materials used. These must be accurate. The goods must also be of satisfactory quality – and should be fit for their purpose. An example of this is when you buy sports equipment that breaks on first use and is therefore not fit for purpose.

Consumer Protection Act 1987

This says that only safe goods should be put on sale (watch out for that sauna with the broken thermostat).

It also prohibits misleading price indications. Customers have a right to complain to the trading standards office if they are charged more at the till than the price on the shelf or advert.

Supply of Goods and Services Act 1982 (amended with Supply of Goods and Services Act 1994)

This states that work covered by the contract – which exists as soon as you agree to provide a service (note issuing a ticket is in effect a contract) – must be carried out with reasonable skill and care, within a reasonable time, and for a reasonable price (if that's not stated). Note, what is reasonable is not defined by law.

If something goes wrong, the customer can ask you to rectify it. If you are unable to do so, then he or she is legally entitled to employ another contractor to rectify the problem and claim the costs from you.

Unfair Contract Terms Act 1977 (and Unfair Terms in Consumer Contracts Regulations 1994)

If terms in pre-printed contracts are unreasonable the Office of Fair Trading can make the company change the contract. The regulations apply only to standard (pre-printed) contracts.

Consumer Credit Act 1974

If purchasers sign a credit agreement at home, they are given a cooling-off period (usually of 28 days) during which they can change their mind and cancel the agreement. Most reputable companies extend this to all credit agreements.

Check it out

1 What is self regulation and statutory control? Give an example of each.

2 What do you need to do if you are 'professionally' interviewing people in a survey?

3 Who are the controlling bodies for market research and advertising?

4 Describe the principles behind the advertising code of practice?

5 Why is Carlsberg lager only 'probably the best lager in the world'?

6 You sign a credit agreement for a new sound system but change your mind on getting home. Which law protects you and allows you to withdraw from the contract?

7 You buy a computer that breaks down after a month. The company wants to charge you a £100 inspection charge. What law are they breaking?

Sources of information and further reading

Most books on marketing are somewhat academic and are probably best used to dip into to expand your knowledge. You may find more serviceable companions in the AVCE Business textbook and the Sage publications. It is also worth looking at the various BBC business programmes as many of these give a practical and lively insight into marketing. A good magazine to look at is *Leisure Week* which provides a mine of information on corporate leisure.

Websites tend to be poor and are designed largely to promote the businesses rather than to educate. Government sites are improving all the time, and visits to Office for National Statistics or Statbase may throw up tables you are looking for. Research information is best found in specialist business libraries.

Cowell, D., *The Marketing of Services*, Heinemann

Davies, E. and Davies B., *Successful Marketing in a Week*, Hodder and Stoughton, 1998

Farby A.D., *How to Produce Successful Advertising*, 2nd edition, Kogan and Page, 1998

Fink, A. and Kosecoff, J., *How to Conduct Surveys*, Sage, 1998

Gabuy J., *Teach Yourself Copywriting for Creative Advertising*, Hodder and Stoughton, 1998

Morgan, D. L., *The Focus Group Handbook*, Sage, 1997

McDonald, M., *Marketing Plans*, Butterworth Heinemann, 1995

Needham, D. and Dransfield, R., AVCE *Business Advanced*, Heinemann, 2000

Sport England, *Model Survey Package*, 1999

Veal, A.J., *Research Methods for Leisure and Tourism*, second edition, Financial Times, Prentice Hall, 1996

Walsh, K., *Marketing in Local Government*, Longman, 1989

Useful websites

The Data Protection Registry: **www.dataprotection.gov.uk/dprhome.htm**

Advertising Standards Authority: **www.asa.org.uk**

Office of Fair Trading: **www.oft.gov.uk**

Office for National Statistics: **www.statistics.gov.uk**

This unit is organised into eight sections. You will learn about:

- the importance of excellent customer service
- personal presentation
- types of customers
- dealing with customers
- selling skills
- customer service situations
- handling complaints
- assessing the quality and effectiveness of customer service.

Introduction

'The customer is king' is a much voiced slogan and it is true. If you don't look after your customers they will leave you, the business will fail, and you will lose your job. If you work in the industry your primary aim will be to produce what the customer wants. Delivering good customer service is the core of any service industry and relating to and thinking of your customers is a lot if fun. If you can deliver what the customers want and you can see them benefiting from your efforts, you will almost certainly have a great deal of job satisfaction.

As you will see in this chapter, customer service is more than just being friendly and smiling (although these are essential). It requires planning and forethought and attention to your own interpersonal and communication skills. In addition, like any modern management process, customer service needs to be assessed to evaluate what is being done and how it can be further improved.

You can learn a lot from books and you would be well advised to expand your knowledge by reading around the subject. There are many readable books on the market. You will also learn a lot by looking at yourself. This can mean literally (in the mirror or on video) or by asking yourself and others how you handle situations and how you appear to others. Another excellent way of learning about customer service is to analyse how you are treated when you are the customer. Every day you buy products and use services. Get into the habit of identifying when you are pleased or unhappy with service and then analysing why. Work out how the service could have been improved. The chances are that many other customers will have the same reactions as you. Learn from your experience and apply it when you provide your own customer service.

Britain has lagged behind other countries in standards of customer service, although in the last ten years things have begun to change. In many areas of the leisure industry managers are now particularly concerned to improve customer service, and this concern has been reflected at national level with the establishment of the Institute of Customer Care (www.ics.nto.com).

When studying customer service it is always fun to look at bad practice. This is why The Brittas Empire, Fawlty Towers and Hi de Hi were such good comedies and were used to train people in customer service and management. If you watch videos of these series you can legitimately say that you are researching customer service. The Theme Park computer game is worth playing also as it shows how physical design can add to customer satisfaction.

In this chapter there are a good number of simulations. They are worth practising because as John Wellemin (1998) says, 'Customer care is not a spectator sport'.

5.1 The importance of excellent customer service

Introduction

The forerunner of modern active leisure provision was the Public Baths, which made washing facilities available to the Victorian working classes. The function of these baths

The forerunner of modern leisure provision was the Public Baths – these were designed for public health not recreation

was therefore public health and not recreational. The core of their operation was to provide hot water from coke-fired boilers which resembled those in the boiler room of a steam ship. Not surprisingly, many of the staff who worked at the baths were retired stokers and ship's engineers. Their aim was to run an efficient 'ship' and provide the hot water for washing or swimming in. Needless to say the operation was run on naval standards and the brass was kept shining and the engine room in peak condition. Users of the baths were of secondary importance; at best they might be greeted by the manager, at worst they were seen as pests who would spoil all the hard work of the staff in maintaining a spotless baths. This was an attitude that persisted as baths evolved into swimming baths, and could even be found at a few pools up to a decade ago.

The early 1900s saw the start of the development of recreation grounds to meet the growing demand for games of soccer, rugby football and athletics races. Players needed to change and wash, so changing rooms were built on the same sites. These were, with only a few exceptions, purely functional and basic. The message was clearly 'change and do not linger'. In the voluntary sector things were not much better. Sports for the well-off often reflected the spartan conditions of the public schools where many had learned to love sport, but also to consider any comforts or conveniences as 'soft'. For the rest of society, small sports clubs and drama societies with only the most basic facilities formed the backbone of recreational life.

The third type of recreational provision from this same period were the pubic libraries and assembly rooms. While grand in their architecture, they were like the sports facilities in that they were essentially functional. In the private sector, the emphasis was also on entertainment with a huge number of theatres, music halls and cinemas, where there might be an usherette to show

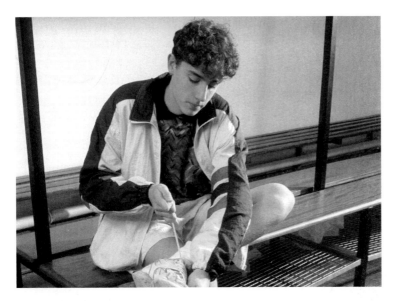

Change and do not linger!

The major leisure activity for the British between 1930 and 1960 was going to the cinema. What was it like? You would almost certainly have to queue for tickets outside the cinema (often in the rain). Cinemas often had an audience of several hundred for a big film and a long wait was not unusual and could end with no tickets if the cinema was full. In the front of house there would often be an imposing commissionaire dressed in livery or ex-serviceman's uniform, whose main purpose was to give authority rather than hospitality. Tickets were cheap, sweets were expensive. On entering the auditorium your first impression was the warm smell (of damp clothes, scent and sweat from a large crowd not yet introduced to modern hygiene products), coupled with a fog of cigarette smoke. You would be ushered to an empty seat (no choice of where you would like to sit). Those in the back rows would be subjected throughout the performance to the blinding beam of a torch as the usherette made sure you were behaving. At the end of the performance the National Anthem was played and everyone stood to attention. In the bigger cinemas an organist bathed in soft lights played background music before and after the 'show'. It was considered a great night out and even after a fish and chip supper you still had change out of half a crown (the equivalent today of twelve pence)!

Think of a trip to the cinema today and see how customer care has reduced the inconveniences described here.

you to your seat and a manager to deal with misbehaving customers.

The 1970s and change

Up to this point leisure providers were not greatly concerned with service for their customers. Things began to change in the 1970s. The creation of the first leisure centres demanded a new type of manager that had not existed before. These were often PE teachers who had quite a different attitude. They were interested in attracting young people into playing sport (many managers of the old pools saw children as nothing but a nuisance) and in developing sports where everyone could have lessons.

The 1980s and 1990s then saw the arrival of professional managers with specialised leisure management qualifications.

There was also a change in society. People had increasing amounts of disposable leisure income. They were going abroad for their holidays and learning what happened in other countries. Businesses which were more attentive to the needs of their customers found that this brought more customers and more profits. Cinemas which had been failing for some years found that if they made the seating more comfortable, allowed telephone bookings and provided car parks, they could attract back an audience.

The influence of the Americans has been enormous. American society has a different view of customers. 'The customer *is* king' and if the customer has paid for a service he/she expects value and will complain if it isn't up to standard. The pattern of many of the leisure operations now established in Britain came from America and was founded on the basic principle of excellent customer service. Themed restaurants started life there as did theme parks and the multiplex cinema, created as the answer to the same decline in film-going as had been seen in Europe.

And of course there is the fitness revolution. The British attitude to sport until recently was that if it didn't hurt or you weren't wearing some tatty old shorts then it was not doing you any good. The American view was if you want to feel good you want to look good and enjoy doing it. Thus health and fitness facilities and country clubs arrived and sport for the first time was taking place in a luxurious and up-market setting. Hand in hand with this came customer service – customers are treated with respect, courtesy and interest.

As the private sector changed, so there were developments in the public sector. In the late 1980s government funding of local authorities was shrinking. Leisure facilities were put under the spotlight. On the one hand, their high running costs were challenged and pressure was put on them either to close or reduce costs. On the other hand, they were one of the few council services capable of providing an income and profits. The message was for many authorities to abandon the idea of subsidised leisure for the majority and to start to increase income. However, to do this the providers had to compete with the private sector and adopt its standards of provision and customer service, which meant increasing

value for money. The last ten years have seen major changes, and the adoption of the Best Value system will no doubt complete this revolution in customer standards.

Finally, there is the voluntary sector, where, it seems, many clubs have failed to catch up with the standards and efficiency now being offered by their professional competitors. Even this is changing now, largely due to Lottery funding which is providing the means for new and luxurious designs for facilities. The Lottery also requires clubs to adopt a more open attitude to the community and welcome members who may previously have been excluded.

What is customer service?

Customer service involves putting the customers and their needs at the heart of an organisation's policies and methods. This sounds, and is, very similar to the marketing approach which we have already discussed. Customer service can be seen as the front-of-house delivery of marketing. It is the business of ensuring that the customers gets exactly what they thought they were going to get, or more, from the marketing promotion.

Figure 5.1 shows some aspects of customer service that organisations should try to supply if they are to win their customer's loyalty.

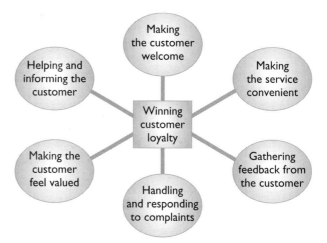

Figure 5.1 Aspects of customer service needed to win customer loyalty

Customer service has two components and these always need to be kept in mind:

- staff and their attitude and performance with customers
- design of systems and facilities to help the customer.

We shall deal at length with the personal aspect of customer service. You should, however, keep in mind that design and the physical nature of a facility are also very important in that they provide ambience, access and information. Here are some key features of the physical aspects of customer service:

- easy access to and around the facility
- pleasant and hospitable décor and atmosphere (air conditioning, plant, lighting)
- quick, efficient and simple purchasing system
- effective friendly signing and information points
- a product which has been promised in good working order
- clean facilities, especially toilets and catering areas.

Both the staff and the physical components have two aspects:

CASE STUDY — Customer service at the cinema

1 There are two films showing at the local cinema and Jane is not sure which will be suitable for the family. She would like some advice, but when she phones up she is answered by an automated booking system that does not contain a loop out to a live person. She has to look up another number and re-dial. This cinema is trying to reduce staff costs and also keep the customer happy, but by eliminating the staff component and providing only a physical customer service, it causes an unfriendly, irritating feeling and Jane feels rejected and unwanted as well as being annoyed and frustrated because she cannot get the necessary information to make her choice. Moreover, older customers quite often feel threatened by modern, automated booking systems and therefore would fail to persevere, thus losing the cinema sales.

2 Jeff goes to a small independent cinema that does not have pre-booking to see a popular film. There is a queue and when he finally reaches the ticket office he finds out that the cinema is full. The salesperson is extremely sympathetic and suggests Jeff watches the other film. However, Jeff feels that it would have been a good idea for someone to have told the queue earlier that the tickets were sold out. He appreciates the concern of the receptionist, but why was there a problem in the first place? His impression is probably 'nice people but really unprofessional – in future I am going to the multiplex'.

3 The multiplex Jeff goes to has got it right: it has an automated system for booking beforehand by phone for all the screens, but immediately offers two other options – firstly, to go to a recorded message that describes the films or secondly, to talk to a staff member. Jeff can pre-book and when he arrives walks into a smart, welcoming building with good décor, plants and welcoming signs. The multiplex seems to have got it right, which is perhaps why they are dominating the movies industry.

Question

What else can you think of in the way of facilities and customer care that would make a trip to the cinema pleasant?

What are the tangible and non-tangible effects of this centre?

- tangible – the things which customers perceive through the senses (touch, taste, smell, sight)

Try it out

	Tangible	Non-tangible
Staff	Uniform, personal presentation	Friendliness, concern, interest
Physical	Information signs, disabled ramps	Ambience, atmosphere

The design of facilities and other physical provision can make or break the leisure experience. Think of some features that might create a pleasant visit for:

- a parent taking a toddler to a tots gym session at a sport centre
- a pensioner going to a bingo night at a local community centre
- a disabled person going to the theatre.

- non-tangible – the emotional effect on customers.

Table 5.1 Aspects and components of customer care

Action	Staff	Design
Making the customer welcome	Staff who know booking systems and how to welcome.	Quick, efficient booking tills and booking systems. Welcoming reception area. Adequate reception to avoid queues or bottlenecks.
Helping the customer	Staff who understand the product and can communicate.	Equipment and services that are easy to use and reduce the need for explanation or information. Signs, recorded messages.
Making the customer comfortable	Staff who enquire about needs, offer hospitality.	Weather-proof walkways from car park to reception. Rest areas and comfortable seating.
Making the customer valued	Staff who can give 'positive' strokes or suggest ways the customer would expand their enjoyment. Thanking the customer. Reassuring the customer.	Tokens such as free gifts, follow-up letters, requests for customer opinion of the service. Loyalty schemes, newsletters or notice boards that focus on customers.
Handling complaints	Staff who can apologise to and calm the customer. Solve the problem.	Defined complaint procedure which is easy for the customer to use. Areas where customer can complain out of the public eye.
Gathering feedback from the customer	Staff who can talk to the customer and encourage suggestions.	System to record and analyse feedback.

Check it out

1 Give three reasons for the slow development of customer service in Britain.

2 Give an example of how physical and staffing features are combined to provide customer service.

3 How can a non-tangible component affect customer care?

4 Provide examples you have experienced of four aspects of customer service.

5 Look at the catering facilities in your school or college. Using the matrix shown earlier, give examples of ways in which the service gives good customer care. Can you think of ways in which it could improve?

Think it over

Think back to when you had an enjoyable time at a leisure facility and also to an occasion when you had a bad time. Now identify the various ways in which customer service was provided, using the terms you have learnt. What conclusions can you draw about the importance of customer service from your experiences? What was the impact on the company as a result of your subsequent response?

Customer types

Providing excellent customer service means giving a good service to **all** customers. We will look at different types of customer in detail in section 5.3 Types of customers (page 292). There are two main types of customers:

- internal – colleagues and other people involved in the production process
- external – the people who use the products your organisation provides.

Internal customers

In a leisure organisation, people working in various departments are all providing services to each other in order to produce the service for the external customer. They are acting as providers and customers for each other. They are 'internal' customers. The AVCE specification does not refer to internal customers and you will probably not refer to them in your assessed work. Despite this, it is worth while keeping the importance of internal customer service in mind when working in the industry. You should remember that although

CASE STUDY – A question of communication and consideration

An accounts department bills external customers by sending out formal routine invoices which have not taken into consideration customer variations.

A customer who has had an excellent time using the facility and built up a friendly relationship with operations staff does not want to receive a pompous letter asking for payment. The accounts department needs to liaise with operations staff, and perhaps lighten up their approach to external customers. Likewise, operations staff can help accounts staff by processing membership application forms and payments quickly and by checking that forms and cheques were completed correctly.

Marketing departments lead the promotion of services. If they are going to serve the operation's 'internal customers', they should make sure they consult them on the practicality of the products they plan to offer. They should also tell them about promotions – who they are targeted at – and provide information and training for the operations staff so that they can help the promotion.

Question

Identify three checks a marketing department should make with 'front-of-house' staff when developing a promotion.

when dealing with internal customers there are many similarities in approach and technique to dealing with external ones, there are also differences. This is evident in, for example, telephone manner or the way you address customers or present yourself.

External customers

What is an external customer? The obvious answer is someone who buys or uses your goods or services. However, there are various conditions of customers each requiring a different customer service:

- prospects
- current customers
- lapsed customers.

Prospects: These are the customers who have still to decide to use the product you provide. They are expressing an interest, and this is a crucial moment as not only are they sizing up the material aspects of a service but they are also open to influence. A badly handled, inattentive reception by a member of staff can be immediately off-putting. This is an important moment of staff, non-tangible customer care (see Think it over).

Even when you have turned a prospect into a customer who is using your service you need to work hard at the next stage – keeping their custom. When customers come to you they are expecting:

Think it over

Imagine a telephone conversation like this:

Prospect: 'Hello, is that Flops Gym? I am interested in finding out about membership.'

Giggling receptionist: 'Oh I am sorry, Gavin here was telling us about his night out last night. Membership? Yes I am sure we can help you – now the best thing is for me to send you some information. Unfortunately, our new publicity is not back from the printers until next week so could I send you the details then?'

This is clearly not very good – with an unprofessional start and a failure to meet the prospect's immediate need for information. What might be the result?

Are cheap goods a substitute for good customer service?

CASE STUDY – Cheap at half the price

Have you ever gone to buy trainers from a sports shop and found the place crowded and a queue a mile long because someone is arguing with the manager and the shop is short of staff? If you have, the chances are you left and went to different shop, where you may have paid a little more but at least you were served. What were you? A lost prospect.

Question

The first shop had got both the physical and staff components wrong. They probably thought that offering cheap goods was sufficient to pull in the customers. Were they right?

CASE STUDY – Winners Health Club

Here are some of the customer service features that Winners Health Club carry out with their existing customers:

Staff keep an eye on new members and give them special attention to help them get used to the club. They make a point of introducing them by name to other members. The club newsletter features a new member every month. All new members receive a letter after their first month inviting them to drop by and talk to the manager to say how they are enjoying themselves and to offer any suggestions. All members get sent a birthday card. Staff take note of the customer's fitness progress and advise on how it can be developed to suit the needs of the customer.

Question

What do you think Winners Health Club is trying to achieve by sending birthday cards to its members? Do you think that the benefits would justify the cost?

- a welcome and attention
- advice on how to get best use from the service
- help if they are having problems
- information on new products and services
- equipment and service that do what is expected of them.

If any of these things go wrong the customer will become dissatisfied and will be less likely to rejoin or buy again, and may go away to your competitors and tell others about your poor service, thus putting off new prospects. On the other hand, if you get it right the customer will enjoy coming to you, may use other services you offer, visit more frequently, praise you to his/her friends and bring them along.

Lapsed customers: The third stage is when customers cease using the service and become lapsed customers. Often this is not because they are dissatisfied but because their life-style has changed or their needs are different. For example, a woman may give up playing tennis when she becomes pregnant and does not renew her membership of the club. A good club secretary will check up on why she left the club and why she did not return. The

questions could have different answers. The answer to the first was because she physically did not feel like playing and was preoccupied when the baby arrived. The answer to the second might have been that she had considered coming back the following season but as the club had no crèche it was difficult to organise.

If the club wants to keep members it is important that it finds out why they leave and follows up with more enquiries at a later date. The club may be able to adapt the service in some way to make it more suitable (e.g. provide a crèche, or have a toddlers' activity session). Or an element of motivation may be required to rekindle the customer's interest – for example ten per cent off membership or free toddlers' activity group. In other words, customer service not only tries to keep its customers but aims also to get them back if they leave.

Good customer service from all the staff

Customer service is a continuous process that should be offered by all staff and not just by reception or other 'front-of-house' staff. In many organisations the technicians and 'back-

277

of-house' staff play a vital role in making sure facilities work and are safe. In certain cases maintenance staff and cleaners are also in regular contact with external customers, and will be approached for information and help by customers. Their behaviour and attitude will be judged by customers, and will need to conform with the image of the service as a whole. It is important then that they can give good customer service and do not fall back on the immortal lines, 'Don't ask me, luv, I only do the maintenance here'.

Thought for the page

Loyalty to the organisation and your colleagues is essential when handling a complaint. Although it is right to sympathise with a customer who is making a complaint, it is poor practice and disloyal to side with the customer and start to criticise your own employer or your colleagues – even if you agree with the customer. You are also giving the customer fuel for their complaint when they find the manager. You have to get the balance right.

The commercial benefits of good customer service

A smile costs nothing, it is said. While a smile is essential to customer care it is about the only free thing there is. Customer care involves considerable expenditure by providers in terms of:

- design
- information materials
- training
- research.

There is also the cost of lost sales if you don't give good customer care. The number and constancy of customers is vital to the success of an operation, and Figure 5.2 shows why it is worth while to make the financial investment.

Figure 5.2 Benefits of good customer service

As you can see from the diagram (Figure 5.3), these interact to produce:

- increased income – happy customers come back, come more frequently and bring their friends. Unhappy customers do not
- reduced costs – the extra cost of providing customer care is outweighed by the savings made as a result of it.

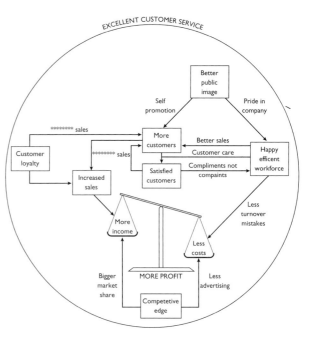

Figure 5.3 How the benefits of good customer service interact to increase income and reduce costs

More first-time customers

How do people find out about a product or an organisation? There are three main ways – advertising, public relations and promotion, and recommendation. Companies who have good customer care can use this as promotion for the whole organisation. An advert may feature aspects of customer care which show that the provider wants the customers to have an enjoyable, hassle-free, safe time. For instance:

- 'no-fuss' refund policies
- special features (disabled access, facilities for children)
- easy booking (credit card bookings, easy payments)
- easy access (car parking, park and ride)
- welcoming facilities (pictures of reception areas, attentive staff)
- attention to health and safety ('all our staff are trained first aiders')
- quality standards (Investors in People, reply guarantees).

It is well known that a mention in the mass media is worth thousands of pounds of local advertising costs, but this is of course true only if the mention is favourable! These days there is increasing interest within the media in consumer affairs and customer care. A company that upsets its customers runs the risk of being criticised publicly which will damage its image and future custom. Yet a company that is well written up stands the chance of gaining many new customers.

Following customer service through

Good customer service not only attracts new customers it is also an essential factor in holding them. To do this the customer service offered must carry out what was promised in the promotion or recommendation. Staff therefore have to:

- live up to expectations (i.e they are welcoming and helpful)

- be able to sell the product (meaning they know what has been promoted to the customer and can relate it to the customer's needs).

Savings

Advertising budgets are a major item in the running costs of many companies. Attracting new customers is particularly costly because they need to advertise more powerfully and more frequently to create in the customer the desire to buy. If a company can establish a positive public image and customer loyalty, there is less need for advertising and so company costs can be reduced.

A less obvious cost benefit of good customer care is the reduction of overheads. These are the costs a company spends on such items as buildings, administration and marketing. These costs stay the same regardless of how many customers the company has. If there are plenty of customers these overheads can be spread thinly, meaning that they are more easily recovered. Few customers means less income from which to recover the overheads. Price increases to make up income often deter both new and existing customers, whereas if a facility is attracting as many customers as it can handle it may be possible to put prices down and still recover overheads. Thus one can say that good customer care keeps prices down and covers the cost of overheads.

Customer satisfaction and repeat business

Once a customer has used the product for the first time they will have experienced the customer service that goes with it. This means the staff will have:

- given a warm welcome and hospitality
- made purchasing easy and pleasant
- provided information
- attended to any special or individual request or needs of the customer

- demonstrated the product
- handled any complaints or queries
- asked the customer about their experience of the product
- said goodbye to the customer.

All these actions achieve something we all like – to be welcomed, valued, and understood. A satisfied customer is one who will return. In the health and fitness industry, exit polls have shown that customers come back more frequently if staff have been helpful and friendly.

Repeat business

In the leisure business our customers tend to be creatures of habit. Once they find something they like they will stay with that activity for some time, be it sub-aqua or going to the cinema. To encourage this excellent habit, we have to make sure that their experience each time is as good as or better than the last one. In other words, repeated satisfaction establishes a buying habit or repeat business. As we have seen, good customer care is continuous, from the customer's arrival to departure, and to be effective must be seen to give satisfaction. This means that the staff need to become skilled at handling different types of people and quick to pick up on what is popular with one customer that may not be so popular with another. For nearly all leisure providers repeat business is the core to success. In leisure centres and health clubs it is normal to find that eighty per cent or more of customers are regular customers while in successful residential outdoor activity centres repeat sales may account for nearly all sales.

Generally speaking, when assessing a service, you should be looking for high total sales or applications and high repeat sales as a guide to broad customer satisfaction. Customer satisfaction and repeat business have knock-on effects within the company.

Thought for the page

A note of caution. High repeat sales coupled with low new sales can denote several things:

- It may represent a product past its sell-by date. In other words, it attracts its old diehards but not new customers. The few Turkish Baths left in the country are good examples of this and attract fantastic customer loyalty from a small and dwindling band of customers and excellent customer care from the staff who work in them.
- It may represent a popular product with excellent customer care service but a limited capacity. You will find this typically in membership clubs like health clubs. A long waiting list is the sign that the service falls into this category.
- It may represent a facility where the only customers left are the ones who for some reason find the service to be what they want and use it often. Very often the reason is that they like the facility because it is empty or because they can meet people like themselves there. Often when a provider like a local authority tries to revamp such centres there is a huge outcry from the small core of regular users.

- Staff and customers get to know each other and staff find new ways to satisfy the customer.
- Satisfied customers will praise staff and give them job satisfaction.
- The company gets a better understanding of the product that is wanted. It may therefore be able to spend less on developing experimental or new products. More likely, it will be able to make better buying and programming decisions to improve the product for the customer. For example, baby-changing stations were first invented to go in female toilets. Managers who knew their customers well soon realised that what they really wanted was a changing station for both parents, and not in the toilets which were associated with dirt.

"THE THING I LIKE ABOUT FLOPS GYM IS THAT THERE ARE NEVER TOO MANY PEOPLE AROUND"...

Some customers may like a facility because it is always empty, but this probably wasn't the managements intention . . .

- Advertising costs can be greatly reduced and in the case of limited capacity facilities such as health clubs almost eliminated.

Customer loyalty and referred business

Over time, the more customers are satisfied, the more they will build up a *customer loyalty* to the organisation. This is when customers prefer to buy your services to that of the competition and tell their friends how good your service is. This may be because they establish friendly relationships with the staff or they grow used to the design, services and practices offered to them. Growing customer loyalty produces two things.

1 A growing commitment to the organisation

Customers like what they have and become committed to it. They begin to defend it against competition and justify any faults the service has. In other words they are reluctant to change loyalty. This is excellent for repeat sales but there may be a down side in that such customer may resist change by the management. This is often seen in voluntary sports clubs where a core group of established members will block many changes. For example, in some golf clubs women members do not have the same privileges as the men.

Resistance to change is a major headache for managers in the public sector who will often receive stiff opposition if they try to change programming or facilities in a way loyal core users do not approve of.

2 Referred business

Referred business is important. It is expensive to create and advertise. Referred business comes from your existing customers referring their friends and contacts to your organisation. It is an outcome of customer loyalty. The histogram below is hypothetical and shows how customer loyalty grows as a customer develops from being a new or occasional customer into a regular or established customer and then finally a committed, long-standing customer. This sort of pattern has been referred to as the loyalty ladder.

As loyalty grows, so does the customers' enthusiasm and commitment and this is passed on to their friends. It is probably in the first stages of being a customer that the person enthuses most and will be telling everyone how good the service is and how they should buy it. This is the 'evangelist' stage (Figure 5.4). As time goes by their knowledge of the product increases, which means they will be regarded as more expert on the subject by people they talk to and therefore a reliable source. However, at the same time they feel less need to tell people about it, so referred sales may dip. Finally, they become expert on the service and are seen as a bit of a 'guru', people will approach them to find out about becoming a customer and referred sales will rise. The 'gurus' may

281

also instinctively tend to 'poach' customers from the competition.

Referred customers will probably have a greater understanding of the product through discussion with your existing customers, and they are also likely to be accompanied by the person who referred them. This means less time will be required to explain how the product

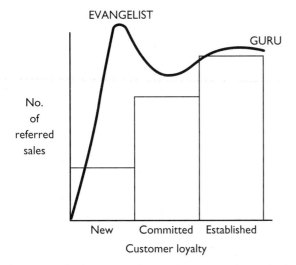

Figure 5.4 Customer loyalty produces a customer 'sales force' who will promote and sell your service

works (although of course you would not skimp on induction and introduction procedures).

The power of referred business

Referred sales are important in all sectors of the industry but especially so where the use by a particular customer is likely to be only one-off or occasional – for example, the Millennium Dome, and most theme parks and heritage attractions. Live performance and cinema is another area where people tend to make one visit, but then tell their friends about it.

Just how powerful the network can be is easy to demonstrate. If the average customer to a theme park tells ten of his/her friends about the experience and then those ten tell five others each, fifty extra people will know about that theme park. It is therefore glaringly obvious that the original customer needs to tell good things, not bad! And have you noticed how a story about a bad/boring/inefficient experience seems to be told more often, and louder, and to become more exaggerated in the telling than the good news?

CASE STUDY – Customer loyalty as a marketing device

Tom and Adrian are discussing their clubs. Tom complains that members at his club have to pay £800 a year up front and that he is finding it hard to find the money. Adrian says 'You should come along and see my club, it's got more equipment than yours. They charge only £750 and they charge you by direct debit on a monthly basis. They really appreciate new members as well – in fact, they give ten per cent discount in the first year to a new member who is introduced by a friend. What's more you will be doing me a favour because I would get a discount as well. Besides which, I think you would enjoy Winners. It strikes me that the people that go there are more your sort of person than you find at Flops.'

It's hard to resist, isn't it? Winners has given Adrian some useful marketing devices to make best use of his loyalty and to encourage his services as an 'unpaid salesman'. The discount scheme and direct debit system established an advantage over the competition. The organisation have not only achieved a customer but an 'unpaid salesman' who is trusted by the prospect.

Question

Think of some other ways in which leisure facilities can encourage their members to be 'unpaid sales people'.

Increased sales

We have seen that first, repeat and referred sales can all be increased by good customer service. However, both the value of sales and the price can also be affected.

Cost and value of sales

Customer service 'oils the wheels' of a sale. No one likes spending money and we all seem to have an in-built urge to stop ourselves buying something even if we want it. Therefore, any slight irritation or obstacles in the sales process can serve to derail it. It could be a chance remark by the salesperson, a queue or a complicated purchasing procedure. On the other hand, if the customer service is working, not only will you buy the service as an initial or *first sale*, but you will feel good about it and inclined to make further purchases or *repeat sales.*

Repeat sales are very important to a business because they cost the organisation less. First sales are expensive to make. This is because they usually require product development and an expensive marketing promotion to attract the customer. At the point of sale, even when the sales procedure is good the sale will take longer (thus costing more) as the salesperson has to explain, inform and motivate the customer.

Repeat sales are far cheaper as customers know what they are getting and do not need to be 'sold' to again. This is one of the strengths of branded products. Some companies link their brand image with their customer service. Customers therefore feel confident that if they walk into any branch of that company they can expect a similar quality of service. Likewise, they will enjoy the same service if they purchase a different range of products with the brand image. For example, Apollo Leisure manages theatres and cinemas. If a customer likes the service he receives in a cinema, he may be more likely to book a show in a theatre run by Apollo.

Think it over

Have you noticed how a good salesperson will round off the sale with a 'feel good' remark that matches your feeling? For example, 'I am sure you are going to love it here, I know we are going to enjoy having you' or 'You have made a wonderful choice, you are really going to improve your game with this one'. A less competent salesperson might say 'Well, I hope you find it is what you wanted', or 'If you have any problems, bring it back'. What problems? He has just been telling you what a wonderful product it is!

Think back to when you last considered buying a leisure item that you were unsure about. What comments or actions by the salesperson convinced you to buy it or put you off buying it? How good was the customer service?

The same branding strategy applies to chains. For example, Living Well is a major health club chain. It is unlikely that they will have a customer who is member of two clubs in the chain. However, it is likely that a customer will refer a friend living elsewhere to join their local club with the assurance that the friend will find the same quality of service.

Pricing and ancillary sales

Most people have a band of prices they can afford when they enter a sale. If the price of the product gets to the ceiling of the band or exceeds it, the decision to buy weakens. This effect can be counteracted by adding value to the product, and persuading the customer to pay more. Good customer service and expertise add value to the product and will be reflected in the price. A comment you will hear frequently from a salesperson is 'We are not the cheapest provider in the area, but I can guarantee that our customers are satisfied and stay with us. Customer service can also play a vital role in pointing out the value of the product to the customer, or even 'feeding back' to management the need to increase value to encourage wavering customers – such as giving a 'let-out' option to an unsure customer in the form of a two-month trial period and a promise of a refund if not happy.

Ancillary or secondary sales are those that are additional to the main product; for instance, drinks, food, cosmetics, equipment and programmes. Good customer care will increase these in two ways.

- If customer service adds value to the core sale, there is a psychological effect on the customer who feels he has saved some money, and may well then purchase another item. The situation is familiar in sports shops when a customer has just bought a bargain price racquet and so decides to buy some new balls or shoes to go with it.

- Good staff will get to know their customers' needs and interests and be able to recommend new and/or helpful products. This applies particularly to sports equipment, when customers are willing to be influenced by staff they like and whose opinion they respect.

Better public image

Sophisticated companies will promote good customer care to catch the public eye and build up a good public image. For example, they may:

- have a celebration for their thousandth customer
- publicise their customer care award
- publicise a charitable act, like raising money for treatment for an ill customer
- promote new customer care features (disabled access, crèche).

Thought for the page

Public image is one of the influences on new customers. It is also important in reinforcing customer loyalty. For example, a customer is pleased when viewing the London Marathon to see the manager of his leisure centre in the race – 'That's Chris, the manager of my leisure centre – we are always doing things for charity'.

Sometimes these promotions may be cold-blooded publicity stunts, but in most cases they reflect the fact that organisations who do care about their customers will spontaneously seek to make gestures like organising fund-raising events. And it is not just customers who benefit from the enhanced public image. Staff will take real pride in seeing their

The Trafford Centre
Customer Services
Committed To Excellence

Help & Assistance If you need help of any kind whilst you are in The Trafford Centre, ask one of our team. Their red uniforms make them easy to pick out and you will find plenty of them on duty in the malls, around the Orient and out in the car parks.

Services for Children There is a children's entertainment programme in the Wonder World. Situated above the Festival Village there are regular performances from The Trafford Centre Bears, real-life magicians, jugglers and a host of other entertainment. More fun is available in Kidz Klub – a soft toy play area and crèche and specially decorated party rooms which are available to hire for special celebrations. We can even arrange the catering and entertainment. Our on-site crèche caters for 65.

Services include:
Crèche for two up to eight year olds.
Children's buggies available from Customer Services Desk and security wrist bands.
Unisex parent and child toilets.
Baby changing facilities and breast-feeding rooms.
Babies bottles can be warmed up in a special unit in the food court within the Orient.

Customer Comfort If you find it hard to manage in the food court - or you are in a wheelchair or juggling with children, shopping and lunch - then ask the catering staff to page one of our Orient team members who will be on hand to carry your tray and see you comfortably seated.
Most of our team are fully trained First Aiders, so whether you suffer a simple cut or serious emergency, all you have to do is alert one of our staff. The meeting point for lost persons is at the Dome Customer Services Desk.
The Operations Room links our customers, stores and staff on the ground with each other and the outside world. It monitors the traffic on the surrounding roads so that when you finally have to tear yourself away, we can help you find the easiest route home.
Hourly visits to our Viewing Gallery will be conducted by a member of The Trafford Centre team, highlighting safety and security procedures for your comfort.

Shopmobility There are car park facilities for visitors with disabilities around the Centre and 65 spaces next to the Centre's Festival Village entrance. Inside, you can pick up a battery-operated scooter or manual wheelchair from the Shopmobility unit. All the public areas, toilet blocks and elevators are designed for wheelchair use.
Two forms of identification are required for equipment hire, one must show the customers current address. Orange badges, drivers licence or similar are acceptable.
Lenses for the visually impaired are available free of charge at the Customer Services Desk and the Shopmobility unit.

Parking The Trafford Centre provides 10,000 free spaces for customers' cars, plus 300 coach spaces.
The Operations Room is in constant touch with our car park staff and with the Traffic Police. So when you arrive at The Trafford Centre, electronic signs on the motorway slip roads will start directing you to a section of car park where space is available.
For more information on buses and taxis please contact our Customer Services Desk.

(Reproduced with kind permission from the Trafford Centre)
Customer service leaflets provide an opportunity to promote new customer care features

CASE STUDY – The Dome

Many journalists and VIPs were invited to the opening of the Millennium Dome. Invitations were sent out late. The management had expected these guests to make their own way using the Underground system – which inevitably became jammed with the New Year crowds. Hence, many guests were late, many others had to queue to get in, and as a result too many missed much of the evening. The following days saw a tidal wave of negative referral from the press that in the end contributed both to disappointing sales and to the change of senior management. In hindsight, this mishap was an oversight of a simple customer care principle – get the design right as well as the staff attitude. And access is a major part of the design component.

Later, ironically, there was relatively little criticism of the customer service at the Dome; in fact, much was heard about the friendly, loyal young staff who had trained specially for it. But that one mistake created a public image which was hard to shift and so critics looked negatively at all other aspects of the experience.

Questions

1 Identify ways that customer care could have better avoided the problem.
2 How could the Dome management, using customer care, have rectified the damage done on the first night?
3 Do you know, or can you find out, what they did do?
4 Could the Dome management have foreseen what happened and prevented it?

company and their colleagues being featured in the media or being congratulated by their customers on their efforts.

We mentioned earlier the power of referral. The most powerful agent for referred sales is not individuals but the media. For years the critic's review in the media – newspapers, magazines, radio and television – has been enormously influential. They are one customer who can influence thousands of prospects, many of whom will have come to rely on that critic's recommendations. No wonder many leisure providers have a healthy respect for the power of the critics. Apart from restaurants where service is usually commented on, the critic's comments are restricted to the core product, such as the film. However, a critic, like the rest of us, will be affected by customer service and a poor piece of customer service can shift the critic's mood and affect his/her experience and the review he/she writes.

Enhanced public image can have other effects. For example, it will often make negotiation and development easier, in the sense that local authorities and politicians are more likely to be receptive to planning applications from a company with a reputation for treating its customers well.

Satisfied customers mean a happier and more efficient workforce

Walk into any leisure facility that prides itself on good customer service and you will notice that the staff breathe 'good attitude'. One reason for this is simply that the management have been careful in their choice of staff. However there are other reasons.

- Customer service training will provide staff with the skills to handle many different situations. They will be able to handle, and not be upset by, complaints. They will have the confidence to achieve successful sales. Training can also raise the staff members' own self-esteem, and there is a good chance that they will be

CASE STUDY – Getting the edge over competitors

Two multiplex cinemas in the Northwest are much the same in design and show similar films. Staff are friendly and well trained in both. However, one has a covered path from the car park to the foyer – providing protection from frequent, wet, blustery weather. The manager also makes a point of standing in the foyer when films start and smiling and greeting customers. Ticket desk staff always give a free 'goody', such as a badge, for all child visitors. These three small extras might give the edge to this cinema over its competitor.

Question

Suggest some ways in which this cinema's competitor could improve its customer service.

---

complimented by customers on various aspects of their work. If these things happen, it is no wonder staff feel good about themselves.

- Part of providing good customer service is working in a team. Remember that you are serving your internal as well as external customers. If management is doing its job, staff will be involved in knowing how the organisation is performing as a whole and be able to contribute. Staff will feel valued and this will show in their performance.
- People work in the leisure industry usually because they enjoy the product and want to see their customers find equal satisfaction. When a facility is working well staff enjoy seeing their customers having a good time, and if there is a problem they will also get satisfaction from solving it. Either way they will feel good about working there.
- Good customer service will mean that the business grows and this may result in cash bonuses for staff. Or there may be development of new products in which they may be involved; or there may be a reward scheme such as 'employee of the month'.
- Employees who are getting customer service right will be recognised by management and tend to be promoted or given extra responsibility.

Satisfied staff who enjoy their work are less likely to leave, thus reducing the expense of recruitment and retraining. This is a saving for the company. There is also likely to be a reduction of disciplinary issues. This saves money and time in grievance procedures and appeals. It also means that staff morale is kept high – which in turn leads to greater productivity.

Having the edge on the competition

The leisure industry, like any other, is highly competitive and all organisations want to maintain and improve their market share. There is a general rule in the business: 'Don't knock the opposition, they can do it perfectly well by themselves'. The philosophy behind this is that if you do things better than the competition, you will gain customers anyway without having to criticise, and as the competition make mistakes they will lose their customers.

Why do other organisations lose their customers?

Sometimes because the product is wrong or often because they have poor customer care. If the product is wrong, it should not be difficult to rectify. It is more common for organisations to lose customers as a result of poor staff attitude, poor concern for their well-being and small oversights in design or service.

! Check it out

1   What are the three types of external customer?

2   What are the costs of customer care?

3   Why are repeat and referred sales so important?

4   Give two examples of internal customers and the services they might provide.

5   Why can customer service make an organisation more competitive?

6   How do loyal customers boost business?

7   How might the pattern of sales reflect customer care?

8   Describe the loyalty ladder.

9   Give three reasons why customer satisfaction and staff satisfaction go hand in hand.

5.2 Personal presentation

Psychologists have shown that the impression made in the first few seconds is very influential. This is known as the primacy effect and, once formed, it is extremely hard to shift. It is created by our initial interpretation of what we see, hear and smell, so the physical appearance and presentation of the staff will significantly affect the impression made on the customer.

The primacy effect influences:

- the customers' attitude to the staff, and then to the rest of the facility – in other words 'sloppy staff means sloppy management means sloppy product; I am not going to enjoy my visit here', or 'smart efficient staff means efficient management means good product; I shall enjoy this'.

- the interaction between staff member and customer. Inevitably both staff member and customer judge each other. However, the member of staff is trained to react well and also trained to cope with any unfortunate reactions from the customer, such as exercising self-restraint in the face of aggressive or rude customer behaviour.

- the customers' attitude to the product. This is even more important. A customer will transfer first impressions of a member of staff to all aspects of the service.

Although we are going to concentrate on personal presentation in this section you should remember that the customer's first impression of a product is of its physical

CASE STUDY – Keeping the customer in mind

Many dual-use sports centres were designed by school architects whose primary concern was for the school users who knew their way around the site. At one such centre in Cornwall the disadvantages to the outside customer were plain: firstly, you have to know to follow the signs to 'school'; you then have a choice of car parks with no signs at all. Heading towards a building that looks like a sports hall, you cannot initially find a door. Once you do, there is no one around. The changing rooms have obviously just been used by a class and are full of odd shoes and pools of water. However, the sports hall is probably much cheaper than any club within easy reach.

Question

What would you suggest to improve the customer care for outside users, given the restrictions of school use and limited funds?

What are your first impressions of this leisure centre?

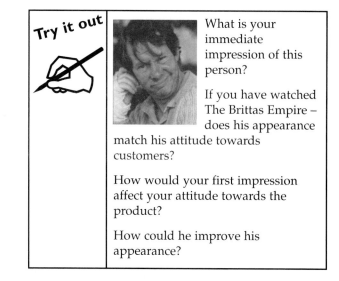

Try it out

What is your immediate impression of this person?

If you have watched The Brittas Empire – does his appearance match his attitude towards customers?

How would your first impression affect your attitude towards the product?

How could he improve his appearance?

appearance. Well-managed landscape, clean and tidy buildings and pathways, and a welcoming reception area will create a good first impression before the staff are even encountered.

With staff, the primacy effect is created largely by four aspects of personal presentation (Figure 5.5).

offence and be appropriate to your role. For example, the FCUK logo might be a fashion icon but it would not be suitable on a garment worn by a receptionist in a leisure centre. Problems can arise if staff are allowed to wear what they like; managers and staff do not always have the same ideas as to what is suitable and what is not, and staff cannot be distinguished from customers. A solution to the second problem is for staff to wear identity badges giving name and role (Figure 5.6).

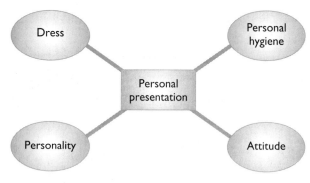

Figure 5.5 The four aspects of personal presentation which create the primacy effect

Figure 5.6 The purpose of identity badges

Dress

Your clothes say a lot about you personally and also about the organisation you represent. Obviously, basic rules apply to your appearance: clothes should be clean and ironed, cause no

Some organisations suggest a 'house style' for their staff, who wear their own clothes chosen according to this 'code of dress' which might

Criteria for dress options

- *Does it identify the wearer as an obvious point of contact?* Customers need to recognise staff in order to make enquiries, seek help or make a purchase.

- *Does it reflect the status of the wearer?* This can be useful to customers and save them embarrassment if they want to be able to recognise the difference between someone at manager level and an assistant.

- *Is it functional?* Some uniforms are designed for a specific job. If staff are wearing the right clothes for the job the customer will have confidence that they are in the right hands. If a manager had come from the plant room you would accept seeing him or her in an overall with a stain on it, whereas if she or he had a stain on their shirt the customer would judge them to be sloppy and dirty. It is good practice, therefore, for staff to change uniforms if they are doing a task with a different function.

- *Does it reflect the role of the wearer?* Uniforms can denote the role of the person wearing it; for example, in museums and heritage centres the attendants often wear police-style uniforms indicating their security role. In theme parks and visitor attractions staff sometimes wear costumes that invite the customer to interact.

- *Does it reflect the professionalism and image of the organisation?* The choice and quality of uniform says a lot about the organisation. Generally speaking, well-dressed staff in up-to-date uniforms will indicate investment in staff by the management and the likelihood that they will be trained and effective.

be, for example, black trousers or skirts and a white shirt or blouse, with the company tie or scarf supplied by management. House style may also demand that jewellery is removed and tattoos covered. The general opinion within the industry is that uniforms are the best means of conveying a positive image. They give a consistency to staff appearance, they can be designed to fit in with other aspects of the company's image (such as its logo), and it means the company can select clothing that is suitable for the jobs involved. While some staff take pride in their uniform, others find the uniforms don't suit them. Increasingly, uniforms are not uniform. They come in all shapes and sizes and frequently appear as fashion garments in their own right. Good employers will often provide a choice of styles to allow staff to choose what suits them best. Nor are uniforms necessarily formal; formality in the wrong place can be off-putting to clients (at activity centres for example). In contrast in other circumstances, a formal uniform is traditional, respected and looked for (such as

The dress code at The Tower of London pulls in the visitors, so would it be a good choice for the staff of all leisure and recreation facilities?

commissionaires at the Centre Court at Wimbledon). Whatever dress option is selected it should satisfy the following criteria for good customer service.

> **Try it out**
>
> Think of examples of when a member of staff could cause embarrassment to a customer by being too casually dressed or too formally dressed.
>
> Why does knowing a person's status help a customer?
>
> Think of as many different 'uniforms' as you can that would be functional for different jobs.

Personal hygiene

Occasionally, an eccentric can get away with being less than one hundred per cent clean and tidy – usually in the field of interpretation or performance art. There are also some real characters around, demonstrating country crafts for example, who breathe a heady mixture of horse dung, cider and tobacco over their customers. However, in the main such practice is to be discouraged. People working in leisure should conform to the normal rules of hygiene; that is to say, they look and smell clean and pay particular attention to their hands, nails and hair. Too much scent is not a good idea as not all customers will share your particular taste.

Fashions in haircuts, jewellery and tattoos that are extreme can create problems. Some of your customers may think such 'way-out' styles are 'cool', while others think they look terrible and even seem dirty. In some cases customers may feel intimidated – for example, old age pensioners arriving for an indoor bowls session might be concerned by a shaven-headed, nose-pierced and tattooed body-building attendant.

Some organisations set their own standards which employees need to follow. Disney for many years had a ban on employees with facial hair and other companies discourage extreme hairstyles or body piercing. If no rules are in effect it is best to be on the conservative side and then no one can be offended.

> **Think it over**
>
> Sometimes staff members find themselves doing a job they do not usually do; for example, a manager might visit the plant room. It is good practice to wear overalls or change into clothes suited to the job in these circumstances – the manager could easily get dirt on his shirt from the plant room which would then give the wrong impression to customers in reception.
>
> Think of three other examples of poor personal presentation which would give the wrong impression to customers.

> **Think it over**
>
> A common issue in customer service is drinking. It affects health and safety, but also affects the appearance of the person. If you are hung over it is hard to look 'bright eyed and bushy tailed'; if you are under the influence your behaviour will be unacceptable. Most leisure professionals these days avoid even social drinking either before coming on duty or in their breaks. The reason for this is that:
>
> - your breath smells and is unpleasant to customers (the same applies to smokers)
> - it can give cause to accusations of drunkenness
> - it does not reflect well on the company image, especially in the health and sports sectors.
>
> Bad breath is a problem that most of us are unaware of, especially if it is only temporary and the result of last night's curry. It is good practice as a matter of habit to start your shift with a squirt of breath freshener.
>
> Think about a time you have met and talked to someone with a breath problem (halitosis, alcohol or smoke). How does it affect your impression of that person and how does it affect the way you interact with them?

Personality

General disposition

There is a myth that you have to be an extrovert to work in leisure. In fact anyone with a pleasant personality can work in the business. Often it is the quieter ones who are good listeners who can handle customers best. Being pleasant, open and honest, courteous and slow to show irritation are obvious traits which it is essential to have. Staff who are good with customers will be able to maintain their poise at all times, even if they are feeling ill or a customer is being unreasonably rude.

Shyness

A lot of younger people are shy of talking to customers. But in the vast majority of cases gradual exposure to customer service builds up their confidence and they find that they have developed personal skills they never knew they had.

Humour

Humour is more problematical. Being cheerful is a positive attribute but you should be aware of your customer's mood and the effect of your cheerfulness and of your own sense of humour. Misplaced humour can be as damaging as a deliberate insult. Generally speaking, unless you are very sure of your customer, it is best to avoid jokes and witticisms in case they backfire.

Intimacy with the customer

Being friendly is fine, being too friendly may be regarded as being impertinent. Personal comments may be all right providing you know the customer and the comments are positive and not judgemental.

Attitude

There are three key beliefs that help to create a positive customer service (Figure 5.7).

Figure 5.7 Three key beliefs in creating positive customer service

Someone who believes in the values and aims of their employer will be enthusiastic. This enthusiasm will be infectious and will be picked up by the customers. Someone who runs down the manager, or tells the customer about all the things that go wrong behind the scenes, is not only damaging the organisation but spoiling the day for the customer.

Respect for the customer

Good customer care is about having a genuine concern for the customers. It may mean offering one of them a free coffee if he comes in after a particularly bad journey; it may be remembering their children's names; or spotting that they are having difficulty with equipment and helping them. There are organisations that do this naturally and have never trained anyone in customer care. They are usually small organisations where the 'boss' has the right idea and selects only staff who share it. On the other hand, there are organisations that train their staff but never really believe in their customers. You will hear remarks behind the scenes like 'Customers! Life would be a lot nicer without them', or joke signs like 'You don't have to be mad to work here, but it helps'. The ethos of customer care has to be total within an organisation, and not just superficial. Any leisure provider has a surprising variety of customers – from different ethnic or cultural groups, from different social and economic backgrounds, young, old, and people with particular needs. It is essential that staff do not fall into the 'primacy trap' and pre-judge their customers by letting any stereotyped attitudes or predispositions affect their response to them.

It is not uncommon among front-line leisure workers to feel unease when working for the first time with customers with a disability. Usually, basic training (on the guiding principles and on how the customer is feeling) coupled with a gradual build-up of interaction eliminate such inhibitions. And frequently, sports leaders who have experienced these problems end up by enjoying their work with these customers the most.

> **Think it over**
>
> Few of us can say honestly we do not have likes and dislikes, that we do not either 'take to' or 'take against' people that we meet. Most people have feelings and prejudices they find difficult to control, and that they know they should not allow. It is a good exercise to:
>
> - recognise these weaknesses in our attitudes towards others
> - note what our behaviour is like when subject to these weaknesses
> - identify ways that we can reduce these feelings and responses.
>
> Have a go – and be honest with yourself.

Customer fatigue

At major visitor attractions staff can lose the personal touch with their customers if they are having to process hundreds of visitors an hour. A smile and freshness can last only so long without fading or becoming false. Attractions with good customer service will rotate receptionists on a half-hourly basis like lifeguards.

Belief in yourself

Taking the trouble to project a belief in yourself is also important. The British have had a reputation for playing themselves down, for being reserved and looking on the gloomy side, but this is changing with many influences from abroad and from the cultural mix of people in Britain. The Americans, who are the masters of customer service, adopt what they call Positive Mental Attitude (or looking on the bright side) which they reinforce with unabashed enthusiasm. Many people believe that adopting a positive mental attitude has a self-fulfilling element. You feel good about yourself and good things happen to you. Whether or not you believe this, it is certain that this attitude is frequently appreciated by the customers.

> **! Check it out**
>
> 1 What is the primacy effect and how does it affect customer care?
> 2 What are the key components of personal presentation?
> 3 Give four criteria of dressing for work and explain, giving examples, how these affect customer service.
> 4 What are the main points you would attend to in your personal appearance if you were working in a leisure service?
> 5 Explain how attitude affects customer service.

5.3 Types of customers

While it is always important to treat customers as individuals it is a help if you can recognise typical characteristics of certain types of customers. However, you must be careful not to stereotype people and not to make assumptions about how customers will behave just because they appear to be representative of a certain type.

Let's look now at some of the ways by which we can classify customers as:

- individuals
- groups

- people of different ages
- people from different cultures and/or speaking a different language
- people with special needs.

Individuals

Using the customer's name

Two golden rules of customer service are: firstly, to show that you know something positive about the customer and, secondly, to make him or her feel an individual. The first and strongest way of following both these is to find out and use the customer's name correctly. If this does not happen naturally, registration or payment details will give the details.

Formal or informal

First name terms are more and more frequent these days, but it is advisable to use the formal title Mr or Mrs (or Sir or Madam if you do not have the name) until you are told the first name and asked to use it. Older people in particular are not always happy with the instant use of first names and also like to know who you are, and both your names, not just your first name.

Identifying any particular needs

Staff should be on the alert and check as a matter of course that all is well with the customer. They can be helpful, as long as

Think it over

If you are addressed by your name, you appreciate the fact that someone has taken the trouble to find it out, even if you are not aware of having told anyone what it is. Sometimes people who want to impress a client will ask staff in advance (in a restaurant, for example) to address them personally. How would you feel if you were that member of staff?

they do not pre-judge a situation and thereby cause offence. If someone looks worried, or is obviously new to the facility and shy about asking where to go, then a couple of tactful questions will probably identify the problem (for example, 'Can I help you?' 'Have you been here before?' 'Is everything all right, Sir?' are perfectly acceptable, whereas 'Is everything all right, Sir? You seem a bit upset.' is not advisable.)

Welcoming individuals

When individuals arrive at a facility for the first time they are often anxious about fitting

Table 5.2 Strategies for welcoming individuals

Action Issue	Description
Pre-welcome	If customer makes an enquiry about health club membership over the phone, invite him/her to come in to meet a senior staff member at an arranged time. This shows that the prospect is valued. It will also avoid the customer being 'ignored' when and if he/she arrives at a busy time.
Initial welcome	Welcome sign and have a notice board in reception with staff photos and names on it.
Isolation	Member host scheme. New members are introduced to an existing member who acts as a guide and host in the first few visits to make the new member feel at home.
Reassurance	Staff note who are the new members and make a special effort to talk to them and ask how they are getting on.
Reassurance, familiarity	Induction: where staff member gives customer a guided tour and demonstration. This can be used as a vehicle to introduce the customer to other new customers.
Follow-up	Staff enquire of customer on departure if the visit or session has been enjoyed, what the customer expected and wanted.

Receptionists should make a special effort to make new customers particularly welcome

in and meeting other people. Staff should be aware of this and act as good hosts. For example, receptionists can make a special effort to tell or show a new customer where to go. Even better, find other customers and introduce them if it is appropriate.

Table 5.2 shows the various strategies that can be used. They are obviously more suited to facilities such as sports centres and clubs where customer and staff contact is high. However, even in a cinema there is nothing to stop a receptionist from asking 'Is this your first time here?', or from having a display board of staff members.

Groups

Groups are good for business. Every booking involves less sales time and reduced staff time than would the same number of individuals. Organisations who want to cater for groups often provide incentives such as discounted booking, privileges and sometimes specialised services. For example, a staff member may go out to welcome a coach when it arrives, the organisation may provide a 'goody bag' for the group members or arrange for fast-track entry.

On the other hand, groups can be disruptive or threatening to individual visitors (see Think it over). Group members can also be irritated if their visit is not managed well. Imagine how you would feel if you had paid to go on a tour, only to find you had to wait for thirty minutes in a queue as an individual to get your admission ticket.

There are several ways of managing groups and individuals in order to avoid irritations (Table 5.3):

Table 5.3 Ways of managing groups

Feature	Description
Access and design	Separate parking for coaches avoids blocking individual visitors. Group-only entrances to the facility. This values the group by processing them speedily. It also prevents crowding and the slowing down of customer flow.
Advance booking	This reduces point-of-sale transaction and bottlenecks. It also provides better customer service in that the group customer may receive information and promotions such as vouchers in advance of their visit.
Communication design	Identify group leader through whom to communicate. If possible provide information in advance. Provide clear signing and information (e.g. where to go, price tariffs) – if possible place these out of the main areas to avoid crowds building up.
Be aware of group benefits and needs	Remind them of group discounts or advise on best combination of prices. Be aware of collective needs. For example, point out to OAP group where rest places and toilets are. At a cinema, ensure that the group is in the same row. On a cycling expedition, ensure that suitable bikes are issued for each individual in the group.

You will find that looking after groups of people calls for different skills to dealing with individuals

> **Think it over**
>
> You are visiting a major attraction such as the British Museum, and while you are minding your own business looking at an exhibit you are hit by a tidal wave of a coach party who has thirty minutes to 'do' the national heritage. If you worked at the museum, how would you try to organise entry and timing in these circumstances so as to lessen the disruption to individuals?

Communication style

It is a good idea to concentrate on the leader or spokesperson when seeking information or making a sale but there are also times when you want to communicate with the whole group, to receive information from each individual. With individual communication you should be fairly close to the person and your voice conversational. For group communication you need to adopt a different physical stance, raise your voice and keep the group within earshot and eye contact. You also need to catch and keep people's attention.

In formal situations phrases like 'Ladies and gentlemen, can I have your attention' are acceptable. In many recreational situations you can be lighter – 'Hey guys/gang, listen up' or similar. Invariably people in a group carry on talking, and the best way to get their attention is simply to stop talking yourself, look at them and wait. About ten seconds does it normally!

People of different ages

Age affects people's behaviour and needs. Good customer service will take account of this.

Children

Recreational facilities can be big and scary for small children. Staff should be aware of this and be extra friendly. Remember you are much less frightening squatting down next to a child to start with, rather than standing up. Facilities can be designed to be child-friendly, with high chairs, baby-changing stations preferably in their own space (and not in the toilets), and brightly coloured signs. In sports activities there has been a boom in the development of games and equipment that is suitable for small children, such as short tennis or toddlers' gymnastics.

Lost children

As soon as children can walk they can get lost and they are particularly good at getting lost in a leisure facility where they and their parents are relaxed and distracted. Leisure providers must be able to reassure parents that lost children will not only be spotted but looked after in an easily identifiable place. This provision is a major customer service in that it will reassure parents that their children are safe. Children will often be scared and suspicious of strangers, so staff should:

- identify themselves by giving their first name

- show that they work in the facility
- explain what they are going to do to find the parents/carers.

When you identify that a child is lost, look after the child and call for the carers either by sending messages to all departments or on the PA system.

Thought for the page

It is sensitive to refer to the designated collection point for lost children as something other than 'lost children' since this only reinforces the 'lost' feeling for the children.

Entertaining children

These days the larger leisure facilities can offer a variety of experiences for all ages. There are some activities which adults enjoy which children cannot take part in, and good customer service provides alternative options for children while the adults follow their own pursuits. For younger children this would ideally be a crèche or play park, and for older ones a film show or interactive activities of the kind you would find in some museums.

Keeping control: There is always a possibility of dangerous or antisocial behaviour with a group of children and staff have to know how to handle these situations. If the children are with the adults the correct procedure is to ask the adults and not to discipline the children directly. It is best always to explain why the behaviour is not allowed rather than simply to demand that it ceases; for example, 'Excuse me, Sir, could you please ask your children to stop throwing sticks at the elephant, it is upsetting for the animal and may cause it to become violent.' If the children are unaccompanied, in the swimming pool for instance, staff need to establish their authority right from the start and list with reasons all actions or behaviour that will not be acceptable. Children are naturally high-spirited and 'misbehaviour' is sometimes intended, as a 'dare' for instance, and sometimes not. In most cases it is best to approach the kids and explain why their behaviour is not acceptable. If they persist, the 'three strikes and you're out' method often works.

Older people

Changes in society and advances in medicine are pushing back the definition of the elderly. Twenty years ago the over-60s were seen to have reached the age when infirmity and old age began; nowadays it is probably the over-70s. And in fact you should always keep in mind that leisure is a life-long experience and even the very old enjoy leisure activities.

The traditional stereotypes often do not apply any more. Older people generally like to think young and do not like to be reminded of their age. People in their sixties are eligible for concessionary pricing, and are usually fully aware of this, so it is wise to be cautious in

How can leisure and recreation centres assure parents that their children will be safe while in their care?

mentioning concessions if they do not. An obvious notice about concessions is a good idea.

However, some older customers do have requirements traditionally associated with their age:

- mobility problems
- health problems (raised blood pressure)
- hard of hearing or poor sight
- forgetfulness or confusion
- deteriorating communication skills (for example, as a result of a stroke).

Maintaining respect and patience are the key customer service issues. Try to find out what older people like to be called; some may prefer to follow modern customs of the young and use first names and others may still

prefer to be called by their surnames or 'Sir' or 'Madam'. For anyone with physical difficulties it is important to assess how much assistance, if any, is required and whether the activity needs tactful modification. Older people may also want a greater degree of privacy if they feel self-conscious about their appearance.

Thought for the page

In many theme parks and zoos, for example, wheelchairs or electric 'trains' are available for customers who, while not actually disabled, might find a long walk tiring or difficult. You can point out the availability of these to old and young alike in a way that will not offend those who love walking and pride themselves on being fit enough to do so.

In facilities where there are access problems, such as in older cinemas or theatres, it is excellent service to escort an elderly person to his/her seat and support an arm if required, but ask permission first.

People from different cultures

Customers from ethnic communities and foreign visitors may speak English but have different ways of doing things. Such differences need to be recognised and accommodated if we are to provide a full service to these customers. Handshakes vary from nationality to nationality both in style and meaning, as does body language (including nodding of the head and bowing), and other mannerisms and habits mean different things to different peoples.

Four rules apply to cross-cultural communication that may help you:

- always assume that someone from another culture has good intentions and is not being rude or arrogant and respond accordingly

Many traditional stereotypes of older people do not apply any more

> **Think it over**
>
> The English are, on the whole, good at saying 'please', 'thank you' and 'excuse me'. These are not necessarily standard phrases or customs in other cultures. We must therefore try not to apply English customs to other nationalities and cultures and think people rude who do not do as we do. 'The customer is king' and it is our responsibility to avoid or reduce misunderstandings as far as possible and ensure the customer has an enjoyable time, without prejudicing the enjoyment of other customers.

- find out about other cultures through reading or, even better, talking to friends and acquaintances from other cultures
- do not ingratiate yourself or go over the top in recognising a customer's cultural customs – it can appear patronising and you may get it wrong
- stay within your own cultural mode unless you know it will be offensive for some reason.

Religion is a one of the strongest factors that affects culture and it is a human right that religious customs should be tolerated. Generally speaking, Christianity has lost its influence on recreational patterns; the Sunday Trading Act allowed retailing on Sundays, all sports are now played on Sundays, and there has been a relaxing of censorship on entertainment. There are exceptions to this which tend to go unnoticed by the general public. Licences and planning permission are issued locally, and in areas where there is a strong Christian tradition, local politicians and magistrates will not permit the sale of alcohol on a Sunday or grant licences for gambling houses or strip clubs. Those who are strict followers of certain religions do not drink (Muslims) or go to the cinema (Orthodox Jews). In sport, both religions have beliefs that affect hygiene, exposure of the body and, most importantly, the participation of women. Sport is not

forbidden to Muslim women but there are religious or cultural conventions that may need to be followed. Contact between providers and the community is often best initiated through a community spokesperson such as the Iman or priest, or a community worker. For reasons of modesty, women will want to be assured that they will not be seen by male staff or members of the public, which will mean making special arrangements and changing staff shifts, and that the session may have to be screened or curtained off.

There are other areas where good customer service involves changes in the product to accommodate cultural differences; for instance, the stocking of foreign-language newspapers, books and videos in libraries. Library staff will be trained to know about these materials or sources for multi-cultural reading and entertainment.

> **Think it over**
>
> As with other aspects of customer service, working with people from different cultures is not simply a case of being nice; it takes training and practice. Many local authorities run racial awareness courses and the English Tourist Board run a suite of courses called 'Welcome Host' that provide a training for receiving tourists and understanding the different customs.

Non-English speakers

English is the language most used with customers. Around the world, 310 million people are thought to have English as a first language and a similar number speak it as a second language. This explains why in Britain people are poor at speaking other languages, which is a pity because there are still many visitors to Britain who cannot speak English comfortably. In 1998, for example, nearly 26 million visits were made by overseas visitors which generated something like £13 billion. Many of these tourists are here on holiday and visit leisure attractions and recreational facilities such as

1 How would you prepare yourself for receiving customers who cannot speak English? How would you prepare your workplace for non-English-speaking visitors? Make a list or chart of your work-place step by step from the visitors' arrival to their departure so as to formulate your ideas. (Key words: map, manners, phrases, speaking, pictograms.)

2 You are helping at the swimming pool and you have a group booking. The group consists of teenagers, none of whom speak much English. They are noisy and cheerful and pay little attention to you. How are you going to communicate with them and how will you make them listen to you quickly if the need arises?

BLENHEIM PALACE

Full-colour guidebook available here

Sixty-four pages of high-quality photographs and informative text

£3.50

- Farbig bebilderter Schloßführer hier erhältlich

- Guide en couleurs en vente ici

- Guida a colori disponibile qui

- Solicite aquí su guía turística a todo color

- カラー・ガイドブックあります。

Multilingual signs are common at most visitor attractions

Think it over

The Celtic Games is a multinational Youth Games for countries speaking Celtic languages. It is held in a different host country each time it is run. Explain what actions you would take if you were the manager of the leisure centre in Cornwall that had just been chosen as the venue for the Games. You may need to do a little research here.

national parks or major sporting events. It is up to the industry to make their visit as pleasurable as possible. In their home countries, the Celtic languages of Welsh and Gaelic are officially promoted. It is therefore common for staff to be bilingual where they are spoken.

Customers with special needs

Catering for different needs – women

For many years leisure facilities were mostly managed and designed by men for male customers. This is said to be one reason why women have not until recently participated in sport as much as men; it can be uncomfortable for them in a male-dominated setting. In recent years there has been a tremendous breakthrough in providing better customer service to what amounts to over 50 per cent of the market. This has occurred in various sectors – for example, pubs have been changing to become more attractive to women and families. However, it is in the sports sector that there has been most change.

In 1994 the Sports Council formally recognised the 'Brighton Declaration' that stated that 'Providers [are encouraged] to acknowledge diversity and recognise that the different needs of women may require different solutions from those traditionally adopted.'

Confidence

Physical: Locate and design facilities in non-threatening environments (e.g. well lit, no hidden alleys, safe access, CCTV and alarms) which are well staffed and where there is a flow of users.

Staffing: treat female customers with equal respect and courtesy, provide activities designed for women, provide professionally run crèches, train staff on equity issues, employ female staff.

Comfort

Physical: have suitably designed changing rooms (e.g. sanitary towel dispenser, hairdriers), have female-designated areas such as bars, provide screens from activities. Have buggy- and child-friendly design, such as automatic doors or ramps.

Staffing: Relax dress codes (e.g. all whites at tennis). Have female as well as male staff; staff to be child-friendly, organisation to display its code of conduct towards female users.

Choice

Physical: offer female-only areas or sessions such as saunas; offer single-booth showering and changing as well as communal.

Staffing: offer women's events and tournaments, offer recreational as well as competitive sport. Develop a wider choice of activities that are more attractive to women, such as yoga.

Convenience

Physical: locate facilities near or in place that women use, such as health centres or shops.

Staffing: have access to female staff and female users, programme opening times that suit women.

Consultation

Physical: consult women on the design of equipment and facilities.

Staffing: consult women on service issues and policies.

The 'Brighton Declaration' – raising the standards of confidence, comfort, choice, convenience and consultation

The 'Brighton Declaration' was concerned to raise the standards of:

- confidence
- comfort
- choice
- convenience
- consultation

Catering for special needs – disabled

People with disabilities form the major group of customers with special needs. Of these it is those with limited mobility who may use a wheelchair, and the deaf and visually impaired who are the most frequently seen. The aim behind the provision for people with disabilities is that they should be as independent as possible during their visit. This is achieved largely by careful design of the facility, which means taking into account wheelchair users with the inclusion of ramps, lifts, sliding or automatic doors, designated car parking and disabled toilets. At theme parks and country parks there may be wheelchairs for those who need one to cover some of the distances, or there may be a bus or electric train travelling around the site for use by everyone.

Many deaf people have hearing aids or cochlear implants that can be linked up by radio waves to a transmitter. With this, they can hear a public address system, stage performer, guide, coach or presenter. Similarly, broadcast sound such as in the cinema or an interpretive recording in a museum can all be transmitted. When this is not possible the use of visual information is important; for example, the large-screen formats used at professional sports grounds which show information that has been given on the public address system. Another example is in the

It should also be remembered that British Sign Language is recognised as a language for the deaf community. It is good practice (although often not followed) to have at least one member of staff, preferably on reception, who can sign.

home entertainment industry where DVD films are increasingly provided with subtitles.

Visually impaired people can also be helped by well-thought-out design details. Clear access routes are important, the use of Braille information signs set into handrails, large-letter signs, well-lit areas, and surface markings such as bands on steps are all helpful. The use of sound is of course of great importance, and in sport there are various clever devices such as a bell in the ball to indicate its whereabouts, and the use of radio in sub-aqua to allow the coach to direct a blind diver.

In other areas of the industry there are devices that help visually impaired people. Computers have an 'accessibility option' which can change the screen setting to larger print and greater contrast. For many years the

Many visitor attractions provide automated transport for getting around

library services and charities have produced 'talking books' that are audio tapes of popular books, and in museums and other visitor attractions the use of sound wands (radio-controlled tape guides) are as useful to blind people as they are to the sighted.

Good service by staff also helps the visitor with a disability. Some organisations train their staff in disability awareness. The golden rule is to show the same respect and consideration as you would for any other customer.

- Talk directly to the disabled customer and not his/her helper.
- Use your usual customer service style.
- Adapt, if appropriate, your communication. For example, don't shout at deaf people as it often distorts your words or can be painful. It is better to talk to them in a quiet place, where there is no other noise, particularly people talking.
- Remember disability is not a sign of mental handicap.
- Ask if they need any assistance, don't assume that they do.
- Bring to their notice any service that they might find useful (e.g. mention the presence of a hearing loop, or a listening wand).
- Avoid embarrassing gestures such as offering to lift a person in their wheelchair.
- Welcome companions such as helpers or guide-dogs. For example, offer a dish of water to the dog; offer assistance to a companion who is having difficulties.

Disability Discrimination Act

The **Disability Discrimination Act** (1995) (DDA) and the **National Tourism Strategy** (1999) are legislation and guidelines respectively which cover customer service for people with disabilities or specific needs.

The DDA has been in operation since 1995 and is being phased in in stages. By 2004 it will include service providers who will have to make substantial changes to serve the needs of disabled customers. For example, it is possible that theme parks will need to provide adapted seats on rides for disabled people.

Access for the disabled is one of the guiding principles of 'Tomorrow's Tourism', the National Tourist Strategy launched by the Government in 1999. The Strategy looks at further raising the standards of service and provision by the tourist industry, which not only includes travel and accommodation, but also the places people visit. It is estimated that 14% of the population has a disability of one sort or another and due to the lack of suitable access approximately £19 million of tourist income is lost per year. In response to the Strategy, the English Tourism Council has produced a guide 'Accessible Britain 2000' which lists accommodation and visitor attractions with suitable disabled access. This may direct you to sites in your area where there is good practice. In terms of training, the regional tourist boards run, as part of Welcome Host, a 'Welcome All' scheme, that focuses on catering for customers with particular needs including the elderly and people with disabilities.

! Check it out

1 Identify five examples of customer types.

2 Give examples of two ways individual children can be helped to join in activities.

3 Give examples of five different ways which improve customer service to groups.

4 Identify three ways in which you can provide better customer service for children.

5 What customer care considerations might you anticipate when working with older customers?

6 How would you improve customer service for foreign-language speakers?

7 What design features might assist people with disabilities?

5.4 Dealing with customers – the art of communication

At the heart of all customer service is communication. No matter how much you know about the principles of good customer service it will not help you if your communication skills are not up to scratch.

Communication is 'the sending of information and the confirmation that it has been received as intended'. It is essentially a two-way process. There are four stages:

- encoding information (that is putting it into a communicable form such as words)
- sending it through a channel or medium (in words – face to face, or on the telephone, in writing, or by signs and expressions)
- decoding (interpretation) by the receiver
- returning feedback that the message has been understood.

As the message travels there may be 'noise' that distorts it. Noise is unwanted information from distractions, or other, contradictory messages. 'Noise' could be the sender's personal mannerisms which can distract from what he/she is saying; for example, biting a lip or covering the mouth. Excessive use of 'filler phrases' is another example, such as 'at this moment in time', 'as it were'. Try to lose them to make the message clearer. There are other reasons why the message is not received

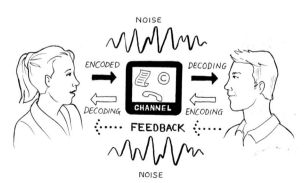

Background noise, poor speech and unclear sentences are all noise that distort the message and feedback

and understood. Encoding may be poor (poor use of language), and so may be the decoding (the sender has used words that the receiver does not understand), or the channel may not be effective (poor diction, illegible writing). Staff with good customer care practice minimise 'noise' and match encoding to the customer's ability to decode. In other words keep things clear and simple.

This model is clearly summarised on page 304. It combines the communication process with the type of medium used and shows possible causes for communication breaking down.

> **Try it out**
>
> Get a friend to read a message of about fifty words to you. Write down what was said. Now get two friends to read to you at the same time similar but different messages and try to write down one of them. Compare the accuracy of both records.
>
> Next, get a friend to read a new message to you and record it. Now get the friend to write the message, using longer and more technical words and record that. Again, compare the two records. Explain any differences or similarities you find between each pair of records.

There are essentially three means of communication (Figure 5.8).

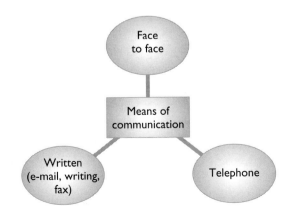

Figure 5.8 The three means of communication

Face-to-face communication

This consists of verbal and non-verbal communication.

Verbal communication

Verbal communication requires both listening and talking. While most of us can talk and be understood, some of us are less effective at listening, and this is a skill that often needs developing.

Even talking, something that may seem to be second nature, will need practice to be effective, particularly to a group or in front of others.

Speaking
- Know what you are going to say – prepare your information.
- Keep the channel open – make sure your speech is clear and audible.
- Keep it lively – modulate your voice by using tone and emphasis.
- Make sure you are using language that will be understood.
- Stress what is important by repeating key phrases and words.
- Keep it simple by avoiding speech mannerisms and unnecessary words.

> **Try it out**
>
> To communicate effectively, you need to pitch your level of language appropriately. You need to assess the receiver and alter your message accordingly, e.g.:
>
> Start at normal: *You will be given a demonstration and after that Karen here will design a personal schedule for you.*
>
> Up a level: *First, we will give you an induction on the CV stations and then Karen will work with you developing a training and personal fitness programme that fits your physiological profile.*
>
> Down a level: *First we will show you how things work and then Karen will show you what to do.*

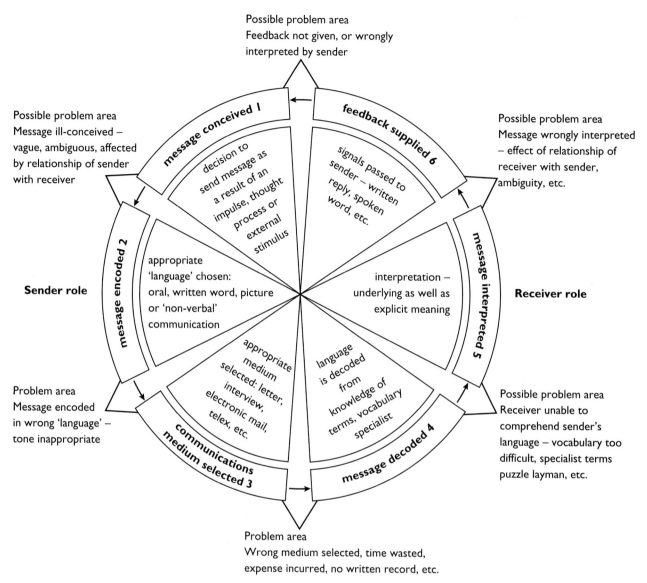

The communication process and possible causes of communication breakdown
Source: Evans

Listening

- Focus – concentrate only on what the person is saying.
- Look at the speaker and observe gestures.
- Interpret the meaning – be alert to his tone and speech patterns.
- Eliminate confusion by asking questions and seeking clarification.
- Show understanding by giving regular brief feedback and recognition.
- Try to avoid interrupting – be patient and wait to ask a question without losing concentration on what is being said.

If you are to communicate well you must always assess customers as the receivers of your message, and adapt your style and message to suit them, whether they are children, hard of hearing, non-English speakers, etc. This means trying to choose an appropriate level of language. Start by using everyday language which everyone will understand (no jargon, no big words), and as the customer gives you feedback you can adjust the level accordingly.

When talking to a customer you will be sending more than one message at a time.

Good customer service means putting the customer at ease

Giving information is most probably one, but there is also one of hospitality, known as making small talk, used to put the customer at ease. Comments on the weather, the traffic, or a question as to how the customer heard of the facility, are all standard small talk. If the customer feels like responding then he/she may enjoy the conversation. If the customer doesn't respond, then don't continue. In any event, keep to neutral comments, and avoid judgemental remarks as they can lead to trouble.

Making communication easier – putting the customer at ease

Transactions are often short in a leisure setting and an effective introduction is often all that is required. For longer transactions 'primacy' affects the interaction. A good start means smoother communication throughout. The first thing to do then is put the customer at ease. Smile on first meeting, keep smiling, finish with a smile. Practise your handshake, it communicates confidence and trustworthiness. Introduce yourself and your job and use the customer's name, to create a friendly, personal link, but make sure you are using the form of name that the customer prefers – if in doubt, use a formal greeting.

Personal space

All cultures have unconsciously established customs on how close people stand to each other – this is known as personal space. Imagine two circles around a person. The outer zone is for strangers, or virtual strangers (i.e. member of staff and customer). The inner zone is reserved for family and close friends. The distance of these zones varies with culture, gender and age, and from person to person. Remember that it is better to be too far away than too close.

Sports coaches or play workers frequently have to work close to customers. It is good practice to:

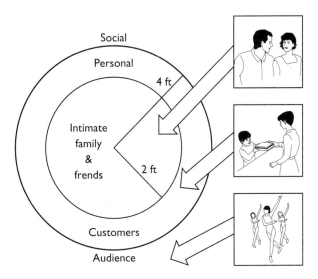

Personal space zones

- ask permission to come close (e.g. 'May I have the use of your arm to demonstrate this to the class?')
- restrict any contact to non-threatening areas of the body (e.g. hands, elbows and shoulders).

In dance sessions where close physical contact is required, the leader will often start the session by breaking down personal space with 'ice-breaking' activities such as holding hands or waists.

Using language

Leland and Bailey (1999) in *Customer Service for Dummies* show that words play a small part in communication and it is tone, speed, rhythm, and emphasis of the voice that are largely influential (Figure 5.9).

- Keep the volume down. A raised voice sounds aggressive. Beware of unconsciously copying the raised voice of a customer.
- Use stress. Stress can indicate concern and emotion. If you want to hear stress and volume used well, listen to an experienced aerobics coach talking to a class.
- Copy the customer. It can be effective to use the same words and expressions as the customer. Try to identify and reflect the customer's style of speech. This behaviour is the basis of neuro-linguistic programming (NLP), an important theory which you may find worthwhile exploring further.

> **Think it over**
>
> Start to notice what people do around you – watch a couple of people having a conversation and see how close they stand to each other, and whether the distance is comfortable for both. They may have different ideas about personal space, which will tell you something about them, and their interaction.
>
> Are there reasons for the custom of having a receptionist's desk other than the convenience of somewhere to put things?
>
> Look at yourself and work out what your own preferred 'space ' is when talking to a selection of different people – a close friend, an acquaintance, a stranger, an assistant.
>
> What would you say was the norm for personal space between staff and customer ? How does this vary between different nationalities that you have noticed?

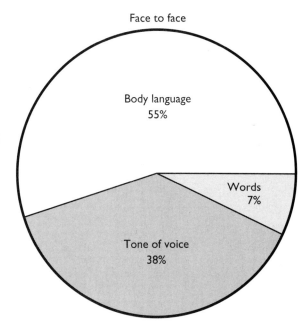

Figure 5.9 Relative importance of verbal and non-verbal factors in face-to-face communication

Thought for the page

It can be difficult, for receptionists in particular, to have to repeat the same information, say on prices or opening times over and over again. Without realising it your voice goes dull. To get round the problem smile a little more, slightly exaggerate the stress and the rise and fall in your voice. In addition vary your routine with each customer. Don't chant 'Flops Gym Centre, Karen speaking, how may I help you?' Simple variations like 'This is Flops Gym' or 'How can I help?' will keep you fresh.

Non-verbal communication

Because sight is a more developed sense than hearing, non-verbal communication or 'body language' is a more powerful face-to-face communication. Figure 5.10 shows what face-to-face communication is made up of.

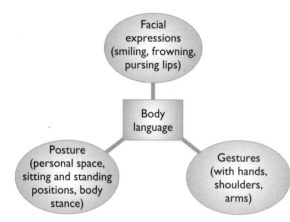

Figure 5.10 Components of face-to-face communiction

We have already seen how simple body language like smiling influences verbal communication, and the combination of all the above components produces hundreds of other pictures that tell us about the emotions, the mental state, and the physical state. Often body language tells us someone's real state of mind at the same time that they are saying something quite different.

Remember that, like all communication, non-verbal communication is a two-way

Body language often communicates a more powerful message than what is actually being said

process. You should be able to read the body language of your customer and you should be aware of the messages your own body language is sending.

Expressions

'You could read in her face that she was upset' is a typical illustration of the importance of expressions. The response to what you are saying may be silent, but the facial expression should tell you the degree to which your message has been understood or if it has met with agreement.

Eye contact

Eye contact, or looking the person in the eye, is a major signal of interest, concentration and trustworthiness. In Britain, eye contact should start immediately two people meet; after that it should be regularly maintained. If you are with a group, make sure you share eye contact around the group. When looking at a customer, your eyes should be the same as they would be when talking to friends or family. Once again, if you smile the eye size will be naturally welcoming. Avoid frequently looking away or, even worse, looking over the customer's shoulder. Customers will feel rejected or annoyed.

Thought for the page

Some people who are used to communicating with large groups become expert at looking at everyone all the time – or so it seems. Conductors (of orchestras, choirs, bands) are particularly clever at continuous eye contact, and if you are in the choir or band it can feel as if the conductor is looking only at you, but you will find out that everyone feels the same!

Nodding

The other important expression is the nod –it shows you are listening. Think about nodding and make sure it reflects what the speaker is feeling as well as what they are saying. Beware also that a nod is not used as an automatic response to cover for inattention.

Gestures and posture

The way we move and position our body:

- expresses our inner feelings
- reinforces what we are saying
- reflects our status alongside the other person.

In customer care the usual role of the staff is to ensure that the customers are relaxed and calm. This is normally a straightforward process (we will talk about complaint handling later) and body language helps.

Controlling communication

Handling customers is a bit like being a conductor and there is much evidence to show that by simply using body language you can relax the customers, make them feel valued, calm them down, and so on. There are some basic rules to note.

Speak the same body language

Two people who are getting on well reflect each other's positions and gestures. When dealing with a customer you should consciously copy their gestures and posture (unless they are hostile ones). You can then either maintain this if things are going well, or introduce elements that you think will improve the interaction and which the customer will start subconsciously to copy.

Reinforce behaviour

Use your own body language to show approval or concern for that of the customer. For example, if a customer starts to raise his/her voice cast your eyes down, drop your smile, look hurt, and step back slightly. When they become calmer turn the smile and eye contact back on, and nod.

Manage space

Body language varies according to the physical circumstances. It is more likely that a person will start pointing a finger (hostility) if she is within intimate personal space or taller than the person she is talking to. That is why reception desks and bars are often raised – so that both parties are at eye level and a distance is created between customer and receptionist. Generally speaking, you should try to encourage a customer to adopt a relaxed physical position where you can both talk on an equal footing.

Telephone

So far you have been concentrating on face-to-face personal skills. However, in many aspects of working life the telephone is also a major channel for communications. It is important to develop good telephone skills including:

- quick, efficient explanations
- accurate recording of bookings or cancellations
- ability to reach the right people in large organisations
- ability to transfer calls quickly
- ability to end calls politely when necessary (another line ringing, a customer arrives to talk to you).

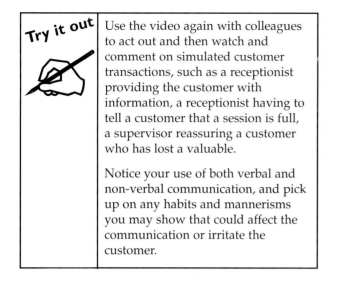

Use the video again with colleagues to act out and then watch and comment on simulated customer transactions, such as a receptionist providing the customer with information, a receptionist having to tell a customer that a session is full, a supervisor reassuring a customer who has lost a valuable.

Notice your use of both verbal and non-verbal communication, and pick up on any habits and mannerisms you may show that could affect the communication or irritate the customer.

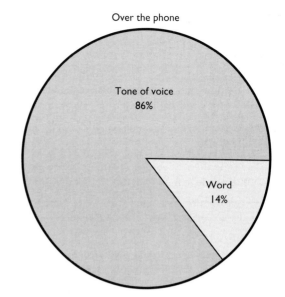

Over the phone

Tone of voice
86%

Word
14%

Figure 5.11 Relative importance of tone of voice to what is said in telephone conversation

Quick and efficient the phone may be, but it does have a major drawback in that the major communication tools (your face and body) are no longer part of the equation. Your voice is the only way that you can communicate. Compare the pie chart (Figure 5.11) for telephone communication with the one on page 306 for face-to-face communication and see how the importance of the tone of voice has increased. Without body language you now need to make sure you use your voice creatively.

Check it out

1 How can you maximise your listening skills?

2 Explain how you would stand or sit in relation to the customer.

3 Explain how you might modify your speech for different customers.

4 What are the components of non-verbal communication?

5 Explain why tone is important in communication.

6 What expression might a customer show if he/she was not understanding you?

CASE STUDY – Dealing with customers effectively

A customer walks into a video shop and returns a tape to an assistant who is looking at a film on TV.

The assistant looks up and looks at the tape, sighs and says 'You should rewind the tape before returning it'. The assistant then checks on the computer and says 'That's £2 please'.

The customer says, 'What do you mean? I paid last night'. The assistant looks at a colleague and says 'That can't be the case, if you had it would be on the computer'.

The customer replies 'What do you mean – "can't" – are you saying I didn't pay?'

Questions
1 What went wrong?
2 Access this situation in terms of communication and rewrite a more effective handling of the situation.

Tips for good telephone practice

- *Speak clearly:* This may seem obvious but eating, resting your hand on your chin, holding the phone under your chin, or looking away are all common habits that distort the message, and can be irritating.
- *Speak reasonably slowly:* Because your listener has no body language to support your meaning, concentration on words and inflexion are very important.
- *Modulate your voice:* Without body language you need to place more emphasis on tone, stress and rhythm.
- *Break the message:* If the conversation is very one-sided, try to break it up either by asking questions or making verbal nods ('Yes, I see', 'that's great'), or allow the other person to speak. Silence is an effective way of bringing a monologue to an end, as the talker will quickly want to know if you are still on the line.
- *Manage the conversation:* The copycat approach to verbal communication is the same as that with body language. If you adopt the same speed of conversation as your customer and use similar vocal devices such as stress, you will fall into a mutual communication.
- *Understand the machinery:* Telephone systems are now so technically sophisticated and can do so many different things that it is important to familiarise yourself thoroughly with the system you are using. Breakdowns in telephone communications cause great irritation and lead rapidly to breakdowns in customer relations.
- *Know who is who in the facility:* This is vital for referring customers to the right people – customers quickly get annoyed if they are put through to the wrong people and have to be rereferred and repeat their requests.

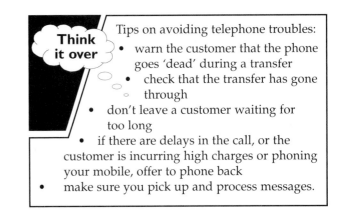

Think it over

Tips on avoiding telephone troubles:
- warn the customer that the phone goes 'dead' during a transfer
- check that the transfer has gone through
- don't leave a customer waiting for too long
- if there are delays in the call, or the customer is incurring high charges or phoning your mobile, offer to phone back
- make sure you pick up and process messages.

Conventions vary

Many organisations use a standard formula that often becomes a cliché. If you are allowed, vary your use of words around the above theme. Get a 'handle' on the customer. Even if you are acting only as a transfer point it helps to get the customer's name. 'I am transferring you now, Mrs Beckham' is so much friendlier and caring than 'I am transferring you now, caller... click'.

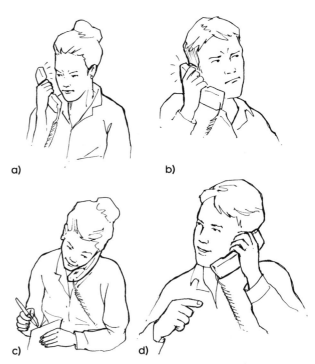

a) b) c) d)

Telephone communication is not just about talking down the phone – position and emotional state affect the way we communicate. Which of the above pictures shows the best telephone communication?

Having information at your fingertips avoids delays and inefficiency in answering a telephone call

Good telephone practice applies just as much to internal calls as to external ones.

Completing the call and follow-up

While business calls should be pleasant they should also be efficient and brought to a conclusion when sufficient information has been gathered and appropriate actions decided.

- Finally clarify and record information such as spelling of names or addresses.
- Summarise and confirm the main points and define the actions that will be taken

Does answering a call with your mouth full give a good impression?

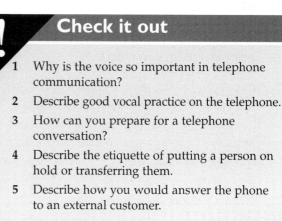

Message: When you were out		
Date: 12 June	Urgent Yes ☑	No ☐
Time: 1310		

Message from: John Knightly
Message to: Emma Woodhouse
Taken by: Jane Fairfax

Action

Telephoned ☑	Came in ☐
Will phone back ☐	Will come back ☐
You to phone back ☑	Wants to see you ☐

Message: Mr Knightly from Austens phoned about the new location for the corporate hospitality event – seemingly they want to have an open air picnic at Box Hill. Can you phone him back on 0205673456 today

Figure 5.12 A telephone message form like this makes it easier to recall the details of a call

(when and by whom). Many organisations have a form for doing this on, like the ones shown here (Figure 5.12) for taking a message and for recording the outcomes of a conversation.

- Thank the caller, exchange pleasantries and hang up.

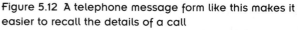

! Check it out

1 Why is the voice so important in telephone communication?
2 Describe good vocal practice on the telephone.
3 How can you prepare for a telephone conversation?
4 Describe the etiquette of putting a person on hold or transferring them.
5 Describe how you would answer the phone to an external customer.

Written communication

Written communication has none of the communication devices we use in interpersonal contact. The importance of the written word is that it should mean exactly what it says and once written is there, unchanging, for all to see – which is why it is often used as evidence or confirmation. With writing you can't say 'What I meant to say was this'. The way an individual or an organisation presents written information says something about both the writer and the organisation – so it is important to get it right. Figure 5.13 shows the various formats available.

Figure 5.13 Written communication devices

All these except for e-mail can be hand-written, so make sure your writing can be read otherwise use the keyboard, except for sticky notes. Faxes, e-mails and memos are the life-blood of daily business and require less formality than letters. All of them have the same advantages in that:

- they contain the same message for who-ever reads it and when ever it is read
- they can be copied and sent to other people
- they are evidence, thus making it difficult to change or deny messages after they have been sent.

Faxes

are a convenient way of sending documents (especially with artwork) over a telephone line. Their great advantage is that they are more or less instant to send and allow last-minute transfer of documents, or even allow editing/alterations to made between two distant places. Traditionally, the channel for faxes was fax machines but increasingly they are integrated into a computer, which has the advantage that text can be edited directly. The downside is that if the work is not generated on the computer it has to be scanned in and filed – which takes time. It is normal practice when sending a fax to attach a cover sheet to it which gives the company logo, address and further details (including the number of pages being faxed – important in case one page fails in transmission) plus a short (often informal and hand-written) note from the sender.

E-mails

are generated on a computer and are messages that are sent though a web server. Computer files can also be sent as attachments. They are faster and cheaper than faxes. There is a whole new etiquette to sending e-mails, and people in business are still learning all the nuances. It is best therefore to write e-mails in an informal but conventional style until you are certain of the style of your receiver. Because of its novelty there are new ground rules for e-mail:

- keep them snappy and use plenty of bullets
- cut the formalities (e.g. further to your e-mail of).
- the writing still reflects the image of your workplace so don't get sloppy on spelling and grammar. Use the spell checker and read your message before sending it.
- e-mails are lasting documents, so don't get into the habit of using them to send jokes or comments about colleagues and customers. Staff have been dismissed for this.
- they are a source of computer viruses. To reduce this worry it is always good practice to describe the subject matter of the e-mail in a straightforward way and identify yourself as the sender.

- do not send large files (including art work) unnecessarily. A file of several hundred kBs may take a long time to send through, resulting in high charges and a blocked system for the receiver.

Memos

are short messages summarising instructions, information or comments – their purpose is to remind us of conversations or instructions. Basic information to be included is

- name of sender and recipient(s)
- date
- subject.

New or more complex information should be put in a structured report (a far more complex area not covered here, but it can be studied in Mort 1992). They are increasingly being replaced by e-mail because memos are slower to send, more time consuming and expensive to produce, and bulkier to store. They are still used, however, and one advantage they maintain is that they are useful for mass display such as on notice boards. Although they are conventionally longer than e-mails they should still be kept short – one side of A4 is usually counted as being good practice. In non-IT offices the memo is still the mainstay of written communication. The 'shuttle' memo is often used which is a hand-written triplicate form. The sender writes the message and keeps back a copy and sends the other two; the receiver writes a reply and returns one copy. A classic case of encode, decode and provide feedback!

Who writes?

It was said when computers first entered offices that typists would become a thing of the past. Not so, the typists' skills of speed, accuracy, knowledge of machinery, layout, style and procedure still make them valuable contributors, especially for external communication. In most offices typists are

kept busy by senior staff so if you want to send a message quickly, it is better to do it yourself. As with the telephone you should know how to use the machinery involved and be able to identify and rectify problems – not create them.

Letters

are the normal means of written communication for external customers, although faxes and e-mails are increasingly being used. Letters should be typed for all external correspondence and should be printed on headed notepaper, giving all the details of the organisation. The quality and design of a letter is important as it indicates the professionalism of the organisation.

Notices

The other type of written communication to customers is the notice. In most organisations notices for health and safety and other common occurrences will probably be pre-designed. However, frequently, temporary notices are needed: notice to congratulate a team for winning a competition, to say that a court is being repaired, to announce a BBQ later in the week, etc. Notice boards are often the place where people congregate and customers like to know what is going on and usually check as they arrive and leave for new notices. Thus it is worth while taking care that the notices look good and are written in a friendly way that reflects the ambience of the organisation. They can be written or computer generated, and be

Thought for the page

Good notice board practice
- Keep them uncluttered and give each notice a clear display.
- Remove out-of-date notices.
- Remove unauthorised notices.
- Decide on the relevance of a notice for the people who are going to be reading it in that place.

CASE STUDY – Written communication

Emma, from Churchill Corporate Hospitality, has talked on the telephone to Austen Publishing about their centenary picnic.

She now writes to confirm their conversation and to report on follow-up action.

Churchill Corporate Hospitality   a

Northanger House
Mansfield Business Park
Basingstoke
Hants RG21 5FT

b   Mr John Knightley
Operations Manager
Austen Publishing
Weston Square
Highbury
London N5 6TH

Tel 01256 34561 (ext 2987)   c
Fax 01256 239874
e-mail emma.w@cch.org.uk

Attn Ms E Woodhouse   d

e   21st June 2000

Ref: Austen Centenary Celebrations/ EW/JFA1287   f

Dear Mr Knightly   g

It was good to talk to you yesterday by telephone. I have now followed up the various points arising from our discussions and I am pleased to confirm the following items for your centenary picnic to be held on Tuesday 15th August for 250 guests.   h

The trip to Box Hill is feasible in that the Local Authority has given clearance to erect a marquee and fencing and have a picnic for up to 300 guests.

I have contacted the various service providers involved and can confirm that all services will be available – although the catering charge will be increased by approximately 15% per person. Perhaps you could let me know within the next week if this is acceptable or if you wish to reduce the scale of catering. I will then be able to send you the contract and start arranging the day for your guests.

I am sending a copy of this letter to Jane Fairfax whom I believe you know and who will be responsible for the guest list.

I look forward very much to working with you over the forthcoming months.   i

Yours sincerely,   j

Emma Woodhouse

Emma Woodhouse (Ms)
(Conference and Entertainment Manager)   k

cc Jane Fairfax   l

CASE STUDY (Continued)

a/b Logo and company details (address communication numbers). These are often pre-printed so the normal convention of placing your name and position here is omitted if space does not allow.

The traditional convention is to put the sender's details at top right and the receiver's top left. Modern logos and layout mean that this can sometimes be altered but the receiver's name, title and address should be somewhere at the top of the page.

c Letterheads usually give the main number of an organisation, so you may want to add your extension or direct line number.

d Sometimes letters sent by one person are replied to by another person. This inclusion clarifies the situation.

e Always put the date in this position.

f The 'Ref' refers to the subject in hand plus any filing references so that the letter can be traced later.

g Remain conventional – 'Dear John', or 'Mr, Mrs, Ms' not 'My dear' or 'Hi'. 'Dear Sir' or 'Dear Madam' are used only if you are writing to an organisation and have no name (although it would be better to ring the organisation and try to find out a name to write to from the receptionist).

h The first paragraph should briefly refer to any contacts you have had and what the letter is about. Keep any pleasantries short. You should then proceed with the main points you need to make, keeping each to its own paragraph. Bulleted lists are acceptable.

i The last signing-off paragraph can often be left purely as a pleasantry. Even a demand letter can finish 'I do hope we can settle this matter favourably and that we can look forward to your continued membership.'

j Be conventional: 'Yours sincerely' (if recipient is named), 'Yours faithfully' if not. You may use your full signature or just your forename, depending on the stage of formality and familiarity with your customer. Avoid initials as it makes you appear too busy to value the customer.

k Repeat or identify your name and role for the first time. Identify your gender and title as it saves the recipient of letter the embarrassment of having to decide and perhaps having to reply Dear Sir/Madam.

l cc refers to the other people to whom a copy of the letter has been sent.

Questions

1 Emma has made a sloppy mistake. Can you spot it?

2 Can you give two reasons why she may have made it?

suitably decorated. If you are saying something negative, try to put it in a positive way ('Be aware', not 'Beware'; see Thought for the page).

Thought for the page

Good notice practice

Be positive – do not put *'Don't park your cars here. The Manager'*.

Instead put *'For the convenience of all customers please park your car in the marked areas. Thank you, Rodney Stewart, Manager'*

! Check it out

1 Identify three conventions in sending e-mails.

2 What basic information should be on a written message?

3 Give three personal details about yourself that you should include in a written letter to someone you do not know. Explain why they are useful.

4 'Be aware' not 'Beware'. Why is this good customer service?

5.5 Selling skills

Many people still have a stereotyped picture of a salesman – a caricature like Danny de Vito in the film *Matilda* – oily, greedy, shifty and just plain crooked. Nothing could be further from the truth as successful salespeople usually have:

- a liking for their customers and people in general
- a liking for their product (this may be a material product or a service)
- excellent interpersonal and selling skills.

This sounds just like someone who is good at customer care and so it is – as many of the skills we have referred to so far in this section are also sales skills.

Sales are a major activity in the leisure industry. Everyone who works in it, not just the designated sales staff, has a part to play in selling the product to the customer. For example, in the cinema or theatre there are booking personnel who will advise you on the

CASE STUDY – Customer care standards

The ultimate customer care notice is the Customer Standards Notice. This should be prominently displayed at reception and other suitable places such as changing rooms or catering areas. It tells customers that:

- they are valued ('We never forget that you are our customer')

- the standards they can expect to receive in service (all complaints will be replied to within 24 hrs) and material products (e.g cleanliness, heating)

- how the customer can get redress if standards fail

- how the customer can make suggestions to improve the service

- Here is the notice at Kingsbridge Leisure Centre:

CUSTOMER CHARTER
We are committed to providing a high quality service every time you visit our Centre.

We promise that:
– the time and availability of services will be as published in our customer information leaflet;
– any foreseen change will be duly notified to our customers by the display of an appropriate notice within the Centre;
– any unforeseen (emergency) interruption to services that have been booked will result in refunds and/or an offer of alternative services where possible.

The swimming pools at South Dartmoor Leisure Centre and Totnes Pavilion will be:
– maintained at a minimum of 30 degrees indoors and 27 degrees outdoors at SDLC and 28 degrees at Totnes Pavilion;
– balanced chemically and tested regularly to ensure customer comfort and safety;
– supervised by the recommended number of qualified and trained staff;
– kept in a warm, clean, safe and hygienic condition.

The dry sport/activity areas will be:
– clean and safe to use;
– furnished with equipment which is in good working order and checked and maintained regularly;
– set out in accordance with the requirements or the governing body of the sport where necessary;
– ready for use within 5 minutes of the commencement of the booked period where equipment changeovers are necessary;
– illuminated, heated and ventilated to ensure comfort, good play conditions and safety.

Staff will be:
– trained and appropriately qualified;
– easily identifiable by earing their uniforms and badges;
– helpful, experienced and informative to ensure that your visit is safe and enjoyable.

All ancillary area, including changing rooms, showers and toilets, will be:
– clean, hygienic and in good working order;
– checked by staff every hour and remedial action taken where necessary.

In general we will:
– ensure the Centre is clean, safe and well maintained;
– listen and be responsive to comments, complaints and suggestions;
– maintain a balanced programme of activities and services which cater for the needs of all section of the community;
– publish up to date and accurate customer information for all activities;
– have clear technical standards for all important features of the service and meet them;
– make prices competitive and fair to ensure value for money;
– undertake regular surveys of our customers to ensure that we continue to meet their stated priorities.

best film to see, suggest the best seats, and ensure that the product you get is the one you want. In a health club it may be a receptionist or recreation assistant who tells the prospective customer ('the prospect') all about the club and shows them round. If they are doing a good job they will find out what the customer wants to do, pick up on their interests and create the impression that the club is the sort of place the customer wants to belong to.

Raising customer awareness

- Making a sale is not necessarily about taking money. For example, in libraries or country parks where many activities are free, staff will still be carrying out similar work that will persuade the prospect to use the product and select from the choice on offer.
- Making a sale is not necessarily directed just to your present customer. For instance, most people visit theme parks only occasionally and probably won't return to the same one for a long time, but on their visit the staff will be welcoming and helpful and say that they are looking forward to the customer's return. They are selling to *referred* sales –

Not all selling situations involve immediate purchase. Staff may encourage prospects to use a product

the friends the customers will recommend to come.

- Selling is not just to customers from the general public. In leisure many of our customers are other businesses who may be interested in sponsorship deals or who want our organisation to provide a special service. Can you sell your organisation to them and convince them it would be able to deliver the right sort of service?

The sales process is usually most apparent at the point when the customer decides to part with his/her money and buy the service. However, the process continues throughout the whole time the customer uses the service. This 'hidden' selling is not only influencing the customer to become loyal to the service but will also bring to their notice other products which might be available.

At its best, the leisure industry has certain characteristics that make it a good sales environment.

- The customer will be relaxed and is usually happy to trust the provider.
- The staff usually love their work and the product it creates.
- The staff are naturally 'people's people' with good interpersonal skills.
- The staff genuinely want the product to be what the customer wants.

In addition, customers have already made the decision to participate to some extent. They are:

- already interested in the product and other products associated with it
- often relaxed or have time to spare to consider a sales offer
- often significantly motivated by the marketing and merely wish to confirm their expectations and purchase the product.

With this situation it is likely that you can make a sale of some sort. Your goal, though, is to maximise a sale – not only in terms of immediate income, but also in terms of customer satisfaction, which is the key to increased usage and repeat sales and referred sales.

The stages of making a sale – the AIDA technique

Making a sale goes through the same stages every time although sometimes in a different order:

Attention – poster, product, advertisement, loudspeaker

Interest – brochure, product to handle, staff assistance

Desire – customer wishes to buy, so the member of staff checks that customer has the right product; the customer then cannot decide which product is best or which suits them

Action – member of staff turns desire into reality, by making the product available immediately, or

Making a sale using the AIDA technique

by making the purchase easier, e.g. option to buy now and pay later.

There are also associated techniques.

Establishing rapport

If customers are suspicious that they are being 'sold to', dislike the salesperson or feel tense in any way, they become sales resistant. It is essential therefore to put customers at ease and establish a good relationship with them. The interpersonal skills that have been described above are all important in rapidly establishing rapport:

* the smile and welcome
* good presentation skills (appearance, eye contact, body language)
* identifying the customer type (matter of fact, amiable, etc)
* reflecting their verbal and body language
* share the same ideas and interests as the customer (see Thought for the page).

Pleasant environment

Is the selling area warm and dry? Selling in a comfortable and pleasant setting usually gets the best results. For example, don't linger outside on a cold wet day showing every tennis court; describe the set-up inside the club.

Thought for the page

Rapport is also about sharing the same ideas and feelings as the customer. Few customers want to know the technical definitions and rebound co-efficient of an artificial court – even though you have spent months researching which specification would give the best play. Find out what they are interested in and what they want to get out of the product and concentrate on that. If the customer likes the décor of the gym or is interested in nutrients, talk about them.

Is it difficult to talk against noise? For example, don't try to discuss membership in a fitness suite with the noise of MTV and the machines; go to a quiet corner.

Investigate customer needs

This requires some on-the-spot research. Look at and listen to the customers and ask them questions about themselves. Maslow (1943) suggested a hierarchy of needs (Figure 5.14).

- Basic needs such as food, drink, sex and comfort are the most powerful. Think how many adverts feature these.
- Less basic needs become important when the basic needs are satisfied. This is why better-off people are more concerned with safety or enhancing their physical and mental state through leisure.
- Unnecessary needs become desires. Some people find it difficult to recognise that a need is satisfied and will demand more, and even when satisfied can become addicted. This may result in excessive consumption or a demand for new products. It is one reason why the health business is constantly offering new variations on the fitness theme to satisfy already fit customers.

Personal appeal and image

are both major influences on many people. 'Do I look attractive to people I find attractive?', 'Do my "role models" use this product?' or 'Am I likely to meet a partner in this club?', are all questions which influence customer actions. The products themselves do not have to be obviously attractive ones for this to apply. For example, a person who wants to be attractive to intellectuals or appear clever will read books from the library that will help her to do this. A person who wants to appear active may buy all-terrain shoes and a diver's watch even though the nearest he gets to the activities is watching a documentary on TV. What they are buying is an image not an activity.

Safety

is a constant source of concern for customers and is probably always worth promoting to:

- parents, with a strong parental instinct to protect their children and to protect themselves so as to be able to protect their children and set a good example
- women and elderly people, who often want to be assured of personal protection and secure premises.

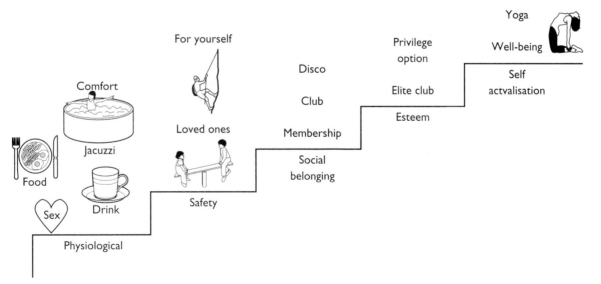

Figure 5.14 The hierarchy of customer needs

Think it over

High-risk sport activists will want to know that risk has been assessed and as far as possible eliminated in a product and that there are fail-safe options. In all areas, customers will also want to know if staff are trained and experienced, or if a facility is insured or licensed. Safety is not just about personal safety but also about financial security. They will want to be assured of money-back guarantees on faulty goods or the insurance if, for instance, an activity holiday is cancelled. In other words, whenever you are selling the product, have the safety features at your fingertips.

Belonging to a group and social contact

are important aspects of leisure activities. Many people who want to use a service do so because they want to meet people like themselves or people who are different from them, or they want to be part of a group. These people will respond with interest to the mention of the social programme of a club or the availability of products, such as sweatshirts bearing the club logo. At the same time, the fear of not fitting in, of not being good enough at a sport, or general shyness can act as a demotivator, and the successful salesperson will identify (but rarely refer to) these demotivators and then sell the points of the product that reduce them; for example, the friendliness of the club, the special welcome for beginners. Good follow-up practice would be to ensure that these selling points are indeed in place for these particular people should they become customers.

The need for esteem or status can drive people to buy products such as designer-label sportswear. The desire to buy the product is largely driven by the need to be seen as someone who has the money or connections to use such an elite product or service. People may want to belong to expensive health or country clubs because of what that membership says about them. The importance of self-image means that people collect possessions and activities that show what sort of people they are. This can help the leisure staff as their dress, car and manner will identify which aspects of their product will fit the customer's image.

Self-actualisation

is the need to recognise yourself as a fulfilled person. Genuine interest and love of an activity may be the foremost reason for participation and is in fact very common in leisure. In sport, fitness and health the feeling of understanding oneself is often mentioned as being one of the great rewards for the individual. For a gardener or a walker the feeling of being one with nature may be all-important.

Leisure staff should be able to do two things in relation to these needs.

CASE STUDY – Identifying subconscious needs and motivations

A male customer walks into a health club saying he is in search of a health-based programme. He in fact talks more about his shape, and glances particularly at the members rather than at the equipment.

Questions
1 What do you think his needs are?
2 Imagine what you would recommend to him.
3 What questions would you ask him, to find out more about what he really wants so as to suit his needs best?

- Identify the product consciously wanted by the customer. If this is not made clear by the customer you can ask questions as to what is wanted, and why, or for what purpose.
- Identify the subconscious needs and motivation. This is done largely by listening and observing (see case study).

Once you have discovered the customer's motivation, you will need to find a product that has the right characteristics to satisfy the customer's motivation and needs. Sometimes you will find that the product the customer wants is not the one best suited to him/her, or that what the customer wants is going to be too expensive. It is then up to you to try to resolve the conflict (see Thought for the page).

Presenting the product or service

Customers often need to be satisfied about the product itself and its value in terms of its selling points. These include for

Material products:

- life expectancy and quality of the product

Thought for the page

Money is one common cause of customer/product conflict. Rosie wants to buy a good racquet, but the one she likes and knows about is out of her price range. She is disappointed and cautious about buying anything else. You will need to convince her of the value to her of the expensive racquet, or you should try to find out how and how much she plays, and find one that will suit her equally well if not better, and at her price.

Jason wants to join an expensive health club and you suspect that he will have problems paying a one-off annual fee. You can (as long as you have the management's permission) suggest that he pays by monthly direct debit even though it will cost him slightly more in the long run.

- after-sales costs such as maintenance, repair, guarantees.

Activities:

- will the product satisfy desire (make the customer fitter, let the customer meet new people, appear well-off)?
- withdrawal if the product is not suitable (e.g. trial membership, refunds)
- professionalism, safety and security (are staff qualified, is the centre licensed and/or insured?)
- availability and programming (timing, frequency of courses)
- sales support (will staff help development, in and out of hours?).

Once the customer's motivation and needs are discovered, he/she can be presented with the

When presenting information you will often find that creating 'pictures' can be effective. In other words rather than simply describing the product you should describe the outcome, which is what the customer is often seeing in his own mind

product. This will hopefully trigger his/her desire to buy it, and in fact this may already be well under way – demonstrating various products is an extremely useful way of discovering what the customer does and does not like, and why. It is essential that a sales-person is fully aware of the product's selling points and can give information and answer questions:

- about the product (what it does, how it is made and how long it will last, where it comes from, its price, its availability)
- about the competition (why this product is better than others)
- about the industry (background knowledge, points of reference with the customer).

There may also be unique selling points (USPs). This is a quality about the product which is either unique or of which the organisation is particularly proud. For example, your organisation may be the only one in the area that offers a total refund to customers should they decide they want to withdraw from the sale. Or you might offer a free repair service for the first year's use of a piece of equipment. Or your organisation has won an award for its service. Praise your product, but resist the temptation to criticise the competition (even if asked by a customer to compare) as this only reflects badly upon you. Customers will have to make up their own minds.

Let the customer experience the product if possible. The more you can let the customer experience a suitable product, the more he will be committed to it. Photographs and videos are useful, as is a tour of the facilities or an introduction to staff. Perhaps the strongest experience is to let the customer use the product for a trial period.

Closing the sale

There is a point in the sale when the customer will decide to buy. You can often

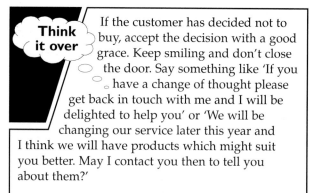

Think it over
If the customer has decided not to buy, accept the decision with a good grace. Keep smiling and don't close the door. Say something like 'If you have a change of thought please get back in touch with me and I will be delighted to help you' or 'We will be changing our service later this year and I think we will have products which might suit you better. May I contact you then to tell you about them?'

tell by the body language (a nod, sitting back relaxed, a smile). Very often people say directly 'Yes, I'll have it'. They may simply start using a lot of appropriate words ('Fine, okay, looks good').

Now is the time to 'wrap up' by stopping the presentation and confirming that the customer wants to buy. If you carry on selling there is a risk of boring the customer or saying something to undo the sale. (For example, 'You will have the green one then – mind you, the red one was nice too'. This has just resurrected the doubts you have spent ten minutes trying to sort out!)

Now all you have to do is ask how the sale will be processed (cash, credit card) and if any formalities have to be completed such as a reference or a credit agreement. Customers can

Thought for the page
Don't raise expectations. Experienced sellers do not tell the customer anything that they cannot deliver. So don't get carried away – there should be plenty of things you can say without inventing any. Raising expectations is always risky, but can be incredibly damaging especially with corporate customers. For example, you sell a sponsorship deal to a customer by saying that you will have an entry of two thousand participants. If in reality this number is very unlikely, your sponsor is not going to be pleased to see a much smaller gathering.

find parting with money or being checked out for credit stressful so you should help by being quick and efficient, making any checks away from the customer and offering hospitality such as a cup of coffee if appropriate.

In leisure, many of the products sold are used in the future and not at the point of sale (e.g. membership, advance bookings). In these circumstances you can save any embarrassment and build up good relations by declining bank cards or not phoning through for clearance. This tells the customer that you trust him or her and it carries no risk because if there are any irregularities they will be discovered before the customer uses the product.

Delivering after-sales service

Finally, you should remember that the sale does not finish when the customer buys the product. In many cases there will be an after-sales service. This normally includes one or more of the following:

- providing repairs and maintenance
- refunds or replacement if product is faulty or does not suit the needs of the customer
- follow-up by the organisation to see that the customer is still satisfied with the product.

In some organisations this service may be handled by someone other than the salesperson. Normally it is far better for the salesperson to follow up personally. This is because it re-establishes a successful link and allows the salesperson to answer directly any criticisms or receive praise about the product.

Furthermore, because of the trust that has been established, it is easier for the existing salesperson to develop new sales. For example, if a golf professional sold a customer a set of clubs he could later ask the customer how her game is improving, might suggest that he watches her play with the clubs and

at some point might suggest a further sale of a new golf bag or an additional club that was not in the original set.

Check it out

1 Why is the leisure industry conducive to selling?
2 How might you interest a customer in a product?
3 Explain how you might apply Maslow's theory in selling a swimming session to a retired person, a circuit to a teenage male, a climbing course to a woman in her twenties.
4 How might you persuade a customer to buy a more expensive product?
5 What do you need to know when selling?
6 Why is it important to close a sale quickly?
7 What are after-sales?

5.6 Customer service situations

Introduction

In this section and the next we are going to look briefly at various situations that customer service covers:

- providing information (for example, about products/services, directions)
- giving advice (for example, about appropriate products/services, equipment, safety)
- taking and relaying messages (for example, in person, on the telephone)
- keeping records (for example, of financial transactions, customer details)
- providing assistance (for example, help with access to buildings)
- dealing with problems (for example, stolen personal belongings, injuries)
- handling complaints (for example, timetable delays, cancelled services).

'Be prepared' is the motto for leisure providers as well as Boy Scouts. Customer service can have difficult moments and it helps greatly if you have anticipated what might happen and have taken measures to ensure things run smoothly. You will need to:

- know and understand your systems and service
- listen to what the customer is saying
- match needs to service
- take action
- check on satisfaction.

Understanding systems and services

You should know who does what in the organisation or anything connected with it. For many customer service situations there are forms to complete or set procedures to follow, for securing valuables for instance. You should be aware of these and have them to hand. Accurate and up-to-date information is essential. Information can be complex at times and often printed materials are preferable to spoken information.

Thought for the page

Josie phones the Midway Leisure Centre and asks to speak to someone who deals with the arrangements for school sessions in the pool. The switchboard operator takes a long time to decide who Josie should speak to and then transfers her to the wrong person, who in turn doesn't know how to re-route the call and promptly cuts her off. Infuriating, isn't it?

Listen to the customer

Customers should have your complete attention, and you should concentrate on listening to them to make sure you know exactly what is wanted. Most customers are clear in what they want, but some are undecided or obscure or just uncommunicative. If their needs are unclear you should ask questions to get a better idea.

Match customer and service needs

Often the transaction affects only the customer. But sometimes the organisation needs to be involved; for example, if there is an incident of some sort it will need to be recorded and, perhaps, other authorities informed. Bookings or cash transactions should be recorded.

Take action

In many cases you will be able to sort out any queries yourself. If you are unsure of your competence or remit to act, you should not just hazard a guess and then get it wrong, which will be irritating for the customer. However, as your aim is to produce customer satisfaction you will want to do your best to find a solution. Depending on circumstances you can:

- seek someone who can help (e.g. I will have to get the manager to sign this refund slip)
- offer the customer something to occupy time (e.g. offer coffee, if there is a delay)
- take the customer's details and say you will find out the answer – make sure you do
- if all else fails, apologise and admit defeat (this, after all, is better than fudging the answer).

If you need to fetch someone else it is worth checking first on their availability. If a senior manager is absent or unavailable there should be someone to take his place temporarily. Specialised people are often more elusive and it is a good idea in an organisation to keep a signing in and out book so that such people can be easily traced. It is also good manners for that person to come to the customer. If this is not possible, arrange for yourself or someone else to take the customer to them. Not only is this good manners but it will prevent the customer getting lost or breaching security rules.

If the customer has to wait for more than, say, a minute or so, it is good manners to offer a chair, some refreshment or something to read. You may notice that an increasing number of facilities where people wait (bars, reception) often have the day's papers to read or maybe even the TV on as part of their general customer service.

Check on satisfaction

Finally, there should be some way of checking that your service has met with the customer's satisfaction. At the end of any customer interaction the member of staff should ask something like 'Have you found everything you wanted to know?' or 'Are you happy with everything we have discussed?' It's that simple.

Providing information

Providing information, whether by telephone, face to face or in writing, is often time consuming and may involve customers waiting. It is often a good idea to also have self-select information sources such as brochures, posters, notice boards, and signs.

Customer information is often restricted to the categories in Figure 5.15.

Figure 5.15 Information required by customers

Complex information is condensed into a useful-sized card, which customers can take home

It is advisable, therefore, to know these and have support materials such as change for machines (better still have a change machine), local maps, and summaries of opening times.

> **Think it over**
>
> A new customer is being shown round a gym and says that he has a knee problem and wants to know what will be the best equipment to use. It would be irresponsible to say something like 'Well, I reckon the bicycle would be the best item to start with and then see how it goes.' The correct procedure would be to suggest that the customer has a medical assessment of the injury and then a professional assessment of what exercise was needed. What other advice might you be cautious about giving?

Giving advice

Providing information and giving advice (for example, about appropriate products/services, equipment, safety) are very similar except that when you give advice you are taking responsibility and influencing customers' actions. If you do this, you must be sure that you have the authority and competence to advise.

Even when you do give advice remember that the final choice is up to the customer, otherwise you may be accused by an unsatisfied customer that you led him/her into the decision.

Any information kept on file or computer is confidential and subject to the Data Protection Act. Any request by a third party for any such information must be refused. Even if the only record is your memory you must refuse all requests for personal information. The polite way to do this is to say 'I am sorry, Sir, but that is confidential information that I am not allowed by law to give you. However, if you would like to leave your name and a contact point, I will see if we have a Mr Lucan on our database, and if so I'll pass your message on to him.'

Taking and relaying messages

We have already seen how best to record messages from the telephone. The face-to-face situation is exactly the same, and the important thing is to make sure the message is delivered to the right person as soon as possible.

- Keep all the messages in an agreed place (desk diary, notice boards) where everyone knows where to look.
- Immediately deliver the message to the person – either by phone or in person, and leave a written message in a prominent place if he/she is out.

Voice mail is another way of recording messages.

- Your receiving message should include your name and/or company plus simple instructions to the caller how to leave a message.
- If you are leaving a message, speak slowly, give your name and company, who you are calling, the date and time of your call, and your message. It is good manners to say your contact number slowly at both the beginning and end of the message.

Keeping records

Keeping records is essential to:

- monitor the performance of an organisation
- account for money and materials
- provide evidence and details of past transactions and incidents.

Every organisation has its own records and ways of keeping them on computer or on paper. They should include:

- health and safety records (accident report form, near-miss records, incident book)
- lost property/deposited valuables records

- financial records (till receipts, cashing up, bank deposit forms, petty cash slips)
- customer comment forms
- customer records.

Points to notice about records:

- *Explain to the customer why they need to be completed*
- *Complete them immediately – delay and you will forget*
- *Complete them accurately and completely*
- *secure them*
- *Follow all procedures (such as giving a receipt)*

Providing assistance

Customers often need help other than the provision of information or advice. At the most basic level some customers may find themselves restricted in what they can do.

The following are some typical situations where assistance may be needed:

- an elderly person with a mobility problem who finds it difficult to walk up stairs
- a customer with learning difficulties who does not understand how to use the vending machine
- a non-English speaker who cannot read directional signs
- an event organiser who has hired a sports hall and needs to bring in extra equipment from the car
- a parent carrying a young child and bags
- a pregnant woman who is feeling faint
- a person with reading difficulties who is having a problem reading information materials.

When you realise there is a problem, your usual response is likely to be: 'Could I give you a hand there?' It can sometimes be embarrassing to the customer to refer to his/her specific problem, so a simple offer of help is sufficient. For example, a blind person might be sensitive if you said: 'Could I give you a hand there – you seem to be having a problem?' Similarly a dyslexic person will not thank you for bringing his disability to people's attention. It is much better to assist him by summarising the information you have given him verbally. You could say something like 'As you can see, Sir, there are three types of membership'.

In any situation you have two options. The first is to remove the cause of the difficulty. The second is to support the customer.

In the first case you might offer to help carry or store bags or equipment. For example: 'I think you might find the lockers too small for your shopping, would you like to leave it here and I will put it in the manager's office?'

In some cases, such as infirmity or disability, the customer needs support. You may offer a steadying arm or offer the use of a wheelchair. For customers with a learning difficulty, a language problem or visual impairment you might escort them or carry out the problematic action yourself (e.g. operate the vending machine or instruct a taxi driver where to take them).

Most assistance provides immediate solutions to minor problems. Sometimes the problem is more stressful to the customer – for example, someone may have lost her car keys and cannot pick up her child from school, or another may have left tickets or sports kit at home. In such situations your role is to do your best to solve the problem and minimise the stress or inconvenience caused to the customer. You might:

- offer the customer free use of the telephone or even make calls for them
- seek useful information for them
- provide comfort and reassurance (e.g. a cup of tea, rest area)

- offer to take care of other problems that may have resulted from the initial problem (e.g. pass messages to other members of the customer's group)
- provide transport (e.g. give the customer a lift home)
- with your line manager's consent, lend the customer money – most people are very honest and will return it
- provide the customer with missing resources (e.g. a tie in a fancy restaurant, swimwear in a pool)
- in the case of lost tickets, check records and ask the customer for ID.

You should try to provide the customer with the kind of assistance you would expect to receive yourself in such situations.

Dealing with problems (for example, stolen personal belongings, injuries)

Providing assistance is usually concerned with minor problems. Sometimes problems are more serious, for example:

- personal attacks on staff or customers
- allegations or incidence of theft
- lost possessions
- injury
- unruly behaviour.

In terms of customer care it is important to realise that the customer may be agitated, in pain, upset or even hysterical (e.g. a parent with an injured or lost child).

- The first priority is to try to calm and reassure the customer. If you cannot and the situation worsens, you will have to call for assistance from a colleague. If the problem involves a violent person, someone who has a mental health problem, or someone you suspect is under the influence of drink/drugs, you should call assistance or security immediately.
- The second is to set procedures in process. These will invariably be in

'operating procedures' and you will have been trained how to implement them.

- The final stage may be to make a record of the problem and how it was dealt with. If you have to complete a record, do not let the process get in the way of solving the problem.

Sometimes you are part of the problem. For example, a customer may think you have been rude or short-changed him. Ask him what he means and if you cannot resolve it immediately do not continue, as an argument will inevitably result. Instead call your supervisor.

Handling complaints

This topic is dealt with in Section 5.7 below.

Check it out

For two of the following situations:

- a cinema booking
- a mother at a theme park who has lost her child
- offering advice to a middle-aged person wanting to se a health suite
- a customer in a a swimmimg pool who has had his clothes stolen.

Make a list of the:

- information about the service you would need to serve a customer
- the people in the organisation who could help
- how these people could be contacted
- what you would do if they were not present
- what you would do if you could not satisfy the customer's request.

Now get a friend to play the above roles. Discuss and evaluate your performance.

5.7 Handling complaints

No matter how good your customer handling skills and the quality of your service, there will come a time when you receive a complaint. It may be as a result of something you have done but it is as likely to be about something a colleague has done or not done, the behaviour of other customers or simply a breakdown in the system. Although there will be times when you need to pass the complaint on, your first responsibility as an employee is to see if you can handle the complaint yourself, thus minimising the inconvenience to the customer.

A complaint is a criticism, and no one enjoys receiving criticism. As adults we hope that we have left the childish reactions to criticism behind and can handle complaints in a rational and calm manner. It does happen that those making complaints revert to childish behaviour and lose their tempers, which makes it all the more important for staff not to lose theirs.

- Remember that both you, as the staff member, and the customer are equals and have a right of opinion and reply.
- Show genuine interest in the person and her complaint.
- Do not be influenced by the customer's childish behaviour.

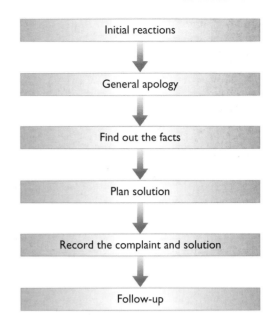

Dealing with complaints – the 6-stage plan

- Remain calm and assertive, and request the other person to be so if she is not.
- Repeat your comments and behaviour until you get an adult response.
- React favourably to calmer behaviour, but beware of being patronising.

Initial reactions

Complainants often approach you in a public place, sometimes because there is no other, but also because they may want to show off in front of other people. Public complaints are bad for business, especially if they get out of control. So you want to get the person to a quieter, private place and into a non-aggressive position – sitting down to discuss the matter is best. The same applies when handling telephone complaints. If the complainant is shouting, speaking fast or swearing, you will need to ask the person to slow down and adopt a clearer, quieter tone if you are going to handle their complaint. This may initially make matters worse, but if you keep repeating yourself the customer will eventually understand that he/she is not going to get anywhere until speaking normally.

> **Think it over**
>
> A director of leisure often had to deal with angry, complaining people on the phone. Some of them just seemed to need to 'get it off their chests'. After his opening pleasantries had been brushed aside he would place the receiver on the desk. Occasionally he would pick it up and say 'Yes' or 'I see', until eventually the customer went quiet. He once wrote an entire committee report during a customer tirade before the customer ended up by meekly asking 'Can you see my point?' The director now had control of the conversation and was in a position to deal with the complaint.
>
> Think about how and why this method works. Would it work face to face?

General apology

It is always useful to apologise at this stage. But you should apologise for the stress or inconvenience the customer is feeling rather than apologise for the incident that has caused the complaint. After all, you don't know the facts of the matter yet, so you can say, for example, 'I am sorry to see that you are so upset, Sir, please have a seat and let me know exactly what has happened.'

Find out the facts

Rational customers will be able to give you a clear picture of their complaint. Angry, uncontrolled customers may find it difficult: they will swear, make all sorts of irrelevant comments, try to get you to agree that your organisation is rubbish, insult you and so on. Extreme patience is needed on your part not to be drawn in to defend your organisation or yourself, nor to lose your own temper in the face of childish behaviour. Try to build up a picture of the relevant facts and then give back to the customer a summary of what she is saying and ask her to confirm it:

'Thank you, madam. Now from what you have been saying it seems to me that the main points are ...' You need to be objective in this and while you should not criticise your colleagues or employer you should be able to accept that there could be faults. Try at this stage to be neutral, and recognise that the customer has a right to have a view.

Plan solution

At this point you will be in position to plan a solution. Hopefully, the facts will be self-evident and you can propose a course of action immediately. For example, the customer has torn a tracksuit on a rough surface. If you feel the complaint is justified, you can apologise specifically for the incident and propose a course of action, such as paying for a mending

or for replacing the suit, or compensation in kind such as book of vouchers. In some cases, an apology and a promise to rectify the problem may be sufficient.

In other cases you will need to delay a final solution and propose a temporary measure. For example, if the complaint is about a colleague you may decide that it is up to the manager to investigate the matter. In which case you would say to the customer: 'This is a serious matter, Sir, and one which the manager needs to decide. I now have sufficient information to pass on to him and he will contact you as soon as he has established the situation. Is that acceptable to you?'

Whenever you agree a plan of action with a customer you should also specify realistic time-lines that can be achieved by the organisation and are acceptable to the customer.

Record the complaint and solution

Many leisure organisations have a complaint book in which customer details and the nature of the complaint and how it was resolved are recorded. With more serious complaints a supplementary report may be required that details the complaint and describes how the complaint was handled. The reasons for this are that it:

- supplies other people involved in the process with details
- is a record for any legal use
- supplies data for analysis and review of the complaint handling procedure.

Follow-up

Usually it is good practice to follow up a complaint you have handled yourself. This means you can be sure that the complaint process has been completed correctly. It also means that the customer is not being further inconvenienced by having to establish contact with another member of staff. Sometimes you will need to pass the complaint on to someone else, because you do not have the authority to make a decision or the area of complaint is not within your normal range of work. If you do this, it is a good idea to check that action has taken place, and at the time and in the way you agreed with the customer. It is surprising how often complaints get 'lost' when passed on. And if they do, you will be the last point of contact that the customer had, and will be in the firing line for the renewed and increased complaints.

> ### ! Check it out
>
> 1 What are the six stages of the complaint process?
> 2 Why should you record a complaint?
> 3 Why do you follow up complaints?

5.8 Assessing the quality and effectiveness of customer service

Organisations that pride themselves on customer service want to improve all the time. They realise that it is important to measure what is going on and to identify where the service is good or poor and what methods of customer service are effective. Customer service is measured by *performance indicators* which are statistics derived from records or primary research. They measure various aspects of the performance of a leisure service; for example, financial, sales, political, environmental. In this case we are going to concentrate on customer service. The performance indicator is used in three main ways.

- To define standards and inform customers of these. For example, 'Winners Health Club assure its customers that all enquiries will be answered within the hour' or 'Our toilets are inspected every two hours'.

- To define the targets that all staff are aiming to achieve.
- To allow comparison with other organisations or with the past performance of your own.

There are three types of performance criteria (Figure 5.16):

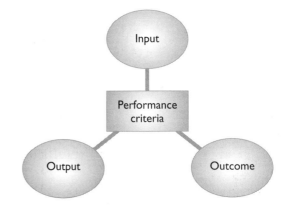

Figure 5.16 Performance criteria

Input indicators

Input indicators are measures of the resources we *provide* for an activity to occur; for example, number of seats, pool water, staff. There is an assumption when using them that the fact they have been provided means that the customer will be satisfied. In other words, provision automatically creates a standard. For example, if you provide twenty places on a course, you will create twenty happy customers. Input indicators have the advantage that they are easy to measure. Their downside is that they are based on an assumption that isn't always true.

Thought for the page

There is a Monty Python sketch where a customer comes into a shop, asks for an item and is told 'Sorry we don't keep that, there's no demand'. As the customer leaves the shop the shopkeeper says to himself, 'Funny, that's the third person this week who wanted that, when are they going to learn?'

Think it over

A squash centre is fully booked through telephone bookings and this is taken as a sign of satisfied customers. However, what about the customers who could not get through on the phone and had to make several phone calls before booking, or the customers who gave up in disgust and went elsewhere? And what about customers who have difficulty in getting to a telephone and may not even become a member of the club for that reason? Therefore, do you think that booked courts are in fact a good indicator of customer satisfaction?

Output indicators

Output indicators provide a balance to the picture given by the input indicators. These are measures of what happened as a *result* of provision. They are in numerical form, such as user figures which, if possible, should be divided into first visits, repeat and referred visits. They may be the actual opening hours of the service, or the proportion of the population using the service, or numbers of enquiries following an advert.

Output indicators measure the customers and the service they receive. This tells us nothing about people who may have been put off by the service and are lost. Nor does it tell us if existing customers liked what they got. To investigate these, we need to use *outcome indicators*. These may be derived from data such as number of rings before a phone is answered, numbers of phone calls where the service was engaged, proportions of enquiries that became customers, number of lost enquiries.

Very often they are derived from primary data gained from observation or questioning the customer – and sometimes the lost customer.

As you know from the marketing chapter, qualitative data can be turned into a numerical form and this can be used as outcome indicators – usually as a percentage or ratio.

For example, 'percentage of customers rating cleanliness as excellent', or 'ratio of repeat sales to first visits'.

Customer service needs to satisfy various criteria. When assessing customer services, we need to ask, 'How does it satisfy?' We shall look at the main criteria (Figure 5.17).

Price and value for money

Prices are easy to quantify and can be used as an input measure. Value is far more difficult as it is relative to customer needs and disposable income. Sometimes value will be measured as the number of service options available to a customer. However, output indicators that the customer has assessed are probably the most reliable guide to value. You may, for example, ask customers to rank value for money. In that case the output indicator may be a percentage of customers who regard value of the service to be good or excellent.

Consistency/accuracy

Most services have an outcome in terms of what the customer expects to get from the activity. It is important that the provider can describe and then provide the service in

Figure 5.17 Some of the main criteria for assessing customer service

accordance with the description and intended outcomes. For example, there is no point in a health club saying a member can lose 20 kilos in two months if that is unlikely. If a sub-aqua instructor says a novice diver will be able to dive in the sea after four lessons, then that should be achieveable by every customer.

Consistency/accuracy can be measured in terms of inputs and outputs. In week one of an 'Introduction to Tennis' course the *inputs* may include: health and safety induction and holding the racquet. The resulting *outputs* may therefore be: participant awareness of health and safety and the participant can catch and throw the ball and play simple strokes.

To measure consistency and accuracy there has to be a measure of the extent to which the inputs were done and the outputs achieved. For example, the water in a swimming pool was, as stated in the customers' charter, to be at a temperature of between 28° and 31°C. A consistency rate would be the number of pool readings that were outside this range/all pool readings – e.g. 95% readings were inside the standard range.

Reliability

This is very important for good customer practice. Customers do not like to be let down. Imagine how annoying it is to cross town for a swim only to be met by a notice saying 'Sorry, closed for repairs'. Have you seen what happens when two customers have booked the same seat at a theatre or an event? Reliability applies to any aspect of the service where the provider says something will happen and it doesn't. A normal general indicator would be times when something did or did not happen.

Staffing levels and quality

If a service is understaffed things start to go wrong. Staff become overworked and stressed,

there are omissions in service standards, and customers may find it difficult to be served or find staff; the service may even have to close. A simple way of measuring staffing levels is to use outputs such as staff records, including sickness records. Sometimes using ratios is more relevant (e.g. one staff: x customers) as is done in swimming pool life-guarding.

If staff are unqualified or inexperienced, they will find it harder to provide the expected service to the customer. There are a variety of records that could be used here. Some are fairly crude such as amount spent per member of staff on training. Or they may be more specific, such as proportion of staff with Level 3 NVQ. In many companies there are appraisal schemes that will set training and achievement targets for individuals. A useful indicator would be the percentage of all staff achieving their training targets.

Customer enjoyment

At a show the audience tells us exactly how much it is enjoying itself. For the facility manager, attendance rates are a simple indication of customer enjoyment especially if repeat, referred and first visits can be separated out.

There are also certain observed indicators that can be easily measured and affect customer enjoyment either adversely, such as queues and waiting time, or advantageously such as the use of specially provided rest places. Customer enjoyment is complex and the total experience will be an amalgam of the good and not so good. It is therefore useful to probe customers' feelings. Increasingly we ask customers to fill in simple surveys such as 'exit forms', or encourage them to fill in comment forms about their good and bad experiences, as well as suggestions they may have for improved services. As usual, the results from these can be put into numerical form. For example, the ratio of positive to negative comments, the average satisfaction score for various service aspects.

Health and safety

An accident can seriously mar a customer's enjoyment or impression of a service. It is important therefore to keep and fill out accident report forms. You should also remember that in any facility there will be many more 'near-misses' or non-serious accidents that need not be reported by law. A service that is customer-orientated will try to record these as well.

Cleanliness and hygiene

Clean facilities are very important. As with other indicators this can be measured by inputs such as the frequency and rigour of cleaning. It may be observed every day, and in a well-run facility the desired outcome would be zero rubbish and dirt.

Accessibility and availability

The new economies such as Web-orientated trade aim to give customers what they want when they want it. The leisure industry is moving towards this concept as well. Health clubs and swimming pools put on early-morning and late-evening activities, theme parks open all year and pubs are soon to lose licensing hours. Access and availability are particularly relative to the customer group. That is to say, what is available (daytime opening hours) to one group (e.g. housewives and pensioners) may not be available to another (e.g. people at work, shift workers). A performance indicator of access is to take the proportion of users who come from a certain group and divide this by the proportion of that group in the population as a whole. For example, if fifteen per cent of users and ten per cent of the population are Afro-Caribbean, then a ratio of 1.5 shows that Afro-Caribbean people have good but

unbalanced access to the service. In the same service the white population makes up seventy per cent of users and the population as a whole; representing a ratio of 1, which shows that the service is providing good and balanced access. On the other hand, only 2 per cent of the Asian community uses the service compared with being twenty per cent of the population. This gives a ratio of 0.1 which shows poor and unbalanced access for this community.

Obviously, inputs such as opening times and the presence of aids for the disabled are also important input indicators. You need to be sure that the input relates to actual usage. For example, there are pools that have pool lifts for wheelchairs which are hardly used because the customers do not like the fuss and bother of using one. In terms of input these pools looks as though they are doing a good job but are in fact failing to satisfy that disabled group. Provision of shallow entry steps may be a better choice where the group has some mobility.

Access and availability can have subcomponents to them. For example, how much you enjoy a swim is partly due to the amount of water available to you and the time you can spend in the pool. Area of water per customer and time available in the pool are two input indicators. Although few pools do, it might be good customer service to turn away customers when the pool exceeds the desired levels for an enjoyable swim although it is still below Health and Safety maximum levels.

Provision for individual needs

In any service there may be services and products that only a few users require but which make their stay more enjoyable. For example, nursing mothers may prefer some privacy to feed their babies that is not in the same place as the toilet. Disabled people obviously require modified changing areas and toilets. A sports club may welcome the use of a bar area for after-session planning.

Making sense of indicators

Anyone who has got performance data together usually comes up against the problem of trying to work out whether the data indicates good or poor performance. In other words, you need a yardstick to compare your performance against. There are three methods.

Self-comparison

By comparing data over time it is fairly easy to see if you are improving or declining in performance. The trouble is you don't know how you compare with the industry as a whole. For example, you might find that bookings for a sports hall have increased from twenty per cent to forty per cent use of capacity over the past year. Doubling use in a year? Pretty impressive?! However, as most other centres will be operating above sixty per cent use of capacity, your service is simply not as bad as it used to be. Again, if you find that fifty per cent of enquiries are not resulting in sales and think 'We must be a failure', you need to talk to other organisations in your field and find out what their lost-sales rate is – it might be nearer eighty per cent! It is important not to work in isolation. But internal data still has great strengths because we can easily generate it, when we want it and in the form we want.

Similar organisations

Very often we can find out information about other organisations. This is particularly so in the public sector where the Chartered Institute of Public Finance and Accountancy (CIPFA) publishes annual tables of the leisure facilities, their expenditure and usage, from all authorities. In the private sector you may get information out of company reports. We can also observe other organisations or we can use them and find out their prices and the types of service and resources they offer.

Benchmarking

The latest trend is to look at examples of best practice in the industry and match performance against these. This is going to be a big area in the near future. In the public sector especially the policy of 'Best Value' means that Councils need to show that they are providing good service to their customers. To be able to judge this, benchmarks are needed to be able to make the comparison. The creation of benchmarks is already going ahead. Sport England has recently published performance tables for leisure centres and pools in the UK. These will give providers a benchmark for comparison.

You may be able to use these benchmarks to make your own assessments of customer service. If they are not available it may be a good idea to simulate one. To do this, select and assess the performance of an organisation that you feel to be strong on customer service. Then you can compare other facilities against it.

Assessing service

Assessing a service is a fairly straightforward process as shown in the spider diagram below (Figure 5.18).

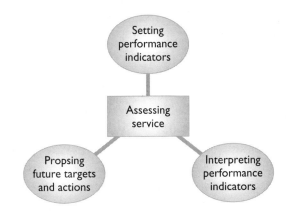

Figure 5.18 Assessing service

The choice of performance indicators is largely determined by the data that is available and the area which is being focused on. Performance indicators are useful in comparing changes and target achievement. You should also use simple questions and answers. For example, find out and describe what the system is for booking, making comments, reception and hospitality. Ask how are customers valued, what the staff attitude is like. Describing the service in this way will quickly reveal where the organisation is doing things well, and where there are omissions in the service.

When it comes to interpreting the data you need to ask various questions including:

- are customers happy with the service?
- how does the organisation compare with others?
- how is it improving in relation to its own past performance?
- is it achieving its current targets?
- what are the causes of good or of poor performance?
- what might improve customer satisfaction?

Having come up with answers, you are now in a position to propose changes to the system if they are required. With good service the old adage 'If it ain't broke, don't fix it' may have an element of truth – although it is rare to find total perfection and some small improvements may be worth while. Most organisations can, however, make significant improvements. Very often it will be about:

- setting higher standards and letting the customers and staff know about them
- developing new methods of delivering customer service
- setting targets that can be achieved
- introducing methods to monitor performance
- introducing consultation and meetings to discuss customer service.

Primary research methods

Performance indicators have been used significantly in the leisure industry for about ten years. When they were first introduced it was apparent that the data that was available was extremely limited. Ticket sales, physical measurements, letters of complaints and financial measures were often about the extent of it. The initial response of managers was frequently 'Nice idea but not practicable'. In fact many established managers were highly suspicious of the approach, saying that they could get more insight into customer service by simply talking to and watching customers and staff in action.

While 'walking the job' will always be a major part of a manager's job it does have its drawbacks in that managers will often have prejudices and preferences that they are often not aware of. They may be biased towards a member of staff or they may avoid talking to troublesome customers and, besides, staff may go on to their best behaviour when the 'boss' is around.

Objective analysis of performance is therefore vital to get the full picture. Luckily, modern technology has advanced so much in the past ten years that many of the obstacles to measuring and recording performance have been overcome. Computer spreadsheets and databases now allow for rapid and complex manipulation of data, and software is available that will generate and analyse surveys.

Telephone systems have a whole bunch of electronic wizardry that can tell us who phoned us and for how long, who failed to reach us and so on. The introduction of CCTV gives the opportunity to observe both staff and customers and witness the causes of customer care problems.

One of the breakthroughs in facility management has been the development of the smart card in conjunction with the computerised till. Because it can link the details of the members to their usage and expenditure patterns it allows for detailed analysis of customer behaviour. This is sophisticated output analysis. For example, we might be able to show that certain coaches attract different groups of user or that the introduction of specific customer service benefits affect usage. Despite such technology, it is the outcome data of customer experience that gives us the greatest insight. Here are some of the methods that are used to do this.

Informal feedback and observation

This is 'walking the job'. Good managers will constantly observe or chat to their staff and customers to find out:

- how customers are enjoying the service
- suggestions they might have to improve the service
- any problems there might be and how they are dealt with.

Managers will also talk to non-customers about their perception of the service and the leisure activities they do and enjoy. It is an easy and cheap method of collecting data. It can also be done at any time, thus allowing the manager to focus on unusual occurrences which would be missed with more formal methods such as surveys.

Surveys

Surveys have to be planned and structured in order to produce meaningful analysis. This is specialist work and until recently was time consuming and expensive because either an outside survey company had to be employed or staff time was needed to design, distribute and analyse the results.

Surveys often take up customer time and although most people are happy to help once, they will respond less and less if they are constantly questioned. Because of these limitations surveys tend to be used only occasionally and to focus on particular areas of concern or interest. Recently, the cost and time involved has been reduced by the development of 'off the peg' questionnaires by organisations such as Sport England or ILAM. Software packages are also available that allow instant questionnaire generation. Some of these are specialised but some general office packages (e.g. Lotus) have 'survey wizards' in their databases for this purpose.

Given the constraints of cost and time, surveys can be an excellent way of getting high-quality, meaningful information about

---

SOUTHBRIDGE LEISURE CENTRE

Customer Survey 2000

What age range do you fall into?

Under 16 ☐   16–24 ☐   25–34 ☐

35–44 ☐   45–60 ☐   Over 60 ☐

What facilities at the centre did you use today?

_____

What other facilities do you use on a regular basis?

_____

How frequently do you visit the centre?

Daily ☐   2–3 times per week ☐   Weekly ☐

Monthly ☐   Other (please specify) _____

What level of customer service did you experience?

Very good ☐ Good ☐ Satisfactory ☐ Poor ☐ Very poor ☐

Surveys can provide high-quality, meaningful information about both customers and non-customers

not only customers but also non-customers. This last group is particularly important as they represent the group that may have experienced customer service that was highly unsatisfactory. Some providers will therefore track customers who do not come back and mail them with a short informal survey that focuses on the reasons why they left and what would attract them back again.

Suggestions

The suggestion box has been around for many years. Unfortunately, it was often a place where only complaints and insults were placed or where small boys put their sweet papers. The key to making suggestions work as a source of information and feedback is to develop a 'culture' where customers know that their comments will be put to use. Over the past decade, for instance, many hotels have started to leave a customer pack in all rooms. This will include a description of the standards in the hotel, a letter appreciating

the customer's business and welcoming him or her, perhaps a token gift and, finally, a short feedback slip where the customer can express his perceptions of service quality. Packages like this greatly improve the response rate.

This method is being used in many other leisure situations these days. Probably the most common is at the end of courses where the course leader will ask people to complete a form about the course itself and the customer service they received. To preserve anonymity, it is a good idea to provide an unmarked envelope or collecting box to put the forms in. The suggestion culture is now being adopted and promoted by many leisure providers especially in the public sector. Good practice is shown in the spider diagram below (Figure 5.19).

When done well, this method can make a great difference to a service with little cost or time. It does have limitations, however, in that the information may be selective and it

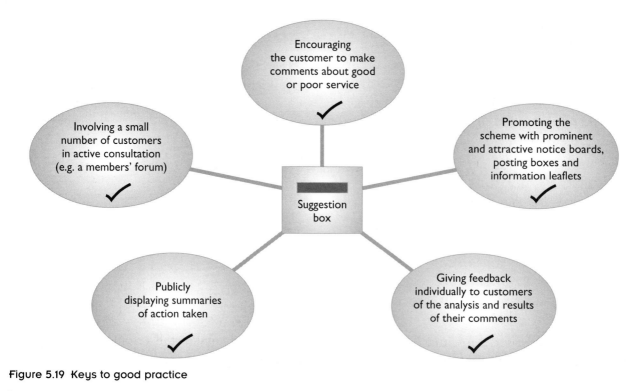

Figure 5.19 Keys to good practice

focuses only on the customer and not on the non-customer or lost customer.

Focus groups

Focus groups are small groups of customers or non-customers who are invited to meet on a couple of occasions to give their opinions and feelings about a service. It is important the group leader is impartial in leading the group and objectively analysing the results. To be done properly, focus groups really need a specialist company leading them, or a staff member who has researched and rehearsed the methodology involved. There is plenty of guidance around; one good series of books is by Krueger and Morgan (see Further reading).

The great value behind focus groups is that they can go into depth about issues. It is good practice not to ask more than twelve key questions in a two-hour meeting, so that everyone can make a contribution. It also allows customers to make associations. For example, you might ask customers 'Imagine your perfect cinema; what smells come to mind when you think of it?' People might answer 'Flowers – especially roses'. In that case, you might decide to have a flower display in reception, perhaps a rose motif in the décor, and rose fragrance dispensers in the washrooms and reception.

Or you might ask them to describe their perfect receptionist. Most probably the group would identify the things they don't like about receptionists before concentrating on what they like. These results would allow you to identify if there were faults in your service and replace them with the desired service.

Mystery shoppers

As we have seen, observation and feedback when done by staff can be subject to selectivity, or provoke untypical behaviour by the staff. A growing method of observation is to use firms that observe leisure providers in action. These firms use 'mystery shoppers'. This is an old technique used for many years by restaurant and hotel guides and by consumer groups (e.g. Egon Ronay, CAMRA, *Which?*) and which is now being used throughout the industry. These are people who are trained to be able to assess many of the features of a service such as customer skills, cleanliness, equipment and available service. They visit the service as an ordinary member of the public, sometimes alone or with others such as their children or elderly relatives. Sometimes they may simply observe normal practice, but they may also provoke situations such as a complaint or asking for wheelchair access to test staff skills.

Some mystery shoppers will make the assessment using their memory according to a predefined schedule, others will make secret notes or recordings. On their return the firm writes up a report based on their assessment and then discusses this with the management.

It is important and ethical that staff know that mystery shoppers are being used on a regular basis and that they are given an explanation of the benefits of this method. If not, staff will feel that they are being spied on. It is also a good idea to reward or praise good staff practice that the mystery shopper identifies.

As it is with any of the above methods, it is also good practice to let staff know the results and involve them in consultation on how things can be further improved. The results should be discussed in general terms, however, as witch hunting (identifying culprits) will make staff resentful of the mystery shopper approach.

1 What are performance indicators used for?

2 What are the three types of performance indicator?

3 Identify three areas of leisure performance that indicators can measure. Give an example of each type of indicator for each case.

4 What are the three methods of interpreting performance indicators?

5 What questions would you ask to assess customer service performance?

6 Give examples of how you could improve future customer service performance.

7 What purpose does 'walking the job' serve?

8 What are the advantages of the mystery shopper over 'walking the job'?

Sources of information and further reading

Adler, H., *NLP for Managers,* Piatkus, 1995

Cava, R., *Dealing with difficult people,* Piatkus, 1990

Evans, D.W., *People Communication and Organisations,* Pitman, 1992

Fink, A. & Kosecoff J., *How to conduct surveys,* Sage Publications, 1998

Harvey, C., *Successful selling in a week,* Institute of Management, Hodder and Stoughton, 1998

Krueger, R.A., Morgan D.L., *The Focus Group Kit* (six-volume series), Sage Publications, 1997

Leland, K. and Bailey K., *Customer Service for Dummies,* IDG Books, 1999

Linton, I., 25 *Tips for excellent customer service,* Pitman, 1995

Mort, S., *Professional report writing,* Gower, 1992

Sport England Factfile 1, *Women Friendly Sports Facilities,* 1999

Sport England Factfile 1, *Performance Indicators,* 1995

Sport England, *Best value through sport* series, 2000

Stewart, I. and Joines, V., *TA Today a new introduction to transactional analysis*, Lifespace, 1989

Wellemin, J., *Successful customer care in a week*, Institute of Management, Hodder and Stoughton, 1998

Useful websites

Institute of Customer Care
www.ics.nto.com

English Tourist Council
www.travelengland.org.uk

This unit is organised into four sections. You will learn about:

- feasibility of the project
- teamwork
- carrying out the project
- evaluating the project

Introduction

In the previous chapters in this book you have read about marketing, health and safety, customer care and the structure of leisure and recreation including funding and resources. In this chapter we will see how these can be combined with some new knowledge to design and execute a project. To do this you will need to know how to select and manage teams and organise the project. These are not difficult skills to learn initially but developing them through experience so that you are fully effective and efficient is a lifelong process.

You need also to consider the type of project you are going to do. Various criteria will influence your decision.

Time

The guidance in the AVCE specification suggests that the project starts after the marketing and customer care units have been completed. In most schools and colleges this will mean the project will take place towards the end of the course. This will almost certainly restrict you in terms of what you can do and place pressure on you to meet deadlines. Alternatively, it may mean that you can plan only a simple activity, with which it will be difficult to achieve high grades. To widen your options you can start the planning process much earlier and at the same time as the other units. This would allow you time for team building, research and outline planning. You can also discuss and give examples that relate to the project you have in mind when studying the other units – for example, if you were planning a sports course for single mothers, your marketing research could be targeted at this group, and a questionnaire created to assess their needs. While studying the customer care unit you might identify the particular needs of this group and think of ways to provide good customer service.

If you start to plan your project earlier in the course you can initially sketch a plan without committing yourself to it or looking at the finer details. For example, you might write to potential sponsors to find out if they give sponsorship, where their interests lie and how you can apply for funding. Or, if you were creating a team, you might pull together a 'working' group that would look at what its final makeup should be to produce a project of the type chosen.

Choice of activity

This is important if you want to achieve high grades in assessment. Simple activities offer less opportunity for initiative, less likelihood of creating problems that will challenge you and less opportunity for working with colleagues. Activities based on college or school will be limited to sport or drama and not really stretch you to discover your potential. You will also be familiar with your customer groups and the resources will be available to you. It is far more rewarding to go for activities that are achievable but also challenging. For example:

- reducing loneliness among old people
- raising awareness on drug-related issues in sport
- fundraising campaign for a local charity
- fundraising campaign to support a voluntary sports club
- organising a major charity event for a college or a community (e.g. Red Nose Day)
- staging a healthy living exhibition
- developing a roadshow for playgroups
- staging an open-air concert
- putting on a college film festival
- staging a complex sports event (a taster day, competition)
- producing a show.

No doubt such projects will bring headaches, conflicts and even mistakes. But after all, that is exactly what working in the world of leisure is about. It is your recognition of these issues and your ability to deal with them that will allow you to get high grades in your assignments.

> **Think it over**
>
> Practical experience is as important as learning the theory and studying the techniques of running leisure businesses. The two go hand in hand, and working in leisure demands common sense, attention to detail, imagination and good skills with people. The sooner you can start working in the industry, part time, or as a trainee or on work experience, the more you will learn about the way it works, and you may even earn some money! Think about opportunities you may wish to pursue in the leisure industry. How are you going to gain the necessary experience?

Resources

In many cases AVCE projects are kept 'in house' with most resources being in kind or donated. If so, you will learn less about security and money management. The best approach is to have a cash-funded project. This will almost certainly mean raising sponsorship or funding from charities or local firms or the college or school. It may mean charging your customers. It may also mean opening a bank or building society account. Whatever the case, money cannot be realised overnight and you will need to plan and cost your project at an early stage, and then set about raising that money before you start to run the activity itself. Raising the money also requires planning, and it may be that the scope of the project will depend upon how much you can raise. If you have the money to pay for a resource there should in principle be no problem about accessing it, whether it be hiring a microphone or booking the Wembley Arena! In practice, you will be restricted in your use of resources by the quality and size of your team, and the availability of suitable resources such as facilities and equipment in the area.

6.1 Feasibility of the project

There is an unwritten law in the leisure industry – 'poor planning leads to poor performance'. The more you plan the less will go wrong and if something does go wrong, you will have contingency plans to put it right.

Planning also has the great advantage that it means team members have been involved and have *ownership* of the project. Ownership is recognised as a strong factor in making projects work and developing team cohesiveness. Team members can make better decisions if they know exactly what their team mates are doing. Planning also provides a 'map' for team members to use. It means they know what they should be doing, and why they are doing it, and it shows the problems they might encounter and the ways in which they can deal with them.

This knowledge is also helpful when communicating with customers and stakeholders – it means you will be competent and well informed, which will inspire confidence and respect. For example, sponsors may ask you why you think old people will want to come to the self-defence classes you are planning to start. They will be unimpressed if you say, 'well there's lots of muggings around here and lots of old people so we thought they would be interested'. However, they will be impressed if you can say, 'we have sent out a survey to various pensioner groups which showed that a majority in each group liked the idea of courses on self-defence'. Similarly, the sponsors might say, 'if people are so afraid of being mugged aren't they going to avoid coming along to an evening class at night'? Compare the impression of an unplanned answer such as, 'oh, we hadn't thought of that' with a planned one such as, 'yes, we thought about that and so we have

arranged a minibus service to pick our customers up'.

Information for planning

You need information in order to plan. When the plan begins to form you will need detailed information for its development (for example, product information, market research) and this level of information will be essential in developing a business plan. However, in the early stages of planning when you are fixing goals and objectives, most of the information you need will be at your fingertips. You will already have beliefs and values which will drive your interest in the project and you will have a vast array of information that you have gathered quite naturally and without research. In the early stages the trick is to release this information and encourage the team to use it in a creative way.

One way you can do this is to hold a formal meeting where everyone makes their suggestions in an ordered fashion. Or you can have an informal meeting where everyone chips in. This may be the more dynamic occasion, but meetings like this can end in lots of ideas and no results. An excellent way to encourage creative and usable ideas is *brainstorming*. This is when group members, using a series of pre-arranged questions, are encouraged to come up with any suggestion or idea they want. These ideas can include the sensible, the facetious, the outlandish or the just plain stupid. The rule of the group is that no one can criticise or put down an idea but can add to it or go off on another tangent. Participation should be encouraged and if people don't put suggestions forward they should be asked to do so. The idea is for the suggestions to be spontaneous and quick-fire – so no more than five to ten minutes are usually needed, during which the co-ordinator should try to write down every response on a flipchart or whiteboard. People

Thought for the page

Not only do you need to plan your project, you also need to plan key meetings with your suppliers and funding partners. Remember the lessons of customer service and sales. If you want to achieve the objectives of the meeting, you need first to define these and then rehearse how you want the meeting to go. You need to anticipate the type of questions you will be asked and come up with answers that will satisfy the questioner. You also need to convince your 'customer' that you are well informed and have planned what you doing.

can be cautious about entering into the spirit of brainstorming, or they can overreact and get argumentative, so a co-ordinator should be in control and be like a compere on a game show. Their job is to:

- whip up excitement and enthusiasm
- involve everyone in the group
- lead the group through the agenda for the session
- record ideas and comments.

At the end of the brainstorming you should have a list of suggestions that the group can now discuss. A good way to do this is to ask a series of questions about each suggestion to measure what the group thinks of it in terms of, say, practicality, popularity, value, and profitability, or any other criteria relevant to the project. It is also a good idea to ask how problems could be turned round as this can make initially poor ideas become good ones or eliminate hopelessly optimistic ones. If your team is Belbin balanced you will find a

Brainstorming is an excellent way to encourage creative ideas

mix of pessimists who find fault in anything and optimists who can put a new slant on a previously unattractive idea (see the case study below).

CASE STUDY – Several points of view provide better solutions

Co-ordinator Shaper (SH) or Chairman (CH)	'Why do you say a sports day for children of working mothers would be too costly?'
Complete-finisher (CF)	'Because they would not be able to pay entry fees that would pay for our cost.'
Co-ordinator	'That seems a good point, can anyone think of a way we can get round that?'
PL	'Well I don't see why we need to charge them – why don't we make it free?'
CF	'Yeah, so where does our money come from to pay for our production costs? We make a loss – get real.'
MI	'I don't see why it couldn't work. My uncle works in the Council, and he reckons they will give grants for leisure projects for people who are hard up. If we got a grant then we could afford to subsidise them'.

(The meaning of the initials is revealed in the table on p367)

Questions

1 Why does this group need a co-ordinator?

2 How would the sports day be run if CF was working on it alone?

When the pros and cons of all the ideas have being discussed the group can then vote for each of them. This can be a simple 'for' or 'against' or can be some form of scale, such as a conventional 'good', 'average' or 'poor'. This will show which ideas are going to be accepted by the group as a whole. Brainstorming can be used at any stage of the project from deciding what to do at the beginning to evaluating how to improve performance next time.

You may also want to use the SWOT analysis you looked at in the marketing chapter. This is really a variation of brainstorming which concentrates on strengths, weaknesses, threats and opportunities. You might want to assess the strengths and weaknesses of the team and the implications of this for the type of project that is selected.

Try it out	Rudyard Kipling wrote a poem about what are known as the 'journalists' friends' – they are 'why, who, what, when, where and how' questions and they are also invaluable for research of any sort. So always ask them.
	Think of a community you live or work in and ask the above questions about it. Try to identify something that is missing from it (e.g. opportunities for making friends, lack of community pride). From your answers, identify projects that could be undertaken to improve the situation.

Now think about what that community likes to do, where it would do it, what money it has to do it and so on. You should also ask the question about yourself as finding something that you will enjoy organising means you will do it much better.

When you have decided what to do, repeat the questions again. What will we need to do it? Where shall we put it on? When is the best time? Why are certain things stopping us? How will we organise ourselves? Who can we have in our team?

Planning – the first stages

Action planning is the first stage in developing a project. You need to identify:

- what you want to achieve
- the most direct route to get there.

When you have done this you will need to fill in all the details and check that the original plan is still feasible. You will almost certainly have to make modifications before finalising it in a business plan. You may also find that you fail to reach your objectives or that circumstances have made it difficult to use the plan. In either case you may have to adjust the plan during the project. In other words, action planning is an ongoing process that will be renewed several times in the life of a project because:

- conditions change
- you fail to carry out the plan
- the plan turns out to be flawed.

Plans are like maps, they show you where you want to go and you work out the route.

In order to organise a project you need to construct a plan which will serve as a 'map' for your team. This map will tell them:

- where you want to go (goals or aims)
- the route you want to take (objectives)
- the means by which you will travel (tasks)
- what you will need along the route (resources)
- when they have arrived (targets)
- a timetable for the plan.

To do this you need to identify:

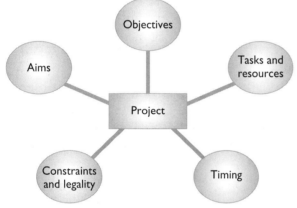

Figure 6.1 Considerations in project planning

Aims

The aims or goals of any project are best seen as 'the change you want to make in the world' rather than just a simple physical outcome. For example, you are organising a holiday tennis course for children. Don't just consider the functioning of the tennis course as your goal; consider also what it will achieve. In other words, you will try to see that the children enjoy themselves, become fitter and begin to improve their tennis skills. All of these goals show a change from a present state to a future one.

To continue to use the example of a tennis course, the goals for this project could be:

- to make holidays a happy time for children

Thought for the page

Sometimes goals are created to avoid an outcome you do not want; for example, in the early 1990s Leisure Departments were told by the government that under CCT regulations they would have to be able to compete successfully for contracts to do the work they were already doing. In other words, if they carried on as they were they would become redundant. To avoid this they had to adopt a new goal which was 'to become a successful and competitive commercial business'. The period saw a huge amount of energetic reorganisation and planning to make the changes in time.

- to develop health and fitness in children
- to develop the tennis skills of children.

A goal should be qualified by the service or product you are going to use, which is in this case a five-day tennis course.

From now on all your thinking and planning will be designed to achieve these goals. For example, when selecting a coach you will not only want someone who can develop tennis skills but who is also going to make the course fun and who may be in a position to encourage opportunities for regular play after the course. When you design your publicity you can stress the fun, skill and fitness themes in a way that attracts children.

Any goal you choose needs to be supported by a system of beliefs and values which provide the reason for achieving the goal. Sometimes these are personal beliefs; for example, if you strongly believe that children will be happier if they learn to play better tennis, then that belief will fuel your desire to pursue the goal of helping them to play. You may be fired by personal goals such as becoming rich, loved or famous. For example, if you want to be famous you will not try for jobs that are usually regarded as boring but will try for ones that will lead you towards the limelight – your goal will be to become a

In the 1980s 'mission statements' became popular. These are short statements produced by organisations to sum up what they are trying to achieve through their work. It is a great idea in that it gives all the workers in the organisation something to focus on and encourages them to work out how their own work can best contribute to the overall goal. The mission for the example we have used earlier could be 'making children's lives better through sport'.

Unfortunately mission statements have often been badly produced. They are sometimes a paragraph long, which no one can remember, or short snappy slogans that have no real meaning.

The place where you are studying will probably have a mission statement. Why not find out what it is, and also if your lecturers know what it is. Depending on their reply you could then discuss:

- how they contribute to achieving it
- how students are involved in the mission
- alternative statements or how the existing one could be improved.

tennis player rather than a sports scientist. More often, though, we tend to attach ourselves to organisational values and policies which generally reflect our personal ones. For example, if you are a tennis development officer you will adopt goals that reflect the policies of the Lawn Tennis Association.

Objectives

Having decided on your goal the next stage is to work out what you need to do to get there.

Have you ever wondered why lesser-known teams in sport sometimes become 'giant killers' in major competitions? One reason is that they have greater belief in their goal than the major teams they play. Every time the lesser-known team plays it is achieving new and greater goals. For a major team and its superstars it is far harder to maintain their belief in the goal and their position at the top.

Think of a journey that involves several stages. Your objectives are to reach each stop and then travel on to the next in order to complete the journey. Project objectives are far more complex than this, and you need to package them into various groups. The standard classification was devised by Peter Drucker, a guru of management, and these groups are:

- *Market standing*: This is the market you intend to reach, the marketing mix or the outcomes, such as customer satisfaction and customer loyalty (for example, participants ask for another competition)
- *Innovation*: This encompasses new ways to provide the service or to organise the business (for example, find an all-weather pitch, design the course so that any child will enjoy it)
- *Productivity*: Efficient use of resources (for example, divide project team into specialist subgroups who can work in parallel)
- *Resources*: These include finance, buildings, equipment and who is going to be involved in the project (for example, an objective might be to find a sponsor)
- *Profitability*: Defines what profits need to be made over what period of time (for example, the project team may decide to make a small profit that will be invested to be used by next year's project team)
- *Management*: This defines the managerial role (for example, the project team might decide that the manager must be fully participative and follow the wishes of the team as a whole)
- *Worker performance*: This covers employee relations, staff morale
- *Public responsibility*: This involves the role of the project within society and the law (for example, you will ensure that local neighbours are not put to any inconvenience by the course – parents

. dropping their children off or parking in front of local houses – maintaining legal coaching ratios, complying with health and safety).

Drucker's views were established for American heavy industry in the middle of the 20th century. They may seem a little remote for your project and indeed some of these categories will have little to do with it. They are, however, useful areas to focus on and will ensure that you have considered your project in the fullest perspective.

Using a functional system like this Figure 6.2 shows a suitable series of core objectives.

Figure 6.2 Core objectives

Whatever system of groups you adopt you will now need to define the objectives that work within the groups. To do this, simply ask yourself the following questions in relation to your goal. In the first instance you should ask questions about the goal itself and this will give you a series of objectives about which you will then ask the same questions. Planning objectives is therefore usually about working back from

where you want to go to where you are at present. For example:

- what do I need to know to get there?
- what actions can I take to get there?
- how am I going to take them?
- what materials can I use?
- what money will I need?
- when will I need to achieve objectives by?
- who can do the work involved?

Concentrate on a core objective group (service delivery in this case), and you will find as you work back though a timeline of events and actions that are required that you will automatically be led into the other groups. For example, at some point during the consideration of the development of the course someone in the group will ask 'How are our customers going to get to know about it?' or 'If we are going to design a course to attract children, we need to ask some children what they like'.

This method works well because it quickly gives you an indication as to whether the plan is practical or needs to be discarded or postponed. Sometimes an idea for a goal appears to be a good one and then when tested against the questions it is shown to be not possible in the near future, although it may be worth developing in the longer term when there has been time to address its weaknesses. Lack of money is often a reason for the shelving of a goal. If this is so, then the first objective might be to make funds available in next year's budget for the project.

You may even like to consider a two-year plan containing two project plans. If you carry out your project in the second year and involve the incoming first-year students, they can take over the plan in their second year. Theoretically this could result in an ongoing programme that would allow for long-term planning of a leisure programme for a particular community.

| Define job description for coach |
| Advertise and recruit for suitable coaches |
| Interview and select coach |

How do you know you are writing a good objective?

In Unit 4 we discussed SMART as the criteria for a good objective, and now it can be applied to a project. To run through it again: to test the validity of an objective you ask the critical questions – is the objective SMART:

Specific
Measurable
Achievable
Realistic
Timed.

Specific? Does it refer to definite actions and outcomes rather than vague ones? 'Hire appropriate physical resources' is vague. 'Hire all-weather pitch, soccer equipment and p.a. system' is more specific.

Measurable? You need to be able to measure an objective if you are to know that you have achieved it. These measurements will be your *targets* and we shall discuss them later, at the end of this chapter. The tennis courts are easy to measure as you can see them, assess their condition and keep the booking confirmation. But to measure something like customer satisfaction you may need to do some research; for example, 'to achieve 75% of customer satisfaction'.

Achievable? Can an objective be achieved with the time and resources available? For example, if you have planned to run a promotion campaign from start to finish in six weeks, it

---

Try it out

Permanent organisations often have a series of plans which fit into each other like Russian dolls. Long-term planning may consider what needs to be done in the next five years or more. Within that, come a series of annual plans and within these, detailed short-term plans which often cover projects and work programmes created to achieve the annual programmes. During the year the team will come up with new ideas as they review their current work or identify new opportunities. These are often recorded in monthly meetings. Likewise, throughout the year there are monthly reports on finance. At about half way through the financial year there is sufficient information to estimate the following year's budgets. After this a series of planning review meetings is held when the existing 'next year's plan' is reviewed in the light of the current achievement of objectives and the budget. At this point new ideas may be included in the plan or objectives that are no longer feasible are dropped. Projects are often prioritised as high, medium or reserve priority so that there can be automatic replacement of projects that fail to materialise. This entire process is known as the *planning cycle*.

For the project you are going to undertake try to identify the stages in the planning cycle that will be involved.

Objectives will start to form family trees. Working back along each objective group you will define one layer of sub-objectives and then in turn define the layer beneath. These lower sub-objectives or departmental objectives can also be called 'milestones', which gives the impression of making a journey to your objectives and goals. Thus an objective such as *interview and select coach* might require the following milestones to achieve it:

Thought for the page

All objectives must be fitted into a timescale with a date by which they will be achieved. Time is the only resource that cannot be replaced. A missed deadine will hold up and delay other objectives with the risk that the project may disintegrate.

is not achievable, as the times required to design and print posters and for the market to respond will be far longer than this.

Realistic? There is no point in writing an objective if it does not stand much chance of being achieved. 'To have all children playing at Wimbledon' would be unrealistic, 'to ensure that all participants can demonstrate four basic strokes and understand the rules of the game' is realistic. Unrealistic objectives can also involve underachieving. For example, if your objective for the course was that the children could hit a ball – then you have not achieved very much change and your work will have been largely wasted.

Surya Lovejoy (1993) has an alternative system of assessing objectives using a series of questions.

Have you checked or have you assumed that your objective serves its goals?

The customer test: How will this objective help the customer? It is the customer you are trying to serve. For instance, if you are providing a sports day for single parents the objective 'hiring sports facilities' is not as customer friendly as 'hire facilities including sports facilities, play equipment and crèche'.

The means test: Does the objective give the means by which the objective will be achieved? For example, 'to achieve 75 per cent customer satisfaction' would read better as 'to achieve 75 per cent customer satisfaction through booking procedures, and training officials to be customer friendly'.

The identity test: Does the objective identify who is doing it? 'Steve to hire facilities.'

The measurement test: This is the same as SMART – can you measure the objective?

The sufficiency test: Will the objective achieve the goal in all circumstances? Will it do the job? Hiring a tennis court may be fine but what if it rains? Perhaps the objective should read 'hire courts with dry facilities'.

The assumption test: Have you assumed or do you know that the objective will result in a desired change? For example, if a goal of the tennis course is to increase fitness will the objective 'provide tennis course' result in this? Or should it also have an objective that 'creates after-course playing opportunities'? Supposing you choose to put on a tennis course because you enjoy tennis. Can you assume that children will also enjoy a tennis course? Perhaps market research will show that children are unenthusiastic about tennis and prefer soccer? If that is the case and you really want to stick to tennis then you will have to make your new goal 'to popularise tennis with children'. Alternatively you could stick to the old goals 'to make children happy' but achieve them through a soccer course.

The jargon test: Can everyone reading the objective understand it? If not, everyone will interpret it differently. For example, 'to acquire economically participative material resources' really means 'hire the courts at the lowest price'.

Whatever criteria you use you will now be able to set your goals and objectives. Your next step is to set your targets, but we will leave these for the moment and discuss them at the end of the chapter. Then you should start to fill in the details of how you will achieve the milestones, and what you need to achieve them.

Try it out Here is an objective: 'In order to raise the health of the nation we intend to ensure that all primary treatment centres provide service to all patients within twenty-four hours'. Assess this objective and then rewrite it.

Tasks

By now you will have a family tree of objectives which you are confident will get you from where you are now to the achievement of your goal. You now need to make a shopping list of all the things (resources) you will need and how you will get them and use them (tasks). Think of going on holiday – you make a list of things you need to take with you and decide if you already have them or need to go out and buy them. You also think about the best place and time to buy them – at home, because it is needed now; on holiday, because it is cheaper, and so on. These considerations will determine your tasks – either to go shopping or to surf the Web, or to wait.

These same simple considerations apply to project planning. List the resources needed and the tasks to be done. For example, one of the milestones for your marketing programme may be '*to produce publicity*

brochures'. The tasks for this might include '*design artwork*', '*deliver finished artwork to printer*', '*collect brochures from printer*'.

You should record every task on a separate form so that they can be shuffled around and assigned to objectives and times as required. If you plot out your objectives on a white board and then 'Blu-Tack' the tasks to the appropriate places, everyone can see what is happening and may spot opportunities to short-cut some of the work. Or you may find that tasks need to be shifted around; for example, one team member may see a task form to buy tennis balls and say 'I'm going to the printers next Monday, I could pick up the tennis balls at the same time as the supplier is on the way – stick your task form on mine to remind me'. You will find when identifying resources that many of them will be used time and time again across the objectives.

Each task form should include:

- what the task is
- what objective it serves
- the resources it will use and if they are available

A timetable seen by all the teams is an ideal place to put tasks and objectives

Thought for the page

Tasks are the work that will be needed to achieve the objectives. The work in a task should be familiar to the people doing it and they should be competent to perform it. If they are not, then you will automatically create a new objective which is 'to find competent people to do tasks'.

In other words you have created a personnel objective group. Two of its milestones are going to be either to recruit competent people or train existing team members. For example, in the tennis project you may not have any tennis coaches on the team. In that case you would be probably best advised to recruit a qualified coach, because to train existing staff would take several months. On the other hand, several of the team may be acting as helpers on the day and in this case it would sensible to have a training session for them to familiarise themselves with the event, customer handling and evaluating customer satisfaction.

- who will be doing the task
- how long the task will take
- when it has to be completed by.

Contingencies

Every project will go wrong from time to time and the team's job is to alter their tasks and resources to get the project back on course again. You can make *contingency plans* to deal with the things most likely to go wrong. Although they are called 'plans' they are usually a small series of tasks or processes which can be put into place easily. Think of them as small detours on your route to the objective – if the road is blocked then you can quickly get round the problem and return to the road at a later point. Here are some common examples which you should have included in your plan, but always think afresh and decide what could go wrong in your particular project.

- Accidents (always have within reason the emergency services' contacts and nearest locations, plus access to telephone, accident report forms, and if possible a first aider).
- Weather – identify alternative activities and facilities that could be used.
- Travel failure (strikes, traffic jams, breakdowns). Can you provide alternative transport or delay the event?
- Participants/officials not turning up. Can you delay or rearrange activity, substitute alternatives?

CASE STUDY – Contingencies

Look at the following scenarios:

- A Youth Games weekend tournament in the middle of July is hit by a torrential cloudburst that floods all the pitches – it will take four hours for them to drain back to a playing condition.
- A one-day local soccer competition. The referee refuses to start the competition because the ball is sub-standard.
- A residential outdoor activities expedition for twelve schoolchildren led by two leaders. One mile into their hike one of the children becomes sick and obviously needs medical treatment.
- A film night at a college film club. The guest speaker who was going to introduce the programme phones in to say that his train has been delayed and he will arrive an hour after the performance begins.

Questions

1 Could the problem have been avoided?

2 What contingencies would you have made to cope with these scenarios?

Weather, particularly in Britain, should always be taken into account when planning an outdoor event

- Equipment failure: have repair kits and parts on hand, have repair/supplier contact; have provider contacts who could lend you replacements, use personal resources (are they insured?).
- Facilities being closed: have key holder contact.
- Utilities failure (do you have backup such as a generator or mobile telephone?).
- Forgotten resources. This should not happen if you use checklists. If there is failure then act as for equipment failure.

Resources

At this stage of the planning process you need not worry too much about financial resources as these can often restrict your creativity and project development. Your main aim at this stage is to develop a product that does the job. It can be reviewed in financial terms at a later stage.

Having said this you should have a rough idea of the size of your budget and allow this to guide the scope of the project. Concentrate on time and the human and physical resources you need to create a good product

and then you can then review it financially. You then may decide:

- to reduce the resources you are using
- negotiate better prices
- develop a strategy to raise money to fill any shortfall.

Physical resources

Finding the right equipment, materials and facilities for the job is important. Any resource you use should be *'fit for purpose'* which means you must know:

- what it will be used for
- the conditions it will be used in (environmental, technological, aesthetic)
- the profile of the user (either team members or participants and their needs and competence).

Resources can be obtained in various ways.

Borrowing is widely used (but if you borrow, make sure you have agreed the conditions of use and allow for any damage or loss in your contingency budget). Hiring is normal practice if it is cheaper than purchasing the resource. It is especially used with equipment, transport and facilities. If you hire you will want to avoid unnecessary charges by starting the hire as late as possible, but make sure you have a margin for late delivery by the previous hirer. Buying is also common. Make sure you have a legitimate source, and that you have got a competitive price. And then we all contribute our own equipment from time to time. However, you must be prepared to accept wear and tear to whatever you have lent. You should also check your personal insurance policy as the organisation's policy will probably not cover personal equipment being used for project purposes.

When acquiring resources you should question:

- is this the best price?
- when is it available?

When hiring allow time for contingencies or setting up

- when can it be delivered or collected?
- about the supplier – are they reliable, do they have a good track record?
- are there guarantees or penalty clauses for damage or loss to hired resources?

Staffing

Good staff are essential. At the planning stage you need to decide:

- the tasks required and the time needed for them

- the number of people required and the time they can give
- the types of people needed (e.g. administrators, leaders)
- organisation and structure of the workforce.

Staff come in many forms – paid or voluntary, part time or full time, team members of external contractors.

Time and timescales

After people, materials and finance, the fourth resource you have is time, and on any project it is the most difficult to use and control. Furthermore, unlike other resources you cannot buy in extra supplies to achieve your goal. Time is the ultimate unsustainable resource – once gone it cannot be re-created.

When planning you should first ask when you want to carry ou the activity. This should be a time:

- which is appropriate for the activity (for example, tennis without floodlighting would have to be during the day, a holiday course has to be in the holidays)
- which is available to the market (office workers may prefer courses after work or during lunchtimes or evenings and weekends). Any competing events (TV,

CASE STUDY – Resources

You need a video camera and recorder to be used throughout a four-month-long drama production. You have the following options:

- buying them second-hand in a car boot sale
- purchasing them through your college-buying consortium
- hiring them from a high-street hire company

- borrowing them from another college department
- buying new items from someone in your rugby club who gets them from abroad
- buying them from an electrical retailer's sale on a credit agreement.

Question

1   What are the advantages and disadvantages of the options?

sport) may affect the attractiveness of the project
- when resources are available
- which allows sufficient time for the plan to be achieved. Look out for time blocks that slow down work (e.g. facilities closed for refurbishment, a team member is on holiday).

Critical path analysis

You need a grid where the columns represent time periods and the rows the main objectives. You can buy wallchart versions of these from office shops or you could mark one up on a whiteboard. On the rows in the right-hand column write the main objectives or categories of objectives (e.g. promotion, course development). Each of these categories may contain several lines as each line within an objective will represent the series of tasks required to meet groups of milestones. If you find that major tasks are overlapping, give each one a separate line. In the left-hand column write the names of the team members who will be handling these tasks. Each of the remaining columns will represent a time period (in this case, a week).

At appropriate cells along each row you write in a milestone. Where you place it will depend on three things:

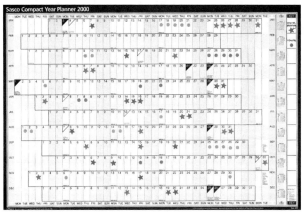

Critical path analysis using a wall display chart can help with time planning

- how long the tasks involved will take. Remember to allow for contingencies such as delays (e.g. the printer not sending back brochures on time).
- available time. The team will have other things to do besides the project, so allow for other work, social events, and holidays.
- dependence on another milestone being reached before it can be activated. For example, you cannot distribute brochures until they have been printed. You can do nothing in a project until you have secured sufficient funds. Milestones like these are known as *critical points* and they need to be highlighted on the chart. You may also want to draw a red line down to the milestones on other lines that are triggered by its completion. The process of charting the timetable like this is called *critical path analysis.* Although the method used here is a simple one you will be quite justified in impressing your backers by saying that your project is based on critical path analysis.

Finally, two major points:

Some tasks have very long lead times with critical points long before they are actually implemented. The best example is facility hire. In this sample project you will need tennis courts on the day of the event at the end of the project, but because they are crucial you need to make sure that they are booked at the beginning of the project. Your critical milestone is therefore 'provisionally book tennis courts'.

The main event of your project is not going to be in the last column on your chart. This is because after the main event there are other project objectives and tasks such as clearing up, thanking helpers, returning equipment, researching and evaluating the success of the project.

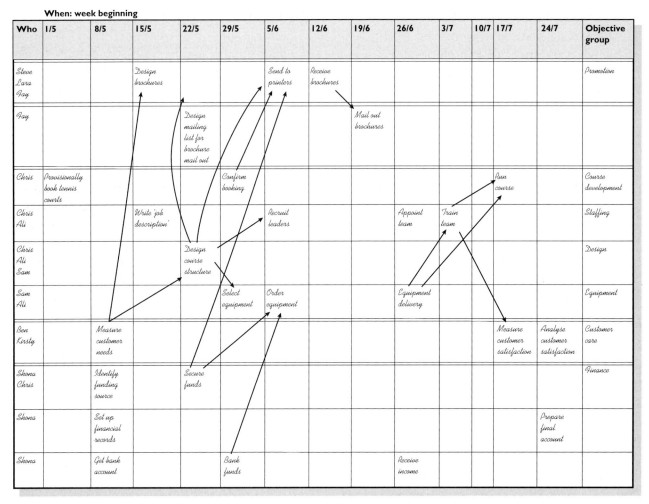

When: week beginning

Who	1/5	8/5	15/5	22/5	29/5	5/6	12/6	19/6	26/6	3/7	10/7	17/7	24/7	Objective group
Steve Lara Fay			Design brochures			Send to printers	Receive brochures							Promotion
Fay				Design mailing list for brochure mail out				Mail out brochures						
Chris	Provisionally book tennis courts				Confirm booking							Run course		Course development
Chris Ali			Write 'job description'			Recruit leaders			Appoint team	Train team				Staffing
Chris Ali Sam				Design course structure										Design
Sam Ali					Select equipment	Order equipment			Equipment delivery					Equipment
Ben Kirsty		Measure customer needs										Measure customer satisfaction	Analyse customer satisfaction	Customer care
Shona Chris		Identify funding source		Secure funds										Finance
Shona		Set up financial records											Prepare final account	
Shona		Get bank account			Bank funds		Receive income							

Critical path analysis shows what needs to be done, how it affects other tasks and who is responsible

Good practice

Your project will need to work within the codes of society and the law. For example:

- cultural: the project may not fit into the culture of the community or authorities. For example, male and female strippers are a popular and legitimate part of the entertainment industry, but it is unlikely that your college or school would allow you to put on a show featuring such entertainment.
- nuisance: projects can often annoy local communities because they generate noise or crowds. While this may not be of a level to be illegal it can still bring complaints which will not do your project any good.

Legal aspects

The feasibility of a project will often depend on the capability of the team to find the required resources and have them in the right place at the right time. However, all this will be wasted if the project has not been designed to meet laws and other regulations. Here are some of the key factors that you will need to check:

- Health and safety. The key consideration here is the 'duty of care' for your co-workers and your customers. In many cases you will be using resources provided by other organisations. By law they should have **a)** public liability insurance that protects you as a user if they fail in their duty of care; **b)** health and safety checks and systems that minimise the risk of incident. With large organisations you can probably assume these precautions are in place but this should not stop you doing your own assessment when you inspect the resource.

- Premises. You should make it a golden rule to inspect the site before booking it. This ensures that you will get what you need, and you can personally assess risk, and the health and safety arrangements.
- Equipment and other resources should be inspected before you take possession; for example, check wiring on an amplifier or inspect cleanliness of catering equipment.

Large or reputable suppliers will usually have quality assurance certificates that indicate good health and safety practice. Smaller traders may be less convincing. If you are in doubt then check – for example, ask to see the service record for a hire vehicle. When dealing with individuals you should always ask to see original copies of any legal documentation that shows they are legally qualified – for example, first aid and lifeguarding certificates, public service or private driving licences, governing-body-recognised coaching certificates.

When it comes to using your own resources – and that includes the behaviour and performance of the team – you are unlikely to be fully responsible for health and safety regulations as your school or college will have overall responsibility. You should nevertheless follow good practice in accordance with the regulations. This includes:

- risk assessment
- management of health and safety (e.g. having only transport with safety belts, good supervision ratios, providing a first aid box)
- checking and removing defective equipment.

Licences and permissions

There may be other precautions to take if you are involved in the following areas:

- selling alcohol – this requires a liquor licence
- running a lottery (but not raffles and competitions) – this requires a licence from the local authority
- any event that might cause a disturbance needs to be checked with the authorities, including the police and environmental health. This includes amplified music, floodlighting, processions, large crowds and traffic disturbance. If they judge the effect to be significant, certain orders may need to be applied for
- any aerial activity (including fireworks which also come under COSSH and the Explosives Act) should be approved by the Civil Aviation Authority
- trading (e.g. car boot sales) will often require a traders' licence
- making a street collection for fundraising requires permission from the council
- public entertainments such as rock concerts require a public entertainments licence
- events with a fire risk (e.g. bonfires) should be approved by the fire services.

Aerial activity comes under COSHH and the Explosives Act. Permission is also needed from the Civil Aviation Authority

You should treat these licences as resources in their own right and they need to be planned into the project. They are rarely immediately available and may take some months to get. It is also likely that the authorities may ask you to modify your event before they will give permission. If you fail to get these permissions sorted at an early stage, you may have the embarrassment of being unable to fulfil your promises.

Advertising and sales

It is likely that your project will conform with the legislation and standards set out in Unit 5. Remember to keep your advertising decent, legal and honest. Likewise keep any personal information about your customers secure and do not divulge it to others. You should always ask for receipts, and when possible get terms and conditions and contracts from those supplying you with services and resources. For example, if you hire something you should know in advance what will happen if you damage or lose it. Likewise your customers should be informed of relevant terms and conditions such as 'refunds in case of cancellation'.

Insurance

Even with a small project there is always the possibility of an accident that may cause serious injury or massive damage to property. As an organiser of an event you may be held personally liable for compensation for injured parties, so it is essential that the event is covered by Public Liability Insurance. Businesses are required by law to be insured but smaller businesses and some voluntary clubs may evade this. You should check that the premises you are going to use are covered. The insurance certificate is displayed in reception or the manager's office.

The premises you use may be covered but this does not mean to say that you are covered for activities either inside or outside these premises; for example, coaching, transporting and escorting clients. You are obliged to insure the project team for its work. In most cases this will simply require you to make enquiries of your college or school and ensure that your project and the members of the team are covered by its policy. If you were working independently of an organisation, you would need to approach an insurance broker to take out your own policy.

Other insurances are often required for events or long-term provision of leisure – for example:

- motor insurance: it is obvious that you will need to be insured to drive. If using your own car will need to check whether it is insured to be used for the purposes of the project.
- cancellation insurance: some events can be insured against loss of income if they are cancelled. Insurance for 'rained off' events goes by the name of pluvious insurance.
- employers' liability: both paid workers and volunteers are classified as employees. You need to be insured against damage to the employee's health or livelihood caused by your organisation. Again your college will be insured for you.
- professional indemnity: If you are going to instruct or lead customers, or employ someone who does, there may be a need for professional indemnity. This is insurance that covers the person giving professional advice against damage or injury to the people being advised, or their property. You are unlikely to need it in your project. If you hired a professional coach to lead the tennis course, you would expect him or her to have professional indemnity insurance. It is always worth while to check this.

CASE STUDY – White Knuckle Adventure

Here is the 'flyer' for an outdoor activities centre you are thinking of using for your project – which is to take a party of thirty children away for the weekend.

White Knuckle Adventure

Established in 1997, we are the best outdoor activity centre in Yorkshire. Using experienced leaders, we provide canoeing, climbing, and high rope activities on the coasts and in wilderness areas. Our emphasis is on safety and we can guarantee that all our leaders will be responsible for fewer than 15 participants on all expeditions.

Accommodation is fantastic. Participants share bunkhouse-style rooms in our recently decorated centre which was, until 1997, a three-star hotel. Our grub is great and just what hungry trekkers need: a packed lunch of pies or sandwiches, while in the evening there's lashings of home-prepared food for even the hungriest person.

So why not contact us and make that booking right now?

Questions

1 Assess the centre in terms of legislation and advertising.
2 What checks would you want to make before booking it?

! Check it out

1 What two things does a plan identify?
2 Why do you need to review and adjust the plan throughout the project?
3 What are the five components of a plan?
4 Draw a family tree of how missions, goals and objectives relate.
5 What does SMART stand for?
6 Explain two contingency plans in your project.
7 What does 'fit for purpose' mean?
8 What are critical points?
9 Identify three types of insurance that a project might need.

6.2 Teamwork

Team selection

As we have seen the success of any project depends largely on identifying suitable resources and then making the best use of them. Foremost of these resources are the human resources or the people involved in the project. There is always the temptation when selecting the people to work on a project to choose people you like. This is a flawed method. Think about NeuroLinguistic Programming (NLP) and remember who you are attracted to … it's the people who reflect your own thinking and behaviour. A team selected on this basis will tend to consist of people who react and think in similar ways, and will therefore tend to exaggerate your strengths but also multiply your weaknesses.

Selecting a team is usually far more successful if you analyse what the tasks will involve and the type of person who will do them best. Hopefully you will still be able to look at your friends and find a suitable selection of types to choose from. After all, a really successful team usually consists not only of people who are suited to their tasks but who also get on with each other.

CASE STUDY – Everyone has something to offer

Tarik is a quiet sort of person whose strong point is attention to detail. He finds loud, disorganised extroverts annoying and thinks they are unreliable although he has a sneaking regard for the way they can come up with new ideas. He starts the project by teaming up with other people like himself who appreciate the need for good order and planned activity. The project starts off well. The team develops objectives and a business plan and knows exactly what needs doing. They send an excellent letter to a sponsor and are given an appointment, but now things go wrong – an inability to enthuse and motivate the sponsor results in rejection. At the same time they find that some resources that they thought were available are withdrawn.

Tarik and the team find it difficult to react quickly to the changes and the deadline is coming closer.

With a crisis looming, think about who the team need to get them out of the hole. Yes, it is that loud extrovert who can never be bothered to plan because new ideas and activities are much more exciting.

Questions

1 What lessons can be learnt from this situation?

2 Look at Table 6.1 on page 367 and decide, according to Belbin's classification, what team roles are represented here.

The purpose of a team

Synergy

One of the great advantages of working in a team is that the team is more effective than the same individuals working by themselves. This has been described as 'the output of a team is greater than the sum of the output of its individual members'. A current buzzword for this is 'synergistic' which means that by putting components together you release energy. For example, if you take a lump of phosphorus (which is usually stored in oil) and let it dry out in the air, the oxygen and phosphorus combine and explode and catch fire.

How does synergy work?

- *Physical:* Two or more people can handle equipment which an individual cannot.
- *Creative:* The ideas of one person spark off another individual's train of thought to produce a solution.
- *Delegation:* A person who is more competent with certain tasks can take on the work of others less competent, thus saving time and mistakes.
- *Time:* A team can operate around the clock and in several places at once. For example, when meeting sponsors the team can divide up and different members visit sponsors on the same day.
- *Fitness:* Because a team can rest its members it can ensure that the members who are on duty are performing at their best. For example, if you are setting up an event you may rest the person who will meet the VIPs at the event because you want him or her to be fresh and looking good, and not exhausted after spending six hours setting up a stage and marquee.
- *Motivation:* Individuals working alone often become depressed or deterred by problems and apparent lack of success. A team on the other hand gives support and encouragement to its members to push on and overcome problems. A true team is far more able to go 'the extra mile' than a group of individuals.

A team is more effective than the same individuals working by themselves

- *Support:* Few people are totally competent and most have weaknesses as well as strengths. Very often, pairing members with different strengths and weaknesses means that the task can be done well.

Team building

Teams can be formed in two ways. The best way is for the task and objectives to be formed first and then analysed to see what sorts of people are best suited to make up the team. For example, Sport England created the Millennium Youth Games in 1999 and then distributed the policy and structure of the scheme out to its regional offices where it was decided how to organise the games at regional level. In many cases, a local authority took the lead role and a sports development officer was appointed manager and given the task of selecting and running local teams to set up and run the Games.

CASE STUDY – Balanced teams succeed

Suppose we have two small teams faced with the same two tasks of putting together a sponsorship package and then personally selling this to sponsors. Both teams know nothing about what defines a good sponsorship package nor have they tried to sell anything. Both teams contain members who are good at carrying out research by talking to people who have been successful in raising sponsorship, and reading some of the publications on the subject; both teams are therefore quite capable of achieving the first task. In other words, the teams have been able to use their existing skills.

Faced with the second task the teams are very different. The first team has no problems in selling. Two of its members work in part-time sales jobs and know the importance of good interpersonal and presentation skills. Given the sponsorship package they know they can run with it. As with the first task this team realises it can take on the task within it's existing makeup.

The second team consists entirely of people who have a problem with selling. Some members have poor presentation skills, are shy or appear unenthusiastic, while others refuse to adopt a 'good' presentation or personal appearance. After a critical assessment of itself the team recognises that it would be difficult to achieve a sufficiently rapid change in their skills. Their best option is to invite in a new member who can act as spokesperson and promote the sponsorship deal.

Question

What problems are the second team likely to encounter by recruiting a new team member at a late stage?

The other way is that you already have a team which takes on projects. This is a far more common situation and is typically found in existing organisations that have departments to take on certain types of work. For example, a personnel team may be given the job of developing an appraisal system for the organisation, while a sports development team may be responsible for investigating sources of grant aid. This may be the situation you find when developing your project as the team will be made up from the members of your course.

If this is the case, you need to analyse the tasks and determine who can best do the job. Normally what happens is that the group will decide or adopt a goal and will do two things (Figure 6.3):

- decide if it can achieve that goal using the existing talents of the team
- identify tasks that require skills that do not exist in the team. Then decide if

Think it over

Sometimes teams 'cheat' in choosing goals based on activities that they know and like. For example, everyone in your team likes netball so you decide to run a netball tournament. This method often produces a good product but in some ways its goal is weak. If you are honest the goal may not be 'to run a netball competition' but better summed up as 'to allow the team to do what it enjoys best'. This approach can occur in the workplace. Leisure Development Officers may put their personal preferences forward rather than objectively analyse the needs of the community. Thus, someone who enjoys working with children may do a lot of child-based activities, ignoring the fact that the group that is recreationally deprived in that community is the elderly.

Imagine you are to work with a group of pensioners. What activities would you choose to do that they would enjoy and that you would also enjoy?

members of the team can acquire these skills through training or other methods, or if new members with these skills need to be recruited.

Identifying all the tasks needed for a project is not always easy and you will probably have to review your choice along the planning route as new objectives and roles become apparent. For most teams there will be tasks that involve:

- planning (setting goals and then deciding what resources are needed, when they are needed and how they will be acquired, and who will do the work involved)
- administration (this is the paperwork, such as writing letters, filing, keeping records of customers and contacts)
- financial control (monitoring of expenses and income and ensuring that budgets are kept to target)
- office management (making sure that the project has adequate space, materials (paper, stamps, envelopes) and services (telephones) to be able to operate)

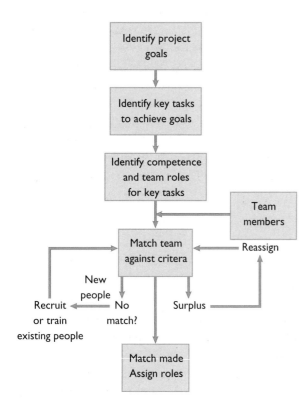

Figure 6.3 Flow chart for team selection

- marketing (relating the product to its market and then promoting and selling it)
- fundraising (identifying and contacting sources of funding to set up and run the project – loans, sponsorship, subsidy)
- public relations (convincing authorities and general public to support your project, and running the event on the day)
- research and evaluation (providing information that will help the project, devising and using systems to measure if the plan is on course).

Roles and responsibilities of team members

Not everyone can do every task. Some people are better suited in character to perform certain tasks than others, and a wrongly chosen individual can actually be detrimental – for example, a person who is forgetful and poor at figures will not be happy in charge of financial control.

> **Try it out**
>
> Learning to work in a team requires being able to give and receive critical appraisal. Here's your chance to start. Link up with a friend and, using the form, decide on four task areas that will be involved in your project. You should now do both a self-assessment and an assessment of each other. Compare the results and respond to the other's comments. Decide who would be best for each task.

There is a school of thought which says that everyone in a team should be included in all of the tasks. We disagree with that view as it misses the point of having a team, which should be made up of individuals doing different tasks to provide for the common goal of the team. Selection of members and the allocation of tasks is therefore an essential process for an effective team. It is rare to get a perfect match between every member and every task. Often you will find that there are certain jobs that everyone wants to do or for which everyone is suited. And then there are others that no one wants to do, even though they may be competent.

If there is a significant lack of skills amongst the team, you may have to deselect some members and recruit other more suitable people. For example, you are planning an activity day for an exchange visit of German students, and as no one in the team speaks German, it would be sensible to recruit someone who does. In a leisure-based team it might be that no one in the team has suitable graphic skills to design promotions. You could pay to buy in this service, or even link up with the Art AVCE course and invite someone from there to join your team as the graphics expert. They in turn could use the experience to supply examples for their own assessment. And although it is usual for projects to be carried out by course students there is nothing to stop you inviting people from outside your course to become members of your team. For example, if you were working on a community project like a play day, it would be highly productive to invite a play worker from the area. Such a team member would have a wealth of knowledge about playwork and local circumstances that would make your project more effective. Remember effective management and good teamwork is not about 'doing it yourself' but about manipulating resources to produce the best outcome.

The practice of using people from outside organisations in your team is widespread in the workplace and is called *partnership*. Sometimes partners will work together to decide what their organisations will do to assist in a particular project. In other cases they will actually work on the task team itself. When this is a long-term placement it is called *secondment*.

There are two criteria for selecting people for teams and for allocating jobs to the members (Figure 6.4).

Figure 6.4 Criteria for team selection

Competence

To be fully competent at a task a person needs to be competent in five areas:

- knowledge: they know how to do the job

- application: they can apply knowledge and perform the task
- focus: they can concentrate without distraction on what is important to get the job done
- attitude: they are positive about doing the job
- communication: they can express their views and observations.

All these factors are essential and if any one is missing the task may not get done.

Competence appraisal

When you are assessing a team member's competence all the information you gather can be confusing so you may want to use a form like the one on p356. On the left-hand

CASE STUDY – Competence

A sports centre manager is recruiting a new team. Here are some of the candidates for the jobs as recreation assistants.

- Steve has a degree in sports science (knowledge) but has no practical experience (application). He is keen (attitude) to start. He appears somewhat disorganised (focus) and is constantly changing from one idea to another (focus and communication).
- Gemma has worked well (application, focus) as a casual recreation assistant at another centre. She has an NVQ (knowledge and application), she can talk well (communication). She has a sarcastic nature and an explosive temper and tends to criticise the centre (attitude).
- Wesley has just left school with no qualifications (knowledge) but is really keen to work in the centre. He is practical (application), cheerful

(attitude) and sticks to the job in hand (focus).

As you can see the candidates above all have their strengths and weaknesses. As is very often the case, the manager needs to select the best of an imperfect bunch. If so, then certain questions should be asked:

- 'Are any of the weaknesses so serious that they will damage the performance of the organisation? If so the candidate would not be suitable and should not be selected.'
- 'Can any of the weaknesses be reduced by training, guidance or doing the job?'
- 'Can any of the weaknesses be balanced by the strengths of other team members?'

Question

Who would you select for the job and why?

CASE STUDY – Selecting the best job for a person

Here is an extract from an assessment for Lara who is in a team where the project will need, among other tasks, fundraising, sports leadership and budgeting skills. As you can see, sometimes she is being judged on her experience and knowledge (does a Saturday job), while on other occasions she is being judged as others see her (bossy). Sometimes when there is no evidence directly related to the task you can use related evidence such as her general time-keeping as an indication that she will be focused in the task as well.

From the scores we can see that she would not be competent in sports leadership but would be well suited to financial control. We can also see that in fundraising it is her attitude that is a weak point together with the lack of experience. She is enthusiastic, though, so why not encourage her to get involved as a back-room person? She could be involved in developing the funding package where her attitude problem (which would affect her sales technique) would not be so much of an issue and could be worked on over time.

Question

Why was Lara's average score low for leadership?

Team member

Lara Croft **Competence Criteria**

Task	Knowledge	Application	Focus	Attitude	Communication
Fundraising	Top marks in marketing assignments. Knows about fundraising 4	No experience 2	Track record of getting work assignments done on time. Good organiser 4	Enthusiasm, commitment but can appear arrogant and pushy 3	Good interpersonal skills. Good telephone skills. Good letter-writing skills 4 **Average score 3.4**
Sports leadership	Knows rules of several games 3	Plays netball 2	Good time-keeping 3	Not too interested – more interested in sports science 2	Good interpersonal skills but bossy and impatient 2 **Average score 2.4**
Financial control	Understanding of basic account keeping, knowledge of security 4	Has kept accounts or handled money (e.g. Saturday job) 4	High attention to detail. Methodical 4	Enthusiasm and commitment. Assertive and honest 4	Good numeracy skills. IT skills. Clear handwriting 4 **Average score 4**

side you write in the tasks or areas of work required for the project and then note what evidence there is of a candidate's competence to do that job. If you wanted to, you could score each box as:

1	incompetent	(novice)
2	not very competent	(improver)
3	competent	(team player)
4	highly competent	(champion)

365

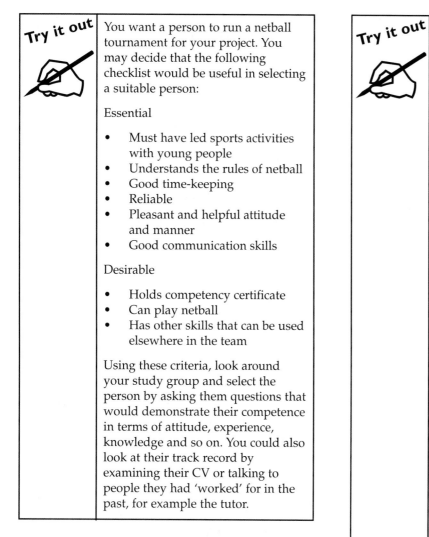

Try it out

You want a person to run a netball tournament for your project. You may decide that the following checklist would be useful in selecting a suitable person:

Essential

- Must have led sports activities with young people
- Understands the rules of netball
- Good time-keeping
- Reliable
- Pleasant and helpful attitude and manner
- Good communication skills

Desirable

- Holds competency certificate
- Can play netball
- Has other skills that can be used elsewhere in the team

Using these criteria, look around your study group and select the person by asking them questions that would demonstrate their competence in terms of attitude, experience, knowledge and so on. You could also look at their track record by examining their CV or talking to people they had 'worked' for in the past, for example the tutor.

Try it out

In the business world competence assessment can be a formal process and a bit intimidating. In your project, formal interviews of the team members may be inappropriate and you may assess members in another way. Team discussion where members describe their own skills and other team members add to these or qualify them. This can be effective, for example:

Kirsty says, 'Our criteria specify that someone with good graphics skills needs to handle the promotions – Well I could do that'. Natalie supports her by saying, 'Remember that great poster you did for the disco'. Shelley then adds, 'Let's not forget she also raised £200 for charity on Red Nose Day – maybe Kirsty should be in charge of fundraising as well'. Sam then chips in, 'But don't you remember she had that problem with losing £50 as well, our criteria say that it is desirable that the fund-raiser is reliable with money. As Kirsty is good at fundraising maybe we should split the job and have someone who handles the money which Kirsty raises?'

In a team, set up your own similar discussion for tasks that you have identified in your project.

(The titles in brackets are alternatives you could use to avoid hurting people's feelings should the form be seen – it is better to be called a novice than incompetent.)

Another way of selecting people is to list the characteristics that are required for a task and to score each as:

- essential – the person must have this competence or cannot be selected
- desirable – it will help if the person has this competence but absence of it will not prevent selection.

Only people with all the essential skills can be selected. The 'desirable' scores can be used to determine the best candidate if more than one has all the essential skills.

Team roles

Another way of constructing teams is to look at the personality types of the individual members. Experienced managers often find that they select a group of highly competent people for a team but somehow the team does not work. You might find that everyone is having good ideas but the team is poor on doing the paperwork. In another group everyone likes to discuss all the things they could do but no one is prepared to make hard decisions or actually put the ideas into practice. In other groups everyone wants to be the leader and all start arguing.

In 1981 RM Belbin, a management analyst, looked at this problem and suggested that teams have:

- tasks – which is what people do and which are largely controlled by their competence
- processes – which is the way people do their tasks.

Belbin thought that the processes were fundamental to why teams fail or succeed in doing their tasks. He felt that people have behavioural patterns that are closely associated with their personalities and which they find hard to change. He called these *team roles* and they are:

- company worker (CW)
- shaper (SH)
- resource investigator (RI)
- team worker (TW)
- chairman (CH)
- plant (PL)
- monitor – evaluator (ME)
- completer-finisher (CF).

Table 6.1 shows the features and qualities of these types. You can often recognise these types in yourself and your team-mates.

Table 6.1 Useful people to have in teams

Type	Symbol	Typical features	Positive qualities	Allowable weaknesses
Company worker	CW	Conservative, dutiful, predictable.	Organizing ability, practical common sense, hard-working, self-discipline.	Lack of flexibility, unresponsiveness to unproven ideas.
Chairman	CH	Calm, self-confident, controlled.	A capacity for treating and welcoming all potential contributors on their merits and without prejudice. A strong sense of objectives.	No more than ordinary in terms of intellect or creative ability.
Shaper	SH	Highly strung, outgoing, dynamic.	Drive and a readiness to challenge inertia, ineffectiveness, complacency or self-deception.	Proneness to provocation, irritation and impatience.
Plant	PL	Individualistic, serious-minded, unorthodox.	Genius, imagination, intellect, knowledge.	Up in the clouds, inclined to disregard practical details or protocol.
Resource investigator	RI	Extroverted, enthusiastic, curious, communicative.	A capacity for contacting people and exploring anything new. An ability to respond to challenge.	Liable to lose interest once the initial fascination has passed.
Monitor-evaluator	ME	Sober, unemotional, prudent.	Judgement, discretion, hard-headedness.	Lacks inspiration or the ability to motivate others.
Team worker	TW	Socially orientated, rather mild, sensitive.	An ability to respond to people and to situations, and to promote team spirit.	Indecisiveness at moments of crisis.
Completer-finisher	CF	Painstaking, orderly, conscientious, anxious.	A capacity for follow-through. Perfectionism.	A tendency to worry about small things. A reluctance to 'let go'.

(Reprinted with permission from Belbin R.M., *Management Teams: Why They Succeed or Fail*, Heinemann (1981) p. 78.)

Sometimes people fit the picture exactly; more often they will have a variety of roles in their nature. To be more accurate you can use a questionnaire that measures someone's profile more exactly.

The Belbin model has four major implications for team success.

1 A team works on various tasks which require certain skills and competence. Team roles affect how well people can do these tasks. For example, if you need new ideas then SHs in the group will come up with the answers, if you want to see if the ideas are feasible then you would need some MEs. It is likely though that these two 'opposites' would start arguing so you might need a CH or an SH to take control of the process. On the other hand if you need to make sure that letters go out and receipts are kept and recorded then a SH will be useless while the CF would revel in the task.

The lesson to be learnt here is to match the profiles of the team members to the type of task they will do.

2 Tasks change as the project develops. In the early stages there will be a great deal of planning and creativity which means the SHs and RIs will operate at full strength. Next there will be a need for the hard graft and getting on with the routine jobs and so the company worker (CW) roles come to the fore. Later on, dealing with the customer may be important and the team workers (TW) show their worth.

The lesson here is that different members of the team will be able to show their strengths at different times. In some cases the circumstances might change drastically and you might wish to use the best member for that moment; for example, if you are running behind a deadline you might put a powerful shaper (SH) in charge of the team to cut out wasting time on seeking perfection.

The other lesson is that not all members have to be active all of the time. Team members quite frequently accuse someone else of not pulling his/her weight. Team members must realise that they will come in and out of play according to their abilities and the demands of the current task. For example, putting a PL or an RI on administrative duties with a CF is going to lead to annoyance and irritation.

3 Selecting your team by matching tasks to roles will make it more effective, but it can be a social minefield. One way to avoid the minefield is to let the team into the secret. Everyone should know what roles they fit and why they will be doing certain tasks. The possibility of conflict should be discussed and the team should be consulted on what methods are going to be used to minimise this. It should be made clear that members will work more or less on different tasks or at different stages of the project. It is also a good idea to emphasise that the team should recognise their differences, and control any annoyance, and concentrate on recognising the positive achievements of others.

Try it out

One way to promote team openness is to suggest that the team members who will be working together arrange to discuss the following:

- the goals they share and how they intend to contribute to the achievement of those goals
- their strengths and weaknesses and how they can support each other
- how they can recognise or cope with behaviours that irritate the others.

A discussion like this will help members to work together and it may add to their commitment. Each person could write down what he/she has agreed.

The manager is often thought of as 'the boss' and somehow more important than the rest of the team. You may be reluctant to assume this role for fear that the rest of the team will think you are being bossy in wanting to take on the job. Good managers do not see themselves like this but merely as another member of the team whose task is to keep things moving in the right direction. You may well decide at a certain point of the project or when there is a change of circumstances that another team member would be more suitable. There is no shame in 'resigning' and in fact it shows you are a better manager for being able to recognise the need for change.

Think about your own strengths as a manager. What stages of a project would benefit best from these strengths?

4 You can create sub-teams within the team that will make the best use of members. This will complement the negative weaknesses of some members with the positive qualities of others. You can then allocate appropriate tasks.

For example in the earlier example of the team meeting, Kirsty is a typical PL or RI and will be great at selling ideas to sponsors. She may come back with a cheque, but being the type she is she may, despite her best intentions, forget to bank the cheque, leave it lying around or lose it. Sam's suggestion to split the role was a sensible one. Far better to bring a CF into the picture who will handle the money. You can also establish a procedure that relieves Kirsty from handling money whereby she can ask the sponsor to send the cheque directly to the CF who will efficiently record and bank it and send a receipt and letter of thanks back to the sponsor.

Team structure and formation

So far we have largely concentrated on the individuals who make up the team and on their role in it. What about teams as a whole? How do they work? What about their strengths?

- Teams spread the workload: difficult or unpopular tasks can be rotated or given to members who do enjoy them.
- They provide social support which helps members overcome personal difficulties or helps the group as a whole face external threats.
- They set standards for work and the behaviour of the members.
- They provide a structure for communication.
- They set objectives and find out ways to achieve them.

Informal groups

In any organisation or social setting there are groups which come together simply because people have similar interests or because circumstances put them together. For example, in your class there will be a group of people who play a sport, there will be some who smoke and meet outside to do so, there will be others with shared political or religious interests. This type of group is called an *informal group.* It has no defined structure or purpose but exists as long as its members retain the characteristics that drew them together.

Informal groups exist throughout work and society. They have a great strength in that they overlap and so members will belong to many groups at once. This very often leads to what is shown as *networking* where members have contacts in other groups that can support the first group in a variety of ways such as providing resources and finding contacts. For example, you are putting on an outdoor play. You might know someone in an informal group who knows someone else in the building trade who can provide staging, and they know someone who belongs to a dressmaking class who can recruit several volunteers to help with the costumes.

Informal groups may be influential in the workplace. For example, if a manager wants to change the hours of the staff you may find that the internal groups agitate other informal groups such as customers to make the changes unfeasible. Because informal groups have no structure they can network far more quickly than formal groups, which have limited communication channels. Have a look at your college and identify informal groups that exist both among the staff and students. Can you think of ways in which they affect the college policies or programme?

Formal groups

The usual type of group in the workplace is the *formal* one. Figure 6.5 shows the differences from the informal group.

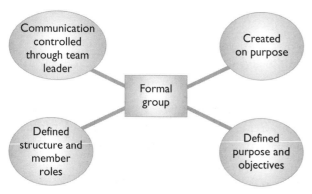

Figure 6.5 Criteria for a formal group

You will find that for the purposes of your project the formal structure (mixed by utilising informal networks) will probably be the most effective one to adopt.

Roles and responsibilities

If you are to work as a formal group you will need to define the roles and responsibilities of team members and how they relate to the rest of the team. Most people like to know who they are (job title), where they are (their relationship to colleagues, who they report to) and what they are meant to be doing.

In the workplace these are laid out in a *job description* which will:

- give the person a title: e.g. fundraiser
- describe the job and objectives: e.g. to raise funds for the project and ensure that the funding of partners' needs is satisfied

---

Think it over

When does a group become a team? You will find in textbooks that the term group is used more often than team and sometimes it is used instead of team. Some clarification may be useful here.

Teams are strong, well-developed groups. They are characterised by:

- a sharing of common goals and objectives
- an ability to resolve differences without splitting up
- a sharing of the workload
- a high degree of pride and team identity
- being small enough for members to know each other well
- high trust in the team leader
- an ability to recognise threats and weaknesses in the team and its members and cover them
- an ability to recognise opportunities and strengths in team mates and play to these
- full participation by members.

Look at your group and, using these criteria, decide if it has become a team.

- provide details of the work involved:
    - to identify and contact funding partner
    - to prepare a sponsorship package
    - to ensure funding criteria are met
- give communication and reporting lines:
    - to liaise with event organiser on funding
    - to report all income to finance controller
    - to report back to the team on funding issues
- map organisational structure: e.g. a chart showing reporting lines and position in the organisation.

(In paid employment there would be a section on terms and conditions such as pay, holidays and hours.)

In this project it is a good idea to write a brief job description for all team members. These should be short and to the point. Remember that there may be occasions when an individual has more that one role or job, and in that case he/she will have more than one job description.

Communication

A great deal of work has been done on the structure of teams, especially on how information is communicated and directions given. In many ways this will be academic to your project as your team may be too small to divide up. But here are some options (Figure 6.6).

Hierarchy
Here there is an overall manager with managers beneath him at various levels. Each

is directed by the manager above. This is not a very productive option as lower-level workers do not get much job satisfaction and tend to be left 'in the dark'. But it can be effective, as it is clear who is responsible for what actions and miscommunication is minimised.

Wheel
Here task groups work independently and are directed from a central point by a manager through whom all communication and direction flows. This can work well for a small project if you have trust in one person as leader. Perhaps a better way is for the centre of the wheel to consist of a 'board' of task team leaders who make decisions collectively. But in situations where the task groups on the rim of the wheel are physically separated, this can lead to a feeling of isolation from the team as a whole.

Web
Here communications exist between all task teams. This is a likely structure for a project where all the team will be close to each other and it means that there is lots of communication and synergy. The downside is that decisions will be made after communication between some and not all the team members, which can cause confusion. If a web exists then you need to decide how you are going to make sure everyone is aware of what is going on and agree a system for making decisions and giving directives.

Team development

Teams, like individuals, go through a development process in which they change from a loose collection of individuals into a well-formed team. Tuckman (1965) suggested that they go through four stages in which they develop and define their behaviour and communication and the way

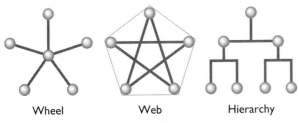

Wheel   Web   Hierarchy

Figure 6.6 Group structure options

they work. It is likely that your project team will be a new one even though many of its members may have already been part of an informal group (e.g. your class). Don't be surprised if the team goes through a stage of arguments and rows and even changes of purpose and structure as it matures. Don't give up, but try to find ways to resolve the issues as they arise.

As a team you will probably go through:

Forming

Individuals come together with the purpose of taking on the task or project. The first thing they will need to do is to decide the group's structure and roles. The members will be unsure and apprehensive as they start to work together and jockey for position within the group. Some will try to impose themselves on the group and test the other members, and all will be experimenting with relationships

Storming

Members become more relaxed and certain about their strategies. They will start to question what has been decided in the forming stage and challenge, attack or support each other. This will be the time when there will be walkouts or major revisions of what has been decided earlier on. For example, this is the time when an extrovert leader whom the group initially felt would be good at managing them turns out to be ineffective and is asked to step down

Norming

The air is now cleared and the group settles down to work on what has been agreed and discover what work styles suit them best. The group starts to develop its standards, such as dress codes, or what is acceptable behaviour. This is the time mascots or team names start to appear and be accepted by

the group. The group is now becoming a team

Performing

The team is now fully formed and gets on with the job. Success will tend to reinforce the team's belief in itself and it attaches itself more strongly to its values and ways of working. The team now starts to gel and strong bonds are formed to make the team cohesive.

Factors influencing team performance

Team strength and performance depend on other factors as well as group development (Figure 6.7). These are:

- membership
- work environment
- organisation.

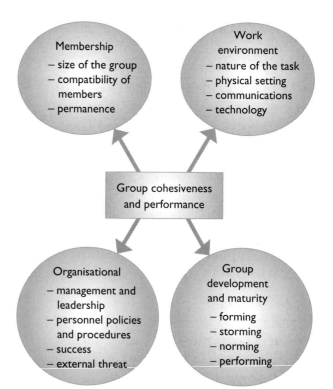

Figure 6.7 Factors contributing to group cohesiveness and performance.
Source: Mullins 1994

Membership

The bigger the group the more it will tend to fall apart. It becomes harder for members to maintain good communication with each other and to form bonds. It is generally held that twelve people are about the maximum, with natural groups usually consisting of about six people. It is interesting to note that rugby teams of fifteen can be hard to keep together and often there is a subgrouping into forwards and backs.

Likewise, if you decided your project should involve your entire class you would have to devise a structure of smaller subgroups; for instance, you might have a small promotions team or administration team each with a team leader. Your project would automatically become more sophisticated and produce new management challenges which would earn it extra grading points.

Personalities

Personalities can make or break a team. Leadership skills, sense of humour, perseverance or concern for others can all make a team stronger. However, if strong personalities clash or overrule less strong ones then the team can start to fragment.

Performance

In long-term situations groups perform better when there is little change amongst their members. In a short-term project it makes little difference.

Work environment

Generally speaking, groups are more cohesive if members are doing similar work. This feeling of the shared experience is especially heightened if the task is difficult or challenging. Think for instance about sports you play and the difference you may have felt towards your team when you have won a league game and when you have won a championship.

Competition

If a team cannot get the resources it needs it will often become more cohesive and thus more able to get resources from its competitors. In large organisations with many departments this can be detrimental as subgroups start to fight each other for resources such as space or money.

Physical setting

A team that works together stays together. Doing the work in physical proximity to each other helps cohesiveness. There are many reasons for this:

- communication is shared and more direct. Members will hear what was said at the time and can respond directly. This means that there will be less rumour and gossip and members can be 'up front'.
- there will be no sense of 'us and them' as might be felt if part of the team at headquarters appeared to be more favoured than a part of the team in a branch office. Shared location means it is less easy to blame the other part of the team for failures.
- the team can work more effectively in sharing tasks, supporting each other and responding to common threats and challenges. This gives both a greater sense of achievement as well as loyalty to each other.

Communication

People not only like to talk, they also like the freedom to say what they feel. A team that communicates well within itself will be cohesive.

Technology

In industries where machines 'control' the work process, studies have generally shown that group cohesiveness is reduced. In the leisure industry, with its high 'people' content, this factor is rarely present.

> **Think it over**
>
> Often in the modern workplace teams are split up. Members may be located in different places, out doing the job or even working on an e-mail basis. All these factors weaken team identity. To overcome this, organisations often encourage events that bring the team together. This may be simply meeting down at the pub after work on a Friday, or it may be a programme of social events. Sometimes the team is taken away on a 'bonding meeting' in a hotel where they will get a chance to renew social links as well as confirm their team values and objectives. How would you create a strong team identity?

Organisation

Leaders and managers try to build up cohesiveness in teams. Support, fairness, clear decisions and understanding of the job are all factors that will bond the group. On the other hand, insensitive management can break it down. One paradox in the workplace is that managers need to be owned by the team, while at the same time they are under an obligation to meet the objectives of the organisation as a whole. If the organisational objectives threaten or do not lie within those of the team, then the team is likely to disown its manager whom they will see as siding with the enemy. Without a manager the team may lose effectiveness. It is more likely, though, to elect its own leader who will resist the manager.

Although there are organisations where teams work to the orders of managers, there are an increasing number of organisations that work successfully because managers are good leaders and encourage team cohesiveness and bonding. Here are some ways good managers carry this out:

- they have a good record of personal delivery (e.g. they deliver what they say, hand work in on time, are on time themselves, don't avoid work, can do the job they expect their team to do).

- they have good organisational skills (e.g. they make lists or notes, they put things into categories, their presentations and work are ordered and tidy).

- they can communicate with others effectively (this does not mean that they are necessarily lively and witty but they can put their thoughts across clearly to their workmates, and to people in authority). In class these people will ask questions and give clear answers without being 'clever' or seeking an audience.

- they can use symbols to motivate, such as a 'team member of the week' trophy that sits on the winner's desk.

- they can use praise to motivate and even when criticising good managers will still praise (e.g. 'I am really impressed by the way you are handling the sponsor but I think you will find it will work even better if you stick to the package we agreed. Can you do that?' In a project meeting the manager might say, 'Dave did a great job at getting the hall at that price. But I'm afraid buying a microphone from a bloke in the pub was a mistake that has cost us. Can we all agree as a team that we will only work to plan in future?'

- they encourage others to give feedback and listen. Good managers will say things like 'What do you think?', 'How do you see the plan going?', 'Let's hear from Dave'. Good listeners will not only take in what is being said, they will also show that they have understood what has been said. For example, 'Just to summarise what Dave has being saying'. They will also refer back to conversations at a later date: 'I would like to remind you that Dave pointed out this problem a couple of weeks ago'.

- they will give credit where it is due. Good managers will remind others in the group where ideas or actions have come from. Poor managers take the credit for themselves. Good practice would be: 'I must stress that although I am making this presentation, what I am going to say is the result of the whole team working really well together over the past two months'. If you are looking for inspiration look at the winners' speeches at the Oscars.

- they are fair. People do not mind tough decisions if they are fair. Good managers delegate and praise on merit. In your class, watch for people who select teams on the basis of skills and not popularity or include everyone when sharing out something.

Personnel

In workplaces personnel practice can build up or breakdown groups. Good personnel practice includes support and recognition of success, appraisal of members and development of fair disciplinary procedures, all in order to aid cohesiveness.

Success

Success builds on success. Success rewards a group for its efforts and makes it more cohesive which makes it more effective which results in success and so on.

Threat

If a team is threatened it will close ranks and become more cohesive. This is a defence mechanism since, as it becomes more cohesive, it becomes more effective at getting rid of the threat.

Factors influencing team building

Team building can happen naturally through group development and the coincidence of other factors such as good personalities. However, this cannot be relied on and active team building is often more productive. This is the case where you have a short-term project to achieve and where the building process may need to be accelerated.

If you look at the diagram on page 372 you can see that some of the factors such as personnel or technology are not particularly important. Neither is it a good idea to use threats to build a team as this often requires very sophisticated management techniques which can easily backfire.

Personality

Keep an eye on the obvious pitfalls by avoiding personality clashes. For example, if you can, put likely enemies in tasks where they won't come into much contact or affect each other's work. Providing they can do the job, existing friends will often work well together. If clashes cannot be avoided the team needs to have a fair way to decide such disputes and ask the offending members to alter their behaviour or attitude.

More positive is to reward or promote team-building behaviour. Laughter is a great cement for teams and it is often a good idea to encourage humorous team members. Another type of person is the member who has the respect of the team, and such people should be encouraged to give their opinions to motivate the group when it is under pressure or threatened.

Size

Keep size down to small groups if possible. Once a team goes above ten it starts to lose cohesiveness. This effect can be reduced by breaking the team down into sub- teams responsible for specific tasks. These may be as small as pairs (for example, two people designing the publicity materials). This way you may be able to build up a large team and still maintain cohesion.

Location

Try to encourage the team to work in the same room if it is feasible. Make sure you bring in as often you can members of the team who may work away from the main group (e.g. set makers for a play, poster designers for a sports event).

Success

Even with a short-term project you can have lots of successes, all of which should be celebrated. The team can vote for a 'worker of the week' award, you might have a small party every time a significant objective is achieved (e.g. sponsorship) or you might get a mention of the project in the College news-letter or on the radio. When you finish the project recognise the achievement with an award ceremony.

Communication

The more people contribute and communicate the more they will bond. In the early stages of the group people will not know each other well so why not have some social events (e.g. a silly games tournament, a disco, or a spaghetti eating contest) that will bring the group together? If you work hard at this, the stormy period in the life of the team may be just a passing breeze!

As soon as the project starts it is a good idea to have regular meetings to update everyone. Have a notice board where people can put up dates, jokes, and suggestions, anything they want.

Check it out

1 Explain the differences between a group and a team.

2 Explain, with examples, the differences between formal and informal groups.

3 What does a job description contain?

4 Describe three team structures and give advantages and disadvantages.

5 Describe the four stages of team development.

6.3 Carrying out the project
The business plan

Planning should result in a document called a business plan which has three purposes:

- It sets out the thinking of the team and allows flaws and omissions to be identified. Perhaps most importantly it identifies problems that may arise in the future and hinder the project. In other words, it makes sure that the project is *feasible* – that it can achieve its goals and objectives with the resources and time available.

  A well-known example of a problem that can be identified in a business plan is *cash flow*, which often occurs and can ruin flourishing businesses. This problem occurs when the business has to spend more to expand (for example, to buy bigger premises or employ more staff). Once the business has made this investment there will be a delay before the increased income comes back to it. If the gap is too long the firm may become bankrupt as it has insufficient funds to pay its debts or continue spending on essential resources. Business plans will often be able to locate when these problems will occur and alternative solutions are found to get round them, such as borrowing or staggering expenditure by buying on credit or in instalments.

- Business plans are used to persuade *stakeholders* to become involved in a project. Stakeholders are the organisations and people affected by a project, from the customers through to the people who authorise or fund the project. Stakeholders also include people in the community who may be affected by the project and whose co-operation will help it succeed. For example, in the public sector a sports development officer may set up a coaching scheme funded by Sport

England, which uses resources from the partners in the scheme including the local authority, a sports club and local schools. In the private sector the owner of a health club will almost certainly have to see a bank manager or a venture capitalist to borrow money for a new project. The bank manager will expect to see a business plan that shows likely returns on the loan. Other stakeholders would be the shareholders of the company and the staff who aim to make it a success. Even in the voluntary sector business plans are important. For instance, a sports club hoping to build a new clubhouse will have to present a similar business plan to its members to convince them that this will be a project in their interests and within the club's resources.

- Business plans allow the project team to see if they are reaching their objectives and keeping within the budget.

CASE STUDY – Using a business plan

A hockey club had the opportunity to sell their old and dilapidated ground and clubhouse for housing and with the money buy a new site nearby. The club was faced with the decision as to what sort of facilities to build and how to use these to maximise income. The club membership was split on how to use the facilities. Some members wanted the facilities only to be used by members, others felt the artificial pitches could be used by footballers who would pay for it. There was even a choice as to whether to go for a high-tech 'water-based' pitch complex making the club a centre of excellence or to go for a more modest 'sand-based' pitch.

The club decided to develop a business plan that compared all the options. The results were surprising and steered the club away from options that initially had looked appealing, but which on closer inspection would have ruined the club.

- There was a lack of financial support from the governing body for a Centre of Excellence even though it was encouraging the club to go in that direction.
- The running and long-term maintenance of the water-based pitches meant they would have been a financial drain on the club because of their high replacement costs.

- A single sand-based pitch would give the lowest risk and highest return.
- Footballers would almost certainly be needed to ensure that there was sufficient income to cover costs. This was not popular with some members who did not want to open the doors to soccer players.
- Members' subscriptions would have to go up to pay for the running costs and replacement costs of the pitches. Many members had not realised that new facilities often bring higher costs that have to be paid for.
- Substantial income could be made by designing the clubhouse to accommodate daytime hires for business meetings. This is known as ancillary income and the club had not realised they could raise so much from this source.

Questions

1 What sources of income did the plan identify for building the club and running it?

2 If the club had decided to go with the idea of developing a Centre of Excellence, what would have been the outcome?

377

You now know where you want to go and what you want to achieve. Now you need to know how you are going to do it. This is the business plan, and it will not only confirm if you can do what you want to do with the resources at your disposal, but it will also be the main tool in persuading other people that your ideas are feasible.

Research

Unlike the early stages of planning the business plan relies on detailed information that is accurate and valid. Sometimes, as in the case of the hockey club, the information will be put into spreadsheet format and various calculations run through to find out what the results would be of changing certain factors such as membership subscription. In order to do this the information needs again to be accurate and in a form that can be manipulated in this way. In other words, the business plan is putting hard facts up against the values, beliefs and creativity first put forward when fixing goals and objectives.

To achieve this you will also want to use the research methods that we talked about in Unit 4, Marketing. You may use these to develop the business plan or to measure and evaluate the project when it takes place (e.g. exit surveys). Modern project planning is market orientated and it is important that you have researched the market and its needs. You will also need to carry out business research in order to investigate sources of funding, the best suppliers of resources, and how other organisations provide similar projects.

Here are some areas you might want to investigate:

- what is on the market already? Look around and see what is happening in the marketplace, what products there are, how much they are, where and when are they situated

- what do the customers want? Ask them through focus groups or interviews
- what works and what fails? Look at the success of past schemes
- where are the sources of funding?
- what new opportunities are there? Look around for new resources and markets
- how have others approached similar projects? Talk to teachers and past students, look at their project files.

In the business world a great deal of time and effort is put into researching feasibility studies, using demographic and mathematical models as well as survey research. Remember, however, that simple questions often need simple answers. In other words, if you can identify your market by simple desk research such as looking through the *Yellow Pages* or talking to a group of students that reflects the interests of the school or college, this may be all you need to ascertain whether what you are going to do will work. You don't need rocket science to organise a disco.

Don't let stereotyped ideas cloud your research or lead to false assumptions.

Getting the right information at the start is important. You may go to a residential home and find that the residents are a lively bunch and would like to do a bit of hill walking – thus confounding any stereotypes you may have had. If you hadn't done your research you would have found that the indoor croquet session you had intended to organise would have been a disaster.

Remember to stick to the principles of survey research. Do not think that because your project is small or short that you can forget about the methodology of questionnaire writing, running an interview or sampling. If you do not apply these basic rules, your results will be open to error and the project may start off on a false premise and fail as a result.

Creating the business plan

Figure 6.8 shows the components of a business plan.

Figure 6.8 Business plan

It is a series of short reports that describe the project. The reports must be kept:

- clear – anyone who reads them should understand the plan

Think it over

You are going to send out a mail-shot to local schools and you get a list from the Education Authority. Have you checked that it is complete? If you have not, you may find that the list has omitted schools outside the state sector – in an affluent area the private schools may contain a significant number of children. How are you going to locate these schools to maximise your promotion?

- accurate – base the report on facts not fancy
- brief – for a project of this size, two sides of A4 will be ample for most of the sections.

Creating the business plan is not a one-off process. You will find that an initial draft plan will inevitably have flaws in it and will need to be modified. In some cases you will find that the business plan shows that your goal and objectives are not feasible, in which case it is back to the drawing board. Even when you have a finished plan which is acceptable you will need to make sure that you are keeping to it when the project gets under way. Using the business plan is like referring to your map and taking compass bearings as you go along your route. With the project, the compass bearings will take the form of meetings which must be held regularly and frequently throughout.

We will look at each section of the plan in detail.

Thought for the page

While a business plan will be used formally it does not have to be a formal document. You may well want to develop a style that reflects your project. For example use illustrations, develop a project logo, and use plain English and not business jargon. You may prefer to present the whole package on disk as a computer presentation or as an audio-visual display using several members of the team.

Introduction and purpose

The introduction should give a brief background to the plan including:

- *a brief description of the area* where the project is based (eg demographics, cultural, socio-economic, transport and communications)
- *definition of the industry* you will be working in and the opportunities and issues that exist
- *the reasons why you are interested* in setting up your 'business'.

All this leads to a summary of your purpose in running this business. This is where you state your beliefs and values, and the goal and the main objectives that will achieve this. This is your *declaration of intent* and the rest of the business plan is entirely focused on how you will deliver this.

Business description (people, skills, location)

You now need to say what the business (project) consists of and this will include:

- *The structure of the organisation*: This will give the titles, roles (and names) of its people. If there are reporting lines these can be shown as a diagram like a family tree. In large organisations it would be normal to show structure in a depersonalised form giving department names or numbers of people doing the same task. In your project the team will small enough to personalise – why not include photos of them looking happy and enthusiastic?
- *Brief descriptions of key posts*: This should describe the function of the post, the skills required for it and the key responsibilities of the person doing it.
- *CVs of key staff*: These may be full CVs (one side of A4) or perhaps summary paragraphs describing the person, his/her

relevant experience and skills. These are often put in an appendix.
- *Physical nature of the business*: Where it is located, what its premises are, and what physical resources it has. For your project you could refer to any resources that you have access to in, say, your school or college. For example, 'We are based in Bash Street College where we have use of classrooms, workshops and gyms'.
- *The history and function of the business*: This should include how long the business has run and its track record and the type of work it has done. In the case of a project you could legitimately say 'The Bash Street Festival Group is a business that has been formed specifically to stage this festival'. Your function could be 'BSFC produces community leisure events'.

A marketing plan

You now need to define your market and how you are going to reach it. Much of what you need to know about how to do this you have already read in Unit 4, Marketing. However, to reiterate, you might consider:

- identifying your customers and their needs
- developing a market mix which will supply those needs
- assessing competition and how you will deal with it (e.g. other events)
- showing how you will respond to the environment
- summarising your marketing strategy
- describing how you will train sales staff.

It is again worth remembering that in the first attempt your marketing plan will probably deal in ranges rather than absolutes and may need revising. For example, you might find that your customers are willing to pay between £5 and £8 for the service you are offering. At a later stage you will need to match this against what it will cost you to provide the service and what your profit objectives are. You may find then that you will charge £6 as this will return an acceptable profit and undercut the competition. Or you may find that you cannot deliver at that price and will have to revise the product, if this can be done without adversely affecting demand.

The end-product of marketing is making a sale. This may mean selling the proposal to sponsors and authorising authorities and, of course, selling the service to the consumer – the customer. We have seen from the unit on customer service that sales don't happen naturally and any member of staff involved with customers will need to:

- have appropriate selling skills
- know about the service you are offering
- be able to process any sales
- develop a sales plan for each type of customer (e.g. sponsors, participants).

Your plan will therefore have to show how you intend to get team members fit to sell, for example by introducing sales training sessions.

> **Think it over**
> Consider your own project. How are you going to achieve sales? They may be achieved through promotion and personal selling. Identify the USPs that may be important to your sales.

Personal selling is a hard road to follow as it is often lonely and can result in personal rejection. In businesses with large sales forces the selling process is not only about training sales staff but keeping their motivation and self-belief and confidence. This is often achieved by sales meetings that show sales staff how well they are doing, how important they are and how valued by the company

which may offer them incentives to achieve more sales. Why not introduce motivators into your team? What about a big cake to celebrate finding a sponsor?

Environmental assessment

Remember PEST in the Marketing Unit? (See page 220) Now is the time to use it. This is not just in the marketing context but for the business as a whole. Analysing the environment is essential if the project is going to work, as is finding out about any constraints that will hinder it. With longer-term projects it will also allow you to identify threats and opportunities that might crop up in the future.

Political

The most likely implication here for your project is legislation and, in particular, health and safety legislation. You need to consider if what you intend to do is legal, and if it requires authorisation or licensing. You should find out if there are any changes taking place that will affect your plan – for example, in the year 2000 licensing laws were changed. Your business plan should list the main areas of legislation that affect you and a brief declaration of how you intend to comply with these. You should be able to back up this declaration with details about how you have complied.

For example, you should:

- have prepared a risk assessment of the event
- be able to refer to health and safety inspections on your premises (don't worry, your school or college will have already done these – so a quick word with the health and safety officer will alert you to any special requirements)
- have a checklist of the specific requirements of relevant legislation (e.g. Children Act)

- have details of licensing and permits that you will require (e.g. performing rights, police permission).

Another political factor to take into account could be the policies of your college or school which, for example, may not wish college projects to make a profit and may not want students to get involved in controversial areas – you may have thought about having a fundraising day for a local 'Rehab' unit for heroin users and this might not be acceptable to the college.

You also need to think ahead and identify any political changes that may occur; for example, licensing laws are currently being changed and a project that involves these may have an opportunity to do something different when the legislation comes into effect.

Economic

Can you assume that any subsidies that your cash-strapped college gave for projects will be available this year? Will your customers have varying amounts of disposable income throughout the year? For example, if you survey students in the autumn term about how much they would spend, it may be that by the the summer when the project takes place they will have run out of money.

Remember that the economic environment will affect all sorts of items in your plan. For example, the disposable income of your customers, the competition, and the cost of resources will all combine to affect your pricing which in turn will affect the feasibility of the project. The availability of income from sponsorship, grants and subsidies will affect the timing of the projects, your choice of market and the partners you may be able call upon.

Social

A simple social factor is annoyance of your neighbours. Have you worked out if there is

anything in your project which will annoy them? Irritations such as parking noise and obstructions, floodlighting, noise of music and crowds may come under the Environment Act or Noise Control regulations. But even if they don't, they may still be sufficiently annoying to cause bad public relations. How are you going to cope with this problem? Have you considered if your team's involvement in the project is going to be affected by social pressures such as holidays or exams? While these might not stop the project they would almost certainly require you to extend your time schedule to accommodate such pressures.

Technology

Technology has a huge part to play in the leisure industry whether it be the development of 'e-commerce' or the various technological developments such as digital broadcasting, the use of lasers in special events and concerts, or the sophistication of new fitness machinery. All these changes challenge the suitability of existing technology and open up new opportunities for the future. Your project will be affected similarly. Can you use computer projection and presentations to strengthen your appeal to sponsors? Can you use mobile phones to keep in touch during an event or would radio be more suitable? Can you go for paperless office systems or arrange 'chat rooms' or video conferencing for the team to stay in touch?

! Check it out

1 What should the introduction of a business plan consist of?
2 What should your marketing plan achieve?
3 What are the opportunities for selling in your project?
4 Describe the market mix for your project.
5 What opportunities does technology provide for your project?

Financial planning

The financial plan is the cornerstone of any business. Great ideas that could have been successful in the long term can often fail because set-up charges were underestimated or business was slow in picking up. A well-known cause of failure is a problem with cash flow. This is where delays in payment by people who owe you (debtors) means you do not have enough available cash to pay people you owe (creditors), or acquire resources when you want them. Cash flow analysis and budget creation are the two principal features of the financial plan.

The following stages are essential to develop a simple financial plan:

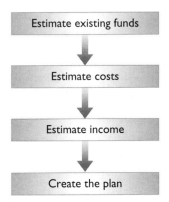

Stages in a financial plan

Estimate existing funds

How much you have and will have for a project depends on various criteria:

Earned income: This will include what you will charge for the service (core income) and what you will get from associated sales (such as refreshments, programmes and merchandising). This sort of income will come in later on in the project and may not be available until after the project has been completed. In other words, for new projects earned income will not normally be available to pay for the *start-up costs* – that is getting the service ready for consumption.

Unearned income: There are several ways you can fund a project from income that does not come from sales and therefore can be used to start up and develop the project. These contributions will go into your *cash reserves.*

- Sponsorship: this will involve selling a sponsorship package to a sponsor. If successful it should bring you a free source of money provided you stick to your contract with the sponsor – usually mentioning their name at agreed intervals on your public address system, or placing promotions on clothing, point of sale material and brochures, etc.
- Grants: these require an application process which is often complex and drawn out. The authorising bodies often require you to match the funding in some way. However, this can be a free source of money.
- Donations: these are another way of funding your project and can be useful particularly if the project is a charitable one. However, the law can be complicated on what proportion of a donation can be used for internal administration. Fundraising events such as sponsored runs are a good way of raising project funds.
- Shares: if you are feeling really ambitious and intend to make money out of the project, you may wish to offer 'shares' in the project. The shareholders pay an amount for a share in the project on the understanding that they will receive a share of the profit back plus their original investment. Of course you should always remember the old caveat 'the value of shares may go down as well as up'. The other disadvantage of shares is that the major shareholders can dictate how your business is run.

Other sources of income include:

Cash reserves: Many businesses that are up and running will put aside part of their profits to set up new projects. This money is the 'cash in the bank'. New businesses, such as your project, do not have a reserve to set up the project and this can be a major problem.

Investing your own money: Exactly what it says. This is putting your money where your mouth is and it will guarantee that you won't come up with sloppy plans or indulgent spending.

Borrowing: This is expensive, as it is not often that you can find an interest-free loan. Even so, borrowing is an essential and normal part of many businesses. To be a successful borrower you will have to have a good business plan to convince the lender to lend.

Thought for the page

Grant aid from public bodies like local authorities and the Lottery are two major sources of unearned income. In the past, grant aid was given but not rigorously monitored. Even when a project was a failure it was often politically embarrassing to do anything about it except note that any further applications would be rejected. In the past ten years evaluation has become far more rigorous and the influence of a convincing business plan is often the success of the application. Furthermore, evidence that the business plan is adhered to by the organisation is becoming the acid test for evaluation. There are now cases where organisations that did not spend the grant as they intended may be asked to return the grant and even be subject to prosecution.

Underwriting: Sometimes you can be lucky and find an organisation or person who believes in your idea and will offer to pay or 'write off' any shortfalls of your budget. For example, you are holding an outdoor event that depends on a certain number of people turning up for it to make a profit. The weather is bad and you fail to make the expected income. The underwriter would make up the difference between your estimated profit and your actual loss. In the commercial world such benefactors do exist; they are called insurance companies and you have to pay for that service. With your project you may find your college or school will provide such a service.

Subsidies: Sometimes you will find that the parent organisation will provide a cash reserve for the purposes of the project. They may stipulate conditions such as that the money has to be paid back. A subsidy is often given without the threat of financial penalties if the project fails. However, there may be non-financial penalties in that the project team may be considered incompetent if they cannot give good reason for their lack of success.

Try it out

Raising cash is fraught with problems. You may be too young to sign contracts or you may get into debt if the project goes wrong. It is essential that you establish the ground rules with your college or school on what actions on your part they will support or allow. You will also often need a long lead-in to raise start-up funds. It is essential that you discuss the principles of funding long before the project starts its operational stage, otherwise you will be trying to raise funds at the same time as you need them to spend on the project.

Find out at what age you can:

- open a savings account
- take out a loan
- become a director of a company.

Estimate costs

Estimating income always suffers from uncertainty because of the whims of the market. Estimating how much a project is going to cost can on the other hand be

CASE STUDY – Wages can go up or down

In the early 1990s local government leisure services were faced with tough competition from the private sector. A major element of the fixed costs of these government services was staff salaries, since many of the staff were permanent, full-time, and enjoyed benefits such as enhanced overtime and payment for working unsocial hours and holidays. The private sector did not do this. To become competitive many local authorities have moved towards fixed-term contracts and greater use of casual staff who do receive enhanced pay.

In the world of professional football, players' wages form a major part of the fixed costs of a club. Since the supply of top players is limited and there is competition from other clubs to sign them, wages and fixed costs escalate. For smaller clubs with fewer fans, ticket sales increasingly fall short of wages and therefore, these clubs are unable to sign star players. For the larger clubs, broadcast fees provide income to pay fixed costs and therefore, players' fees and fixed costs continue to escalate.

Questions

1 Apart from wages what other overheads does a football club have?

2 Identify the variable costs that a football club incur.

---

relatively accurate, providing you think carefully about it. There are two types of cost:

Fixed costs or overheads: These are the costs you incur even if no customers use your service (e.g. equipment and facility hire, licences). In many leisure projects these costs often take up most of the budget. For example, in leisure facilities such as sports centres, rates and insurance, energy and staffing costs will often make up over 80 per cent of the budget. It makes good business sense to work constantly at these and keep them as low as possible by looking for new suppliers or decreased charges, reducing staff or controlling wages, limiting expenses for staff and controlling the built environment.

Variable costs: These are costs that are a result of the customer using the service. For example, the costs of consumables like food which the customer uses. Some energy costs may be a direct result of customer use, such as the use of hairdriers or lighting for a hired pitch or squash court.

Some variable costs are not incurred if customers do not use certain resources (e.g. lighting, laundry charges). Costs are incurred, on the other hand, if the resource has to be purchased in anticipation of customer use. If the resource has a short shelf life, the provider is faced with the problem of wastage and unnecessary expense, or undersupplying the resource and not satisfying the customer.

There are solutions to the problem. A simple method is 'supply and return'. For example, you are running a Teddy Bears' Picnic for children in a park and will be giving each child a 'goody bag'. You don't know if five children will turn up or a hundred. You therefore purchase 100 goody bags with an agreement that those that are not used can be returned to the supplier and refunded. This method works well with items that are not perishable and are not associated with an event or date. Sports equipment is a good example.

Another method is a secondary purchase option. You place a minimum order with the supplier with the agreement that they will be

385

able to supply extra items at short notice. Thus, if bookings are going well or the weather looks set fine, you can accommodate the last-minute demand. This method is best used where the manufacturer has complex set-up procedures but once these are done can produce finished goods quickly, as with anything to do with printing (e.g. T-shirts, programmes). Similar to this is a standby option where you arrange to have a reserve of supplies available should there be a surge in customers. Casual staff or reserve transport (such as a reserve minibus) are good examples.

A fourth method is to have pre-booking which will give you information with which to forecast customer numbers before committing yourself to new orders.

Handling costs: These are costs that service providers charge for carrying out certain transactions. They are charged per transaction or per customer and are particularly common in the travel and tourism industries (e.g. travel agent's commission and airport charges). They are not so common in the

Financial charges are often made for handling cheques and credit card transactions, so often a minimum payment is set.

leisure and recreation industries, with one notable exception being commission charged by ticket agents. Financial charges are often made for handling cheques, withdrawing money and on credit card transactions. These may be as much as £1 per transaction, so for example, a small payment by cheque can incur a significant variable cost. As a result many companies try to encourage cash sales.

Your project faces a problem in that it is 'one-off' and the purchase of items such a racquets is very much related to use by a small number of customers. The racquets therefore become a significant part of the budget which may stop you reaching your desired profit levels. To avoid this you will need to find a strategy to reduce these costs. One way is to borrow them from the college store or a similar provider. Another way is to expect the customers to supply their own. A third option is to hire rather than purchase them.

Scenario building: If there is uncertainty attached to customer numbers it is usual practice when estimating variable costs to work out three scenarios. These are:

- worst case: highest costs you could expect
- likely case: costs you would be likely to expect
- best case: the lowest costs you could expect.

Keep in mind that fixed costs can usually be estimated accurately and don't require a scenario calculation. However, there are cases when you might want to calculate them on a scenario basis. You would usually do this for items that might change their prices over the time of the project. For example, petrol costs for a project could increase after the next budget, so you might cost the best case on the current price plus the rate of inflation, the likely scenario as current price plus five per cent and the worst case to include a ten per cent rise.

CASE STUDY – Getting more customers – a nasty shock

When calculating extra costs incurred by increasing customers we can use the formula:

extra fixed cost + (the expected number of customers x extra variable cost incurred by each customer) = total extra costs.

A tennis coach costs £100 a day (original fixed cost) and the governing body code of practice says that a coaching ratio of 10:1 (pupils to staff) is the maximum. Under your duty of care you need to stick to this. You are now faced with a dilemma. If you go above ten customers, you have to pay for another coach £100 (extra fixed cost). If you get twenty customers in all, the second coach generates the same cost per customer as the first (i.e. £100/10 customers = £10 per customer). In other words, you can spread the costs. However, if you succeed in attracting only eleven customers, that one extra customer is costing you the full £100 that the coach is charging. That extra £90 might wipe out all your profit if your profit target (i.e. income less costs) is less than £90 for the day.

There are variable costs as well. While you had tennis racquets available from store for the first ten customers you will now need to purchase a racquet at a cost of £15 for each extra customer. Thus, one extra customer incurs a variable cost of £15 while ten would cost the project £150 extra.

You now need to relate this back to your income. Each customer pays £10.

For the first ten customers you will receive £100 and spend £100. You break even.

For one extra customer you will receive £10 and spend £105. You are making a loss overall of £95.

For ten extra customers you will receive £100 and spend £150. You are still making a loss of £50.

Question

In this case expanding the course means you will increase your losses. What two strategies could you take to allow expansion of the course without incurring losses?

It is usual to allocate various types of expenditure to well-defined categories. Both fixed and variable costs fall into the same cost category and therefore will need to be combined to give your final estimate. Figure 6.9 shows some of the main categories a business would use, some of which will apply to your project costs.

Finally, it is time to combine the fixed and variable costs. If you think your project is pre-planned and is likely to show no variation in customer numbers then add them together. Where there is some doubt on variable costs you should use the scenarios and have a total for each. The reason for this is that you and/or your

Figure 6.9 Different types of costs incurred by businesses

CASE STUDY – Financial planning – a dim view

The solar eclipse as an event in Cornwall in 1999 was a classic case of variable costs not being offset by income. Several event organisers thought that there was an opportunity for staging events which would attract thousands of spectators.

To put on a festival of this sort costs many thousands of pounds in fixed costs. For example, advertising and promotion, renting sites and booking all the equipment for them, as well as bands and catering facilities. All these services work on a fixed basis and, once booked, the event organiser is committed to paying them even if they are not used. On top of that were the considerable variable costs of merchandising, such as T-shirts and souvenirs.

A PEST analysis of the environment would have suggested that there were good reasons why people might not come. These included:

- Cornish weather often throws up mist and rain in August
- TV technology is now so good that many people might stay at home to watch the eclipse
- It was in the middle of the holiday season, so would people give up other holidays to come to Cornwall?

There was room for doubts about the feasibility of the eclipse as an attractive event for customers. However, the organisers thought that they could afford a slightly risky plan. An unexpected development then arose in that the County Council became worried about the impact of up to a million extra tourists coming into Cornwall for the one day. Their worries about how to manage this problem were quickly picked up by the media and turned into a negative public relations programme which most probably discouraged a great many people. There were advance warning stories of a grid-locked Cornwall, rip-off prices, lakes of human waste and sewage, and pitched battles with New Age travellers.

As it happened, everything that could go wrong went wrong. The weather was bad, the TV films were great and the publicised nightmare of a grid-locked Cornwall on the day kept the public away. And so the income did not offset the fixed and variable costs that had been spent and huge amounts of money were lost. Some firms went bankrupt, including the illustrious Harvey Goldsmith Organisation which had been a leading festival promoter for over thirty years.

Questions

1 How could the organisers have reduced their costs?

2 What action could the organisers have taken to cover their loss of income?

3 What two factors will most seriously affect the outcome of a business plan?

4 Give another example of a business plan that has come to grief due to lack of income.

backers will know exactly what you are letting yourselves in for.

On a short-term project where availability of cash was a problem you might want to work on a weekly basis (see Table 6.2). Note you would not put explanatory text on the form as there is here, just the figures.

Table 6.2 is an extract and in the full version there would be all the cost categories and possibly more time periods. For a new business, start-up projections would be made over, say, three years on a monthly basis.

Having worked out your costs and when they will need to be paid for, you will now:

- know how much money you will have, at which times, and be able to keep the project out of the red
- be able to inform your financial backers about the cost of the project and when you will require loans and other income
- be able to manipulate payments to suit your ability to make them. For example, if you were short of cash in weeks one and two you might be able to schedule your purchase of equipment to week three.

Try it out

Here are some of the costs for Lymbridge Squash Club, a private sector sports club. The owner has made few changes to the club over the years, using the same suppliers and employing the same staff. Membership income is dropping away fast and something needs to be done.

Rates	£15,000
Permanent staff including bar staff	£70,000
Casual staff	£5,000
Cost of catering	£20,000
Lighting	£15,000
Heating	£10,000
Insurance	£5,000
Licences	£900

Now decide which of these are fixed costs and which are variable costs and total each. Make notes explaining why you have made each choice. Indicate two ways the club can reduce its overheads.

What you now need to know is: will you be able to pay for the project?

Table 6.2 Cost flow form: worst scenario

	Week						
Cost item	1	2	3	4	5 Day of event	6	7
Staff					2150 (wages)	50 (expenses)	
Equipment	60 (purchase 1)	70 (purchase 2)		100 (hire)			75 (penalty charge)
Facilities	50 (deposit)						150 (pay invoice)
Catering							120 (pay invoice)
Transport	150 (pay in advance)						
Total	260	70	0	100	2150	50	345

CASE STUDY – Estimating costs

Here is a layout for a form you might use for a sports leadership project involving a Teddy Bears' Picnic to which you transport children. Each child will be given a £3 meal voucher. If it is raining you expect 40 children, but if the weather is really sunny, there may be only about 30. You reckon that 35 would be a reasonable expectation.

We have restricted fixed costs to one scenario; if there were variable fixed costs, extra columns could be added.

Here are some interpretations of the figures in this form:

- with staffing you know that the five play leaders you will use will work for £50 each (fixed). However, you have agreed to pay their expenses up to £10 a head (variable). In the worst case the leaders have spent up to their limits, in the other cases they have been more frugal or perhaps have not had to travel so far.
- equipment has been both bought and hired (fixed at a cost of £230). The hire agreement has a clause that you will pay up to £75 if it is lost or damaged (variable). In the worst case you might lose the equipment. We have assigned

this to a variable cost as damage is most likely to result from customer use.

- the charge for facilities are for the hire of a hall for indoor games. This is a one-off charge – so a fixed cost of £200.
- catering: there are no fixed charges, each child is given a voucher so this is a variable cost.
- transport: hire of a coach will cost £150 and is a fixed cost.

Now for the final step you need to estimate these costs against a time frame – you will see why later. Unlike the action plan which works on calendar time (e.g. week beginning), financial plans work on periods. A normal time-span is to work on a monthly basis and then summarise for the year or quarter. Many people work on a thirteen-period year as opposed to calendar months as this avoids distortion due to long and short months. If you look in your diary you will see that the weeks are numbered 1–52, a thirteen-period year would be weeks 1–4, 5–8 and so on.

Questions

1 Why is there only one column for fixed costs?

2 Which item is most affected by sales?

Cost estimating sheet

Costs

Cost item	Fixed costs	Variable costs: worst	Variable costs: expected	Variable costs: best	Total costs: worst	Total costs: expected	Total costs: best
Staff	250	50	30	10	300	280	260
Equipment	230	75	0	0	305	230	230
Facilities	200	0	0	0	200	200	200
Catering	0	120	105	90	120	105	90
Transport	150	0	0	0	150	150	150
Total	830	245	135	100	1075	965	930

Estimate income

Remember income comes from two sources (Figure 6.10).

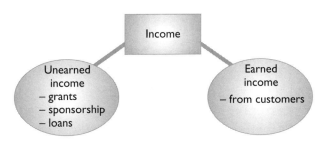

Figure 6.10 Sources of income

Once you have negotiated unearned income you will know when you will be receiving the money and how much. Like a fixed cost it is usually simple to estimate and put in the plan.

For earned income, you need to calculate the number of customers and visits they will make. You then multiply these customer numbers by any fees you are going to charge (e.g. membership). You also multiply number of visits by the usage charges (e.g. entrance fee), and by the estimated amount of ancillary income (e.g. food, souvenirs) that the customers will spend. Next, add the three together and you know how much you are going to earn.

Earned income = equals number of customers $\times$ fees + number of visits $\times$ usage charge + number of visits $\times$ estimated ancillary spending.

Try it out

Here is a simple example for a health club with an annual membership of 1,000. Annual membership is £100 and members pay £1 each time they go. The club knows that on average its members spend £1.50 on ancillary expenditure such as drinks. Over the year there are 100,000 visits.

What is the earned income of the club?

Note here that you take the number of *customers* when a charge is a one-off charge to a customer, and for other estimates use the number of *visits* (this takes into account the problem of some customers making frequent use of the facilities and others only occasional use). For one-off events such as a pop concert, visits will be the same as customers.

Unfortunately, there are complications which you will have to do your best to estimate.

- Supposing the customers don't turn up? Or supposing they come in droves? The three-scenario scheme has to be put into operation again.
- What price package are the customers going to use? Will they go for family discounts, concessions, free children schemes or any of the schemes that you have ingeniously invented in the marketing plan?
- When will they make their purchase? If you can get them to pay for the service in advance you are getting cash in to pay your bills. If they pay on account it may be some time after they use the service that you see your money.
- How do they pay? Cash is convenient (although it may incur extra costs for security), cheques can be a security risk, and credit cards may take longer to process and will also incur extra charges.
- What will they spend on drinks, refreshments and souvenirs? You can ask other people who have run similar activities and use that as a guide (e.g. £2.50 per customer). Circumstances on the day may cause variations from this estimate. Poor sales staffing may result in long queues which means that customers give up waiting for a drink or a snack.

Don't get too worried over these complications as they are more likely to occur

Thought for the page

Many health clubs offer heavy reductions on advance membership. Although this may have a marketing outcome in increased membership, its main purpose is often simply to get cash into the system. This sort of promotion does not necessarily mean that profits are lost in the long term because the reduction is made in the knowledge that the lifespan for a member for many clubs is short. This is because customers' good intentions (for example to get fit) often fade away.

with major projects. It is good that you know they exist as it will allow you to appreciate how projects like the Millennium Dome or the Royal Armouries have run into difficulties, largely because they miscalculated income.

For your project things will be much more manageable because:

- customer numbers are likely to be controlled by the capacity of the facilities and so you will have a good idea of the maximum number of customers
- your project is likely to have only one price, or maybe a couple of variations
- your customers are likely to pay up front or on the door
- ancillary income will fairly limited.

Having said this, it would still be sensible to make a sales forecast in your business. It should:

- describe the various sales options and pricing scheme
- explain your estimates of customer numbers and types
- give evidence if possible to justify your estimates of income (e.g. attendance at similar events).

Create the plan

The following is a worked example to show how costs and income are combined to produce a cash flow forecast.

Project, a disco, as planned and directed by Melanie.

'This project involves an end-of-term disco for students at our college. The maximum number of customers is 450 as determined by fire regulations. Previous discos of this sort have attracted on average 350 people, but occasionally numbers have been as low as 200 and at other times at maximum levels. We feel that this variation has been largely due to timing and the quality of the DJ. We have chosen a good night for the disco and have a top-line DJ. We feel that 350 would be our lowest audience, with 450 being attainable.

Pricing will be £5 in advance and £6.50 on the night and the week before. We expect 50 per cent of tickets to be sold at the lower price.

There will be little ancillary income as the hall owners retain the right to sell refreshments. However, we intend to sell £1 raffle tickets to 50 per cent of the audience.'

Fixed costs

Unlike the costs example earlier on, this project has largely restricted itself to a fixed cost schedule.

- Hire of hall   £200
- DJ   £250
- Printing tickets and posters   £100
- Hiring a light show   £50

We have decided to put on a buffet that is free to customers and the cost of which works out at £2 per head. This is the only variable cost.

Its financial success is now therefore dependent on accurate income estimates.

Income

'We have secured sponsorship of £200 from Fulskins Brewery which will add to our reserves of £100.'

We have estimated income on a scenario basis. There are two variables:

- *variation on discount ticket uptake:* shall allow 20 per cent variation each way of the 50 per cent
- *size of audience:* take 350 as a low, 400 as expected and 450 as the maximum.

We have calculated the amounts taken for each combination of variables by using a matrix like this:

	Advance/on-door sales		
	Audience size		
Ticket price	350	400	450
30% @ £5 70% @ £6.50	[(30/100) x 350 x 5] + [(70/100) x 350 x 6.50]= 525 + 1592.50 = **£2117.50**	[(30/100) x 400 x 5] + [(70/100) x 400 x 6.50]= 600 + 1820 = **£2420**	[(30/100) x 450 x 5] + [(70/100) x 450 x 6.50] = 675 + 2047.50 = **£2722.50** **best**
50% @ £5 50% @ £6.50	[(50/100) x 350 x 5] + [(50/100) x 350 x 6.50] = 875 + 1137.50 = **£2012.50**	[(50/100) x 400 x 5] + [(50/100) x 400 x 6.50] = 1000+1300= **£2300** **expected**	[(50/100) x 450 x 5] + [(50/100) x 450 x 6.50] = 1125 + 1462.50 = **£2587.50**
70% @ £5 30% @ £6.50	[(70/100) x 350 x 5] + [(30/100) x 350 x 6.50] = 1225 + 682.5 = **£1907.50** **worst**	[(70/100) x 400 x 5] + [(30/100) x 400 x 6.50] = 1400 + 780 = **£2180**	[(70/100) x 450 x 5] + [(30/100) x 450 x 6.50] = 1575 + 877.50 = **£2452.50**

The raffle income has been calculated in the same way. Allow 10 per cent variation on the expected sales of fifty per cent.

Worst= 40 per cent of 350= £140

Expected= 50 per cent of 400 = £200
Best= 60 per cent of 450 = £270

On this basis, income can be forecast as in the table below:

Income estimating sheet

		Income					
Income source	Unearned income	Earned income: worst	Earned income: expected	Earned income: best	Total income: worst	Total income: expected	Total income: best
Sponsorship	200				200	200	200
Tickets		1907.50	2300	2722.50	1907.50	2300	2722.50
Raffle		140	200	270	140	200	270
Total	200	2047.50	2500	2992.50	2247.50	2700	3192.50

Melanie is now in a position to make a cash flow analysis. This time combine costs and income using the time chart. It needs to be done for each of the three scenarios, and assume that ticket income is equally spread up to the disco.

You should also note that the timescale is shortened for the example; in the real project you would probably want six weeks or more to print and distribute publicity.

This is a cash flow forecast. It is probably the most important document you will produce for your business plan and will be referred to throughout the project to see if you are keeping to plan.

A feature that you must be aware of is the 'carry forward'. This is the cash you have in reserve (i.e. in the bank or in petty cash). In this case Melanie started the project with £100 – maybe the team all chipped in. The amount remaining after each time period is then carried forward to the top of the next column. You will see in this forecast that it is positive in all but one case – which means she has sufficient cash to pay for her costs. The exception to this is in week one where

Cash flow forecast: Melanie's disco – expected scenario

| | Week | | | | | | |
	1	2	3	4	5 Day of event	6	7
Cash in reserve/ brought forward	100	−100	+100	+600	+1050	+1500	
Income							
Sponsorship		200					
Tickets			500	500	1300		
Raffle					200		
Total income	0	200	500	500	1500	0	
Costs							
Facilities (hall hire)	100					100	
Staff (DJ)					250		
Equipment (light show)				50			
Catering (buffet)					800		
Printing	100						
Total costs	200	0	0	50	1050	100	
Surplus/deficit (income − costs)	−200	200	500	450	350	−100	
Cash in reserve + total income − total costs	−100	+100	+600	+1050	+1500	+1400	

the start-up money was not enough to pay that week's cash demands.

To avoid this she would review the business plan. She could:

- change the time that she purchased resources.
- obtain different credit terms. For example, ask to be invoiced rather than pay at the time. This can give her extra time to pay. Because she has the plan she knows in advance what the cash situation will be, so she can find a printer who will accept delayed payment rather than the cash-in-hand payment scheduled in the first draft of the plan.
- arrange with the sponsor to make payment earlier than originally agreed so that she starts the project 'cash rich'.

The first attempts at cash flow forecasts often reveal problems. If so, you may have to make changes to your original feasibility plan – by choosing alternative resources, charging more, generating more customers and so on until you get a plan that is both realistic and viable.

One final point to consider is *financial contingencies*. No matter how hard you plan, it is likely that some things will cost more than you expected. Perhaps due to an accident, or something getting broken, or because the supplier has increased the price. It is normal practice to allow for a financial contingency as a percentage of the expenditure budget. A reasonable amount would be five to ten per cent. Using three scenarios in effect provides a built-in contingency so it has been left off the analysis above. If there is only one cash flow analysis or budget, the normal way to express this is as an item at the bottom of the expenditure column.

A word of warning! Contingencies and best scenarios should not be used as a replacement for your spending limits or a way of upping your budget. Their purpose is to allow for a rescue line if you get into trouble. If you are cutting into contingencies, you should be examining future expenditure and income to see if you can get your financial objectives back on to plan.

Budgets and income targets: A budget is the amount of expenditure you have for a given period of time for the various cost categories. For a one-off project it will be the total costs of the project. For an ongoing work programme it will normally be for the financial year. In either case the budget is simply the final column of the cost estimating sheet.

Income is often not included in a budget but allocated to a divisional 'pot' from which allocations are made to pay for each budget. This does not mean to say that a budget holder is not interested in income and, where he or she is expected to produce income as well as spend it, there will be income targets, which are in effect the right-hand column of the income estimating sheet.

Profit and loss: While the cash flow analysis will give you a detailed plan and forecast you will need a summary document to show to your backers and to use in summarising the financial outcome of your project. This is called a profit and loss account (Figure 6.11).

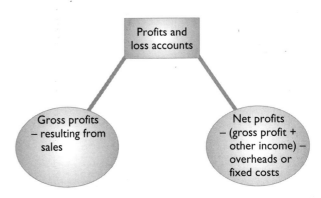

Figure 6.11 Profit and loss account

This division can be useful as it can indicate where an organisation needs to improve to increase its profits. For example, it is not unusual to find that an organisation is trading very well and making good gross profits but that these are drained out by excessive overheads to produce a net loss. This is particularly so with a new organisation which will have high set-up costs in the first stage of its development.

For your project, the purpose of a profit and loss account will largely be as a convenient summary to persuade backers to support you. You will also produce a second version at the end of the project that shows actual rather than estimated figures.

Calculating profit and loss is simple.

Sales give *Gross turnover*

Subtract from gross turnover the variable costs (*Cost of sales*)

This gives you the *Trading profit* or *Gross profit*:

> *Gross turnover – cost of sales = Trading profit or Gross profit*

You now add in *Other income* such as grant aid, sponsorship, sales of old equipment.

You now need to subtract the fixed costs or *Expenses*

And this gives the *Net profit or loss*

> *(Gross profit + other income) – expenses = Net profit or loss*

Here are the calculations using the disco cash flow:

Profit and loss account for the disco

Income

Sales		2,500
Gross turnover/income		2,500

Cost of sales

Buffet	800	
Total cost of sales	800	
Gross profit		**1,700**

Other income

Teams donation		100
Sponsorship		200
Total other income		300
		2,000

Expenses

Facilities	200	
Staff	250	
Equipment	50	
Printing	100	
Total expenses	600	

Net profit 1,400

The final document you would normally find in a full-scale business plan is a *balance sheet*. This is basically a snapshot of an organisation at a given point in time – often the end of the financial year.

Essentially it shows:

- what an organisation owns – fixed assets (buildings, vehicles)
- what it is owed – current assets (bank accounts, stocks, debtors)
- what it has borrowed in the short term – current liabilities (creditors)
- what it has borrowed in the long term – long-term liabilities (loans)
- where its money comes from – finance (capital, profits).

Balance sheets show the financial health of an organisation, but it is unlikely that you will need to produce one for your project as most of the categories will show no entry – since you own nothing, will have cleared your debts and will have received payments. You should have only current assets in the form of your profits now safely deposited in the bank.

Funding sources: Now you know the size of your budget and any shortfalls within it, you need to include in your business plan a short section on how you intend to fund the project. This section in the plan describes the ways in which you intend to raise the money (e.g. loans, grants, sponsors) and possible sources (e.g. named banks or sponsors). You should also include any implications resulting from obtaining the money. For example, the sponsor may request that you use their logo on all publicity. Another factor may be the conditions of payback such as interest rates.

Professional support: Commercial firms would identify their accountants and other professional services in a plan. For your project you should give details of:

! Check it out

1 What information is needed to create a financial plan?

2 Why is earned income not a source of funds for a new project?

3 Give three methods of finding start-up funds – what are their advantages and drawbacks?

4 What is the difference between fixed and variable costs?

5 Why do you need to produce more than one cash flow analysis?

6 How can a cash flow analysis be used to help the business plan?

7 Why is unearned income easier to estimate than earned income?

8 Explain some of the options you might have if you found a cash flow problem in a cash flow analysis.

9 What is the difference between gross and net profits?

10 Give examples of professional support.

- your bank or how you intend to secure and or process money
- insurers (you will certainly need 'public indemnity' and possibly other insurances against loss, theft, damage of items)
- your legal support (e.g. college solicitors)
- the names and addresses of the people who will sign cheques (normally two signatures are required on a project check – that way you can go on a long holiday to Rio with a friend!)
- details of how you are going to present financial records (a simple ledger showing expenditure and income details (amount, date, paid by whom, received by whom would be sufficient, but a ready-made computer package such as Intuit Quick Books makes life easy).

Special factors

Sometimes a project will depend upon special conditions for it to be able to go ahead. For example you may need approval to use facilities, as would be the case when you are trying to get free use of the college sports hall. Or you may need a licence to run a lottery or have a licensed bar. Many projects in the community rely on Lottery and other grants and cannot proceed until they have received the go-ahead that they will receive a grant.

These special factors must be seen as priorities in the plan and need to be solved before any other work can go ahead.

Administration

Administration is the glue of a project. It is the paperwork and systems that are used to make sure the project goes smoothly and that the project can provide evidence that it is doing the work effectively, legally and honestly.

- It makes the project efficient by ensuring that all tasks are completed and not forgotten or duplicated (e.g. two people do not visit the same sponsor to raise money).

- It ensures security by recording where cash and resources are and securing them.
- It maintains good customer and supplier relations by ensuring that bookings are made and services delivered and that bills are paid.
- It allows effective monitoring and evaluation.

In your business plan you would briefly describe the following:

- handling of correspondence and communication
- monitoring of work
- evaluation procedures
- the meetings you would hold and how they would be recorded.

In practice, however, you need to know and apply much more.

Administrative medium

The main choice is between paper systems (e.g. filing cabinets, memos) and computers (desktops and e-mails).

Computers are extremely useful in tracking and manipulating large amounts of information or for keeping filing systems. These benefits increase with the size of the project, the longer it lasts or the more repetitive it becomes. The standard packages you use are shown in Figure 6.12.

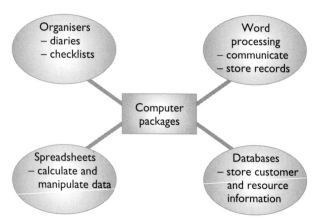

Figure 6.12 Standard computer packages

> **Think it over**
>
> Computerised administration is a mixed blessing and you should not assume that computers are superior to paper systems. For example, if you have 200 customers to contact a word processor and database will allow you to write one letter and the computer will do the rest, individually addressing each letter and inserting sentences which are relevant to that customer alone. This is evidently a wonderful saving in time and work.
>
> But if you have only five customers the time taken to create the database will probably be far longer than the time needed to write five individual letters.
>
> Think of some other situations within the leisure and recreation industry where computers are not necessarily superior to paper systems.

Also available are software packages for booking and project management. However, both of these are more suited to large-scale projects and you may find them a hindrance for your project.

With small projects you will need to make a decision – whether it is worth taking the time to set up computerised systems or more efficient to rely on paperwork. Remember also that the your team members will either have to be competent or need to be trained in using hi-tech tools and be able to access them. For example, to receive an e-mail you need to have access to the Web (which many people do not have); but to receive a phone call you need only to be on the phone (which most people are).

You will be well advised, however, to use word processors for any correspondence with customers and other people outside the team with whom you need to communicate. This is simply because typed letters look far more professional and reflect your project image.

Many of us like computer filing because it does away with the time-consuming job of filing many pieces of paper or searching for

	Date and time	From	To	Message	Contact No	Received	Action
	12.2.00 12.30	Chris	Sam	Mr Hardy from Victory Marine phoned about sponsorship for the regatta	013567 234576	**13.2.00** **11.35**	Phoned back and will visit Mon next

An office diary

misplaced documents, but if your computer crashes or is stolen you will have lost your entire administrative system, so always back up at the end of each session.

If we assume that you use computerised systems for outgoing correspondence and paper systems for all other administration, what are you going to need apart from a PC?

Communication and open information are essential in a project. An office diary or wall planner to show when meetings are, where people are and key dates in the plan is vital.

Computers are extremely useful in tracking and manipulating large amounts of information

Similarly, you will want to get a pad of carbonised message forms or an A4 message book (a page-to-a-day diary is fine) and rule it like the above example.

Records of meeting

After a meeting you can spend a long period of time making notes about who said what to whom. Why bother? The purpose of meetings is to find out what is happening and to decide what to do.

Decide what you are going to discuss before the meeting and send everyone in the team an agenda a few days before to allow them to prepare for the meeting. This will say:

- who is to come to the meeting
- where it is
- when it is
- main points to be discussed.

After the meeting simply give a list of action points for each of the agenda items, who is going to action them and by when. It is also a good idea to refer the action back to the objective it is fulfilling and provide some comments saying what the person is going to do or pointing out any problems there may be.

Book-keeping basic requirements

Book-keeping is the recording of money coming into and out of a project. It is important in order to keep track of money and also because it is evidence that those handling money have been honest and can account for it. Under company law it is a legal obligation.

Team meeting action notes

When: 20 April   Place: in the Canteen

Present: Jim, Steve, Lara, Warren, and Ali   Absent: Tamsin

Agenda item	Action points	Objectives	Who?	Deadline	Comments
Promotion	Finalise artwork for poster	M1 (design posters)	Jim Whistler	4 May	Jim will present team with 3 versions of the poster to choose from
"	Finalise printing costs and dates	M2 (print and distribute publicity)	Lara Clarke	5 May	Lara will get three quotes from printers and pass artwork to the best
Resourcing	Book pitch	R4	Asif Patel	3 May	Asif will make a provisional booking but will confirm later when entries are known

There are simple rules for handling money:

- always give a receipt for a sale (a numbered ticket, a till record or a written invoice are all acceptable)
- never pay out money unless you have an invoice or receipt. This includes giving your friends money for goods they have bought
- always make a record of money you have paid out
- keep all money secure (in a bank, a safe, or a locked drawer)
- never leave money without securing it
- never let money accumulate
- never borrow project money for your own use – even for buying a Mars Bar in the canteen

Here is your list of initial tasks to do with money:

- open a bank account
- buy a cash book or computer software programme
- buy a petty cash book so that team members can sign out small amounts of money to make purchases
- buy a receipt and invoice book with carbon copies
- find a secure place for temporarily storing money and cheques (desk and lockable cash box, or safe).

Booking systems

Some project like courses and theatre seating require places to be reserved (and possibly data to be kept about customers). Bookings may be recorded (on computer or in a book) from application forms or booking forms.

Monitoring

The other side to financial administration is monitoring the budget; in other words, seeing that you are keeping to the budget. Traditional methods such as double entry book-keeping are recognised for accountancy purposes but difficult to learn in a short time. Lovejoy suggests a simple form that for all practical purposes does the job. We have modified it (Figure 6.13). If you want to use his entire system you need to read Chapter 3 in his book.

When you are drawing up your budgets you will have calculated what you will need and how much each item will cost. Each of these items needs to be given a number and put on a master list. Next, you need to work out which items will be used for each of the project objectives (e.g. marketing, administration). For example, one milestone or objective might be to 'equip course' and this might involve items such as purchasing tennis balls or buying sweatshirts for the leaders.

At the start of the project, for each milestone, put all the items on the form, and in the budget column put what you expect to pay for them. At the bottom of that column in the projected budget box **B** put the total cost of the column. This will remain constant as it is your target budget.

Now make plenty of copies of this master form and then record actual expenditure on it (say on a weekly basis) in the 'actual' column. If you have not spent anything on an item that week then leave that line blank. Now mark off on the budget column those items which you have spent on this week. Add up these budget items and put the total in box **A** – this is the amount you should have spent this week if you are on budget. Now total up the actual column and put the sum in box **C**, this is what you spent for that week. Now add this to last week's box **D** and enter the amount in this week's box **D**. This is your total spending to date.

It is also a good idea when you spend on an item to tick it off in the item column and to carry these ticks over to the next week.

Finally, write in the final column, 'variance,' the difference between the budget and actual columns for each item you have spent on in the current week. If the difference is a positive you are under budget (well done); if it is negative, you are over budget (look out).

Now add these up and put the sum in box **E**. This is how much you are above or below budget for the week. If you add this to last week's box **F** and enter that in the current box **F** you get the total variation to date.

Now for the final stroke – colour code all variations. Use the traffic lights:

Green for all positive variations. You are on course no action needed

Orange for minuses that are within contingency levels (e.g. the variation is less than five per cent of the budget). Note to get back on course

Red for minuses above contingency level. Serious problem – seek action as to how you can get back on course.

The great thing about this system is that it allows each person who is responsible for objectives to be fully aware of his/her spending actions. It also allows the person in charge of the budget as a whole to see how the entire project is progressing. To do this,

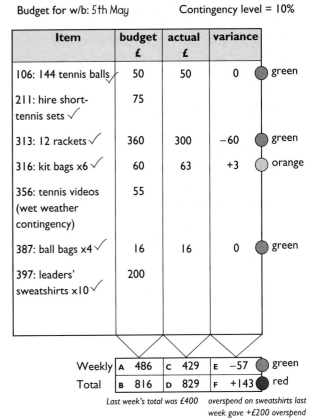

Milestone: equip course

Budget for w/b: 5th May   Contingency level = 10%

Item	budget £	actual £	variance	
106: 144 tennis balls ✓	50	50	0	green
211: hire short-tennis sets ✓	75			
313: 12 rackets ✓	360	300	−60	green
316: kit bags x6 ✓	60	63	+3	orange
356: tennis videos (wet weather contingency)	55			
387: ball bags x4 ✓	16	16	0	green
397: leaders' sweatshirts x10 ✓	200			

Weekly	A	486	C	429	E −57	green
Total	B	816	D	829	F +143	red

Last week's total was £400   overspend on sweatshirts last week gave +£200 overspend

Figure 6.13 A budget monitoring sheet allows personal and up-to-date control of the budget by all team members involved in purchasing

all the team members will give their totals to the co-ordinator, who enters these on a master list that contains all the milestones and their estimated total expenditure.

Have a look at the completed form (Figure 6.13) for the order equipment milestone.

You can see from this that the actual spend this week has been well within budget (–£57). But because the bottom row keeps a track on the total or cumulative spend to date we can see that a large overspend the previous week on sweatshirts (due to a misunderstanding with the supplier) has meant that the budget is heading for a serious overspend.

Action is needed to get back on budget. A glance at the ticks shows that only the videos and short-tennis sets remains, so if you spend on neither you can retrieve the budget. You go back to the team and explain the problem. You decide to cancel the videos and use some from the college library. A phone call to the Tennis Development Officer who is supplying the kit results in her waiving the hire charge.

Action plan

The preceding stages of business planning have provided detailed evidence for and against the original action plan. Throughout the business planning you will have been modifying the action plan in response to this information. This modified plan will become the final plan and will be at the team headquarters. For the purposes of the printed business plan you will probably simply write a summary in a series of paragraphs, each of which describes the main objectives and the tasks involved and how they will be staged.

Another way is to describe it in project stages:

- planning and securing finance
- event preparation
- event implementation

- evaluation and review
- further developments/long-term plans.

Implementation

If you have planned well, implementation of the project should go well. Certainly things will go off course sometimes, or you may feel stressed because you cannot meet a deadline for a milestone or have to put in extra effort to get there. But overall the plan, if followed, will take you to your goal. Much of the success of what you do as a team will depend on the degree to which you have committed yourself to:

- *the project and its goals*: If you have, your enthusiasm will enable you to 'sell' the project to customers and stakeholders. It will also fuel your resolve to get through the bad times and succeed.
- *being a team player*: This means you will accept your role in the team even if it is not one of the 'star roles', you will be proud to be part of the team and get satisfaction from its overall success. Get used to talking in a team way – use 'we' instead of 'I'. Support, don't gloat over others' failures or the problems of your team-mates. When you have individually

A hectic social life can interfere with your ability to work and let down the team

succeeded, don't take all the credit for your success but thank your team-mates for what they have done.

- *customer service*: Working in a team is going to test your service to your internal customers and you will find the skills you picked up earlier very useful. Working in a team can get heated and people can annoy you easily. If they do, here is a tip that works: breathe very slowly and count to ten and use the time to think about what that person is thinking or feeling.

- *being fit for purpose*: When you are working in a team you need to be fit for purpose just as much as any piece of equipment. You need to be alert and be able to make decisions and behave in an effective and attractive way. Not being up to the job means you let your team mates down and keeping fit is entirely your responsibility. Good team workers will always make sure that whatever happens in their social life they will be fully fit to work. Some people have a heroic ability to ignore how they feel and turn in a top performance, even if they are nursing a terrible hangover and have just broken up with their partner. While this is truly professional, it is much simpler to plan your life a bit better. If you know that you are involved in a task: get rested, leave off any abusive habits and make sure the rest of your life and study is not going to interfere.

- *the systems*: If you have designed administrative or communication systems, they apply to you just as they do to the rest of the team. If you don't adhere, you will be causing a point of conflict every time you decide not to conform. High on the list of annoying habits are failing to keep receipts for expenditure, losing petty cash, putting things back in the wrong place or not putting them away, forgetting to give messages, and turning up late.

With these thoughts in mind, let's look briefly at some of the points featured in the AVCE specification.

Task completion

We all have a tendency not to finish what we are doing. There are two ways round this problem. Grit your teeth and get on with it but promise yourself a reward when you have done it. This is why it is good for the team to be rewarded when a milestone has been achieved. The other way is to team up with a person who has good finishing skills (remember Belbin). 'Don't put off to tomorrow what can be done today' is an old saying and one which every project worker should follow.

Deal politely with your team mates

This is basic customer care as applied to the internal customer. In teams things can get stressed so remember to remain 'adult'. Be open. Statements like this are helpful:

'I don't feel we are achieving too well – how does everyone else feel – what are we not getting right?'

'I don't feel I am coping very well here, can someone help me?'

'Do you know that when you do that it is making it difficult for me to do my tasks?'

Sometimes you may find that people will not try to adapt to the group or are a liability. If so, this needs explaining to them, and if they will not change or cannot be found another role it is permissible to ask them to leave the group.

Supporting the team

The action plan you are working to is designed to be a guide, not a set of regulations. A team works far better if people are flexible about their tasks. If you have finished one task, offer to help someone who might be flagging. Or you may be more efficient by offering a team member a lift or doing one of their tasks because it is convenient for you when you are doing one of your own.

There are times when motivation flags. The team joker can often raise spirits with a joke but sometimes this is misplaced. A more constant spur to motivation is to concentrate on what has been achieved and how the team has overcome similar problems in the past. Remind the team what their goal is and paint a picture of how the customers are going to feel if you fail and how they will feel if you succeed.

Like the Three Musketeers, teams are 'all for one, one for all'. Be sure that you do not run down team members in front of other team members or to your customers. If you have a gripe, air it in an adult way within the group with the person present. If you are deviating from the plan or you can see difficulties ahead don't bottle it up but tell the team at the earliest opportunity as this will give greater time to solve the problem as a group.

Getting help and advice

Neither team members nor the team as a whole can be expected to know everything they need to. It is normal practice to seek advice and information. In many large companies there is a recognised system of mentors where senior managers (who are meant to know everything!) visit other senior managers to discuss their problems and how they can handle certain situations.

In your project your course tutor could agree to take on such a role or you may want to enlist the help of students on a more advanced course such as an HND. There are other sources of advice. If you are using professional services, a bank manager or

accountant will advise you. Do any of the team have such a person in their family?

Many new businesses use advice services and training provided by regional development programmes. For your project you may be able to find similar sources by going to other departments such as Psychology or Business Studies. For example, the former may be able to do a Belbin test on the team, while the latter may have computer software for accounting.

The Development Officers from local councils and members of the Governing Bodies of Sport would be able to advise you on sources of funding, planning and programming problems. Because of the potential importance of what they can offer it is wise to seek their advice early on and even before you start the project. This is because they are busy people and their cycles of work are long. If you approach them early there may be time for them to find funding for you or even allow you to incorporate your project into their programme of activities.

Check it out

1 What administrative procedures would you describe in the business plan?

2 Give advantages and disadvantages of computer and paper-based systems.

3 What would you include in an agenda – what is its purpose?

4 What would you record in the minutes of a meeting?

5 Give two methods of monitoring the budget.

6 What should be included in an action plan for the business plan?

7 Explain ways in which you can show commitment to the team.

8 Assess your ability to complete tasks – how could you improve your performance or overcome weaknesses?

6.4 Evaluating the project

Setting targets and monitoring

Look back to when you were first setting up the project. You will remember that when you set your objectives you tested them to see if they were sound and measured them to see if they were realistic and achievable. We measure the success of an objective by setting targets. You have already read about these in Unit 5 on customer service. They can be measured in terms of:

- inputs (e.g. your project supplied a top coach and good-quality courts and equipment)
- outputs (e.g. 25 people attended the course)
- outcomes (e.g. 85 per cent of participants have taken up tennis).

Try it out

Think of the last time you went to a live entertainment event or the cinema. Identify indicators that would measure the following objectives:

- to optimise the market mix to attract 90 per cent capacity audiences
- to provide customers with a highly enjoyable experience.

At the planning stage you will have looked at all your milestones and main objectives and decided:

- what measurement can be used to measure what you are aiming for
- how much of that measure will indicate that you have achieved the goal
- when the target should be reached.

Many of these will be quite easy to decide. For example, if your milestone is to produce 100 posters by 5 May, you either have or have not achieved that target on that date.

Things become harder when you start to qualify your objectives by using adjectives like sufficient, effective, quality, greater, less. Your objectives become *relative* in their meaning and you have first to decide what you mean by that objective and what will measure it. For example, you may have an objective 'to promote the tennis course effectively'. To promote effectively presumably means that you would expect the promotion to result in customers. So your measurement might be the number of customers who come on the course. However, in marketing terms you might want it to produce an over-demand. So maybe the number of enquiries is a better measurement? At what level it becomes effective is a matter of discussion – some of you may decide that a full course is the target level while others may say it should be a full course plus a waiting list of ten per cent to allow for dropouts. The more ambitious might go for a waiting list that is big enough to turn into a second course. The choice is yours but remember to be SMART.

A final point on setting targets is that you are looking for *change* when achieving objectives. To be able to measure change you will need a reference point of what things were like before you started the programme. For example, with the goal 'to develop the tennis skills of children' you need first to know how skilled the children are before the course so that you can say if they have developed by the end of it. Two assessments are therefore needed. One at the start and one at the end.

Reference points are needed for any evaluation, so don't forget to include them in your planning, otherwise you may have nothing with which to compare.

Customer evaluation

The purpose of a leisure experience is usually enjoyment or self-development. The more our objectives are focused on the customer experience the harder it is to define measures

405

as they usually rely on outcomes or outputs. For example, take the first goal in the tennis course 'to make holidays a happy time for children'.

Input: The fact that we have provided a course with a qualified coach tells us little about what the customer gained from the project.

Output: Repeat bookings or requests for another course would be good output measurement. The logic here is that happy children book extra courses. Can this assumption be justified? You should be aware that some children get put on courses, others go because their friends are going, some book because there is nothing else to do – for these children their happiness button has not been pushed – even though the outputs would suggest it has.

Outcomes: Subjective assessment can be used. Listen out for comments like 'This is the best holiday I've had in years' and look out for smiling faces. Written or spoken *testimonials* are quite often used as indicators of target achievement. They are, however, like a

snapshot, pretty selective and difficult to quantify. You and your team mates' shared perception may be as good an indication as can be obtained.

Exit and entrance surveys

Surveys are by far the best way of accurately measuring outcomes. You can reduce the cost and time needed for doing them by carrying out surveys of your customers at the time of the course. Exit surveys ask people questions about their experience at its conclusion. You could ask them 'How much has this course increased your enjoyment during these holidays?' A lot, a bit, not much, not at all. You can also carry out entrance surveys which ask the customer questions such as what they expect to get out of the experience. If you carry out both, you have a reference point to measure change.

Surveys have two important functions:

- they actually ask the customer what he/she has experienced (rather than you making assumptions)
- the results can be quantified and matched against targets. If the target is narrowed so that we expect 80 per cent (for example) of customers to be happy or very happy with the course, the results can be matched to indicate whether we have achieved our objective.

Repeat bookings do not always mean everyone is happy

Think it over Think of some questions you might ask in an entrance and exit survey for an outdoor leisure facility

Team performance

Team outcomes

As is usual with an outcome, you will probably need to ask team members to assess their feelings about how the team has changed or what it has achieved. You could ask questions such as 'Do the team members have confidence in each other?', 'Is the team now more capable of taking on other challenges?', 'In what way does the team show that it has matured as a team?' Sometimes observation alone may indicate how well the group is working. For example, do members of the team turn up when they don't have to, or does the team get together outside the project?

Team output

There may be output measurements that will indicate how the team is performing. For example, the number or length of meetings it needs (these normally reduce if the team is working well – although if they go below a certain level they may indicate that the team is fragmenting). The speed and accuracy of passing on messages to other members of the group might also reflect a cohesive group that is working well. While the number of conflicts or people refusing to work with others are indicators of the extent of cohesiveness and therefore stage of group formation that has been reached.

Financial targets are also usually measured in terms of indicators. There are various measures of profitability, such as the amount of money made or income versus expenditure, while profit versus expenditure is an indicator of efficiency. You may also want to compare your financial performance to that of other projects. The Audit Commission's guides are a useful source for financial indicators.

Team output, like other measures, needs reference points. If measures are made continuously, these outcomes will also serve as monitoring measurements to see if the team is on target.

Financial objectives are a good example. Using the variance-based form described earlier, the budget can be measured weekly

and actions taken if the programme is going off target. Quality standards also need to be tracked continuously if they are promising a continuous level of performance. For example, you may have introduced into your project a guarantee to customers of a 24-hour response time to bookings; if you have, you would keep a log and note if there was a deviation from the standard, and then take steps to rectify it.

To summarise, the following decisions need to be made at the planning stage:

- how an objective can be measured
- when it should be measured
- what level of measurement indicates the achievement of the objective.

It is important to remember that once you have set your targets you must not change them. If you do, you are moving the goalposts and cheating yourself. It is surprising how often people do this in work – for example, only four people turn up and the course is suddenly judged a success because those who came enjoyed themselves.

Evaluation

The final stage of the project is evaluation and review. We have reached the end of the event.

The first thing to do is take a break. Everyone is hyped up on the day itself and afterwards, over the next few days, everyone feels a bit flat and tired. This combination means that feelings and opinions can be distorted or exaggerated. If the event was a success everyone thinks they can take on the world next time and that everything they have done has been perfect – savour the moment. If it did not go so well then the opposite applies. Whatever the outcome, now is not the time to have an inquest.

Think of a stressful or important day you spent recently – such as taking an exam.

Think how you felt the night before, immediately you went into the exam, your reaction after the exam and then how you felt the next day when you had thought about all the mistakes you had made. Your feeling after running an event will probably be very similar. So give it a few days and then get down to the business of evaluation.

In order to get a balanced and full assessment the project and team achievement must be analysed as a team. If the team is supportive it can also be a powerful means of helping individuals realise how they have contributed, how they have developed and how they could improve their performance.

There are three stages to evaluation:

Stages of evaluation

Evaluation will occur at three levels:

- project achievement
- team achievement
- personal achievement.

Preparation

First get your data together. Some information you will have been recording and sorting out throughout the project and at the event itself and will be ready to use – for example, customer enquiries, bookings, attendance numbers. Other data will need to be collected or put into some order. For example, there may be a need to analyse questionnaires and put the results into tables or histograms. Financial data is almost certainly going to need tidying up and a final account created.

Evaluation

There will be members of the team who will have been busy finishing off or analysing data and they will have been busy after the event, but the evaluation of this data and the review of the project are best done by the whole team. Just as you all started the project with planning so you finish it with a team meeting that looks at the project from all angles. Because evaluation will often entail criticism, and some of it may be personal, you need to use the rules of engagement that you should be familiar with by now:

- everyone gets a say and those who are naturally quiet should be encouraged to give their views.
- be honest – don't try to fudge the results. You will get more credit from spotting non-achievement and suggesting improvement than from trying to claim success where there was none.
- don't cast blame – it will only throw people on to the defensive and tempt them to attack back. Remember the 'all for one' code. If someone has let the team down, the team should have been alert to it and can be collectively at fault if it has let poor performance go unchecked. If, for example, you criticised Lara by saying 'Of course Lara not turning up until halfway through the day didn't help things at all', you can expect Lara to respond with an accusation of some poor performance on your part or go into some sob story asking the team how they could be so cruel. Neither gets the evaluation very far. The correct way to approach this is to adopt your best transactional analysis skills from customer care and start a discussion with 'staffing on the day – we had a problem in the morning because we were understaffed, what were the reasons for this and what can we do about it in future?'
- learn to take criticism. This can be difficult, especially when you feel you

have given your best shot in your work. It is good practice not to respond immediately but to probe and clarify the criticism. Lara could ask:

'Why do you think my being late affected our overall performance?'

'When you say I turned up halfway through the day could you be a bit more specific about how late I was?'

'Are you aware that I telephoned Steve to say I would be late?'

Staying in 'adult' mode Lara could now respond 'Yes I am very sorry about that. It couldn't be helped although I can see it must have been annoying if my message did not get through. I am glad we have cleared up the matter that I was only 30 minutes late and I would ask you all if you think that my lateness affected the achievement of the day?'

Of course it may be that Lara should take a more positive approach. 'Yes, I did oversleep and I am sorry if I let you down – I really shouldn't have gone to the disco the night before. You did all warn me. Can I suggest though that in future we keep a list of all our numbers so that if anyone is late again someone could phone to find out what is happening?'

- appoint a chairperson. As with any meetings things will get out if order if there is no one leading the group. The chairperson's role is to:
  - make sure only one person talks at a time
  - make sure everyone gets a chance to contribute
  - keep the group on the subject and not digress
  - ensure that the above rules are kept to
  - summarise the outcomes of the meeting.

Project evaluation

The team needs to focus on the achieving of goals and objectives, and the reasons for success or failure. The first task is to decide if you achieved the objectives and their targets in terms of the time and performance. This should be quite simple if you have devised an effective measuring system. You should also ask questions about the objectives themselves, particularly if the outcome is way off target. If the results are unclear, it is likely that the objective did not lend itself to measurement or the measure you used was not suitable. Think about how you would write the objective next time or what other measure you could have used.

If the outcome is way off target you need to ask if the objective was realistic or achievable or whether you got the milestones wrong. For example, if you had sent out 30,000 leaflets for a course for 12 it would be the promotion objectives that were unrealistic rather than the course itself. In contrast, if one poster had produced 300 applicants it would seem likely that you misjudged market demand. Next time you would aim to have a series of courses to meet this demand.

You also need to examine what failings of critical points may have resulted in objectives not being reached. Financial management is a classic critical point in most projects. Until you have cash to spend, nearly all other tasks will remain provisional or not possible. For example, even though you may have found a sponsor early on in the project, the actual funds may not have come through for a while. This resulted in a delay in sending promotional artwork to the printers, so that there was inadequate time to distribute the brochures. Customers had little time to respond or fit the event into their diaries, meaning that the event was a failure. By tracking back to the critical point you would identify this weakness and realise that in future you

409

would need either to make sure that the sponsor delivered as promised or allow more time to raise the funding before starting on the project.

Focusing on the reasons for success or failure is important, because we can find out how to improve performance next time or learn from good practice this time. Where there have been successes or problems you need to ask 'why?' The real reason why something has happened is not always obvious and you need to be analytical. For example, one of your milestones was to 'promote the course effectively' and this was measured by the number of applications you received. Fine, you hit the target so you achieved your goal. However, supposing the applications had started coming in before you launched the promotion, or when you asked applicants how they had heard about the course they said 'from someone on your team'. These applications were clearly not a result of promotion and on further investigation you find out that the applicants turned out to be friends of the team members who had been inadvertently selling the course to them. With this information you can now say that you did

not achieve the marketing objective or at least not using the method you thought would work. The implications of this are that next time you could save your printing bill and use personal selling as your preferred promotional technique.

Team evaluation

Discovering the reasons for success or failure of the project as a whole often lies in understanding the process that produced it and the performance of the team. For example:

What worked well or poorly?	
What actions or systems helped the team get around problems or difficulties?	
What threats or opportunities occurred and did we respond appropriately to these?	
What were our team's strengths or weaknesses?	
Did we get the timing right?	
Were we economical and were there also times when we penny-pinched and lost effectiveness?	

Think it over

Although we are talking about the final evaluation here, it is worth noting that these are questions that you should be asking yourself throughout the life of the project, whether at weekly meetings or when you are doing your tasks. Furthermore, the answers you get are not just academic but may demand immediate action. Although you cannot change your objectives or deadlines you can change the tasks or use of resources to meet them. Your answers to these questions will tell you what you should be doing.

When you have completed your project come back and ask yourself the above questions. Did you have to change your tasks or use of resources to meet your objectives and deadlines?

Personal performance

One of the important things about working in a team is that it gives you an insight into yourself and your personal capabilities, and also the opportunity to develop yourself. Although you may prefer to evaluate yourself by yourself, it is far better to take advantage of the support and feedback of a team meeting or of talking to colleagues to get a balanced picture of yourself. Some people who are very confident may collect comments that will surprise them. However, most of us tend to undervalue ourselves and will find group insight an experience that builds confidence and brings rewards. For example, Gavin hates being in the limelight and opts for the tasks he sees as easy, such as book-keeping. At the team meeting he expects the 'stars' to get all the praise and is surprised to find that several team members feel that he has held the project together by his conscientious approach to finance and his iron will in not letting funds be misspent. He is even more surprised to find that the team finds his dry sense of humour really funny. Their only criticism is that he doesn't join in – though with his new-found self-confidence he now knows he won't find it so difficult to join in with the team.

Questions about self-development often centre around such issues as:

- how did I work and get on with the rest of the team?
- what did I find hard or easy and why?
- what did I do best or least well and why?
- what have I learnt about myself from working in the team?
- how could I achieve better in terms of my personal characteristics?

Review

At this stage the project is 'water under the bridge' and no matter how good or bad it was we can do nothing to alter the situation. Adopting the motto 'onwards and upwards', we now need to look at what the next project will be and decide how we can improve our team performance or widen or raise our goals. The lessons of the past are a major consideration here and to conclude evaluation we need to review what we have done and how we would do it better next time.

The review process will therefore ask questions on issues such as:

- what are the implications of this project for future goals and objectives?
- what changes would we make to the tasks and resources we use?
- how could we make better use of time?
- what changes would we make to the systems we used?
- what changes would we make to the team structure and membership?
- how do we need to develop the team for new work and goals?

> ### Check it out
>
> 1. What are the categories of performance indicators?
> 2. What is a reference point used for?
> 3. What are testimonials?
> 4. What is the importance of surveys in measuring customer-related targets?
> 5. What should you do immediately after the event?
> 6. Why are team and personal evaluation important?
> 7. What is the difference between review and evaluation?

411

Sources of information and further reading

Audit Commission, *Audit Guide Special Study Series,* HMSO, 1990

Clark S., *The Complete Fundraising Handbook,* Directory of Social Change, 1993

Evans D. W., *People, Communication, & Organisations,* Pitman, 1992

Handy C., *Understanding Organisations,* Penguin, 1985

Johnson R., *The 24 hour Business Plan,* Hutchinson Business Books, 1990

Lovejoy S., *A Systematic Approach to Getting Results,* Gower Publishing, 1993

Mullins L. J., *Management and Organisational Behaviour,* Pitman Publishing 1994

Passingham S., *Organising Local Events,* Directory of Social Change, 1993

Shibli S., *Leisure Managers' Guide to Budgeting and Budgeting Control,* Longman/ILAM, 1994

Sport England, *Best Value Series* (6 vols), Sport England, 2000

Sport England, *Model Survey Packages for Measuring Sports Participation*

Woods M., *The New Management,* Element Books, 1988

A special mention should be made of Sport England's series 'Running Sport'. Although geared primarily at voluntary sports clubs it provides a wealth of practical and easy-to-read ideas about running and organising teams and events.

Many of the high-street banks provide support material for starting up businesses which apply to a project e.g. free books, industry profiles and business fact sheets.

Index